MENNONITE COUNTRY~STYLE RECIPES

&

Kitchen Secrets

MENNONITE COUNTRY~STYLE RECIPES

&
Kitchen Secrets

Esther H. Shank

Art by Susan K. Hunsberger

Herald Press
Scottdale, Pennsylvania
Kitchener, Ontario

Library of Congress Cataloging-in-Publication Data

Shank, Esther H.
  Mennonite country-style recipes and kitchen secrets.

  Includes index.
  1. Cookery, Mennonite.   I. Title.
TX715.S527   1987   641.5'088287   87-8518
ISBN 0-8361-3442-7

MENNONITE COUNTRY-STYLE RECIPES
AND KITCHEN SECRETS
Copyright © 1987 by Herald Press, Scottdale, Pa. 15683
  Published simultaneously in Canada by Herald Press,
  Kitchener, Ont. N2G 4M5. All rights reserved.
Library of Congress Catalog Card Number: 87-8518
International Standard Book Number: 0-8361-3442-7
Printed in the United States of America
Design by Susan K. Hunsberger

92 91 90 89 88   10 9 8 7 6 5 4 3 2

Dedicated to
our three dear daughters,
Linda, Donna, and Nancy,
sharing all the practical assistance that I can
to help them be successful in their cooking—
and to enjoy it as well!

ACKNOWLEDGMENTS

I have always tended to be inquisitive by nature. If my friends made an unusually flaky pie crust, or their bread was extra light, I often asked if they minded sharing their secret. Almost always, the persons seemed delighted. Occasionally I even went to the home of someone and took "lessons." Through the years I have benefited greatly from information I otherwise would never have come by.

I've also kept an open eye for tips in newspaper columns and in other books and magazines.

After deciding to compile my own cookbook, I did a lot of research and testing to make certain the information I offer is accurate and that the tips are reliable. I also contacted various companies and manufacturers about their products and questions I had concerning them. I studied through numerous books on various aspects of food science and food preparation including:

Food Science, by Helen Charley. New York: John Wiley & Sons, 2nd ed., 1982.
Butchering, Processing, and Preservation of Meat, Frank G. Ashbrook. New York: Van Nostrand Reinhold Co., 1955.
Beverage Handbook, by Thorner and Herzberg. Westport, Conn.: AVI Publishing Co., 1979.
Cooking with Understanding, by Herbert L. Nichols, Jr. Greenwich, Conn.: North Castle Books, 1971.
The Art of Fine Baking, by Paula Peck. New York: Simon & Schuster, 1984.
Fundamentals of Quantity Food Preparation, by Geraline B. Hardwick and Robert L. Kennedy. New York: Van Nostrand Reinhold Co., 1982.
The Basic Cook Book, by Heseltine and Dow. Boston, Mass.: Houghton Mifflin, 1967.
For the Love of Cooking, by Sturges. Birmingham, Ala.: Oxmore House, 1975.
So You Are Ready to Cook, by Mary Ann Duffie. Minneapolis: Burgess Publishing Co., 4th ed., 1974.
Joy of Cooking, by Irma S. Rombauer and Marion R. Becker. New York: Bobbs-Merrill Co., rev. ed., 1975.
The Fannie Farmer Boston Cooking School Cookbook, by Wilma Perkins. Boston, Mass.: Little, Brown and Co., 1959.

I also received information from:

The American Egg Board
The U.S. Department of Agriculture
The National Livestock and Meat Board
The Virginia Co-operative Extension Service
Amana Refrigeration, Inc.
The Ball Canning Corporation
The Kerr Manufacturing Corporation

I was pleased many times to discover tips and information that I had learned by experience and from friends years ago. I was also delighted to find new information that I wished I could have benefited from knowing long ago.

The list of persons who contributed to my cooking experience through the years and more specifically in developing this book is too long to mention in detail. I'm grateful for my mother, Fannie B. Heatwole, and the tradition of good cooking which she passed on to me. A special thanks to the following:

To my husband, Rawley, and to our three daughters, Linda, Donna, and Nancy, who encouraged me in so many ways and willingly sampled and evaluated much experimental cooking! To our son-in-law, Ron Shenk, who taught me word processing, and helped with computer work on the book.

To Doris Bomberger, former professor of home economics at Eastern Mennonite College; Susan Offerdahl, home economist and instructor in living sciences at James Madison University; and Andrea Schrock Wenger, an EMC graduate and new homemaker—each of whom reviewed the manuscript and gave numerous helpful suggestions.

To Paul M. Schrock, general book editor at Herald Press, who edited the manuscript and helped in many other ways to make the book possible. To Susan Graber Hunsberger for the artwork, and to Miriam Martin for the diagrams.

Also to the following family and friends, several of whom also reviewed parts of the book, and others who shared in a special way with information and recipes:

Ruth Heatwole	Mae Shank	Margaret Brubaker
Carolyn H. Reed	Marie Shank	Barbara Bowman
Elizabeth H. Yoder	Gladys Harman	Rhoda S. Wenger
Kathryn Heatwole	Shirley Shank	Dorothy Slabaugh Grove
Fannie S. Heatwole	Bertha Shank	Ruby Petersheim
Louise Heatwole	Nancy Heatwole	Gloria Snider
Doris Heatwole	Dorothy Shank Showalter	Harriet Steiner
Mary Ann Heatwole	Lois B. Wenger	Alice Trissel
Donna Lou Heatwole	Jerry and Diane Horst	Wanda Good
Jeanne Heatwole	Minnie Carr	Annie Weaver
Mabelee Blosser	Gladys and Brownie Driver	Dorothy Suter Showalter

Although the recipes are basically from Mennonite families and friends, I wish to acknowledge the contribution of some non-Mennonite friends. Their recipes are of the same type usually passed along in Mennonite circles.

I have indicated at the end of recipes the name or names of persons who contributed them. I am especially grateful to each one who shared recipes with me!

Above all, I wish to thank the Lord for his many blessings to us, including the abundance of food he has given us to enjoy, and for the opportunity to share information in this way which he graciously allowed me to discover.

CONTENTS

Introduction 13
Recipe Abbreviations and Ingredients 17
Definitions of Food and Cooking Terms 18
Daily Nutrition Guide 21

1. BEVERAGES 25
   Tips for Beverages 29
   Recipes—
   •Cold Drinks 30
   •Hot Drinks 38
   •Milk Shakes 41

2. BREADS, COFFEE CAKES, AND CEREALS 43
   Procedure for Making Bread 45
   Quick Breads 48
   Rolls and Sweet Breads 48
   Cereals 51
   Tips for Breads, Sweet Breads, and Cereals 51
   Recipes—
   •Yeast Breads 53
   •Sweet Breads 62
   •Quick Breads 68
   •Fruit Breads and Coffee Cake 79
   •Pancakes and Miscellaneous 85
   •Cereals 88

3. CAKES, FROSTINGS, AND COOKIES 91
   Cakes 92
   •How to Make Angel Food Cake 96
   Cookies 97
   •Quick Checklist for Failures with Cakes and Cookies 99
   Tips for Cakes, Frostings, and Cookies 100
   Recipes—
   •Miscellaneous Cakes 104
   •Cake Mix 137
   •Cupcakes 138
   •Frostings and Fillings 141
   •Bar Cookies 147

• Drop Cookies and Miscellaneous Cookies *158*
• No-Bake Cookies *174*
• Rolled and Filled Cookies *176*

4. DESSERTS, FRUITS, SNACKS, AND CANDY............*183*
Homemade Ice Cream *185*
Melting Chocolate *186*
Popcorn *187*
Testing Candy and Icing for Doneness *187*
Tips for Desserts, Fruits, Snacks, and Candy *188*
Recipes—
• Fruit Desserts *192*
• Puddings and Soft Desserts *209*
• Frozen Desserts *222*
• Sauces and Toppings *229*
• Snacks *230*
• Candy *236*

5. EGGS, MILK, AND CHEESE *243*
Tips for Eggs, Milk, and Cheese *248*
Recipes—
• Eggs *249*
• Milk and Cream *252*
• Cheese *255*
• Eggs, Milk, and Cheese Dishes *257*

6. MAIN DISHES AND VEGETABLES.......................*263*
Vegetables *264*
• Chart for Cooking Vegetables *268-272*
Potatoes *273*
Cooking Dry Beans *274*
Cooking Pasta (Macaroni, Noodles, and Spaghetti) *274*
• Create Your Own Casserole Chart *275*
Tips for Main Dishes and Vegetables *276*
Recipes—
• Dishes Containing Meat *278*
• Vegetable and Miscellaneous Dishes *312*

7. MEATS, POULTRY, AND SEAFOOD *339*
Meat *340*
• Charts on Common Cuts of Beef, Pork, Veal, and Lamb *345-348*
Wild Meats *349*
Poultry *349*
Fish *354*
Stock for Soup *357*
Gravy *358*
• Approximate Timetable for Roasting Meats *361*

Tips for Meats, Poultry, and Seafood *362*
Recipes—
  •Sauces and Seasonings *364*
  •Beef *367*
  •Pork *372*
  •Poultry *376*
  •Seafood *383*
  • Variety Meats and Wild Meats *388*

8. MICROWAVE COOKING.................................*393*
Tips for Heating Leftovers *398*
Do's and Don'ts *398*
Uses for Your Microwave Oven *399*
  •Flower Drying Chart *402*
  •Microwave Heating Chart *403-404*
Recipes—
  •Beverages *405*
  •Muffins *405*
  •Meats *406*
  •Main Dishes *409*
  •Miscellaneous *419*
  •Soups and Stew *420*
  •Desserts *421*
  •Cakes and Cookies *423*
  •Snacks and Candy *428*
  •Jam and Jelly *432*

9. PASTRY AND PIES *433*
Procedure for Making Pastry *436*
How to Make Meringue *440*
Cream Pies *440*
Tips for Pastry and Pies *442*
Recipes—
  •Pastry *444*
  •Pies *448*

10. SALADS, SANDWICHES, AND SOUPS.....................*467*
About Gelatin *468*
Ideas for Sandwiches *469*
Tips for Salads, and Soups *471*
Recipes—
  •Fruit Salads *473*
  •Vegetable Salads *488*
  •Miscellaneous Salads *498*
  •Salad Dressings *500*
  •Sandwiches *505*
  •Soups *510*

11. ENTERTAINING, QUANTITY COOKING,
AND PARTY FOODS.......................................*523*
    •Approximate Amounts for 100 People *526*
    Party Ideas *527*
    Recipes—
        •Appetizers *529*
        •Dips *537*
        •Sandwich Spreads *540*
        •Miscellaneous *542*

12. QUICK-FIX SECTION *545*
    Tips for Quick-Fixes *551*
    Recipes—
        •Beverages and Breads *552*
        •Main Course *556*
        •Mixes *575*
        •Salads *577*
        •Desserts *580*

13. CANNING, FREEZING, AND PRESERVING................*589*
    Canning *591*
    Freezing *595*
    Processing Fruits *597*
    Processing Vegetables *602*
        •Approximate Yield per Bushel of Fruits and Vegetables *609-610*
    Processing Meats *610*
        •Timetables for Processing Fruits, Vegetables, and Meats *611-612*
        •Timetable of Approximate Blanching Time for Freezing Vegetables *612*
    Storing Vegetables *613*
    Tips for Canning, Freezing, and Preserving *614*
    Recipes *615*

14. NON-FOOD RECIPES AND MISCELLANEOUS TIPS........*633*
    Ideas for Leftovers *634*
    Soap Making *637*
    Ways to Save *640*
    Gardening Tips *644*
    Miscellaneous Tips *644*
    Non-Food Recipes *650*
    Removing Stains from Fabrics *655*
        •Equivalent Measures *658*
        •Substitutes for Ingredients *660*
        •Weights and Measures *662*
        •Commercial Container Sizes *662*

General Index 663
Canning, Freezing, and Preserving Index 679
The Author 680

INTRODUCTION

With all the multitudes of cookbooks on the market, I never imagined that someday I would be writing one. The idea for this project came about quite unintentionally.

I've always felt it was unfortunate for a mother to raise children (especially daughters) and not teach them how to cook, knowing full well that most of us usually eat three meals a day, 365 days a year, and that this skill is a necessary part of everyday living. Many young adults have expressed considerable frustration over suddenly being out on their own, facing major responsibility for meal preparation without much of a clue on how to cook. We send our children to school to learn all the other skills they need for getting along well in life, but this one is often thoughtlessly neglected. The assumption seems to be that one will automatically know how to cook when the time comes to do it! And because of this lack of know-how, many young persons end up buying large amounts of convenience foods which they may scarcely be able to afford and which often are not very nutritious.

Many of the older generation (including myself) grew up on a farm, often in large families, with continual opportunity for learning gardening, canning, and cooking. The young women often worked at home until they were married and by that time were quite experienced and confident in most areas of homemaking.

Today many young people are growing up in an urban setting, often with mother also holding down a job away from home. The music lessons, jobs, social functions, and many other extracurricular activities that modern families are involved in allow little time for food preparation.

When I suddenly found my own daughters starting to venture out on their own, I began to wonder if I had really taught them the things I wanted them to know before they left home. My concern in this area came when one of them moved in with a group of other college students (along with a sponsor) to live on campus. They took turns cooking the evening meal. When it was her turn to cook, she cooked for a group of 13 persons! Often she would call home saying, "Mother, could you quickly give me the recipe for your Chicken and Vegetable Stir-Fry," or whatever.

When another one of our daughters left with a group of college students for a summer work experience in another state, I felt more concern. How would she manage to cook for 16 when it was her turn? She wouldn't be able to call home easily for a few tips! She was the youngest of the students, and her experience in the kitchen hadn't been nearly what I had intended it to be before she left home. (All three of the girls had helped to milk the cows on weekends if they had any spare moments from school and their many other activities, rather than taking over the cooking.)

When I talked to her on the telephone several weeks later, one of my anxious questions was, "How is it going cooking for 16 people at once?"

"Very good," she replied. "Mother, you won't believe this, but someone told me yesterday that I was the best cook in the group!"

"Really?" I must have sounded shocked.

"Didn't you think I could cook?" she said.

"Well, yes," I said, "but I wasn't sure about cooking for a group of 16 all of a sudden."

"I'm trying to be creative," she said. "I made homemade biscuits and I added grated cheese to the casserole. It was so hot today, I put the mixed fruit in the freezer to make slush, and they all loved it."

"Oh, ye of little faith," I thought to myself, and breathed a prayer of thanks!

The whole experience, however, set me to thinking of how helpful it might be to them to have a book with all the tips and helpful hints included that I have learned through many years of experience. My own collection of favorite recipes that I had been adding to for 25 years was badly in need of updating and organizing, so I decided to type them into a notebook. Many of the directions for recipes were incomplete, and some called for a 6-oz. bag of this or a 12-oz. bag of that. With the coming of bulk food stores, this wasn't very helpful for a young inexperienced cook.

Actually, it was incredible what I discovered in my collection. For instance, one recipe from an elderly friend called for half of a 19-cent bag of miniature marshmallows. When I called her up and asked if she realized that her 19-cent bag of marshmallows was now 79 cents, we both had a good laugh! Beside all of this, I did not even have recipes for many of the things I prepared. I hadn't realized how many times I just put in a scoop or smidgen of this or that! My daughters found it difficult to know just how much that was! I had no idea how much work the project would be until I found myself bogged down in the middle of it. By then I was determined not to leave the task unfinished.

When a number of my friends learned what I was doing, they began asking if I would please run off a copy of it for them also. I gladly agreed until I went to several different printers and discovered what it would cost to run off a few copies. They all said if I would order a large number, the cost per copy would be about half. Well, I decided that was it! I didn't feel I could go into any large project, and the cost was prohibitive for a small one. So the project was put on the shelf for a year or two while we were extremely busy with another venture.

In the meantime, several people strongly encouraged me to consider having a book published. They felt there was a real need for this type thing. If we Mennonites intended to hand on to the next generations our tradition of "good country-style cooking," we needed to give them more help than is usually found in a recipe collection. I was also personally receiving an increasing number of calls from young persons and others about how to prepare certain foods, and especially how to can and freeze various foods. It seemed there was definitely a lack of easy access to this type of information.

So I began to pray about it, and to do a little research to see what others' reactions might be. I could not believe the response I received. Every mother I checked with was enthused about the possibility of being able to buy such a book for their own daughters and most of them expressed the desire to have this type of information for themselves!

There are many young men and some older ones, too, who are finding it a challenge and a pleasure to master meal preparation. This is especially true for married men whose wives work outside the home also. They are grateful for practical cooking information. If I have given the impression that the information in this book is only for feminine use, it is probably because we have three daughters and no sons; and the book, of course, is written from their perspective. I am hoping the book will be just as beneficial to men. I think it's great that they are interested also.

Even though there are many excellent cookbooks on the market, the intent of this book is not to compete, but to supply useful tips that are not found in many other books. I have tried to include the kinds of practical information that would have been helpful to me when I began cooking many years ago. My prayer is that you will find it helpful also!

I have also tried to give many options for using home processed foods in recipes calling for commercial products. In my own cooking experience, there are few recipes that I don't end up changing at least slightly. I often try to make them a bit more economical, or less laden with fats, or seasoned to please the taste of my own family. It is surprising what a little extra effort can do to make food more appealing, and what a little bit of extra spice or flavoring will do to perk up an otherwise ordinary dish! I encourage all young cooks to experiment and to be creative with their cooking. I think cooking is challenging and fun. I hope you find it that way too!

Esther H. Shank
Harrisonburg, Virginia

RECIPE ABBREVIATIONS AND INGREDIENTS

The following abbreviations have been used:

env. – envelope	*pkg.* – package
approx. – approximately	*pt.* – pint
gal. – gallon	*qt.* – quart
lb. – pound	*sec.* – second
med. – medium	*tbsp.* – tablespoon
pk. – packet	*tsp.* – teaspoon

In recipes calling for 3 teaspoons (1 tablespoon) of an ingredient such as baking powder, I have used the 3 tsp. indication to prevent error. Even though it is the same as 1 tablespoon, experience has shown that this is a frequent point of oversight. Many cooks when in a hurry are so accustomed to baking powder being in teaspoon amounts that they will put in 1 teaspoon instead of 1 tablespoon!

Explanation of usage of terms in the recipes:

Clearjel Always means the regular Clearjel unless instant Clearjel is specified. The regular form of Clearjel needs cooking and is used just like cornstarch. The instant Clearjel must not be cooked. Flavor is not as good with the instant Clearjel, since starches improve in flavor with cooking. Instant Clearjel must be mixed well with sugar before adding to liquid and then needs to be stirred very briskly while adding slowly to avoid lumping.

flour For any recipe calling for yeast, use bread flour. For all other recipes (except cakes), use all-purpose flour. I use all-purpose flour for many cakes, using cake flour only for delicate cakes. Flour is usually sifted, or at least stirred until very fluffy before measuring, and should then be spooned lightly into cup.

fruit pectin Commercial fruit pectin for jelly making comes in powder form such as Sure-jell or in liquid form such as Certo.

gelatin Flavored gelatin comes in various brands such as Jell-O. Plain gelatin, such as Knox, is usually sold in a box of small packets.

oatmeal Means quick uncooked (in dry form) unless otherwise stated.

rice Means regular white rice (uncooked) unless otherwise stated.

shortening Means a good solid shortening such as Crisco.

sugar Means white granulated sugar (any other kind will be specified).
yeast Use the granular yeast in the same amount as dry yeast. For 1 pk. dry yeast, use 1 tbsp. granular yeast, if desired.

All measures should be standard size, and should be level. Use a spatula or knife to level off measures of dry ingredients. Check liquid measures at eye level. Brown sugar should be packed into the cup. Spoon powdered sugar lightly into a cup.

Several brand names have been used simply to identify a product (such as Bisquick, Cool Whip, and Dream Whip). Other brands may be used as desired.

The use of saachrin is optional and may be substituted with other artificial sweetener, or with sugar.

Casseroles are usually baked uncovered unless a cover is specified.

The term "Low Cal." or "Lower Cal." is used to indicate recipes that are lower in calories than the usual recipes for that specific food. Rather than making a separate chapter of recipes for weight watchers, these recipes have been identified throughout the book. See page 22 for tips for lower-calorie cooking.

The amount of yield is not given for cookies and cakes baked in pans where pieces may be cut in varying sizes according to individual preference. The pan size indicates the yield.

DEFINITIONS OF FOOD AND COOKING TERMS

A la king Served in rich cream sauce usually seasoned with mushrooms, green pepper, and pimiento.
A la mode Served in style, served with ice cream.
Au gratin Food mixed with cream or white sauce and topped with crumbs or grated cheese or both, and browned in the oven or under broiler.
Baste To spoon liquid or fat over food while it is cooking. This prevents drying out and adds flavor.
Beat To combine with a regular over-and-over or circular motion, or with electric mixer, either to make smooth or to incorporate air into batter.
Blanche To cook briefly in boiling water to destroy enzymes or to loosen fruit or vegetable skins. Food is then usually chilled quickly to stop cooking process and maintain quality.
Blend To combine thoroughly (e.g., as melted chocolate would be incorporated throughout the dough).
Bouillon Clear meat broth, may be made with bouillon cubes.
Broth The rich liquid in which meat was cooked.
Canapé An appetizer of a seasoned mixture of meats, olives, fish, or cheese, served on small pieces of bread, toast, or crackers.
Caramelize To heat or melt sugar in a skillet over low heat stirring constantly until it turns brown and caramel flavored.
Caviar The salted roe (eggs) of sturgeon or other fish. An expensive delicacy.

Clearjel A modified food starch derived from hybrid waxy maize corn. It is more highly refined than cornstarch and, therefore, gives better cooking results, especially when food isn't used the first day. It is excellent for thickening fruit pies and fruit desserts. It is not sold in most grocery stores, but is usually carried in bulk food stores. In the regular form it is used like cornstarch. It also comes in an instant form. (See page 17 for more information on using it.)

Compote Stewed fruit—usually more than one kind—cooked in sugar syrup, usually served cold.

Condiment Seasoning served at the table.

Consommé A Clear soup stock, usually double strength.

Cream (verb) To soften and make creamy by beating against bowl with spoon or with electric mixer. To beat sugar and fat together to make creamy and to incorporate air into the mixture.

Croutons Little dried bread cubes, often seasoned with herbs.

Cubed meat Cut part of the way through on both sides by machine to tenderize.

Cut in To combine solid shortening with flour or flour mixture by repeated cuts through both substances, using two knives (scissor-fashion), or two forks, or a pastry blender, or by working it together with your hands.

Dash A few sprinkles from a shaker, about half of ⅛ tsp.

Deep fat fry To cook food in hot fat deep enough to completely cover food being cooked.

Dredge To coat with flour, or mixture of seasoning and flour or crumbs.

Dot To drop little chunks over the top of food, as to dot with butter.

Fat Butter, lard, shortening, oils, or rendered grease from fat tissues of meat. (Margarine is a substitute.)

Flake To separate lightly with a fork into small pieces.

Fold To use a spatula or rubber scraper to gently blend one ingredient with another in a down-over-up-over motion, usually egg whites, without damaging air cells in whites.

Fondue A dish often made of melted cheese, butter, or sauces, into which small pieces of food are dipped and eaten.

Fruit pectin A water-soluble substance in fruit yielding a jelly. Commercial fruit pectins are used frequently to make jelly, such as Sure-jell, which is in powder form, or Certo, which is in liquid form.

Garnish To decorate one food with another.

Gelatin Flavored gelatin comes in various brands, such as Jell-O. Plain gelatin, such as Knox, is usually sold in a box of small packets.

Giblets The liver, heart, and gizzard of poultry.

Hors d' oeuvres A French term (pronounced "or derv") meaning an assortment of appetizers or dainty finger foods.

Julienne To cut into long, very thin strips.

Knead To work dough by stretching, folding, and pressing it with palms of hands to develop strands of gluten and make dough smooth and elastic.

Kosher Processed and sanctioned according to strict Jewish law.

Lukewarm Not hot or cold—approximately 95 to 100 degrees.

MSG Monosodium glutamate, a concentrated form of sodium in a white powder form sold under different brand names such as Accent. It has no flavor of its own, but greatly enhances the flavor of certain foods, especially meats.

Marinate To let food stand in a mixture which usually contains vinegar (or lemon juice). This improves flavor and tenderizes. Mixture may include spices.

Mince To chop food very fine with a chopper or sharp knife.

Mix To combine ingredients using any technique suitable to the ingredients involved.

Mocha A combination of coffee and chocolate flavors in beverages and desserts.

Molasses A thick dark sugar syrup usually referring to sorghum or cane molasses which are the same. It is stronger flavored than corn syrup.

Parmount crystals Crystals of partially hydrogenated palm kernel oil, with lecithin added for use in making confections. Can usually be purchased at confectionary shops.

Parboil To partially cook food in boiling water similar to blanching, but cooking time is usually longer. Cooking is usually completed by another method.

Parfait A dessert in which ice cream is layered with syrup or crushed fruit, etc., and whipped cream, served in tall-stemmed dessert glasses.

Puree To press food into thick, mushy pulp through a sieve or strainer, or by processing in electric blender.

Roe Eggs of fish.

Sauté To lightly brown or cook in small amount of fat in skillet.

Scallions Another term for green onions.

Scald To heat to just below the boiling point as when scalding milk. Or to rinse with boiling water to sanitize.

Score To make cuts or gashes partially through fibers, as in meat.

Skewer A long pin, usually metal, on which food is browned; or pins used to fasten meat and poultry together while cooking.

Soufflé A puffy, airy baked dish made light with beaten egg whites folded in with white sauce or other ingredients, usually cheese, meat, fish, or vegetables richly flavored.

Steep To soak in hot water just below the boiling point to extract flavor.

Stir To combine, usually with a spoon with a circular or rotary motion, or to move the position of food being heated to mix and prevent burning.

Stir-fry To fry quickly over high heat in a lightly oiled pan (as a wok) while stirring continuously.

Stock The richly flavored liquid in which meat, fish, or vegetables have been cooked, usually used in soups and sauces.

Torte Rich layers of cake, often made with crumbs, eggs, and nuts. Thin layers of custard or jelly may be spread between layers, and whipped cream over the top and sides. Or a meringue baked in the form of a cake.

Toss To mix ingredients lightly without mashing them.

Veal The meat of calves up to 6 months of age.

Whip To beat rapidly to incorporate air and increase volume.

Wok A skillet-type appliance with a rounded bottom used to stir-fry foods.

DAILY NUTRITION GUIDE

As you plan your meals, keep in mind the four basic food groups:

Milk Group 3 or more glasses for children each day
4 or more glasses for teenagers
2 or more glasses for adults
(Cheese, ice cream, and other milk-based foods can supply part of the milk.)

Meat Group 2 or more servings each day
(Meats, fish, poultry, eggs, dry beans and peas, lentils, nuts, peanut butter, etc.)

Vegetable and Fruit Group 4 or more servings each day.
(Include dark green or yellow vegetables, citrus fruits or tomatoes.)

Breads and Cereals Group 4 or more servings each day
(Enriched or whole grain. Includes rice, grits, macaroni, crackers, cooked cereals.)

Milk Group Milk and most milk products are calcium-rich foods. They also contribute riboflavin, protein, and vitamins A, B-6, and B-12. Some of these products are fortified with vitamin D. This group includes whole, skim, lowfat, evaporated, and nonfat dry milk, buttermilk, yogurt, ice cream, ice milk, cheese, cottage cheese, process cheese foods, and process cheese spreads.

Meat Group These foods are valued for protein, phosphorus, iron, zinc, vitamin B-6, and still other vitamins and minerals. Included in this group are beef, veal, lamb, pork, poultry, fish, shellfish (shrimp, oysters, crabs, etc.), dry beans, dry peas, soybeans, lentils, eggs, seeds, nuts, peanuts, and peanut butter. It's a good idea to vary your choices in this group. Each food has a distinct nutritional advantage. Red meats are good sources of zinc. Liver and egg yolks are valuable sources of vitamin A. Dry beans, peas, soybeans, and nuts are worthwhile sources of magnesium. All foods of animal origin contain vitamin B-12; foods of vegetable origin do not.

Vegetable and Fruit Group   Vegetables and fruits contribute vitamins A and C and also fiber. Peels and edible seeds are especially rich in fiber. Dark-green and deep-yellow vegetables are good sources of vitamin A. Most dark-green vegetables, if not overcooked, are also reliable sources of vitamin C, as are melons, berries, tomatoes, and citrus fruits (oranges, grapefruit, tangerines, lemons, etc.). Dark-green vegetables, in addition, are valued for riboflavin, folacin, iron, and magnesium. Certain greens—collards, kale, mustard, turnip, and dandelion—provide calcium. Nearly all vegetables and fruits are low in fat, and none contain cholesterol.

Bread and Cereal Group   Whole-grain and enriched breads and cereals are important sources of B vitamins, iron, and protein. They are a major source of protein in vegetarian diets. Whole-grain products contribute magnesium, folacin, and fiber, in addition. Foods in the bread and cereal group include all products made with whole grains or enriched flour or meal.*

TIPS FOR LOWER CALORIE COOKING

With many more people becoming aware of the importance of proper weight to maintain good health, a few tips for weight watchers may be helpful.

An important key in maintaining proper weight is to learn to eat smaller portions of many foods rather than to go on strict diets depriving yourself of many foods that you really enjoy and which may be good for you. It seems the more you determine you should not eat something, the more you crave that very thing! After losing a few pounds, many people overindulge again, going up and down on a constant seesaw of weight gain and loss. Rather than to be continually going on and off of diets, more people are finding they have much better long-range success by simply cutting back on serving sizes. With this method, you may regularly include small portions of your favorite foods without having a guilt complex.

Several friends told me that they and a group of their weight-watching friends had agreed they would rather eat smaller portions of food that really tastes good than to be able to fill up on food that isn't very tasty which is often quite typical of low calorie recipes. They had passed around some low calorie recipes among themselves and weren't satisfied with most of them. These recipes often call for special ingredients that are usually much more expensive when they actually should be cheaper because they contain a lesser amount of expensive fat and sugar. One of the easiest ways to cut back in calories is to eat raw vegetables and fruits, and you do not need recipes for these. I have included a limited number of recipes throughout the book which are lower in calories than the usual recipes for these foods, and which I feel are good. These are identified by "(Low Cal.)" following the recipe title.

Special diet plans are often quite expensive. It seems ironic that many people run up gigantic special-food and diet-plan bills while they are cutting back on their

---

*The paragraphs on the four food groups are reprinted courtesy of the U.S.D.A.

food consumption. This should be the time to save on the grocery bill! It makes so much more sense to cultivate the habit of moderation as a regular routine.

It is important to eat nutritionally balanced meals which include a good variety of foods. Don't cut out foods such as potatoes, whole-grain bread, and rice. These foods furnish many nutrients and important roughage. It is usually the butter, sour cream, and spreads we pile on these foods that make them calorie laden.

Be sure to include plenty of fruits and vegetables—the things that help keep your body in shape. Omit the cream sauces and other dressings and toppings that are high in calories.

The consumption of sugar-sweet desserts and candies are major culprits for weight watchers. Many recipes can have the amount of sugar cut back considerably. Every teaspoon of sugar contains 17 calories! Part artificial sweetener may be used in place of part of the sugar in many foods. The texture of baked goods may be adversely affected if too much artificial sweetener is substituted, however. Popcorn is a good non-sweet snack for weight watchers if a lot of salt and melted butter are not added.

Another important area to watch is in the use of fats. Especially animal fats are high in saturated fat and contain cholesterol. Bacon, for example, is mostly fat and calories. Even though bacon grease makes an excellent seasoning for a number of dishes, it can be a real hazard for the calorie-conscious. The polyunsaturated fats from plant origin which are liquid at room temperature are considered best for low calorie cooking. Two exceptions are coconut oil and palm kernel oil. Broil or cook foods instead of frying them to cut back in calories. By all means avoid deep fat fried foods. Stir-frying foods has become quite popular, and is an excellent method if you use a skillet or wok with a non-stick finish and coat it with nonfat vegetable spray rather than with fat.

Remove as much fat as possible from meats. Ground meat should be sautéed and drained thoroughly before adding it to recipes. Fish, chicken, and turkey are good sources of protein. Poultry skin is high in fat, however, and may be removed to reduce calories.

• A number of people with high cholesterol are finding they are able to reduce their cholesterol level by simply eating oatmeal or oat bran cereal regularly. If you are having a problem with high cholesterol, this is certainly worth trying.

There are numerous other ways that can make a tremendous difference over a period of time with a very small amount of effort such as using lowfat milk and other dairy products. Lowfat yogurt and cottage cheese are good substitutes for sour cream and other dressings. Replace soft drinks with fruit juices, other nutritional beverages, or water. If you have a special weakness for chocolate, cocoa powder has less calories than solid chocolate and is the lesser of two evils. Avoid junk foods, and also snacks between meals, especially bedtime snacks! This seems to be another major culprit for many people.

It is not good to skip meals, especially breakfast, thinking that you can then fill up on the next meal. Your body needs energy to begin the day and you usually end up eating more later because of increased appetite and lack of energy. The largest meal of the day should not be served late in the evening. It is not good to go to bed with a full stomach. Have regular mealtimes if possible, and you'll find your body develops a routine of craving food at these regular times and not in between!

It takes extra discipline to change any bad habits that have gradually developed over a period of time. But if you are persistent for a few weeks, it is amazing how a preference can also be developed for lower calorie foods. Your appetite seems to shrink so that a smaller amount of food will satisfy you as much as the larger amount you formerly consumed!

An important thing to remember is that it is much better to avoid nutritional problems than to try to correct them after suffering the consequences of bad habits years later.

CHAPTER ONE ....

BEVERAGES

BEVERAGES

One would wish the most popular beverage in the United States would be milk, since milk is considered by many authorities to be the most complete natural food available. Coffee, however, takes the lead with tea coming in second. Even though coffee and tea have little, if any, nutritional value, they top the list in popularity. This is probably partly because milk is much more perishable and, therefore, often more inconvenient to have readily available. Herb tea is much prefered over caffeinated tea.

Since milk contains so many of the nutrients we need for growth and good health, it should be included as often as possible in the diet in place of other non-nutritional drinks. It is also an especially good source of calcium. There are a number of delicious ways to serve milk drinks such as milk shakes, egg nog, chocolate milk (either hot or cold—without too much chocolate!), flavored hot milk, and even just plain good cold milk! Experiment with adding various flavors or fruit to suit your taste.

There are numerous good recipes for punches or drinks containing fruit juices that are excellent to use instead of the popular soft drinks and coffee. See recipe section for these. Several are also included in the Quick-Fix section. These are much better for your health, and are usually easier on the pocketbook as well! My family prefers garden teas over commercial teas. If you don't have a garden, a little space in a flower bed could furnish you with a nice supply. Concentrate can be made in season and frozen to use over winter.

In spite of the fact that it isn't particularly good for you, many people feel that nothing quite replaces a good hot cup of coffee, occasionally at least. Since the coffee break has become such an integral part of the establishment in the business and social world coffee seems to be here to stay. Much happy socializing is done around hot cups of coffee and tea.

Various factors affect the quality and flavor of these two beverages. First, you must purchase a good quality product if you want a good beverage. The shelf life of coffee is not nearly as long as that of tea. Coffee should be kept in an airtight container, and if not used fairly promptly, it can be stored in the freezer to retain freshness. Tea can be stored in a tight container indefinitely.

When making coffee and tea, all utensils should be thoroughly clean. Deposits in the coffeepot and teapot have an adverse effect on taste. Water used for brewing should be freshly boiled, beginning with fresh cold water. Hot water which stands for an extended period of time tends to give a flat and stale taste. Do not use hot tap water. Water that has been softened by chemicals or heavily chlorinated water affect the flavor of coffee and tea. It is also more difficult to obtain good full flavor when using very hard water. Very hard water is more likely to cause cloudiness in tea.

When making coffee and tea for a group, be sure to consider the size of the cups you plan to use. Most coffee cups and teacups hold about 5 or 6 ounces. Since a 1-cup measure holds 8 ounces, you can figure at least 20 servings to each gallon of beverage. Keep in mind that a limited amount of water is absorbed into the coffee grounds. Coffee does not need to be made quite as strong when making larger amounts, especially if it stands for a while. It becomes stronger as it stands.

Making Coffee
1. Most automatic coffee makers or percolators use the regular grind of coffee. Vacuum coffee makers use fine grind. Be sure to follow the manufacturer's directions. Use cold tap water in the coffee maker.
2. Temperature for brewing coffee should come to approximately 200 degrees. Never boil coffee (boiling will make it bitter).
3. Coffee should be freshly made. It can be held at 185 to 190 degrees for up to 1 hour. After this, it becomes bitter and stale and is not good reheated.
4. Varying amounts of coffee are used depending on the strength you prefer, but recommended amounts are as follows:
   —Use 1 slightly rounded tbsp. coffee for each individual cup.
   —Use 2 cups coffee and 6 qts. water for 25 cups.
   —Use 1 lb. coffee (approximately 4½ cups) and 14 qts. water for 60 cups.
5. Coffee improves in flavor if held at serving temperature for 3 to 5 minutes. After that it deteriorates. Basket containing coffee grounds should be removed from coffee maker as soon as coffee has brewed (to prevent an off flavor).

Making Hot Tea (from commercial dried tea):
1. Do not use metal container to steep tea. Use earthenware, china, or granite. Container should be small enough in diameter to permit hot water to completely cover tea bags or container holding tea.
2. Preheat container by pouring in boiling water before making the tea.
3. Place tea in heated pot and pour boiling water over tea. Stir to immerse all leaves. Allow to steep from 3 to 5 minutes for small amounts. For larger amounts, cover to retain heat and aroma, and steep from 6 to 7 minutes. Water temperature should be between 185 and 200 degrees for entire steeping time. Never boil tea—this makes it excessively astringent and also causes cloudiness.
4. Varying amounts of tea are used depending on the strength you prefer, but recommended amounts are as follows:
   —Use 1 tsp. loose tea or 1 tea bag for each individual cup.
   —Use 1 oz. (about ⅓ cup) tea leaves to 1 gallon water to serve 20. (This makes 16 [8-oz.] cups or approximately 20 teacups.)
   —Use 5 oz. (about 1⅔ cups) tea leaves and 20 qts. of water for 100 teacups.
5. Remove tea bags or strain if loose tea was used, and serve.

6. Cloudiness in tea may be caused by steeping it too long, by boiling the tea, or by hard water. It may also be caused by tea being stronger than the water can absorb or by chilling strong tea in refrigerator. Hot tea should be allowed to cool at room temperature. Cloudiness does not affect the flavor of tea and may be cleared by adding a small amount of boiling water. The addition of a little lemon juice while brewing the tea may also help to avoid cloudiness.

Iced Tea

To make 1 gallon iced tea, pour 1 qt. boiling water over 2 oz. (about ⅔ cup) tea. Steep for 6 minutes. Stir and strain into 3 qts. of cold tap water. Sweeten to taste and serve over ice cubes. Iced tea can be held for 3 to 4 hours without harming flavor. (Iced tea is prepared double strength because melting ice dilutes the tea to serving strength.)

Instant Tea

Iced tea can be made quickly using instant tea. It is not necessary to boil the water as the tea granules will dissolve instantly even in cold tap water. Follow manufacturer's directions on container. For each single serving, use approximately 1 rounded tsp. for a 6-oz. glass of cold water, or about 2 tbsp. for each quart of cold water. (Variation: For *spiced tea,* I like to keep a small jar of water, with about 1 tbsp. whole cloves added, in the refrigerator to add to iced tea. Add the amount desired. If you need the spice water right away, simply pour boiling water over cloves in jar and let steep about 5 minutes. After using clove water, you can add more water to the same cloves and refrigerate for next time. The same cloves can be used several times. One cinnamon stick may also be crumbled into the jar if desired.)

Garden Tea

Many people like to grow their own tea in a corner of the garden. If you don't have a garden, the edge of a flower bed makes a good place. Tea is usually quite prolific, so if you can get a friend or neighbor to dig up a start for you, it is easy to have fresh tea on hand all summer long. Concentrate can be made and frozen for winter usage as well. Keep well watered for a tender abundant crop. Spearmint, balsam or applemint, and peppermint are popular homegrown teas. Thelma Showalter prefers the applemint tea (it has fuzzy leaves that are shaped like an apple leaf) for the following recipe:

(Do not use very hard water, soft water makes better tea.) Combine 1 ½ to 2 cups sugar and 4 cups water in stainless steel saucepan or granite pan and boil for several minutes. Remove from heat and add 2 tightly packed cups garden tea (use leaves and small stem ends). Make sure all leaves are covered with water. Cover pan and let steep for approximately 6 hours. Strain and refrigerate. This makes a concentrate which should be mixed with 3 parts (or more if desired) ice and water to 1 part tea concentrate to serve. It can be used immediately or the concentrate can be poured into ice cube trays and frozen for later use. Makes 4 cups concentrate which makes 3 qts. tea.

Tea Lemonade

Use preceding recipe, but add 1 cup lemon juice and 1 cup orange juice to strained concentrate. Dilute concentrate as directed to serve. Makes 6 cups concentrate which makes 4 ½ qts. tea lemonade.

TIPS FOR BEVERAGES

•To prevent the formation of a film on top of hot milk beverages, heat only to 165 degrees. Higher temperatures cause a film to form. Another way to prevent formation of film and to garnish hot milk beverages is to top them with a marshmallow or a dab of whipped cream. Whipped cream may be sprinkled with cinnamon or nutmeg. Coffee garnished with whipped cream is delicious also.

•The flavor of nonfat powdered milk is improved by adding 2 tbsp. coffee creamer to each quart of reconstituted powdered milk. Dissolve 2 tbsp. coffee creamer in 2 tbsp. hot water and add to milk. For improved flavor, refrigerate milk overnight before using.

•To pasteurize raw milk, heat to 162 degrees and hold at that temperature for 15 seconds. Then cool immediately by setting container in a larger pan of cold, slowly running water.

•Hot milk is nature's sleeping aid. For a relaxing bedtime treat, try a cup of flavored hot milk—mint flavored, with butterscotch chips, chocolate, or crushed fresh or frozen fruit, or vanilla flavoring, with a small amount of sugar added.

•To keep beverages hot when serving a group, place in the crockpot.

•To cut back on the amount of sugar in beverages, I prefer using 1 cup sugar and 4 whole-grain saccharin per 1 gallon rather than all sugar. Crush saccharin with back of spoon and dissolve in small amount of water before adding to mixture.

•For elegant serving, frost the rims of glasses for cold drink by dipping rim in slightly beaten egg white, then into granulated sugar, white or tinted.

•To make attractive ice ring for punch bowl, fill ring mold ¾ full with water and freeze. Arrange lemon slices or red and green maraschino cherries and sprigs of mint on top of frozen ring. Fill to top with water and freeze again. Unmold and float on top of punch bowl. Or to prevent weakening punch with addition of water, use some of punch mixture instead of water to make ice ring, or to make ice cubes. Colored ice cubes are an attractive addition to the punch bowl.

•Freeze ice cubes in muffin pans for large, long-lasting cubes for punch. For larger blocks of ice, set water-filled ½-gallon milk cartons or cottage cheese containers in freezer.

•Do not put instant coffee and creamer in the cup together before pouring in hot water. Creamer blends in better if put on top of hot coffee after coffee is dissolved.

•If you have coffee left over from a group, freeze it in ice cube trays for iced coffee. Do this as soon as possible, however, since coffee begins to turn bitter after an hour. Tea cubes can be frozen in the same way to chill iced tea without diluting the strength.

•The addition of a little salt helps to sweeten slightly bitter coffee.

•For an easy way to make tea with dried garden tea leaves, place loose tea leaves in top of a drip coffee maker and follow the same procedure as for making coffee. Use slightly less tea than when making it in teapot. (Flavor may not be quite as good, but this is a handy way to serve a small group.)

•If instant tea is not used promptly, keep partly used jar in freezer to avoid having granules harden in jar.

BEVERAGES RECIPES
COLD DRINKS
Almond-Lime Punch

2 small pks. lime Kool-Aid
1½ to 2 cups sugar
2 qts. water
1 (46-oz.) can pineapple juice
1½ tbsp. almond flavoring

Mix until sugar is dissolved and serve. (Sherbet may be added to garnish.)

. . . .

Variation: Instead of almond flavoring, add 1 qt. ginger ale.

Yield: 1 gal.   *Fannie B. Heatwole—my mother*

. . . .

Banana Punch

3 cups sugar
3 cups water
3 or 4 bananas

Put in blender and process until well blended.

. . . .

1 (12-oz.) can frozen orange juice
   concentrate
1 (46-oz.) can pineapple juice

Add and chill well.

. . . .

2 qts. ginger ale, and ice and water
   enough to make 2 gals.

Add just before serving.

. . . .

Variation: Omit ginger ale and add 2 tbsp. almond flavoring instead.

Yield: 2 gals.   *Evelyn Kratz*

. . . .

Banana Fruit Punch

1 (46-oz.) can pineapple juice
4 bananas

Process bananas in blender with enough of juice to puree well.

. . . .

2 small pks. orange Kool-Aid
1 (6-oz.) can frozen lemon juice
   concentrate
2 (12-oz.) cans frozen orange juice
   concentrate
3 to 4 cups sugar
2 qts. ginger ale (optional)

Add these ingredients plus water and ice enough to make 2 gals. Stir until sugar is dissolved. Serve immediately.

. . . .

Yield: 2 gals.   *Thelma Showalter*

Breakfast-in-a-Glass (Low Cal.)

1 cup cold skim milk
½ cup orange juice
1 egg
⅛ tsp. salt
1 tbsp. sugar or artificial sweetener to taste

Combine all ingredients in blender and process until frothy.

Yield: 1 serving

Christmas Punch

2 (46-oz.) cans Hawaiian Red Punch
1 (46-oz.) can pineapple juice
2 ½ to 3 cups sugar
1 (32-oz.) bottle ginger ale
2 qts. water and ice

Mix until sugar is dissolved and serve.

Yield: 1 ¾ gals.

Coffee Punch

1 gal. strong cold coffee

Brewed as directed on coffee can.

2 cups sugar

Add to hot coffee, then cool.

1 gal. vanilla ice cream

Stir half of ice cream into coffee. Then pour into punch bowl. Dip remaining ice cream over the top to garnish.

1 pt. whipping cream

Whip cream and place a dab on top of each cup as you serve.

Yield: 1 gal.

Dorothy Suter Showalter

Cranberry Punch

1½ qts, cranberry juice
1 (6-oz.) can frozen orange juice concentrate
1 (6-oz.) can frozen lemon juice concentrate
1½ cups sugar
1 qt. ginger ale

Mix all ingredients with enough water and ice to make 1 gal.

Yield: 1 gal.

Dieter's Delight (Low Cal.)

1 (6-oz.) container yogurt
1 egg
1 tbsp. honey
2 tbsp. dry milk powder
1 banana
1 orange, juiced
1 tsp. wheat germ

Combine all ingredients in blender and process until smooth. (This makes a good thick drink. A little water or skim milk may be added if desired.)

Yield: 1 serving

Easy Punch

1 (46-oz.) can Hawaiian Punch
1 small pk. strawberry Kool-Aid
1 qt. ginger ale
1 cup sugar
4 whole-grain saccharin

Mix all ingredients with enough water and ice to make 1 gal.

Yield: 1 gal.

Eggnog

For each glass of eggnog, use 1 well-beaten egg, 1 tbsp. sugar, ½ tsp. vanilla, and 1 cup or more of milk to fill glass. Sprinkle nutmeg on top. (For richer eggnog, use ½ cup evaporated milk or cream in place of ½ cup of whole milk. Cream may be whipped and folded in for a rich effect. Or top with a little ice cream.)

Eggnog (or Fruity) Liquid Breakfast

1 cup whole milk
1 tsp. vanilla
1 tbsp. honey
1 egg
½ cup instant dry milk powder
¼ tsp. nutmeg
dash of salt

Combine all ingredients in blender and process until smooth and frothy.

Variation: For Fruity Liquid Breakfast, omit egg and nutmeg, and add 10 strawberries or 1 banana instead.

Yield: 1 serving

Fruit Slush Mix

2 cups sugar
4 cups water

Combine in saucepan and heat just until sugar is dissolved.

1 (6-oz.) can frozen orange juice
   concentrate (see next page)

| ½ cup lemon juice
1 (46-oz.) can pineapple juice | Add and mix thoroughly. Fill 6 or 7 ice cube trays and freeze. Remove from trays and store in plastic bag. Use within 6 months. |

Fruit Slush: For each serving, fill glass with cubes and also fill with ginger ale or club soda. Let stand 15 minutes. Stir and serve.

Variation: Add 5 or 6 mashed bananas, mashed peaches, or other fruit. These may be pureed in the blender with part of the liquid.

Yield: approximately 100 cubes   *Gloria Snider*

Lemonade Syrup

| 6 lemons | Juice lemons, and cut the rind of two of them into very thin strips. |
| 1 cup water
2 cups sugar
⅛ tsp. salt | Combine in saucepan. Add strips from two lemons and boil for 3 to 5 minutes. Cool and add lemon juice. Strain and store in refrigerator in covered jar. |

Use 2 tbsp. syrup to 1 glass ice water or carbonated water to serve. Or add entire amount of syrup to 1 gal. ice and water for 1 gal. lemonade.
Variation: May add 1 tbsp. syrup and 2 tbsp. orange juice or pineapple juice to 1 glass water or carbonated water to serve.

Yield: 1 gal.

Lemonade Mint Drink

For a refreshing drink, combine 2 qts. lemonade and 1 pt. garden spearmint tea.

Lime-Light Banana Crush Punch

6 cups water 2 cups sugar 5 bananas	Process in blender until bananas are pureed and sugar is dissolved.
1 (46-oz.) can pineapple juice 1 (12-oz.) can frozen lemonade concentrate 2 (12-oz.) cans frozen orange juice concentrate	Add to mixture. Ladle into freezer containers, cover and freeze.
2 qts. lime-lemon carbonated beverage, or Sprite, or 7-Up	To serve: thaw to mush consistency in refrigerator. Pour in bowl or glasses and add soda.

Yield: 6 qts.   *Ruth Weaver*

Orange Float (Low Cal.)

1 cup skim milk
2 tbsp. frozen orange juice
  concentrate
4 ice cubes
1 tsp. artificial sweetener
½ tsp. vanilla

Combine all ingredients in blender and process until thick and frothy. Serve immediately.

Yield: 1 serving

Orange Jubilee

(Similar to Orange Julius)

1 (6-oz.) can frozen orange juice
  concentrate
2 cups milk
1 egg (optional)
1 tsp. vanilla
½ cup sugar
12 ice cubes

Combine all ingredients in blender and process on high speed until well mixed. Serve immediately. (Great on a hot summer day!)

Yield: 5 servings   *Carolyn Shank*

Orange Punch

1 gal. water
2 small pks. orange Kool-Aid
1 (12-oz.) can frozen orange juice
  concentrate, or 1 qt. pineapple
  juice
2 cups sugar

Mix until sugar is dissolved.

1 qt. ginger ale (optional)

Add just before serving.

½ gal. orange sherbet (optional)

Dip over the top with ice cream dipper. Serve immediately. (Very refreshing!)

Yield: 1 ½ gals

Delightful Rhubarb Punch

(The concentrate can be made in quantity during rhubarb season, and can then be frozen or canned the same as apple cider for use all year long.)

2 qts. rhubarb, cut in ½-inch pieces
2 qts. water

Combine in large saucepan, and cook 10 minutes. Let set ½ hour to allow juice to absorb more flavor. Then sieve.

This yields 2 qts. plus 1 cup juice. Add the 1 cup juice to the remaining rhubarb pulp for eating. Use the 2 qts. juice for punch.

Punch:

2 qts. rhubarb concentrate
1 (6-oz.) can frozen pineapple juice concentrate
2 cups ginger ale
2 cups sugar
2 qts. water and ice (or more if desired)

Mix until sugar is dissolved.

Variation: Add 1 (6-oz.) can frozen orange juice concentrate and ½ cup lemon juice, in place of pineapple juice concentrate.

Yield: 1 ¼ gals.

Emma Beachy

Strawberry Milk Punch

16 oz. crushed frozen strawberries
¾ cup sugar

Mix in punch bowl.

½ gal. strawberry ice cream, softened

Add, stirring well.

1 gal. chilled milk
½ tsp. almond flavoring
few drops red color to make pink

Add. Serve immediately.

Yield: 1 ½ gals.

Strawberry Sparkle

1 (12-oz.) can frozen orange juice concentrate
1 (46-oz.) can pineapple juice
2 small pks. strawberry Kool-Aid, or 2 or 3 cups frozen strawberries, crushed
1½ cups sugar
4 whole-grain saccharin
red color as desired
1 qt. ginger ale

Mix all ingredients together with enough water and ice to make 1 ½ gal. Serve immediately.

Yield: 1 ½ gals.

Summer Shower Punch

1 qt. vanilla ice cream **3 cups pineapple juice** **½ cup orange juice** **1 tbsp. lemon juice** **½ cup sugar**	Blend in mixing bowl.

5 cups cold milk	Add and serve immediately.

Yield: 3 qts.

Super Peach Drink

1 qt. peaches, undrained	Puree in blender.

2 scoops (6 tbsp.) orange breakfast
  drink powder (such as Tang)
1 scoop (3 tbsp.) lemonade mix
  (such as Countrytime)
1 cup sugar
4 whole-grain saccharin
	Mix all ingredients together with enough water and ice to make 1 gal..

Yield: 1 gal.

Gladys and Brownie Driver

Tea Concentrate for a Group

Add 1 ⅔ cups dried tea leaves to 1 gal. boiling water. Continue to heat until almost boiling again. Let steep 3 minutes, then strain. While tea is hot add 5 cups sugar and 3 tbsp. artificial sweetener. This concentrate makes 5 gals. of tea. To serve, mix 2 tbsp. concentrate to an 8-oz. glass of water.

Iced Tea Syrup

1 cup (packed) fresh mint garden
  tea
2 tbsp. or more loose black tea
  (English breakfast tea is good)
	Place in a stainless steel, glass, or ceramic container.

3½ cups boiling water	Add, being sure to cover tea. Steep 8 minutes. Strain into jar.

1½ to 2½ cups sugar	Add, stirring with wooden spoon to dissolve. Refrigerate when cool.

Use 1 cup syrup to 4 cups water to serve.

Yield: 1 qt. syrup yielding 5 qts. tea

Berdella Stutzman

Wedding Punch (Pink)

5 cups sugar 5 cups water	Combine in saucepan. Heat to boiling stirring until sugar is dissolved.
2 small pks. strawberry Kool-Aid	Add to mixture while hot. Then cool.

1 (6-oz.) can frozen orange juice
   concentrate
1 (6-oz.) can frozen lemonade
   concentrate
1 (46-oz.) can pineapple juice
2 qts. ginger ale
	Add, along with enough water and ice to make 3 gals..

Yield: 3 gals.   *Bertha Shank*

Wedding Reception Punch

2 small pks. cherry or lime Kool-Aid 4 qts. water and ice	Dissolve Kool-aid in water.
4 ripe bananas 3 or 4 cups sugar	Puree in blender with part of above water.

1 (6-oz.) can frozen lemonade
   concentrate
1 (6-oz.) can frozen orange juice
   concentrate
1 (46-oz.) can pineapple juice
1 qt. ginger ale
	Add, mixing well and serve immediately.

Garnish with 1 (10-oz.) pkg. frozen strawberries (half-thawed) if desired. (Use Kool-Aid according to the color you wish the punch to be. If using cherry, add a few drops red color also.)

Yield: 2 gals.

Zesty Fruit Cooler

3 oranges 3 lemons	Juice and strain into blender container.
3 bananas 1½ cups sugar	Add and blend only until thoroughly pureed. Pour into ice cube tray and freeze.

To serve: Place one ice cube in each glass and fill with ginger ale.

Yield: 12 to 14 cubes.   *Alice Trissel*

HOT DRINKS

Butterscotch Steamer

¼ cup butter **½ cup brown sugar**	Melt together in saucepan.
2 qts. milk	Add, heating until hot, but not boiling (about 165 degrees). Serve in hot mugs sprinkled with cinnamon.

Yield: 8 cups   *Wanda Good*

Hot Cranberry Punch

3 cups sugar **2 cups water**	Heat until boiling.
⅓ cup red cinnamon candies	Dissolve in hot syrup.
2 qts. cranberry juice **2 cups lemon juice** **2 cups orange juice**	Add and heat thoroughly. May add an additional qt. or two of water depending on strength desired.

Yield: 1 to 1 ½ gals.

Hot Chocolate Mix

8 cups dry milk powder **1 (16-oz.) can hot chocolate mix** **(such as Nestle Quik)** **1 (8-oz.) jar coffee creamer** **2 cups sugar** **½ tsp. salt**	Mix well. Store in cool, dry place. To serve: fill cup ⅓ of the way with mix and then finish filling with boiling water.

Yield: approximately 14 cups mix which makes 42 cups hot chocolate

Hot Cocoa Mix

4 cups dry milk powder **½ cup cocoa powder** **2 cups powdered sugar** **⅔ cup coffee creamer** **⅓ cup malted milk powder (optional)** **¼ tsp. salt**	Mix all ingredients well. To serve: add ¼ cup mix to 1 cup boiling water. Top with a marshmallow.

Yield: 7 ½ cups mix which makes approximately 30 cups cocoa

Chocolate Syrup

(This syrup is similar to Hershey's canned syrup)

1 cup cocoa powder
3 cups sugar
¼ tsp. salt
2 cups hot water

Mix dry ingredients in saucepan with a small amount of the water, stirring until smooth. Add remaining water and boil 3 to 5 minutes. Remove from heat.

. . . .

1 tbsp. vanilla

Add. Pour in jar, cover tightly when cool and store in refrigerator.

. . . .

To serve: Use approximately 2 tbsp. syrup per cup of milk or as desired. Serve hot or cold.

Yield: about 1 qt. *Edith Branner*

. . . .

Spicy Cider

1 qt. apple cider
½ of a 3-inch stick cinnamon, crushed
⅓ tsp. whole allspice
½ tsp. whole clove
⅛ tsp. salt

Combine in saucepan. Crumble the cinnamon. Simmer 10 minutes.

. . . .

⅓ cup brown sugar

Add. Strain and serve hot.

. . . .

Yield: 5 servings

. . . .

Delicious Maple Milk

Mix 1 cup cold milk, 2 tbsp. maple syrup, and 1 tsp. vanilla. Serve chilled or hot.

. . . .

Hot Mocha Drink (Low Cal.)

1 tsp. sugar substitute
1 tsp. cocoa powder
1 tsp. instant coffee granules
2 tsp. coffee creamer

Mix in cup.

. . . .

1 cup boiling water

Add. Serve immediately.

. . . .

Yield: 1 serving

. . . .

Spicy Milk Steamers

Spiced Syrup:
2 cups water
¼ cup whole cloves
½ cup red cinnamon candies
½ cup sugar

Combine in saucepan. Simmer 15 minutes, stirring occasionally. Strain. Use 2 tbsp. syrup per each cup of hot milk

....

2 qts. milk
1 cup spiced syrup
⅛ tsp. salt

Heat together just until hot. Serve in mugs topped with marshmallow or a dab of whipped cream.

....

Wanda Good

....

Hot Spicy Punch

2 qts. apple cider or apple juice
1½ qts. cranberry juice
1 cup sugar
½ cup brown sugar
1 tsp. whole cloves
1 tsp. whole allspice
3 sticks cinnamon, crumbled

Combine in saucepan. Add 2 cups water and simmer approximately 10 minutes. Strain and serve hot.

....

Yield: 1 gal.

....

Hot Rhubarb Punch

2 qts. rhubarb concentrate (see recipe on page 34)
2 sticks cinnamon
4 whole cloves

Simmer 20 minutes. (Either tie spices in gauze bag, or strain after heating.)

....

1½ to 2 qts water (to taste)
1½ to 2 cups sugar (to taste)

Add and serve hot.

....

Yield: 3 ½ to 4 qts.

Emma Beachy

....

Liquid Russian Tea

(This tea is often enjoyed by persons who usually do not care for Russian tea. Green tea bags give a better flavor in the tea than the black tea bags.)

1 tsp. whole cloves
1 tsp. crushed stick cinnamon
3 green tea bags
1 qt. water

Combine in saucepan. Simmer 10 minutes. Strain.

....

1 (6 oz.) can frozen orange juice concentrate
juice of 3 lemons
2 to 2¼ cups sugar

Add, stirring until dissolved. Store in refirgerator. Will keep several weeks.

To use: Combine half water with half or less concentrate. Heat until hot, but do not boil. (Tea is better if not made too strong.)

Yield: 6 cups concentrate which makes 3 or more qts. tea   *Berdella Stutzman*

Instant Spiced Tea Mix

2 cups instant tea with lemon
2 cups orange-flavored instant
breakfast drink powder
1 cup sugar
1 tsp. ground cinnamon
½ tsp. ground cloves

Mix well. To serve: place 2 tbsp. mix in a cup and fill with hot water.

Yield: 5 cups mix which makes approximately 40 cups tea

MILK SHAKES

Banana Shake

2 cups milk
1 ripe banana, cut in chunks
1 tbsp. sorghum molasses
1 tbsp. sugar
2 scoops vanilla ice cream
1 tsp. vanilla

Combine all ingredients in blender and process until smooth and frothy. Serve immediately.

Yield: 3 large glasses

Banana Shake (Low Cal.)

2 frozen bananas, cut in chunks
1½ cups skim milk
2 tsp. vanilla
½ cup orange juice (optional)
artificial sweetener to taste

Combine all ingredients in blender and process until smooth.

Yield: 2 servings

Orange Milk Shake

2 cups milk
6 tbsp. (3-oz.) frozen orange juice
concentrate
¼ cup sugar
1 cup vanilla ice cream

Combine all ingredients in blender and process until smooth and frothy. Serve immediately. (Garnish with orange slices if desired.)

Yield: 3 or 4 servings

Chocolate Shake

2 cups milk
3 tbsp. chocolate syrup
3 drops peppermint extract
3 tbsp. sugar
½ tsp. vanilla
2 scoops vanilla ice cream

Combine all ingredients in blender and process until smooth and frothy. Serve immediately.

Variation: For chocolate malt, omit peppermint and add 2 tbsp. malted milk powder.

Yield: 2 or 3 servings

Fruity Milk Shake (Low Cal.)

4 ice cubes
1 cup skim milk
2 tsp. coffee creamer, dissolved in 1
    tbsp. hot water
½ to ¾ cup fresh fruit
1 to 3 tsp. artificial sweetener
½ tsp. flavoring (vanilla or rum)

Combine all ingredients in blender and process until frothy.

Yield: 1 serving

Strawberry Shake

2 cups milk
½ to 1 cup frozen strawberries
2 tbsp. sugar
2 drops red color
½ tsp. vanilla
2 scoops ice cream

Combine all ingredients in blender and process until smooth and frothy. Serve immediately.

Variation: For peach shake, use peaches instead of strawberries and omit color.

Yield: 3 or 4 servings

Thick Pudding Shake

3 cups milk
1 (3½-oz.) pkg. instant pudding
    (chocolate or vanilla)
2 scoops ice cream

Put all ingredients in blender in order listed. Process until smooth and thick.

Variation: For a lighter shake, use flavored gelatin instead of pudding.

Yield: 3 or 4 servings

CHAPTER TWO

BREADS, COFFEE CAKES, & CEREALS

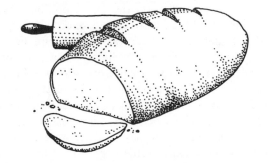

BREADS

Baking bread brings a real sense of satisfaction and pleasure to the creative cook. There is nothing quite like delicious slices of warm homemade bread spread with apple butter or jelly to settle your appetite on a cold winter evening. Just the aroma is enough to delight your family with your efforts to please their taste buds!

To make good yeast-raised bread requires time and patience. Once you've mastered the technique, however, I'm sure you'll agree it is well worth the effort to surprise your family at least occasionally with this special treat.

Yeast breads freeze well and are a much enjoyed item to have on hand for guests.

If you are inexperienced in bread baking, begin early in the day. Give yourself plenty of time to avoid rushing the dough or not having it ready when you plan to serve it. Allow a minimum of at least five hours for the whole mixing, kneading, rising, and baking process.

A hard wheat flour rich in gluten makes the best bread. Lighter milled and softer wheat all-purpose flours can be substituted if necessary, but are not as good for bread. Unfortunately, the labeling of all-purpose flours is a bit confusing—some are harder wheat flours than others. Never use self-rising flour in yeast breads. (I prefer Robin Hood flour for any baking using yeast.) There are special bread flours on the market which are excellent.

If you don't bake bread regularly, keep in mind that flour deteriorates in quality with age. Flour should not be kept in a warm pantry for many months since it will lose its freshness and will not produce the best baking results. If you bake regularly, there should be no problem. However, if you buy special bread flour and bake only occasionally, store the unused portion in the freezer where it should keep indefinitely. Flours also vary in moisture content, so the exact amount needed each time you bake can vary slightly. If dough is sticky after full amount is added, this could be the reason. Simply add a little more flour.

Yeast is available in two types—active dry yeast in either pellet or granular form, and compressed yeast in cake form. The dry yeast stays fresh in a cool dry place until the expiration date on the package. I feel the compressed yeast gives slightly better results, but is very perishable and must be kept refrigerated at all times. It should be used within a few days of purchase. It can be frozen, however, and will keep up to four months in the freezer. Be cautious when buying cake yeast—some grocery stores are not as careful as they should be about keeping their stock fresh. If it is dark and hard around the edges, it will have poor rising ability. Granular dry yeast seems to work quite well, and I prefer this for all-around use. It can be kept in the freezer so you will always have it on hand and do not need to be concerned about freshness.

You can use milk, water, or potato water (the water in which you have cooked potatoes) as liquid in bread dough. If using raw milk, it should always be heated to the boiling point to kill enzymes which may interfere with the rising action of the yeast. Failure to scald the milk makes poor quality bread. It must be cooled to lukewarm before adding to the yeast mixture. Pasteurized milk does not require scalding.

It is important that water for dissolving yeast is at the correct temperature. If not hot enough, it will not dissolve and activate the yeast properly. If too hot, it will kill the yeast cells. For compressed yeast cakes, water should be 95 to 100 degrees. For dry or granular yeast, it should be a little hotter—110 to 115 degrees.

Any good solid shortening, butter, lard, or margerine can be used for the fat in baking bread.

All ingredients for making bread should be at room temperature when you begin to mix the dough.

Procedure for Making Bread

1. Sift flour into large bowl or dishpan.
2. Sprinkle dry yeast or crumble cake of yeast into warm water, stirring until dissolved. Add at least 1 tsp. of the sugar called for in the recipe to the yeast-water mixture. This helps to activate the yeast much more quickly. Stir again until sugar is dissolved. Then let mixture set while you measure other ingredients.
3. If recipe calls for milk, heat milk to the boiling point. Remove from heat and add shortening, salt, and remaining sugar, stirring until dissolved. Then cool to lukewarm before adding to yeast mixture.
4. Combine yeast mixture and liquid/shortening mixture in electric mixer bowl. Add flour, 1 cup at a time, beating *well* after each addition until you have added about half of the total amount of flour called for in the recipe. It is important to beat mixture thoroughly at this point to obtain light tender bread. Then cover and let rest for approximately 20 minutes. This resting time can be omitted, but will give you a lighter, nicer textured bread. It also makes the bread easier to knead without working in too much flour.
5. Add additional flour with a heavy spoon until very stiff. Then use your hands to work remaining flour into the dough until stiff enough to knead. Sprinkle flour over sticky surface as you work to keep your hands and the bowl from getting too sticky. Add the minimum amount of flour possible to obtain a workable dough.

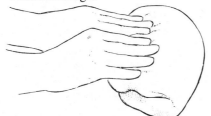

6. Turn dough out on floured surface to knead. Knead the dough by (1) folding the ball of dough over double, (2) pushing it away from you with the heels of your hands, and (3) drawing it back toward you with your fingertips. Give the ball a partial turn, and repeat these motions until dough is smooth and elastic with a satiny appearance. You may continue to sprinkle lightly a little flour over any sticky areas as you knead to keep dough from sticking to hands or table surface, but add sparingly to obtain as light a dough as possible. If too much flour is worked into the dough, the bread will be firm and heavy rather than soft and light.

The kneading process is important. It develops the gluten structure of the dough so that the gas produced by the yeast will be trapped. Kneading takes from 5 to 15 minutes, depending on how large a batch of dough you have, how energetically you work, and your skill. Thorough kneading gives uniform grain, fine texture, and good volume.

7. Grease bowl generously, place dough in bowl. Contact with the greased bowl quickly greases the top of the dough. Turn it over. The generous amount of grease will be sufficient for both the top and bottom of dough. Cover with lid or plastic wrap and let rise in a warm place, preferably from 80 to 85 degrees until double in size. This usually takes about one hour.

For a warm place, turn on oven at lowest setting for 2 or 3 minutes and then turn it off. Place bowl of dough in warm oven. You may need to turn oven on again a time or two for 1 or 2 minutes during rising time to maintain warmth, but don't accidentally leave it on! The lowest setting on most ovens is too hot and will cause a yeasty taste in the bread, or even kill the yeast. Some persons place a pan of hot water in the oven beside the dough and change it several times to maintain warmth. On a sunny day, you can set the bowl of dough in the sunlight. Some people even set it on a heating pad turned on medium!

It is important for the dough to rise properly. It should rise until double in size. Do not let dough overrise. This will greatly damage the quality of the bread. The yeast cells stretch beyond their capacity and break. Dough will not rise properly the second time and bread will have poor volume, a course texture, and a yeasty taste when baked. Dough that did not rise enough tends to be heavy and soggy. To test dough, quickly press two fingers deeply into dough. If the indentation remains, the dough is ready to be punched down.

8. To punch down dough, plunge your fists into the center of the dough, fold over edges of dough from all sides, and punch down again. Do this several times to break up the large gas pockets in the dough. Then turn dough over so smooth side is up. Let rise until double again. (This second rising time makes a nicer finer-textured bread. It does not take quite as long for the second rising as the first. If you need to delay baking the bread because of your schedule, it may be worked down another additional time. This additional rising does not improve nor hinder the quality of the bread. It may also be placed in refrigerator tightly covered to retard rising. Be sure to let it rise until double, however, when removing from refrigerator.) When dough has doubled again, it is ready to shape into loaves.

9. Remove dough from bowl onto a greased counter and divide into desired portions. This is done most easily with a knife. Flatten each portion and press out all the air either with your fists, with the heels of your hand, or with a rolling pin. Fold over each end of rectangle, pressing dough firmly as you proceed. Then roll up loaf from the side. Slap loaf onto the table several times to help remove air bubbles. Place in well greased pan, smooth side up.

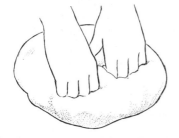 

10. With sharp fork, make deep pricks over loaf to remove all air bubbles. Grease top with shortening or oil and let rise until doubled again. (This is the third rising.)

 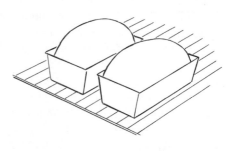

11. Preheat oven to 350 degrees. Jarring the pan on the way to the oven could cause dough to fall slightly. Place pans on lower oven rack so tops don't overbrown, and leave air space around each loaf for even browning. Bake at 350 degrees for approximately 40 minutes until golden brown and it sounds hollow when crust is tapped.

12. Remove bread from pans immediately and grease tops again with butter or shortening. Cover loosely with cloth and let cool away from draft. As soon as bread has cooled, place in plastic bags and close tightly. Store loaves to be used promptly at room temperature. Otherwise, store in freezer.

Quick Breads

Quick breads require an entirely different procedure for mixing than yeast breads. For most quick breads (such as muffins, pancakes, and corn bread) the dry ingredients and liquids are each mixed separately first. Sift dry ingredients together thoroughly to ensure even distribution since liquid is only mixed in for a very short time. Blend beaten eggs and milk thoroughly without beating up excessive foam. The two mixtures are then combined quickly, mixing only until dry ingredients are moistened. Overmixing causes toughness and tunnels. (Many inexperienced cooks overmix these breads in an attempt to make them fluffy and light, and end up with the opposite results!) Muffins can be removed from pans more easily if they are allowed to cool a minute or two after they are taken from the oven. Some cooks prefer baking muffins in cupcake papers for easy handling.

Biscuits are slightly different in that solid shortening is used and is cut into the dry ingredients as in the procedure for pastry. The liquid is then stirred into dry ingredients just enough to mix through so dough can be made into a ball. Dough should be turned out on a floured surface and kneaded approximately 10 times to develop a desirable amount of cohesiveness. It is then rolled out and cut into biscuits.

Waffles are usually mixed in the same manner as pancakes except that in many recipes the beaten egg whites are folded in last to make a lighter batter.

Rolls and Sweet Breads

Rolls and sweet breads are usually made with yeast. Therefore, the procedure is much the same as for baking bread. Bread dough can be used for rolls or sweet rolls if desired. However, it usually does not contain quite as much sugar and yeast. With additional sugar, a little more yeast is needed. (A little sugar activates yeast more rapidly, but a large amount of sugar slightly retards the action of the yeast. This adjustment in amount of yeast needed should be made in recipe.)

The primary difference in bread, rolls, doughnuts, and sweet breads is the final shaping of the dough before the last rising and the adding of additional sugar, butter, and spice to sweet rolls. Dough can be shaped into most any imaginable form—from braids, baskets, and crescents to tea rings, cloverleaf, or Parker House rolls, knots, or simply into balls. The main thing to watch is that you don't have long thin areas of extended dough which will become overdone and hard during baking until thick center areas are done. The easiest way to divide dough evenly for rolls is by cutting portions in half several times until you get down to small amounts which may be cut into thirds or halves, depending on whether it comes out evenly. Brush a small amount of vegetable oil over tops of rolls before baking for a soft crust.

There are many ways to be creative with sweet roll decorations for special oc-

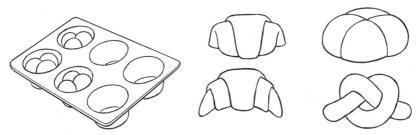

casions. Combinations of raisins, nuts, candied cherries, spices, and coconut, with and without icings, are numerous.

Cinnamon rolls are made by rolling out sweet bread dough into a rectangle.

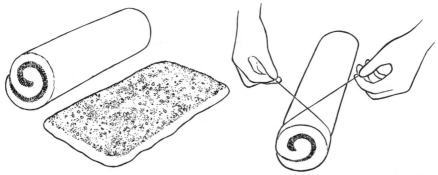

Spread with brown sugar and cinnamon. May also be sprinkled with nuts or raisins if desired. Roll up dough jelly-roll fashion and slice in approximately 1-inch thick slices. Lay slices in greased pans to rise. Slices may also be cut with a strong thread or dental floss. This works easier than you may think!

A brown sugar syrup may be placed in the pans before adding slices of rolls. (See recipe on pages 66 and 67.) When hot rolls are turned out of the pans, this gooey syrup coats the tops. These are often called **sticky buns.**

Tea rings are made from sweet roll dough. Roll up as for cinnamon buns.

Instead of slicing roll, form dough into a ring. Place in pan and seal the two ends together. With a sharp knife or kitchen shears, cut slits ¾ of the way through the dough at 1 to 1½-inch intervals all around the ring being careful to keep center intact. Slightly twist each section spreading apart enough to see filling inside. Let rise until double. Bake as for cinnamon buns. Baking time may need to be slightly longer, depending on the thickness of the ring.

Doughnuts are, of course, rolled out and cut with a doughnut cutter. They are usually fried in hot fat rather than baked.

Deep Fat Frying: A deep fat fryer is excellent to use for frying a variety of foods because of the built-in thermostat which keeps fat at temperature you set. However, any deep heavy saucepan or kettle can be used on top of the stove.It is important that the container be large enough for the amount of fat you are using. Never fill much over half full to allow for bubbling up when food is added to hot fat.

An electric skillet filled half full of fat may be used for frying doughnuts and other dry foods since there is little bubbling up with dry foods. Foods containing moisture, however, such as potatoes for french frying, often bubble up and need extra space to prevent bubbling over. These foods should be patted as dry as possible before frying to avoid excessive bubbling and spattering. A 3- or 4-qt. kettle should be used for approximately 3 or 4 pounds of fat.

Use a good solid shortening or oil for deep fat frying. Butter and margarine are not considered good for deep fat frying because of their low smoking point. Do not skimp on the amount of fat used. It should be deep enough to cover food and to allow food to move around.

Fat is usually heated to approximately 375 degrees (recipes vary from 365 to 385 degrees). If fat is not hot enough, food will absorb too much fat until it is cooked. If fat is too hot, the outside will become too brown until the center is done.

Never heat fat to the smoking point. This breaks down and damages the fat, spoiling it for reuse.

Grease utensils used for transporting food to the fat by dipping in the hot fat first, to avoid having food stick to utensils.

Never let fat dribble down the sides of the kettle onto the burner of the stove. This could cause a fire. If kettle of fat should catch on fire, quickly cover it with a lid to extinguish the blaze and turn off burner. Never throw water on flames (this would only scatter the fire). If a fire extinguisher is not handy, throw dry baking soda or salt on any surrounding flames.

Do not put large amounts of food in at once.This will cool the fat too much and food will take too long to cook. Doughnuts or other food will become very greasy. It will also cause boil-over with foods containing moisture. With food such as french fries, fill basket only about ¼ full. After removing one batch of food, let fat reheat to desired temperature before adding next batch. When draining foods on paper towels to absorb grease, place newspaper underneath towels to help soak up grease and save on amount of towels needed.

After using fat, cool to safe temperature to handle. Then strain to remove any particles of food. Fat can be reused a number of times if properly handled.

Clarifying Fat: If needed, fat can be clarified to remove any odors from previously cooked strong-flavored food such as onions. To clarify fat, peel and slice one medium-size raw potato and add to cooled fat. (Use 4 or 5 thin slices of potato for each cup of fat.) Heat slowly, stirring occasionally until potato slices are browned—approximately 20 minutes. Remove potato and discard, cool fat slightly, and strain it through a fine strainer. Fat should be stored in covered container in cool place.

For next batch of food to be french fried, additional new fat may be added to give volume needed.

Cereals

Home-cooked cereals are much more economical than ready-to-eat boxed cereals. They are easy to prepare and are very nutritious.

Manufacturers tend to give minimal cooking times for cereals since many persons are sold on quick-fix products. However, a little longer cooking time often produces a better flavored cereal. Cooking times vary, of course, depending on whether the grain is whole or crushed, or finely or coarsely milled. Finely milled cereals usually take from 5 to 10 minutes to cook, and coarsely milled or whole wheat cereals from 20 minutes to 1 hour.

For cooking most cereals figure approximately 3 or 4 times as much water as cereal. Fine granular cereals take a little more, and flaked cereals a little less. For longer cooking time, slightly more water is needed. About 1/4 tsp. salt per cup of cereal should be added.

Cooked cereal may be varied in a number of delicious ways. Use milk for cooking instead of water. The starch will swell slightly more when cooked in milk. Sweeten with brown sugar instead of white sugar, or use honey or molasses to sweeten. Add raisins, chopped dates, or any dried fruit. Coconut or nuts may also be added as well as cinnamon or other spices. Chopped raw apples also make a delicious addition to oatmeal. Cook cereal according to directions, add chopped peeled apple, and cook several additional minutes.

Leftover cooked cereal should not be wasted. It can be sliced when cold and fried in a little fat in skillet. Serve with syrup or apple butter. It can also be used in recipes that call for bread crumbs, such as meat loaf.

TIPS FOR BREADS, SWEET BREADS, AND CEREAL

•To test whether yeast is still active (if in doubt) mix small amount of yeast in ¼ cup warm water in which ¼ tsp. sugar has been dissolved. Yeast should begin to foam and bubble within 5 to 10 minutes. If it doesn't, yeast should be discarded since it obviously is dead.

•To reduce rising time of bread, the amount of yeast may be increased. One package dry yeast to 2 cups liquid will rise in approximately 1 hour. Two packages yeast to 2 cups liquid will rise in ap-proximately 35 minutes. Extra yeast does not make a yeasty taste. A yeasty taste is caused by dough being too warm during rising or by rising too long. Bread will have a nicer texture, however, with slower ris-ing. When doubling recipes or for large amounts of bread, the amount of yeast does not need to be doubled. Usually 1½ times the single amount is sufficient.

•The addition of a little ground ginger to the dry ingredients when mixing bread dough seems to improve the rising ability of the yeast. Add ¼ tsp. for a two-loaf recipe.

•If whole wheat flour is sifted, bran from flour will remain in sifter. Be sure to return to flour mixture after any lumps are removed.

•Bread recipes which do not include eggs and milk usually turn out better and will dry out less quickly than those that do—especially bread with eggs included. Recipes using potato liquid or water for the liquid usually make better bread.

•Bread keeps best stored in a cool dry place, but *not* in the refrigerator. If weather is warm, store extra bread in the freezer, then thaw when needed.

•Bread is more moist if allowed to thaw slowly. To serve a large loaf of frozen homemade bread for Sunday dinner, remove it from the freezer and place it in the refrigerator Saturday night. Then remove it from refrigerator on Sunday morning and place it on the counter top until noon.

•Do not overbake breads and especially rolls, muffins, and biscuits. Overbaked breads are dry and crumbly, and rolls become hard.

•The amount of flour needed for breads and pastries can vary, depending on how much moisture the flour already contains. This depends on how the flour was handled and stored both before and after you purchased it and on weather conditions. Flour keeps best in a cool dry place.

•The use of granite or heavy black pans for baking bread causes it to burn or turn too dark on the bottom. Use shiny aluminum pans for best results. Allow air space around each pan in the oven so heat can circulate properly.

•To avoid last-minute rush when making muffins for guests, mix dry ingredients and liquids separately ahead. They can be combined quickly at the last minute and baked.

•To cut biscuits in a hurry, roll out dough and cut in squares or triangles with a knife instead of using biscuit cutter.

•If you do not wish to heat up the oven for baking a few biscuits on a hot summer day, try cooking them in a skillet on top of the stove. Grease skillet. Use very low heat, cover tightly, and cook about 2 to 4 minutes on each side until lightly browned.

•If you do not have muffin tins, use cupcake papers placed inside regular canning jar rings to hold them in place. Place on cookie sheet. Large quantities can be baked at once with this method.

•Muffins will release from pans more easily without tearing if allowed to cool a few minutes in the pans before removing. For nicely shaped muffins that do not have a rim around the top, do not grease the sides of the muffin tins. Grease only the bottoms.

•The addition of 1 tsp. jelly or peanut butter on top of muffins before baking adds a delicious touch.

•Freeze any leftover pancakes to be popped in the toaster or microwave for quick use later.

•If you don't use a lot of corn meal, buckwheat flour, etc., store partly used container in the freezer to prevent contamination with weevils.

•Heat waffle iron hot before pouring in batter to prevent sticking. A small amount of fat may be needed to coat iron for first batch. Do not scrub iron with soap or abrasives between use. Use damp cloth or paper towel to wipe iron so coating remains. If thorough cleaning is needed, season with extra fat before using.

•For novelty pancakes that children love, first drop small amounts of pancake batter into skillet forming eyes, nose, and mouth, or other design. Let fry several seconds to set design; then pour regular amount of batter over top. When turned over, pancake will retain clown face.

BREADS, COFFEE CAKES, AND CEREALS RECIPES

YEAST BREADS

Angel Biscuits

½ cup warm water 2 pks. dry yeast 1 tbsp. sugar	Combine and stir until dissolved. Set aside.
5½ cups flour 1 tsp. baking soda 2 tsp. baking powder 2 tsp. salt 3 tbsp. sugar	Sift together.
1 cup shortening	Cut in.
2 cups thick sour milk or buttermilk	Make a well in dry ingredients and add buttermilk and yeast mixture. Blend thoroughly.

Turn out on floured surface and knead several times. Roll out to ½ inch thickness and cut with biscuit cutter. Place on greased baking sheet and let rise until double, approximately 1 hour. Bake at 350 degrees for about 12 minutes

Yield: 32 to 36 biscuits

Angel Flake Rolls

4 pks. dry yeast ⅔ cup warm water 1 tbsp. sugar	Combine and stir until dissolved. Set aside.
2 ½ cups milk	Scald in large pan.
¼ cup sugar 1 tbsp. salt ⅔ cup shortening	Add, stirring until dissolved. Then cool to lukewarm and add yeast mixture above.
6½ cups flour or more if needed	Add, and knead until smooth and elastic.

Let rise until double. Punch down and let rise again. Then shape into 48 rolls and place in greased pan. For softer crusts, grease tops with vegetable oil. Bake at 350 degrees for approximately 20 minutes. Brush tops with butter or margarine while hot. (For whole wheat rolls, use 2 cups whole wheat flour in place of 2 cups of the white flour.)

Yield: 48 rolls

Fannie Heatwole, my mother

Batter Bread

¾ cup warm water 1 pk. dry yeast 1 tbsp. sugar	Combine and stir until dissolved. Set aside.
1 cup hot water ⅓ cup shortening ¼ cup sugar 1½ tsp. salt	Combine and stir until melted. Cool to lukewarm.
1 egg, slightly beaten	Combine with yeast mixture. Then add to shortening mixture.
4½ to 5 cups flour (divided in half)	Gradually beat in half the flour. Beat thoroughly, then let rest 10 minutes..

Then stir in remaining flour—enough to make a stiff, but still stirable dough, stirring as thoroughly as possible. (A heavy-duty electric mixer is great for mixing this bread.) Grease top of dough, cover, and let rise until double. Stir down, and pour in greased round 2-qt. casserole dish. Grease top with vegetable oil. Let rise until double again. Bake at 350 degrees for approximately 40 minutes. Remove from dish and brush top with butter or margarine while hot. (For whole wheat bread, use 2 cups whole wheat flour in place of 2 cups of the white flour.)

Yield: 1 loaf

Cinnamon Swirl Bread

½ cup warm water 2 pks. dry yeast (1 tbsp. sugar)	Combine and stir until dissolved. Set aside. (Use 1 tbsp. of the sugar listed below.)
1 cup milk, scalded ½ cup shortening ½ cup sugar 2 tsp. salt	Combine and stir until melted. Cool to lukewarm, then add to yeast mixture.
1 egg, slightly beaten ⅔ cup orange juice 2 cups flour	Add, beating until smooth. Let rest 10 minutes.
5 to 5½ cups more flour	Add and knead until smooth and elastic.

Grease top and place in greased bowl. Cover and let rise until doubled. Punch down. Divide dough into two balls. Let rest 10 minutes. Roll each ball into a 7 × 15 rectangle ½ inch thick.

½ cup brown sugar 1 tbsp. ground cinnamon	Mix.
2 tbsp. melted butter	Spread over dough. Then sprinkle with brown sugar mixture above.

Roll up rectangles jelly-roll fashion and place in 2 greased 9 × 5 loaf pans sealed side down. Grease tops with oil or melted butter. Let rise until double again. Bake at 350 degrees for 35 to 40 minutes. Grease tops with butter while hot. (May omit orange juice and use additional milk instead.)

Yield: 2 loaves

(Refrigerator) Crescent Rolls

1 cup warm water **1 pk. dry yeast** **1 tbsp. sugar** **3 eggs, beaten**	Beat together and let stand 10 minutes
½ cup sugar **½ cup soft margarine** **1 tsp. salt**	Add.
5 cups flour	Add, and knead until smooth.

Place in large covered container and refrigerate overnight, or up to one week. Divide dough in half. Roll each half in a 12-inch circle and cut into 16 pie wedges each. Roll up each wedge starting at wide end. Place in greased baking pans and let rise 2 or 3 hours or until double. Bake at 350 degrees for 12 to 15 minutes.

Yield: 32 rolls

Joyce Heatwole

French Bread

½ cup warm water **2 pks. dry yeast** **2 tsp. sugar**	Combine and stir until dissolved. Set aside.
2 cups boiling water **2 tbsp. shortening** **2 tsp. salt** **2 tbsp. sugar**	Combine and stir until melted. Cool to lukewarm and add to yeast mixture.
6½ to 7 cups flour	Beat in 2 cups with electric mixer. Then add remaining flour with spoon stirring well.

Let rise until double. Punch down and let rise until double again. Divide dough in half and roll up each half like a jelly roll. Place on greased cookie sheet. Make about 5 slashes across top of each loaf about ¼ inch deep. Let rise until double. Beat together 1 egg and 2 tbsp. milk slightly. Brush over tops of loaves. Sprinkle with sesame seeds. Bake at 350 degrees for 20 to 25 minutes.

Yield: 2 loaves

Kathryn Forrester

Delicious Dill Bread

½ cup warm water 2 tbsp. dry yeast 1 tbsp. sugar	Combine and stir until dissolved. Set aside.
2 cups cottage cheese	Heat until lukewarm.
2 eggs, beaten	Add to warm cheese, beating well.
2 tbsp. sugar 2 tbsp. oil 2 tsp. salt 4 tsp. dill seed 2 tbsp. dry minced onion ½ tsp. baking soda	Add to cheese mixture. Then add yeast mixture.
2¼ cups flour	Add with electric mixer, beating well.
2¼ cups more flour	Stir in with heavy spoon.

Cover and let rise in bowl until double in size, about 1 hour. Stir down and turn into 2 well-greased 1 ½-qt. casserole dishes for round loaves, or two 9 × 5 pans. Spread 1 tsp. oil over top of each loaf smoothing out roughness. Let rise until double again. Place on lower rack in 350 degree oven and bake approximately 40 minutes. Brush tops with butter while hot.

Yield: 2 loaves

Top-Notch Dinner Rolls

1 cup warm water 2 pks. dry yeast (2 tbsp.) 1 tbsp. sugar	Stir together until dissolved. Let set until foamy.
1½ cups hot water ½ cup shortening ½ cup sugar 2½ tsp. salt	Stir together until melted. Cool to lukewarm and add to yeast mixture.
approximately 10 cups sifted flour (8 cups unsifted)	Gradually add half of flour, beating well. Then work in just enough more flour to make a soft but not sticky dough.

Grease top and place in greased bowl. Cover and let rise until double. Punch down and let rest 10 minutes. Shape into rolls and let rise until double. Bake at 350 degrees about 25 minutes until lightly browned.

Yield: about 32 large rolls   *Ruby Petersheim*

Oatmeal Bread

½ cup warm water 2 pks. dry yeast 1 tsp. sugar	Combine and stir until dissolved. Set aside.
1 cup quick oats ½ cup whole wheat flour ½ cup brown sugar 1 tbsp. salt	Mix in bowl.
2 cups boiling water 2 tbsp. margarine	Add, stirring until well mixed. Cool to lukewarm and add yeast mixture.
1 cup grated sharp cheese 1 med. onion, minced or 1 tbsp. granulated onion	Add.
5 cups flour	Add, and knead until smooth and elastic.

Grease, cover and let rise until double. Punch down and let rise again. Then divide dough in half, shape into loaves and place in two greased 9 × 5 pans. Grease tops of loaves with oil and let rise until double again. Bake at 350 degrees for 30 to 40 minutes. Brush tops with butter while hot.

Yield: 2 loaves

Dorothy Shank Showalter

Pepperoni and Cheese Loaf

Thaw a 1 lb. loaf of frozen bread dough and allow to rise according to package directions. Divide dough in half and set one portion aside. Turn out remaining half of dough on lightly floured surface. Roll into a 10-inch circle.

1 egg, beaten ½ cup grated Parmesan cheese	Combine and spread half of mixture over circle of dough, leaving a ½-inch margin at edges.

2 (3 ½-oz.) pkgs. sliced pepperoni
   (reserve half)
2 cups shredded mozzarella cheese
   (reserve half)
	Layer half of each over egg mixture. Reserve other half.

¾ tsp. dried crushed oregano (reserve half)	Sprinkle half over cheese. Reserve half.

Roll up dough jelly-roll fashion. Seal edges and fold under ends. Place loaf, seam side down, on an ungreased baking sheet. Brush top with butter. Repeat procedure with other half of dough and reserved half of ingredients. Bake at 375 degrees for 30 minutes. Slice and serve.

Yield: 6 to 8 servings

Donna Lou Heatwole

Unleavened Bread (or Communion Bread)

*(According to some research I've done, it seems unleavened bread has not tradi-
tionally been used to a large extent in the Mennonite Church. Some congregations have preferred to use a large loaf of leavened bread, breaking it apart sym-
bolically of the way Jesus must have broken bread. Others cut the loaves of bread
into long strips prior to the service for convenience in breaking off a portion for
each person. There does seem to be more interest in using unleavened bread in
recent years, however, in light of the symbolism of leaven in the Old Testament
referring to sin. The cracker-like bread sticks here are made much like pie
dough. The strips are pricked with a fork to make it easy to break off a small
portion for each person.)*

4 cups flour **¼ cup sugar** **¾ tsp. salt**	Mix together and reserve ¾ cup of mixture.
¾ cup margarine	Cut into remaining mixture until crumbly.
¾ cup rich milk (evaporated milk or light cream)	Mix with the reserved dry mixture making a batter. Then add to dry crumbly mixture tossing with a fork until moist. Shape into a ball of dough.

Roll out into a ¼-inch thick rectangle. Use a pizza cutter to cut into 1 ¼ × 6 inch strips.
Prick each stick with a fork at 4 even points using a ruler to measure. Place on ungreased
baking sheet and bake at 425 degrees until just beginning to brown on the bottom.

Yield: 200 servings

Evelyn Kratz
Lois Wenger

Pita Bread (or Pocket Bread)

*(This recipe was slightly adapted from one our daughter brought home from a
term in the Middle East with a group of Eastern Mennonite College students.
Young people especially enjoy filling the bread pockets with a variety of fillings.
Use one of the recipes following, or fill with chili, or with the taco sauce used with
the Navajo Tacos on page 299.)*

1 pk. dry yeast **1½ cups warm water** **1 tsp. sugar**	Stir together until dissolved. Let set until bub- bly.
1 tbsp. vegetable oil **1 tbsp. sugar** **1 tsp. salt** **1½ tsp. ground cumin seeds** **1½ cups whole wheat flour**	Add, beating thoroughly until very smooth.
2 cups flour*	Add. Knead until smooth and elastic.

Place in a greased bowl and grease top. Cover and let rise until double, about 1 hour. Punch down dough. Cut into 6 parts. Shape each into a ball. Cover with plastic wrap and let rise until double, about 30 minutes. Sprinkle 2 large baking sheets lightly with wheat bran or cornmeal. Roll each ball into a 6- or 7-inch circle and place on baking sheets. Cover and let rise 30 minutes more. Bake at 450 degrees for 12 minutes, or until puffed and lightly browned. Cut each in half and fill. (*The Middle Easterners like to also use about ¾ cup rye flour in place of ¾ cup of the white flour.)

Filling:

1 lb.hamburger **1 small chopped onion**	Sauté in skillet and drain.

1 (10-oz.) can chicken gumbo soup **⅓ cup chili sauce** **1 tbsp. chopped parsley** **½ cup cooked rice or instant rice** **1 tsp. salt**	Add, and cook several minutes. Spoon into bread shells.

Yield: 6 servings of 2 halves each

Optional Filling:

6 slices* Swiss or provolone cheese **6 (1-oz.) slices* ham**	Cut each slice in half and insert in bread pockets. Heat in microwave or in oven until cheese is slightly softened.

7 cups shredded lettuce **4 hard-cooked eggs, coarsely** **chopped (optional)** **2 med. tomatoes, chopped** **⅓ cup diced green onions**	Combine and spoon into pockets.

¾ cup Thousand Island or Italian **dressing**	Drizzle in.

(*Instead of heating the slices in the pockets, cheese and ham may be cut into julienne strips and added to lettuce mixture if desired.)

Dorothy Shank Showalter

Basic White Bread

1 cup warm water **3 pks. dry yeast or 1 large yeast cake** **2 tbsp. sugar**	Combine and stir until dissolved. Set aside.
2 cups boiling water **⅓ cup shortening** **⅓ cup sugar** **4 tsp. salt**	Combine and stir until melted.
2½ cups cold water	Add. When mixture is lukewarm, add yeast mixture.
6 cups flour	Add, beating well with electric mixer. Let rise ½ hour.
6½ to 7½ cups more flour	Add, and knead until smooth and elastic.

Place in greased pan, grease on top, cover, and let rise until double, approximately 1 hour. Punch down and let rise again. Then divide into 4 portions, shape into loaves, and place in 4 greased pans. Grease tops with oil. Let rise until double again. Bake at 350 degrees for 40 minutes. Brush tops with butter while hot.

Yield: 4 loaves   *Anna Mae Weaver*

Basic Whole Wheat Bread

1 cup warm water **2 pks. dry yeast** **2 tbsp. sugar**	Combine and stir until dissolved. Set aside.
1½ cups milk, scalded **½ cup margarine** **⅓ cup brown sugar** **2 tbsp. sorghum molasses** **4 tsp. salt**	Combine and stir until melted.
2½ cups water	Add. When mixture is lukewarm, add yeast mixture.
8 cups flour **4½ cups whole wheat flour**	Combine flours first, then add 5 cups flour to mixture beating well with electric mixer. Let rest 15 minutes.

Add remaining flour and knead until smooth and elastic. Place in greased pan and grease top. Cover and let rise until double. Punch down and let rise again. Then shape into 4 loaves. Grease tops with oil and let rise until double again. Bake at 350 degrees for 40 minutes. Do not overbake.

(May add 1 cup natural [miller's] bran if desired. Use ½ cup less flour.

Yield: 4 loaves

Christine Burkholder

Whole Wheat Orange Bread

½ cup warm water **2 pks. dry yeast** **1 tbsp. sugar**	Combine and stir until dissolved. Set aside.
1½ cups hot water* **¼ cup butter or margarine** **⅓ cup brown sugar** **½ cup honey** **2 tsp. salt**	Combine and stir until melted. Cool to luke-warm.
1 egg, lightly beaten **grated rind of 1 orange**	Add, then combine with yeast mixture.
4 cups flour **2 cups whole wheat flour**	Combine flours, then add 2 cups of flour beating well with electric mixer. Let rest 10 minutes.

Add remaining flour and knead until smooth and elastic. Place in greased bowl, and grease top. Cover and let rise until double. Turn dough out and knead lightly. Cover and let rest 10 minutes. Shape into two loaves and place in two greased 9 × 5 pans. Let rise until double again and bake at 350 degrees for 40 minutes. (*Juice of the orange may be included with water if desired.)

Yield: 2 loaves

Betty Rossheim

SWEET BREADS

Cream Cheese Danish

Dough Recipe:

½ cup warm water 2 pks. dry yeast 1 tsp. sugar	Combine and stir until dissolved. Set aside.
1 cup commercial sour cream	Heat on low just until barely bubbly.
½ cup butter ½ cup sugar 1 tsp. salt	Add, stirring until dissolved. Cool to lukewarm.
2 eggs, beaten	Add. Then combine with yeast mixture.
4 cups flour	Add, mixing well! Cover and refrigerate overnight.

Cream Cheese Filling: 2 (8-oz.) pkgs. cream cheese, softened ¾ cup sugar	(Make filling the next morning.) Beat together well.
1 egg, beaten ⅛ tsp. salt 2 tsp. vanilla	Add, mixing well.

Divide dough into 4 equal portions. Roll out each portion on floured surface into a 12 × 8 rectangle. Spread ¼ of cream cheese mixture in the center of each rectangle. Fold over dough and pinch edges together. Place rolls on a greased baking sheet with seam side down. Slit each roll on top ½ way through dough at 2-inch intervals resembling a braid. Cover and let rise until double. Bake at 350 degrees for 12 to 15 minutes. Do not overbake.

Glaze: 2 cups powdered sugar 4 tbsp. milk 2 tsp. vanilla	Mix until smooth. Spread over loaves while they are still warm.

Yield: 4 loaves   *Patty Showalter*

Easy Cinnamon Buns

(These buns are delicious and are easier than most since the dough is not kneaded. It is handled like batter bread.)

1 cup warm water 4 pks. dry yeast 1 tsp. sugar	Combine and mix until dissolved. Set aside.

3½ cups hot water **1 cup margarine** **1 cup sugar** **4 tsp. salt**	Combine and stir until melted. Cool to lukewarm and add to yeast mixture.

10 to 12 cups Robin Hood flour	Beat in enough flour to make a thick, but still sticky dough—not stiff enough for kneading.

Place in greased bowl, grease top, and let rise until double in size. Sprinkle flour on counter and roll dough into a rectangle 8 × 42 inches ½-inch thick. Spread ⅓ cup melted butter over dough.

2½ cups brown sugar **1½ tbsp. ground cinnamon** **¾ cup chopped nuts (optional)**	Mix and sprinkle over dough.

Roll up like jelly roll and cut into about l-inch slices. Place in greased pans. Let rise until double again. Bake at 350 degrees for 15 to 20 minutes until lightly browned. Do not overbake.

Glaze:

4 cups powdered sugar **1 tsp. vanilla** **about ⅓ cup hot water**	Mix with enough hot water to make of drizzling consistency. Drizzle over buns while they are hot.

Yield: about 6 pans (8 or 9″ cake pans)   *Shirley Shank*

Soft Cinnamon Rolls

½ cup warm water **2 pks. dry yeast** **2 tbsp. sugar**	Combine and stir until dissolved. Set aside.

1 (3½-oz.) pkg. instant vanilla **pudding**	Mix according to package directions.

½ cup margarine, melted **2 eggs, beaten** **1 tsp. salt**	Add. Then add yeast mixture.

6 cups flour	Add and knead until smooth.

Place in greased bowl and grease top. Cover and let rise until double. Punch down and let rise again. Then roll out and spread with 2 tbsp. melted margarine. Sprinkle with ½ cup brown sugar and 1 tsp. cinnamon. Roll up and cut in about l-inch slices. Place in greased pans and let rise until double again. Bake at 350 degrees for 15 to 20 minutes. Drizzle with powdered sugar glaze while still warm, or frost with caramel frosting.

Yield: two 9 × 13 pans   *Miriam Basinger*

Bakery Doughnuts

(This is a good basic recipe that can be used for dinner rolls or for cinnamon buns if desired. Omit spice if using for rolls.)

4 cups warm water **4 pks. dry yeast** **1 tsp. sugar**	Combine and stir until dissolved. Set aside.

1½ cups soft shortening **1 cup sugar**	Cream together.

4 eggs, beaten **1 tsp. vanilla** **1 tbsp. salt** **1 tsp. mace (optional)** **1 tsp. nutmeg (optional)**	Add and beat well. Then add yeast mixture.

13 to 14 cups flour	Add, and knead until smooth and elastic.

Place in greased bowl and grease top. Cover and let rise until double. Then roll out to ½-inch thickness and cut with doughnut cutter. (Or shape into rolls or make buns.) Let rise until double again. Fry in hot fat—about 360 degrees. Dip in powdered sugar or glaze and drain on rack.

Yield: approximately 9 dozen doughnuts   *Mary Shank, my mother-in-law*

Glaze:

1 lb. powdered sugar (3½ cups) **6 or 8 tbsp. boiling water** **1 tsp. vanilla**	Mix until smooth.

Optional Honey Glaze:

⅔ cup powdered sugar **½ cup honey**	Mix until smooth. Spread on warm doughnuts.

Baked Doughnuts

(If you don't like all the grease with fried doughnuts, try this recipe.)

½ cup warm water **3 pks. dry yeast** **1 tsp. sugar**	Combine and stir until dissolved. Set aside.

2¼ cups milk, scalded **½ cup shortening** **1¼ cups sugar** **1½ tsp. salt**	Combine and stir until melted. Cool to lukewarm.

3 eggs, beaten **¾ tsp. vanilla** **½ tsp. mace** **1½ tsp. nutmeg**	Add, and then combine with yeast mixture.

3 cups flour	Beat in thoroughly with electric mixer. Let rest 10 minutes.
4 additional cups flour	Add, kneading until smooth.

Place in greased bowl and grease top. Cover and let rise until doubled—about 1 hour. Turn out on floured board, roll to ½-inch thickness and cut with doughnut cutter. Lift carefully onto greased baking sheet with spatula. Brush tops with oil and let rise until double. Bake at 375 degrees for approximately 10 minutes until golden brown. Immediately brush tops with melted butter and lightly press buttered side in cinnamon-sugar mixture (1 cup sugar to 1 tbsp. cinnamon), or in powdered sugar, or dip top side in glaze used in previous recipe. (If you don't have enough baking sheets, lay doughnuts on greased sheets of foil to rise. When ready to bake, very carefully slip baking sheet under foil so you do not cause raised doughnuts to fall. You can use one baking sheet to bake many batches of doughnuts.)

Yield: 3 ½ to 4 dozen

Potato Doughnuts

(This is a good basic recipe to use for rolls, cinnamon buns, or doughnuts.)

1 cup warm water **3 pks. dry yeast or 1 large yeast cake** **1 tbsp. sugar**	Combine and stir until dissolved. Set aside.
4 cups milk, scalded **1 cup mashed potatoes** **4 tsp. salt** **1 cup sugar**	Combine and stir until sugar is dissolved. Cool to lukewarm. Combine with yeast mixture.
12 cups flour **1 tsp. baking soda** **1 cup shortening**	Work together as for pie dough. Then add to yeast mixture. Knead until smooth. Add a little more flour if needed.

Place in greased bowl and grease top. Let rise until double, punch down, and let rise again. Then shape into rolls or cinnamon buns, or make into doughnuts as desired. (For cinnamon buns, bake at 350 degrees for 18 to 20 minutes.)

Yield: approx. 9 doz.

Dorothy Shank Showalter

Lemon Bubble Ring (or Pluck-It Bread)

2 cups flour **½ cup sugar** **1 tsp. salt** **2 pks. dry yeast**	Combine.
1 cup milk **½ cup water** **¼ cup butter**	Heat until very warm—l20 to 130 degrees. Gradually add to dry ingredients mixing well.
2 eggs	Add and beat 2 minutes.
½ cup soft butter	Add and beat well.
3 cups flour	Add enough to make soft dough, and knead until smooth and elastic—l0 minutes..

Place in greased bowl and grease top. Cover and let rise until doubled, about 1 hour. Punch dough down and turn out on lightly floured surface. Cut dough in half. Cover with bowl and let rest 15 minutes.

½ cup sugar **grated peel of 2 lemons or 1 orange** **¼ tsp. mace**	Combine.
2 tbsp. melted butter	Have ready.

Cut each half of dough into 16 pieces. Shape each piece into a ball by tucking ends under. Place half of the balls in a buttered tube pan. Brush with half of the melted butter and sprinkle with half of the sugar mixture. Repeat with other half of balls. Cover and let rise until doubled again. Bake at 350 degrees for 35 minutes. Cool in pan 5 minutes. Then remove from pan and cool on rack.

Evie King

Oatmeal-Nut Sticky Buns

⅓ cup warm water **1 pk. dry yeast** **1 tsp. sugar**	Combine and stir until dissolved. Set aside.
1 cup milk, scalded **⅓ cup shortening** **½ cup sugar** **1 tsp. salt**	Combine and stir until melted. Cool to lukewarm.
2 eggs, beaten	Add, and combine with yeast mixture.
1 cup quick oatmeal **1 cup flour**	Add and beat well with electric mixer.
3 to 3½ cups more flour	Add, and knead until smooth and elastic.

. . . .

Place in greased bowl and grease top of dough. Cover and let rise until double in size. Punch down, cover, and let rest 10 minutes. Then divide dough in half and roll out each half into a 12-inch square. Brush with melted butter.

. . . .

Filling:

½ cup sugar
½ cup brown sugar
2 tsp. ground cinnamon

Combine for filling and sprinkle each square with half of filling. Roll up as for jelly roll. Cut each roll into 12 one-inch slices.

. . . .

Sugar Syrup:

Melt 2 tbsp. butter in *each* of 3 round 8 or 9-inch cake pans. Stir 2 tbsp. dark corn syrup or maple flavored syrup, and ¼ cup brown sugar into butter in each pan. Sprinkle ¼ cup nuts in each pan. Place 8 rolls in syrup in each pan. Cover and let rise until double again. Bake at 350 degrees for 18 to 20 minutes until lightly browned. Invert on plates soon after removing from oven so topping will not stick in pan.

Yield: 24 buns.

. . . .

Sour Cream Twists

½ cup warm water
1 pk. dry yeast (1 tbsp.)
1 tbsp. sugar

Combine and stir until dissolved. Set aside.

. . . .

1 cup thick sour cream*
¼ cup sugar
1 tsp. salt
2 eggs, beaten
½ cup soft margarine

Mix, then add to yeast mixture.

. . . .

5 to 5½ cups flour

Add gradually, mixing well.

. . . .

Knead until smooth. Grease, cover, and let rise until double. Then roll out into a rectangle 36 × 8 inches. Spread with 3 tbsp. melted butter. Mix together ½ cup sugar and 2 tsp. cinnamon. Sprinkle over half of the dough, a 36 × 4-inch portion. Then fold uncovered half of dough over sugared half pressing together lightly. Cut into 1 × 4-inch strips. Holding strips at both ends, twist in opposite directions. Place on greased baking sheet. Let rise until double. Bake at 350 degrees for 12 to 15 minutes. Ice with orange icing. (*You may substitute thick sour milk if desired. Increase margarine to ⅔ cup.)

Yield: 36 twists.

. . . .

Orange Icing:

2 cups powdered sugar
2 tbsp. soft shortening
3 tbsp. orange juice

Mix together until smooth. Spread on twists while still warm.

. . . .

QUICK BREADS

Biscuit Mix

(This mix is similar to Bisquick, and may be used in any recipe calling for biscuit mix. It may also be used as a pancake mix.)

8 cups all-purpose flour (may use one-third whole wheat if desired)	Mix together thoroughly.
⅓ cup baking powder	
2 tsp. cream of tartar	
3 tbsp. sugar	
1 tbsp. salt	
1½ cups dry milk powder	

. . . .

2 cups vegetable shortening	Cut in until mixture is fine uniform crumbs.

. . . .

Store in airtight container in cool dry place.

Yield: 13 cups mix which makes 45 to 50 biscuits.   *Cynthia Harman*

. . . .

USES FOR MIX

For Biscuits:
or Basic Dough: Blend together 3½ cups mix and ⅔ cup water. Stir just until liquid is mixed into the dough. Form into a ball and knead slightly. Pat or roll out to ½-inch thickness. Cut with biscuit cutter. Place on greased baking sheet and bake at 375 degrees for 12 to 15 minutes. Makes 12 large biscuits. (To make up full amount of mix at once, add 2½ cups water to the 13 cups mix.)

. . . .

For Cinnamon Rolls:
Roll dough into a rectangle and brush with melted butter. Sprinkle with brown sugar and cinnamon. Roll up as for a jelly roll. Slice, place in greased pans, and bake approximately 15 minutes. Drizzle with powdered sugar glaze while warm.

. . . .

For Pancakes:
Beat 2 eggs. Add 1 cup milk. Stir in 2 cups or more of biscuit mix just until blended. Fry on hot griddle until lightly browned on each side. Makes approximately 12 pancakes.

. . . .

For Pizza:
Pat dough ⅛ inch thick in pan. Cover with desired topping and bake 15 to 20 minutes.

. . . .

For Meat Pinwheels:
Roll out dough to ⅓ inch thickness. Spread with finely chopped meat and gravy. Roll up as for jelly roll. Bake and serve with gravy, chicken or mushroom soup, or cheese sauce.

. . . .

For Potpie or Meat Pie:
Roll to ¼ inch thickness and top chicken or meat pie.

. . . .

For Fruit Shortcake:
Beat together on low for ½ minute: 1½ cups mix, ½ cup sugar, 2 tbsp. soft butter or margarine, ½ cup milk or water, 1 tsp. vanilla, and 1 egg. (May omit egg if desired.) Then beat

4 minutes at medium speed scraping bowl occasionally. Pour into a greased 9-inch cake pan, and bake for 25 to 30 minutes. Partially cool and top with crushed fruit and whipped cream.

. . . .

Buttermilk Biscuits

Sift together into bowl.

3 cups flour
¾ tsp. salt
4½ tsp. baking powder
1 tbsp. sugar
¾ tsp. baking soda

. . . .

6 tbsp. shortening   Cut in until crumbly.

. . . .

1 small egg, slightly beaten   Combine and then stir into mixture.
1⅓ cups thick sour milk or
  buttermilk

. . . .

Knead slightly. Roll to ½-inch thickness and cut with biscuit cutter. Place on greased baking sheet and bake at 350 degrees for 10 to 12 minutes.

Variation: For cheese biscuits, add 1 cup grated cheese and 1 tsp. Italian seasoning to dry ingredients.

Yield: 24 large biscuits

. . . .

Sweet Potato Biscuits

2½ cups flour   Sift together into bowl.
½ cup sugar
5 tsp. baking powder
1 tsp. salt
¼ tsp. cream of tartar
1 tsp. ground cinnamon (optional)

. . . .

½ cup shortening   Cut in until crumbly.

. . . .

1¼ cups cooked mashed sweet   Combine and then stir into mixture.
  potatoes
⅓ cup milk (more or less*)

. . . .

(*Amount of milk may vary slightly depending on how stiff the sweet potatoes are. Potatoes should be mashed without adding any liquid.) Knead slightly. Roll to ½-inch thickness and cut with biscuit cutter. Place on greased baking sheet and bake at 375 degrees for 12 to 15 minutes.

Yield: 18 to 20 large biscuits

. . . .

Corn Bread

1 cup cornmeal
1 cup flour
2 tsp. baking powder
1 tsp. baking soda
½ tsp. salt
2 tbsp. brown sugar

Sift together and mix thoroughly in bowl.

2 eggs, beaten
1 cup thick sour milk
¼ cup oil

Combine and then stir into dry ingredients just until moistened.

Pour into greased 9 × 9-inch pan and bake at 375 degrees 15 to 20 minutes. Serve hot.

Corn Bread Puff

(Mixing procedure is different for this cakelike corn bread.)

½ cup sugar
½ cup butter or margarine

Cream.

2 eggs

Add and beat well.

1 cup yellow cornmeal
1¼ cups flour
3 tsp. baking powder
¼ tsp. salt
1 cup milk

Add combined dry ingredients alternately with milk.

Pour into greased 9-inch square pan and bake at 350 degrees for 35 minutes.

Mexican Corn Bread

1 cup cornmeal
⅓ cup flour
2 tbsp. sugar
1 tsp. salt
2 tsp. baking powder
½ tsp. baking soda

Sift together and mix thoroughly in bowl.

2 eggs, beaten
1 cup buttermilk
½ cup vegetable oil
1 cup cream-style corn
⅓ cup chopped onion
2 tbsp. chopped green pepper
½ cup grated cheese

Combine, then stir into dry ingredients only until moistened.

Pour into greased 9-inch square pan and bake at 350 degrees for 30 minutes.

Taco Crepes

8 to 10 cooked crepes. (For a crispy taco, place cooked crepes on cookie sheet. Fold each crepe in half with crumpled foil inside to hold it open for filling. Heat in 325-degree oven with foil inside for about 10 to 12 minutes or until crisp.) Meanwhile, prepare filling:

1 lb. lean ground beef	Brown, stirring until crumbly and drain.
1 (1¼-oz.) pkg. taco seasoning mix **1 cup water**	Stir in. Bring to boil and simmer uncovered 15 to 20 minutes stirring occasionally. Spoon into crisp shells.
1½ cups grated cheddar cheese **2 cups shredded lettuce** **2 small tomatoes, chopped** **Taco sauce (optional)**	Add to shells and top with sauce if desired.

Yield: 8 to 10 taco crepes   *Elizabeth Yoder*

Basic Dessert Crepes

4 eggs **1 cup flour** **2 tbsp. sugar** **¼ tsp. baking powder** **1 cup milk** **¼ cup water** **1 tbsp. melted butter**	Combine all ingredients in blender container and process for 1 minute. Scrape down sides with rubber scraper and blend 15 seconds more or until smooth.

Refrigerate batter at least 1 hour. Cook in buttered omelet pan until browned. (See detailed directions in recipe for Basic Crepes.) Dessert crepes may be filled with fresh fruit or pie filling. Or fill with instant pudding, or spread with jelly. Top with whipped cream and chopped nuts if desired.

Yield: 20 to 25 crepes.

Basic Crepes

3 tbsp. butter	Melt in omelet pan or crepe pan (teflon pan is good).
3 eggs, slightly beaten **½ cup milk** **½ cup water**	Beat together with electric mixer or rotary beater, beating in melted butter also.
¾ cup flour **½ tsp. salt** **¼ tsp. baking powder**	Blend in until mixture is smooth.

(Blender method of mixing: Combine all ingredients in blender container. Blend for 1 minute. Scrape down sides of container with rubber scraper. Blend for another 15 seconds or until smooth.)

Refrigerate batter at least 1 hour. Heat buttered pan on medium-high heat just hot enough to sizzle a drop of water. For each crepe pour a scant ¼ cup batter in pan. Quickly tilt pan in all directions so batter spreads out thinly. Cook until lightly browned on bottom. Remove from pan, or if desired, turn and brown other side. (Crepes to be filled need browning only on one side. Use unbrowned side for filling.) Stack between sheets of waxed paper or paper towel until ready to use. (NOTE: Crepes should set to a thin lacy pancake almost immediately. If too much batter is poured into pan, pour off excess immediately. If there are holes, add a drop or two of batter for a patch. Crepes may be frozen.) Crepes may be filled with creamed chicken or other meat or sauces; or spread with jelly, apple butter, or pancake syrup. Roll up, or fold in each side ⅓ of the way to serve.

Elizabeth Yoder

Creamed Chicken Filling:

1 fryer-sized chicken **1 small onion** **1 stem celery, chopped**	Simmer together in about 2 cups water until tender—approximately 1 hour. Remove chicken from bones and chop meat. Reserve broth.
3 tbsp. butter or margarine **1 lb. sliced mushroms (fresh or canned)**	Sauté in skillet. Remove from skillet. Divide amount in 2 portions and set aside.
4½ tbsp. butter or margarine	Melt in skillet.
⅓ cup flour **¾ tsp. salt.**	Add.
1½ cups reserved broth **3 eggs yolks, slightly beaten** **1½ cups milk**	Combine and stir in slowly, cooking just until thickened.
1½ cups shredded Swiss cheese	Stir in. (Reserve ¾ cup cheese sauce).
1 (10-oz.) pkg. frozen chopped broccoli, cooked	Add to remaining sauce.

Combine mixture with chicken mixture, and half of mushrooms. Pour ⅓ cup of filling into each crepe. Roll up and place in bake dish. Stir 3 tbsp. milk into reserve cheese sauce, and add remaining half of mushrooms. Spoon over the center of the top of each crepe. Bake at 325 degrees for 20 minutes. Garnish with a sprig of parsley to serve.

Yield: filling for 20 crepes   *Dawn Showalter*

Dumplings

1 cup flour	Sift together.
½ tsp. salt	
2 tsp. baking powder	
(1 tbsp. sugar if using over fruit)	

1 small egg, slightly beaten	Combine, and quickly stir into dry ingredients
⅓ cup milk	just until smooth.

Drop by spoonfuls on top of boiling stew or fruit. Cover tightly at once and simmer 18 minutes. Do not remove cover until done or dumplings will fall! (Simmer only; too high heat will cause toughness.)

Yield: 6 to 8 dumplings

Hush Puppies

1¼ cups cornmeal	Sift together and mix thoroughly in bowl.
¾ cup flour	
1 tbsp. sugar	
½ tsp. salt	
½ tsp. baking soda	
2 tsp. baking powder	
¼ tsp. garlic powder	

1 egg, beaten	Combine, and stir into dry ingredients just until
1 cup thick sour milk or buttermilk	moistened.
3 tbsp. finely chopped onion	

Drop by tablespoonfuls into hot oil (375 degrees) in deep fryer and fry until golden.

Yield: 1 ½ to 2 dozen

Cheesy Spoon Bread

1 cup cornmeal **1 tsp. salt** **½ tsp. dry mustard or 1 tsp.** **prepared mustard** **¼ tsp. black pepper** **3 tbsp. sugar**	Combine in saucepan.
3 cups milk	Stir in gradually to avoid lumps. Then cook and stir constantly until thickened.
1 cup grated cheddar cheese	Stir in until melted. Remove from heat.
6 eggs, beaten	Stir small amount of hot mixture into eggs first, then add to hot mixture, mixing thoroughly.

Pour into a greased 2-qt. casserole dish. Bake at 350 degrees for 45 to 50 minutes until puffy and browned.

Yield: 10 to 12 servings

Southern Spoon Bread

1 cup cornmeal **¼ cup sugar** **1 tsp. salt**	Combine in saucepan.
4 cups milk **½ cup melted butter or vegetable oil**	Stir in gradually to avoid lumps. Then cook and stir constantly until thickened like mush. Remove from heat.
4 egg yolks, slightly beaten	Add small amount of hot mixture to yolks first, then add to hot mixture, mixing well.
4 egg whites, beaten stiff	Fold into mixture.

Pour into a greased 2-qt. bake dish, and set the dish in a 9-inch square or other dish of hot water to bake. Bake at 375 degrees for 35 to 40 minutes.

Yield: 8 servings

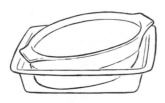

Blueberry Muffins

2 cups flour **3 tsp. baking powder** **½ tsp. salt** **½ cup sugar**	Sift together into bowl and mix thoroughly.
1 egg, beaten **1 cup milk** **¼ cup butter or margarine, melted**	Combine, then stir into dry ingredients only until moistened.
1 cup fresh blueberries, sweetened **(drain, if using canned berries)**	Fold in.

Fill greased muffin cups ½ to ⅔ full. Bake at 375 for 15 to 20 minutes.

Yield: 12 muffins

Carrot-Raisin Muffins

3 eggs	Beat well.
⅓ cup brown sugar	Gradually add, beating until fluffy.
½ cup honey or molasses **⅔ cup vegetable oil**	Blend in.
1 cup chopped raisins **1 cup shredded carrots** **2 cups natural bran** **½ cup wheat germ**	Add.
2 cups flour **2 tsp. baking powder** **1 tsp baking soda** **1 tsp. salt** **1¼ cups milk**	Add sifted dry ingredients alternately with milk.
Topping: **2 tbsp. brown sugar** **2 tbsp. chopped walnuts**	Combine.

Fill greased muffin cups ¾ full. Sprinkle with topping. Bake at 375 degrees for 18 to 20 minutes.

Yield: 18 muffins   *Evelyn Basinger*

French Brunch Puffs

1 egg, beaten ⅓ cup soft shortening ½ cup sugar	Beat together thoroughly.

1½ cups flour 1½ tsp. baking powder ½ tsp. salt ¼ tsp. nutmeg ½ cup milk	Sift dry ingredients together and add alternately with milk.

Fill greased muffin cups ⅔ full. Bake at 375 degrees about 20 minutes. Then while hot, dip tops in melted butter (2 tbsp.) and then lightly press in mixture of cinnamon and sugar (¼ cup sugar and ½ tsp. cinnamon).

Yield: 12 puffs

Cheese-Stuffed Pumpkin Muffins

(These muffins have a surprise center of cheese that gives the effect of pumpkin pie.)

1 (3-oz.) pkg. cream cheese, cut in 12 cubes cinnamon and sugar to garnish	Have ready.

2 cups flour ½ cup sugar 3 tsp. baking powder 1½ tsp. pumpkin pie spice ½ tsp. salt ½ cup chopped pecans	Combine in bowl.

2 eggs, slightly beaten ¾ cup canned pumpkin ½ cup melted butter or margarine ¼ cup sour cream	Mix, then add to flour mixture, stirring just until moistened.

Fill greased muffin cups ⅓ full. Place a cheese cube in center of each. Add remaining batter to fill cups ⅔ full. Sprinkle with cinnamon and sugar. Bake in 375 degree oven 18 to 20 minutes.

(For coffee cake, spread half of batter in a greased 9-inch square pan. Arrange cheese cubes evenly spaced over the batter. Top with remaining batter. Sprinkle with cinnamon and sugar. Bake approximately 30 minutes.)

Yield: 12 muffins

Carolyn Reed

Oatmeal Muffins

1 cup flour **¼ cup sugar** **3 tsp. baking powder** **½ tsp. salt** **1 cup quick oatmeal**	Sift together into bowl.
½ cup chopped raisins	Add.
1 egg, beaten **1 cup milk** **3 tbsp. oil**	Combine and add, stirring only until moistened. Fill greased muffin cups ⅔ full.
Topping: **2 tbsp. sugar** **2 tsp. flour** **1 tsp. ground cinnamon** **1 tsp. margarine, melted**	Mix well and sprinkle over each muffin before baking.

Bake at 375 degrees for about 20 minutes.

Yield: 12 muffins

Old-Timey Raisin Muffins

1 cup raisins **¾ cup water**	Combine in saucepan and simmer 20 min. Drain, and reserve liquid.
½ cup soft butter or margarine **¾ cup sugar**	Cream well.
2 eggs	Add, beating until fluffy.
1½ cups flour **1½ tsp. baking powder** **½ tsp. salt** **½ tsp. ground cinnamon**	Sift together. Add water to reserved raisin liquid to make ½ cup liquid, and add alternately with sifted dry ingredients. Stir in raisins.

Spoon into greased muffin cups, filling ⅔ full. Bake at 375 degrees for 15 to 20 minutes.

Yield: 18 muffins

Refrigerator Raisin Bran Muffins

(Large Batch)

4 cups all-bran cereal 2 cups boiling water	Pour boiling water over cereal and let stand 15 minutes.
1 cup soft shortening 3 cups sugar	Cream thoroughly.
4 eggs, beaten	Add, beating until fluffy. Then add bran mixture.
5 cups flour 5 tsp. baking soda 1 tbsp. salt 1 qt. thick sour milk or buttermilk	Add sifted dry ingredients alternately with milk.
1½ cups raisins	Fold in.

May store mix in refrigerator for several weeks in covered container. To use: Fill greased muffin cups ⅔ full. Bake at 375 degrees for 20 to 25 min.

Yield: 6 dozen muffins   *Mae Shank*

Sugary Orange Muffins

2 cups Bisquick ½ cup sugar ½ cup chopped nuts	Combine in bowl.
1 egg, beaten ½ cup orange juice ½ cup orange marmalade 2 tbsp. salad oil	Combine, then stir into dry ingredients just until moistened. Fill greased muffin cups ¾ full.
Topping: ¼ cup sugar 1½ tbsp. flour ½ tsp. ground cinnamon ¼ tsp. nutmeg 1 tbsp. butter	Combine thoroughly and sprinkle on muffins before baking.

Bake at 375 degrees for 15 to 20 minutes.

Yield: 12 muffins   *Alice Trissel*

FRUIT BREADS AND COFFEE CAKES

Banana Oatmeal Bread

½ cup shortening 1 cup sugar	Cream thoroughly.

2 eggs ½ tsp. vanilla	Add, beating until fluffy.

1 cup flour 1 cup quick oatmeal 1 tsp. baking soda ½ tsp. salt ½ tsp. ground cinnamon 1½ cups mashed bananas (3 medium) ¼ cup milk	Add sifted dry ingredients alternately with bananas and milk.

½ cup chopped raisins	Fold in.

Pour in greased 9 × 5 loaf pan and bake at 350 degrees for 50 to 60 minutes. Cover 5 minutes after removing from oven to cool. (This keeps moisture in cake.)

Carrot-Pineapple Bread

3 cups flour 2 cups sugar 2 tsp. baking powder 2 tsp. baking soda 2 tsp. ground cinnamon ½ tsp. salt	Sift together in mixer bowl.

4 eggs, beaten 1⅓ cups vegetable oil 1 tsp. vanilla 2 cups shredded carrots 1 cup crushed pineapple, undrained	Stir in. Then beat at medium speed of electric mixer for 2 minutes.

Pour into two greased 9 × 5 loaf pans. Bake at 350 degrees for 50 to 55 minutes, or until toothpick inserted in center comes out clean.

Cranberry Nut Bread

2 cups flour
1 cup sugar
1½ tsp. baking powder
½ tsp. baking soda
1 tsp. salt

Sift together into bowl and mix thoroughly.

1 egg, well beaten
¾ cup orange juice
1 tbsp. grated orange rind
¼ cup vegetable oil

Combine, then stir into flour mixture just until moistened.

1 cup chopped cranberries
½ cup chopped nuts

Fold in.

Pour into a greased 9 × 5 loaf pan and bake at 350 degrees for 45 to 50 minutes.

Pumpkin Bread

3 eggs, well beaten
¾ cup vegetable oil
2¼ cups sugar
2¼ cups canned pumpkin

Beat together.

2½ cups flour
2 tsp. baking powder
1½ tsp. baking soda
1 tsp. salt
1 tsp. ground cinnamon
½ tsp. ground cloves
½ tsp. nutmeg

Sift together and blend in.

½ cup chopped nuts
½ cup chopped dates or chopped
  raisins

Fold in.

Pour in 2 greased 9 × 5 loaf pans and bake at 350 degrees for 45 to 50 minutes.

Strawberry Bread

2 eggs, well beaten
½ cup vegetable oil
1 cup sugar
½ tsp. vanilla
½ tsp. almond extract

Beat together well.

1⅔ cups flour
½ tsp. baking powder
½ tsp. baking soda (see next page)

Add sifted dry ingredients alternately with strawberries.

½ tsp. salt
1½ cups frozen strawberries,
   thawed and *lightly* drained

. . . .

½ cup chopped nuts   Fold in lightly.

. . . .

Pour into a greased 9 × 5 loaf pan and bake at 350 degrees for 50 to 60 minutes or until done.

. . . .

Zucchini Bread (or Cake)

3 eggs, well beaten   Beat together until fluffy.
2 cups sugar (or half brown sugar if
   desired)
1 cup vegetable oil
2 tsp. vanilla

. . . .

2 cups grated raw zucchini   Blend in.

. . . .

3 cups flour   Sift together and add.
1 tsp. baking powder
1 tsp. baking soda
1 tsp. salt
1 tsp. ground cinnamon
½ tsp. nutmeg

. . . .

½ cup chopped nuts   Fold in.
½ cup chopped raisins

. . . .

Pour into 2 greased 9 × 5 loaf pans and bake at 350 degrees 45 to 50 minutes. For **Zucchini Cake** fold in 1 cup undrained crushed pineapple along with nuts and raisins and bake in 9 × 13 pan for 35 to 40 minutes.

Marie Shank

. . . .

Blueberry Coffee Cake

1 egg, well beaten **⅔ cup sugar** **½ cup oil** **½ tsp. vanilla**	Beat together until fluffy.
1½ cups flour **2 tsp. baking powder** **½ tsp. salt** **½ cup milk**	Add sifted dry ingredients alternately with milk.
1½ cups blueberries (fresh or well drained)	Fold in. Pour into a greased 9-inch square pan.
Topping: **½ cup brown sugar** **⅓ cup flour** **½ tsp. ground cinnamon** **¼ cup melted margarine** **½ cup chopped nuts**	Combine thoroughly and sprinkle over the top.

Bake at 350 degrees for 25 to 30 minutes. Serve warm.

Fruit-Filled Coffee Cake

1 cup margarine **1¾ cups sugar**	Cream together thoroughly.
4 eggs **1 tsp. vanilla**	Add and beat until fluffy.
3 cups flour **1½ tsp. baking powder** **½ tsp. salt** **¼ cup milk**	Add sifted dry ingredients alternately with milk.
2 or 3 cups pie filling or 21-oz. can (blueberry, strawberry, cherry or raspberry)	Have ready.

Spread half of batter in greased 10 × 15 jelly roll pan. Spread pie filling over next. Top with remaining batter. (Drop little mounds of dough all over and gently rake together with fork.) Bake at 350 degrees for about 30 minutes.

Icing: **1 cup powdered sugar** **½ tsp. vanilla** **2 tbsp. milk or more to mix**	Mix until smooth and drizzle over warm cake.

Serve warm.

Elizabeth Yoder

Buttermilk Coffee Cake

2½ cups flour ½ tsp. salt 1 tsp. ground cinnamon ¾ cup sugar 1 cup brown sugar ¾ cup vegetable oil	Mix thoroughly with hands until crumbly. Reserve 1½ cups crumbs.
1 egg, beaten ½ cup thick sour milk or buttermilk 1 tsp. baking powder 1 tsp. baking soda	Combine and add to remaining flour mixture. Beat 2 minutes.
another ½ cup thick sour milk or buttermilk	Add and beat 2 minutes more.

Pour into greased 9 × 13 pan. Sprinkle reserved crumbs over the top. Bake at 350 degrees for 30 minutes. Serve warm.

Variation: Before sprinkling on reserved crumbs, sprinkle chopped nuts, coconut, or finely chopped dates over the top. Then sprinkle on crumbs and a little additional cinnamon.

Harriet Steiner

Orange Coffee Cake

1 cup sugar ½ cup shortening	Cream thoroughly.
2 eggs	Add, beating until fluffy.
2 cups flour 1 tsp. baking powder 1 tsp. baking soda ½ tsp. salt ½ cup thick sour milk or buttermilk ½ cup orange juice	Add sifted dry ingredients alternately with combined liquids.
⅔ cup chopped raisins	Fold in.

Pour into greased 9 × 13 pan and bake at 350 degrees for 25 minutes.

Topping: ¼ cup margarine, melted ½ cup brown sugar 1 cup angel flake coconut ¼ cup orange juice	Combine and spread over hot cake. Broil a few minutes until lightly browned.

Serve warm.

Raspberry Coffee Cake

2 cups Bisquick 1 (3-oz.) pkg. cream cheese 2 tbsp. butter or margarine 2 tbsp. sugar	Mix together as for pie dough until crumbly.

. . . .

1 egg, beaten ¼ cup milk	Combine and stir in with fork just until moistened.

. . . .

½ cup raspberry preserves or ¾ to 1 cup pie filling	Have ready.

. . . .

Turn dough out on floured surface and knead several times. Roll into a 12 × 8 inch rectangle on waxed paper. Spread with preserves or pie filling, leaving ½-inch margin around edges. Fold each side to center of dough. Pinch ends to seal. Transfer to greased baking sheet. Make 1½-inch cuts about 1 inch apart on each side of coffee cake, cutting ⅓ of the way through the dough at each cut. Bake at 360 degrees for 20 to 25 minutes.

. . . .

Glaze: ¾ cup powdered sugar ½ tsp. vanilla 1½ to 2 tbsp. milk to mix	Mix until smooth and pour over cake while still warm.

. . . .

Serve warm.

. . . .

Yummy Any-Cake

(This is a delicious yeast-raised coffee cake and can vary with different kinds of fruits.)

1 pk. dry yeast ¼ cup warm water 1 tsp. sugar	Combine, stirring until dissolved. Set aside.

. . . .

⅔ cup milk, scalded ¾ cup margarine 1 cup sugar 1 tsp. salt	Combine, stirring until melted. Cool to lukewarm.

. . . .

2 eggs, beaten	Stir into yeast mixture and then into milk mixture.

. . . .

3 cups flour	Beat in until smooth.

. . . .

2 cups or a 21-oz. can pie filling apple, cherry, blueberry, etc.	Have ready.

Let rise until double in size. Spread half of dough in greased 9 × 13 pan. Spread any kind of pie filling over dough. Spread remaining dough over top. Let rise again until double. Bake at 350 degrees for 25 to 30 minutes. May be drizzled with powdered sugar glaze, or serve with whipped cream or ice cream. Best served warm.

PANCAKES AND MISCELLANEOUS
Basic Pancakes

1¾ to 2 cups flour 1 tsp. baking soda 1 tsp. baking powder ½ tsp. salt 2 tsp. sugar	Sift together into bowl and mix thoroughly.
2 eggs, beaten 1¾ cups thick sour milk or buttermilk ⅓ cup oil	Combine first, then stir into dry ingredients only until moistened.

Fry on hot griddle until browned on each side.

Variations: For **corn cakes,** add 1 cup cornmeal in place of 1 cup of flour. For **whole wheat cakes,** add 1 cup whole wheat flour and ¾ cup white flour.

Yield: 14 to 16 pancakes

Oatmeal Pancakes

¾ to 1 cup flour 1 tsp. baking soda 1 tsp. baking powder 1 tbsp. sugar 1 tsp. salt 1½ cups quick oatmeal	Sift dry ingredients into bowl, and mix in oatmeal thoroughly.
2 eggs, beaten 1¾ cups thick sour milk or buttermilk ¼ cup oil	Combine first, then add to dry ingredients stirring only until moistened.

Fry on hot griddle until browned on each side.

Yield: 14 to 16 pancakes

Old-Fashioned Buckwheat Pancakes

(Mix the night before.)

½ cup warm water 1 pk. dry yeast 1 tsp. sugar	Combine, stirring until dissolved. Let set several minutes.
1½ cups cold water	Add.
1½ cups flour 1½ cups buckwheat flour 1 tsp. salt	Combine, then beat into yeast mixture until smooth. Cover and place in refrigerator overnight.
2 tbsp. sorghum molasses ¼ cup butter or margarine, melted 1 tsp. soda, dissolved in ½ cup very warm water	(The next morning) Stir in.

Let stand at room temperature for 30 minutes. Then fry pancakes on hot griddle until browned on both sides.

Yield: 18 to 20 pancakes

Waffles

2 cups flour 2 tbsp. sugar 1 tsp. salt 3 tsp. baking powder	Sift together, set aside.
2 eggs, separated	Beat whites until stiff, then beat yolks separately.
¼ cup melted shortening or oil 1¾ cups milk	Combine with egg yolks, then stir into dry ingredients.

Fold in stiffly beaten egg whites last. Bake in hot waffle iron until lightly browned.

Variation: After pouring batter in waffle iron, sprinkle with blueberries, crumbled bacon, or chopped nuts before baking.

Yield: 10 to 12 waffles

Quick Pancake Syrup

1 cup brown sugar **1½ cups water** **1 tbsp. cornstarch**	Combine in saucepan. Cook just until slightly thickened, stirring constantly. Remove from heat.
1 tsp. maple flavoring	Add.

Serve on pancakes, waffles, or scrapple, etc.

Old-Fashioned Cornmeal Mush

1 cup cornmeal **1 cup cold water** **1 tsp. salt**	Mix together.
3 cups water	Heat to boiling in saucepan.

Slowly add cornmeal mixture to boiling water, stirring constantly over medium heat until thickened. Lower heat, cover, and cook 10 to 30 minutes, stirring occasionally. (The longer the cooking time the better!) Serve warm with milk and sugar, or pour into a pan to cool. Refrigerate overnight. Slice and fry in a little fat in skillet until browned on each side. Serve with apple butter or syrup

Variation: To make **scrapple,** add ¾ lb. pork pudding meat while mixture is cooking. Cook the full 30 minutes or longer for best flavor. Cool, slice, and fry as above.

Yield: 6 to 8 servings   *Phyllis Martin Bayse*

Old-Fashioned Ponhoss

(Aunt Annie always said, "Just use your own judgment" about the amounts of ingredients needed! Recipe was acquired by measuring as she stirred in ingredients for her family specialty! You will need 8 cups of broth for the ponhoss which is obtained by cooking approximately 5 lbs. of spareribs or other pork—or beef if preferred—in water to cover. Cook for 2 or 3 hours until tender. Drain off broth, and use meat at another meal. These make delicious barbecued spareribs. If amount of broth isn't quite sufficient, add water to make 8 cups.)

8 cups pork (or beef) broth **2½ cups pudding meat (more or less)**	Heat in heavy cooker.

. . . .

2 cups cornmeal **½ cup flour** **1 tsp. sugar**	Combine first, then slowly mix into broth stirring constantly. (Add before broth gets hot to avoid lumping.)

. . . .

Cook for 1 hour, stirring constantly at first, then less often the longer it cooks just to keep it from sticking. (The secret of good ponhoss, she says, is in the long cooking!) Remove from heat, let set a few minutes to collect excess fat. Skim off all you can, add a little salt if needed, and pour into 2 small loaf pans. When chilled, cut in slices. Flour, and fry in a little margarine in skillet. Serve with eggs, or with syrup or apple butter.

Yield: 12 to 14 servings   *Annie Weaver*

. . . .

CEREALS

Granola Cereal

4 cups quick oatmeal **2 cups raw wheat germ** **1 cup hulled sunflower seeds** **¾ cup chopped nuts (walnuts or pecans)** **1 cup flaked coconut**	Combine in large bowl.

. . . .

1 cup brown sugar **¾ cup cooking oil** **⅓ cup water** **1 tsp. ground cinnamon (optional)** **½ tsp. salt** **2 tbsp. vanilla**	Blend together until smooth. Pour over cereal in bowl stirring until evenly mixed.

. . . .

Spread on large baking tray and bake at 275 degrees for 1 hour stirring every 15 minutes. Cool before storing in airtight container.

Yield: slightly over ½ gal. cereal   *Ella Ruth*

. . . .

Maple Granola

6 cups oats
1½ cups coconut
2 cups raw wheat germ
1 cup chopped walnuts or almonds
½ cup sesame seeds

Combine in bowl.

. . . .

¾ cup brown sugar
⅓ cup honey
2 tbsp. sorghum molasses
½ cup oil
2 tbsp. water
3 tsp. maple flavor
½ tsp. salt

Blend together until smooth. Pour over cereal in bowl, stirring until evenly mixed.

. . . .

Spread on large tray and heat in 325-degree oven for 30 minutes, stirring every 10 minutes until very lightly toasted. Cool and store in airtight container.

Yield: 3 qts. cereal

. . . .

Grape Nuts

3½ cups whole wheat graham flour
1 cup brown sugar
1 tsp. baking soda
1 tsp. salt

Combine in mixing bowl.

. . . .

2 cups thick sour milk or buttermilk
1 tsp. maple flavoring

Add, beating until smooth.

. . . .

Spread dough in 2 greased 9 × 13 pans and bake at 350 degrees for 20 to 25 minutes until golden brown. Crumble cake with hands while warm. When cool run through coarse blade on food grinder or grate through very coarse sieve. May also use bottom of glass jar to mash into coarse crumbs after cake is dry. Spread on trays and heat in 325 oven for 15 to 20 minutes until crisp. Store in airtight container.

Yield: about 7 cups cereal

. . . .

How to Cook Oatmeal

1¼ cups water	Bring to rapid boil.

¾ cup quick oatmeal	Stir in slowly, so water keeps boiling as you stir.
¼ tsp. salt	Cover and cook 1 to 3 minutes.
2 tsp. brown sugar	

A little longer cooking develops better flavor. Raisins, dates, or coconut, or a little cinnamon may be added if desired. Or add a peeled chopped apple and cook several additional minutes.

Yield: 2 servings

Baked Oatmeal

(This is a nice way to serve oatmeal to breakfast guests. Baking it adds to the flavor.)

2 eggs, beaten	Mix together thoroughly.
1 cup milk	
½ cup vegetable oil	
1 cup brown sugar	
2 tsp. baking powder	
1 tsp. salt	

3 cups quick oatmeal	Stir in.

Pour into a greased 8 × 12 baking dish. Bake at 350 degrees for approximately 25 minutes. Serve warm with milk.

Yield: 6 to 8 servings   *Mildred Bucher*

CHAPTER THREE

CAKES, FROSTINGS, & COOKIES

CAKES, FROSTINGS, AND COOKIES

Cake baking can be as simple these days as whipping up a mix. Or it can be an elaborate art of creating a masterpiece from scratch to honor the most special occasions that come along.

Many young persons' aspirations for baking are initiated by the desire to be able to bake a cake successfully.

I well remember the first attempt my sister and I made years ago when my parents were away from home one day. We decided to surprise my mother with a cake upon her return. In those days many recipes listed only the major ingredients, assuming that anyone would know the procedure and the pan size as well as the necessary temperature and the baking time.

We must have done quite well with the mixing. However, when we peeped into the oven while it was baking and saw a beautiful tall cake, we were so delighted we took it out immediately. Much to our dismay, it soon began to fall. By the time it had cooled, it looked so sad we invited our hungry brothers to help sample the specimen! Even though the center was doughy, the outer edge was quite delicious. By the time Mother returned, the cake had been devoured except for a sample plus the soggy center portion!

We were apprehensive about what Mother might say, since cakes were a specialty in those days that we didn't bake for just "everyday." The amount we could have at mealtime was also rationed since the family was large. We were pleased that she seemed quite impressed. She told us we had done a very good job except that we had taken the cake from the oven much too soon. This stirred our ambition to master the art.

Recipes are much improved today, however, with exact measurements for all ingredients as well as pan sizes, baking time, and temperature. With a knowledge of correct procedure and good ingredients, you should be able to achieve excellent results. Even though some persons feel the ability to bake well is a matter of good luck or being born with a knack at it, this certainly is not the case!

For youngsters, it is helpful to master cookie baking first, and then proceed with cake baking. If you do have a failure with cookie baking, often you can remedy it with the second panful without ruining a complete batch of dough.

To make a good cake, you must have good ingredients. It is important to patronize a grocery store that has a good turnover of products. If not, you could easily end up buying ingredients or mixes that are too old for best results when purchased. Since you also will probably store them a while before using them, you could be unaware of how old they actually are. Not only do eggs and milk spoil when they are kept too long, but baking powder can lose its effectiveness and flour can become too stale to give best results, especially if stored where it is damp and warm. If you purchase ingredients that you know you will not be using for some time, store them in the freezer until used. Cake mixes also keep well in the freezer if you prefer using those.

All ingredients should be at room temperature when used unless otherwise specified in the recipe. This is important for good blending of the ingredients. Removing the ingredients from the refrigerator one-half hour ahead of time should be sufficient.

Use standard measuring cups and spoons. Measure accurately by scraping off tops of measures with a knife or spatula. Flour should be sifted before measuring or stirred until fluffy and spooned very lightly into a cup. Use cake flour for delicate cakes. All-purpose flour may be used for other cakes. Do not use bread flour. Bread flour has high gluten content and it is difficult not to develop too much of it in the mixing process. This results in a cake of coarser texture that will not be as light. If all-purpose flour needs to be substituted for cake flour, use 2 tablespoons less per cup of flour and add 2 tablespoons of cornstarch in its place. Sift dry ingredients together before adding to batter. Always use double-acting baking powder unless otherwise specified. Use a good-quality margarine or solid shortening. Poorly refined margarines do not give the best baking results. Do *not* use whipped margarines for baking! Do not substitute oil when recipe calls for margarine or solid shortening.

Use clean shiny pans so a dark crust does not form on the cake. I much prefer shiny aluminum pans for baking. Stainless steel is a poor conductor of heat and stainless steel pans do not give the best baking results. Glass pans or dark metal pans will result in excessive browning. If you prefer using glass or dark pans, reduce oven temperature by 15 degrees for the same amount of baking time. Pans that are dingy or have an accumulation of burned-on grease tend to burn or brown the contents before the inside is done.

It is important to use the correct size pan. Pans should be filled at least half full, but not over ⅔ full for best results. Loaf or tube pans are an exception as well as sponge cake batters. If a pan is too full the texture will be more coarse and the outer part of the cake will be overbaked before the center is done. Often these cakes fall in the center while cooling. The batter should be at least one inch deep in the pan for a velvety texture.

Prepare pans before mixing cake. Pans for sponge or angel cakes should not be greased. Pans for shortened cakes should either be greased or lined with waxed paper. Do not use margarine or vegetable spray to grease pans since this may result in sticking. Use lard or a good solid shortening. Pans may be dusted lightly with flour after greasing. Remove excess flour by tapping pan over flour container. If you prefer waxed-paper lining for easy removal of the cake after it is baked, set pan on the waxed paper for a pattern, and mark around it using the point of the shears or a pencil. Cut out and lay in bottom of pan.

Read the recipe carefully before you begin so you understand the procedure to be used with the type cake you are making. There are basically two types of cakes—cakes with shortening (called shortened cakes) and cakes without. The procedures for mixing the two types are different.

Cakes without shortening are called foam-type cakes and include angel food and sponge cakes. They mainly depend on air which is beaten into the egg whites for leavening. A folding motion is used to combine the beaten egg whites and yolks with the other ingredients so that the incorporated air is not lost in the mixing process. See directions for angel food cake on page 96.

The conventional method for mixing cakes with shortening is to first cream the shortening until soft. Then gradually add sugar and beat until light and creamy. Add the eggs and flavoring next and beat very well, until mixture is fluffy. Add sifted dry ingredients in three portions alternately with liquid ingredients in two portions beginning and ending with dry ingredients. Do not overmix at this point; mix only until blended, scraping bowl thoroughly while mixing.

Some recipes call for eggs to be separated and the beaten whites to be added last. If this is the case, beat whites in separate bowl until soft peaks form. Then gradually add about one-fourth of the sugar the recipe calls for, beating into stiff peaks. Cream the remaining sugar with the shortening. Gently fold egg whites into batter after last addition of flour. Beaten egg whites should set for only a minimum amount of time before being incorporated into the batter, however, as they deteriorate quickly. If you wish to beat them first, have everything else measured out and ready so they do not need to set long.

There is also a quick-mix method for shortened cakes. However, this method should be used only with recipes that are adapted for it. Most of these recipes call for all dry ingredients to be sifted together into bowl. Then add shortening and half of the milk. Beat at medium speed for 2 minutes. Add remaining milk, eggs, and flavoring. Beat 2 minutes longer, scraping bowl thoroughly while mixing. These batters are usually thin and should be poured into pans immediately. Some quick-mix recipes call for placing all ingredients in bowl together. Beat on low speed for approximately one minute scraping bowl thoroughly. Then beat on medium-high speed for two or three minutes. Be sure to follow directions given for specific recipe when making these cakes.

Cake mixes should also be prepared carefully according to directions on the package. There are many variations people use with cake mixes to obtain all kinds of results. But if you are experimenting, beware that results could be a bit tricky. For instance, I have found that I can obtain a much lighter cake from a regular cake mix if I separate the eggs and fold the beaten whites in last. The mixing time needs to be cut down slightly. With the change to pudding mixes however, the body of the cake is heavier and some of these mixes cannot hold the delicate frame the beaten whites incorporate into it. Therefore, what works great for one type mix may not work so well with another. The moral of the story is—if you are experimenting, do not do it for guests. Sometimes to make food more special, we alter a recipe in a way we have not tested and the results are disappointing!

Always preheat oven to correct temperature before placing cake in oven. It usually takes from 5 to 10 minutes to heat. Place pans in the oven so they do not touch each other or the sides of the oven to obtain even baking.

Cakes should be baked undisturbed. Do not open oven door until time to test for doneness. This could cause the cake to fall. It is also important not to jar the stove during baking, especially with delicate cakes. For instance, to open and then bang shut the stove drawer beneath the oven while the cake is baking could cause the cake to fall.

Cake is done when top springs back when lightly touched with finger, or when a wooden pick inserted in the center comes out clean. It may be just beginning to shrink away from the sides of the pan. Do not overbake as this will cause cake to be dry and crumbly.

Cakes should be cooled 5 to 10 minutes before turning out of the pan to avoid breaking cake apart. Cake is difficult to remove when too cool, however, without part of it sticking in pan. If pans were lined with waxed paper, cut around edge of pan with knife to loosen warm cake from sides. Then turn out cake and carefully peel off waxed paper.

If you wish to totally cool cake in pans, purchase pans with a narrow metal insert that you simply slide around the pan to loosen the entire cake.

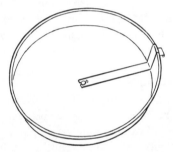

Angel food or sponge cakes should be inverted over a funnel to cool. Let hang until entirely cold. Two-piece pans allow for easiest removal of cake. Cut around edge of cake with long narrow knife to loosen from sides of pan. With two-piece pan you can also then cut around bottom of pan. With one-piece pan, after cutting around edge, rap pan sharply with hand to loosen bottom while holding over a plate.

Icing the Cake: Ice cake as soon as it is cool to seal in moisture and freshness. Do not try to ice a warm cake, however. Icing may slide off cake, or harden too quickly to spread properly, depending on the kind of icing you are using.

Place bottom layer upside down on cake plate so smooth flat side is up. Spread with filling or frosting. If using filling, be sure to keep it back from the edges slightly so it will not ooze out into icing. Add top layer top side up so smooth straight sides are together. If cake is too rounded on top, a thin slice can be removed to level it off. In this case, raw edge should be put down because it would be difficult to spread icing onto it without pulling up cake.

Brush off loose crumbs. Spread icing on sides of cake first. Depending on the thickness of the icing, it sometimes helps to go around entire sides of cake with a thin layer of icing first to seal in crumbs. Then add a second coat of desired thickness. Bring icing up high on the sides of the cake to make a good sharp edge at top of cake. Pile remaining icing on top. Spread lightly and then swirl or make ridges with knife to look attractive.

Add any garnishes such as coconut, chocolate curls, or chopped nuts while icing is soft so they will stick better. Fluffy icings can be made attractive by using the back of a spoon to create a hobnail effect. Or sprinkle powdered sugar over top of cake to give a finished touch without icing. For decorative look, lay a lace paper doily on top of cake and sift a generous amount of sugar over and around it. Be careful to fill in small cut-out sections. Then carefully lift doily from cake and dump the sugar on it back into container. This gives a very attractive appearance.

How to Make Angel Food Cake

Making angel food cake is not really difficult. However, there are several important steps that can determine the difference between success and failure. Excellent results can be obtained by mastering the simple art of knowing how long to beat the egg whites, the ability to lightly, yet quickly and thoroughly, incorporate the sugar/flour mixture into them, and baking the cake undisturbed at correct temperature.

As mentioned elsewhere in this book, eggs separate best when refrigerator cold. But they must be warmed to room temperature before beating them. Do not get a single speck of yolk in the whites as this will reduce volume considerably. Also, the bowl and beaters must be thoroughly clean and free of grease.

Always use cake flour to obtain a top-quality angel food cake. Sift the flour and half of the sugar together three times to ensure a very fine well-blended mixture that will easily combine with the beaten whites. Set flour mixture aside.

Measure egg whites, salt, and water into large mixer bowl. Turn electric mixer to highest speed and beat until foamy. Sprinkle in cream of tartar. Then reduce speed slightly and gradually sprinkle in sugar. Quickly increase to highest speed again and beat just until sugar is dissolved and *very* stiff peaks are formed. Underbeating will cause poor volume and a gummy texture, and may cause cake to fall out of pan while cooling. Overbeating, however, can also cause reduced volume since the cells are no longer elastic and will break instead of rising the optimum amount during baking. Stop beating as soon as peaks stand very stiff when beater is lifted out of bowl.

With spatula or large spoon, gently and quickly fold sugar/flour mixture and flavoring into whites in a down-over, up-over motion. Either sprinkle mixture in with spoon or sift with one-hand sifter while you are folding with the other hand. It helps to set bowl on a damp dishcloth to keep it from scooting around while you work. Fold only until flour mixture all disappears.

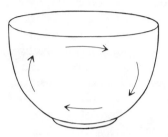

Gently push batter into ungreased tube pan. (Any greasy film on pan may cause cake to fall out of pan while cooling.) Cut through the batter in circular fashion with table knife to remove any air pockets, starting at outside edge of pan and ending at the center tube.

Place cake on lower rack in preheated 360-degree oven and bake undisturbed approximately 35 to 40 minutes until top springs back when lightly touched. Immediately invert pan over a funnel to cool. When cold, cut around edges with sharp knife to loosen cake. (See recipe on page 104.)

COOKIES

Cookies come in such a variety of types, kinds, and sizes that they will fit most any occasion. Directions are usually easy to follow so that an amateur can enjoy good results.

As with any other baking, just remember that different kinds of flour and the different brands of margarine and shortening can give considerably different results. It is simplist to find a good brand that works well for you and then stick with it. All-purpose flour should be used for cookies.

Bar cookies are usually the easiest and quickest to make since they do not require additional time for dropping or cutting out. They are baked in a pan much like cake and are cut into bars when partially cooled.

Drop cookies are made from a soft dough and are usually dropped or pushed from a spoon with rubber scraper onto cookie sheet. Cookies should be placed at least one inch apart on cookie sheet to allow for spreading during baking. To minimize spreading, dough may be chilled before baking.

Cookies should be baked on sheets rather than pans with tall sides which would hinder the heat from flowing evenly throughout the cookies. If you only have a pan with tall sides, turn it over and place cookies on the top. The baking sheet or pan should be small enough to allow at least two inches on all sides of the oven for a good flow of air around it. Baking sheet should be cold when cookies are placed on it so they will not melt down and spread too much during baking.

To speed up the process if you have only one baking sheet, cut two sheets of foil to fit baking sheet. Place cookies on foil and slide baking sheet under it to bake. Fill second sheet of foil with cookies while the other one is baking. To remove baked cookies, simply slide foil and cookies onto rack to cool slightly. Slip baking sheet under second batch of cookies and return to oven. Remove baked cookies from foil and reuse for next batch. If you like soft cookies, do not overbake them. Remove from oven when they are barely set. Overbaked cookies are hard and crumbly.

Rolled cookies take the most time, but are great for decorating for special occasions. The dough must be chilled at least an hour for successful handling without adding too much flour to the dough. Too much flour makes dry, hard cookies. Rolling too thin and baking too long also makes dry cookies. If you like a softer cookie, roll to a scant ¼-inch thickness and bake just until set.

Our three daughters used to love to help make and decorate cookies for Christmas or for other special occasions. One year when they were in grade school, we baked and decorated a Valentine Day cookie for each of their classmates including their names. We made over 100 cookies one evening. We didn't do three grades at a time every year!

Cookies may be iced and decorated after baking. While icing is soft, colored sugar may be sprinkled on cookies, or any of a number of other garnishes such as cinnamon candies, tinted coconut, nuts, or chocolate sprinkles. Or they may be sprinkled with colored sugar, or a design may be painted on them *before* baking. For paint, mix 1 tsp. water and half of both the white and the yolk of one egg. Beat slightly and add several drops of food color to achieve the desired shade. Use a clean watercolor brush to paint the design.

Filling may be added to rolled cookies for filled cookies. Cut out cookies as desired. Place a rounded tsp. of filling on one cookie. Top with second cookie. Filled cookies need to be baked longer than single cookies.

Refrigerator cookies are made by forming the dough into a roll. Wrap in plastic wrap or foil. Chill dough several hours until firm. Unwrap and slice dough crosswise into at least ¼-inch thick slices and bake.

QUICK CHECKLIST FOR FAILURES WITH CAKES AND COOKIES

Common Problems	Usual Causes
Holes in cake	overbeating too high oven temperature dry ingredients not sifted
Fallen cake	underbaking too low oven temperature baking powder too old using too small a pan insufficient flour overbeating
Cake cracks on top or is peaked on top	oven too hot too much flour
Coarse-grained cake	undermixing too much baking powder shortening too soft (do not melt shortening for cakes)
Dry, crumbly cake	overbaking overbeating too much flour
Cake sticks to pan	pan not greased properly (did not use solid fat for greasing) left in pan until too cool
Cake is sticky	too much sugar baking powder too old underbeating
Cake rises unevenly	batter not spread evenly in pan pans placed too close to side of oven or too close together
Cake burned on sides or bottom	oven too full dark or glass pans used without reducing temperature slightly oven too hot

Common Problems	Usual Causes
Cookies burned on bottom	pan too large for oven dark or dingy pan used pan too deep
Cookies burned around edges	oven too hot oven too full
Cookies hard and crumbly	overbaking too much flour cut-out cookies rolled too thin
Cookies flattened out	placed on hot cookie sheet not enough flour dough not chilled poor quality margarine

TIPS FOR CAKES, FROSTINGS AND COOKIES

•There are several quick easy methods for greasing pans for baking to avoid getting your hands greasy. Slip hand into a sandwich bag and grease with it. Or keep a small paintbrush or pastry brush in a plastic bag to use for this purpose. Store brush in refrigerator or freezer between bakings to keep it from getting rancid. If brush has a short handle, you could put it in a tall narrow jar of grease and keep the covered jar in the refrigerator. If you store it in a small heat-proof container, this can be placed in the oven a short time while you are preheating it to soften grease slightly. Another method is to use a rubber plate scraper or an empty margarine wrapper to apply the grease. Do not use margarine or vegetable spray to grease baking pans as the contents will often stick. Use lard or solid shortening.

•When adding such ingredients as apple slices, cherries, berries, candied fruits, or raisins to dough, dust fruit first with a little of the flour called for in the recipe. This will help keep it from sinking to the bottom of the cake. When adding dried fruit such as raisins or currants, it helps to heat fruit until very warm to prevent sinking in batter. Place in microwave or in preheating oven.

•Raisins will be much more flavorful if chopped before adding to batters. Pile on cutting board and cut through pile in all directions several times with a long, sharp knife.

•When using the ground-up date pellets that are now popular at bulk food stores, keep in mind that they are coated heavily with flour. Therefore, the amount of flour or other thickening called for in a recipe should be reduced slightly to compensate.

•To soften hard margarine quickly for baking, slice into mixer bowl and place bowl for a short time under the broiler in the oven which needs preheating anyway. Do not overdo this—shortening should not be melted for cakes and cookies unless recipe specifically calls for it. Don't forget to turn oven control back to bake instead of leaving it on broil for baking!

•Measure the shortening before molasses when recipe calls for both and molasses will not stick to cup.

•To measure shortening accurately, for 1 cup shortening, use a 2-cup glass measuring cup. Fill with water to the 1-cup level, then add shortening until water reaches the 2-cup level. Drain off water.

•When baking something that takes both eggs and shortening, break an egg into the measuring cup first and tilt cup around enough that all of the interior has been dampened with egg white. Empty egg into bowl and measure shortening in same cup. Shortening will slip right out!

•To chop sticky foods such as dates, marshmallows, dried prunes, or apricots, use wet kitchen shears. Or rub shears with butter or margarine.

•Soften candied fruit peels by heating briefly in a preheating oven.

•Dip spoon or measuring cup in hot water before measuring shortening. It will slip out easily.

•The more sugar and shortening a cake contains, the longer the mixing time should be when mixing it.

•If angel food cake pan was used for something greasy, it is very important to have it totally grease free before baking an angel food cake in it. Hot water with ammonia added is effective for removing any greasy film.

•For a nicer lighter cake from a cake mix, sift mix into bowl. Blend water in with mix on low speed only until totally moistened. Let mixture set at least 1 or 2 minutes to soften thoroughly. Then mix according to package directions. Also, if you suspect that a cake mix may be a little old, add ½ tsp. baking powder to the dry ingredients before mixing. Baking powder deteriorates with age, and an additional amount may be needed.

•For a throwaway cake plate, cover a circle of cardboard with foil. This is also especially nice for freezing cakes so plate isn't tied up in the freezer, or when taking a cake to someone, so they don't need to bother with returning the plate.

•When packing sheet cake squares with sticky icing for a lunch, cut square in half and stack the two halves with iced sides together forming a sandwich-type piece with icing in the middle. This eliminates having icing stick to the waxed-paper wrapping.

•In many cakes, the egg whites can be beaten separately and folded in last to obtain a lighter cake.

•For special cupcakes, cut the top out of each cupcake in a cone shape and put a spoonful of pudding in each one. Replace cone, and dust with powdered sugar. (Chocolate pudding in yellow cupcakes is delicious.)

•To frost cupcakes quickly, swirl top of cake in a bowl of fluffy frosting. To keep cupcake papers from loosening on the cakes after they are baked, spread icing well to the edge of cakes "sealing" it onto the paper edges.

•For children's party, fill cup-type ice-cream cones half full of batter and bake. Ice when cool and sprinkle with colored sugar.

•For an extra moist cake, cover cake tightly about 5 minutes after removing it from the oven. Keep covered until cool. The steam will soak back into the cake adding moisture. (Do not do this with sponge or delicate cakes since it would cause sogginess in these types of cakes.)

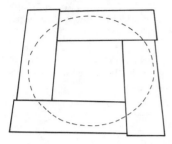

•Place 4 narrow strips of waxed paper on plate under cake before icing it. These can easily be pulled out after cake is iced to remove any mess and leave clean edge on plate around cake.

•If layer cake sticks to pan, return to warm oven briefly, or place on a warm (not hot) burner a short time and it should come out intact.

•For easier removal of fruitcakes or loaf cakes from pans, line pans with aluminum foil. Foil should be greased just as you would grease the empty pan. Pan does not need to be greased when using foil.

•Do not stir old-fashioned boiled icings while they are boiling. This causes roughness and sugaring in the finished icing. Stir only until mixture comes to a full boil.

•If boiled icing doesn't beat to spreading consistency, it can be salvaged. Place it over boiling water in double boiler and heat while continuing to beat it to desired consistency.

•Dip knife in hot water to heat it to help smooth icing that is difficult to spread.

•A corn syrup glaze makes an attractive addition to fruitcake. To make glaze, combine equal parts of light corn syrup and water in saucepan. Boil 1 minute. Cool to lukewarm. Brush cooled cake with glaze. Then arrange nuts and candied fruit over the top to decorate. Brush another coat of glaze over fruit.

•To add to the appearance of a plain cake, tint white frosting a pastel shade with a small amount of food color. An attractive effect may also be obtained by leaving half the frosting white. Then frost the cake with a marbleized effect with the two colors.

•For quick frosting for sheet cakes or cupcakes, place peppermint patties, pieces of chocolate bar, or marshmallows on hot cake. Let candy melt and spread with knife.

•Any cake with pudding filling or whipped cream topping should be served promptly or refrigerated until served.

•To slice fresh cake more easily, dip knife in hot water first. Wipe knife with towel.

•Use mint patties or other colorful candy as candle holders on birthday cake. "Drill" hole in candy just enough to hold candle by twisting tip of sharp-pointed knife in center of candy.

•If you do not have enough muffin tins to hold cake papers when making cupcakes, use a cookie sheet and regular metal canning jar rings to hold the papers in place. You can bake a large quantity at once with this method.

•To make heart-shaped cupcakes, simply place small balls of foil between muffin pan and paper cup to indent them into the shape of a heart. Use a cake decorator to pipe the outline of a heart with icing on top of cooled cakes.

•The addition of 1 tsp. vinegar along with the flavoring to boiled frostings will keep them from becoming brittle and breaking when cut.

•To make black frosting for decorating cookies or cake, add blue color to chocolate frosting.

•Set cake on a turntable for easy turning while icing.

•When rolling out the dough for cut-out cookies, try sprinkling counter with granulated sugar instead of flour. Cookies can be turned over to place on cookie sheet and they will have a sugary top.

•Remove cookies from baking sheets immediately because they will continue to cook on hot sheet for a short time.

•For extra flavor and crunchiness, toast the oatmeal for cookies. Spread on tray and place in oven while it is preheating to bake the cookies.

•Use tuna cans or other small cans for cookie cutters when you need odd sizes. These can be bent into various shapes as desired. Plastic bottles can be cut in half and used also. Or tear the metal edge off discarded boxes of waxed paper and plastic wrap and bend into any desired shape.

•For refrigerator cookies, pack dough in empty juice cans or other cans. If you don't have the lid, cover the open end with plastic wrap secured with a rubber band. To remove for easy slicing, use can opener to cut bottom end and push dough through can with lid, slicing as you push.

•Leftover icing can be spread between graham crackers for an after-school snack.

•For a clever design on children's cookies, press animal cookie cutters lightly into the soft icing to make a slight imprint. Remove cutter, and outline indentation with colored sugar.

•To avoid damage to icings or toppings, especially on soft cookies which you wish to stack for storage, place a tray of cookies in freezer a short while first to harden. Then pack in plastic bags or containers and return to freezer.

•Don't throw away leftover icings. Little dabs can be placed in plastic wrap with rubber bands around them and frozen. Accumulate enough for a rainbow effect icing on a sheet cake, or ice cookies with different colors. Light colors may be mixed. Use your imagination. Icing must be warmed to room temperature to use again. Microwave is excellent for softening it to good spreading consistency.

•See method for testing doneness of candy and cake icings on page 187, in Desserts, Fruits, Snacks, and Candy chapter.

CAKES, FROSTINGS, AND COOKIES RECIPES
MISCELLANEOUS CAKES

Angel Food Cake
(See information about angel food cakes on page 96.)

1¼ cups cake flour **¾ cup sugar**	Sift together three times.
1½ cups egg whites (about 12) **1 tbsp. warm water** **¼ tsp. salt**	Beat until foamy.
1½ tsp. cream of tartar	Add and beat into soft peaks.
1 cup sugar	Gradually add, beating into very stiff peaks.
1 tsp. vanilla **½ tsp. almond flavoring**	Carefully fold in. Then gradually sift in flour-sugar mixture, gently folding just until blended.

Gently push batter into ungreased 10-inch tube pan. Carefully cut through batter with a knife to remove any air bubbles. Place on lower rack in oven so top doesn't get too dark. Bake at 360 degrees for 30 to 35 minutes. Invert pan on a funnel to cool.

Variation: For chocolate angel food cake, remove 3 tbsp. flour from cup and replace it with 3 tbsp. cocoa powder. Or add several drops of peppermint flavoring and a little green color instead of vanilla for a mint cake. Ice this cake with chocolate icing.

Apple Cake

¾ cup margarine **1½ cups sugar**	Cream thoroughly.
2 eggs	Add, beating until fluffy.
1¾ cups flour **1 tsp. soda** **½ tsp. salt** **1 tsp. ground cinnamon** **¼ tsp. nutmeg**	Sift together and add.
¼ cup flour **4 cups raw apples, diced** **½ cup chopped walnuts**	Dust apples and nuts with flour, then fold in.

Pour into greased and floured 9 × 13 pan and bake at 350 degrees for 45 minutes. Delicious served warm or cold with ice cream or whipped cream topped with buttermilk sauce—recipe on page 229.

Mary Shank, my mother-in-law

Variation: Serve warm with whipped cream or ice cream and rum-flavored sauce.
Rum-Flavored Sauce:

½ cup butter ½ cup half and half 1 cup sugar	Cook over boiling water in double boiler for 10 minutes. Remove from heat.

½ tsp. rum flavoring	Add, then pour over cake while hot.

Wanda Good

Apple Dapple Cake

3 eggs	Beat well.

1¼ cups oil 2 tsp. vanilla 2 cups sugar	Add, beating well.

2¾ cups flour 1 tsp. baking soda 1 tsp. salt 1 tsp. ground cinnamon ¼ tsp. nutmeg	Sift together and add.

¼ cup flour 3 cups apples, chopped 1 cup nuts, chopped 1 cup coconut	Mix together, then fold in.

Pour into a greased 9-inch tube pan or bundt pan and bake at 350 degrees for approximately 70 minutes.

Topping:

⅓ cup margarine 1 cup brown sugar ¼ cup milk 1 tsp. vanilla	Mix in saucepan and boil 2 or 3 minutes. Pour hot toppng over cake about 5 minutes after removing cake from oven.

(If sheet cake is desired, may be baked in one 9 × 13 pan, plus a 9 × 5 loaf pan. It is too much batter for a 9 × 13 pan only. Bake sheet cake for 40 to 45 minutes.)

Louise Heatwole
Pat Hertzler

Optional Topping: Mix 1 cup powdered sugar and 2 tbsp. milk, and spread over hot cake.

Margaret Keller

Applesauce Cake

2 cups sugar ¾ cup shortening	Cream thoroughly.
3 eggs 1 tsp. vanilla	Add, beating until fluffy.
3 cups flour 1 tsp. baking powder 1 tsp. baking soda ½ tsp. salt 1 tsp. ground cinnamon ½ tsp. ground allspice ½ tsp. ground cloves 1 cup crushed pineapple, drained 1¼ cups applesauce	Add sifted dry ingredients alternately with combined pineapple and applesauce.
1 cup chopped raisins ½ cup chopped nuts ½ cup angel flake coconut	Fold in.

Pour into a greased and floured 10-inch tube pan. Bake at 350 degrees for 50 to 60 minutes. Remove from oven and cool 5 minutes. Then remove from pan and cover to finish cooling.

Filled Banana Cake

¾ cup shortening 1½ cups sugar	Cream thoroughly.
2 egg yolks ½ tsp. vanilla 1 cup mashed bananas (2 medium)	Add, beating thoroughly.
2 cups flour 1 tsp. baking powder 1 tsp. baking soda ½ tsp. salt ½ cup thick sour milk or buttermilk	Add sifted dry ingredients alternately with milk.
½ cup chopped pecans or walnuts	Fold in.
2 egg whites, stiffly beaten	Fold in gently, and pour into 2 greased and floured 9-inch layer pans.
1 cup angel flake coconut	Sprinkle over layers.

Bake at 350 degrees for 25 to 30 minutes. Cool 10 minutes in pans, then remove and cool completely.

Filling:

½ cup sugar (see next page)	Combine in saucepan and cook until thickened.

3 tbsp. flour
⅛ tsp. salt
½ cup rich milk
2 tbsp. butter

. . . .

½ cup chopped pecans   Add. Cool.
1 tsp. vanilla

. . . .

Frosting:
1 egg white   Cream together until well blended.
½ cup soft shortening
½ tsp. coconut extract
½ tsp. vanilla

. . . .

2 cups powdered sugar   Gradually add, beating until light and fluffy.

. . . .

To assemble cake: Place first layer on plate with coconut side down and spread with filling. Top with second layer, coconut side up. Swirl frosting on sides. Leave top unfrosted.

. . . .

Banana Nut Cake

2 cups flour   Measure all ingredients into large mixer bowl.
1⅔ cups sugar   Blend on low speed for 1 minute. Then beat on
1 tsp. salt   medium-high speed for 2 minutes.
¾ tsp. baking powder
1½ tsp. baking soda
⅔ cup soft shortening
⅔ cup thick sour milk or buttermilk
3 eggs
1 tsp. vanilla
1 ½ cups mashed bananas
⅔ cup chopped nuts

. . . .

Pour into a greased and floured 9 × 13 pan and bake at 350 degrees for 35 to 40 minutes.

Wanda Good

. . . .

Black Cherry Forest Cake

1 (18-oz.) chocolate cake mix   Blend all ingredients on low speed of electric
  (without pudding)   mixer for 1 minute. Then beat on medium-
1 (21-oz.) can cherry pie filling   high speed for 2 minutes scraping bowl
¼ cup vegetable oil   frequently.
1 tsp. almond flavoring
3 eggs

. . . .

Pour into a greased and floured 9-inch bundt pan and bake at 350 degrees for 45 minutes. Cool in pan 10 minutes. Then turn out on rack to finish cooling. Serve with whipped cream and spoon additional pie filling over the top. (Cake may be baked in a 9 × 13 pan for approximately 30 minutes if desired.)

Barbara Bowman
Harriet Steiner

. . . .

Banana Pudding Cake

1 (18-oz.) yellow cake mix 1 (3½-oz.) pkg. instant vanilla pudding ¼ tsp. ground mace 4 eggs 2 tbsp. water 1 cup commercial sour cream 2 medium bananas, mashed ½ cup vegetable oil	Measure all ingredients in large mixer bowl. Blend on low speed 1 minute scrapping bowl often. Beat 2 minutes at medium-high speed. Do not overmix.

Pour into a greased and floured 9-inch tube or bundt pan. Bake at 350 degrees for 40 to 50 minutes. Cool in pan 5 minutes. Then turn out to cool completely.

Frosting:

1 (3-oz. pkg.) cream cheese, softened 3 tbsp. butter, melted ½ tsp. grated orange peel 1 tbsp. orange juice 1½ cups powdered sugar	Beat all ingredients together until smooth. Spread on cooled cake.

Black Walnut Coconut Pound Cake

(This is a very delicious moist cake that freezes exceptionally well.)

2 cups sugar 1 cup vegetable oil 4 eggs, beaten	Beat together well.

3 cups flour ½ tsp. baking powder ½ tsp. baking soda ¼ tsp. salt 1 cup thick sour milk or buttermilk	Add sifted dry ingredients alternately with milk. Beat well after each addition.

1 cup chopped black walnuts 1 cup angel flake coconut 2 tsp. coconut flavoring	Blend in.

Pour in greased and floured 10-inch tube pan. Bake at 325 degrees for 1 hour and 15 minutes or until cake tests done. Remove from oven, and pour hot coconut syrup over cake.

Hot Coconut Syrup:

½ cup water 2 tbsp. butter 1 tsp. coconut flavoring 1 cup sugar	Combine in saucepan. Boil 5 minutes. Remove from heat and pour over hot cake.

Leave cake in pan 3 hours to absorb syrup well. Then wrap tightly to store.

Edna Kagey

Carrot Gold Cake

2 cups sugar **1½ cups vegetable oil**	Beat together thoroughly.

4 eggs, well beaten	Add, beating until fluffy.

2 cups flour **2 tsp. baking powder** **1½ tsp. baking soda** **1 tsp. salt** **2 tsp. ground cinnamon**	Sift together and blend in.

2 cups finely grated raw carrots **1 cup crushed pineapple, drained** **1 cup angel flake coconut** **½ cup chopped nuts**	Fold in.

Pour into 3 greased and floured 8-inch layer pans and bake at 350 degrees for 25 to 30 minutes. Or bake in a 9 × 13 pan for 40 to 45 minutes. Ice with cream cheese frosting on page 142 when cool. (If making sheet cake, use only half recipe of frosting.)

Variation: Omit crushed pineapple and add ¾ cup chopped dates instead.

Jean Horning

Delicious Chocolate Cake (Basic)

2 cups flour **2 cups sugar** **½ tsp. salt** **1 tsp. baking powder** **2 tsp. baking soda** **⅔ cup cocoa powder**	Sift together into bowl.

⅔ cup vegetable oil **1 cup milk** **2 eggs** **1 tsp. vanilla**	Add, beating for 2 minutes at medium high speed.

1 cup hot coffee (already brewed)	Blend in. (Batter will be thin.)

Pour into 2 greased and floured 9-inch layer pans or a 9 × 13 pan and bake at 350 degrees for 30 to 35 minutes.

Ida Heatwole

Yellow Chiffon Cake

2¼ cups cake flour 1½ cups sugar 3 tsp. baking powder ½ tsp. salt	Sift together in larger bowl. Make a well in center of mixture.

½ cup cooking oil 5 egg yolks, unbeaten ¾ cup water 1 tsp. vanilla 1 tsp. lemon flavoring	Place in well, and then beat with spoon until smooth.

1 cup egg whites (7 or 8) 1 tbsp. warm water ½ tsp. cream of tartar	Beat egg whites with water until foamy. Add cream of tartar and beat into very stiff peaks.

Slowly pour egg yolk mixture over beaten whites, gently folding just until blended. Pour into ungreased 10-inch tube pan. Circle through batter gently with knife to remove air bubbles. Bake at 325 degrees for 55 minutes. Then turn to 350 degrees and bake 10 minutes more. Invert pan on funnel to cool.

For Anniversary Chiffon Cake: Instead of 1½ cups sugar, use ¾ cup sugar and ¾ cup brown sugar. Omit vanilla and add 2 tsp. maple flavoring. Very gently fold in 1 cup finely chopped pecans at the last. When cake is cool, frost with whipped cream (whip 1 cup cream and sweeten with ⅓ cup brown sugar).

Ella May Miller

For Orange Chiffon Cake: Omit lemon and vanilla flavoring, and add 1 tsp. orange flavoring and grated rind from one orange. Ice with Quick Fluffy White Icing, except use pineapple juice in place of water. Sprinkle ½ cup well drained pineapple over the top of iced cake and ¾ cup toasted coconut onto the sides.

For Spicy Chiffon Cake: Omit lemon flavoring, and add 1 tsp. cinnamon, ½ tsp. nutmeg, ¼ tsp. cloves, and ¼ tsp. allspice. Ice with 2 cups Cool Whip with ½ tsp. cinnamon added.

For Walnut Chiffon Cake: Omit lemon flavoring and add 1 tsp. walnut flavoring. Very gently fold in ¾ cup finely chopped walnuts at the last.

Chocolate Brownie Cake

2 cups sugar 2 cups flour	Mix in bowl. Set aside.

½ cup margarine ½ cup Crisco ⅓ cup cocoa powder 1 cup water	Combine in saucepan and heat to boiling, stirring until dissolved. Remove from heat and pour over sugar flour mixture. Beat well.

2 eggs ½ cup thick sour milk or buttermilk 1 tsp. vanilla 1 tsp. baking soda 1 tsp. salt 1 tsp. ground cinnamon (optional)	Beat in until blended.

Pour into greased 11 × 15 pan and bake at 400 degrees about 20 minutes. Or bake in a 9 × 13 pan for 35 minutes at 375 degrees.

Icing:

½ cup margarine **¼ cup cocoa powder** **6 tbsp. thick sour milk or buttermilk**	Combine in saucepan. Heat to boiling, stirring until dissolved. Remove from heat.
2½ cups powdered sugar **1 tsp. vanilla**	Beat in until smooth. Pour over hot cake soon after removing it from oven.
¾ cup chopped nuts (optional)	Sprinkle over icing while soft.

Louise Heatwole

Chocolate Cherry Valentine Cake Torte

1¾ cups flour **1¼ cups sugar** **½ cup cocoa powder** **¾ tsp. baking soda** **½ tsp. salt**	Sift together into bowl.
½ cup vegetable oil **1 cup buttermilk or thick sour milk** **2 egg yolks** **1 tsp. vanilla**	Add, beating until smooth.
2 egg whites	Beat until foamy.
¼ cup sugar	Gradually add, beating into stiff peaks. Fold into batter.

Pour into 2 greased heart-shaped pans, or 9-inch layer pans. Bake at 350 degrees for 20 to 25 minutes until cake springs back when touched lightly. Cool 5 minutes. Remove from pans and cool completely.

Cream Filling: **1 cup whipping cream** **2 tbsp. sugar** **1 tsp. vanilla**	Combine in chilled bowl and whip until stiff.
Chocolate Whipped Cream: **1 cup whipping cream** **½ cup sugar** **¼ cup cocoa powder**	Combine in chilled bowl and whip until stiff.
1 cup cherry pie filling **¼ tsp. almond flavoring**	Mix and have ready.

Place 1 layer of cake on plate. Spread with half of cream filling, reserving other half. Add second layer of cake. Spoon pie filling on top leaving a 1-inch edge around cake. Frost sides of cake with chocolate whipped cream, piping an edge at bottom of cake. Pipe a decorative edge around top of cake with reserved cream filling. Chill until served.

Rhoda Bennett

Superb Chocolate Chip Cake

1 (18-oz.) yellow cake mix (without pudding) 1 (3½-oz.) pkg. instant vanilla pudding ½ cup Crisco (or other) oil ⅓ cup water	Stir together.

4 eggs	Add, one at a time, beating well after each addition.

1 cup commercial sour cream	Add.

1 cup tiny chocolate chips or grated semisweet chocolate 1 cup angel flake coconut ¾ cup chopped pecans (optional)	Fold in.

Pour into greased and floured 9-inch bundt pan and bake at 350 degrees for 40 to 45 minutes. Cool in pan 5 minutes, then invert to cake plate to finish cooling.

Chocolate-Marshmallow Cake

1 (18-oz.) German-Chocolate cake mix (without pudding) 1 (3½-oz.) pkg. instant vanilla pudding 1½ cups milk 3 eggs	Blend together on low speed of electric mixer 1 minute. Then beat at medium high speed for 2 minutes.

Pour into greased 11 × 15 sheet cake pan. Bake at 350 degrees for 20 to 25 minutes.

3 cups white miniature marshmallows	Sprinkle over hot cake immediately upon removing from oven so marshmallows will melt slightly.

Icing: ¾ cup sugar ¼ cup margarine ¼ cup milk	Heat to good rolling boil. Remove from heat.

½ cup chocolate chips	Stir in until melted.

Immediately drizzle over marshmallows on hot cake.

Wanda Good

Chocolate Mayonnaise Cake

4 eggs	Beat well.

1⅔ cups sugar 1 tsp. vanilla	Add, beating until fluffy.

| 1 cup mayonnaise | Blend in. |

| 2 cups flour
⅓ cup cocoa powder
½ tsp. baking powder
1½ tsp. baking soda
½ tsp. salt
1¼ cups water | Add sifted dry ingredients alternately with water. |

Pour into 2 greased and floured 9-inch layer pans and bake at 350 degrees for 30 to 35 minutes.

Fresh Coconut Cake

| ¾ cup butter
1½ cups sugar | Cream thoroughly. |

| 3 egg yolks
1 tsp. vanilla | Add, beating until fluffy. |

| 2¾ cups cake flour
3 tsp. baking powder
½ tsp. salt
¾ cup coconut milk* | Add sifted dry ingredients alternately with coconut milk. |

| 1 cup freshly grated coconut | Blend in. |

| 3 egg whites, beaten stiff | Fold in gently. |

Pour into 2 greased and floured 9-inch layer pans and bake at 350 degrees for 25 to 30 minutes.

Icing:
Make one recipe of Quick Fluffy White Icing, page 143. Place one layer of cake on plate. Spread with ½ cup raspberry jam or orange marmalade. Then spread with icing. Add second layer and ice entire cake. Sprinkle with an additional ½ cup fresh coconut. (*The liquid inside the fresh coconut.)

Alice Trissel

Special Day Coconut Cake

| 1 (18-oz.) yellow cake mix | Bake according to package directions in a 9 × 13 pan. Poke holes all over cake with sharp fork while still hot. |

| ½ cup powdered sugar
½ cup milk
3 tsp. coconut flavoring | Mix thoroughly and pour over hot cake so it will soak in holes. Cool. |

| 2 cups Cool Whip
1 (9-oz.) pkg. frozen coconut, thawed | Spread with Cool Whip and sprinkle with coconut. Chill several hours. |

Luscious Coconut Cream Cake

1 cup margarine **2 cups sugar**	Cream thoroughly.

1 tsp. vanilla **½ tsp. coconut flavoring** **5 egg yolks**	Add flavorings and egg yolks one at a time, beating well after each addition.

2¼ cups flour **1½ tsp. baking soda** **½ tsp. salt** **1 cup thick sour milk or buttermilk**	Add sifted dry ingredients alternately with milk.

¾ cup angel flake coconut	Blend in.

5 egg whites, stiffly beaten	Fold in.

Pour into 3 greased and floured 9-inch layer pans. Bake at 350 degrees for 20 to 25 minutes. Cool.

Icing: **½ cup soft margarine** **8-oz. softened cream cheese** **½ tsp. vanilla** **¼ tsp. coconut flavoring**	Cream together.

3 cups powdered sugar	Gradually add, beating until smooth. Spread between layers and on top of cake. Do not ice sides.

¾ cup angel flake coconut	Sprinkle over top.

Sour Cream Coconut Cake

(So moist and luscious!)

1 (18 oz.) butter-flavor yellow cake mix	Bake according to package directions in two 9-inch layer pans. Cool.

Cut each layer into two layers horizontally.

Filling and Topping: **2 cups sugar** **2 cups commercial sour cream** **1 (12-oz.) pkg. frozen coconut, thawed**	Mix together. Reserve 1 cup. Spread remainder between layers of cake.

3 cups Cool Whip	Mix with reserved sour cream mixture. Spread over top and sides of cake.

Refrigerate several hours or a day before serving. (May use a 9 × 13 pan. Cut in half horizontally and use half of recipe for filling and topping.)

Dream Cake

1 (18-oz.) yellow cake mix (without pudding)
1 (11-oz.) can mandarin oranges, including juice
4 eggs
½ cup vegetable oil

Combine all ingredients and beat on low speed 1 minute. Then turn to medium-high speed and beat 2 minutes more.

Pour into 3 greased and floured 9-inch layer pans and bake at 350 degrees for 18 minutes. Cool.

Topping:
1 (9-oz.) Cool Whip or 2 pkgs. topping, whipped
1 (3½-oz.) instant vanilla pudding
1 cup crushed pineapple, drained

Combine all ingredients (add pudding mix dry). If too thick, add small amount of pineapple juice. Spread between layers and on top of cake.

Variation: Use 1 ⅓ cups crushed pineapple with juice instead of mandarin oranges.

Gail Campbell

Candied Orange Fruit Cake

1 cup shortening
2 cups sugar

Cream thoroughly.

4 eggs
1 tsp. vanilla
1 tsp. orange flavoring

Add eggs, one at a time, and flavoring beating until fluffy.

⅔ cup thick sour milk or buttermilk
1 tsp. baking soda
2½ cups flour

Combine soda and milk, and add alternately with sifted flour.

1 ½ cups orange candy slices, chopped
½ cup flour
1 cup chopped dates
1 cup chopped nuts
1 cup flaked coconut

Mix well, then fold in.

Pour into greased and floured 10-inch tube pan or bundt pan. Bake at 325 degrees for 1 ½ hours.

Glaze:
½ cup orange juice
1 cup powdered sugar

Combine in saucepan and heat just until clear.

Pour over hot cake as soon as you remove it from the oven. Cool 10 minutes, then remove from pan. Cover tightly to finish cooling. Best to store in tight container one day before serving.

Applesauce Fruit Cake

1 cup shortening 1 cup sugar 1 cup brown sugar	Cream thoroughly.
2 eggs 1 tsp. black walnut flavoring	Add eggs, one at a time, and flavoring, beating until fluffy.
2 cups flour 2 tsp. baking soda 1 tsp. salt 1½ tsp. ground cinnamon 1 tsp. ground cloves ½ tsp. nutmeg ¼ tsp. ginger 2 cups applesauce	Add sifted dry ingredients alternately with applesauce.
1 lb. mixed candied fruit 1 cup flour 1½ cups chopped raisins 1 cup chopped nuts	Mix well, then fold in.

Pour into greased and floured 10-inch tube pan and bake at 325 degrees for 1 ½ hours. Or use two 9 × 5 loaf pans and bake at 350 degrees for 45 minutes.

Dorothy Shank Showalter

Fruit Cocktail Cake

2 cups flour 2 tsp. baking soda 1½ cups sugar ½ tsp. salt	Sift together into bowl.
¼ cup vegetable oil 2 cups fruit cocktail with juice (16 oz. can) 2 eggs 1 tsp. vanilla ½ tsp. coconut flavoring	Add, and beat 2 minutes with electric mixer.

Pour into a greased and floured 9 × 13 pan. Bake at 350 degrees for 35 to 40 minutes.

Topping: 6 tbsp. margarine ½ cup evaporated milk ¾ cup sugar	Combine in saucepan. Heat to boiling, stirring constantly. Boil 3 minutes. Remove from heat.
¾ cup angel flake coconut ½ tsp. vanilla	Add. Pour over hot cake.

Holiday Cake

2 cups sugar **1 cup shortening**	Cream thoroughly.

4 eggs **1 tsp. vanilla**	Add, beating until fluffy.

3 cups flour **1 tsp. baking powder** **1 tsp. baking soda** **½ tsp. salt** **1½ cups thick sour milk or** **buttermilk**	Add sifted dry ingredients alternately with milk.

¾ cup chopped raisins **1 cup coconut** **¾ cup chopped nuts**	Fold in.

Pour into 2 greased and floured 9 × 5 loaf pans and bake at 350 degrees for 45 to 50 minutes, or in 3 round 9-inch layer pans and bake about 30 minutes.

Icing: **2 cups sugar** **1 cup milk**	Heat in saucepan stirring until sugar is dissolved. Boil until mixture reaches soft-ball stage (232 degrees). Remove from heat.

½ cup chopped nuts **½ cup chopped raisins** **½ cup coconut**	Quickly stir in and spread over loaves, or between and on top of layers. (If icing wants to set up too quickly, add a very small amount of milk.)

Soft Gingerbread

1 cup brown sugar **1 cup soft margarine**	Cream thoroughly.

2 eggs, well beaten **½ cup sorghum molasses**	Add.

2 cups flour **½ tsp. baking powder** **½ tsp. salt** **½ tsp. ground cinnamon** **½ tsp. ground ginger** **1 cup boiling water** **2 tsp. baking soda**	Sift dry ingredients together and add alternately with combined water and soda.

Pour into greased and floured 9 × 13 pan. Bake at 350 degrees 30 to 35 minutes. Serve warm with whipped cream or topping.

Glorified Gingerbread

½ cup margarine 2 cups flour 1 cup sugar ½ tsp. ground cinnamon ½ tsp. ground ginger	Mix like pie dough until crumbly. Reserve ⅔ cup.
1 tsp. soda 1 cup thick sour milk 1 egg, beaten 2 tbsp. sorghum molasses ½ tsp. salt	Dissolve soda in milk first, then combine with other ingredients. Stir into flour mixture.

Pour into greased and floured 9 × 13 pan and sprinkle reserved crumbs over the top. Bake at 350 degrees about 20 to 25 minutes. Best served warm with whipped cream.

German Chocolate Cake

1 (4-oz.) pkg. German Sweet Chocolate ½ cup water	Combine in saucepan. Heat just to a boil, stirring until chocolate melts. Set aside to cool.
1 cup butter or margarine, softened 2 cups sugar	Cream thoroughly.
4 egg yolks 1 tsp. vanilla	Add yolks, one at a time, and vanilla, beating until fluffy. Blend in chocolate mixture.
3 cups sifted cake flour 1 tsp. baking soda ½ tsp. salt 1 cup thick sour milk or buttermilk	Add sifted dry ingredients alternately with milk.
4 egg whites, stiffly beaten	Fold in.

Pour into 3 greased and floured 9-inch layer pans. Bake at 350 degrees about 30 minutes. Cool in pans 10 minutes, then remove and cool completely.

Coconut-Pecan Frosting:

1 cup evaporated milk 1 cup sugar 3 egg yolks ½ cup margarine	Combine in saucepan. Heat over medium heat for 12 minutes, stirring constantly. Remove from heat.
1⅓ cups angel flake coconut ¾ cup chopped pecans 1 tsp. vanilla	Add. Stir until cool and of good spreading consistency.

Spread between layers and on top of cake.

Honey-Pecan Cake

1 cup quick oatmeal 1 cup boiling water	Combine and let set 15 minutes.

....

½ cup soft shortening ¾ cup sugar	Cream thoroughly.

....

2 eggs 1 cup honey 1 tsp. vanilla	Add, beating until fluffy.

....

1½ cups flour 1 tsp. baking soda ½ tsp. salt ½ tsp. ground cinnamon ¼ tsp. ground ginger ¼ tsp. ground nutmeg ⅛ tsp. ground cloves	Add alternately with oats mixture.

....

Pour into a greased 9 × 13 pan and bake at 350 degrees for 30 to 35 minutes.

....

Topping:

¼ cup melted margarine ⅓ cup honey ¾ cup chopped pecans ½ cup flaked coconut	Mix and spread over hot cake. Broil just until lightly browned. (Watch carefully—it browns fast.)

....

Alice Trissel

....

Hummingbird Cake

3 cups flour 2 cups sugar 1 tsp. baking soda 1 tsp. salt 1 tsp. ground cinnamon	Sift together into bowl.

....

2 cups finely chopped bananas ¾ cup chopped nuts 1¼ cups vegetable oil 3 eggs, beaten 1 tsp. vanilla 1 (8-oz.) can crushed pineapple, undrained	Add, stirring until mixed. Do not use electric mixer.

....

Pour into greased and floured 9 or 10-inch tube pan and bake at 350 degrees for 70 minutes, or bake in three 9-inch layer pans for 25 to 30 minutes. Frost with Cream Cheese Frosting (on page 142) when cool.

Brenda Rhodes Fluharty

Imagination Cake

1 (18-oz.) yellow cake mix 1 (3-oz.) pkg. flavored gelatin (any flavor you wish)	Mix in bowl.

4 eggs ¾ cup vegetable oil ¾ cup water	Add at once, beating 2 minutes with electric mixer. Scrape bowl often.

Pour into greased 9 × 13 pan and bake at 350 degrees for about 30 minutes. While cake is hot, prick holes over the top with sharp fork.

Topping:

1½ cups powdered sugar ⅓ cup fruit juice*	Mix together and pour over hot cake so it soaks into the holes.

(*Use any kind of juice that would blend with the flavor gelatin you choose. Use your imagination for combinations! I like to use orange-pineapple gelatin and pineapple juice. Orange juice or juice from frozen strawberries is also de-lish!)

Jell-O Cake

1 (3-oz.) pkg. cherry or raspberry Jell-O ¾ cup boiling water	Stir together until dissolved.

½ cup cold water	Add, and set aside at room temperature.

1 (18-oz.) white cake mix	Mix and bake in 9 × 13 dish according to package directions.

Cool cake 25 minutes. Then pierce holes in cake at ½-inch intervals with sharp fork. Pour Jell-O over cake so it soaks into the holes. Refrigerate.

Topping:

1 envelope Dream Whip 1 (3 ½ oz.) pkg. instant vanilla pudding 1½ cups cold milk	Whip until stiff—about 5 minutes, and spread over cake.

For a lovely Christmas cake:

Dissolve 1 pkg. raspberry Jell-O and 1 pkg. lime Jell-O separately in 1 cup boiling water each. Do not add cold water. Set aside and bake cake in two 8 or 9-inch layer pans. Prick holes as directed. Pour the red Jell-O over the one layer and the green over the other. Refrigerate until set. To remove cake from pans you may need to set in hot water a few minutes to loosen. Use a 9-oz. bowl of Cool Whip to frost cake. Decorate with red and green gumdrops. Flatten with rolling pin and cut into holly leaves and berries.

Linda Shenk

Lady Fingers or Sponge Drops

(Measure all ingredients ahead so egg whites do not need to set after beating.)

4 egg whites **¼ tsp. cream of tartar** **⅔ cup powdered sugar**	Beat egg whites until foamy. Add cream of tartar and beat at highest speed into soft peaks. Gradually add sugar, beating into very stiff, but not dry peaks.
4 egg yolks **½ tsp. vanilla** **¼ tsp salt**	Beat together well.
⅔ cup cake flour	Add, beating thoroughly. Then gently fold into egg whites.

Spoon into well-greased lady finger tins, or onto cookie sheet covered with greased unglazed paper. May use pastry bag to pipe batter onto cookie sheet in 3 ½ or 4-inch × 1 to 1 ½-inch oblongs. Bake at 350 degrees about 12 minutes. Peel paper from warm cakes.

Yield: 25 to 30

Nameless Cake

¾ cup shortening **1½ cups sugar**	Cream thoroughly.
3 eggs, well beaten **1 tsp. vanilla** **½ tsp. lemon flavoring**	Blend in.
1¾ cups flour **1 tsp. baking powder** **½ tsp. baking soda** **½ tsp. salt** **¾ tsp. ground cinnamon** **½ tsp. ground nutmeg** **2 tbsp. cocoa powder** **¾ cup thick sour milk or buttermilk**	Add sifted dry ingredients alternately with milk.

Pour into 2 greased and floured 9-inch layer pans and bake at 350 degrees for about 30 minutes.

Icing:

½ cup butter or margarine **1 egg yolk** **3 cups powdered sugar** **1½ tbsp. cocoa powder** **1 tsp. ground cinnamon** **3 or 4 tbsp. hot coffee to mix**	Beat together until smooth.
½ cup chopped walnuts	Sprinkle over top before icing sets.

Oatmeal Cake

1 cup quick oatmeal 1¼ cups hot water	Combine and set aside to cool for 20 minutes.
½ cup margarine 1 cup sugar 1 cup brown sugar	Cream thoroughly.
2 eggs 1 tsp. vanilla	Add, beating until fluffy.
1⅓ cups flour 1 tsp. baking soda ¼ tsp. salt 1 tsp. ground cinnamon	Sift together and add alternately with oatmeal mixture.

Pour into greased 9 × 13 pan and bake at 350 degrees about 35 minutes.

Topping: ¼ cup soft margarine ½ cup brown sugar ¼ cup cream or 3 tbsp. rich milk 1 cup angel flake coconut ½ cup chopped nuts (optional)	Mix together thoroughly and spread on top of hot cake. Broil a few minutes until slightly brown.

Peanut Butter Cake

¼ cup soft margarine ¼ cup peanut butter 1½ cups brown sugar 2 eggs ½ cup warm water 1 cup thick sour milk 2 cups flour 1 tsp. salt 1 tsp. baking soda	Blend on low speed of electric mixer for 1 minute, scraping bowl frequently. Then beat at medium-high speed for 2 minutes.

Pour into 2 greased and floured 9-inch layer pans or a 9 × 13 pan. Bake at 350 degrees for 25 to 30 minutes.

Frosting: 1 oz. unsweetened chocolate, melted 2 tbsp. soft margarine 2 tbsp. peanut butter 2 cups powdered sugar ½ tsp. vanilla 3 or 4 tbsp. milk to mix	Beat together until thick and creamy. Spread on cooled cake. (Use half this amount for sheet cake.)

Elizabeth Yoder

Party Cake

1 (18-oz.) yellow cake mix (without pudding*)
1 (3½-oz.) pkg. instant vanilla pudding
4 eggs
½ cup oil
¾ cup water
2 tbsp. vinegar
1 tsp. rum flavoring

Blend all ingredients in mixing bowl on low speed 1 minute. Then beat on medium-high speed for 2 minutes.

⅔ cup chopped pecans or walnuts

Sprinkle over bottom of well-greased 9 or 10-inch tube or bundt pan.

Pour batter in pan and bake at 350 degrees for 35 to 40 minutes.

Glaze:
¾ cup sugar
⅓ cup margarine
¼ cup milk

Combine in saucepan. Heat and stir until dissolved. Boil 2 minutes. Remove from heat.

1 tsp. rum flavoring

Add. Pierce holes in hot cake with sharp fork and pour glaze over hot cake.

Cool cake in pan 15 minutes, then remove to finish cooling. Delicious served with or without whipped cream. (*If using pudding cake mix, omit pudding and use 3 eggs instead of 4, and ⅓ cup oil instead of ½.) May also be baked in 9 × 13 pan for sheet cake. Bake sheet cake 25 to 30 minutes.

Lucy Helmick

Pecan Crunch Cake

¼ cup butter, melted
1 cup brown sugar
1 cup chopped pecans

Pat over bottom of greased 9 × 13 pan.

1 (18-oz.) yellow or white cake mix

Prepare according to package directions and pour over mixture in pan.

Bake at 350 degrees for approximately 35 to 40 minutes. Let cool in pan 5 minutes, then turn out on tray to cool. Cut in squares and serve warm with whipped cream and lemon sauce.

Lemon Sauce:
1 cup water
2 tbsp. lemon juice
½ cup sugar
2 tbsp. cornstarch
1 tbsp. margarine
½ tsp. grated lemon peel

Combine in saucepan and cook until thick and clear, stirring constantly. Cool.

Pineapple Delight Cake

1 (18-oz.) yellow cake mix (without pudding)	Bake in 9 × 13 pan according to pkg. directions.
1 (16-oz.) can crushed pineapple **½ cup sugar**	Combine in saucepan and boil 5 minutes. Pour over hot cake. Cool cake well.
3 bananas	Slice over cake.
1 (3½-oz.) pkg. instant vanilla pudding **1 ½ cups milk**	Mix according to pkg. directions. Chill 5 minutes. Spread over cake.
2 cups Cool Whip	Spread over next.
1 cup coconut **½ cup chopped pecans**	Sprinkle over top. Chill until served.

Ruby Petersheim

Variation: Mix 8-oz softened cream cheese with the Cool Whip, and combine mixture with the prepared pudding before spreading on cake.

Dorothy Slabaugh Grove

Prize Pineapple Sponge Cake

(This is one of our favorite cakes)

1⅓ cups flour **1 cup sugar** **½ tsp. baking powder** **½ tsp. salt**	Sift together. Set aside.
6 egg whites **2 tsp. warm water** **1 tsp. cream of tartar** **½ cup sugar**	Add water to whites. Beat until foamy and add cream of tartar. Beat at highest speed into soft peaks, then gradually add sugar beating into very stiff, but not dry peaks.
6 egg yolks **¼ cup pineapple juice** **½ tsp. vanilla** **½ tsp. lemon flavoring**	Measure into bowl with dry ingredients and beat at medium-high speed until light and fluffy—about 4 minutes. Then fold yolk mixture gently into the beaten whites just until blended.

Pour into ungreased 10-inch tube pan and bake at 350 degrees for 45 minutes. Invert pan on a funnel to cool.

Creamy Pineapple Frosting:

½ cup soft margarine **1 cup *well-drained* crushed pineapple** **¼ tsp. vanilla** (see next page)	Beat together just until creamy and spread on cooled cake.

¼ tsp. lemon flavoring
2 or 3 drops yellow color (optional)
3 cups powdered sugar

. . . .

Swedish Pineapple Cake
(Another favorite!)

2 cups sugar
2 cups flour
2 tsp. baking soda
1 tsp. vanilla
2 cups crushed pineapple
   (undrained)
2 eggs
1 cup chopped walnuts (optional)

Measure all ingredients in large bowl. Mix on low speed of electric mixer about 1 minute until blended. Then beat on medium-high speed for 2 minutes.

. . . .

Pour into greased and floured 9 × 13 pan. Bake at 350 degrees for about 35 minutes.

. . . .

Frosting:
½ cup soft margarine
8 oz. cream cheese, softened
1½ cups powdered sugar
1 tsp. vanilla

Beat together until smooth and spread on cooled cake.

. . . .

½ cup chopped walnuts

Sprinkle over frosting before it sets.

. . . .

Evelyn Borntrager
Jewel Shenk

. . . .

Pistachio Cake

1 (18-oz.) white cake mix
3 eggs
1 (3½-oz.) pkg. instant pistachio
   pudding
1 cup vegetable oil
1 cup ginger ale
½ cup chopped nuts

Measure all ingredients into bowl. Blend on low speed for 1 minute. Then beat on medium-high speed for 2 minutes.

. . . .

Pour into 2 greased and floured 9-inch layer pans or a 9 × 13 pan. Bake at 350 degrees for 30 minutes.

. . . .

Topping:
2 pks. Dream Whip
1 (3½-oz.) pkg. instant pistachio
   pudding
1¼ cups milk

Mix and beat until very stiff. This makes enough for layer cake. I use only half this amount for sheet cake.

. . . .

Polka Dot Cake

1¼ cups chopped dates 1 cup boiling water	Combine and set aside to cool.
¾ cup butter or margarine 1 cup sugar	Cream thoroughly.
2 eggs 1 tsp. vanilla	Add, beating until fluffy.
2 cups flour 1 tsp. baking soda ½ tsp. salt	Sift together and add alternately with date mixture.
1 cup chocolate chips (reserve half) ½ cup chopped nuts (optional)	Fold in half of chips and nuts.

Pour into greased and floured 9 × 13 pan. Sprinkle reserved chips over the top. Bake at 350 degrees for about 30 minutes. **Variation:** Omit chocolate chips, and pour the following icing on hot cake instead.

Optional Icing:

¼ cup brown sugar ¼ cup cream 2 tbsp. margarine	Heat in small saucepan, stirring constantly until boiling. Boil 2 minutes. Remove from heat and immediately spread on hot cake.
½ cup angel flake coconut ¼ cup chopped walnuts (optional)	Sprinkle over top.

Poppy Seed Cake

(Since this cake takes so many bought ingredients, I almost didn't include it. However, it is excellent for that special occasion when you want something different and special! Poppy seeds can usually be bought more inexpensively at bulk food stores.)

¼ cup poppy seeds ½ cup boiling water	Combine and let set 5 minutes.
1 (18-oz.) Duncan Hines butter cake mix 1 (3½-oz.) pkg. instant vanilla pudding 1 cup (8-oz.) commercial sour cream ¼ cup sugar ¼ cup vegetable oil 4 eggs 1 tsp. vanilla	Add to poppy seed mixture, blending on low speed of electric mixer for 1 minute Then beat on medium-high speed for 1 minute.
1 cup angel flake coconut ½ cup flour	Add, and beat 1 minute more.

Pour into greased and floured 9 or 10-inch bundt pan. Bake at 300 degrees for 1 hour and 25 minutes. Cool 10 minutes in pan. Then remove from pan and prick holes all around cake with meat fork.

Glaze:

½ cup sugar	Combine in small saucepan. Cook 3 or 4
1 tsp. vanilla	minutes. Pour over hot cake so it will soak in
¼ cup buttermilk	holes.
1 tsp. butter	
1 tbsp. light corn syrup	
¼ tsp. soda	

Esther H. Wenger

Five Flavor Pound Cake

1 cup margarine	Cream thoroughly.
½ cup vegetable shortening	
3 cups sugar	

5 eggs	Beat until lemon colored, then add.

3 cups flour	Add sifted dry ingredients alternately with
½ tsp. baking powder	combined milk and flavorings.
¼ tsp. salt	
1 cup milk	
1 tsp. each of coconut, rum, butter, lemon, and vanilla flavorings	

Very gently push batter into greased 10-inch tube pan. Bake at 340 degrees for about 1¼ hours or until cake tests done.

Glaze:

1 cup sugar	Combine in saucepan. Heat to boiling, stirring
½ cup water	until dissolved. Boil 1 minute. Pour over hot
1 tsp each of coconut, rum, butter, lemon, and vanilla flavorings	cake. Let cake set in pan until cool.

Gladys and Brownie Driver

Variation: For **Coconut Pound Cake,** omit 5 flavorings and add ½ tsp. almond flavoring and 1 tsp. coconut flavoring. Fold in 1½ cups of angel flake coconut last. Omit glaze on coconut cake.

Betty Lahman

Lemon Pound Cake

1 (18-oz.) Duncan Hines yellow cake mix
1 (3½-oz.) pkg. lemon instant pudding
½ cup vegetable oil
4 eggs
1 cup water
1 tsp. butter flavoring
1 tsp. vanilla

Blend all ingredients together in large bowl. Beat for 2 minutes. Don't overmix.

Pour into a greased and floured 9-inch bundt pan and bake at 350 degrees for 35 to 40 minutes. Cool 10 minutes in pan. Then remove and cover tightly to finish cooling. Serve plain, or sprinkle with powdered sugar, or drizzle with glaze.

Variation: For **Poppy Seed Pound Cake,** add 3 tbsp. poppy seeds to the water which should be hot instead of room temperature. Omit vanilla and add ½ tsp. almond flavoring. Blend in water mixture last after mixing all remaining ingredients for 2 minutes.

Glaze:
1 cup powdered sugar
2 tbsp. lemon juice or milk
½ tsp. butter flavoring
2 drops yellow color

Blend until smooth. Drizzle on warm cake.

Luscious Pound Cake Torte

(You may bake your own pound cake. Use recipe for 10-inch tube pan below and bake in two 9 × 5 loaf pans. Freeze one for later use.)

8 oz. pkg. cream cheese
1 cup powdered sugar
½ tsp. vanilla

Beat together until smooth.

1 oz. square unsweetened chocolate

Melt over low heat and blend in.

¾ cup whipping cream
¼ cup powdered sugar

Whip the cream, add sugar, and fold into cream cheese mixture.

1 (10¾-oz.) frozen pound cake, thawed

Slice cake horizontally into 3 layers.

Spread cream cheese mixture between layers and on sides and top of cake. Chill.

Yield: 8 servings

Sour Cream Pound Cake

1 cup butter
2½ cups sugar

Cream together thoroughly.

6 egg yolks	Add one at a time beating well after each addition.

1 tsp. vanilla **1 tsp. almond flavoring, or 2 tsp. lemon flavoring**	Add.

3 cups flour **½ tsp. baking soda** **½ tsp. salt** **1 cup thick sour cream**	Add sifted dry ingredients alternately with sour cream.

6 egg whites, stiffly beaten	Fold in.

Pour into greased and floured 10-inch tube pan and bake at 350 degrees for approximately 60 to 75 minutes. Or bake in two 9 × 5 loaf pans for 50 to 55 minutes. Cool cake 10 minutes, then turn out of pan and cover tightly to finish cooling. Dust with powdered sugar to serve.

Prune (or Plum) Cake

1 cup vegetable oil **1½ cups sugar**	Beat together until well blended.

3 eggs	Add one at a time, beating well after each addition.

2 cups flour **1 tsp. baking powder** **1 tsp. baking soda** **½ tsp. salt** **1 tsp. ground cinnamon** **½ tsp. ground nutmeg** **½ tsp. ground allspice** **1 cup thick sour milk or buttermilk** **1 cup cooked chopped prunes or plums***	Add sifted dry ingredients alternately with milk and prunes.

¾ cup chopped walnuts	Blend in.

Pour into a greased and floured 9 × 13 pan. Bake at 350 degrees for 35 to 40 minutes.

Caramel Glaze:

½ cup sugar **¼ cup thick sour milk or buttermilk** **1 tbsp. light corn syrup** **2 tbsp. butter** **¼ tsp. baking soda** **½ tsp. vanilla**	Combine in saucepan and cook over medium heat, stirring constantly until mixture boils. Turn on low and boil 5 minutes, stirring occasionally. Remove from heat.

Cool cake 5 minutes, then make deep pricks over it with fork so glaze will soak into cake. Pour glaze over hot cake. (*You may use an 8-oz. junior size jar of baby food prunes or plums, if desired.)

Pumpkin Cake

4 eggs, well beaten 2 cups sugar 1 cup oil	Beat together thoroughly.

. . . .

2 cups flour 1 tsp. baking powder 2 tsp. baking soda ½ tsp. salt 1 tsp. ground cinnamon ¼ tsp. ground nutmeg ¼ tsp. ground cloves 2 cups canned pumpkin	Sift dry ingredients together and add alternately with pumpkin.

. . . .

1 cup angel flake coconut	Fold in.

. . . .

Pour into 2 greased 9-inch layer pans or a 9 × 13 pan and bake at 350 degrees for 35 to 40 minutes. Frost with Cream Cheese Frosting on page 142. Then sprinkle with coconut.

. . . .

Basic Cake Roll

(Prepare pan ahead—line an 11 × 15 jelly roll pan with waxed paper. Be sure eggs are at room temperature!)

¾ cup cake flour ¾ tsp. baking powder ½ tsp. salt	Sift together; set aside.

. . . .

4 egg whites 2 tsp. water ½ cup sugar	Combine egg whites and water and beat into soft peaks; add sugar gradually beating into very stiff, but not dry peaks. Set aside.

. . . .

4 egg yolks 1 tsp. vanilla	Beat until light and lemon colored.

. . . .

¼ cup sugar	Slowly add, beating well.

. . . .

Mix in dry ingredients just until blended. Then gently fold in egg whites. Spread batter in prepared pan. Bake at 375 degrees for 15 minutes or until top springs back when lightly touched. Run a knife around the edge of pan to loosen sides of cake. Invert IM-MEDIATELY onto a clean towel sprinkled with powdered sugar. Gently and quickly peel off paper. Roll up hot cake and towel together. Cool completely. Unroll and fill as desired. Reroll and chill.

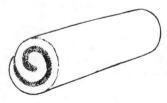

Fillings:
Spread with any kind of jelly. Or use 1 (3 ½-oz.) pkg. chocolate or vanilla instant pudding prepared according to package directions, except use 1 ½ cups milk instead of 2 cups. Or whip 1 cup cream, add 3 tbsp. sugar, and ½ tsp. vanilla; then add sliced fresh strawberries or peaches, or drained frozen fruit. Or add 3 tbsp. cocoa to cream and increase sugar to ⅓ cup. Or add ½ cup fresh or angel flake coconut and ¼ tsp coconut flavor to cream. Or fold 1 (8-oz.) can well-drained crushed pineapple into cream. May also be filled with different flavors of ice cream softened just enough to spread. Reroll quickly and freeze.

Creamy Chocolate Cake Roll

¼ cup margarine	Line an 11 × 15 jelly roll pan with foil. Melt the margarine in the pan.
¾ cup chopped pecans 1 cup angel flake coconut	Sprinkle evenly in pan.
1 (14-oz.) can sweetened condensed milk	Drizzle over mixture in pan. Set aside.
4 eggs	Beat at highest speed until thick and lemon colored—about 5 minutes.
½ cup water	Gradually blend in at lowest speed.
1 (18-oz.) devil's food cake mix	Add, blending 1 minute.

Pour batter over condensed milk in pan, spreading evenly. Bake at 350 degrees for 20 to 25 minutes until center springs back when touched lightly. Dust a clean dish towel with powdered sugar. Remove cake from oven, cover it with towel, and immediately invert pan. Remove foil from cake. Roll up cake with filling inside. Wrap towel around cake to cool. Serve as is, or ice with chocolate frosting. (For Christmas, comb icing with a fork to give appearance of a log. Decorate with cinnamon candies and gumdrops.)

Shoo Fly Cake

4 cups flour ½ tsp. salt ½ tsp. ground cinnamon	Sift together.
2 cups brown sugar	Mix in.
1 cup shortening	Cut in until fine crumbs. Reserve 1 ¼ cups crumbs for topping.
2 cups boiling water 1 cup sorghum molasses (may use half dark corn syrup) 3 tsp. baking soda	Combine, and add to remaining crumbs.

Pour into greased 9 × 13 pan. Top with reserved crumbs. Bake at 350 degrees for approximately 25 minutes. (This makes a very thick cake. I like to put part of the batter into a 9 × 5 loaf pan also, so cake isn't so thick. Bake the 2 thinner cakes about 20 minutes.)

Pumpkin Cake Roll

3 eggs	Beat at highest speed for 5 minutes.
1 cup sugar	Gradually beat in.
⅔ cup canned pumpkin **1 tsp. lemon juice**	Stir in.
¾ cup flour **1 tsp. baking powder** **½ tsp. salt** **2 tsp. ground cinnamon** **½ tsp. ground ginger** **½ tsp. ground nutmeg**	Sift together and fold in.

Spread in waxed-paper-lined 11 × 15 jelly roll pan. Bake at 375 degrees for 15 minutes or until top springs back when touched. (Follow directions for basic cake roll.)

Filling:

6 oz. cream cheese, softened **¼ cup soft margarine** **½ tsp. vanilla** **1 cup powdered sugar**	Beat until smooth and creamy. Fill cake and reroll. Dust with additional powdered sugar or serve with whipped cream.
½ cup chopped pecans (optional)	Sprinkle over top.

Fluffy Yellow Sponge Cake

(This cake is delicious iced with Quick Fluffy White Icing with ¼ tsp. coconut flavoring added, and then sprinkled generously with coconut.)

1½ cups cake flour **1 cup sugar** **1 tsp. baking powder** **½ tsp. salt**	Sift together. Set aside.
5 egg yolks	Beat well.
½ cup sugar	Gradually add, beating until thick and lemon colored.
½ cup warm water **½ tsp. vanilla** **½ tsp. lemon or vanilla flavoring**	Combine, and add alternately with dry ingredients.
5 egg whites **¾ tsp. cream of tartar**	Beat whites until foamy. Add cream of tartar and beat into very stiff, but not dry peaks. Gently fold into batter.

Pour into 2 greased and floured 9-inch layer pans, or a 9 × 13 pan, and bake at 350 degrees for approximately 25 minutes. Or bake in a tube pan for approximately 1 hour.

Hot Milk Sponge Cake

(This is a good multipurpose cake. We like to use it for strawberry shortcake. Or for a quick topping, use broiled topping below.)

4 egg yolks	Beat well.
2 cups sugar **1 tsp. vanilla** **1 tsp. lemon flavoring**	Gradually add, beating until light and thick.
1 cup milk **¼ cup butter or margarine**	Heat together just to boiling point. Then slowly blend into mixture.
2 cups flour **2 tsp. baking powder** **½ tsp. salt**	Sift together and blend in.
4 egg whites	Beat until stiff, then fold in gently.

Pour into 2 greased 9-inch layer pans and bake at 350 degrees for 25 to 30 minutes. Or bake in 9 × 13 pan. This makes a thick cake. For thinner cake, use 9 × 5 loaf pan also.

Topping (optional):

⅔ cup brown sugar **1 cup angel flake coconut** **3 tbsp. soft butter or margarine** **3 tbsp. cream**	Mix thoroughly and spread on hot cake. Broil just until lightly browned.

Lillian Shickel

Blueberry Upside-Down Cake

¼ cup butter or margarine	Melt in 9 × 13 pan.
½ cup sugar	Sprinkle evenly over butter. (If berries are sweetened, omit sugar.)
2 cups fresh, or frozen blueberries, thawed **1 tsp. grated lemon peel or ½ tsp. lemon flavoring**	Mix, then sprinkle over sugar.
1 (18-oz.) yellow cake mix **1 tsp. lemon peel**	Prepare according to pkg. directions, stirring in peel at end of mixing.

Spread batter over berries. Bake at 350 degrees approximately 30 minutes. Let stand 5 minutes. Then turn out on platter. Serve warm with whipped cream.

Southern Special Cake

(This cake is really special! Make the filling first, so it can cool while you bake the cake.)

Filling:

6 egg yolks	Beat well.
¾ cup sugar **¼ tsp. salt**	Gradually add, beating until thick and lemon colored.
⅓ cup margarine	Melt in saucepan on medium heat.
½ cup milk	Add along with egg yolk mixture to melted margarine. Heat, stirring constantly until thickened. Remove from heat.
1 tsp. almond flavoring **½ cup chopped pecans** **¾ cup chopped raisins** **1 cup angel flake coconut**	Mix in until blended. Cool well, then refrigerate.

Cake:

3 cups flour **2¼ cups sugar** **5 tsp. baking powder** **1 tsp. salt** **¾ cup soft shortening**	Measure into mixer bowl. (Sift dry ingredients.)
1 cup milk **1 tsp. vanilla** **½ tsp. almond flavoring**	Blend in ½ minute on low speed, scraping bowl while blending.
6 egg whites **an additional ½ cup milk**	Add. Beat 2 minutes at high speed.

Pour into 3 greased and floured 9-inch layer pans. Bake at 360 degrees about 25 minutes. Spread filling between layers and on top of cooled cake. Frost the sides with the Quick Fluffy White Icing on page 143. Use the back of a teaspoon to make a hobnail effect in the icing. (See page 96 for sketch.)

Strawberry Cake

1 cup fresh or frozen strawberries	If berries are fresh, sprinkle with ¼ cup sugar. Let stand 1 to 2 hours. Then drain. If frozen, thaw, then drain. Reserve juice.
1 (3-oz.) pkg. strawberry flavored gelatin **½ cup boiling water**	Combine, stirring until dissolved. Then cool.
¾ cup vegetable oil **4 eggs**	Combine with gelatin and strawberries.

1 (18-oz.) white or yellow cake mix	Sift into mixer bowl, and add above mixture blending on low speed. Then beat on high speed for 4 minutes.

Pour into 2 greased and floured 9-inch layer pans and bake at 350 degrees for 25 to 30 minutes.

Icing:

½ cup soft butter or margarine **3½ cups powdered sugar** **about ⅓ cup strawberry juice**	Beat until smooth using enough juice to make of good spreading consistency. Ice cooled cake.

Ina Heatwole

Upside-Down Chocolate Nut Cake

¼ cup butter **¼ cup brown sugar**	Heat in saucepan until bubbly.
⅔ cup light corn syrup **¼ cup cream**	Add, and heat just until boiling. Pour into greased 9 × 13 pan.
¾ cup chopped walnuts	Sprinkle over sugar mixture in pan.
1 (18-oz.) chocolate cake mix	Mix according to package directions.

Pour over mixture in pan. Bake at 350 degrees for approximately 30 minutes. Cool in pan 5 minutes, then invert onto tray. Serve warm with whipped cream.

Fluffy White Cake (Basic)

½ cup soft shortening **1½ cups sugar**	Cream thoroughly.
1 tsp. vanilla **½ tsp. almond extract** **1 egg white**	Add, beating until fluffy.
2½ cups cake flour **2½ tsp. baking powder** **½ tsp. salt** **1 cup milk**	Add sifted dry ingredients alternately with milk.
3 egg whites, stiffly beaten	Fold in gently.

Pour into 2 greased and floured 9-inch layer pans or a 9 × 13 pan and bake at 350 degrees for 25 to 30 minutes.

Fluffy Yellow Cake (Basic)

¾ cup soft shortening 1½ cups sugar	Cream thoroughly.
3 egg yolks 1 tsp. vanilla 1 tsp. butter flavoring	Add, beating until fluffy.
2¼ cups flour (or cake flour) 1½ tsp. baking powder 1 tsp. baking soda ½ tsp. salt ¾ cup thick sour milk or buttermilk*	Add sifted dry ingredients alternately with milk.
3 egg whites, stiffly beaten	Fold in gently.

Pour into 2 greased and floured 9-inch layer pans or a 9 × 13 pan and bake at 350 degrees for 25 to 30 minutes. (*May use sweet milk, but omit soda and increase baking powder to 3 tsp. instead.)

Zucchini Chocolate Cake

½ cup margarine ½ cup vegetable oil 1¾ cups sugar	Cream thoroughly.
2 eggs 1 tsp. vanilla	Add, beat well.
2½ cups flour ¼ cup cocoa powder ½ tsp. baking powder ½ tsp. baking soda ½ tsp. salt ½ tsp. ground cinnamon ½ tsp. ground cloves ½ cup thick sour milk	Add sifted dry ingredients alternately with milk.
2 cups grated raw zucchini	Blend in. Pour into greased and floured 9 × 13 pan.
1½ cups chocolate chips	Sprinkle over the top.

Bake at 325 degrees for 40 to 45 minutes.

Harriet Steiner

CAKE MIX
Basic Make-Your-Own Cake Mix

9½ cups all-purpose flour **6 cups sugar** **¼ cup baking powder** **1 tbsp. salt**	Sift together.

2¼ cups shortening (use a good **solid shortening)**	Cut in until very fine crumbs.

Divide mix into 4 equal portions (4 ½ cups each). Place in airtight containers and store in cool, dry place up to 2 months. Or place in freezer containers, and freeze up to 6 months. To use, allow mix to come to room temperature.

Chocolate Cake from Mix

Follow directions for yellow cake except add ¼ cup cocoa powder to cake mix before adding the milk.

Chocolate Chip Cake from Mix

Prepare batter as for yellow cake. Then pour ¼ of batter into each of the 2 pans, and sprinkle ¼ cup finely chopped semisweet chocolate pieces, or tiny chocolate chips over batter. Add remaining batter to each pan and sprinkle another ¼ cup chocolate pieces over batter. Bake as directed.

Pineapple Upside-Down Cake from Mix

Prepare pan as follows:

⅓ cup butter or margarine	Melt in a 9 × 13 cake pan.

⅔ cup brown sugar	Stir into butter.

8 slices pineapple **8 maraschino cherries**	Arrange in pan with cherries in center of each pineapple slice.

Then prepare batter for a yellow cake and pour over the top. Bake at 350 degrees for 30 to 35 minutes. Cool in pan 5 minutes, then invert on plate. Serve warm. Delicious with ice cream or whipped cream.

Spice Cake from Mix

Prepare batter as for yellow cake except add 1 tsp. cinnamon, ¼ tsp. allspice, and ¼ tsp. cloves to cake mix before adding the milk.

White Cake from Mix

Prepare batter as for yellow cake except use 3 egg whites instead of 2 whole eggs. Whites may be beaten separately and folded in last for a fluffier cake. Bake as directed.

Yellow Cake from Mix

4½ cups (1 portion) basic mix
1 cup milk
1 tsp. vanilla
2 eggs

In mixer bowl, combine all ingredients. Beat at low speed until moistened, about 1 minute. Beat 2 minutes at medium-high speed.

Pour into 2 greased and floured 9-inch layer cake pans or a 9 × 13 pan and bake at 350 degrees for 25 minutes.

Portions for One Quick-Mix Cake

2⅓ cups flour
3 tsp. baking powder
¾ tsp. salt
1½ cups sugar

Sift together into bowl.

½ cup + 1 tbsp. shortening

Cut in until fine crumbs.

2 eggs
1 cup milk
1 tsp. vanilla

Add, beating at low speed 1 minute scrapping bowl often. Then beat at medium-high speed for 2 minutes.

Pour into 2 greased 9-inch layer cake pans or a 9 × 13 pan and bake at 350 degrees for 25 to 30 minutes.

CUPCAKES

Little Cream Cakes

These are not cupcakes, but is an idea for a very handy lunch item that is quite similar to Twinkies. It seemed to fit best here with the cupcakes. Bake a yellow cake in a 9 × 13 pan—the Fluffy Yellow Cake on page 136, the Fluffy Yellow Sponge Cake on page 132, or a yellow cake mix. Cut cake in half horizontally making two layers. Fill cake between layers with the Boiled Flour Icing on page 143. Then cut little cakes 4½ × 1½ inches in size, and wrap each individually in plastic wrap. Freeze for quick use.

Carrot-Pineapple Cupcakes

Mix batter for Carrot Pineapple Bread on page 79. Fill paper-lined muffin cups ¾ full. Bake at 375 degrees for about 20 minutes. When cool, frost with cream cheese frosting. Yield: 24 cupcakes

Mini Date Cakes
(This is a Christmas favorite!)

4 eggs	Beat.
2 cups sugar **1 cup melted margarine** **1 tsp. grated orange rind**	Gradually beat in.
2 cups flour **1 tsp. baking powder** **1 tsp. salt**	Sift together and add.
2 cups chopped dates **¾ cup chopped maraschino or candied cherries**	Stir in. Fill paper cups ½ to ¾ full.
pecan halves to garnish	Place 1 on top of each cake.

Bake at 325 degrees for 25 to 30 minutes.

Yield: 20 to 24 cupcakes

Donna Lou Heatwole

Never-Fail Cupcakes

2 eggs **⅔ cup cocoa powder** **1 cup shortening** **3 cups flour** **1 cup thick sour milk or buttermilk** **2 tsp. vanilla** **2 tsp. baking soda** **2 cups sugar** **1 cup hot water**	Measure all ingredients into mixer bowl in order listed. Beat until smooth, approximately 2 minutes, scraping bowl often.

Pour into cupcake papers and bake at 350 degrees for 20 to 25 minutes. Cool and frost as desired.

Yield: 24 cupcakes

Raisins and Spice Cupcakes

1 cup raisins 1¼ cups water	Combine in saucepan, and simmer 10 minutes. Drain and reserve liquid. If needed, add water to liquid to make 1 cup.
1 cup butter or margarine 1½ cups sugar	Cream thoroughly.
2 eggs	Add, beating until fluffy.
2½ cups flour 1 tsp. baking powder 1 tsp. baking soda ½ tsp. salt 1½ tsp. ground cinnamon ½ tsp. ground nutmeg	Sift together and add alternately with reserved raisin liquid.
¼ cup flour ¾ cup chopped walnuts	Mix with raisins until well dusted. Stir in.

Pour into paper-lined muffin cups filling ⅔ full. Bake at 375 degrees for 18 to 20 minutes or until done. (May be dusted with powdered sugar or iced with caramel icing.)

Yield: 36 cupcakes

Yummy Cupcakes

Creamy Filling: 8 oz. softened cream cheese ⅔ cup sugar 2 eggs ¼ tsp. salt	Beat together well.
1½ cups chocolate chips	Blend in. Refrigerate while mixing cake.
Cake Mixture: 3 cups flour 2 cups sugar 2 tsp. baking soda ½ tsp. salt ½ cup cocoa powder	Sift together.
⅔ cup vegetable oil 2 tsp. vanilla 2 tsp. vinegar 2 cups water	Add and beat until well blended.

Fill cupcake papers ½ full with cake mixture. Add about 2 tsp. filling to each cake. Bake at 350 degrees for about 25 minutes. Do not overbake. (May add a tsp. of cherry pie filling in slight indentation in top of cakes after cakes are cooled if desired.)

Yield: 34 to 36 cupcakes.

Pam Weaver

FROSTINGS AND FILLINGS

Quick Fluffy Brown Sugar Icing

1½ cups brown sugar
¼ tsp. cream of tartar
¼ cup water
2 egg whites, unbeaten
⅛ tsp. salt

Combine in top of double boiler. Beat over rapidly boiling water with electric mixer until icing holds fairly stiff peaks. Remove from heat.

½ tsp. vanilla

Blend in, beating into very stiff peaks.

Quick Caramel Frosting

½ cup butter or margarine
1 cup brown sugar

Melt together on low heat, and boil 2 minutes, stirring constantly.

¼ cup milk

Add, and heat just until boiling again. Remove from heat and cool slightly.

2 cups sifted powdered sugar

Stir in until smooth.

Old-Fashioned Chocolate Frosting

2 cups sugar
3 tbsp. light corn syrup
½ cup milk
½ cup evaporated milk
1½ or 2 (1-oz.) squares
   unsweetened chocolate

Combine all ingredients in saucepan. Heat, stirring constantly until dissolved. Cook to soft-ball stage (235 degrees). Remove from heat. Cool slightly, then beat until of spreading consistency.

If icing sets too quickly, add a little hot water to thin. Spread on cake immediately.

Quick Chocolate Frosting

1 (1-oz.) square unsweetened
   chocolate
2 tbsp. butter or margarine
¼ cup milk

Heat together in saucepan on low heat just until chocolate melts. Remove from heat.

approximately 2 cups powdered
   sugar

Stir in until of desired spreading consistency and until smooth.

Chocolate Peanut Butter Frosting

½ cup peanut butter
⅓ cup cocoa powder

Cream together.

. . . .

2½ cups powdered sugar
1 tsp. vanilla
⅓ to ½ cup cream or evaporated
   milk

Add, beating until smooth. (Use enough cream to make of good spreading consistency.)

. . . .

Coating Icing

½ cup water
2 tbsp. light corn syrup
¼ tsp. vanilla
5½ cups powdered sugar

Heat together to a lukewarm temperature. Spoon over pieces of cake or confections on a rack so excess can drain off.

. . . .

Cocoa Fluff

1 cup whipping cream
3 tbsp. cocoa powder
⅛ tsp. salt

Mix in chilled bowl and beat until stiff.

. . . .

⅓ cup sugar

Gradually add just until blended.

. . . .

Cocoa Frosting

¼ cup soft margarine
2 cups powdered sugar
¼ cup cocoa powder
¼ cup evaporated milk or cream
½ tsp. vanilla

Beat together until smooth and fluffy.

. . . .

Cream Cheese Frosting

8 oz. softened cream cheese
½ cup soft margarine
1 tsp. vanilla
3 cups powdered sugar
small amount of milk to mix

Combine all ingredients with 1 tbsp. milk or more and mix until smooth.

. . . .

Decorating Icing

½ cup Crisco
1 lb. powdered sugar (about 3 ½
   cups) (see next page)

Beat all ingredients together until smooth.

5 tbsp. milk
½ tsp. vanilla

May use half vanilla and half almond flavoring if desired.

Geneva Bowman

Boiled Flour Icing

(This is a good creamy icing that isn't so sweet.)

5 tbsp. flour **1 cup milk**	Mix together in saucepan and cook until thickened, stirring constantly. (Mixture will be very thick.) Cool thoroughly.
1 cup Crisco or margarine **1 cup sugar** **½ tsp. vanilla**	Beat together. Then add flour mixture and beat until very fluffy—5 or more minutes!

Variation: Add 2 ½ tbsp. cocoa powder in flour mixture for chocolate icing.

Diane Burkholder

Quick Fluffy White Icing

(Sometimes called 7-minute icing, because it takes about 7 minutes to make.)

2 egg whites **¾ cup sugar** **⅓ cup light corn syrup** **2 tbsp. water** **¼ tsp. salt** **¼ tsp. cream of tartar**	Combine in top of double boiler. Cook over rapidly boiling water, while beating with electric mixer at highest speed until mixture stands in stiff peaks. Remove from heat.
1 tsp. vanilla	Add, continuing to beat into very stiff peaks.

Maple Cake Topping

(Delicious on chocolate or yellow cake.)

1 cup brown sugar **3 tbsp. flour**	Combine in saucepan.
¼ cup margarine **1 cup milk**	Add, and cook until thickened. Remove from heat.
1 tsp. maple flavoring	Stir in.

Cool 10 minutes. Then pour over cooled cake and cover tightly.

Broiled Pineapple Frosting

¼ cup butter or margarine, melted
1 cup brown sugar
1 cup angel flake coconut
1 cup crushed pineapple, drained
½ cup chopped walnuts

Blend together thoroughly and spread on hot cake. Broil about 2 minutes or until frosting is lightly browned. Enough for a 9 × 13 cake.

Creamy Peanut Butter Frosting

3 oz. softened cream cheese
¼ cup peanut butter
2 cups powdered sugar
2 tbsp milk
½ tsp. vanilla

Beat together until creamy.

Quick Powdered Sugar Frosting

¼ cup Crisco or margarine

Heat just until softened and beginning to melt. Do not overheat!

2 cups powdered sugar
½ tsp. vanilla
approx. 3 tbsp. milk

Beat in until smooth.

Satiny Beige Icing

⅔ cup brown sugar
3 tbsp. water
⅓ cup light corn syrup

Heat together in saucepan stirring until dissolved. Boil rapidly until syrup spins a thread (242 degrees).

2 large egg whites (⅓ cup)

Beat until very stiff. Slowly pour hot syrup into white, beating constantly.

1 tsp. vanilla

Add, beating into very stiff peaks.

Sour Cream Chocolate Frosting

2 (1-oz.) squares unsweetened
   chocolate
¼ cup butter or margarine

Melt together on low heat. Cool several minutes.

½ cup commercial sour cream
1 tsp. vanilla

Beat in until smooth.

3 cups powdered sugar

Add, beating until creamy.

White Mountain Frosting

(To prevent formation of sugar crystals around edge of pan which can make icing gritty, cover pan for first 2 or 3 minutes of boiling time to melt down crystals. Then uncover, cautiously insert thermometer, and boil to 240 degrees.)

¾ cup sugar ¼ cup light corn syrup 3 tbsp. water 1 tsp. vinegar	Combine in saucepan & heat to boiling, stirring until dissolved. Boil rapidly until mixture spins a thread (240 degrees).
¼ cup egg whites (2 large)	Beat into stiff peaks, then slowly pour hot syrup into whites, beating constantly until very stiff and fluffy.
1 tsp. vanilla	Blend in.

For marshmallow frosting—drop 6 large marshmallows over the top of hot syrup as soon as it reaches 240 degrees. Turn off burner and cover pan tightly. Let set to soften while you beat egg whites. When beating hot syrup into egg whites, hold back marshmallows with rubber scraper until last. Then add to egg white mixture, beating until thick and fluffy. **For chocolate frosting**—grate a 1-oz. square of unsweetened chocolate and sprinkle on the hot boiled syrup. Cover just until melted, then beat syrup into egg whites.

Fillings

Fillings always help to make a cake moist and special. My family often enjoys having a sheet cake spread with filling rather than a sweet icing. There is so much variety with fillings. Try the orange filling in a cake iced with fluffy white icing to which you have added ½ tsp. orange flavoring instead of vanilla. Then sprinkle with toasted coconut. Or ice an orange-filled cake with cream cheese frosting. Instant puddings also make delicious cake fillings. Use 1½ cups milk instead of the 2 cups called for on a 3½ oz. package of instant pudding when using for a filling. There are many delightful combinations with the many flavors of puddings, using basic chocolate, yellow, or white cakes. (Cover the following fillings while cooling so a film doesn't form over the top.)

Chocolate Cream Filling

3 tbsp. cornstarch ¾ cup sugar 3 tbsp. cocoa powder	Mix together in saucepan.
1 egg yolk 1 cup milk	Add, and cook until thickened, stirring constantly. Remove from heat.
1 tbsp. butter ½ tsp. vanilla	Blend in. Cool thoroughly.

Date Filling

(For a delicious combination, bake the cake part of the Chocolate Cherry Valentine Cake Torte on page 111. Fill with Date Filling, and ice with the Sour Cream Chocolate Frosting on page 144.)

1½ tbsp. cornstarch ½ cup sugar 1 egg, lightly beaten ⅔ cup chopped dates or raisins 1 cup milk	Combine in saucepan, and cook until thickened, stirring constantly. Remove from heat. Cool.
½ cup chopped nuts ½ tsp. vanilla	Blend in. Cool thoroughly.

Fruit Filling

½ cup sugar 1½ tbsp. cornstarch 1 cup crushed pineapple, undrained 1 cup cooked dried apricots, diced 1 tbsp. grated orange rind 1 cup flaked coconut	Combine in saucepan and cook until thickened, stirring constantly. Cool.

Orange (or Lemon) Filling

¾ cup sugar 3 tbsp. cornstarch	Combine in saucepan.
1 egg yolk ½ cup water ½ cup orange juice 1 tsp. grated orange rind	Add, and cook until thickened, stirring constantly.
1 tbsp. butter	Blend in. Cool.

(For lemon filling: use ¼ cup lemon juice and ¼ cup water instead of orange juice. Omit rind.)

Pineapple Filling

½ cup sugar 3 tbsp. cornstarch 1½ cups crushed pineapple, undrained 1 egg, slightly beaten	Combine in saucepan. Cook until thickened, stirring constantly.
1 tbsp. butter	Blend in. Cool.

Variation: May add 1 cup angel flake coconut.

BAR COOKIES

Brownies

1 cup margarine, softened **1¾ cups sugar**	Cream thoroughly.
4 eggs **1 tsp. vanilla**	Add, beating until fluffy.
2 (1-oz.) squares unsweetened **chocolate, melted**	Blend in.
1 cup sifted flour	Add.
½ cup chopped nuts	Fold in.

Pour into greased 9 × 13 pan and bake at 325 degrees for 35 minutes. Cut into squares.

Mint Brownies

¼ cup margarine **1 cup sugar**	Cream thoroughly.
4 eggs	Add, one at a time, beating well.
1 (16-oz.) can chocolate syrup, **(such as Hershey's)**	Blend in.
1 cup + 1 tbsp. flour	Add.
½ cup chopped nuts	Blend in.

Pour in greased 11 × 15 pan. Bake at 350 degrees for 20 to 25 minutes. Cool.

Frosting:

2 cups powdered sugar **½ cup margarine** **2 tbsp. milk** **½ tsp. peppermint flavoring** **2 or 3 drops green food color**	Beat together until smooth and creamy. Spread over completely cooled brownies. Place in refrigerator or freezer to chill.
1 cup chocolate chips **¼ cup margarine**	Melt together. Spread over chilled green frosting. Store in refrigerator.

Cut in bars.

Edith Branner

Chocolate Chip Blonde Brownies

¾ cup margarine 2 cups brown sugar	Heat together until melted stirring constantly. Cool slightly.
2 eggs 2 tsp. vanilla	Add, beating well.
2 cups flour 1 tsp. baking powder ½ tsp. baking soda ¾ tsp. salt	Sift together and add.
¾ cup chopped dates ¾ cup chocolate chips	Blend in.

Pour into greased (but not floured) 11 × 15 pan. Bake at 350 degrees 20 to 25 minutes. Do not overbake. Cut into squares.

Nancy Heatwole

Peanut Butter Brownies

⅔ cup sugar 2 cups brown sugar ½ cup shortening ½ cup peanut butter	Cream together thoroughly.
4 eggs 1 tsp. vanilla	Add, beating until fluffy.
2⅔ cups flour 3 tsp. baking powder 1 tsp. salt	Sift together and blend in only until smooth. Spread dough in two greased 9 × 13 pans.
1 cup chopped peanuts	Sprinkle over top.

Bake at 350 degrees approximately 20 minutes. Do not overbake. Cut into bars.

Betty Jane Brenneman

Chewy Granola Bars

½ to 1 cup brown sugar ⅔ cup peanut butter ½ cup light corn syrup or honey ½ cup margarine, melted 2 tsp. vanilla	Mix together until well blended.
3 cups quick oatmeal ½ cup coconut ½ cup sunflower nuts ½ cup raisins (see next page)	Stir in.

⅓ cup wheat germ
2 tbsp. sesame seeds
1 cup chocolate or butterscotch
   chips

. . . .

Press mixture in a greased 9 × 13 pan. Bake at 350 degrees for 15 to 20 minutes, or until lightly browned. Cool completely. Cut into 24 bars.

Carolyn Shank

Deluxe Chocolate Marshmallow Bars

(A family favorite!)

¾ cup margarine 1½ cups sugar	Cream together thoroughly.
3 eggs 1 tsp. vanilla	Add, beating until fluffy.
1⅓ cups flour ½ tsp. baking powder ½ tsp. salt 3 tbsp. cocoa powder	Sift together and add.
½ cup chopped nuts (optional)	Fold in.

Spread in greased 11 × 15 pan. Bake at 350 degrees for 15 to 18 minutes.

4 cups miniature marshmallows	Sprinkle evenly over chocolate layer as soon as you remove it from oven. Return to oven for 2 minutes to slightly melt. Use knife to spread evenly.* Cool.
Deluxe Topping: 1⅓ cups chocolate chips 3 tbsp. butter or margarine 1 cup peanut butter	Combine in saucepan. Stir constantly over low heat until melted. Remove from heat.
2 cups Rice Krispies cereal	Stir in. Spread over top of bars.
Optional Chocolate Topping: 2 cups powdered sugar 3 tbsp. cocoa powder 3 tbsp. soft margarine 3 or 4 tbsp. hot coffee to mix ¼ tsp. vanilla	Beat together until smooth. Spread over bars.

(*Dip knife in water occasionally to aid in spreading if necessary.)

Coconut-Chip Meringue Squares

(This is another family specialty.)

¾ cup margarine ½ cup sugar ½ cup brown sugar 3 egg yolks 1 tsp. vanilla	Beat together for 2 minutes.
2 cups flour 1 tsp. baking powder ¼ tsp. baking soda ¼ tsp. salt	Sift together and mix in thoroughly. Pat dough in greased 9 × 13 pan.
1 cup angel flake coconut ¾ cup chocolate chips	Sprinkle over dough.
3 egg whites ¼ tsp. cream of tartar	Beat into soft peaks.
¾ cup brown sugar	Gradually add, beating at highest speed into very stiff peaks. Spread over top 'sealing' to edges of pan.

Place on lower rack in oven and bake at 350 degrees for 30 minutes. Cool completely, then cut into bars. If meringue wants to tear, dip knife in hot water occasionally while cutting bars.

Evelyn Borntrager

Crispy Date Bars

1 cup flour ½ cup brown sugar ½ cup margarine, softened	Mix together until crumbly. Press in an 11 × 7, or a 9-inch square bake dish. Bake at 350 degrees for 10 minutes.
1 cup chopped dates ½ cup sugar ½ cup margarine	Heat together in saucepan, stirring constantly until boiling. Simmer 3 minutes.
1 egg, well beaten	Add a little of hot mixture to egg first, stirring well, then add to mixture in saucepan. Heat to a good boil again. Remove from heat.
3½ cups Rice Krispies cereal ½ cup chopped nuts 1 tsp. vanilla	Stir in, and spread over baked crust. Cool completely.
Frosting: 2 cups powdered sugar ½ tsp. vanilla 3 oz. softened cream cheese	Beat together until smooth. Spread over top. Cut into bars.

Congo Squares

⅔ cup margarine **2¼ cups brown sugar**	Melt together. Cool slightly.

3 eggs	Add, one at a time, beating well.

2¾ cups flour **2½ tsp. baking powder** **½ tsp. salt**	Sift together and add.

¾ cup chocolate chips **½ cup chopped nuts (optional)**	Fold in.

Pour in greased (but not floured) 9 × 13 pan. Bake at 350 degrees 25 minutes. Or bake in 11 × 14 pan for 20 minutes. Cut in squares when cool.

Dorothy Shank Showalter

Fruit-Filled Oatmeal Squares

½ cup butter or margarine **1¼ cups flour** **1 cup brown sugar** **1½ cups quick oatmeal**	Mix together until crumbly. Press ⅔ crumbs in a 9-inch square pan. Reserve other ⅓ crumbs.

1 (21-oz.) can fruit pie filling (cherry, blueberry, etc.)	Spread with pie filling. Sprinkle with reserve crumbs.

Bake at 325 degrees for approximately 20 minutes. Cool and cut into squares.

Lemon Bars

1 cup margarine **2½ cups flour** **½ cup sugar**	Mix together until crumbly. Pat into a 9 × 13 pan. Bake at 350 degrees for 15 minutes or until brown on edges.

4 eggs	Beat well.

1½ cups sugar	Gradually add, beating well.

⅓ cup flour **½ tsp. baking powder** **6 tbsp. lemon juice** **¼ tsp. salt**	Blend in. Pour over baked crust.

Bake for 18 minutes more or until set. Cool and sprinkle with powdered sugar.

Arneida Gaines

Date or Raisin-Filled Oatmeal Squares

(If using raisins, run through coarse blade on food grinder for best flavor.)

2 cups chopped dates or chopped
  raisins
¼ cup flour
⅔ cup brown sugar
1 tsp. vanilla
1½ cups water

Combine in saucepan and cook just until thickened. Set aside.

2 cups flour
1 tsp. baking soda
¼ tsp. salt
3 cups quick oatmeal
1½ cups brown sugar
1 cup margarine

Mix together in bowl until crumbly. Pat half of mixture in 11 × 15 pan. Spread with filling. Sprinkle with remaining crumbs. Pat down with fork.

Bake at 350 degrees for 20 minutes. Cut in squares.

Oatmeal Delights

1½ cups shortening
1 cup sugar
1 cup brown sugar

Cream thoroughly.

4 eggs
2 tsp. vanilla

Add, beating until fluffy.

2 cups flour
½ tsp. salt
1 tsp. baking powder
2 cups quick oatmeal

Sift together (except oatmeal) and add.

¾ cup raisins
¾ cup chocolate or butterscotch
  chips

Fold in.

Spread in greased 11 × 15 pan. Bake at 350 degrees for approximately 25 minutes. Do not overbake.

Optional Topping:
1½ cups chocolate chips

Sprinkle over hot bars. Spread when soft.

¾ cup chopped nuts
¾ cup shredded coconut

Sprinkle over soft chocolate. Cut in bars when cool.

Oatmeal Fudge Bars

1 cup margarine
1 cup sugar
1 cup brown sugar
2½ cups flour
1 tsp. salt

Mix together as for pie crust until crumbly. Reserve 2½ cups crumbs.

2 eggs **2 tsp. vanilla** **1 tsp. baking soda** **3 cups oatmeal**	Add to remaining crumbs. Press into greased 11 × 15 pan. (Spread with filling.)

Filling:

1½ cups chocolate chips **2 tbsp. margarine** **¼ tsp. salt** **1 (14-oz.) can sweetened** **condensed milk**	Combine in saucepan. Heat until dissolved, stirring constantly. Remove from heat.

2 tsp. vanilla **½ cup chopped nuts**	Blend in. Spread over crumbs in pan, and sprinkle with reserved crumbs.

Bake at 350 degrees for 25 minutes. Cool and cut in bars.

Peanut Butter Bars

½ cup margarine **½ cup sugar** **½ cup brown sugar**	Cream together thoroughly.

1 egg **½ tsp. vanilla** **⅓ cup peanut butter** **½ tsp. baking soda** **½ tsp. salt**	Beat in.

1 cup flour **1 cup quick oatmeal** **2 tbsp. milk**	Stir in.

Spread in greased (but not floured) 9 × 13 pan. Bake at 350 degrees for 20 to 25 minutes. Do not overbake.

Frosting:

¾ to 1 cup chocolate chips	Sprinkle over hot bars immediately after removing from oven to melt.

½ cup powdered sugar **¼ cup peanut butter** **2 tbsp. milk**	Combine thoroughly, then spread over hot bars, blending into melted chocolate as you spread.

Cut into bars when cool.

Ruth Ann Horst

Favorite Peanut Squares

¾ cup margarine ½ cup sugar ½ cup peanut butter 1 cup quick oatmeal 1 cup flour	Combine and work together until crumbly. Press in bottom of 11 × 15 pan. Bake at 350 degrees 10 to 15 minutes until slightly browned at edges.

Topping:

3 eggs	Beat well.

¾ cup brown sugar 1 tsp. vanilla	Gradually add, beating well.

3 tbsp. flour ½ tsp. baking powder 1 cup angel flake coconut	Blend in. Spread over baked crust.

1 cup peanuts, coarsely chopped	Sprinkle over top.

Bake another 10 to 15 minutes. Cut in bars when cool.

Raggedy Top Bars

1 cup soft margarine ½ cup sugar ½ cup brown sugar	Cream together thoroughly.

1 egg 1 tsp. vanilla	Add, beating until fluffy.

2 cups flour ½ tsp. salt ½ tsp. baking soda	Blend in.

Spread in greased 11 × 15 pan. Bake at 350 degrees for 20 minutes until slightly browned. (Spread with topping.)

Butterscotch Topping:

1 cup butterscotch chips ⅓ cup light corn syrup 2 tbsp. margarine 1 tbsp. water	Combine in saucepan and stir over low heat until melted and well blended. Remove from heat.

1 tsp. vanilla 1⅓ cups angel flake coconut ½ cup chopped nuts	Stir in. Then spread over hot bars and bake 8 minutes longer.

Cut into bars when cool.

Pumpkin Bars
(This is a fall of the year favorite.)

1 cup margarine 2 cups brown sugar	Cream together thoroughly.
2 eggs 1 tsp. vanilla	Add, beating until fluffy.
2 cups flour 1 tsp. baking powder ¼ tsp. baking soda ½ tsp. salt 1 tsp. ground cinnamon ½ tsp. ground ginger ¼ tsp. ground allspice 1 cup canned pumpkin	Add sifted dry ingredients alternately with pumpkin.
1 cup angel flake coconut ½ cup chopped nuts	Blend in.

Spread in greased 11 × 15 pan. Bake at 350 degrees for 25 minutes. Cut into bars when cool.

Anna Mae Weaver

Spicy Raisin Bars

½ cup margarine 1 cup raisins 1 cup water	Heat in saucepan to a good rolling boil. Remove from heat.
1 cup sugar 1 egg ½ tsp. ground cinnamon ½ tsp. ground cloves	Combine, then add to raisin mixture.
2 cups flour 1 tsp. baking soda ½ tsp. salt	Add.

Pour into greased 9 × 13 pan and bake at 350 degrees for 15 minutes.

Icing:

1⅓ cups powdered sugar ½ tsp. vanilla 2 tbsp. soft margarine 2 tbsp. milk	Beat together until smooth. Spread on hot bars 10 minutes after removing from oven.

Jesse Johnson
Sandy Sherman

Rocky Road Fudge Bars

½ cup margarine 1 (1-oz.) square unsweetened chocolate	Melt together on low heat.
1 cup sugar	Add, beating until blended.
2 eggs 1 tsp. vanilla	Add, beating until fuffy.
1 cup flour 1 tsp. baking powder ¼ tsp. salt	Sift together and add.
½ cup chopped nuts (optional)	Blend in. Spread in greased 9 × 13 pan.
Filling: 6 oz. softened cream cheese ½ cup sugar ¼ cup soft margarine ½ tsp. vanilla 2 tbsp. flour 1 egg	Measure into mixing bowl, and beat until smooth and fluffy. Spread over chocolate mixture. Bake at 350 degrees for 25 to 30 minutes.
Frosting: 2 or 3 cups miniature marshmallows	Sprinkle over hot cake as soon as you remove it from oven, to soften.
¼ cup margarine 1 (1-oz.) square unsweetened chocolate	Melt together on low heat.
2 oz. softened cream cheese 3 tbsp. milk ½ tsp. vanilla	Add, beating well.
2½ cups powdered sugar	Gradually add, beating until smooth.

Immediately drizzle over the softened marshmallows. Cool, and cut into bars.

Toffee-Nut Bars

½ cup margarine ½ cup brown sugar 1 cup flour	Mix together and press in 9 × 13 pan. Bake at 350 degrees for 12 minutes.
2 eggs, beaten 1 cup brown sugar 1 tsp. vanilla	Blend together.

2 tbsp. flour **1 tsp. baking powder** **½ tsp. salt**	Mix together, then blend in.

1 cup angel flake coconut **¾ cup chopped nuts**	Add. Pour over crust and bake 20 minutes more.

Cool slightly, then cut into bars. **Variation:** For Christmas, sprinkle ⅓ cup chopped maraschino cherries over coconut mixture just before baking the last time. (For more chewy bars, reduce the amount of brown sugar in topping to ½ cup and add ½ cup light corn syrup.)

Bonnie Knight

Zucchini Bars

1 cup vegetable oil **2 cups sugar**	Beat together well.

4 eggs **2 tsp. vanilla**	Add, beating until fluffy.

2 cups flour **1 tsp. baking powder** **1 tsp. baking soda** **1 tsp. ground cinnamon** **¼ tsp. salt**	Sift together and add.

2 cups shredded raw zucchini **1 cup chopped nuts**	Fold in.

Pour into a greased 11 × 15 pan and bake at 350 degrees for about 25 minutes.

Frosting:

3 oz. softened cream cheese **¼ cup margarine** **2 tsp. milk** **½ tsp. vanilla** **2 cups powdered sugar**	Beat together until smooth and spread on cooled bars.

Turtles

2 cups flour **1 cup light brown sugar** **½ cup butter**	Mix together until crumbly. Pat firmly into a 9 × 13 *glass* dish.
1¼ cups pecan halves	Place evenly over crust.
¾ cup brown sugar **¾ cup butter or margarine**	Heat in saucepan, and boil 1 minute, stirring constantly. Pour evenly over pecan crust, and bake at 325 degrees for 20 minutes.
1 cup chocolate chips	Sprinkle over hot bars immediately after removing from oven.

Let set 2 minutes to soften, then swirl as they melt leaving some whole. Do not spread smooth. Cool and cut into bars.

Carolyn Reed

DROP COOKIES AND MISCELLANEOUS COOKIES

Anise Fruit-Nut Cookies

½ cup butter or margarine **1 cup sugar**	Cream together thoroughly.
2 eggs	Add, beating until fluffy
¼ cup honey **¼ cup sorghum molasses** **1 tsp. baking soda dissolved in ½** **cup warm coffee** **1½ tsp. anise extract or ¼ tsp. oil of** **anise**	Add.
4¼ cups flour **½ tsp. salt** **½ tsp. ground cloves**	Sift together and blend in.
¾ cup chopped walnuts **1 cup chopped dates** **1 cup chopped raisins**	Fold in. Cover and chill dough in refrigerator at least 1 hour.

Lightly flour hands and form dough into 1¼-inch balls. Place on greased baking sheet and flatten slightly. Bake at 350 degrees for 8 to 10 minutes. Cool. Roll in powdered sugar to coat. Store in tight container. Better the next day.

Yield: approximately 7 dozen

Apple Cookies

¾ cup shortening 1½ cups brown sugar	Cream together thoroughly.
3 eggs 1 tsp. vanilla	Add, beating until fluffy.
2 cups flour ½ tsp. salt ¾ tsp. baking powder ¾ tsp. baking soda ¾ tsp. ground cinnamon 1½ cups quick oatmeal	Sift together (except oats), and add.
⅓ cup flour 2 med.-sized peeled apples, chopped ¾ cup raisins or dates, chopped ⅔ cup walnuts, chopped	Stir together, then fold in.

Drop by spoon onto greased baking sheet. Bake at 350 degrees for about 12 minutes.

Yield: 5 or 6 dozen

Basic Drop Cookies

1 cup shortening 2 cups brown sugar (or 1 each granulated and brown)	Cream together thoroughly.
2 eggs 2 tsp. vanilla	Add, beating until fluffy.
4 cups flour 1 tsp. baking soda 1 tsp. salt ¼ cup milk (preferably thick sour milk)	Add sifted dry ingredients alternately with milk.
¾ cup chocolate chips	Stir in.

Drop onto greased baking sheet. Bake at 350 degrees for 10 to 12 minutes.

Variations: For **coconut cookies,** add 1 ½ cups angel flake coconut in place of chocolate chips and ½ tsp. coconut flavoring instead of vanilla. For **raisin cookies:** cook together 1 cup raisins, 2 tbsp. sugar, ¾ cup water, and 1½ tsp. Clearjel or cornstarch just until thickened. Cool slightly. Press a slight indentation in center of each cookie before baking and fill with 1 tsp. raisin mixture. May also use jelly instead of raisins if desired.

Yield: approximately 6 dozen   *Dorothy Shank Showalter*

Banana Chocolate Chip Cookies

1½ cups flour **1 cup sugar** **½ tsp. baking soda** **1 tsp. salt** **¾ tsp. ground cinnamon** **¼ tsp. ground nutmeg**	Sift together into bowl.

¾ cup margarine	Cut in until crumbly.

1 egg, beaten **1 cup mashed bananas (2 medium)** **1¾ cup quick oatmeal** **¾ cup chocolate chips** **½ cup chopped nuts**	Add, mixing well.

Drop by spoonfuls onto greased baking sheet. Bake at 350 degrees for 8 to 10 minutes.

Yield: 5 or 6 dozen

Boy Friend Cookies

1 cup butter **¾ cup sugar** **¾ cup brown sugar**	Cream together thoroughly.

3 eggs **1 tsp. vanilla**	Add, beating until fluffy.

1½ cups flour **1 tsp. baking soda**	Add.

3½ cups quick oatmeal **1½ cups coarsely chopped salted** ** peanuts** **1 cup chocolate chips**	Fold in.

Drop by spoonfuls onto greased baking sheet. Bake at 350 degrees for 8 to 10 minutes.

Yield: 7 to 8 dozen

Jewel Shenk
Gloria Snider

Cherry Winks

1 cup sugar **⅔ cup soft margarine**	Cream together thoroughly.

2 eggs **1 tsp. vanilla**	Add, beating until fluffy.

2 cups flour **1 tsp. baking powder** **½ tsp. baking soda** **½ tsp. salt** **2 tbsp. milk**	Add sifted dry ingredients alternately with milk.
1 cup chopped dates	Stir in.
3 to 4 cups cornflakes cereal	Crush slightly (in plastic bag with rolling pin).

Drop by spoon into cornflake crumbs and roll into balls, coating well. Place on greased baking sheet and press slightly. Place ½ or ⅓ maraschino cherry on top of each to garnish. Bake at 350 degrees 10 to 12 minutes. Do not overbake.

Yield: 4 to 5 dozen   *Emma Horst*

Chocolate Marshmallow Cookies

1 cup shortening **2 cups sugar**	Cream together thoroughly.
2 eggs **2 tsp. vanilla**	Add, beating until fluffy.
4 cups flour **1 tsp. baking soda** **1 tsp. salt** **⅔ cup cocoa powder** **1 cup thick sour milk or buttermilk**	Add sifted dry ingredients alternately with milk. Drop by spoonfuls onto greased baking sheet. Bake at 350 degrees about 8 minutes.
36 marshmallows, cut in half	Top each hot cookie with marshmallow half and return to oven 2 minutes more to soften. Cool and frost.

Frosting:

6 tbsp. butter or margarine, melted **¼ cup cocoa powder** **1 tsp. vanilla** **3½ cups powdered sugar** **5 to 6 tbsp. milk to mix**	Beat together until smooth. Spread over cookies, covering marshmallows. May top with pecan half if desired.

Yield: 6 dozen   *Mae Shank*

Chocolate Chip Pudding Cookies

1 cup margarine ¼ cup sugar ¾ cup brown sugar	Cream thoroughly
2 eggs 1 tsp. vanilla	Add, beating until fluffy.
2⅓ cups flour 1 tsp. baking soda 1 (3½-oz.) pkg. instant vanilla pudding	Sift together, then add.
1 cup chocolate chips 1 cup chopped nuts	Fold in.

Drop by spoon onto greased baking sheet. Bake at 375 degrees for about 7 minutes.

Yield: about 5 dozen   *Sharon Carper*

Chocolate Crinkles

½ cup vegetable oil 3 (1-oz.) squares unsweetened chocolate, melted 2 cups sugar	Beat together well.
4 eggs 2 tsp. vanilla	Add, one at a time, beating well after each addition.
2 cups + 2 tbsp. flour 2 tsp. baking powder ½ tsp. salt	Sift together, and add.

Chill dough several hours or overnight. Drop by spoon into powdered sugar and roll into balls, coating well. Place on greased baking sheet and bake at 350 degrees for 10 to 12 minutes. Do not overbake!

Yield: 5 or 6 dozen

Christmas Ribbon Cookies

1 cup butter or margarine 1½ cups sugar	Cream together thoroughly.
1 egg 1 tsp. vanilla	Add, beating until fluffy.
2½ cups flour 1½ tsp. baking powder ½ tsp. salt	Sift together and blend in. Divide dough into 3 equal portions.

¼ cup chopped red candied cherries	Add to one portion.
¼ cup chopped green candied cherries	Add to one portion.
⅓ cup semisweet chocolate pieces, melted over low heat	Add to one portion.

Line bottom and sides of a 9 × 5 loaf pan with foil. Then layer the dough into the pan, pressing each layer firmly as you go. Put red cherry dough on the bottom, then chocolate next, and green cherry dough on top. Cover and refrigerate several hours. Turn out of pan. Slice in half lengthwise. Then slice each bar into ⅛ to ¼-inch thick slices. Bake at 375 degrees for about 10 minutes.

Yield: 6 to 7 dozen   *Wanda Good*

Christmas Fruit Cookies

1 cup soft margarine 2 cups brown sugar	Cream together thoroughly.
2 eggs ½ tsp. vanilla	Add, beating until fluffy.
3¾ cups flour 1 tsp. baking soda 1 tsp. salt ½ cup thick sour milk or buttermilk	Add sifted dry ingredients alternately with milk.
½ cup chopped pecans 1½ cups chopped candied cherries (red and/or green) 1½ cups chopped dates	Mix in.
pecans halves to garnish	Have ready.

Chill dough at least 1 hour. Drop by spoon onto greased baking sheet. Place pecan half on top of each. Bake at 350 degrees about 10 minutes.

Yield: about 6 dozen   *Gladys and Brownie Driver*

Coconut Cookies
(Soft and good)

1½ cups margarine 1 cup sugar 2 cups brown sugar	Cream together thoroughly.

3 eggs 1 tsp. vanilla 1 tsp. coconut flavoring 2 tbsp. water	Add, beating until fluffy.

4½ cups flour 1½ tsp. baking soda 1½ tsp. cream of tartar ¾ tsp. salt	Sift together and add.

2 cups angel flake coconut	Mix in.

Drop onto greased baking sheet. Bake at 350 degrees for 10 to 12 minutes. Do not overbake.

Yield: 6 ½ to 7 ½ dozen

Chewy Coconut Cookies

1 cup shortening ½ cup sugar 1 cup brown sugar	Cream together thoroughly.

2 eggs ⅔ cup dark corn syrup 1 tsp. vanilla ½ tsp. coconut flavoring	Add, beating well.

4 cups flour 1 tsp. baking soda ½ tsp. salt	Sift together and add.

1 cup angel flake coconut	Mix in.

Drop onto greased cookie sheet. Bake at 375 degrees for approximately 10 minutes. Do not overbake.

Yield: 7 or 8 dozen

Coconut Delights

1 cup instant mashed potato flakes ½ cup sugar 1 cup margarine, softened (see next page)	Beat together thoroughly.

3 tbsp. milk
1 tsp. coconut flavoring

. . . .

2 cups flour   Stir in.
½ tsp. baking powder
½ tsp. salt

. . . .

½ cup angel flake coconut   Blend in.
½ cup finely chopped nuts (optional)

. . . .

Shape into l-inch balls and place on ungreased baking sheet. Bake at 350 degrees for about 12 minutes. Do not overbake. Remove from baking sheet and cool 10 minutes. Then roll in powdered sugar to coat.

Yield: about 4½ dozen

. . . .

Hawaiian Delights

(Attractive and delicious!)

2 cups soft margarine   Cream together thoroughly.
2 cups sugar

. . . .

3 eggs   Add, beating until fluffy.
2 tsp. vanilla

. . . .

4 cups flour   Add sifted dry ingredients alternately with
4 tsp. baking powder   pineapple.
1 tsp. salt
1 (20-oz.) can crushed pineapple,
    drained well (reserve juice)

. . . .

2 cups quick oatmeal   Stir in.

. . . .

Drop onto greased baking sheet. Bake at 350 degrees 10 to 12 minutes. Cool and frost.

. . . .

1½ to 2 cups angel flake coconut,   Have ready.
    toasted

. . . .

Frosting:

½ cup soft margarine   Beat together until smooth. Spread on cooled
3½ cups powdered sugar   cookies, and sprinkle with toasted coconut
¼ cup of the reserved pineapple   while icing is soft.
    juice
2 or 3 drops yellow food coloring

. . . .

Yield: approximately 9 dozen

. . . .

Holiday Specials

3 oz. cream cheese, softened **1 cup shortening**	Cream together.
¾ cup sugar	Add gradually, beating well.
1 egg **1 tsp. almond flavoring**	Add, beating until fluffy.
2¼ cups flour **¼ tsp. baking soda** **½ tsp. salt**	Sift together, and stir in.
1 cup finely chopped nuts **maraschino cherry halves to** **garnish**	Have ready.

Chill dough at least 1 hour. Shape into 1-inch balls and roll in nuts. Place on ungreased baking sheet. Place cherry half in center of each cookie. Bake at 350 degrees for about 10 minutes.

Yield: about 3½ dozen

Chewy Date Drops

2 cups chopped dates **½ cup sugar** **½ cup water**	Combine in saucepan. Cook just until thickened. Set aside to cool
1 cup margarine **1 cup sugar** **1 cup brown sugar**	Cream thoroughly
3 eggs **1 tsp. vanilla**	Add, beating until fluffy.
4 cups flour **1 tsp. baking soda** **1 tsp. salt**	Sift together and add.
½ cup chopped nuts	Add to date mixture and stir in.

Drop onto greased baking sheet. Bake at 350 degrees about 12 minutes. (For Christmas, place ½ maraschino cherry on top of each cookie before baking.)

Yield: 6 to 7 dozen

Jubilee Jumbles

| ½ cup soft margarine
½ cup sugar
1 cup brown sugar | Cream together thoroughly. |

| 2 eggs
1 tsp. vanilla | Add, beating until fluffy. |

| 2¾ cups flour
½ tsp. baking soda
¾ tsp. salt
1 cup evaporated milk | Add sifted dry ingredients alternately with milk. |

| ½ cup chopped nuts (optional) | Blend in. |

Chill dough at least 1 hour. Drop onto greased baking sheet. Bake at 350 degrees about 10 minutes. Frost while warm with Quick Powdered Sugar Frosting on page 144. A couple drops of mint flavoring may be added. (For Christmas, sprinkle with red or green sugar before icing sets.)

Yield: approximately 4 dozen

Monster Cookies

(This is a real novelty recipe that young people love. Our "fresh-air daughter" enjoyed helping make them when she came to the farm from New York City each summer. If you prefer, try the smaller amount given in brackets.)

| 12 eggs, beaten [3]
4 cups sugar [1]
4½ cups brown sugar [1]
1 lb. soft margarine [½ cup]
1 tbsp. vanilla [1 tsp.]
1 tbsp. light corn syrup [1 tsp.]
3 lbs. (6¾ cups) peanut butter
   [1½ cups]
8 tsp. baking soda [2 tsp.]
2 lb. 10-oz. box (or 14 cups) quick
   oatmeal [3½ cups]
2 cups chocolate chips [⅔ cup] | Measure all ingredients in a large dishpan in order given. Mix thoroughly. Dip with ice-cream dipper onto greased cookie sheet. |

| 1 lb. peanut M & M's [l/2 lb.]
1 lb. plain M & M's | Place several on top of each cookie. |

Bake at 350 degrees for 10 to 12 minutes. Do not overbake! These are flat moist cookies. For slightly thicker cookie, include 1 or 2 cups flour.

Yield: 144 monstrous cookies!

Melting Moments

2 cups margarine **1½ cups brown sugar**	Cream together thoroughly.
2 eggs **2 tsp. vanilla**	Add, beating until fluffy.
3½ cups flour **2 tsp. baking powder** **1 tsp. salt**	Sift together and stir in.
quick oatmeal to coat	Have ready.

Drop by spoon into dish of dry oatmeal and roll to coat. Place on greased baking sheet. Bake at 350 degrees for 10 minutes. **Variation:** Roll in angel flake coconut instead of oatmeal. For Christmas, place half of a red or green candied or maraschino cherry in center of each cookie before baking.

Yield: 6 to 7 dozen

Meringue Tea-Party Cookies

¾ cup margarine **1 cup brown sugar**	Cream together thoroughly.
2 egg yolks **1 tsp. vanilla**	Add, beating until fluffy.
2½ cups flour **1½ tsp. baking powder** **¼ tsp. salt** **2 tbsp. milk**	Add sifted dry ingredients alternately with milk. Make balls of heaping teaspoonsful of dough. Place on greased baking sheet. Make indentation in center of each cookie.
½ cup thick jam or jelly	Fill indentations with jelly or jam.
2 egg whites	Beat into soft peaks.
½ cup sugar	Gradually add, beating into stiff peaks.

Top cookies with meringue. Completely cover jelly and seal to edges of cookies. Bake at 325 degrees for 15 to 20 minutes until golden brown.

Yield: approximately 3 dozen

Old-Fashioned Molasses Crinkles (or Ginger Snaps)

1½ cups shortening **2 cups brown sugar**	Cream together thoroughly.
2 eggs **2 tsp. vanilla**	Add, beating until fluffy.

¾ cup sorghum molasses	Blend in.

4 ½ cups flour	Sift together and add.
4 tsp. baking soda	
1 tsp. salt	
2 tsp. ground cinnamon	
1 tsp. ground ginger	
¼ tsp. ground cloves	

Chill dough for 1 to 2 hours. Drop by spoon into a bowl of granulated sugar. Roll into l-inch balls coating well. Place on greased baking sheet and bake at 350 degrees for 10 to 12 minutes. Do not overbake.

Yield: about 7 dozen

Pumpkin Cookies

¼ cup margarine	Cream together thoroughly.
¾ cup vegetable oil	
1 cup sugar	

1 egg, beaten	Combine and blend in.
1 tsp. vanilla	
1 cup pumpkin	

3 cups flour	Sift together and add.
1 tsp. baking powder	
1 tsp. baking soda	
½ tsp. salt	
1 tsp. ground cinnamon	

½ cup chopped dates	Stir in.
½ cup chopped pecans	

Drop onto ungreased baking sheet and bake at 350 degrees for 10 to 12 minutes. Frost while warm.

Frosting:

¼ cup soft margarine	Beat together until smooth. Spread on warm cookies.
½ tsp. orange flavoring	
2 cups powdered sugar	
approximately 3 tbsp. milk to mix	
2 drops each red and yellow color if desired	

Yield: 6 or 7 dozen   *Gladys Harman*

Pumpkin-Oatmeal Cookies

1½ cups margarine 1 cup sugar 2 cups brown sugar	Cream together thoroughly.

2 eggs 1 tsp. vanilla	Add, beating until fluffy.

4 cups flour 2 tsp. baking soda 1 tsp. salt 1½ tsp. ground cinnamon 2 cups quick oatmeal 1¾ cups canned pumpkin	Sift dry ingredients together (except oatmeal) and add alternately with pumpkin.

1 cup chocolate chips	Stir in.

Drop by spoon onto greased baking sheet. Bake at 350 degrees for 8 to 10 minutes.

Yield: approximately 10 dozen

Oatmeal Chip Cookies

1 cup margarine ¾ cup sugar ¾ cup brown sugar	Cream together thoroughly.

2 eggs 1 tsp. vanilla	Add, beating until fluffy.

2 cups flour 1 tsp. baking powder 1 tsp. baking soda 1 tsp. salt 2 cups quick oatmeal 3 tbsp. warm water	Sift dry ingredients together (except oatmeal) and add alternately with water.

1 cup angel flake coconut 1 cup chocolate chips	Stir in.

Drop by spoon onto greased baking sheet. Bake at 350 degrees for 8 to 10 minutes.

Yield: approximately 7 dozen

Old-Fashioned Oatmeal Cookies

1 cup raisins 1 cup water	Combine in saucepan. Simmer 15 minutes. Drain. Reserve liquid. Add enough water to reserve liquid to make ½ cup.

¾ **cup shortening** 1½ **cups sugar**	Cream thoroughly.

2 **eggs** 1 **tsp. vanilla**	Add, beating until fluffy.

2½ **cups flour** ½ **tsp. baking powder** 1 **tsp. baking soda** 1 **tsp. salt** 1 **tsp. ground cinnamon** ¼ **tsp. ground cloves**	Sift dry ingredients together, and add alternately with reserved raisin liquid.

2 **cups quick oatmeal** ¾ **cup chopped nuts**	Mix with raisins and stir in.

Drop by spoon onto greased baking sheet. Bake at 375 degrees for 8 to 10 minutes.

Yield: 6 to 7 dozen

Favorite Peanut Butter Oatmeal Cookies

(Children [and older "children"] really love this favorite cookie!)

1 **cup margarine** 1 **cup peanut butter** ½ **cup sugar** 1 **cup brown sugar**	Cream together thoroughly.

2 **eggs** 1 **tsp. vanilla** 2 **tbsp. water**	Add, beating until fluffy.

1½ **cups flour** 1 **tsp. baking soda** 1 **tsp. salt**	Sift together and add.

2½ **cups quick oatmeal** ¾ **cup chocolate chips**	Stir in.

Drop onto ungreased baking sheet. Bake at 350 degrees for 10 to 12 minutes.

Yield: approximately 6 dozen

Peanut Blossom Cookies

1 cup margarine 1 cup peanut butter 1 cup brown sugar	Cream together thoroughly.
2 eggs 2 tsp. vanilla ¼ cup milk	Add, beating well.
3 cups flour 2 tsp. baking soda 1 tsp. salt	Add.
chocolate kisses to garnish	Have ready.

Shape into l-inch balls and roll in granulated sugar to coat. Place on greased baking sheet. Bake at 350 degrees for 8 minutes. Remove and place a chocolate kiss or star in center of each cookie. Press slightly. Return to oven and bake 2 minutes more.

Yield: approximately 8 dozen

Peanut Butter Chip Chocolate Cookies

1 cup margarine 1½ cups sugar 2 eggs 2 tsp. vanilla	Cream together until fluffy.
2 cups flour ½ cup cocoa powder ¾ tsp. baking soda ½ tsp. salt	Sift together and add.
1½ cups peanut butter chips	Stir in.

Drop onto ungreased cookie sheet. Bake at 350 degrees for 8 to 10 minutes.

Yield: 4 to 5 dozen   *Elaine Schaefer*

Russian Tea Cakes

1 cup margarine 1 tsp. vanilla ½ tsp. almond flavoring ½ cup sugar	Mix together thoroughly.
2¼ cups flour ¼ tsp. baking soda ¼ tsp. salt	Sift together and add.
¾ cup finely chopped walnuts	Stir in.

. . . .

Powdered sugar to coat	Roll in balls and coat well.

. . . .

Place on ungreased baking sheet. Bake at 360 degrees for 9 to 10 minutes. Top may be dusted again with powdered sugar if desired. Do not overbake.

Yield: 3½ dozen   *Margaret Keller*

. . . .

Thumbprint Cookies

1½ cups soft margarine **½ cup brown sugar** **2 egg yolks** **1 tsp. vanilla**	Beat together thoroughly.

. . . .

2 cups flour **½ tsp. salt** **¼ tsp. baking powder**	Sift together and add. Roll into 1-inch balls.

. . . .

2 egg whites, lightly beaten **1 cup finely chopped nuts**	Roll balls in egg whites, then in nuts.

. . . .

jelly to fill thumbprints	Have ready.

. . . .

Place on greased baking sheet. Press thumb deeply into center of each cookie. Bake at 350 degrees for 10 minutes. Remove and cool. Fill thumbprints with jelly. (May be filled before baking if desired.) Store in tightly covered container with waxed paper between layers.

Yield: 3½ dozen

. . . .

Zucchini Chocolate Chip Cookies

¾ cup soft butter or margarine **½ cup sugar** **1 cup brown sugar**	Cream together thoroughly.

. . . .

1 egg **1 tsp. vanilla**	Add, beating until fluffy.

. . . .

2½ cups flour **1½ tsp. baking powder** **¾ tsp. salt** **1 tsp. ground cinnamon** **1½ cups finely grated unpeeled** **zucchini**	Add sifted dry ingredients alternately with zucchini.

. . . .

¾ cup chocolate chips **¾ cup chopped walnuts**	Stir in.

. . . .

Drop onto greased baking sheet. Bake at 375 degrees for 12 to 15 minutes.

Yield: 4 to 5 dozen   *Alice Trissel*

NO-BAKE COOKIES
Boiled Chocolate Cookies

2 cups sugar
½ cup milk
½ cup margarine
3 tbsp. cocoa powder

Combine in saucepan. Heat to boiling stirring until dissolved. Boil 2 minutes. Remove from heat.

. . . .

½ cup peanut butter
1 tsp. vanilla
3 cups quick oatmeal
¼ cup chopped peanuts (optional)

Stir in until well blended.

. . . .

Drop onto waxed paper or baking sheet. Let cool until set firm.

Yield: 4 or 5 dozen

Candy Cookies

½ cup margarine
1 cup sugar
1 egg
1 cup chopped dates
1 tsp. vanilla

Combine in saucepan. Heat to boiling, and boil 1 minute, stirring *constantly*. Remove from heat.

. . . .

4 cups Rice Krispies cereal

Stir in.

. . . .

1 to 2 cups angel flake coconut

Have ready.

. . . .

Drop by spoon into coconut and roll to coat good, shaping into balls. Do not pack too tightly. Place on baking sheet to cool and set.

Yield: 4 or 5 dozen   *Lillian Shickel*

Candy Wreaths

¼ cup margarine, melted
40 large marshmallows

Melt together on low heat, stirring *constantly*. Turn off heat.

. . . .

several drops green color

Blend in.

. . . .

5 cups cornflakes cereal

Stir in until well mixed.

. . . .

red cinnamon candies to garnish

Have ready.

. . . .

Drop onto baking sheet and shape as desired. May drop into individual clusters or into one large wreath. Decorate with candies before mixture is set.

Ruby Petersheim

Church Windows

½ cup margarine 2 cups chocolate chips	Melt together in top of double boiler, or over low heat. Partially cool.
1 (10-oz.) bag colored miniature marshmallows 1 cup chopped nuts (optional)	Stir in until coated.
angel flake coconut to coat (1 to 2 cups)	Sprinkle on waxed paper and shape candy into 2 rolls in coconut.

Chill in refrigerator until set. Then slice.

Rhoda S. Wenger

Nutritious No-Bake Cookies

1 cup dry milk powder 1 cup graham cracker crumbs or quick oatmeal 1 cup honey or corn syrup	Combine.
1 cup peanut butter 1 cup chopped raisins	Stir in until well mixed.

Shape into small balls. Or form into a roll, chill, and slice.

Barbara Bowman

Peanut Butter Quickies

1½ cups sugar ¾ cup flour ½ cup margarine ½ cup milk	Combine in saucepan. Heat to boiling and cook 3 minutes, *stirring constantly*. Remove from heat.
½ cup peanut butter ¾ tsp. vanilla 1½ cups quick oatmeal ½ cup angel flake coconut 1 cup coarsely chopped salted peanuts	Stir in until well mixed.

Drop by spoonfuls onto waxed paper or a baking sheet. Cool until set.

Yield: 4 or 5 dozen

ROLLED AND FILLED COOKIES

Banana Tarts

1 cup shortening 2¾ cups flour 1 tbsp. sugar	Mix together as for pie dough until crumbly.

2 egg yolks, slightly beaten ½ tsp. vanilla ¼ cup thick sour milk	Combine, then sprinkle over crumbs, tossing with fork until moistened.

Press into a ball. Then pull off small pieces and roll into balls about the size of a small walnut. Place in bowl, cover, and refrigerate until chilled.

Filling:

1 cup mashed ripe bananas (2 med.) 2 tbsp. sugar ¼ tsp. lemon flavoring	Mix together well.

½ cup angel flake coconut	Stir in.

Sprinkle counter with powdered sugar and roll out balls individually to ⅛ inch thickness. Place a teaspoon of filling mixture on each round of dough. Fold over and seal edges with prongs of fork. Bake at 375 degrees for about 20 minutes.

Yield: 3½ dozen

Chocolate Whoopie Pies

1½ cups soft margarine 3 cups sugar	Cream together thoroughly.

3 eggs 2 tsp. vanilla	Add, beating until fluffy.

5½ cups flour 1½ tsp. baking soda 1½ tsp. salt ⅔ cup cocoa powder 2¼ cups thick sour milk or buttermilk	Add sifted dry ingredients alternately with milk. Chill dough at least 1 hour.

Drop onto greased baking sheet. Bake at 350 degrees for 8 minutes.

Filling:

2 egg whites 2 tsp. clear vanilla ¼ cup flour (see next page)	Beat together thoroughly.

3 tbsp. milk
2 tbsp. powdered sugar

....

1 cup Crisco 2½ cups powdered sugar	Add, beating until fluffy. Spread between cookies.

....

Optional filling: may be filled with Boiled Flour Icing on page 143, if desired.

Yield: approximately 5 dozen pies

....

Chocolate Animal Cookies

¾ cup butter or margarine 2 cups sugar	Cream together thoroughly.

....

3 eggs	Add, one at a time, beating well after each addition.

....

3 (1-oz.) squares unsweetened chocolate, melted 2 tsp. vanilla	Blend in.

....

3 cups flour 1 tsp. baking powder ½ tsp. salt	Sift together and add.

....

Cover dough and chill for 2 hours. Divide dough in half. Roll out each half ¼ inch thick on floured counter. Keep remaining dough chilled until ready to roll. Cut out with animal cookie cutters as desired—such as rabbits, horses, ducks, and dogs. Amount of cookies varies with size of cutters. (Tip—roll out the dough in a mixture of 1½ tbsp. cocoa to ½ cup flour for dusting counter top to avoid having finished cookies coated with white flour.) Bake at 350 degrees for 8 to 10 minutes. Do not overbake.

....

Graham Crackers

½ cup margarine ½ cup brown sugar ¼ cup honey	Cream together thoroughly.

....

2 cups whole wheat graham flour ½ cup wheat germ ½ tsp. baking powder ½ tsp. baking soda ½ cup milk ½ tsp. vanilla	Add sifted dry ingredients alternately with combined milk and vanilla.

....

Roll out dough to ⅛ to ¼-inch thickness. Cut into 2½ × 5-inch rectangles. Lift onto greased baking sheet with spatula. Crease center of each rectangle with table knife. Prick with fork. Bake at 350 degrees for 10 to 12 minutes.

Yield: 24 double crackers

....

Date-Filled Oatmeal Cookie Pies

1½ cups shortening **1 cup sugar** **1 cup brown sugar**	Cream together thoroughly.
3 eggs **½ tsp. vanilla**	Add, beating until fluffy.
4½ cups flour **½ tsp. baking powder** **1½ tsp. baking soda** **½ tsp. salt** **½ cup thick sour milk or buttermilk**	Add sifted dry ingredients alternately with milk.
3 cups quick oatmeal	Stir in.

Drop by spoon into dish of granulated sugar and roll into balls. Place on greased cookie sheet. Flatten to ¼-inch thickness with bottom of glass. Bake at 350 degrees for 8 to 10 minutes.

Filling: **2 cups finely chopped dates** **¾ cup sugar** **2 tbsp. cornstarch** **1 cup water**	Combine in saucepan. Cook until thickened, stirring constantly. Cool and spread between cooled cookies.

Yield: 5 to 6 dozen pies

Date or Raisin-Filled Cookies

(This is one of our favorite Christmas cookies. We cut out stars and bells, put on filling and top with slightly smaller stars and bells.)

1 cup margarine **1 cup sugar** **1 cup brown sugar**	Cream together thoroughly
2 eggs **2 tsp. vanilla**	Add, beating until fluffy.
4½ cups flour **1½ tsp. baking powder** **½ tsp. baking soda** **1 tsp. salt** **½ cup thick sour milk or buttermilk**	Add sifted dry ingredients alternately with milk. Chill dough for 2 hours. Prepare filling.
Filling: **⅔ cup sugar** **2 tbsp. flour**	Mix in saucepan.
1 cup water **1½ cups chopped dates or chopped raisins***	Add. Cook until thickened, stirring constantly. Cool.

Roll out dough to ⅛ to ¼-inch thickness. Cut out 2½-inch rounds (or other shapes as desired) and place on greased baking sheet. Top with 1 tsp. filling. Cut slightly smaller rounds and place on top of each. Bake at 350 degrees for 10 to 12 minutes. Store in tight containers. Better the next day or after freezing. (*If using raisins, they are best run through the coarse blade on food grinder.)

Yield: 5 to 6 dozen

Optional Pineapple Filling:

1 (8-oz.) can crushed pineapple, undrained **1½ tbsp. cornstarch** **½ cup sugar** **¼ cup chopped candied or maraschino cherries**	Combine in saucepan. Cook until thickened, stirring constantly. Cool.

Gingerbread Men

1 cup margarine **1 cup sugar**	Cream together thoroughly.
1 cup molasses	Heat to almost boiling. Pour over margarine mixture.
1 tbsp. vinegar	Mix in well. Cool to lukewarm.
1 egg, beaten	Add.
4¾ cups flour **2 tsp. baking soda** **½ tsp. salt** **1 tsp. ground cinnamon** **1 tsp. ground ginger**	Sift together and add. Chill dough several hours or overnight.

Roll out dough to about ¼ inch thickness and cut into desired shapes. Decorate as desired. Bake at 350 degrees for 8 to 10 minutes. Do not overbake. (If you don't have a gingerbread man cookie cutter, draw a pattern on paper and lay on top of dough. Cut around pattern with a sharp knife.)

Yield: about 28 6-inch tall gingerbread men　　　　　　　　　*Laurie Miller*

Pumpkin Whoopie Pies

½ cup vegetable oil 1 cup sugar 2 cups brown sugar	Beat together well.
2 egg yolks 1 tsp. vanilla	Add, beating until fluffy.
4½ cups flour 1 tsp. baking powder 1 tsp. baking soda 1 tsp. salt 1 tsp. ground cinnamon ½ tsp. ground cloves ½ tsp. ground ginger 1½ cups canned pumpkin	Add sifted dry ingredients alternately with pumpkin.

Drop onto greased baking sheet. Bake at 350 degrees for about 10 minutes. Fill with the same filling as for Chocolate Whoopie Pies. (Use egg whites in icing.)

Yield: 3 ½ to 4 dozen pies

Spicy Oatmeal Cookie Pies

1½ cups soft margarine 1 cup brown sugar	Cream together thoroughly.
2 eggs	Add, beating until fluffy.
⅔ cup sorghum molasses	Blend in.
2½ cups flour 2 tsp. baking soda 1 tsp. salt 1 tsp. ground cinnamon ½ tsp. ground cloves ½ tsp. ground ginger 1 cup whole wheat flour 3 cups quick oatmeal	Sift together (except wheat flour and oatmeal), and add.

Drop by spoon into dish of granulated sugar and roll into balls. Place on greased baking sheet and flatten slightly with bottom of glass. Bake at 350 degrees about 8 minutes. Fill with the same filling as for Chocolate Whoopie Pies.

Yield: approximately 5 dozen pies   *Louise Heatwole*

Raisin or Date Pinwheels

Filling:

2 cups chopped raisins or dates **1 cup water** **½ cup sugar** **2 tbsp. cornstarch**	Combine in saucepan. (If using raisins run through coarse blade on food grinder.) Cook until thickened, stirring constantly. Remove from heat and cool.

Dough:

1 cup shortening **1 cup sugar** **1 cup brown sugar**	Cream together thoroughly.
2 eggs **1 tsp. vanilla**	Add, beating until fluffy.
4 cups flour **½ tsp. baking powder** **½ tsp. baking soda** **1 tsp. salt**	Sift together and add. Chill dough 2 hours. for easier handling.

Divide dough in half. Roll each half into a rectangle at least ¼-inch thick. Spread each with half of filling. Roll up jelly-roll fashion. Wrap in plastic wrap and chill again. Slice at least ¼-inch thick and place on greased baking sheet. Bake at 375 degrees for about 12 minutes.

Yield: 7 or 8 dozen

Spicy Sugar Cookies

½ cup butter or margarine **1 cup sugar**	Cream together thoroughly.
1 egg **1 tsp. vanilla**	Add, beating until fluffy.
2¼ cups flour **½ tsp. baking soda** **¼ tsp. salt** **1 tsp. ground cinnamon** **¼ tsp. ground nutmeg** **⅓ cup thick sour cream or thick sour** **milk; or ½ cup commercial sour** **cream**	Add sifted dry ingredients alternately with cream or milk.

Chill dough 2 hours. Roll out to ¼-inch thickness and cut as desired. Bake at 350 degrees for 8 to 10 minutes. Do not overbake! (May be sprinkled with colored sugar before baking. Or frost with powdered sugar frosting after baking and decorate as desired.)

Yield: 4 to 5 dozen   *Cathy Miller*

Sugar Cookies

(This is a good recipe for cookies that can be cut out into any shape and decorated for any occasion—Christmas, Easter, Valentine Day, etc. Cookies may be sprinkled with colored sugar before baking, or ice after baking and sprinkle with colored sugar or other sprinkles as desired.)

1 cup shortening **2 cups sugar (may use half brown if desired)**	Cream together thoroughly.

. . . .

4 eggs **2 tsp. lemon flavoring**	Add, beating until fluffy.

. . . .

5½ cups flour **2 tsp. baking soda** **1 tsp. cream of tartar** **1 tsp. salt** **1 cup thick sour cream or thick sour milk**	Sift dry ingredients together and add alternately with cream or milk.

. . . .

Chill dough in refrigerator overnight. Roll out to ¼-inch thickness and cut into desired shapes. Place on greased baking sheet. Bake at 350 degrees for 8 to 10 minutes. Do not overbake! May be iced with Quick Powdered Sugar Frosting on page 144, to which you have added ½ tsp. lemon flavoring.

Yield: 8 or 9 dozen

Dorothy Shank Showalter

. . . .

For Drop Sugar Cookies: Reduce flour to 3 cups only. Drop by spoon onto greased cookie sheet and bake as above.

Mae Shank

. . . .

CHAPTER FOUR

DESSERTS, FRUITS, SNACKS, & CANDY

DESSERTS, FRUITS, SNACKS, AND CANDY

I came from a family of 12 children—7 boys and 5 girls! When I think of all the food that was consumed by such a tribe, I wonder sometimes what a year's supply of it might have looked like! Believe me, we girls got a lot of practice preparing food.

I faintly remember the sugar rationing during World War II. Stamp books were issued for an allotted amount of sugar per person. When that was used, we couldn't buy any more until new books were issued. We used molasses or corn syrup as much as possible to stretch the sugar supply. Even that wasn't plentiful.

Cakes and candies were special treats that were rationed out carefully. Often there was not enough for each of us to have a piece, so sometimes my parents would start with the oldest, passing out whatever there was until the supply ran out. Other times they would start with the youngest, trying to even things out. Since my twin brother and I were right in the middle of the clan, it seemed like the pieces usually did not reach us no matter where they started!

After sugar was plentiful again, I well remember the abundance of desserts we prepared for the weekend. If we weren't invited away for Sunday dinner, we usually invited someone to visit us, so we always tried to be prepared.

We almost always baked 2 large cakes, made custard or pudding, usually some kind of fruit dessert, and often pies or other dessert to go with it. And that usually didn't last very far into the week! With the heavy farm work, 7 growing boys and whoever else might come along, what we thought should be a week's supply often had a way of disappearing almost overnight!

With modern equipment and the lighter physical work loads of today, many people are cutting back on desserts, especially rich ones. Real butter and cream, which was plentiful on the farm, are now treats that we don't often indulge in.

But in spite of modern efforts to reduce calories, many families still do not consider a meal complete without something sweet at the end of the meal. However, the choice in desserts is so wide that one can substitute something light and nutritious without adding too many wasted calories.

My husband especially enjoys warm fruit desserts served with milk or ice cream, but many times all it takes to finish out a meal is some fruit. It can be raw, canned, or frozen, depending on the remainder of the menu, and the season of the year. A few cookies can always be added to help satisfy the "sweet tooth" without having something too rich and sweet. Or some cereal candy gives a little sweetness with nutrition included.

For the average household, elegant desserts are usually reserved for special occasions or guests. It is rewarding, however, to delight your family with something extra special from time to time.

Homemade Ice Cream

Homemade ice cream was something we often enjoyed on the farm. With plenty of milk and cream, it was an economical dessert. As youngsters, we thought store-bought ice cream was much better. Now that we don't have homemade very often, we realize what a treat it was!

With the more recent popularity of homemade ice cream again, detailed directions may be helpful.

1. All parts of ice cream freezer should be thoroughly clean before using to avoid bacteria, especially when using junket which sets at room temperature until thickened. Rinse metal can and dasher with boiling water, then cool by rinsing with cold water before pouring in ice cream mixture.

2. Ice cream mixture should be refrigerator-cold when placed in can for faster, more even freezing. Never fill can over ¾ full to allow for expansion while freezing. Place can of ice cream mixture in freezer tub making sure that it is centered and resting on pivot in bottom of tub. Attach top cranking mechanism. Latch down securely.

3. Pour 3 to 4 cups cold water in tub which helps to give a buildup for brine needed to freeze the ice cream. (If you wait until you add ice and salt to pour in the water, you will wash the salt to the bottom of the can.) Then add layers of ice sprinkled with rock salt between layers, using 5 parts ice to 1 part salt until tub is filled up over freezer can. (If you live on the farm, use coarse salt like you feed to livestock.) It is good to gently stomp ice down somewhat as you go with wooden stick to give a more solid mass of ice around can—not too hard that ice is tightly wedged against can. This also helps to start melting of the ice which forms the brine needed to freeze the ice cream. Be sure the little hole in the side of the freezer tub is open to allow excess brine to overflow, rather than to seep into the can of ice cream.

4. Crank slowly for about the first 3 minutes until mixture is well chilled. Cranking too fast before mixture is well chilled could cause cream to separate or curdle. Then crank vigorously for the next 5 minutes to incorporate all the air possible as mixture begins to freeze. This will give a finer textured ice cream. After this period, cranking can be at a moderate speed until mixture becomes hardened. This usually takes a total of about 20 to 25 minutes. Add additional ice and salt if needed during freezing to keep metal can lid covered. (If using an electric freezer, plug in motor just before adding ice and salt. Let motor run until it labors hard—about 25 minutes. Do not let motor stall—this may cause motor damage.)

5. Remove crank mechanism, wipe all ice and salt from top of can. While holding can down in tub, pull dasher out of can. Scrape ice cream from dasher and pack down in can. Place a cork in the hole of the lid and replace on can. Pack well with additional ice and salt. Cover with newspaper and an old rug or towel. Let

set for one-half hour to harden and improve flavor. (If short on ice, you may remove can, wipe thoroughly to remove salt water, and place in the deep freeze for one-half hour.)

Additional Tips

• If using an electric freezer, be careful not to let salt get sucked into the air vents of the motor. This could cause severe motor damage.

• Too much salt added to the ice when freezing causes the ice cream to freeze too rapidly before enough air is incorporated into the mix. This makes the ice cream coarser in texture.

• A wooden freezer tub is much preferred over a metal or plastic one because of its insulating qualities.

• If adding coarse fruits, nuts, or chocolate chips to ice cream mix, it is best to wait until mixture is just beginning to freeze. Then stop, remove lid, and quickly add to mixture. Continue freezing process as quickly as possible. This will keep ingredients from settling to the bottom of the can.

• Leftover homemade ice cream is usually not nearly as good after storing in the freezer awhile. To make it taste freshly made again (or even better!), let soften slightly, place in chilled mixer bowl, and beat with heavy-duty electric mixer until fluffy. Serve immediately.

Melting Chocolate

When chocolate is stored at a warm temperature, it can develop a grayish film over the outside. This is cocoa butter that has softened and risen to the surface. This does not affect the flavor or quality of the chocolate and will disappear when chocolate is used in baking or cooking. Unsweetened chocolate has a tendency to liquefy when melted. Semisweet, sweet cooking, and milk chocolate will hold its shape when melted until stirred. Squares of chocolate will melt easier and faster when cut into chunks or small pieces.

NEVER add water to thin chocolate when melting. It will cause chocolate to stiffen instead. Chocolate manufacturers recommend using lecithin liquid (1 or 2 drops per 1 lb. of chocolate) for thinning it, or use Paramount crystals (1 or 2 tsp. per 1 lb. of chocolate). Many persons get along well using butter or a good grade of margarine, adding up to 1 tbsp. per 3 oz. of chocolate. And some people like to use paraffin especially for coating. It gives the chocolate a glossy appearance. (Use 1 or 2 tbsp. paraffin to 1 cup chocolate chips.)

ALWAYS use *low* heat for melting chocolate. High temperature will harden the chocolate and ruin it! Chocolate will continue to melt after it is removed from the heat. You can partly melt it, remove from heat, and stir until smooth.

Be aware that imitation chocolate is different from real chocolate. Chocolate is made from chocolate liquor, cocoa butter, and sugar. Imitation chocolate is usually made from a mixture of cocoa powder, palm kernel oil, sugar, dry milk powder, and other additives. Different brands also vary. Chocolate chips are usually lower in fat. Chocolate coating is higher in fat. Tips for chocolate may vary in results with imitation chocolate. Never use extract flavorings in chocolate, which will also harden it. Use oil flavorings instead.

Popcorn

Popcorn must have some moisture in it to pop well. When packages are opened, they should be stored in a sealed container to retain moisture. It is better to store unpopped corn in the freezer until used for maximum popability. If corn has already dried out too much to pop well, add 2 tbsp. water to 1 qt. jar of popcorn, cover tightly, shake, and let stand in refrigerator for several days, or place in the freezer for at least 24 hours.

A heavy cooker may be used on a stove burner for popping corn. Cooker must be hot enough to pop the corn before it dries out too much, and not too hot to scorch it. A practical rule to follow is to have the temperature on the stove regulated so that the corn begins to pop in 1 to 3 minutes from the time you place it on the stove. Once popping starts, all the kernels should pop within 2 minutes so the yield will be maximum.

Add 1 tbsp. fat or oil to ½ cup corn for popping. For a flavor change, try using bacon grease instead of oil for the fat.

Hot-air poppers are a wonderful invention, especially for calorie counters, since you do not need to add fat for popping. However, without the addition of fat, seasonings will not stick to the dry corn. If you like seasoned corn, spray a little nonfat vegetable oil over the popped corn and sprinkle with the desired seasoning such as onion or garlic salt, celery salt, seasoned salt, or Parmesan cheese. Or sprinkle lightly with powdered drink mix. Some people use a fine mist sprayer of water to moisten corn lightly as it falls from popper. Salt and seasonings can be dissolved in the water before spraying. Corn will quickly dry from heat from popping. Do not add too much water, however, or corn may become soggy.

If you don't mind using a little butter, there are many ways to season the melted butter before sprinkling it over the corn. Use 1 tbsp. butter per quart of popped corn. Try adding either a little barbecue sauce or chopped onion, or Worcestershire sauce, or even a chicken or onion bouillon cube dissolved in the butter. Parmesan cheese and garlic powder make a good combination. Chili powder and cheddar cheese are delicious combined. A combination of poultry seasoning and garlic powder is also good. Or try taco seasoning mix.

Testing Candy and Icing for Doneness

In making old-fashioned boiled candies and icings it is important to know when the boiling syrup has reached the desired degree of doneness. It is, of course, easiest to achieve perfect results by using a candy thermometer. However, if you do not have a thermometer, you can test a small amount of the syrup in cold water to determine the degree of doneness. Use a fresh cupful of cold water (not ice water) for each test. Pour about 1 tsp. of the hot syrup into the water. Pick the candy up in your fingers and attempt to roll it into a ball.

In the *soft ball stage* (235 to 240 degrees on thermometer), the syrup will roll into a soft ball which will lose its shape when removed from the water.

In the *firm ball stage* (245 to 248 degrees on thermometer), the syrup will roll into a firm, but not hard ball. It will flatten slightly a few minutes after removing from water.

In the *hard ball stage* (260 to 265 degrees on thermometer), the syrup will form a firm, but still pliable ball.

In the *soft crack stage* (275 to 280 degrees on thermometer), the syrup will form threads in the water which will soften when removed from the water.

In the *hard crack stage* (290 to 300 degrees on thermometer), the syrup will form brittle threads in the water which remain brittle after being removed from the water.

To test for the *thread stage* (230 to 235 degrees on thermometer), do not place syrup in water. Simply dip up a spoonful of syrup and pour it very slowly back into the pan. It will spin into a threadlike string as it is poured from the spoon.

TIPS FOR DESSERTS, FRUITS, SNACKS, AND CANDY

•If making gelatin desserts, see page 468 in salad section for tips about gelatin.

•Do not freeze gelatin molds or custards. They will become watery when thawed.

•In cooked custard desserts, undercooked starch tends to weep or water (liquid separates from custard) when chilled. Custard needs to be cooked several minutes to ensure a good jell. Cook several minutes longer when using a double boiler than when cooking in a saucepan. In baked custard, overbaking or baking custard at too high a temperature causes watering. Underbaking leaves liquid milk in the center of the custard.

•Cooked custards or puddings must be covered tightly while cooling to prevent having a film form over the top. Or sprinkle sugar over the top of hot custard to prevent the formation of a film.

•Do not use raw milk in commercial whipped topping mixes or in instant puddings. This may cause an off flavor. For those on the farm, either keep some instant powdered milk on hand for this use, or pasteurize a little milk for this purpose. To pasteurize milk, see page 252.

•Before heating milk in a saucepan, rinse pan with cold water. This helps to keep milk from sticking and scorching.

•To avoid having milk stick to pan and scorch when making custards in a saucepan rather than in a double boiler, place milk in pan on stove, then pour sugar over the milk letting it sink to coat bottom surface of pan. Do *not* stir. Heat until almost boiling, and then stir in batter to thicken.

•In custards calling for several eggs, one or more may be left out if you add an additional 2 tbsp. cornstarch for each egg omitted. If custard is made in saucepan instead of double boiler, use a little less thickening.

•Use a pancake spatula for stirring sauces and puddings where contents are prone to stick to the bottom of the pan and scorch. This is an easy way to keep entire bottom surface cleared constantly.

•When mixing instant pudding, always put milk in container first, then pour in powdered pudding mix. This will prevent having powdered mix stick to container.

•When you need to cover a whipped cream or other dessert topping with plastic wrap, insert several toothpicks part way into dessert first. Then add plastic wrap. Picks will hold wrap up enough to prevent damage to topping.

•When adding acids such as lemon juice or vinegar to gelatin or starch-thickened foods, keep in mind that the acids will reduce the firmness of the finished product. A little additional gelatin or starch needs to be added to have the same end result. Note also that acid should never be added until the custard has already thickened to prevent curdling. For lemon custard, add lemon immediately *after* custard has fully thickened.

•Custard may become thinner than you'd like from stirring it too much after it has thickened, or from stirring it too vigorously.

•Whenever you are mixing a batter that calls for both sugar and flour, combine the two ingredients thoroughly first. Sugar keeps the flour separated and liquid can then be stirred in easily without lumps.

•Lemons and oranges handle more easily if heated slightly before squeezing them for juice. They even seem to contain more juice! It also helps to roll them around on tabletop with presssure from your hand to soften the inside and free juice from membrane. Lemons with the smoothest skin and the smallest points on each end are better flavored and juicier than the elongated ones with rough skins. When grating rind from lemons or oranges, grate only the outer colored part. The white part often contains bitter-flavored tissue. Always grate oranges and lemons *before* cutting.

•To peel and section oranges and grapefruit more easily, soak fruit in hot water first for 5 minutes. Membrane will easily separate from fruit.

•Sprinkle a small amount of salt on grapefruit halves to help reduce tartness.

•Be sure to remove the entire leaf from each stem when trimming rhubarb. The leaves are toxic.

•Do not store bananas in refrigerator. This causes them to turn dark. Store in cool place in paper or plastic bag to keep air from them for longer shelf life. If you have extra-ripe bananas, mash them, sprinkle with lemon juice, and freeze in portions for banana bread or cake. They must be used immediately after thawing. Or bananas may be frozen whole to eat as a frozen snack. Thaw 5 to 10 minutes before eating. Do not thaw too much, or they will become mushy.

•Use a vegetable (or potato) peeler for quick, easy peeling of apples and pears.

•Avocados need to be ripened at room temperature before refrigerating.

•Be sure to wash all fresh fruit thoroughly before eating to remove any soil and sprays.

•Add a little salt to tart fruit when cooking to decrease amount of sugar needed to sweeten.

•A little vanilla (¼ tsp. per qt.) added to the juice of canned pears enhances the flavor.

•A couple of tablespoons of orange breakfast drink granules or a little frozen orange juice concentrate added to mixed fruit greatly enhances flavor.

•Fresh strawberries do not store well. If necessary to store, the best way is to place unwashed berries in a colander or open basket in refrigerator so air can circulate around them. Do not remove caps until ready to use.

•The thumping test seems to work best for selecting ripe watermelons. A green melon will have a ringing sound, a ripe melon a dull hollow sound. Cantaloupes are tested by a fragrant, but not overipe aroma. The blossom end should be slightly soft when pressed.

• To garnish desserts, cut candied cherries or citron into shapes of flowers and leaves. Flatten gumdrops with rolling pin and cut into flowers or leaves. To soften candied fruit, heat briefly in oven or microwave.

• To roll cracker crumbs without mess, place crackers in a heavy plastic bag and crush with rolling pin. Shake crackers to middle of bag and leave end open slightly to allow air to escape so you don't burst the bag. Extra crumbs may be stored in the bag.

• Freeze extra potato chips to keep them fresh.

• To blanch almonds, cover with water in saucepan and bring to a boil. Remove from heat, drain, and rinse with cold water. Pinch nuts between thumb and finger, and skins should slip off. Lay on paper towels on tray to dry. To sliver, cut with a sharp knife while nuts are still moist and warm.

• For easy removal of the skins on raw peanuts, place in freezer for several hours. Then stir thoroughly to loosen skins. Take outside and pour from one pan to another and let the skins blow away. If it isn't windy enough, use the cold setting of a hair dryer to blow them away!

• If pecans are placed in the freezer for a couple of days, they will be much easier to crack to obtain whole nutmeats. Or pour on boiling water enough to cover the pecans and let stand until water is cold. Then hammer on small end of nut and it should shell out whole.

• To **toast nuts** such as almonds, spread on a tray and heat in a 350 degree oven about 12 minutes until lightly browned. Or toss nuts in a little butter in a skillet on top of the stove until toasted, using low heat.

• To freshen coconut that is dry and hard, put in a strainer over a steaming pan of water a few minutes.

• To remove shell and grate a whole coconut, first drive two nail holes in the "eyes" of the coconut, one to let air in and the other to drain the liquid (milk) out. Drain, reserving the milk. Place coconut in a 350-degree oven until it is hot to the touch or until it cracks—approximately 30 minutes.

Remove from oven and tap all over it with a hammer especially on the ends to loosen the meat. Then give a good hard whack with the hammer and the shell will crack open. Remove shell and peel off brown skin covering the meat with a knife. Cool before grating. Or place the coconut in the freezer for about 1 hour. The expansion in the freezing process will loosen the shell. Do not freeze too long. Remove from freezer and hit sharply in the middle with a hammer to break it open. The shell should then separate easily from the meat of the coconut.

Either grate by hand or in the blender. With blender method, pour reserved milk into blender container. Break meat into small pieces. Turn blender on, and add small pieces of coconut through the small opening in the lid. Grate only a small amount at a time. Pour meat and milk through a strainer, saving the milk to use for the next batch. Spread out on a platter to dry slightly.

• To **tint coconut,** add a few drops of color to a little water in a jar. Half fill jar with flaked coconut. Cover tightly and shake vigorously until evenly tinted. Spread out on tray to dry.

• To **toast coconut,** spread on tray and heat in 350 degree oven until lightly browned, tossing occasionally.

• To **tint granulated sugar,** add several drops of color to a small jar of sugar. Cover tightly and shake until evenly tinted. Spread on plate to dry.

•For no-stick serving of marshmallow creme, dip spoon in hot water for a few seconds before dipping into creme. It will slide right off hot spoon.

•Store partly used bag of marshmallows in the freezer to keep them from becoming sticky or hardened. They will stay fresh as new, and will thaw rapidly when needed.

•For weight watchers—instead of using whipped cream for topping cake or dessert, try beating together 1 egg white, 1 small ripe banana, and ¼ tsp. lemon juice until fluffy. Use immediately, since topping does not hold well.

•See tips for whipped cream on page 248 in the "Eggs, Milk, and Cheese" chapter.

•Refrigerator ice cream will have a much fluffier and nicer texture if you allow it to freeze until half frozen. Then remove it from tray and beat lightly to incorporate more air. Return to freezer section and freeze until solid.

•Make your own ice cream sandwiches by slicing off squares of slightly softened ice cream. Place between cinnamon-sugared graham crackers. Store in freezer for instant snacks on a hot day.

•Commercial ice cream will keep fresh longer if cardboard carton is placed in a tightly closed plastic bag to store.

•For delicious variety with commercial ice cream, soften vanilla ice cream slightly and swirl chocolate or butterscotch sauce, or peanut butter, through ice cream. Or blend in crushed sweetened strawberries, raspberries, or peaches. Crushed Oreo cookies, chopped toasted nuts, or crushed peanut brittle may also be added. For different flavors of ice cream, add ½ tsp. of unsweetened flavored powdered drink mix

(Kool-Aid) to a dish of vanilla ice cream and stir to mix well. Use orange, strawberry, raspberry, or cherry.

•When boiling a sugar-and-water mixture for icings or candy, cover saucepan for the first 3 minutes of boiling time. This melts down sides of pan and prevents formation of sugar crystals. Then remove lid, cautiously insert candy thermometer, and cook to desired temperature.

•It is best to make candy on a cool dry day. Sticky weather makes for sticky candy!

•For a delicious snack, spread peanut butter on apple halves or cabbage wedges, or fill celery with peanut butter.

•For delicious carrot sticks, peel carrots and cut into sticks as desired. Then immerse in tall container of water to which you have added some artificial sweetener (2 grains saccharin to 2 cups water is good). Chill for at least one hour.

•If celery becomes limp, do not discard it. Cut into celery sticks, immerse in cold water, and refrigerate for at least 1 hour. It will regain its crispness.

•When cutting broccoli flowerets, cut just through stem with knife, then pull bud section apart. This prevents cutting buds into fine pieces.

•To make beautiful chocolate curls easily, warm bar of chocolate slightly. Then shave with sharp knife.

DESSERTS, FRUITS, SNACKS, AND CANDY RECIPES
FRUIT DESSERTS
Baked Apples

8 to 10 baking apples	Pare, cut in half, and core. Stand on edge in 9 × 13 bake dish.
1 cup water **½ cup red hot cinnamon candies** **¼ cup sugar**	Combine in saucepan. Heat and stir until candies are dissolved.
2 tbsp. Clearjel or cornstarch **¼ cup water**	Dissolve, then stir in until thickened and clear. Remove from heat.

Pour half of syrup over apples being careful to cover each piece. Bake at 350 degrees until almost tender, about 40 minutes. Then pour remaining syrup over apples covering each piece again. Bake 10 to 15 minutes more until tender.

Yield: 8 to 10 servings

Frances Harman

Spicy Baked Apples

6 or 8 apples	Peel, halve, and core (use melon baller). Arrange in 8 × 13 bake dish.
1¼ cups water **2 tbsp. sugar** **1 tbsp. red hot cinnamon candies** **2 tbsp. minute tapioca**	Combine in saucepan. Cook 1 minute, stirring constantly. Pour around apples in dish.
red hot cinnamon candies	Place two candies in core area of each apple half.
½ cup sugar	Sprinkle over apples so they are well covered.
ground cinnamon	Sprinkle over generously.
ground allspice	Sprinkle over lightly.

Bake at 350 degrees about 50 minutes or until tender. Chill to serve and top each apple with a spoon of whipped cream. Sprinkle with a little additional cinnamon.

Yield: 6 to 8 servings

Apple or Peach Crisp

1 qt. apple pie filling,* **or 1 qt.**
   canned peaches, drained and
   sliced
	(If using peaches, sprinkle with cinnamon.) Spread in 8-inch square bake dish.

¾ cup quick oatmeal **½ cup brown sugar** (see next page)	Mix until crumbly. Spread over top.

½ cup flour
¼ cup margarine

Bake at 350 degrees about 20 minutes. (*If you have fresh apples instead of filling, mix ⅔ cup sugar, 1¼ cups water, 3 tbsp. Clearjel or cornstarch in saucepan. Add 4 cups sliced peeled apples. Heat just until boiling and slightly thickened, stirring lightly. Remove from heat and add ½ tsp. cinnamon and ¼ tsp. allspice.) If fruit is hot, baking time should be reduced to approximately 12 minutes.

Delightful Macaroon Apples

1 qt. apple pie filling, or make pie
filling (recipe on page 448)

Spread in 8-inch square bake dish.

Topping:
1 cup flour
1 cup sugar
¼ tsp. salt
2 eggs
¼ cup melted margarine

Beat all ingredients together at once and pour over apples in dish.

Bake at 350 degrees for 40 minutes. Serve warm with milk or ice cream.

Yield: 6 servings

Applescotch Dessert

1½ cups brown sugar
1 tbsp. cornstarch
2 cups cold water

Combine in saucepan. Cook until slightly thickened.

½ tsp. vanilla
1 tbsp. butter or margarine

Add. Pour into a 9 × 13 baking dish.

2 cups flour
¼ cup sugar
3 tsp. baking powder
½ tsp. salt
⅓ cup shortening

Mix together until crumbly.

3 cups chopped peeled apples

Stir in.

¾ cup milk
½ tsp. vanilla

Combine, and stir into mixture just until moistened. Drop by tbsp. over syrup in dish.

1 tbsp. sugar
½ tsp. cinnamon

Combine and sprinkle over the top.

Bake at 350 degrees for 35 to 40 minutes. Serve warm with ice cream or whipped cream.

Yield: 10 servings

Apple Dumplings

Sugar Syrup:

1¼ cups sugar (may use half brown if desired) 1½ cups water ¼ tsp. cinnamon ¼ tsp. nutmeg 6 to 10 drops red food color	Combine in saucepan. Heat to boiling. Remove from heat.
3 tbsp. butter or margarine	Add. Set aside.

Dumplings:

6 med.-sized apples, pared, and cored (leave whole)	Have ready.
2 cups flour 2 tsp. baking powder 1 tsp. salt	Sift together.
⅔ cup shortening	Cut in until crumbly.
½ cup milk	Add, tossing with fork until moistened. Press into ball.

Roll out on floured surface into a 12 × 18-inch rectangle ⅛ to ¼-inch thick. Cut into 6-inch squares. Place whole apple on each square. Sprinkle each apple with extra sugar (1 rounded tbsp. each) and with cinnamon, and dot with butter. Moisten edge of squares, fold points to center, and pinch edges together. Place 1 inch apart in ungreased 8 × 12-inch baking dish. Pour syrup over dumplings. Sprinkle small amount of additional sugar over top. Bake at 375 degrees for 35 minutes or until done. Serve warm with milk or ice cream.

Variation: Roll dough into rectangle ¼-inch thick. Spread with sliced apples. Sprinkle with brown sugar and cinnamon. Roll up like jelly roll. Cut into 1¼-inch slices. Place in pan, pour syrup over, and bake.

Yield: 6 servings

Ruth Weaver

Optional Sauce:

Prepare and bake dumplings as directed except omit the sugar syrup. Make the following sauce to pour over dumplings after they are baked to serve:

¼ cup Clearjel 1½ cups sugar (may use half brown sugar) 1½ cups water ½ tsp. ground cinnamon ¼ tsp. ground allspice ¼ tsp. ground nutmeg	Combine in saucepan. Cook and stir until thickened and clear. Remove from heat.
2 tbsp. butter.	Add.

Pour over baked dumplings and serve warm with ice cream.

Wanda Good

Blueberry (or Blackberry) Buckle

¾ cup sugar ⅓ cup margarine	Cream together thoroughly.
2 eggs ½ tsp. vanilla	Add, beating until fluffy.
1½ cups flour 2 tsp. baking powder ½ tsp. salt ½ tsp. ground cinnamon ¼ tsp. ground nutmeg ¼ tsp. ground cloves ½ cup milk	Add sifted dry ingredients alternately with milk.
2 cups fresh or 1 (15-oz.) can blueberries, or blackberries, drained well	Fold in. Spread batter in greased 8 × 12-inch bake dish.
Crumbs: ½ cup brown sugar ½ cup flour 3 tbsp. margarine ½ tsp. ground cinnamon	Mix together until crumbly. Sprinkle over top.

Bake at 350 degrees for 35 minutes. Serve warm with whipped cream or ice cream.

Yield: 9 servings

Cherry Delight

2 cups graham cracker crumbs ⅓ cup margarine, melted 2 tbsp. sugar	Combine and press in bottom of 8 × 12 bake dish.
8-oz. cream cheese, softened ½ cup sugar	Cream together until smooth.
1 envelope Dream Whip ½ cup milk	Whip until stiff. Blend together with cheese mixture. Spread over crumbs. Chill until set.
1 (21-oz.) can cherry pie filling or 2½ cups your own filling*	Spread over top.

Variations: Instead of cherry filling, use blueberry, strawberry, or raspberry. (*Or use fruit pie filling recipe on page 456.)

Yield: 6 to 8 servings

Cherry Rolls

2 cups flour 2 tbsp. sugar 2 tsp. baking powder ½ tsp. baking soda ¾ tsp. salt	Sift together.
1 egg, beaten 2 tbsp. sugar ¾ cup thick sour cream (may use commercial)	Combine, and then stir in just until moistened. Turn out on floured surface and knead several times. Roll out into a 15 × 7-inch rectangle.
2 tbsp. soft butter	Spread over dough.
2 cups canned cherries, drained (reserve juice)	Arrange evenly over dough.
2 tbsp. sugar 1 tsp. cinnamon	Sprinkle over cherries, then roll up like a jelly roll. Cut into 1¼-inch thick slices and lay in a greased 8 × 12 baking dish.
reserved cherry juice and water enough to make 1½ cups few drops red color ⅓ cup sugar ⅓ cup brown sugar 1½ tbsp. cornstarch	Combine in saucepan. Heat to boiling, stirring constantly until thickened. Remove from heat.
1 tbsp. butter ½ tsp. almond flavoring	Add, and pour over rolls.

Bake at 375 degrees for 25 min. Serve warm with ice cream.
Yield: 12 rolls

Blueberry Cheesecake Dessert

2 cups graham cracker crumbs 2 tbsp. sugar ⅓ cup margarine, melted	Combine and press in bottom of an 8 × 12 bake dish.
8 oz. cream cheese, softened ½ cup sugar	Beat together.
2 eggs, beaten	Add, mixing well. Pour over cracker crust.
1 (21-oz.) can blueberry pie filling Whipped cream for topping	Have ready.

Bake at 350 degrees for 15 to 20 minutes. Cool. Pour pie filling over cheese cake. Chill. Serve topped with whipped cream.

Yield: 6 to 8 servings

Danish Dessert

3 cups water, including any juice from berries 1¼ cups sugar 1 (3-oz.) pkg. strawberry-flavored gelatin, or 1 small pk. Strawberry Kool-Aid	Combine in saucepan. Heat to boiling.
1 cup water ½ cup Clearjel or cornstarch	Dissolve and stir into mixture, cooking just until thickened. Cool thoroughly.
2 or 3 cups frozen strawberries—half thawed, or fresh berries*	Stir in and chill.

(*If using fresh berries, increase sugar to 1 ½ cups.) Very attractive served in clear dessert goblets layered with whipped cream or whipped topping.

Variation: Use orange Kool-Aid or gelatin, and then a mixture of pineapple, oranges, and bananas in place of strawberries.

Yield: 8 to 10 servings

Curried Fruit

1½ cups pears 1½ cups peaches 1½ cups pineapple chunks 1 cup apricots ½ cup maraschino cherries 1 cup mandarin oranges (optional)	Drain all fruit, reserving juices. Layer fruit in 2-qt. casserole dish.
⅓ cup brown sugar ½ to 1 tsp. curry powder 2 tbsp. cornstarch	Combine with reserved juice in saucepan. Cook just until thickened. Remove from heat.
1 tbsp. margarine	Add. Pour over fruit in dish.

Bake at 350 degrees for 30 to 40 minutes until bubbly. Serve hot or at room temperature.

Yield: 8 to 10 servings

Fruit Pizza

This is a delightful refreshment to serve guests. (If time is at a premium, 1 (17-oz.) pkg. refrigerated sugar cookie dough may be used instead of making your own cookie dough for the crust. Cut dough in ¼-inch thick slices, arrange in pan, and press together to cover bottom. Bake according to directions on container.)

Crust:

½ cup shortening ½ cup white sugar ½ cup brown sugar	Cream together thoroughly.

1 egg 1 tsp. vanilla	Add, beating until fluffy.

2½ cups flour 1 tsp. baking powder 1 tsp. soda ¼ tsp. salt ½ cup thick sour milk or buttermilk*	Add sifted dry ingredients alternately with milk.

Grease 2 large (14-inch) pizza pans and press dough into pans to form crust. It helps to roll dough right in pan. If rolling pin won't fit inside pan because of the edges of the pan, use a tall smooth water glass to roll dough in pan. If you only have one pan, cover pan with foil; grease and shape dough into pan. Then lift off foil and crust onto baking sheet to bake second crust. Bake in 350-degree oven for 8 to 10 minutes. Do not overbake. Cool thoroughly. (*Sweet milk may be used if preferred, but increase baking powder to 2 tsp. instead of 1. Be sure to include soda.) Crusts freeze well, so while you are mixing and baking dough, make the extra crust to use later.

Cream Cheese Base: (use this amount for *each* pizza)

8-oz. cream cheese, softened ⅓ cup sugar 2 tbsp. milk ½ tsp. vanilla	Beat together until smooth and creamy. Spread over cooled crust.

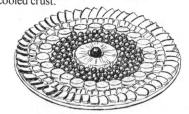

Fruit Topping:

Top with rings of sliced fruit as desired. I like to start in the center with a maraschino cherry, then 1 whole pineapple slice, a ring of blueberries, sliced bananas, pineapple chunks, complete with apple slices around the edge. Dip apple and banana slices in a mixture of half lemon juice and half water and drain before adding to help prevent darkening. In season, fresh sliced strawberries or peaches or halved grapes may be used.

Optional Glaze: (use this amount for *each* pizza)

Pizza is delicious and attractive served without glaze, but glaze may be added if desired.

¾ cup apple juice 2 tbsp. sugar 2 tsp. Clearjel or cornstarch	Combine in saucepan. Cook just until thickened, stirring constantly. Remove from heat.

½ tsp. strawberry extract	Add. Cool slightly and brush over fruit.

Variation: Use all one kind of fruit for pizza. Fresh strawberries sliced in half with cut side down, or sliced fresh peaches, are delicious. For glaze, use water in place of the apple juice, and in place of strawberry extract, add 2 tbsp. of strawberry or peach-flavored gelatin. This may be baked in a sheet cake pan and cut into squares if desired.

Yield: 8 servings

Fruit Cobbler

(This recipe is excellent to use with peaches, cherries, blackberries, blueberries, or black raspberries.)

1 qt. canned fruit or berries, including the juice ½ cup sugar	Heat in saucepan to boiling.
2 tbsp. Clearjel or cornstarch ¼ cup water	Dissolve and add, stirring constantly until thickened. Remove from heat.
1 tbsp. margarine	Add, then pour in an 8 × 12 dish.
cinnamon (optional)	Sprinkle over fruit if using peaches.
2 cups flour 2 tbsp. sugar 3 tsp. baking powder 1 tsp. salt	Sift into bowl.
6 tbsp. margarine	Cut in until crumbly.
1¼ cups milk	Stir in just until moistened. Then drop by spoonfuls over hot fruit.

Bake at 350 degrees for 25 to 30 minutes. Serve warm with milk. May use fresh fruit if desired. Add 1 to 1 ½ cups water to 1 qt. fruit and another ½ cup sugar.

Yield: 8 to 10 servings

Quick-Mix Cobbler

Prepare fruit as above. Use the following recipe for the dough:

2 cups Bisquick ¼ cup sugar ¼ cup oil 1 egg ½ cup milk ½ tsp. vanilla	Measure into bowl. Beat together just until smooth. Pour over hot fruit.

Bake at 350 degrees about 25 minutes.

Frozen Fruit Slush

(This mixture is delightfully refreshing on a hot day. It is a good item for lunches if weather isn't too hot. Cover top of insulated foam cup with plastic wrap fastened with a rubber band. It should be half thawed by dinner time, and just right to eat!)

1 qt. canned peaches, or 4 cups sliced fresh peaches.	If using canned peaches, drain and reserve juice. Mash slightly with potato masher, just so they aren't chunky.
1½ to 2 cups sugar (use less if peaches are sweetened) **3 cups water and reserved juice**	Add enough water to juice to make 3 cups and dissolve sugar.
1 (6-oz.) can frozen orange juice with water added **1 (20-oz.) can crushed pineapple, undrained** **7 or 8 bananas, diced**	Mix all together and freeze until slushy.

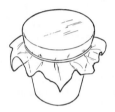

Or fill foam cups and freeze firm. Partially thaw to serve.
(I like to keep a shallow foil-lined cardboard box filled with fruit cups in the freezer for quick use. Tear a sheet of plastic wrap to cover the whole box. They keep indefinitely, and are so handy to have ready for quick use. Just set a cup in the microwave for 1 minute to make almost instant slush! Allow a couple of hours for thawing in the refrigerator.)

Yield: approximately 18 to 20 (7-oz.) cups.

Sara Kreider

Orange Fluff

2 (3-oz.) pkg. orange-flavored gelatin **2 cups boiling water**	Combine and stir until dissolved.
1 (6-oz.) can frozen orange juice, undiluted	Add, stirring until melted. Cool.
1 (16-oz.) can mandarin oranges, drained; or 1 qt. drained canned peaches, crushed **1 (20-oz.) can crushed pineapple, undrained**	Add. Pour into a 9 × 13 glass dish and chill until set.

Topping:

1 (3½-oz.) pkg. instant lemon pudding **1 cup milk***	Beat together until beginning to set. Chill 5 minutes.

2 cups whipped topping	Fold into pudding. Spread over top of fruit.
maraschino cherries to garnish	Arrange over top.

*May add 2 drops each red and yellow color to make orange-colored topping to match fruit. This is a delicious topping that can be used on other gelatin molds.

Yield: 12 servings

Surprise Melon and Fruit Wedges

Chill a medium-sized cantaloupe. Cut in half and remove seeds. Use a small melon baller to remove about half of the fruit leaving an even layer of at least ½ inch over the entire rind. Cut ½ cup of the balls in halves or fourths, and reserve. Place melon halves on a tray in dish fashion. If needed, slice a thin piece of rind from the bottom so they will sit evenly.

1 (3-oz.) pkg. orange or strawberry-flavored gelatin **¾ cup boiling water**	Stir until dissolved. Add a couple of ice cubes to aid in cooling.
½ cup sliced strawberries **½ cup crushed pineapple, or pineapple chunks** **(½ cup reserved melon balls)**	Add to cooled gelatin. Pour into melon "dishes." Chill until firm.

To serve, cut each half into two wedges.

Yield: 4 servings

Broiled Grapefruit

Cut grapefruit in half, crosswise. Flick out seeds with tip of knife. Remove core with sharp knife. Carefully cut around each section to loosen fruit. Sprinkle each half with 2 tsp. brown sugar, dot with ½ tsp. butter or margarine. Place in shallow baking dish and broil under moderate heat until sugar bubbles and edges have browned slightly, about 15 to 20 minutes. May be garnished with maraschino cherry half in center. Serve as first course or dessert.

Filled Grapefruit—Alaska-Style

Trim a thin slice off both ends of each of two grapefruits to make a flat base. Halve grapefruits crosswise (a notched edge is very attractive). Scoop out pulp, reserving pulp, juice, and shells. Discard membranes and seeds. Place pulp, juice, 1 small ripe banana (chopped), and 2 tbsp. sugar in blender and process until smooth. Pour into a shallow pan, cover, and freeze for several hours. Remove, and scrape across frozen mixture with metal spoon, spooning mixture into shells. Place shells in freezer. When ready to serve, beat 1 egg white with ⅛ tsp. cream of tartar into soft peaks. Gradually add 1 tbsp. sugar, beating into stiff peaks. Remove shells from freezer and place a glob of meringue on each, spreading to edges. Place on baking sheet and quickly bake at 500 degrees for about 2 minutes until slightly browned. Serve immediately.

Yield: 4 servings

Peach (or Apple) Strudel

6 or 8 fresh peaches or apples, peeled and sliced	Layer in greased 8-inch-square bake dish.
½ to ¾ cup sugar **ground cinnamon**	Sprinkle over fruit.
Crumbs: **1 cup flour** **1 cup sugar** **1 tsp. baking powder** **½ tsp. salt**	Sift into bowl.
1 egg	Mix in until crumbly.

Spread over peaches and bake at 350 degrees approximately 1 hour until crust is brown. Serve warm with milk, whipped cream, or ice cream.

Yield: 6 to 8 servings

Gladys and Brownie Driver

Easy Pineapple Dessert

1½ cups brown sugar **1 cup boiling water**	Combine in 9 × 13 bake dish.
1 (20-oz.) can crushed pineapple, undrained	Add.
1 (18-oz.) white cake mix	Sprinkle over mixture dry. Do not stir.
½ cup margarine	Slice over mixture.
1 cup angel flake coconut **1 cup chopped nuts**	Sprinkle over top.

Bake at 350 degrees for 50 minutes. Serve warm with ice cream or cold with whipped cream.

Yield: 12 servings

Kathryn Heatwole

Gelatin-Pineapple Dessert

(At Christmas, use lime gelatin instead of orange, for a very attractive red, white, and green dish.)

1 (20-oz.) can crushed pineapple. **1 (10 oz.) bag miniature marshmallows** **3 tbsp. cream**	Mix and refrigerate overnight.

| 1 (3-oz.) pkg. orange or lime-flavored gelatin
1 (3-oz.) pkg. strawberry-flavored gelatin | Mold in separate shallow square dishes according to pkg. directions. Chill at least overnight or longer for a firm gel. Cut into cubes. |

Layer in fancy glass dish or in sherbet dishes.

Yield: 12 to 14 servings

Cooked Prunes

Add water to prunes in saucepan to almost cover. Add sugar to taste (about ½ cup to a qt.) and cook approximately 20 minutes until tender. Or put on stove, bring to rolling boil, turn off heat, and let stand tightly covered overnight. They are ready to eat the next morning. (For flavor change, substitute brown sugar instead of granulated sugar.)

Raspberry or Strawberry Dessert

2 cups graham cracker crumbs ⅓ cup margarine, melted 2 tbsp. sugar	Combine and press in bottom of 8 × 12 dish.
8 oz. cream cheese, softened ½ cup sugar	Beat together until smooth.
1 pk. Dream Whip ½ cup milk	Whip until thick. Blend in cheese mixture. Spread over crumbs. Chill.
1 cup boiling water 1 (3-oz.) pkg. raspberry or strawberry-flavored gelatin	Stir together until dissolved.
1 pt. frozen raspberries or strawberries*	Stir in frozen fruit. Chill until mixture is just beginning to jell. Pour over mixture in dish. Chill until set.

*Fresh fruit may be used instead of frozen. Add ⅓ cup sugar to fruit, and let set to dissolve before stirring into gelatin.

Yield: 6 to 8 servings

Plum Good Dessert

1 qt. canned plums with juice	Remove seeds and puree in blender.
⅓ cup sugar **few drops red color**	Add, and heat in saucepan.
½ cup water **5 tbsp. Clearjel or cornstarch**	Combine until smooth. Then add, stirring constantly until thickened. Remove from heat.
¼ to ½ tsp. almond flavoring	Add. Cool and chill.
2 or 3 cups Cool Whip	Spread over dish, or swirl through fruit.

Yield: 6 to 8 servings

Rhubarb (or Fruit) Dessert

(This dessert is delicious using blueberries or cherries and cherry-flavored gelatin instead of rhubarb. It is also delicious either warm or cold.)

1 qt. sliced fresh rhubarb	Arrange in 9 × 13 baking dish.
1 cup sugar (⅔ cup for fruit other than rhubarb) **1 (3-oz.) pkg. strawberry- flavored gelatin** **1 (18-oz.) white or yellow cake mix (dry mix)**	Sprinkle over fruit in order listed.
2 cups water	Pour over mixture.
½ cup margarine, melted	Pour over top.

Bake at 350 degrees for 50 to 60 minutes. Serve warm with milk or cold with whipped cream.

Yield: 6 to 8 servings

Rhoda Wenger

Favorite Rhubarb Torte

Crust: **¾ cup flour** **1 tbsp. sugar** **⅓ cup shortening**	Mix together until crumbly and press in 9-inch-square bake dish. Bake at 350 degrees for 10 to 12 minutes, until lightly browned.
Filling: **1½ cups sugar** **2 tbsp. flour** **1 or 2 tsp. strawberry Kool-Aid drink powder**	Mix together in saucepan.

⅓ cup milk 3 egg yolks ½ tsp. vanilla 3 cups rhubarb, cut in ½-inch pieces	Mix in. Cook several minutes, just until rhubarb is tender, stirring constantly. Pour into baked crust.
Meringue: 3 egg whites 1 tsp. warm water	Beat until foamy.
¼ tsp. cream of tartar	Add, beating into soft peaks.
6 tbsp. sugar	Gradually add, beating into stiff peaks. Spread over rhubarb mixture, sealing to edges of dish.

Bake at 325 degrees for 12 to 15 minutes until golden brown.
Yield: 8 servings

Elegant Rhubarb Torte

Crust: 1½ cups graham cracker crumbs 3 tbsp. sugar ⅓ cup butter or margarine, melted	Mix well. Reserve ¼ cup. Pat remainder in 9 × 9 bake dish. Bake at 350 degrees for 8 minutes.
Filling: 1 cup sugar 3 tbsp. cornstarch	Mix in saucepan.
½ cup water 4 cups sliced rhubarb few drops red food coloring	Stir in. Cook until thickened, stirring constantly. Reduce heat, and cook 2 to 3 minutes. Remove from heat. Spread in baked crust. Cool.
Topping: ½ cup whipping cream	Whip until stiff.
1½ cups miniature marshmallows	Fold in and spoon over rhubarb mixture.
1 (3½-oz.) pkg. instant vanilla pudding	Prepare according to package directions and spoon over all.

Sprinkle with reserved crumbs. Chill.

Yield: 9 servings   *Gladys and Brownie Driver*

Strawberry-Rhubarb Compote

3 cups diced rhubarb ¼ cup raisins 1½ cups sugar 1 cup water ⅛ tsp. salt	Combine in saucepan. Cook 2 or 3 minutes until tender.
½ cup water 3 tbsp. Clearjel or cornstarch	Dissolve and add, stirring until thickened. Remove from heat.
½ tsp. orange flavoring ⅓ cup flaked coconut	Add. Chill thoroughly.
1 pt. fresh strawberries, each sliced in half; or frozen berries, half thawed	Add.

May be garnished with whipped cream to serve.

Yield: 6 servings

Strawberrioca

(This recipe may be used with other fruit such as peaches, raspberries, or apples.*)

1 pt. frozen strawberries, thawed 2½ cups liquid	Drain berries, and add water and juice to make 2½ cups liquid. Reserve berries.
⅓ cup minute tapioca ½ cup sugar ⅛ tsp. salt	Mix into liquid and let stand 5 minutes. Then heat to boiling, stirring occasionally. Boil 1 minute. Remove from heat. Cool and chill. Stir in strawberries.
whipped cream or topping	Layer in dish with berry mixture.

*If using apples, slice and add to liquid mixture. Boil a couple of minutes until softened, but not mushy. Add ½ tsp. cinnamon and ⅛ tsp. allspice.

Yield: 6 to 8 servings

Strawberry Pudding (Low Cal.)

½ cup water	Pour in blender.
2 env. Knox unflavored gelatin	Sprinkle in. Let stand 3 to 4 min.
1 cup skim milk, heated to boiling	Add, processing at low speed until gelatin is completely dissolved, about 2 minutes.
¼ cup sugar or to taste, (or 1 or 2 tsp. sugar substitute) (see next page)	Add, and process on high speed until strawberries are pureed. Pour into individual

½ tsp. almond flavoring
1 qt. fresh strawberries

dessert goblets or large glass dish. Chill until set.

Garnish with sliced berries or tea leaves.

Yield: 8 servings

Old-Fashioned Strawberry Shortcake

2 cups flour
3 tbsp. sugar
3 tsp. baking powder
½ tsp. salt

Sift together in bowl.

6 tbsp. margarine

Cut in until crumbly.

1 egg, beaten
⅔ cup milk

Combine, then add all at once, stirring just until moistened.

May be rolled out and cut into 6 individual biscuits. Bake at 350 degrees for 12 minutes. Or spread in a 9-inch layer cake pan. Sprinkle a little sugar over the top, and bake for 18 minutes. Do not overbake! Serve warm with crushed berries and whipped cream.

Yield: 6 servings

Orange Tapioca Delight

1 qt. canned peaches, sliced
1 (16-oz.) can mandarin oranges, or
    2 cups diced fresh oranges

Drain and reserve juice. Chill fruit.

4 cups liquid (add water to reserved
    juice to make 4 cups)
1 cup sugar
½ cup minute tapioca

Combine in saucepan and let set 5 minutes. Heat to boiling, stirring constantly. Boil 2 minutes. Remove from heat.

1 (6-oz.) can, or ¾ cup frozen orange
    juice concentrate

Add, stirring until melted. Cool and chill.

3 bananas, sliced

Add.

½ cup whipping cream

Whip until stiff.

2 tbsp. sugar

Add to cream, and spread over top.

Variation: 1 cup halved seedless white grapes may be added.

Yield: 12 servings

Vera Showalter
Julia Witmer

Pearl Tapioca Fruit

½ cup baby pearl tapioca 4 cups water	Soak several hours or overnight.
⅔ cup sugar	Add, and cook about 5 minutes until clear. Remove from heat.
1 (3-oz.) pkg. flavored gelatin*	Add, stirring until dissolved. Cool.
2 or 3 cups frozen fruit or berries*	Fold in and chill thoroughly.

Whipped cream or topping to garnish. Layer in dish or swirl over top. *Use the same flavor gelatin as fruit you choose, or a flavor to compliment fruit. For fruit, choose strawberries, peaches, raspberries, or pineapple and bananas or oranges.

Strawberry Swirl

2 cups sliced fresh strawberries, or 1 pt. frozen berries, half thawed ¼ cup sugar	Sprinkle sugar over berries and let stand 20 minutes. (Omit sugar if using frozen berries already sweetened.) Drain and reserve juice. Chill berries.
1 cup boiling water 1 (3-oz.) pkg. strawberry-flavored gelatin	Combine, stirring until dissolved. Add ice and water to reserved juice to make 1 cup and add to gelatin. Chill until just beginning to congeal.
2 cups Cool Whip 3 cups miniature marshmallows	Combine, and let set while gelatin is being chilled.

Beat slightly congealed gelatin until foamy. Add berries. Swirl berry mixture and Cool Whip mixture in pretty clear glass dish. Chill until set.

Yield: 8 to 10 servings

Watermelon Magnifique

Carefully cut across about ⅓ of the way down on a thoroughly chilled watermelon to make a dish. (If you would like a "handle" on the dish for a basket effect, leave this section intact—cutting in from both ends rather than straight through whole melon.) Scoop out pulp with melon baller and place in a bowl. Discard as many seeds as possible without mutilating balls. Edge of "melon dish" can then be notched if desired. Cut a thin slice from bottom of melon so it will sit evenly on the table. Then layer fruit back into "melon dish" as desired. A delicious assortment may include canteloupe balls, pineapple chunks, and halved white seedless grapes along with the watermelon balls. Do not stir as this would cause it to become mushy. Blueberries may be sprinkled over the top, but should not be put in mixture ahead to avoid bleeding dark juice into mixture. In season, fresh peaches or pears can also be added as well as fresh strawberries and sliced bananas.

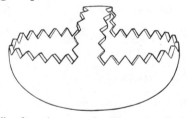

Frozen Melon

Make sugar syrup by boiling for 3 minutes, 1 part sugar to 2 parts water, including any liquid from melon. Cool and chill thoroughly. Cut balls or cubes from cantaloupe or watermelon, and place in freezer container. Cover with sugar syrup and freeze. Serve half thawed. Melon may also be frozen without syrup. Simply sprinkle sugar over layers of melon balls instead. Again, serve only half thawed.

....

PUDDINGS AND SOFT DESSERTS
Boston Cream Pie (Cake)

(Measure all ingredients before you begin mixing cake, so beaten egg whites don't need to stand long.)

2 egg whites	Beat into soft peaks.
½ cup sugar	Gradually add, beating into stiff peaks. Set aside.
2 cups flour **3 tsp. baking powder** **½ tsp. salt** **1 cup sugar**	Sift together.
6 tbsp. vegetable oil **2 egg yolks** **2 tsp. vanilla** **1 cup milk (divided)**	Blend in with ½ cup of the milk, beating 1 minute on medium speed of electric mixer, scraping bowl often. Then add other ½ cup and beat 1 minute more. Fold in egg whites.

Pour into 2 greased or waxed-paper-lined 9-inch layer pans. Bake at 350 degrees for about 25 minutes. Cool in pans 10 minutes. Then remove to cool completely. When cold, cut layers in half horizontally. Spread bottom half of each layer with pudding. Add top half of each layer and pour chocolate glaze over the tops.

Pudding: Mix 1 (3½-oz.) pkg. instant vanilla or banana pudding according to package directions, except use 1¾ cups milk instead of the 2 called for. Chill well.

Chocolate Glaze: Melt together 1½ (1-oz.) squares unsweetened chocolate and 2 tbsp. butter over low heat. Remove from heat and stir in 1½ cups powdered sugar, ½ tsp. vanilla, 1 tbsp. light corn syrup, and 2 tbsp. or more hot water to make a glaze of pouring consistency.

Optional Crumb Topping: For an extra touch, make crumbs for topping. Mix together ⅔ cup crunchy peanut butter and 1 cup powdered sugar until crumbly. Sprinkle half of crumbs over bottom halves of cakes before adding pudding, and the other half on top of the glaze before it sets.

Variation: May use a yellow cake mix in place of above cake if desired.

Yield: 2 desserts of 6 servings each

Baked Vanilla Custard

4 or 5 eggs	Beat.
½ cup sugar **¼ tsp. salt** **1 tsp. vanilla**	Blend in.
4 cups milk, scalded	Blend in slowly. Pour into a 1 ½-qt. bake dish.
nutmeg	Sprinkle over top.

Set dish of custard in larger dish of hot water and bake at 325 degrees for about 50 minutes. Or pour in 8 individual custard cups. Set in pan of warm water and bake 30 minutes. **Variations:** For **coconut custard,** add ¾ cup coconut and ½ tsp. coconut flavoring after adding milk. For **chocolate custard,** mix 2 tbsp. cocoa with the sugar before adding it to the eggs, and increase sugar to ⅔ cup. Then instead of nutmeg sprinkle 1 tsp. sugar over the foam on top of the dish before baking.

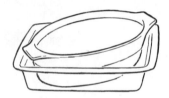

Yield: 6 to 8 servings

Lora Heatwole
Bertha Shank

Caramel Custard

1½ cups brown sugar **6 tbsp. margarine**	Caramelize in skillet until dark brown.
2 tbsp. cold water	Add.
7 cups milk	Add caramel mixture, and heat in large pan to almost boiling, stirring frequently.
¾ cup cornstarch **½ cup flour** **½ cup sugar** **1 tsp. salt**	Stir together in bowl.
3 eggs, beaten **½ cup milk**	Combine, and stir into flour mixture until smooth. Then add to hot milk, stirring constantly over medium heat until thickened. Remove from heat.
2 tsp. vanilla	Add. Cover tightly and cool.

When chilled, it may be processed slightly in blender for very smooth fluffy custard.

Yield: 14 servings

Gladys Harman

Basic Vanilla Pudding or Custard

(Use chilled basic pudding to make luscious layered dessert with graham cracker crumbs, whipped cream, and sliced bananas. Add a few colored miniature marshmallows for an attractive appearance.)

1¼ cups sugar **1 cup flour** **½ tsp. salt**	Mix together in top part of double boiler.

. . . .

6 cups milk*	Stir in 1 cup milk first until smooth, then add 5 cups.

. . . .

Cook in double boiler, stirring constantly until thickened. Then cover and cook slowly for 7 minutes, stirring occasionally.

. . . .

4 egg yolks, slightly beaten	Add small amount of hot mixture to yolks first, then blend into pudding. Cook and stir constantly for 2 minutes more. Re move from heat.

. . . .

2 tsp. vanilla **1 tbsp. butter or margarine**	Blend in. Cover tightly to cool to prevent film from forming over top. Chill thoroughly.

. . . .

*If desired, 4 cups of the milk may be heated in the double boiler first; then the batter using the remaining 2 cups may be added when milk is boiling hot. This saves stirring time

Yield: 12 to 14 servings   *Mary Shank, my mother-in-law*
                                            Mabelee Blosser

. . . .

Variations:
For fluffy pudding: Beat the 4 egg whites as for meringue, adding 2 tbsp. sugar. Then blend hot pudding into beaten whites, slowly at first, then quickly until completely blended. (Mabelee prefers stirring unbeaten egg whites in with sugar/flour mixture before cooking.)

For vanilla wafer pudding: Add 1 tsp. banana flavoring to pudding. Line bottom of 2-qt. bake dish with vanilla wafers. Pour in half of pudding and add another layer of wafers. Top dish with meringue made with the 5 egg whites, ⅛ tsp. cream of tartar, and ½ cup sugar. Spread over dish and bake at 325 degrees for 12 to 15 minutes until browned.

For chocolate pudding: Increase sugar to 1¾ cups and add ⅓ cup cocoa powder to sugar mixture. Add an additional tbsp. of butter after pudding is cooked.

For butterscotch pudding: Caramelize 1 cup brown sugar and ¼ cup butter until very brown, and reduce white sugar to ⅓ cup. Add caramelized mixture to milk mixture. It will melt as you heat and stir mixture.

. . . .

Weight Watcher's Cheesecake (Low Cal.)

1 cup graham cracker crumbs 2 tbsp. margarine, melted	Mix and press in 9-inch pie plate, or round flat dish. Chill in refrigerator.
2 tbsp. cold water 1 env. unflavored gelatin 2 tbsp. lemon juice	Measure in blender container. Process on low 1 or 2 minutes to soften gelatin.
½ cup milk, heated to almost boiling	Add, processing until gelatin is dissolved.
1 egg ⅓ cup sugar 1 tsp. vanilla 2 cups cottage cheese	Turn to high speed, add and process until smooth. Pour into chilled crust. Refrigerate 2 to 3 hours.

May be topped with fresh fruit or pie filling.

Yield: 6 servings

Linda S. Shenk

Petite Cherry Cheesecakes

24 vanilla wafers	Place one in bottom of each of 24 cupcake paper-lined muffin cups.
2 (8-oz.) pkgs. cream cheese, softened ¾ cup sugar 2 eggs 1 tbsp. lemon juice (optional) 1 tsp. vanilla	Beat together until light and fluffy. Fill cups ⅔ full with cheese mixture. Bake at 350 degrees for 15 to 20 minutes until set. Cool thoroughly.
1 (21-oz.) can cherry pie filling	Top each cake with 1 rounded tbsp. pie filling. Chill.

Yield: 24 cheesecakes

Diane Burkholder

Lemon Cheesecake

(Usually this type mixture cannot be frozen, but this one freezes quite well, if thawed in the refrigerator.)

2 cups graham cracker crumbs 2 tbsp. sugar ¼ cup margarine, melted	Combine and press ⅔ of mixture in a 9 × 13 bake dish. Reserve remaining ⅓ crumbs.
1 (3-oz.) pkg. lemon-flavored gelatin 1 cup boiling water	Dissolve, then chill until just beginning to congeal.

1 (13-oz.) can evaporated milk,
    chilled in freezer until icy around
    edge of bowl
	Whip into stiff peaks, about 5 minutes. Blend in thickened gelatin.

| 8 oz. cream cheese, softened
1 cup sugar
1 tbsp. lemon juice
1 tsp. vanilla | Beat together until smooth, then add to milk mixture just until blended . |

Pour over crumbs, and sprinkle with reserved crumbs. Chill for several hours before serving.

Yield: 8 servings

Ruby Petersheim
Vera Showalter

Chocolate Eclair Cake

about 1 lb. graham crackers (not crumbs) (divided)	Grease bottom of 9 × 13 bake dish. Line with whole crackers.
2 (3½-oz.) pkg. French vanilla instant pudding 3 cups milk	Beat together slowly for 2 minutes.
2 pks. Dream Whip	Whip according to pkg. directions, and blend in pudding.

Spread half of pudding mixture over crackers. Add second layer of crackers, then remaining pudding. Cover with third layer of crackers. Refrigerate for 2 hours. Then make frosting.

Frosting:

| 2 (1-oz.) pks. liquid unsweetened chocolate or 5 tbsp. cocoa and 2 tbsp. oil
2 tbsp. light corn syrup
1 tsp. vanilla
3 tbsp. softened margarine
1½ cups powdered sugar
3 tbsp. milk | Beat together until smooth, and spread over top of dessert. Refrigerate for 24 hours before serving. |

Yield: 8 to 10 servings

Mary Ann Heatwole

Chocolate Angel Delight

1 large angel food cake, baked	Break into small pieces. Spread half of pieces in 9 × 13 dish. Reserve other half.
1 (3½-oz.) pkg. instant chocolate pudding **1½ cups milk**	Beat together slowly for 2 minutes. Chill 5 minutes
1 (3-oz.) pkg. cream cheese, softened **2 tbsp. milk**	Beat together until smooth.
2 cups Cool Whip	Blend together with cheese and pudding.
1 cup crushed peanut brittle, or chopped peanuts	Have ready.

Pour half of pudding mixture over cake pieces in dish. Arrange other half of pieces over next, then pour in other half of pudding mixture. Top with peanuts. Chill several hours before serving.

Yield: 12 servings

Chocolate Pudding

1 cup flour **2 tsp. baking powder** **¼ tsp. salt** **¾ cup sugar** **1½ tbsp. cocoa powder**	Sift together in bowl.
½ cup milk **2 tbsp. melted margarine or vegetable oil** **1 tsp. vanilla**	Mix in until smooth. Pour in greased 8 × 12 bake dish.
¾ cup brown sugar **2 tbsp. cocoa powder**	Combine and sprinkle over mixture in dish.
1½ cups hot water	Pour over all.

Bake at 350 degrees about 35 to 40 minutes. Serve warm with whipped cream or milk.

Yield: 8 servings

Karen Eberly

Cinnamon Pudding

1 cup sugar **2 tbsp. soft margarine**	Cream together thoroughly.
2 cups flour **2 tsp. baking powder** (see next page)	Add sifted dry ingredients alternately with milk. Pour in greased 8 × 12 bake dish.

2 tsp. ground cinnamon
1 cup milk

. . . .

1½ cups brown sugar **1½ cups water** **2 tbsp. butter or margarine**	Combine in saucepan. Heat to boiling. Then pour over batter in dish.

. . . .

½ cup chopped walnuts	Sprinkle over all.

. . . .

Bake at 350 degrees approximately 40 minutes. Serve warm with whipped cream.

Yield: 8 servings

Shirley Shank
Pam Weaver

. . . .

Cream Puffs

(Cream puffs are a special treat, especially with the variety of ways you can fill them!)

1 cup water **½ cup margarine** **3 whole-grain saccharin (optional)**	Combine in saucepan. Heat to boiling.

. . . .

1 cup flour **¼ tsp. salt**	Add, all at once, stirring vigorously until mixture forms into a ball, about 1 minute. Remove from heat.

. . . .

4 eggs	Add, one at a time, beating thoroughly after each addition.

. . . .

Drop by tablespoonfuls onto greased baking sheet. Bake at 375 degrees for 30 minutes or until beads of moisture disappear. For tea-size puffs, make only half as large and bake 20 to 25 minutes.

Yield: 12 large puffs.

. . . .

Fillings:
Fill with basic vanilla pudding to which you have folded in ½ tsp. banana flavoring and 1 or 2 cups whipped cream to 2 cups pudding.
Or mix 1 (3½-oz.) pkg. instant banana, vanilla, or chocolate pudding according to package directions. Chill until set. Then fold in 2 cups Cool Whip.
Or whip 1 cup cream, and add ¾ cup fresh fruit (strawberries, raspberries, etc.) and ⅓ cup sugar.
Or fill with vanilla/chocolate ripple ice cream and swirl a dab of chocolate frosting on top.
To make **chocolate frosting**, heat a 1 oz. square unsweetened chocolate and 1 tbsp. butter over low heat until melted. Remove and add 1½ cups powdered sugar and 2 tbsp. or more hot water to make a soft spreading consistency.

. . . .

For Chocolate Eclairs:
Use recipe for cream puffs, but shape into 12 long puffs—about 4 inches long and 1 inch wide. Bake, cool, and fill with chocolate or vanilla pudding. Frost with chocolate frosting made as in preceding recipe.

. . . .

Coconut Cracker Pudding

5½ cups milk 1 cup sugar ¼ tsp. salt 1½ cups crushed saltine crackers (not too fine)	Heat in top of double boiler to boiling.
3 tbsp. cornstarch ½ cup milk	Mix to dissolve. Then add to hot milk, stirring constantly until thickened.
3 egg yolks, beaten lightly	Stir small amount of hot mixture into yolks first, then add to hot pudding. Cook and stir 2 minutes more. Remove from heat.
1 tbsp. butter or margarine ½ tsp. coconut flavoring ½ tsp. vanilla ¾ cup angel flake coconut	Stir in. Pour in 2-qt. casserole dish.
3 egg whites ⅛ tsp. cream of tartar 3 tbsp. sugar	Make meringue of whites. Spread over top of pudding, sealing to edges of dish.
¼ cup angel flake coconut	Sprinkle over top.

Bake at 325 degrees for 12 to 15 minutes until golden brown.

Yield: 8 servings

Fannie B. Heatwole, my mother

Soft Custard

(This is a very soft custard that you can drink from a glass or eat with a spoon. It is especially good for someone who is not feeling too well.)

6 eggs, beaten 6 cups milk 1¼ cups sugar	Combine and cook in double boiler until slightly thickened, and mixture will coat a spoon. Remove from heat.
1½ tsp. vanilla	Add. Cool thoroughly and chill.

Keep covered while cooling to prevent having a film form over top of custard.

Yield: 8 to 10 servings

Hannah Burkholder

Date Pudding Favorite

¾ cup sugar 1 cup flour ½ tsp. salt 2 tsp. baking powder	Sift together.

½ cup milk	Stir in gradually until well mixed.
½ cup chopped dates ½ cup chopped walnuts	Fold in. Pour into greased 8 × 12 baking dish.
¾ cup brown sugar 2 cups water	Heat to boiling. Pour over pudding in dish.

Bake at 350 degrees for 40 to 45 minutes. Serve warm with whipped cream.

Yield: 8 servings

Date Whipped Cream Pudding

1 cup chopped dates 1 tsp. baking soda 1 cup boiling water	Combine and let set until cool.
1 cup sugar 1 cup flour ¼ tsp. salt 1 tbsp. soft margarine 1 egg	Beat together in bowl. Then blend in date mixture. (Batter will be thin.) Pour into greased 9 × 13 pan. Bake at 350 degrees for 15 to 20 minutes. Cool thoroughly and cut into small blocks.
2 cups whipping cream	Whip until stiff.
⅓ to ½ cup sugar	Blend into cream.
2 or 3 sliced bananas chopped pecans as desired	Have ready.

Mix pudding and whipped cream, and layer with bananas and pecans in a glass dish. Sprinkle additional pecans over top.

Yield: 10 to 12 servings   *Wanda Good*

English Trifle

1 angel food cake, baked	Cut into cubes and layer ⅓ of cake in 9 × 13 glass dish.
1 (5½-oz.) pkg. instant vanilla pudding mixed according to pkg. directions 2 (21-oz.) cans cherry pie filling 2 bananas, sliced 1 (20-oz.) can crushed pineapple, drained	Layer ⅓ each ingredient over cake in order listed. Repeat all layers, including cake, twice more.
2 cups Cool Whip grated chocolate maraschino cherries, halved	Garnish over top.

Yield: 12 to 14 servings

Glorified Rice

2 cups cooked rice 1 cup crushed pineapple, undrained ⅓ cup chopped raisins ¼ cup sugar 3 cups miniature marshmallows	Mix together well. Chill for 1 hour.
1 cup whipping cream	Whip until stiff.
¼ cup sugar	Blend into cream.
2 sliced bananas	Fold together lightly with rice mixture and whipped cream in glass dish.
chopped nuts to garnish	Sprinkle over top.

Yield: 12 to 14 servings

Graham Cracker Fluff

2 egg yolks, slightly beaten ½ cup sugar 1 cup milk	Combine in saucepan or in top of double boiler. Cook until thickened, stirring constantly.
1 env. unflavored gelatin (1 tbsp.) ¼ cup pineapple juice	Soak until gelatin is softened. Add to hot mixture, stirring until dissolved. Chill until just beginning to congeal.
1 cup graham cracker crumbs (12 to 14 single crackers) 3 tbsp. melted butter 2 tbsp. sugar	Combine. Sprinkle half of crumbs in bottom of serving dish. (Reserve half.)

2 cups whipped cream (whip 1 cup
cream)
2 egg whites, beaten stiff
1 (8-oz.) can crushed pineapple,
well drained
1 tsp. vanilla

Fold together with gelatin mixture. Pour over crumbs in dish. Sprinkle reserved crumbs over the top.

Variation: For plain vanilla fluff, omit pineapple and use water in place of pineapple juice.

Yield: 6 to 8 servings

Mary Ethel Lahman Heatwole

Pudding Lush

(This is a 4-layer favorite that has a number of delicious variations.)

1. 1 cup flour
½ cup margarine
½ cup chopped nuts (optional)

Mix like pie dough and press in bottom of a 9 × 13 bake dish. Bake at 350 degrees for 15 minutes. Cool and chill.

2. 8 oz. cream cheese, softened
⅔ cup sugar

Beat together until smooth.

1 pkg. Dream Whip, whipped

Blend in and spread over crust.

3. 2 (3½-oz.) pkgs. instant pudding any
flavor desired—chocolate
butterscotch, lemon, etc.)
3 cups milk

Beat together on low speed for 2 minutes. Spread over second layer.

4. 1 pkg. Dream Whip, whipped

Spread over top

½ cup chopped nuts (optional)

Sprinkle over topping. Chill thoroughly.

Yield: 9 to 12 servings

Mary Ann Heatwole

Variations:

For **Coconut Lush,** use vanilla pudding with ½ tsp. coconut flavoring and ¾ cup angel flake coconut added to pudding in third layer. Toast another ¾ cup coconut and sprinkle over top instead of nuts in fourth layer.

For **Oreo Cookie Lush,** make crust in first layer by mixing ¾ cup melted butter with 1 (15-oz.) pkg. crushed Oreo cookies. Do not bake. Use chocolate pudding in third layer. And in fourth layer sprinkle topping with shaved chocolate curls instead of nuts.

For **Peanut Butter Lush,** cream ⅓ cup peanut butter with cream cheese mixture in second layer. Use chocolate pudding in third layer. And sprinkle with chopped peanuts and shaved chocolate in 4th layer instead of other nuts.

For **Pumpkin Lush,** make crust for first layer by mixing 1 cup flour, ½ cup margarine, ½ cup quick oatmeal, and ⅓ cup brown sugar until crumbly. Bake 15 to 20 minutes. In third layer, use vanilla pudding, reduce milk to 2 cups and add 1½ cups canned pumpkin and ½ tsp. cinnamon to pudding. In fourth layer, add ½ tsp. cinnamon, ⅛ tsp. nutmeg, ⅛ tsp. cloves and 2 tbsp. sugar to Dream Whip. Sprinkle with nuts.

Delightful Orange Fluff (Low Cal.)

4 egg yolks, slightly beaten 1 cup orange juice ½ cup sugar, or artificial sweetener	Combine in saucepan. Heat to boiling, stirring constantly. Remove from heat.
1 env. unflavored gelatin (1 tbsp.) ¼ cup cold water	Soak until softened. Add to hot mixture, stirring until dissolved. Place pan in cold water to cool. Chill until just beginning to congeal.
1 tbsp. grated orange rind	Add.
4 egg whites ½ tsp. cream of tartar ⅓ cup sugar	Make meringue. Fold 2 mixtures together.
1 cup graham cracker crumbs (12 to 14 single crackers) 2 tbsp. sugar 3 tbsp. melted margarine	Combine. Place half of crumbs in bottom of serving dish. Pour in orange mixture. Sprinkle remaining crumbs over top. Chill at least 2 hours. before serving.

Yield: 8 servings

Luscious Pumpkin Squares

1¾ cups graham cracker crumbs ⅓ cup sugar ½ cup margarine, melted	Mix together and press in 9 × 13 dish.
2 eggs 8 oz. cream cheese, softened ¾ cup sugar	Beat together until smooth. Pour over crumbs and bake at 350 degrees for 20 minutes. Cool completely.
3 egg yolks, slightly beaten ½ cup sugar ½ cup milk ¼ tsp. salt 2 cups canned pumpkin 1 tsp. ground cinnamon ¼ tsp. ground nutmeg	Combine in saucepan. Heat just to boiling, stirring constantly. Remove from heat.
1 env. unflavored gelatin (1 tbsp.) ¼ cup cold water	Soak until softened. Then add to hot mixture. Cool thoroughly.
3 egg whites ¼ cup sugar	Make meringue. Fold in. Pour over cooled cream cheese layer. Chill at least 1 hour before serving. Cut in squares.
whipped cream to garnish	Put a dab on top of each square.

Yield: 9 to 12 servings   *Louise Heatwole*

Scrumptious Toasted Pecan Pudding

½ cup margarine, melted 1 cup pecans, chopped ¼ cup brown sugar 1 cup flour 1½ cups angel flake coconut	Mix together and spread on tray. Heat in 325-degree oven about ½ hour until lightly browned, stirring occasionally. Cool.
2 (3½-oz.) pkgs. instant vanilla or butterscotch pudding 3 cups milk	Beat together 2 minutes at low speed of electric mixer. Chill 5 minutes.
2 env. Dream Whip	Whip according to pkg. directions and fold into pudding.

Place half of crumbs in 9 × 13 dish. Pour pudding over crumbs. Sprinkle with remaining crumbs over the top. (Best eaten same day as made.)

Yield: 9 to 12 servings   *Ruby Petersheim*

Fluffy Tapioca Pudding

(Chilled pudding may also be layered in pretty glass dish with whipped cream, graham cracker crumbs, sliced bananas, and colored miniature marshmallows.)

3 egg yolks, slightly beaten 4¾ cups milk 6 tbsp. minute tapioca ¼ tsp. salt ⅔ cup sugar	Combine in saucepan. Soak 5 minutes. Heat, stirring constantly until mixture comes to a full rolling boil. Remove from heat.
3 egg whites, stiffly beaten	Pour hot mixture into whites slowly at first, then quickly, stirring vigorously until blended.
1 tsp. vanilla, or ½ tsp. each orange and coconut flavorings	Blend in. Cool 20 minutes and stir again. Chill.

Variation: For chocolate tapioca pudding, add ¼ cup cocoa powder to sugar mixture.

Yield: 10 to 12 servings

Strawberry Angel Dessert

1 10-inch angel food cake, baked	Have ready.
2 cups fresh strawberries* ⅓ cup sugar	Crush berries somewhat and add sugar. Let set 5 minutes. Drain, reserving syrup.
1 (3-oz.) strawberry flavored gelatin 1 cup boiling water	Dissolve. Add reserved syrup. Chill until just beginning to congeal. Then beat lightly until fluffy.
4 cups (12-oz.) Cool Whip	Fold in. Chill until of spreading consistency. Fold in berries.

Slice cake horizontally into 3 layers. Fill between layers with mixture. May ice sides if desired. Chill until serving time. (*May use frozen berries, but omit sugar if already sweetened.)

FROZEN DESSERTS

Frozen Cranberry Dessert

2 cups cinnamon graham cracker crumbs 6 tbsp. margarine, melted	Mix together. Reserve ½ cup crumbs. Press remaining crumbs in 8 × 12 dish.
8 oz. cream cheese, softened 2 tbsp. milk ½ tsp. vanilla ⅓ cup sugar	Beat together until smooth.
1 (16-oz.) can whole cranberry sauce	Fold in.
1 cup whipping cream few drops red color	Whip. Fold in gently. Pour into dish over crumbs. Sprinkle reserved crumbs over the top. Freeze.

Let soften about 15 minutes before serving. Cut in squares to serve.

Yield: 8 to 10 servings

Luscious Oreo Ice Cream Dessert

1 (15-oz.) pkg. Oreo cookies	Crush into crumbs and spread half in bottom of 9 × 13 dish. Reserve half.
½ gallon vanilla ice cream, softened slightly	Spread over crumbs.

caramel ice cream topping*	Drizzle over.
½ cup chopped pecans (optional)	Sprinkle over. Then layer with reserved crumbs.
2 or 3 cups Cool Whip	Spread over top.
shaved chocolate curls to garnish	Sprinkle over topping.

Freeze until firm. Cut in squares and let soften about 15 minutes before serving.

Yield: 8 to 10 servings   *Elizabeth Yoder*

Optional Topping: Cook together 1 cup evaporated milk, 2 (1-oz.) squares unsweetened chocolate, ⅓ cup butter, and 1 cup sugar for 10 minutes. Cool thoroughly. Omit second Oreo layer and caramel topping. Spread over ice cream. Top with Cool Whip and sprinkle with chopped pecans.

Pumpkin Stack-Ups

(It is important to work fast with softened ice cream mixtures. If melted too much, mixture will be icy when refrozen.)

32 or more gingersnaps	Line 8-inch-square dish with half. Reserve other half. Chill dish in freezer 5 or 10 min.
¾ cup canned pumpkin **½ cup brown sugar** **¼ tsp. salt** **½ tsp. ground cinnamon** **⅛ tsp. ground ginger** **⅛ tsp. ground nutmeg**	Combine thoroughly.
1 qt. vanilla ice cream, softened	Blend together quickly. Spoon half of mixture over gingersnaps in dish. Layer reserved gingersnaps over next. Spread remaining mixture over top.
½ cup chopped pecans	Sprinkle over top.

Freeze until firm. Remove from freezer about 15 minutes before serving to soften.

Yield: 6 to 8 servings   *Anna Mae Weaver*

Peanut Butter Ice Cream Squares

2 cups graham cracker crumbs ⅓ cup margarine, melted 3 tbsp. sugar	Mix together. Press in bottom of 9 × 13 bake dish. Place in freezer at least 10 minutes to chill.
1½ cups peanuts, chopped (reserve half) ¾ cup light corn syrup ½ cup chunky peanut butter	Blend together thoroughly.
½ gallon vanilla ice cream, softened slightly (divided in half)	Spoon half evenly over crumbs. Spread peanut butter mixture over next. Then remainder of ice cream. (Work quickly so ice cream doesn't melt!)

Sprinkle reserved peanuts over the top. Freeze until firm. Remove from freezer about 15 minutes before serving to soften.

Yield: 8 to 10 servings

Ice Cream Crunch Dessert

½ cup brown sugar 6 tbsp. margarine	Heat together just until melted.
3 cups coconut, toasted until light brown 3 cups Rice Krispies cereal ⅔ cup chopped slivered almonds or pecans	Add. Spread half of crumbs in 9 × 13 dish. Reserve other half.
½ gallon vanilla ice cream, softened slightly	Spread over crumbs. Top with remaining crumbs. Freeze. Cut in squares to serve.
maraschino cherries or cherry pie filling to garnish	Place cherry half or a dab of pie filling in center of each square to serve.

Let soften about 15 minutes before serving.

Yield: 8 servings

Frosty Strawberry Squares

Crumbs: 1½ cups flour ¼ cup brown sugar ½ cup margarine	Mix together until crumbly.
⅔ cup chopped walnuts	Stir in. Spread in 9 × 13 bake dish.

Bake at 325 degrees about 25 minutes, stirring occasionally until lightly browned. Sprinkle ⅔ of crumbs in bottom of 9 × 13 dish. Reserve remainder for on top. Chill dish in freezer 5 to 10 minutes.

Strawberry Mixture:
2 large egg whites
1 cup sugar (⅔ cup if using frozen berries)
2 cups fresh strawberries, crushed
1 tbsp. lemon juice

Combine in large mixer bowl. Beat at highest speed until stiff—8 to 10 minutes.

1 cup whipping cream
2 drops red color (to make mixture pink)

Whip, and fold in.

Pour over crumbs in dish. Top with reserved crumbs. Freeze 6 hours or overnight. Remove from freezer 15 minutes before serving to soften.

Yield: 10 to 12 servings

Basic Recipe Homemade Ice Cream

4 eggs

Beat well.

2 cups sugar
1 tbsp. vanilla

Gradually add, beating well again.

1 (3½-oz.) pkg. instant vanilla pudding

Mix according to pkg. directions.

½ tsp. salt
2 cups cream, or 1 (14-oz.) can evaporated milk, chilled
1½ qts. milk (approx.)

Combine all ingredients with enough milk to fill 1 gal. freezer can a good ¾ full.

Place can in freezer tub and crank until hardened. See directions on page 185.
Variations: Use 2 cups less milk and add 2 cups **crushed fruit** instead. Use fresh peaches, strawberries, mashed bananas, or strained black raspberries. Increase sugar to 2½ cups when adding fruit.

For **grapenut ice cream:** Use butterscotch pudding instead of vanilla pudding. Then gently pour ¾ cup grapenuts on top of mixture in can just before freezing, so grapenuts don't sink to the bottom of can.

For **maple-nut ice cream:** And ¾ tsp. maple flavoring and ¾ tsp. burnt sugar syrup flavoring* to mixture. Freeze for about 15 minutes. Then stop cranking, quickly open can and pour in 1 cup coarsely chopped pecans or other nuts. Replace lid and continue to crank until hardened.

(*To make your own **burnt sugar syrup,** heat ½ cup dry granulated sugar in heavy pan or skillet, over medium heat, stirring constantly until melted, clear, and a medium-brown color. Add ⅓ cup boiling water carefully so steam doesn't burn your hand. Stir until smooth and clear. Cool, and add this entire amount to ice cream.)

Yield: 1 gal.

Junket Ice Cream

1 (5-oz.) pkg. instant vanilla pudding*	Mix according to pkg. directions.
2 (14-oz.) cans evaporated milk **2 cups sugar** **3 junket rennet tablets, dissolved in a little water** **1 qt. milk or more**	Mix with pudding and enough milk to make 1 gal. freezer can a good ¾ full. Let set at room temperature ½ hour before freezing for junket to set.

Place can in freezer tub and crank until hardened. See directions on page 185.

*For slightly better flavor, use regular pudding instead of instant. Use a 3 ½-oz. pkg. and add 2 tbsp. cornstarch to the dry mix before cooking. Cook according to pkg. directions and cool thoroughly.

Yield: 1 gal.

Kathryn Heatwole

Orange Pineapple Ice Cream

1 (20-oz.) can crushed pineapple*	Drain. Add water to juice to make 1 cup and heat to boiling.
1 (6-oz.) pkg. orange-flavored gelatin	Add, stirring to dissolve. Then cool.
4 eggs, beaten **2 cups sugar** **2 cups cream, or 1 (13-oz.) can evaporated milk** **enough milk to fill freezer can ¾ full—about 1¾ qts.**	Add.

(*Drained pineapple may be pureed slightly in blender with part of milk if desired, to eliminate prominent pieces of pineapple in ice cream.) Place can in freezer tub and crank until hardened. See directions on page 185.

Yield 1 gal.

Soft Ice Cream
(Similar to Dairy Queen)

2 envelopes plain gelatin (2 tbsp.) **½ cup cold water**	Soak until softened.
5 cups milk	Heat until hot, but not boiling—165 degrees. Remove from heat. Add gelatin.
2 cups sugar **½ tsp. salt** **2 tsp. vanilla**	Add, stirring until dissolved. Cool.

3 cups cream (may substitute part evaporated milk) — Stir in. Chill for 4 or 5 hours until set.

Place can in freezer tub and crank until hardened. See directions on page 185.

Yield: 1 gal.

Strawberry Sherbet

1 pt. frozen strawberries, mostly thawed	Drain, and add water to liquid to make 1 ½ cups. (Reserve berries.)
1½ cups sugar 1 env. unflavored gelatin (1 tbsp.)	Mix with liquid in saucepan. Heat to boiling, stirring constantly. Remove from heat and cool completely.
2 cups milk (reserved berries)	Blend in. Pour into 2 refrigerator trays and freeze approx. 1 hour until mushy. Turn into chilled mixer bowl and beat until creamy.
2 stiffly beaten egg whites	Fold in. Return to freezer section and freeze several hours until firm.

Variations: For **pineapple sherbet**, use crushed pineapple in place of strawberries. For **orange sherbet**, add juice and pulp of 3 oranges, 2 tbsp. grated orange rind, and 2 tbsp. lemon juice, in place of strawberries.

Yield: 12 servings

Economy Refrigerator Ice Cream

(This is more delicious than you may think. Make two batches while you are in the process, but the blender container will hold only one batch at a time.)

2½ cups water 4½ cups dry milk powder ½ cup coffee creamer	Place in blender container. Process thoroughly.
1 cup sugar ¾ cup evaporated milk	Process again until smooth.

Pour in 9 × 5 bread pan and place in freezer part of refrigerator overnight or until firm. Just before serving, place in chilled mixer bowl. Add 2 tsp. vanilla, and beat with heavy duty electric mixer until fluffy. Serve immediately.

Variation: For chocolate ice cream, add 3 rounded soup spoons of Nestlé Quik to mixture in blender, or add other flavorings as desired.

Yield: 6 servings   *Gladys Yoder*

Basic Refrigerator Ice Cream

(Refrigerator ice cream is best served fresh when mixture has just frozen solid. It can be "freshened up," however, by scraping the slightly softened ice cream into a chilled mixing bowl, and quickly beating it with heavy duty mixer until fluffy. Bowl should be placed in the freezer for at least 10 minutes to chill before using. If not chilled, ice cream may melt too much. Serve ice cream immediately after beating.)

1½ tsp. unflavored gelatin **¼ cup milk**	Soak until softened.
2 egg yolks, slightly beaten **⅔ cup sugar** **2 tbsp. flour** **⅛ tsp. salt** **1½ cups milk**	Combine in saucepan and heat, stirring constantly, just to a rolling boil. Remove from heat immediately. Add softened gelatin and stir until dissolved.
2 tsp. vanilla	Blend in. Cool mixture. Then pour into 2 ice cube trays or bread pans and freeze until stiff, but not solid.
1 cup whipping cream	Whip until stiff.
2 eggs whites (optional) **2 tbsp. sugar**	Whip egg whites into soft peaks, add sugar and whip until stiff.

Scrape partially frozen custard mixture into a chilled mixing bowl, and beat just until smooth. Then quickly fold all three mixtures together. Pour back into pans and freeze until solid. Egg whites may or may not be included in ice cream as desired. They simply make a little more volume. Whipped evaporated milk may be used in place of the whipping cream if desired. See page 254 for directions for whipping it. To disguise the taste of the evaporated milk, add ¼ cup butterscotch chips, or caramel syrup, or chocolate syrup, to milk mixture before cooking it. For other flavor variations fold 1½ cups mashed and sweetened fresh fruit such as peaches, strawberries, or raspberries into cold mixture along with the whipped cream. Or try ½ cup crushed peppermint stick candy. Or add ½ cup chopped nuts to the caramel or butterscotch mixture.

Yield: 8 or more servings

Snow Cream

1 cup rich milk or cream **1 egg, beaten well** **¾ cup sugar** **¼ tsp. salt** **1½ tsp. vanilla**	Combine thoroughly.
approximately 2 qts. fresh clean snow	Mix quickly. Eat at once.

Yield: 6 servings

SAUCES AND TOPPINGS

Buttermilk Sauce

½ cup sugar
¼ cup buttermilk or thick sour milk
1 tbsp. light corn syrup
½ tsp. vanilla
¼ cup margarine
½ tsp. baking soda

Combine all ingredients in saucepan and boil 3 or 4 minutes. Cool and chill.

Delicious on ice cream or cake, especially spooned over whipped cream on apple cake.

Butterscotch Sauce

½ cup brown sugar
½ cup light corn syrup
1 tbsp. cornstarch
⅛ tsp. salt
1 cup water
1 tsp. vanilla

Cook together until slightly thickened.

1 tbsp. butter
2 tbsp. butterscotch chips

Add, stirring until melted.

Yield: 1 ½ cups

Chocolate Fudge Sauce

(Similar to Shoney's)

2 cups sugar
¼ cup flour
⅔ cup cocoa powder
¼ tsp. salt

Mix in saucepan.

2 cups water

Gradually add, stirring until smooth. Cook, stirring constantly, just until thickened.

2 tbsp. butter
1 tsp. vanilla

Stir in. Cool thoroughly.

Serve over ice cream.

Yield: 3 ½ cups

Chocolate Sauce

1 cup chocolate chips **½ cup light corn syrup**	Heat in saucepan over low heat, stirring constantly until melted. Remove from heat.
¼ cup half and half, or evaporated milk **1 tbsp. butter or margarine** **1 tsp. vanilla**	Stir in until smooth.

Serve warm over ice cream, pound cake, or angel food cake.

Yield: 1 ½ cups

Peanut Butter Sauce

1 cup light corn syrup **¼ cup crunchy peanut butter** **¼ cup butterscotch chips**	Heat together just until melted.

Yield: 1 ¼ cups

Pineapple Topping

1 (20-oz.) can crushed pineapple, undrained **½ cup sugar** **2 or 3 tbsp. Clearjel or cornstarch**	Mix in saucepan. Heat until thickened, stirring constantly. Cool.

Yield: about 2 cups

SNACKS

Caramel Nut Apples (Candied)

6 medium apples (wash and wipe dry) **6 wooden sticks or skewers** **½ cup finely chopped walnuts**	Have ready.
1 cup brown sugar **½ cup light corn syrup** **¼ cup butter or margarine (preferably butter)**	Combine in saucepan and heat to boiling on medium heat, stirring constantly.
⅔ cup sweetened condensed milk	Stir in. Simmer, stirring constantly, to soft ball stage—236 degrees. Remove from heat.

. . . .

½ tsp. vanilla	Stir in.

. . . .

Insert wooden stick into blossom end of each apple. Dip apple in caramel syrup and turn until completely coated. Immediately roll bottom half of coated apple into chopped nuts. Place on waxed-paper-covered tray. Chill until firm.

Yield: 6 caramel apples

Carolyn H. Reed

. . . .

Stuffed Apples

(A nutritious idea that children enjoy—finding the surprise inside their apple!)

Remove core, leaving apple whole. Fill core area with any of the following: dates, peanut butter, cheese, nuts, and raisins, and so forth.

Cleta Gingerich

. . . .

Baked Bananas

See recipe on page 422 in microwave section for baking bananas in a conventional oven.

. . . .

Frozen Bananas

6 or 7 bananas, peeled **6 or 7 wooden sticks or skewers** **½ cup finely chopped peanuts**	Have ready.

. . . .

¼ cup butter or margarine **1 cup chocolate chips** **3 tbsp. evaporated milk**	Combine in saucepan. Heat over low heat until melted and smooth. Remove from heat.

. . . .

Insert skewer into end of each peeled banana. Dip in hot chocolate mixture, coating completely. Sprinkle with chopped nuts immediately before chocolate sets. Lay on waxed-paper-lined tray and freeze. Then store in plastic bags. Remove from freezer 10 to 15 minutes before serving.

Yield: 6 or 7 treats

. . . .

Fudgesicles

1 (3½-oz.) pkg. chocolate instant **pudding** **2½ cups milk**	Mix together according to pkg. directions. Pour into popsicle molds and freeze.

. . . .

Yield: approximately 12

. . . .

Italian Bread Sticks

1 pkg. dry yeast ⅔ cup warm water 1 tbsp. sugar	Combine, stirring until dissolved. Let set until foamy.
1 tsp. salt ¼ cup oil 1 env. onion soup mix	Add, mixing well
2 cups flour	Gradually add, beating well. Knead slightly.
sesame seeds to coat	Have ready.

Grease top, and place in greased bowl. Cover and let rise until double. Cut dough in half. Roll out and cut each half into 24 strips. Roll strips into sticks approximately 4 inches in length. Press in sesame seeds and place on greased baking sheet. Let set 15 minutes. Bake at 350 degrees for about 12 minutes.

Yield: 48

Finger Gelatin

3 env. unflavored gelatin ¾ cup cold water	Soak at least 2 minutes.
2¼ cups boiling water 2 (3-oz.) pkgs. flavored gelatin	Combine also with soaked gelatin and stir until well dissolved and clear.
¼ cup sugar	Stir in until dissolved.

Pour into a 9-inch-square dish and chill until firm—at least overnight or longer. Cut in squares to serve with knife dipped in warm water. For special occasions, use small cookie cutters. Melt "scraps," let set up again and cut in cubes.

Party Mix

6 tbsp. margarine	Melt in large electric skillet at 200 degrees temperature.
1 tbsp. Worcestershire sauce ½ tsp. garlic powder ½ tsp. celery salt ½ tsp. onion salt	Stir in until well blended.
3 cups Cheerios cereal 2 cups Corn Chex cereal 2 cups Rice Chex cereal 2 cups thin pretzel sticks 1 cup mix nuts or peanuts	Add, mixing until well coated. Cover skillet, leaving vents open. Heat at 250 degrees for 20 minutes, stirring occasionally

. . . .

May be heated in 275-degree oven for 20 minutes instead of the skillet if desired. Stir occasionally.

Variation: Use 2 qts. popped corn instead of cereal.

. . . .

Roasted Peanuts

Raw peanuts may be roasted in the oven in or out of the shell. Spread out on a large tray and roast in 300-degree oven until crisp. Do not overheat, as they will darken slightly while they cool. Roast unshelled nuts 45 minutes to 1 hour, and shelled nuts 30 to 40 minutes, stirring frequently. Watch carefully to avoid overbrowning.

. . . .

Gorp Trail Mix

1½ lbs. raisins
2 lbs. mixed nuts or peanuts
½ lb. M&M's
1 cup salted sunflower seeds

Stir together until mixed.

. . . .

Variations: May use other dried fruits or yogurt-covered raisins. Peanut butter or chocolate chips may be added, but these soften in your hand on the trail.

EMC's Colorado Wilderness Seminar Mix

. . . .

Peppernuts

1½ cups shortening
3 cups sugar

Cream together thoroughly.

. . . .

3 large eggs, beaten
½ cup sorghum molasses
½ cup dark corn syrup
1 cup thick sour cream
1 tsp. anise oil

Add.

. . . .

2 cups flour
1 tsp. ground nutmeg
1 tsp. ground cloves
1 tsp. ground cinnamon
1 tsp. ground ginger
1 tsp. ground allspice
1½ tsp. baking soda

Beat in until well mixed.

. . . .

8 additional cups flour

Add.

. . . .

Chill dough several hours or overnight. Cut off small portions of dough and roll into fingerlike rolls. Slice rolls making pieces about the size of a marble. Place pieces close together on greased baking sheet. Bake at 375 degrees for 10 to 12 minutes until light brown.

Yield: approximately 2 gals.

Wanda Good

. . . .

Stuffed Raw Peppers

5 or 6 raw peppers	Cut only around stem end and remove seeds and membrane. Rinse well.

7 cups bread crumbs **1 or 2 cups grated cheese** **1 med. onion, finely chopped** **pepper to taste** **mayonnaise or salad dressing to** **hold mixture together**	Mix together. Stuff peppers.

Popcorn Balls

3 or 4 qts. popped corn	Have ready.

¾ cup sugar **¾ cup brown sugar** **½ cup water** **½ cup light corn syrup** **1 tsp. vinegar** **⅛ tsp. salt**	Combine in saucepan. Heat to boiling, stirring constantly. Reduce heat and cook to hard ball stage—260 degrees. Remove from heat.

¼ cup butter or margarine **1 tsp. vanilla**	Stir in until melted.

Pour over popped corn mixing until well coated. Butter hands and shape into balls. Place on waxed paper to cool. These can be made into various shapes for special occasions.

Variation: add 2 tsp. cinnamon instead of vanilla. Or use all white sugar instead of part brown sugar. Then add a small amount of food coloring and any other flavoring desired—banana, strawberry, butter, etc.

Yield: 12 medium-sized balls

Crispy Caramel Popcorn

8 or 9 qts. popped corn **1 cup peanuts**	Combine in large container. Set aside.

2 cups brown sugar **1 tsp. salt** **½ cup light corn syrup** **1 cup margarine**	Combine in saucepan, stirring constantly until boiling. Boil 5 minutes. Remove from heat.

1 tsp. vanilla **½ tsp. baking soda**	Stir in until foamy.

Pour syrup over corn mixture, stirring until well coated. Pour into 2 large pans and heat in 250-degree oven for 1 hour. Stir occasionally. Remove, cool, and separate.

Peanut Butter Popcorn Balls

3 or 4 qts. popped corn	Have ready.
½ cup sugar ½ cup light corn syrup	Combine in saucepan. Heat to a good rolling boil, stirring constantly. Remove from heat.
½ cup chunky peanut butter ½ tsp. vanilla ⅛ tsp. salt	Stir in until well blended.

Pour over corn, stirring until well coated. Shape into balls if desired.

Soft Pretzels

(This is a fun treat for young people. They like to shape pretzels into all kinds of creations!)

3 pkgs. dry yeast 2¼ cups warm water 1 tsp. sugar	Stir until dissolved. Let rise until foamy.
6¾ cups flour	Add, kneading until smooth. Allow to rise 15 minutes.
½ cup lukewarm water 4 tsp. baking soda	Mix and have ready.

Shape dough into rolls and slice. Roll out each slice into a pencil shape. Twist into pretzel shape. Dip each pretzel into soda-water mixture and place on greased baking sheet. Sprinkle with coarse salt. Bake at 375 degrees for about 15 minutes.

Yield: about 30 pretzels

Roasted Pumpkin Seeds

1½ tbsp. margarine, melted ½ tsp. salt ⅛ tsp. garlic powder 2 tsp. Worcestershire sauce	Combine.
2 cups unwashed pumpkin seeds	Mix thoroughly. Place in shallow baking dish.

Bake at 275 degrees for about 1 hour, stirring occasionally.

Soy Nuts

Soak 1 cup dry soybeans in water overnight. Use 4 cups water for each cup of dry beans. (To soak quickly, boil beans 2 minutes, remove from heat, and let stand 1 hour.) Drain beans thoroughly. Place on absorbent paper and allow to air dry 1 hour. Heat 1 qt. oil in deep fat fryer or a heavy deep saucepan to 350 degrees. Place 1 cup beans in a fryer basket. Lower basket slowly into hot fat. Moisture in beans may cause excessive spattering if lowered too rapidly. Fry 6 to 8 minutes or until crisp and lightly browned. Drain on absorbent paper. Sprinkle with salt. When cool, store in tightly covered container.

Yield: about 2 cups   *Mary Louise Lehman*

Oven Method: Soak beans overnight. Cook 1 hour. Spread on tray and roast at 350 degrees until brown, about 30 minutes. Sprinkle with salt.

. . . .

Strawberry Pudding Popsicles

1 (3½-oz.) pkg. instant vanilla pudding 1 cup milk	Beat together on low for 2 minutes. Chill 5 minutes.
9 oz. or 3 cups whipped topping 2 cups crushed strawberries 1 cup mashed bananas	Fold in.

Spoon into 15 (5-oz.) paper drinking cups. Insert wooden sticks. Freeze until firm. Remove from freezer, peel off paper, and serve.

Yield: 15 servings

. . . .

CANDY

Almond Bark

(All ingredients should be at room temperature.)

2 lbs. almond bark (white chocolate)	Melt in double boiler, or over low heat.
1 cup peanut butter	Mix in thoroughly.
2 cups roasted peanuts, coarsely chopped 2½ cups miniature marshmallows 4 cups Rice Krispies cereal	Stir in until thoroughly coated. Drop by teaspoonfuls onto waxed paper to cool.

Yield: 3½ lbs. candy   *Nancy Heatwole*

. . . .

Butterscotch Crunchies

¾ cup butterscotch morsels ½ cup peanut butter	Melt together over low heat.
4 cups Rice Krispies or Cornflakes cereal	Pour in bowl. Stir in mixture until coated. Drop by teaspoonfuls onto waxed paper.

Or press into 8-inch-square pan. Cut in squares when cool.

Yield: 3 or 4 dozen   *Gretchen McCue*

Candy Bars

(These easy bars remind you of the O'Henry bars)

⅔ cup margarine, melted 1 tbsp. vanilla 1 cup brown sugar ½ cup light or dark corn syrup 4 cups quick oatmeal	Stir together until thoroughly blended. Press in bottom of 9 × 13 pan. Bake at 360 degrees for 12 minutes. Cool.
1 cup chocolate chips	Melt over low heat.
½ cup chunky peanut butter	Stir in until blended. Spread over baked layer. Cool until firm.

Cut into bars.

Yield: 2 or 3 dozen bars

Chocolate Coconut Bars

(A 3-layer treat that tastes similar to Mounds bars.)

2 cups graham cracker crumbs ½ cup melted butter or margarine ½ cup sugar	Mix and spread in a 9 × 13 dish. Bake at 350 degrees for 10 minutes.
2 cups angel flake coconut 1 (14-oz.) can sweetened condensed milk	Mix and spread over first layer. Bake 15 minutes more.
1½ cups chocolate chips 2 tbsp. peanut butter	Melt together over low heat and spread over coconut layer while both are hot.

Cool until firm. Cut into little squares.

Mary K. Heatwole

Chocolate Drops or Easter Eggs

3 cups sugar ¾ cup light corn syrup ½ cup water	Combine in saucepan. Heat, stirring until dissolved. Boil to soft ball stage on candy thermometer—245 degrees.
2 egg whites, stiffly beaten	Pour hot syrup into beaten whites in thin stream, continuing to beat into very stiff peaks.
1 tsp. vanilla	Blend in. Cool slightly.

Shape into little balls or into eggs, of desired sizes. Dip into melted coating chocolate. Cool on waxed paper. May be decorated with icings as desired.

Fannie B. Heatwole, my mother

Fantastic Fudge

3 cups sugar ¾ cup margarine ⅔ cup evaporated milk	Combine in saucepan. Boil 5 minutes, stirring constantly to avoid scorching. Remove from heat.
1½ cups chocolate chips	Stir in until melted.
1 (7-oz.) jar marshmallow creme, or 4 cups miniature marshmallows ¾ cup chopped nuts 1 tsp. vanilla	Add, beating until well blended. Pour into greased 9 × 13 pan. Cool at room temperature. Cut into squares.

Holiday Rocky Road Fudge

3 cups sugar ⅔ cup cocoa powder ½ cup light corn syrup 1 cup milk	Combine in saucepan. Heat, stirring constantly, until boiling. Reduce heat, and cook to soft ball stage—238 degrees, stirring occasionally. Remove from heat.
¼ cup butter or margarine 1 tsp. vanilla	Add, but do not stir. Cool to lukewarm. Beat until creamy.
½ cup candied cherries, cut in fourths 1 cup miniature marshamllows ½ cup chopped nuts ½ cup angel flake coconut	Stir in. Pour into greased 9 × 13 pan. Cool until set. Cut into squares.

Krispy Peanut Butter Drops

3 cups peanut butter ¾ cup margarine, softened 1 lb. powdered sugar (about 3½ cups) 3½ cups Rice Krispies cereal	Work together with hands until well blended. Shape into small balls.

| 1½ cups chocolate chips* | Melt together. Dip balls and place on waxed |
| ½ stick paraffin | paper to cool. |

*Or use coating chocolate.

Fannie S. Heatwole

Party Mints

3 oz. cream cheese, softened	Cream together until well blended.
⅛ tsp. oil of peppermint	
⅛ tsp. butter flavoring	
coloring as desired	

| 2 cups powdered sugar | Add gradually until firm enough to shape |

Roll into little 1-inch balls. Roll balls in granulated sugar to coat. Then press into a mold which has also been dipped in granulated sugar. Or press balls flat with finger, and make an imprint in both directions with a fork to form a grid pattern on top. Serve as is, or they may be dipped in melted chocolate coating.

Yield: approximately 50

For a large amount, use 8 oz. cream cheese and 2 lbs. powdered sugar with flavoring and color—makes 150. These freeze well, and may be made ahead for special occasions, using molds to fit the occasion.

Peanut Butter Cereal Squares

| ½ cup sugar | Combine in saucepan. Heat to boiling. Remove |
| ½ cup light corn syrup | from heat. |

¾ cup peanut butter	Add, stirring until well coated. Press lightly in
1 tsp. vanilla	buttered 8 × 12 dish.
5 cups Rice Krispies cereal, or cornflakes	

Optional Topping:

1 cup butterscotch chips	Melt together over low heat, stirring constantly.
½ cup chocolate chips	Spread over top of candy.
2 tbsp. butter	

Cut into squares when cool.

Peanut Butter Chews

1¼ cups graham cracker crumbs	Mix all ingredients together thoroughly. Press in
1 cup peanut butter	8 × 12 dish. Chill and cut into squares. Or
1 cup honey or corn syrup	shape into balls and roll in crushed cornflakes
1 cup dry milk powder	or additional coconut if desired.
1 cup coconut	

Peanut Brittle

(If pan is covered for first 3 minutes of cooking time, the steam will melt the sugar down around the edge and prevent formation of sugar crystals. After removing lid to continue cooking, insert thermometer carefully in hot syrup to avoid breakage.)

2 cups sugar **½ cup light corn syrup** **½ cup dark corn syrup** **½ cup water**	Combine in saucepan. Cook to softball stage, 236 degrees.

....

3 cups raw peanuts **3 tbsp. butter or margarine**	Add. Continue cooking to 290 degrees until syrup is golden brown. (Stir frequently after adding peanuts to prevent burning.)

....

1 tsp. baking soda **½ tsp. salt** **1 tsp. vanilla**	Stir in well.

....

Pour on 2 greased 11 × 15 cookie sheets, or on greased sheets of foil pulling candy out to make it thin, the thinner the better. Foil is easy to pull away when removing candy. Cool until hardened. Break into pieces as desired.
Yield: about 3 lbs.

Nancy Heatwole
Rosie Weaver

....

Peanut Butter Drops

5¼ cups powdered sugar **1 cup margarine, softened** **2 tsp. vanilla** **2 cups peanut butter (preferably chunky)**	Work together thoroughly with hands until well blended. Shape into rolls the size of a quarter or larger. Chill slightly.

....

Slice into ¾-inch slices, or as desired. Place each on fork and dip in melted chocolate to coat.

Gladys and Brownie Driver

....

Chocolate Coating:

2¼ cups chocolate chips **⅓ cup paraffin**	Melt together in top of double boiler over low heat.

....

Place dipped slices on waxed paper to cool until firm.

....

Peanut Butter Eggs

1 lb. (about 3½ cups) powdered sugar **1½ cups peanut butter** **4 oz. cream cheese, softened** **½ cup margarine, softened** **½ tsp. vanilla**	Mix together with hands until thoroughly blended. Shape into eggs. Chill until firm. Dip in chocolate coating.

....

Rice Krispies Marshmallow Squares

¼ cup butter or margarine	Melt in saucepan.
½ lb. marshmallows (about 38 large)	Add, stirring over low heat until melted.
½ tsp. vanilla	Add.
6 cups Rice Krispies cereal	Stir in until well coated. Press lightly into greased 9 × 13 pan.

Cut into squares when cool.

Variations:

For **peanut butter treats,** blend ¼ cup peanut butter with marshmallow mixture before adding Rice Krispies.

For **chocolate treats,** add 2 (1-oz.) squares unsweetened chocolate or ¼ cup cocoa to marshmallow mixture.

For **spice treats,** add 1 tsp. cinnamon or ¼ tsp. ginger to marshmallow mixture.

For special occasions shape into trees, snowmen, etc. Or may be lightly pressed in shallow layer in dish and cut with cookie cutters into desired shapes after mixture hardens.

Three-Tier Coconut Candy

1.	**2 cups sugar** **1 cup light cream** **½ tbsp. butter** **dash salt**	Combine in saucepan. Heat to boiling, stirring constantly. Boil to soft ball stage—232 degrees.
	1½ tbsp. unflavored gelatin **3 tbsp. cold water**	Soak together 5 minutes. Pour hot mixture over gelatin and beat until creamy.
	1¼ cups fresh grated coconut or frozen coconut* **1 tsp. vanilla**	Stir in until blended well. Pour into greased 9-inch square dish.

2. Make a second recipe, adding small amount of red food coloring to make a pink layer. Pour on top of first layer.

3. Make a third recipe adding 3 tbsp. cocoa to sugar mixture to make a chocolate layer. Pour on top of second layer.

When cool and set, cut into little squares.

(*If using frozen coconut, boil syrup to 235 degrees to compensate for the extra moisture in the frozen coconut.)

Yield: 4 ½ lbs. candy   *Ida Goering*

Taffy

(This is a great treat for a young people's group. Many youth groups have a taffy pull occasionally. Recipe is an amount for 2 couples or 4 persons to pull. An amount for 12 couples, or 24 persons, to pull is given in brackets)

1 ½ tsp. unflavored gelatin [3 envelopes] ¼ cup cold water [1 ½ cups]	Soak together until softened.
2 cups sugar [12] 1 cup dark corn syrup [6] 1 cup milk [6] about 1½ tbsp. paraffin [½ cup or 1 cake]	Combine in saucepan. Boil 15 minutes. Then add softened gelatin and boil to 248 degrees—no higher—stirring occasionally. Remove from heat.

Pour into greased pie pans to cool slightly—not too long. Pull with partner until light. Sprinkle tray with powdered sugar. Stretch into long ropes, snip into desired sized pieces into tray. Shake to coat. Store in refrigerator. (The large amount takes approximately 1 ½ hours of boiling time.)

Fannie S. Heatwole

Toffee Butter Crunch

2 cups butter or margarine 2½ cups sugar 2 tbsp. light corn syrup ¼ cup water	Combine in saucepan. Cook over medium heat to 290 degrees. Remove from heat.
1 cup coarsely chopped almonds, or pecans	Stir in. Spread on buttered baking sheet or foil.
9 oz. milk chocolate candy bar, broken, or 1⅓ cups chocolate chips	Immediately sprinkle over hot candy to melt. Spread evenly when melted.
1 cup finely chopped almonds, or pecans	Sprinkle over top quickly before chocolate is set.

Cool and break into desired size pieces.

Carolyn Reed
Dorothy Schrock Shank

CHAPTER FIVE

EGGS, MILK, & CHEESE

EGGS, MILK, AND CHEESE

Eggs are used in so many ways that they seem to appear in some form at the majority of meals. They are a good source of high-quality protein and many important vitamins and minerals, and yet the per pound price is usually far below that of many foods of much lesser nutritional value.

The color of the shell and the lightness or darkness of the yolk make no difference in the food value of the egg. (The color of the shell is determined by the breed of hens. If hens are let outside the henhouse, the yolks are usually darker in color.)

Purchase only fresh eggs and store them in the refrigerator immediately after purchase. They lose their quality quickly in a hot car or kitchen. If fresh eggs are refrigerated immediately, they should keep in the refrigerator from 4 to 5 weeks without significant quality loss. They will age more in one day at room temperature, however, than in one week in the refrigerator. Store covered since uncovered eggs absorb odors and lose moisture rapidly. Small eggs usually have a thicker shell, and therefore stay fresh longer than larger ones. For those on the farm, do not soak eggs in water to clean them. Eggshells are porous. If needed, either dry-clean with a brush, or rinse quickly with water.

A fresh egg has a dull rather than a shiny shell. A blotchy appearance may occur on eggshells with age. To test the freshness of an egg, place it in a glass of water. A fresh egg will sink to the bottom, an older egg will rise partially at one end, and a stale egg will float. If an egg has any odor or discoloration, discard it. A little fleck of blood occasionally found on the yolk is not harmful, however. The spot can be removed with the tip of a knife, if desired.

The grade of the egg does not affect its food value, but refers to the quality of both the egg and the shell at the time it was packed. The yolk will stand up tall in a fresh A grade egg, and there is a larger portion of thick white than thin. In a B grade egg, the yolk has flattened out and the white is considerably thinner.

Many cooks are much perturbed by the stringy ropelike substance found in the white of the egg. This is not the beginning of an embryo, but is a substance called "chalaza," which serves as an anchor to keep the yolk centered in the thick white. It is a natural, edible part of the egg!

If eggs are very fresh they are quite difficult to peel when hard cooked. They should be at least 3 days old when used for hard cooking. For the first few days the volume for beaten eggs will not be as large. If you must use very fresh eggs for hard cooking, or when volume is important in beaten eggs, let them remain at room temperature for several hours before using.

Another concern of many persons is the safeness of using raw eggs in beverages or other recipes where they remain uncooked. If an egg has been properly stored and the shell is clean and uncracked, the egg should be perfectly safe to use raw if the food is eaten promptly. The shell plus two membranes are the egg's natural protection against bacteria and prevent contamination from entering the egg. It is usually the mishandling of food that causes illness rather than the food itself.

To beat eggs to their greatest volume, warm them to at least room temperature—65 to 75 degrees. Eggs separate more easily at refrigerator temperature, but should then be allowed to warm up before beating. To separate eggs, most old-timers give the egg a hard crack, hold it over a bowl, and pull it apart, keeping the yolk in the larger portion of shell. Then pour it back and forth between the two pieces of shell, letting the white escape into the bowl until only yolk remains. For the less experienced, it is probably easier to break the entire egg carefully into a cup. Then with a spoon, carefully lift the yolk out. It is important not to break the yolk, since the least speck of yolk in with the whites will reduce beaten volume considerably. If this happens, use a spoon to fish out any speck, or moisten a piece of paper towel and try to absorb the speck with the piece of towel. If this is impossible, save the egg to use for another purpose and try another one.

Always use clean utensils for beating egg whites. There should not be the least bit of greasy residue in bowl or on beaters. You cannot first beat the egg yolks and then use the same beater for the whites without washing it. You can, however, beat the whites first and use the unwashed beater for the yolks.

When beating egg whites, the addition of 1 tbsp. warm water to 1 cup of egg whites will help to increase volume. Beat at highest speed of electric mixer until very stiff, but *not* dry, peaks are formed. Do not stop and then beat more later. You will not regain lost volume. Do not fold beaten whites into another mixture with electric mixer as this will break down air cells. Gently and quickly fold in by hand, using a rubber scraper, spatula, or large spoon. Use a down-over, up-over motion, turning the bowl as you work, carefully blending ingredients without damaging air cells.

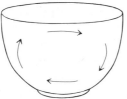

Beaten egg whites begin to deteriorate immediately and rapidly after beating. The oven should be preheated and all other ingredients mixed and ready, to avoid letting the beaten whites sit for any length of time.

Freezing Eggs: If you need only the white or the yolk of the egg in baking, do not waste the other portion of the egg. The whites can easily be frozen without any treatment and used just as fresh ones when thawed. Simply pour in small container, cover tightly, and freeze. Mark quantity on outside for easy reference.

Egg yolks need to be treated first to prevent coagulation when freezing. To each 4 egg yolks, add either 1 tsp. sugar or ¼ tsp. salt. Gently mix and strain into small container. Cover tightly and freeze.

The yolks may also be used in other ways. If not broken, they may be carefully dropped in rapidly boiling water and cooked until hard. Cool and chop for salads, or mash through strainer and use to top sauces or for breakfast. If broken, they may be added to scrambled eggs or custards.

Whole eggs may be frozen by adding either ½ tbsp. sugar or ½ tsp. salt to 1 cup eggs. Stir with fork to mix, but do not whip air into mixture. Strain into container, cover tightly, and freeze.

Frozen eggs are very perishable when thawed and should be used promptly. When thawed they may be used in recipes as follows:

3 tbsp. whole egg for 1 egg called for in recipe

1 tbsp. yolk for 1 egg yolk

2 tbsp. white for 1 egg white

Hard Cooking Eggs: Place eggs in pan and cover with cold water. Cover pan and heat just to the boiling point. Reduce heat to keep eggs just simmering—not a rolling boil. (Bubbles should just break the surface of the water.) Simmer for 18 minutes. Immediately pour off hot water and run cold water over eggs. Peel in just a few minutes for easier peeling. If eggs are cooked at too high a temperature, are cooked too long, or are not cooled immediately, a dark greenish or grayish coating may form on the outside of the yolk. This is not harmful to eat, but spoils the appearance. Overcooking also toughens the white.

Soft Cooking Eggs: Proceed as for hard cooked eggs, except when water begins to boil, turn off burner and remove from heat. Leave covered for 3 to 5 minutes, depending on the degree of doneness desired. When done, immediately run cold water over eggs until just cool enough to handle. Break shell through the middle with knife. Scoop egg out of each half of shell with a teaspoon.

Milk: It is important to include plenty of milk in the diet because of its high nutritional content. It is considered by many authorities to be the most complete natural food available and is an excellent source of calcium.

If your family does not care for plain milk, there are many other ways to incorporate milk or milk products in the diet. Besides flavored milk and milk shakes, you can include many kinds of pudding, yogurt, cheese, and ice cream (made from milk).

Cheese: Eggs, milk, and cheese blend together so well for so many dishes that it is natural to put them together in this chapter. They are rich sources of high-quality protein and can be used as a meat substitute in many meals. Since cheese is so versatile, it is included in recipes from appetizers to desserts. No attempt is made to confine it to this chapter!

Since there are hundreds of kinds of cheeses, it is impossible to describe them all here. The most popular cooking cheese in the United States is cheddar, also called American cheese. It comes in 3 different degrees of ripeness—mild, medium, or sharp—depending on how long it was aged.

Cream cheese (made from light cream) and cottage cheese (often made from lowfat milk) are popular unripened cheeses. They are used in many recipes for salads and desserts.

Mozzarella, Parmesan, and Romano are used in many pasta dishes. Mozzarella is a soft cheese, while Parmesan and Romano are hard ripened cheeses, usually grated.

Swiss is another popular hard cheese. It is a milder, sweeter cheese with a distinct flavor. It is full of holes caused by gases produced by cultured bacteria in processing.

American pasteurized process cheese should not be confused with natural American cheese. This is made by grinding and melting together many different kinds of cheeses. Scraps of cheese and cheeses that were not quite perfect can be combined and used to make process cheese. More liquid and an emulsifier are added. Therefore, it is softer and melts easier. Much of it is used for packaged pre-sliced cheese.

It is important to be aware of the vigorous marketing of cheese foods which are not nearly as high in nutritional content as cheese. Many of these products contain enough cheese for flavoring, along with coloring and additives, to make them look like cheese, but the food value is considerably less. Much of the pre-sliced packages in grocery stores are cheese food rather than cheese. So be sure to read the labels, check prices, and know what you are buying. Many times we pay dearly for processing and packaging without realizing what we are losing in food value.

Cheese must always be kept in a cool place. Unripened cheeses such as cottage cheese are perishable and do not keep long. Semi-hard and hard cheeses last longer, but will develop mold around edges if kept too long. A little dry mold on hard cheese can be trimmed off and does not necessarily indicate spoilage. Cheese should be wrapped tightly for storing to help prevent drying out and molding. To retard molding, cheese may be wrapped in a cloth dampened in vinegar. Or rub the entire piece with a cloth dipped in vinegar and wrap in plastic wrap.

Hard cheeses may be frozen, but will usually be more crumbly when thawed. Freezing adversely affects the texture of soft cheeses such as cottage cheese and cream cheese. Some kinds of hard cheeses freeze better than others. Swiss and cheddar freeze fairly well, but will have better texture if thawed in the refrigerator rather than at room temperature. Smaller blocks will thaw with better texture than large blocks. The best way to freeze cheese is to grate it first. It can be stored indefinitely in the freezer this way and is handy for many uses. So don't let small ends of leftover cheese get lost in the back of the refrigerator and too dried out and moldy to salvage. Keep a bag of grated cheese in the freezer to use from, or add to as desired.

TIPS FOR EGGS, MILK, AND CHEESE

•When breaking eggs, use a quick swish of your finger to clean remaining white out of shell. You'll be surprised at how much remains in the shell.

•Store eggs with broad end up. Yolks are less likely to break stored this way.

•If hard-cooked eggs and raw eggs become mixed in the refrigerator, you can tell which is which by attempting to spin them on the counter top. Hard-cooked eggs will spin easily on their pointed ends. Raw ones will not because of the imbalance of the raw yolk moving around.

•The whites will be more tender if eggs are at room temperature when poached or fried.

•Add 1 tsp. vinegar to water when poaching eggs. This will help whites cover over yolks and retards spreading.

•When adding beaten eggs to a hot mixture, always precondition them by adding a small amount of the hot mixture to eggs first. Blend well, then stir into the remaining hot mixture. Otherwise, you may have particles of cooked egg throughout the hot mixture.

•To keep thin-shelled eggs from cracking while hard boiling, it helps to add a a little vinegar or salt to the water, to have eggs at room temperature, and to start them in cold water.

•When frying eggs, first heat skillet to medium hot, add oil or fat, and then add eggs. This will minimize sticking to the skillet. (Caution: Do not overheat empty Teflon skillet as this may permanently damage the Teflon.)

•If eggs are quite fresh and you think they may be difficult to peel when hard cooked, carefully pierce the large end of each egg with a needle or thumbtack, making only a tiny pinhole. The addition of 1 tbsp. salt or soda per 1 pt. of water in which eggs are cooked helps to make peeling easier.

•If you accidentally break an egg on the floor, instead of trying to mop up all the goop with several cloths or paper towels, simply scrape the egg onto a dust pan with a rubber scraper, then dump out and rinse dustpan. The little remaining residue can easily be wiped up with much less effort.

•Milk and liquid cream may be frozen if desired. Commercial sour cream separates when frozen.

•Flavor is improved with powdered milk by mixing it ahead and with the addition of a little coffee creamer. Dissolve 2 tbsp. creamer in 2 tbsp. hot water and add to 1 qt. milk. Refrigerate overnight before using.

•Always rinse a container for milk with cold water before pouring in the milk to prevent coating of the container. It is especially important to rinse pan with cold water before heating milk to help prevent sticking.

•Drinking hot milk helps to induce sleep. For a bedtime treat try different flavors of hot milk such as butterscotch, chocolate, vanilla with a little sugar, mocha, strawberry and other fruit flavors, or red cinnamon candies. Heat only to 165 degrees to avoid having a film form over the top of the hot milk.

•Very fresh cream does not whip well. Cream should be at least 3 days old for good whipping. For thick cream, retain the milky part which collects on the bottom of the jar and pour only thick portion of cream into bowl for whipping. (This does not apply to commercial whipping cream.) Do not whip cream too long to avoid having it separate and turn into butter. Older cream is more susceptible to this problem. If this threatens, add a little milk and whip again. For easier whipping of cream, place bowl of cream in freezer until ice crystals just begin to form around the edge of the bowl. Sometimes the addition of a little lemon juice to chilled cream will help when cream does not want to whip. It is best not to add sugar until cream is whipped (add ¼ to ½ tsp. vanilla and 2 or 3 tbsp. sugar for each 1 cup chilled cream, which makes approximately 2 cups whipped cream). To keep whipped cream from separating after being whipped, see recipe on page 254 for stabilized whipped cream. Or add a little instant Clearjel. This must be mixed thoroughly with granulated sugar before adding. Add 2 tsp. instant Clearjel to 2 tbsp. sugar for 1 cup whipped cream.

•For a delightful flavor change with whipped cream toppings, sweeten cream with brown sugar instead of white. Add a small amount of maple flavor also.

•For better results with whipped toppings, chill milk in freezer just until ice begins to form around edge of bowl. Then slowly beat in topping mix only until all of it is moistened. Let set at least 1 or 2 minutes to soften thoroughly. Then whip, and it will whip more readily.

•Cheese slices handle much easier without breaking at room temperature rather than refrigerator cold. It also slices more easily with a warm knife. To easily slice soft cheese or blue cheese, use a piece of dental floss. Hold onto each end of the floss tightly and draw it down through the block of cheese.

•Chilled cheese grates more easily. To save time, grate a whole block of cheese at once and store in freezer so you don't need to get out the grater each time you need a little grated cheese.

•To prevent cheese from becoming stringy when cooked, heat at low temperature and do not overcook.

•Cheese tastes best served at room temperature.

•To keep cheese from drying out and molding, wrap in a cloth dampened with vinegar and place in a plastic bag.

•When topping casseroles with cheese for baking, it is best not to add cheese until 5 or 10 minutes before end of baking time to avoid having it toughen or burn. Velveeta cheese is especially prone to burn if added at beginning of baking time.

EGGS

Deviled Eggs

6 or 8 hard-cooked eggs

Cut eggs in half lengthwise, and remove yolks. Be careful not to break the whites. Mash the yolks with a fork.

1 tsp. prepared mustard
2 tbsp. mayonnaise
½ tsp. salt
1½ tsp. sugar
1 tsp. vinegar

Stir into yolks until thoroughly mixed. Use a teaspoon to fill the whites with the yolk mixture.

paprika and parsley, or olive slices
to garnish

Sprinkle or arrange on top of each egg.

Eggs in a Hole

Cut holes in center of slices of bread with a 2½-inch round biscuit cutter. Melt butter or margarine in skillet. Lay slices of bread in skillet. Break an egg in the hole in center of each slice of bread. Fry until lightly browned on each side. Sprinkle egg with salt and pepper and serve immediately. Centers may be browned in skillet along with egg slices and served with eggs.

. . . .

Fried Eggs

Break eggs in a dish. Add 1 or 2 tbsp. water for each egg. Heat skillet to medium hot. Add 1 or 2 tbsp. fat. Pour in eggs and cover tightly. If steam doesn't soon escape from edge of skillet, add another small amount of water. Cook a couple of minutes to desired firmness. Serve immediately.

. . . .

Golden Rod Eggs

5 hard-cooked eggs	Cut in half. Mash yolks through a strainer with the back of a spoon and set aside. Chop whites.
3 tbsp. margarine **⅓ cup flour** **2 cups milk** **1 tsp. salt**	Make white sauce. Add chopped whites.
4 or 5 slices toast	Pour egg white mixture over toast. Sprinkle with sieved yolks.
parsley to garnish	Arrange on top.

Yield: 4 to 5 servings

. . . .

Pickled Eggs

6 or 8 hard-cooked eggs, peeled
1 pint beet pickle

. . . .

Place eggs while still slightly warm in bottom of a widemouthed jar. Pour pickle juice over eggs and then add beets on top to hold eggs down in juice. Place lid on jar and refrigerate 24 hours before using until deep red color. Eggs will keep for a week. If you do not have pickled beets, you may use 1 pt. plain canned beets and pickle them as follows: combine in saucepan the juice from beets and enough water to make 1 cup, ½ cup vinegar, ½ cup sugar, ⅛ tsp. each ground cinnamon, cloves, and allspice. Bring to boil, then add beets and heat to boiling again. Cool slightly. Pour warm beet mixture over eggs in jar. Refrigerate as above. (Beet pickle juice may be used for two batches of eggs by bringing it to a boil again after using it the first time. Cool until lukewarm and pour over second batch of eggs.)

. . . .

Poached Eggs

To poach eggs, heat ½ to 1 inch water in bottom of egg poacher. Spray egg cups with vegetable spray and break an egg into each cup. Place cups in rack in poacher. Cover tightly and simmer for 3 to 5 minutes until firm. If you do not have a poacher, grease the bottom of a skillet and pour in about 1 inch of water and 1 tsp. vinegar. Break eggs individually into a saucer and carefully slip each one into water in skillet. Try to keep yolk in center of egg. Cover tightly and simmer for 3 to 5 minutes. Lift eggs from water with a slotted spoon and drain off water. Or custard cups may also be set in the water in skillet.

. . . .

Poached Eggs Supreme

6 poached eggs **6 slices cheddar, Swiss, or other cheese** **6 slices toast**	Have ready.
¼ cup butter or margarine **¼ cup chopped green pepper**	Sauté in skillet until tender.
¼ cup flour	Stir in.
2 cups milk	Add slowly, stirring vigorously until smooth.

Lay cheese slices on toast and place under broiler just until cheese begins to melt. Remove, and top each with an egg. Spoon sauce over the top.

Variation: In place of white sauce, use 1 can cream of celery soup diluted with ⅓ cup milk.

Yield: 6 servings   *Nancy Shank*

. . . .

Scrambled Eggs

4 eggs, lightly beaten **¼ cup milk or cream** **½ tsp. salt** **⅛ tsp. black pepper**	Beat together until blended.
1 tbsp. butter, margarine, or bacon grease	Heat in skillet.

When skillet is hot enough to sizzle a drop of water, pour in egg mixture. Gently lift through mixture with spatula or rubber scraper as mixture begins to set so uncooked portion will flow to bottom of skillet. Cook just until eggs are thickened throughout, but still moist. Eggs may become watery if stirred too vigorously. Serve immediately.

Variations: Add ½ cup cottage cheese to egg mixture before pouring it into skillet. Or add ¼ cup shredded Swiss cheese or other cheese. Chipped ham or crumbled bacon may also be added. Or sprinkle with parsley, chives, or oregano.

Yield: 2 servings

. . . .

MILK AND CREAM

To Pasteurize Milk

Heat milk to 145 degrees and hold at this temperature for 30 minutes. Or heat to 162 degrees and hold at this temperature for 15 seconds. Cool immediately by placing container in a larger container of slowly running water. Overheating causes a cooked taste in the milk and causes a film to form over the top.

. . . .

To Mix Milk from Instant Dry Milk Powder

⅓ cup dry milk powder and 1 scant cup water = 1 cup milk
1 ⅓ cups dry milk powder and 3 ¾ cups water = 1 qt. milk
2 ⅔ cups dry milk powder and 7 ½ cups water = ½ gal. milk

. . . .

Homemade Sweetened Condensed Milk

⅓ cup boiling water
3 tbsp. margarine, melted
⅔ cup sugar
⅛ tsp. salt
1 tbsp. light corn syrup
1 cup instant dry milk powder

Combine in blender container. Process at highest speed until smooth.

. . . .

This makes the equivalent of a 14-oz. can. It is slightly thinner than the canned; however, it works well for most recipes. You may add 1 tbsp. instant Clearjel, if available, at the end of processing time to thicken more. Process only until blended, since it will be thick enough to pull hard on blender motor.

Vada Swartz

. . . .

Thick Sour Milk

(In baking you will soon discover that recipes calling for thick sour milk or but-termilk are usually better and that it is well worth the effort of having it on hand. In a pinch many people substitute 1 cup sweet milk with 1 tbsp. vinegar or lemon juice added, but this is definitely not as good as the thick sour milk.)

To obtain thick sour milk, all you need to do is to let a jar of milk stand out of the re-frigerator at room temperature and stir 1 or 2 tbsp. of the thick milk from your previous jar into it. Let sit on the countertop approximately 24 hours or more in the wintertime until it thickens or clabbers. Or in the summertime when your kitchen is hotter, it may thicken in about 14 to 16 hours. Place tightly covered jar in refrigerator as soon as it has thickened. Be sure it is thick because it will not thicken more in the refrigerator. It is best not to let it sit too long, however, until it separates and gets watery, even though you may use it when separated—as long as it has not spoiled. If it develops a rotten odor, rather than the usual sour odor, it is spoiled. The thickened milk will keep in the refrigerator for a long time.

When you use it, simply save one tbsp. per pt. of milk for your next jar. (I keep 2 jars on hand most of the time since I use it often for pancakes, biscuits, cakes, and the like.)

For your first jar of milk, you will need to purchase a small amount of buttermilk to stir in for a starter. After that simply save a little from the previous jar.

If you live on the farm and use raw milk, it will thicken much more quickly than pasteurized milk. In fact, you probably will not need a starter to begin. Simply heat milk to lukewarm and let set at room temperature. Lowfat milk may also be used if desired, but will take slightly longer to thicken.

. . . .

Mock Sour Cream (Low Cal.)

(Delicious on baked potatoes)

1 cup (8-oz.) lowfat cottage cheese
3 tbsp. nonfat dry milk powder*
¼ cup cold water
1 tbsp. lemon juice
a dash of artificial sweetener, if
   desired

Process in blender until smooth.

. . . .

*May use 2 or 3 tbsp. skim milk in place of dry milk powder and water.

. . . .

Dieter's Topping (Low Cal.)

½ cup nonfat dry milk powder
½ cup ice water

Combine in chilled bowl, and whip into soft peaks—3 to 4 minutes.

. . . .

2 tbsp. lemon juice

Add, beating until stiff.

. . . .

2 or 3 tbsp. sugar

Fold in.

. . . .

Use immediately. This topping does not hold well.

Yield: about 2 cups

Dorothy Suter Showalter

. . . .

Mock Whipped Cream (Lower Cal.)

(Use as a topping for fresh fruit or other desserts. May be stored in refrigerator up to one week.)

1½ cups (12-oz.) unsalted dry
   cottage cheese
½ cup whipped margarine
1 cup powdered sugar
2 tsp. lemon juice
¼ tsp. vanilla

Combine all ingredients in blender container and process until smooth.

. . . .

Yield: 2 cups

Dorothy Suter Showalter

. . . .

Whipped Evaporated Milk

Evaporated milk may be whipped to use as a topping if desired. It must be thoroughly chilled, however, before whipping. Chill the can of milk overnight or at least 3 or 4 hours in the refrigerator. It also helps to chill the bowl and beaters used for whipping. The addition of 1 tsp. lemon juice aids slightly in whipping, but may be omitted. Then whip as you would cream until stiff. Add vanilla and sugar to taste, beating just until well blended.

. . . .

Stabilized Whipped Cream

Sprinkle ½ tsp. Knox unflavored gelatine over 1 tbsp. cold water. Let stand 1 minute. Heat on stove or in microwave just until melted—120 degrees. Cool, and mix with 1 cup heavy cream. Whip until stiff. Chill.

. . . .

Yogurt with Gelatin

(The addition of gelatin gives a little thicker consistency. It can also be used to salvage a batch that would not thicken properly. To do this, dissolve 1 envelope unflavored gelatin in ¼ cup cold water. Then heat to 120 degrees to melt gelatin. Stir into 1 qt. of yogurt and refrigerate until set.)

1 env. (1 tbsp.) unflavored gelatin soaked in ¼ cup cold water 3 qts. scalded milk	Combine, stirring to dissolve. Cool to luke-warm.

. . . .

1 cup yogurt culture
1 tbsp. vanilla
4 whole-grain saccharin, dissolved
   in a little milk (optional)
1 cup instant dry milk powder*
   (optional)
	Mix in thoroughly.

. . . .

Set in warm place until set. See following recipe for directions. (*Dorothy says the instant milk powder makes it slightly smoother and adds extra nutrition, but is not necessary.)

Yield: 3 qts.   *Dorothy Slabaugh Grove*

. . . .

Yogurt

(Yogurt has a slightly better flavor if some non-instant dry milk is used. This can usually be purchased at a health food store. If not available, use total of 3 cups instant dry milk powder. Yogurt culture is simply plain commercial yogurt which you buy to eat.)

1¼ cups instant dry milk powder
1¼ cups non-instant dry milk
7 cups warm water
4 whole-grain saccharin, dissolved
   in small amount of the warm
   water
1 tbsp. vanilla
⅓ cup yogurt culture
	Mix all ingredients together thoroughly and pour into 2 qt. jars. Place in oven and keep temperature between 110 and 120 degrees until yogurt is set—2 to 3 hrs.* Do not disturb during this time!

Chill immediately when set so mixture does not become too sour or separate. Crushed fruit may be stirred into the yogurt mixture before it sets, but most people like to add the fruit at serving time. Be sure to save ⅓ cup to use for culture for your next batch. In several months, you may need to purchase a new culture if yogurt begins to get more strong and acidic. (*To keep oven at correct temperature of 110 to 120 degrees, you can turn it on and off for a short time occasionally. Or, put a 60-watt bulb on an extension cord in oven. If oven is small, the turned-on oven light provides a good amount of heat. Some persons simply leave the mixture on the countertop overnight, but, depending on the weather, it could set before morning and would not be refrigerated at the proper time. It usually takes about 6 hours at room temperature. Check each half hour after 2 hours to see if mixture is set.)

Yield: 2 qts.   *Gladys and Brownie Driver*

CHEESE

Cheese Ball

8 oz. cream cheese, softened
1 (3-oz.) pkg. dried beef, finely diced
   (reserve half)
1 tsp. MSG (optional)
1 tbsp. dried chives
several drops liquid smoke

Mix all ingredients together thoroughly, except half of beef. Form into a ball. Then roll ball in reserved half of beef to coat outside. Chill.

Yield: 1 ball   *Gretchen McCue*

Chipped Beef Cheese Ball

6 oz. smoked or chipped beef, finely
   diced
2 (8-oz.) pkg. cream cheese,
   softened
8 oz. sharp cheddar cheese, grated
   and softened
2 tbsp. Worcestershire sauce
⅛ tsp. tabasco sauce
¼ cup pickle relish, minced
¼ tsp. onion salt
dash of white pepper

Mix all ingredients together thoroughly. Shape into 2 balls.

Roll in chopped parsley, or grated pecans, or cornflake crumbs to coat. Chill.

Yield: 2 balls   *Gladys Harman*

Ham and Cheese Ball

2 (8-oz.) pkgs. cream cheese,
softened
1 tbsp. finely chopped onion
½ cup finely chopped ham
1 tsp. chopped chives
1 cup grated cheddar cheese
1 tbsp. chopped pimiento
1 tbsp. lemon juice

Mix all ingredients together thoroughly.

Roll in chopped chives, or parsley, or paprika for red and green Christmas effect. Chill.

Yield: 1 large or 2 small balls

Holiday Cheese Ball

2 (8-oz.) pkgs. cream cheese,
softened
1 (8-oz.) can crushed pineapple,
drained well
¼ cup chopped green pepper
2 tbsp. chopped onion
1 tsp. seasoned salt
2 cups chopped pecans (reserve
half)

Mix all ingredients together thoroughly except half of pecans. Shape into 1 large or 2 small balls and roll in reserved pecans to coat. Chill.

Yield: 2 balls

Cottage Cheese

1½ gals. thick sour milk (see page
252 for directions)

Heat slowly to 115 degrees. Cut through milk in both directions with knife while heating to separate curds. Drain overnight in cloth bag. Crumble finely when dry.

1 tsp. salt
1 tbsp. sugar
½ cup cream

Add, mixing thoroughly. Chill.

Serve with apple butter, jelly, or molasses.

Yield: 3 to 4 cups   *Ella May Miller*

Mock Cream Cheese (Low Cal.)

4 tbsp. corn oil margarine
1 cup lowfat cottage cheese
⅛ tsp. salt

Process in blender until smooth.

Yield: 1 ¼ cups   *Dorothy Suter Showalter*

Cream Cheese Made from Yogurt

Make yogurt from one of the recipes on page 254, using whole milk in place of powdered milk. Or use light cream which would give a larger quantity of cheese. Place a colander or strainer in the sink. Line it with several thickness of cheescloth. Add ¼ tsp. salt to 1 qt. yogurt, and carefully pour it through the cloth. Fold the ends of the cheesecloth up and over the top of the yogurt and gently lay a plate or saucer on top to lightly press it down. Let sit overnight to drain out the whey. In the morning, remove cheesecloth and store cheese in covered container in refrigerator.

Yield: 1 qt. yogurt makes approximately 8 oz. cheese

Soda Cheese

1 gal. thick sour milk (see page 252 for directions)	Heat to 115 degrees. Cut through milk in both directions with knife while heating to separate the curds. Drain overnight in cloth bag. Crumble when dry.
½ tsp. baking soda	Mix in and let stand 4 or 5 hours.
3 tbsp. margarine	Melt in heavy skillet and add curds. Heat on low, stirring constantly until curds are melted.
1 cup rich milk	Add, stirring until smooth.
1 tsp. salt **1 egg, beaten** **several drops yellow food coloring.**	Stir in, and heat to boiling again. Remove from heat. Pour in dish to cool. Chill.

Yield: approximately 1 qt. cheese   *Lora Heatwole*

EGGS, MILK, AND CHEESE DISHES

Impossible Cheese and Bacon Pie

10 slices bacon, crisply fried and crumbled **1 cup shredded Swiss cheese** **⅓ cup finely chopped onion**	Sprinkle in greased 10-inch pie plate or bake dish.
2 cups milk **4 eggs** **1 cup Bisquick** **¼ tsp. salt** **⅛ tsp. pepper**	Beat together until smooth—15 seconds in blender on high, or 1 minute with hand beater. Pour over mixture in plate.

Bake at 350 degrees 35 to 40 minutes until knife inserted in center comes out clean.

Variation: Use 1 lb. browned crumbled sausage instead of bacon

Cheese Grits Souffle

1½ cups quick grits 1½ tsp. salt 6 cups boiling water	Combine in saucepan. Cook 5 minutes. (If using regular grits, cook 20 minutes.)
¾ cup melted butter or margarine 2 cups grated cheddar or American cheese 3 eggs, beaten dash of Tabasco sauce 2 tsp. seasoned salt ⅛ tsp. paprika 2 tsp. Worcestershire sauce	Mix together with grits and pour into a greased 2½-qt. casserole dish.

Bake at 350 degrees for 1 hour.

Yield: 8 servings

Dressing (or Dressing Balls*)

(Dried bread makes better dressing than fresh bread. Dressing is also better if you use corn bread for about ⅓ of the bread. I keep leftover corn bread in the freezer just for this purpose.)

6 cups dried bread cubes (preferably part corn bread)	Spread in greased 8 × 12 bake dish.
¼ cup finely chopped celery ¼ cup finely chopped onion	Mix in.
1 tsp. salt ¼ tsp. black pepper	Sprinkle over mixture.
5 eggs, beaten 3½ cups milk 1 tsp. poultry seasoning	Combine thoroughly and pour over mixture.
Italian seasoning (or parsley or sage)	Sprinkle over top.
2 tbsp. butter	Dot over top.

Bake at 350 degrees for about 45 minutes. (*For dressing balls, use only 1 to 1½ cups milk. Shape into balls and place on greased tray. Bake about 25 minutes. This mixture may also be used to stuff a turkey, but I much prefer baking dressing separately so it isn't soggy.)

Variation: 1 cup or more cooked salsify rings may be added to bread cubes for **salsify dressing.**

Yield: 8 to 10 servings

Brunch Casserole

*16 slices white bread (reserve half)	Trim off crusts and lay 8 slices flat in bottom of a greased 9 × 13 bake dish.
8 slices sandwich ham, or Canadian bacon	Place 1 slice on each slice of bread.
8 slices sharp cheddar cheese	Place 1 slice on each slice of ham. Top with reserve bread slices.
6 eggs, beaten **½ tsp. salt** **¼ tsp. MSG (optional)** **½ tsp. dry mustard** **¼ cup minced onion** **¼ cup chopped green pepper** **1½ tsp. Worcestershire sauce** **3 cups milk**	Beat together until blended. Pour over mixture in dish. Cover and refrigerate overnight.
¼ cup butter, melted	(The next morning) Pour over mixture.
1 cup crushed potato chips	Sprinkle over all.

*If you prefer not to trim bread, use 12 slices instead of 16. Bake at 350 degrees for 1 hour.

Yield: 8 servings   *Evie King*

Cheesy Dressing

5 cups dry bread cubes **¾ cup grated cheddar cheese**	Combine in greased 8-inch-square bake dish.
4 eggs, beaten **2½ cups milk** **1 tsp. salt** **½ tsp. dry mustard**	Blend thoroughly and pour over bread.
seasonings	Sprinkle well with Italian seasoning, celery salt, onion salt, and pepper.

May be refrigerated overnight, or bake immediately. Bake at 350 degrees for 45 minutes.

Yield: 6 servings

Eggs with Cheese

6 hard-cooked eggs	Slice and arrange in greased 1 ½-qt. casserole dish.
3 tbsp. butter	Melt in saucepan.
¼ cup flour **1 tsp. salt** **¼ cup grated onion**	Blend in and sauté for 1 or 2 minutes.
2 cups milk	Stir in gradually, cooking until thickened.
¾ cup grated cheddar cheese	Stir in. Then pour over eggs in dish.
1 cup bread crumbs **2 tbsp. butter, melted**	Combine and sprinkle over top.

Bake at 350 degrees for about 20 minutes.

Yield: 5 servings

Ham and Egg Casserole

2 cups small bread cubes **3 tbsp. melted butter**	Combine.
1 cup diced cooked ham **4 hard-cooked eggs, coarsely chopped** **1 (10-oz.) can cream of mushroom soup mixed with ½ cup milk** **½ tsp. salt** **¼ tsp. MSG (optional)**	Combine with bread cubes in greased 1 ½-qt. casserole dish.
⅔ cup grated cheddar cheese	Sprinkle over top.

Bake at 350 degrees for 35 minutes.

Yield: 6 servings

Egg Souffle

½ to 1 lb. sausage, browned and drained (or cubed ham or crumbled bacon) **6 slices bread, cubed** **1 cup grated cheddar cheese**	Combine in greased 8-inch-square bake dish.
5 or 6 eggs, beaten **1 tsp. salt** **1 tsp. dry mustard** **2 cups milk**	Combine and pour over mixture in dish.

3 tbsp. butter, melted	Pour over top. Refrigerate overnight.

Bake at 350 degrees for 45 minutes.

Variation: For heartier dish, spread 1 (10-oz.) can cream of mushroom soup over top. May also use chopped turkey or chipped all-meat bologna in place of other meat.

Yield: 6 servings

Sharon Heatwole
Vera Showalter

Puffy Breakfast Omelet

2 tbsp. margarine **2 tbsp. chopped green pepper**	Sauté in skillet a few minutes until tender.
4 egg yolks **2 tbsp. mayonnaise** **3 tbsp. water** **½ tsp. salt**	Beat together.
4 egg whites, stiffly beaten	Fold into yolk mixture. Pour over peppers in skillet. Cook over low heat without stirring for 5 minutes. Then cover and cook 5 min. longer until set, and browned underneath.
¾ cup shredded cheese **seasoning—basil, oregano, and** **parsley**	Sprinkle over top. Mark omelet lightly through center with the back of a knife. Fold in half and serve immediately.

Variation: Sprinkle with finely chopped ham or browned crumbled sausage.

Yield: 3 servings

Nancy L. Shank

Potato Omelet

2 cups grated raw potatoes **¼ cup chopped green pepper** **¼ cup chopped onion** **2 tbsp. margarine**	Sauté in margarine in skillet until tender.
4 eggs, beaten **½ tsp. salt**	Combine and pour over mixture in skillet. Cover and cook on low heat just until set.
½ cup grated cheese **4 strips bacon, browned and** **crumbled**	Sprinkle over top.

Variation: For **zucchini omelet,** use 1 cup grated raw zucchini instead of potatoes and peppers.

French Toast

2 eggs, slightly beaten **½ cup milk** **¼ tsp. salt** **1 tsp. sugar** **¼ tsp. vanilla** **⅛ tsp. nutmeg (optional)**	Blend thoroughly.
2 tbsp. butter	Heat in skillet.
4 slices bread	Quickly dip in egg mixture one at a time just to moisten, and place in skillet. If there is any mixture left, spoon it over bread in skillet.

Fry on each side until golden brown. Serve immediately with syrup, jelly, gravy, or tomato gravy.

Yield: 4 servings

Tomato Gravy: **¾ cup thick tomato juice** **⅛ tsp. soda** **½ tsp. salt** **½ tbsp. sugar**	Combine in saucepan. Heat to boiling.
¾ cup milk **1½ tbsp. cornstarch**	Dissolve and stir into boiling mixture just until thickened.

May also be served on scrambled eggs or over fried mush.

Quick Quiche

½ cup diced cooked ham or 6 strips
  bacon, browned and crumbled
1 or 2 tbsp. minced onion
1 cup shredded Swiss or sharp
  cheese
	Sprinkle in greased 9-inch deep-dish pie plate.

1½ cups milk **3 eggs** **½ cup Bisquick** **¼ tsp. salt** **½ tsp. dry mustard**	Process briefly in blender, or beat together with mixer. Pour over mixture in plate.
¼ cup melted butter	Pour over all.

Bake at 350 degrees for approximately 40 minutes. Let set 10 minutes before serving.

Yield: 6 servings   *Mary K. Heatwole*

MAIN DISHES & VEGETABLES

MAIN DISHES AND VEGETABLES

Casseroles are probably the most versatile of any main dishes made—and what would we do without them! The advantage of having almost a whole meal all mixed into one dish, prepared ahead, and baking in the oven while you are occupied with other details is a wonderful feeling for the busy cook! A casserole can be placed in the oven and set on time bake while you are away, or frozen ahead and used on a busy day when time is at a premium.

Creative cooks have come up with many ideas for delightfully seasoned casseroles that can please the most discriminating tastes and are also a pleasure to serve to guests. Canned soups have really been a boost in preparing them quickly. Simply add a salad, and if desired, a little fruit or dessert, and you are set for a meal for most anyone.

The content of casseroles may vary from mostly meat and starch, to largely vegetables, or a combination of both. They may even include biscuit or corn bread topping. If vegetables are not included in the casserole, they make a nice side dish to complete the menu.

Other main dishes such as pizza and tacos also practically make a meal in themselves. We can, therefore, have a lot of variety with dishes combining smaller amounts of meat with other foods, rather than having the meat separately, which always increases the amount needed.

Vegetables

Good quality fresh or frozen vegetables properly prepared are full of flavor and nutrition and should be included often in the diet. They complement our meals with variety in color, flavor, and texture. They can be served raw or cooked.

Vegetables need to be harvested when they are young and tender for top quality. Overdeveloped vegetables or vegetables that have grown very slowly in dry weather are often tough and coarse and may even be beginning to dry. They take longer to cook and have lost nutritive value and quality. When vegetables are picked at prime maturity, and are used or processed immediately, the difference in quality and flavor is remarkable.

If necessary to store a short time before using, many vegetables will keep better unwashed. They have a natural protective coating which should not be washed off. If washing is preferred, it is important to dry them thoroughly before storing. Moisture activates bacteria which causes the deteriorating process to accelerate. Vegetables should be stored in a cool place, preferably in the refrigerator. Some vegetables will keep much longer than others.

Asparagus keeps best when placed upright in a widemouthed jar half filled with water in the refrigerator.

Corn is especially perishable and needs to be used or processed promptly for prime flavor. (There is nothing quite like putting a kettle of water on to boil for corn on the cob, while you hurry out to the garden to gather it in for dinner!) If it is necessary to hold it a while, leave shucks on corn until right before cooking to help retain freshness.

Cabbage can be kept a number of weeks in a plastic bag in the refrigerator if dried off thoroughly before storing. Add a paper towel to absorb any moisture.

Carrots can be washed, thoroughly dried off, and stored for many weeks in the refrigerator. The secret for preventing spoilage is to be sure they are thoroughly dry. (After gathering carrots from the garden, I wash them thoroughly and lay them out on newspaper to dry overnight before storing.)

Mushrooms keep better if they are stored loosely in a brown paper bag in the refrigerator unwashed. They will turn yellow if washed and stored damp. Extra ones may be chopped, covered with water, and frozen for use in sauces or soups.

To keep **parsley** fresh, wash in cool water, bunch stems together, and stand the stalks in a jar of cold water like a bouquet of flowers. Slip a plastic bag over the entire glass and store in refrigerator. Parsley will keep for over a week this way. If not needed in this time, chop, place in plastic bag, and freeze. Any amount can be removed as needed.

Vegetables such as **cucumbers, tomatoes,** and **peppers** should be stored unwashed and need to be kept as moisture-free as possible. Some people line the refrigerator drawers with paper towels, changing them occasionally as needed to eliminate moisture. **Broccoli** and **cauliflower** are also best stored unwashed. Other vegetables such as shelled **peas, limas,** and **green beans** can be refrigerated overnight, unwashed if necessary, but will keep better if they are blanched first before storing. Vegetables in pods are best kept unshelled until ready to use. Remember, the sooner most vegetables are used after harvest, the better they will be both in flavor and nutrition.

Cooking Vegetables

When cooking vegetables, keep in mind that the most often made mistake with vegetables is to overcook them! If the bright color, the fresh flavor, and many nutrients are cooked out by the time they arrive on the table, it is no wonder the family is not enthused about eating them. Cook vegetables the minimum amount of time possible, and in a small amount of water to preserve their fresh color, flavor, and nutrients. It is best to add salt near the end of cooking time, since salt added at the beginning lengthens the cooking time in some vegetables. Also, they seem to require less salt after they are cooked.

Popular methods for cooking vegetables are by boiling in water on top of the stove, in the microwave, or in a pressure cooker. They may also be stir-fried.

Boiling Water Method: Vegetables may be cooked satisfactorily in boiling water on top of the stove, but it takes longer. To maintain the bright green color of vegetables when they are cooked in boiling water, leave the lid of the pan slightly tilted to let a small amount of steam escape while cooking. If lid is tightly closed, vegetables will lose their green color. Again, do not overcook. Adding a small chunk of butter to vegetables before cooking will help prevent boil-over which can be a problem, especially with lima beans.

When boiling vegetables, the amount of water needed can vary considerably, depending how high the burner is turned—how much water escapes as steam during cooking. It is usually best to use only as much water as is needed, so water is mostly cooked away by the time the vegetables are tender. A small amount of water usually means to come up ¼ to ⅓ of the way on the vegetables. It always takes a little more when the lid is tilted during cooking than when tightly covered because of evaporation.

Microwave Method: For directions for microwave cooking of small amounts of vegetables, see the chart on page 404 in the microwave section. I feel the microwave is excellent for cooking in small amounts, but not for family-size portions.

The disadvantage with microwave cooking is that you have to stand there and stir the vegetables frequently during the whole cooking process, otherwise you will have very uneven cooking. It is also difficult to know when the entire amount is evenly cooked. In fact, unless you have stirred persistently, it is difficult to attain even cooking with any sizable amount of food. You cannot depend on a precise time chart since there are so many variables in cooking time.

The temperature of the food when put in to cook makes a considerable difference—whether it is partially frozen, or refrigerator-cold, or at room temperature. Just a little larger or smaller amount of food makes a significant difference, and whether the food is chopped finely, coarsely, or cooked whole.

The tenderness and quality of the food is another factor, and whether it is piled in a small container to cook or spread out in a large one. These variables are not too significant with a small amount of food, but make a considerable difference with larger amounts. If you prefer using the microwave, experiment with the size containers, and amounts and types of food you usually prepare to find a formula that works best for you.

Pressure Cooking Method: My favorite way to cook many vegetables is in a pressure saucepan. This works well for maintaining quality and obtaining tenderness at the same time, especially with green vegetables. My family prefers having their vegetables cooked quite tender rather than the crisp stage which has become popular. This can easily be accomplished in a pressure saucepan. Beside the ease with which you can obtain excellent results, pressure cooking is very fast. Most vegetables are only cooked for 1 to 1 ½ minutes after the pressure rises, and there is no stirring!

Some persons fear pressure cookery because of their concern for its safety. Manufacturers have improved cookers with features that are practical and safe if you follow their easy directions. The main concern is to *always* be sure the pressure is down before attempting to open the cooker, and this is not difficult to ascertain. There are a few precautions that are advisable such as not cooking sticky foods like applesauce and rice in the cooker because they tend to clog the stem for venting.

I use the pressure for cooking peas, green limas, green beans, broccoli, brussel sprouts, green soybeans, cabbage, carrots, and cauliflower. It is especially excellent for the green vegetables because the quick cooking preserves color, nutrients, and flavor. The flavor of potatoes is slightly affected when pressured. However, when in a special hurry, it comes in handy for potatoes also.

Precise cooking time is very important for small green vegetables. If cooking time is 1 minute and you allow pressure to remain up for 1 ¼ to 1 ½ minutes, the vegetables will be overcooked. With larger amounts, you do not need to increase pressure time. In fact, I've found it takes slightly less time for a cooker which is ½ to ¾ full, than it does for a small amount. Just as soon as pressure time is up, the cooker should be quickly cooled with cold water (according to manufacturer's directions) and the lid removed IMMEDIATELY. (Do not let cold water run over the handle as this may eventually cause cracking.) If you follow directions, *always* remove the pressure indicator, and make certain the vent is clear before opening, you should get along well with pressure cooking.

Stir-Fry Method: Another way to prepare vegetables is to stir-fry them. A wok or nonstick-finish skillet works best for stir-frying. Heat a small amount of oil or fat in skillet. Add chopped or shredded vegetables. Then toss with spatula and fry on medium high heat until vegetables are just barely tender—a crisp tender stage. You may wish to lower heat slightly and cover skillet between stirring for more tenderness if vegetables do not require constant stirring to keep them from sticking or burning. Frying time is usually about 3 to 8 minutes. If meat is added, it should be cut in very thin pieces and fried first until tender. Then add to vegetables at end of frying time.

The following chart gives approximate cooking time for fresh vegetables. Keep in mind that cooking time will vary with the stage of maturity and tenderness of the vegetables, and whether they are chopped or whole. A little experience soon gives confidence in proper timing. The amount of water given in the "Pressure time" column is for 2 to 5 servings of vegetables. When processing larger amounts, increase amount of water accordingly.

Frozen vegetables take about the same amount of time to cook as young tender raw ones. Even though they are usually blanched before freezing, fresh vegetables are very tender. If raw vegetables are not picked until overly mature, however, they will not be as tender and cooking time will need to be increased. It works best to have frozen vegetables at least partially thawed when put on to cook. A frozen block of vegetables needs to be separated for more even cooking. If vegetables are individually frozen, this is not a problem.

VEGETABLES

Vegetable	Preparation	Cooking Time	Pressure Time	Simple Seasoning
Asparagus	Wash and cut into ½ to ¾" lengths. Discard tough end of stalk. (Using table knife to cut easily identifies point where stalk is tough.)	Barely cover with water. Leave lid slightly tilted and boil 7 min.	Do not pressure-cook.	Add salt to taste. A little MSG greatly enhances flavor of asparagus. Add cream batter and several crushed saltines per each cup of veg. Add cheese if desired. Or drain and serve with Hollandaise sauce.
Beans—green or wax beans	Remove ends and any strings. Break into 1" lengths. Wash.	Time varies with varieties. Add water to come up ⅓ of the way on beans. Cook 30 to 60 min. covered. Best to cook until water is cooked away.	Add ⅓ cup water and process 1¼ to 1½ min. Open cooker. Add fat and seasoning, and cook uncovered until water is cooked away.	Add salt and a small amount of bacon grease or margarine. May add chipped ham or bacon, seasoned salt and dried minced onion, and a little ginger.
Beans—dry	(See recipe in index.)			
Beans—fresh lima	Shell and wash.	Add small amount of water and boil 20 to 25 min. with lid slightly tilted.	Add ⅓ cup water and process 1 min.	Add salt, dash of sugar, and butter. May add cream batter if desired.
Beets (pull while young and tender—will get	May be peeled, washed, and cut in qtrs. or cubes. Or leave 1" stem, wash,	Add water to half cover and boil, covered. Cubes—20 to 25 min.	Add ¾ cup water and process 7 to 10 min.	Add salt, dash of sugar, butter. See recipe for Harvard Beets in index.

Vegetable	Preparation	Boiling	Processing	Seasoning
tough and woody when older)	and cook 15 to 25 min. until peeling will slip off. Then qtr. or cube.	Qtrs. or small whole—30 to 35 min.		
Broccoli	Remove leaves and tough stem ends. Wash and separate into large flowerets.	Add small amt. of water and boil 10 to 15 min. with lid slightly tilted.	Add ⅓ cup water and process 1 to 1¼ min.	Add salt and butter. May also add cheese sauce or Hollandaise sauce.
Brussels sprouts	Cut off stem end and remove any wilted leaves. Wash.	Add small amt. of water and boil 12 to 18 min. with lid slightly tilted.	Add ½ cup water and process 1¼ to 1½ min.	Add salt and butter. May also add cheese sauce or Hollandaise sauce.
Cabbage	Remove outside wilted leaves. Wash and shred or cut into wedges.	Add medium amt. of water and boil covered. Shredded—10 to 12 min. Wedges—15 to 20 min.	Add ½ cup water and process. Shredded—1 to 1½ min. Wedges—1½ to 2 min.	Add salt and butter. May also add cheese sauce or crumbled bacon.
Carrots	Scrape or peel. Wash and cut into slices	Add small amt. of water and boil 15 to 20 min. covered. Varieties vary in cooking time needed.	Add ¼ cup water and process 1½ to 1¾ min.	Add salt, dash of sugar, and butter. Cook dry or drain and sauté ½ min. in butter. May also sprinkle with ginger.
Cauliflower	Trim off leaves and any woody stem. Wash and break into flowerets or leave whole.	Add small amt. of water. Cover and boil. Flowerets—10 to 12 min. Whole—20 to 30 min.	Flowerets—add ⅓ cup water and process 1½ min. Whole—add ½ cup water and process 3 min.	Add salt and butter. May also add cheese sauce.

Vegetable	Preparation	Cooking Time	Pressure Time	Simple Seasoning
Corn	On cob—remove husks and silk just before cooking. Wash with brush. Off cob—wash and cut corn off raw, or boil as for corn on cob. Cool immediately and cut from cob.	On cob—heat water to cover to boiling. Add 5 to 7 ears at a time and leave in water a total of 7 min. Leave burner on high so water soon boils again. After 7 min. quickly rinse in cold water to prevent shriveling of kernels. Do not cool! Off cob—add small amt. of water and heat uncovered just to boiling. Do not cook corn! Stir often for even heating.	Do not pressure-cook. Small amt. of corn on cob may be cooked in microwave—2 min. per ear on high.	On cob—spread with butter and sprinkle with salt. Off cob—add salt, little sugar, and butter. Sprinkle with a little flour while stirring to take up excess liquid.
Eggplant	Wash. Peel if skin is tough. Cut in ¼" thick slices.	Dip in beaten egg and then in fine cracker crumbs and fry in hot fat in skillet until browned on each side.	Do not pressure-cook.	Sprinkle with salt. See recipes in index.
Greens— spinach, beet tops, kale, mustard, etc.	Trim off root ends and discard damaged leaves. Wash several times.	Add no water. Collects its own water. Cover and boil 5 to 10 min. Kale takes a little longer.	Add no water. Process 1 to 2 min.	Add salt and butter. May add crumbled bacon.
Okra	Wash young pods. Cut off stems. Cut in ¼" thick slices. (Discard any woody pods.)	Coat with cornmeal and fry in oil or bacon fat in skillet until tender and lightly browned on both sides.	Do not pressure-cook.	Sprinkle with salt.

Onions	Trim off tops and roots. Remove outer skin. Wash and quarter.	Add small amt. of water and cook covered 15 to 25 min.	Add ⅓ cup water and process 2 min.	Add salt and cream batter.
Peas	Shell and wash. (Varieties may vary in cooking time.)	Add small amt. of water and boil with lid slightly tilted for 12 to 15 min.	Add ⅓ cup water and process ¾ to 1 min.	Add salt, a dash of sugar, and butter. May add cream batter.
Peas—sugar or snow peas	Trim ends and any strings. Wash.	Add small amt. of water and boil with lid slightly tilted for 20 to 30 min.	Add ⅓ cup water and process 1 to 1½ min.	Add salt, a dash of sugar, and butter. May add cream batter.
Potatoes—white (Irish)	Peel, wash, and quarter. (Cooking time varies with age and variety of potatoes.)	Add water to ⅓ cover and boil, covered, for 20 to 30 min. Or grate and fry in fat in skillet with chopped onion, covered, about 20 min., turning occasionally.	Add 1 cup water and process 6 to 8 min.	Add salt and butter. Garnish with parsley. May add cream sauce or cheese sauce to boiled potatoes. Or make mashed potatoes.
Salsify	Peel, wash, and cut into slices.	Add water to ⅓ cover and boil, covered, for 30 to 40 min.	Add ¾ cup water and process 10 to 12 min.	Use for soup, or scalloped salsify. See recipes in index.
Soybeans—green	Heat water enough to cover to boiling and add pods. Boil and stir 2 min. Rinse in cold water. Press on pods to pop out beans. Wash.	Barely cover with water and boil, covered, 1 to 1½ hours.	Add 1 cup water and process 1½ min.	Add salt and sugar to taste and small amt. of browned hamburger, tomato juice, and chili powder.

Vegetable	Preparation	Cooking Time	Pressure Time	Simple Seasoning
Squash—summer (yellow or zucchini)	To cook—peel, wash, and cut in cubes. To fry—wash and cut in ¼" thick slices. Dip in flour, or slightly beaten egg, then cracker crumbs.	Add very small amt. of water (add onions if desired) and boil, covered, 20 to 25 min. Or fry in hot fat in skillet until browned on both sides.	Add ¼ cup water and process 2 to 4 min.	Cooked—add salt and butter. May add crumbled bacon or chipped ham. Fried—sprinkle with salt.
Squash—winter (acorn or butternut)	To bake—wash, cut in half, and scoop out seedy area. To cook—peel, cut in chunks, and wash.	To bake—sprinkle with salt and brown sugar. Dot with butter and bake at 350° for 1 hr. To cook—add small amt. of water and boil, covered, 25 to 35 min.	Add ½ cup water and process 7 to 8 min.	Baked—may sprinkle with cinnamon. Cooked—put in blender or press through sieve or strainer. See index for recipes.
Sweet potatoes	To bake—wash, dry, and grease with butter. Prick skin to allow steam to escape. To cook—peel, wash, and cut in smaller chunks.	To bake—place in 350° oven, uncovered or partially covered and bake 1 hr. or more, depending on size. To cook (same as white potatoes).	Add 1 cup water and process 6 to 8 min.	Baked—cut open. Sprinkle with salt and add a chunk of butter. Cooked—add salt and butter. May add brown sugar or syrup and a dash of nutmeg or cinnamon.
Turnips, rutabagas, and kohlrabi	These vegetables need to grow fast with plenty of moisture to be tender. Discard any woody, strong-flavored ones. May be peeled and eaten raw when young and tender. To cook—peel, wash, and quarter.	Add small amt. of water and boil, covered, 20 to 30 min. (Delicious cooked with half potatoes.)	Add ½ cup water and process 4 to 6 min.	Add salt and cream batter or cheese sauce. Or mash, form into cakes, and fry in hot fat in skillet.

Potatoes

Baked Potatoes: The time it takes to bake potatoes can vary considerably depending on the size of the potato, how old it is, and on the variety of potato. Fresh new potatoes out of the garden can be difficult to bake tender.

The Idaho variety is known to be an excellent baking potato, but they do not produce well in every area. Two popular varieties in Virginia are Kennebec and Cobbler potatoes. The Kennebec variety is considered a good baking potato, but can hardly be baked tender when new. Cobblers are a softer potato and will cook and bake much more easily when new. The Cobblers have lots of eyes in them, while the Kennebec are smoother with fewer eyes. We always plant some of each variety because the Cobblers mature earlier and are best to use right away for cooking or baking and the Kennebec will keep much longer over winter in storage. They will be firm much later in the spring when the Cobblers are shriveled up. Many people like the Red Pontiac variety which is similar to Cobblers in softness. They keep longer over winter than Cobblers, but not as well as Kennebecs. Varieties vary in different areas of the country.

Potatoes may be baked different ways, depending on the results desired. For a softer peeling, rub with butter or margarine before baking. They can be placed in a covered dish or wrapped in foil for a moist potato that is actually steamed rather than baked. For a real baked flavor, do not cover, or only partially cover. (I prefer a partial cover.) Place potatoes in bake dish, or lay on oven rack, or place in muffin tins for easy handling, and bake at 350 degrees for one hour or more, depending on the size. If baked unwrapped, wrap in foil upon removing from the oven to retain heat for serving. Cut an X on top through the foil and squeeze the potato slightly to fluff up the inside. Drop in a chunk of butter or a dab of sour cream and serve.

Mashed Potatoes: Potatoes must be *well* cooked to avoid lumps in mashed potatoes. It is much more difficult to mash new potatoes without having any lumps than older ones, especially some varities.

Liquid added while mashing is usually whole milk, although skim milk works fine. Some cooks use the excess water in which the potatoes were cooked. If you do this, you will have nicer potatoes if you sprinkle in dry milk powder while mashing them. This makes potatoes white and fluffy and adds nutrition. (Use ⅓ to ½ cup powder for 1 cup potato water.) It is easiest to mash potatoes with an electric mixer.

Drain any liquid off hot cooked potatoes and pour potatoes into mixer bowl. Pour milk into hot pan in which potatoes were cooked and quickly heat. While milk is heating, begin mixing potatoes at low to medium speed, scraping bowl often so entire amount is well broken apart and mixed. Slowly pour in the hot milk or liquid, in about three different portions, beating well on medium speed after each addition. Scrap bowl often until mixed thoroughly and potatoes are smooth. The secret for avoiding lumps is to scrap the bowl and mix well after each addition of milk. Add 1 or 2 tbsp. butter for flavor and salt to taste.

After potatoes are smooth and thinned with enough milk to make the desired consistency, fluff them up by turning mixer to highest speed for a few seconds to ½ minute until as fluffy as desired.

(The amount of milk added while mashing varies, depending on personal preference for thinner or stiffer mashed potatoes. A usual amount is approximately 1 cup milk for about 5 medium-size potatoes. It is best to heat milk for mashed potatoes. Hot milk gives nicer consistency and does not cool the potatoes.)

Cooking Dry Beans

Always check through dry beans for any bad beans, stones, or little clods of dirt about the size of a bean. Then wash thoroughly.

To save cooking time, soak beans overnight before cooking. When cooking one pound of beans (approximately 2½ cups), add 5 cups water to soak. The next morning cook tightly covered, in the same water, for approximately 1½ hours on low heat until tender. If not soaked, they will take approximately 2½ hours to cook. If you forget to soak them ahead, add water to beans, heat to boiling, turn off heat, and let sit tightly covered for 1 hour. Then simmer for approximately 1½ hours until tender.

Do not add salt to beans until near the end of cooking time since this prolongs cooking time considerably. The addition of molasses or of any acid such as vinegar or tomato juice also prolongs cooking time. It is best to add any of these near the end of cooking if possible. Do not add cold water to dry beans while they are cooking as this hardens them. If more water is needed, add hot water. It is difficult to cook dry beans tender in very hard water. (If beans tend to disagree with your digestive system there are two methods people use to overcome this problem. Add about ⅛ tsp. ginger to 1 pound beans before cooking. This will not affect the taste. The other method is to bring the beans to a boil. Boil for 1 minute, turn the burner off, and let them sit for 1 hour covered tightly—do not lift lid! Then continue to cook the remaining time until tender. This method could replace the overnight soaking time as mentioned if desired.)

Cooking Pasta *(Macaroni, Noodles, and Spaghetti)*

Most package directions for pasta call for using 3 qts. of water for cooking 8 ounces of pasta. I prefer using about 5 cups for 8 ounces, so there isn't a lot of hot water to drain off.

Heat water to boiling. Add 2 tsp. salt and 2 tbsp. margarine or oil to help prevent sticking together while cooking. Add pasta, stirring well. Place cover on pan in a tilted position to allow steam to escape without boiling over. Boil for 10 to 12 minutes, stirring occasionally. Drain if needed.

For spaghetti: Pour hot cooked spaghetti into a colander. Hold it under fast-running cold water to rinse quickly for just a few seconds—not enough to cool it. It may be rinsed in hot water again, if needed to maintain heat. Drain and place in hot dish to serve. (This little trick will keep spaghetti well separated even when cold!) It may also be used for macaroni that is to be used in macaroni salad, except that it should be cooled completely for salad.

Create Your Own Casserole*

With a variety of canned and packaged foods and a few leftovers in the refrigerator, you can create a casserole in minutes. Mix and match one ingredient from each column to suit your taste and supplies on hand. Choose selections that enhance each other. Simply layer all ingredients except topping in a greased 2-quart casserole dish, adding salt and any other desired seasoning to taste. Bake at 350 degrees until hot through—20 to 25 minutes. Sprinkle on topping and bake until slightly browned—10 to 15 minutes longer.

Protein	Sauce	Cooked Vegetables	Cooked Starch	Topping
1½ to 2 cups	1 can condensed soup and ⅓ cup liquid	1½ cups	1½ to 2 cups	⅓ to ¾ cup
Canned ham, chopped	Cream of celery soup and milk	Sautéed onions, green peppers, and celery	Noodles	Crushed potato chips
Cook chicken or turkey, chopped	Cream of chicken soup and buttermilk	Cooked or canned green beans	Macaroni	Fresh bread crumbs mixed with melted butter
Canned luncheon meat	Cream of potato soup and sour cream	Cooked or canned peas	Rice	French-fried onion rings
Cooked beef, veal, lamb, or pork	Cream of mushroom soup and cream	Cooked or canned carrots	Potatoes	Crushed cornflakes
Hard-cooked eggs	Tomato juice	Cooked or canned asparagus	Spaghetti	Grated cheese
Frankfurters	Cheddar cheese soup and vegetable juice	Cooked shredded cabbage	Corn	Slightly crushed potato sticks
Cheese	Tomato soup and water	Cooked broccoli	Sweet potatoes	Silvered almonds
Canned tuna or salmon				Cracker crumbs

*Adapted by permission from *The Richmond (Va.) News Leader.*

TIPS FOR MAIN DISHES AND VEGETABLES

•A deep rich color usually indicates higher food value in vegetables. Dark green leaves on leafy vegetables have more nutrients than lighter-colored ones. Darker-leafed lettuce will have more nutrients than pale iceberg lettuce. Bright orange carrots contain more vitamin A than pale ones.

•When making casseroles, double the recipe and store one in the freezer for quick use later. In order not to tie up baking dishes in the freezer, line the extra dish with foil before filling. After it is baked and frozen, lift out contents with the foil. Wrap or place in plastic bag for freezing. To reheat, peel off foil, and place in dish again.

•Meat sauces, such as those prepared for casseroles and spaghetti, improve considerably in flavor with longer cooking. This is the reason some recipes give directions to simmer for 20 to 30 minutes, even though a shorter time would seem sufficient.

•When in a hurry, baking time on casseroles can be cut considerably by spreading the ingredients out in a large rectangular dish to about half the usual depth.

•Casseroles are usually baked uncovered, but may be covered to hold in moisture if desired. The sauce on a casserole that is covered while baking will remain thin. Steam escapes on an uncovered casserole and sauce will be thicker. If additional water needs to be added while baking, add hot water. Cold water may cause the dish to break!

•With emphasis on fast cooking, food manufacturers tend to give minimum cooking time for their products rather than maximum. Macaroni and noodles improve in flavor with a little additional cooking time—not so long that they fall apart, however!

•Onions will not burn your eyes nearly as quickly when chopping if they have been refrigerated at least a day before using.

Keep one or two onions in refrigerator in tightly covered container or plastic bag for instant use. Cut onions from the top end instead of the root end to help avoid burning your eyes, or peel under water.

•The addition of a little lemon juice or vinegar to the water when cooking cauliflower or rice helps to retain the snowy white color. Keep in mind that this may prolong cooking time slightly, however.

•Add a little vinegar to the water when boiling cabbage to help prevent odor from permeating the house.

•For a quick thickener for vegetables, work together ½ cup margarine or butter and ½ cup flour. Store in refrigerator in covered container. Add a little to vegetables or sauces as needed. As it melts it will thicken without lumps.

•The addition of a little oil or margarine to water when boiling macaroni or spaghetti will help keep the pasta from sticking together, and also from boiling over.

•Do not waste the large stems of broccoli when cutting it into flowerets for salads or vegetable trays. Peel stems, chop, and add to salad. The inside of stems are tender and delicious.

•To hurry up the baking process for baked potatoes, boil in water for 10 minutes first, then bake. Another method is to cut larger potatoes in half, grease cut side, and place down flat against bottom of baking dish.

•For golden fried potatoes, sprinkle lightly with flour before frying.

•Buttery seasoned salt for popcorn makes an attractive and delicious topping for potatoes and other vegetables.

•Potatoes for mashing may be cooked in the oven in a separate bowl alongside a roast. (This is especially helpful for Sunday dinner when you wish to serve mashed potatoes with a roast, and would like to have them cooked when you get home from church.) Place peeled potatoes in a stainless steel bowl. Add water to cover potatoes so they don't dry out on top, and cover the bowl with foil. Punch a hole or two in the foil with a fork to allow steam to escape. Place in oven beside roast. Do not dump out excess liquid after cooking potatoes. Drain potatoes and add to broth from roast to make gravy. (To cook potatoes in oven will take about triple the cooking time as on top of the stove.)

•To add a more creamy flavor to mashed potatoes without adding too many additional calories, sprinkle in some coffee creamer while mashing them. To add more calcium to the diet, sprinkle in dry milk powder also.

•The addition of acids such as tomato juice, lemon juice, or vinegar to vegetables while cooking prolongs cooking time. It is best to add near the end of cooking time.

•To remove silk from corn on the cob, pull off all that comes easily with your hand, then use a dry vegetable brush and brush diagonally across grains so silk doesn't embed in rows of kernels. Then brush again under slowly running water.

•A small amount of sugar added to canned vegetables such as green beans enhances flavor. Natural sugar of vegetables is often lost in processing.

•To prevent shriveling of the kernels after cooking corn on the cob, dunk the hot ears of corn in cold water or quickly rinse with cold water immediately after removing them from the boiling water. Do not cool the corn—a quick rinse stops the cooking process immediately and kernels remain firm.

•Pick zucchini squash when young and tender, about 8 inches in length for using in soups or to fry. Seedy area will not yet be developed and peeling will be tender and does not need to be removed. More mature squash may be used for breads, cakes, or in pureed form. These should be peeled and seeds removed. Squash may be grated raw and frozen for use in breads and cakes if desired. Freeze in packages the exact size needed for recipe.

•If you scrape new potatoes instead of peeling them, the skins will come off more easily and will not stain your hands if you soak potatoes first in cold salted water.

•If you don't have a food processor, carrots and cabbage can be quickly grated in the blender. Place chunks of vegetables in blender and cover with ice water. Process on and off a few times until shredded. Drain in strainer.

•It is difficult to cook dried beans, dried peas, and lentils tender in very hard water. In fact, most vegetables are easier to cook tender in soft water.

•Add a little lemon juice to margarine in skillet when sautéing mushrooms to help retain their white color.

•To prevent pimientos from spoiling once the jar has been opened, cover with vinegar and refrigerate.

DISHES CONTAINING MEAT

Bacon Quiche

unbaked 9-inch pie crust	Have ready.
6 to 12 slices bacon, fried crisply and crumbled 1 cup shredded cheese (Swiss preferred) ⅓ cup finely chopped onion	Sprinkle in pie crust.
4 eggs, beaten 2 cups light cream (may use 1 cup milk and 1 cup evaporated milk) ¾ tsp. salt ⅛ tsp. black pepper	Beat together and pour over all.

Bake 15 minutes at 425 degrees. Then reduce temperature to 300 degrees and bake 30 minutes more until knife comes out clean when inserted in center. Let stand 10 minutes before cutting.

Yield: 6 servings

Jeanne Heatwole

Beef 'n Bean Casserole

1 lb. ground beef	Brown in skillet and drain.
1 (10-oz.) can cream of mushroom soup 1 tbsp. dried minced onion 1 tsp. garlic salt 1 tsp. onion salt	Add to meat, mixing together well.
1 qt. canned green beans, drained	Have ready.
10 slices cheese	Have ready.

Put half of green beans in greased 1½ or 2-qt. casserole dish. Spread half of meat mixture over beans. Lay half of cheese slices on next. Repeat layers of beans, meat mixture, and cheese on top. Bake at 350 degrees for 25 minutes.

Variation: Place tater tots on top in place of second layer of cheese. Or cook 1 or 2 cups of tiny fresh potatoes until almost tender and put over top. Top these potatoes with cheese slices.

Yield: 8 servings

Marj Heatwole

Delicious Beef-Vegetable Casserole (Low Cal.)

1 lb. ground beef 1 medium onion, chopped ½ cup chopped celery	Sauté in skillet until lightly browned. Drain.

4 cups chopped or shredded cabbage 2½ cups fresh or canned tomatoes, drained and chopped 1 tbsp. flour 1½ tsp. salt 1 tbsp. sugar ½ tsp. black pepper	Have ready.

1 cup soft bread crumbs 2 tbsp. margarine, melted	Mix thoroughly and have ready.

In 2-qt. casserole dish, layer half of cabbage, tomatoes, and meat mixture. Sprinkle with flour and half of seasoning. Then layer with other half of cabbage, tomatoes, meat, and seasoning. Top with crumbs. Bake uncovered in 350-degree oven for at least 1 hour.

Yield: 6 to 8 servings

Cannelloni

(Janet sent this recipe from Italy saying it was one of her favorites.)

15 cannelloni (or manicotti) shells	Cook 5 to 7 minutes in boiling water.

1 (16-oz.) can spaghetti sauce*	Spread ⅔ sauce in a 9 × 13 dish to coat bottom of dish. Reserve ⅓.

½ lb. hamburger, browned and drained ¾ lb. mozzarella cheese, grated ½ lb. ricotta cheese ½ tsp. salt dash of black pepper dash of ground nutmeg ¼ cup bread crumbs 1 egg, beaten	Mix together, and fill shells. Lay shells side by side in sauce in dish. Spoon reserve sauce over top.

¼ cup Parmesan cheese	Sprinkle over top.

Bake at 350 degrees for 40 to 50 minutes. (*If sauce is thick, add a little water to thin it.)

Variation: May add chopped spinach to hamburger mixture if desired.

Yield: 5 to 8 servings

Janet Blosser

Cheeseburger Strata

1 lb. hamburger	Brown in skillet and drain. Spread in bottom of 9 × 13 bake dish.

10 slices bread, cut in cubes **2 cups shredded sharp cheese**	Spread over meat.

6 eggs, beaten **3 cups milk** **1 tsp. dry mustard** **1 tsp. salt**	Combine thoroughly and pour over mixture in dish.

Bake at 350 degrees for 45 to 55 minutes until center is set.

Yield: 9 servings

Country Chicken 'n Biscuits

8 slices bacon, fried and crumbled
2 cups cooked chopped chicken
1 (10-oz.) pkg. frozen mixed
  vegetables or 2 cups peas,
  cooked and drained
1 cup chopped tomatoes (2
  medium)
1 cup shredded cheddar cheese
	Combine in greased 8 × 12 bake dish.

1 (10-oz.) can cream of chicken soup **¾ cup milk**	Combine and pour over casserole.

Bake, covered at 375 degrees for 15 to 20 minutes. Prepare biscuit topping.

Biscuits:

1½ cups Bisquick **1 (2.8-oz.) can French-fried onions** **(reserve half)** **⅔ cup milk**	Combine with half of onions, stirring just until thoroughly mixed.

Drop by spoonfuls to form 6 biscuits around edge of casserole. Bake, uncovered, 15 to 20 minutes more, or until biscuits are golden brown. Top with reserved onions and bake 2 or 3 minutes longer until onions are toasted.

Yield: 6 servings

Chicken-Broccoli Casserole

2 (10-oz.) pkgs. frozen broccoli	Cook 5 minutes and drain. Arrange in a greased 9 × 13 bake dish.
2 or 3 cups chopped cooked chicken	Arrange chicken over broccoli.
2 (10-oz.) cans cream of chicken soup **⅓ cup mayonnaise** **½ cup chopped onion** **1 tsp. lemon juice** **¼ tsp. curry powder**	Mix well, and pour over chicken.
¾ cup grated cheese	Sprinkle over mixture.
1½ cups bread crumbs **2 tbsp. melted butter**	Mix and sprinkle over top.

Bake at 350 degrees for 25 to 30 minutes.

Yield: 10 servings

Beverly Weaver

Make-Ahead Chicken or Dried Beef Casserole

2 cups diced cooked chicken* **1 (7-oz.) pkg. macaroni, uncooked** **(1½ cups)** **1 cup grated cheddar cheese** **1 (10-oz.) can cream of chicken soup** **2 cups milk (or part broth)** **2 tbsp. chopped green pepper** **½ cup celery, finely chopped** **3 hard-boiled eggs, coarsely chopped** **⅓ cup chopped onion** **1 tsp. salt** **½ tsp. MSG (optional)**	Combine all ingredients in an 8 × 12 bake dish and refrigerate overnight. (Or mix it up in the morning, then bake it for the evening meal.)

Bake at 350 degrees for 1 hour. (*For Dried Beef Casserole: Use ¼ lb. dried chipped beef in place of chicken, and mushroom soup instead of chicken soup.)

Yield: 8 to 10 servings

Curried Chicken and Rice

½ cup chopped onion
½ cup chopped celery
2 tbsp. margarine or oil

Sauté in skillet until tender.

. . . .

1 cup tomato juice
2 or 3 cups chopped cooked
    chicken
1 tsp. Worcestershire sauce
1 tsp. salt
½ tsp. MSG
¾ tsp. curry powder

Add.

. . . .

1½ cups chicken broth (or use 2
    bouillon cubes and water)
¼ cup cornstarch

Dissolve and add. Heat, stirring constantly until thickened.

. . . .

Serve over cooked rice (cook about 1 ½ cups rice). Yield 8 servings

. . . .

Chicken and Rice Casserole

1 cup long-grain rice, uncooked
1 small onion, chopped
1 qt. green beans, undrained
1 (10-oz.) can golden mushroom
    soup
¼ cup mayonnaise
¾ cup water
1 carrot, grated
2 tsp. chicken bouillon (or 2 bouillon
    cubes dissolved)
2 or 3 cups chopped cooked
    chicken

Combine all ingredients in large casserole dish.

. . . .

Bake at 350 degrees for 1 hour. Cover at least half of the time, then uncover.

Yield: 8 to 10 servings   *Miriam Haarer*

. . . .

Easy Chicken-Rice Casserole

1¼ cups rice, uncooked
2½ cups water
1 envelope onion soup mix (reserve half)
1 (10-oz.) can cream of mushroom soup (reserve half)

Combine rice, water, half of soup mix and half of mushroom soup in greased 8 × 12 bake dish.

6 serving pieces of chicken

Lay over top of mixture in dish.

Combine reserve onion soup mix and reserve mushroom soup and spread over top of chicken pieces. Cover *loosely* with foil. Bake at 350 degrees for 1 hour. Turn chicken over and bake 45 minutes more uncovered. (Optional: If you don't have onion soup mix on hand, sprinkle well with celery salt, garlic salt, oregano, thyme, minced onion, and paprika.)

Yield: 6 servings

Shirley Shank
Linda Shenk

Favorite Chicken or Turkey Casserole

½ cup chopped onion
⅓ cup chopped celery
⅓ cup margarine

Sauté in skillet until tender.

1 8-oz. pkg. seasoned bread stuffing
2 cups cooked diced chicken, or turkey
1 cup water

Stir in until blended. Pour in greased 8 × 12 bake dish

2 eggs, beaten
1 (10-oz.) can cream of chicken soup
⅓ cup mayonnaise
¾ tsp. salt
¼ tsp. garlic powder
1½ cups milk

Combine thoroughly, and pour over chicken mixture in dish.

1 cup grated cheese

Have ready.

Bake at 350 degrees for 30 minutes. Sprinkle with cheese and bake 10 minutes more.

Yield: 8 to 10 servings

Margaret Brubaker

Chili Casserole

(This is a good dish to serve for a church supper. Amounts for a group of 24 persons is given in brackets.)

1 lb. hamburger [4 lbs.] 1 medium onion, chopped [4]	Sauté in skillet. Drain.

3 cups canned or cooked kidney
   beans, undrained [1 #10 can]
1 (8-oz.) can tomato sauce [32 oz.]
1 cup whole tomatoes, undrained
   (canned or fresh) [1 qt.]
½ tsp. garlic salt [2 tsp.]
½ tsp. salt or to taste [2 tsp.]
1 tsp. chili powder [4 tsp.]
	Add, and simmer 1 hour or less. Add additional water if needed.

¾ cup grated cheese [3 cups] ½ cup crushed corn chips [2 cups]	Have ready.

Pour in 2 qt. casserole dish. Sprinkle cheese and chips over top. Bake at 325 degrees for 20 to 25 minutes.

Yield: 6 servings [24 servings]

Fern Brunk

Chow Mein

¾ cup chopped celery 1 cup chopped onion 2 tbsp. shortening	Sauté in large skillet until tender.

2 cups chopped cooked chicken 1 tbsp. Worcestershire sauce 1½ tbsp. soy sauce ¼ tsp. ground ginger 2 tsp. sugar 1 tsp. salt ¼ tsp. black pepper ¼ tsp. MSG (optional) 2 chicken bouillon cubes dissolved in 1 cup hot water 1 (14-oz.) can bean sprouts, drained	Add, and bring to a boil. Simmer a few minutes.

3 tbsp. cornstarch dissolved in ⅓ cup cold water	Add, stirring until thickened.

Serve over cooked rice (cook about 1 ½ cups rice), and top with chow mein noodles.

Yield: 6 to 8 servings

Chow Mein Casserole

2 cups cooked diced chicken
1 (10-oz.) can cream of chicken soup
2 chicken bouillon cubes dissolved
   in ½ cup hot water
1 cup chopped onion
1 cup chopped celery
½ cup uncooked rice
2 cups water
1 tsp. salt
¼ tsp. black pepper
1 tsp. sugar
½ tsp. MSG (optional)
2½ tbsp. soy sauce
1 (14-oz.) can bean sprouts, drained

Combine all ingredients and pour into a 2-qt. cassserole dish.

1½ cups chow mein noodles

Sprinkle over the top.

Bake at 350 degrees for 1 ¼ hrs. When serving, pass additional chow mein noodles to add on top on each plate.

Yield: 8 to 10 servings

Curried Meat and Rice

(This recipe comes from Japan. Mrs. Yamade served it to our church WMSC group. However, she used 2 tablespoons of curry! That was a 'little' too hot for my family, so I cut the amount back!)

½ cup flour

Heat in skillet until light brown.

1 or 2 tsp. curry powder

Add, and brown a little longer.

1 cup water

Slowly add, stirring constantly until blended. Set aside.

½ to 1 lb. cubed beef (or other meat)
2 tbsp. margarine

Fry in skillet until browned. (I like to then pressure cook meat about 15 minutes for extra tenderness.)

2 carrots, diced
3 med. potatoes, cubed
¾ cup chopped onions
5 or 6 cups water

Add, and cook until tender. Then stir in curry mixture and bring to boil.

1 tsp. salt

Add.

Serve over rice. (Cook 2 cups rice.)

Yield: 6 to 8 servings

Mitsue Yamade

Dinner in a Package

Cut a large piece of heavy-duty aluminum foil for each person. Place a hamburger ball on each piece. This can be a meat loaf mixture shaped into balls, or plain hamburger seasoned any way you wish. Plain hamburger seasoned with a mixture of barbecue sauce or steak sauce, and a few drops liquid smoke, mixed with a little water, and poured over the balls is good.

Add 1 or 2 sliced potatoes in each package, 1 diced carrot, sliced onion, a little shredded cabbage is good—whatever you wish. Sprinkle salt and pepper to taste, and drop some shredded cheese over the top. Seal foil tightly. Lay packages on a baking tray and bake in 350-degree oven at least 1 hour until tender.

These may be cooked on the grill, or half baked in the oven and finished in a charcoal fire. Excellent to put in the oven when you are away. Meat can also be varied. Sprinkle browned crumbled bacon over the vegetables or use diced Spam or luncheon meat.

Eggplant Special

½ to 1 lb. ground beef 1 cup chopped onion	Sauté in skillet. Drain.
1½ cups coarsely chopped peeled eggplant 1 cup coarsely chopped peeled potatoes	Add, and simmer until tender, about 15 minutes. Pour in greased 2-qt. casserole dish.
1 tsp. salt ½ tsp. garlic powder 1 tsp. chili powder ¼ tsp. nutmeg 2 tbsp. flour	Mix and sprinkle over mixture in dish.
½ cup tomato sauce or thick tomato juice	Pour over mixture.
1 tbsp. sugar ½ cup grated cheese	Sprinkle on sugar first, then cheese.
2 eggs, beaten 1 cup milk	Combine and pour over all.

Bake at 350 degrees for 30 to 35 minutes. May be garnished with parsley.

Yield: 6 servings

Frankfurter Casserole

3 med. potatoes, diced	Cook just until tender in small amount of water. Set aside.
1 med. onion, chopped 2 tbsp. butter or margarine	Sauté in skillet until tender.
3 tbsp. flour	Gradually add, stirring until bubbly.
1½ cups milk	Slowly add, stirring until thickened.
6 frankfurters, cut in rings 2 to 4 cups canned green beans, drained	Combine with potatoes in large casserole dish.
⅓ cup mayonnaise 1 tsp. salt ¾ tsp. dry mustard ¼ tsp. black pepper	Add to white sauce first, then pour over mixture in casserole. May be topped with bread crumbs, if desired.

Bake at 350 degrees for 45 minutes.

Yield: 6 to 8 servings

Ground Beef Oriental

1 onion, chopped 1 cup celery, diced 3 tbsp. butter	Sauté in skillet. Remove and set aside.
1 lb. ground beef	Brown in skillet and drain.
1 (10-oz.) can cream of chicken soup 1 (10-oz.) can cream of mushroom soup 1¼ cups water ¼ cup soy sauce ¼ tsp. black pepper	Combine thoroughly, then add to onion mixture and to beef.
1 (14-oz.) can bean sprouts, drained	Fold in.

Pour in greased 2-qt. casserole dish. Cover and bake at 350 degrees for 1 hour. Remove lid the last half hour.

Yield: 8 servings

Nancy Heatwole

Ground Beef Stroganoff Casserole

1 (8-oz.) pkg. medium noodles, cooked	Have ready.
½ cup chopped onion 2 tbsp. butter or margarine	Sauté in skillet.
1 lb. lean hamburger 2 tbsp. flour 1 tsp. salt ½ tsp. black pepper dash garlic powder and MSG (optional) ¼ tsp. paprika ½ cup diced mushrooms-fresh, or canned-drained	Add, and sauté 5 minutes longer.
1 (10-oz.) can cream of mushroom soup 1 soup can water	Add, and simmer 10 minutes longer.
1 cup commercial sour cream	Stir in. Remove from heat.
parsley to garnish	Have ready.

Layer noodles and sauce in 2-qt. casserole dish. Garnish with parsley. Bake at 350 degrees for 30 to 40 minutes until bubbly.

Yield: 8 servings

Nancy Heatwole

Ham and Cheese Bake

1 cup cooked chopped ham ¼ cup minced onion 1 (2½-oz.) can sliced mushrooms, drained 1 med. tomato, chopped ¾ cup Swiss cheese, shredded	Sprinkle in greased 8-inch-square baking dish.
5 eggs ½ cup milk ¾ cup Bisquick ½ tsp. salt ½ tsp. dry mustard ½ tsp. parsley flakes ¼ tsp. black pepper	Beat together until blended. Pour over mixture in dish.

Bake at 350 degrees for about 45 minutes.

Yield: 6 servings

Ham and Asparagus Casserole

(This is also delicious served as only a vegetable dish without the ham.)

3 cups fresh or frozen cut asparagus	Cook several minutes until nearly tender. Drain thoroughly and place in 2-qt. casserole dish.
1 cup diced cooked ham **2 tbsp. minute tapioca** **1 tbsp. dry minced onion** **2 hard cooked eggs, diced** **¼ tsp. MSG (optional)** **¼ tsp. salt**	Sprinkle over asparagus in dish.
1 (10-oz.) can cream of mushroom soup **½ cup milk**	Combine and pour over mixture in dish.
1½ cups dry bread crumbs **2 tbsp. melted margarine**	Combine and sprinkle over top.

Bake at 350 degrees for 35 to 40 minutes until hot and lightly browned.

Yield: 6 to 8 servings

Ham and Broccoli Bake

12 slices white bread	Cut bread with doughnut cutter. Set aside cutouts. Arrange scraps of bread in a 9 × 13 bake dish.
¾ lb. sharp American cheese, sliced	Layer cheese over bread.
1 (10-oz.) pkg. frozen chopped broccoli, cooked and drained **2 cups diced cooked ham**	Layer over cheese. Arrange bread doughnuts and holes over the top.
6 eggs, beaten **3½ cups milk** **2 tbsp. instant minced onion** **½ tsp. salt** **½ tsp. dry mustard**	Combine and pour over all. Cover and refrigerate at least 6 hours or overnight. Uncover and bake at 350 degrees for 50 to 55 minutes. Let stand 10 minutes before serving. Cut into squares.

May sprinkle with shredded cheese 5 minutes before end of baking time if desired.

Yield: 12 servings   *Wanda Good*

Quick-Mix Ham Casserole

1½ cups minute rice
2 cups diced cooked ham (or cubed Spam)
1 qt. green beans, drained
⅓ cup mayonnaise
¼ cup chopped onion
2 tsp. sugar
½ tsp. MSG (optional)
½ tsp. salt
3 chicken bouillon cubes dissolved in 1¾ cups hot water
¼ cup butter or margarine, melted
1 cup shredded cheddar cheese (reserve half)

Combine all ingredients and pour in greased 2-qt. casserole dish. Sprinkle reserved cheese over the top.

Bake at 350 degrees for approximately 40 minutes.

Yield: 8 to 10 servings.

Old-Fashioned Ham Pot Pie

(Use a mixture of ham broth and water to make a rich liquid. Ham broth is often salty, so use an amount that gives a good rich flavor that isn't too strong. A pizza cutter is excellent for quickly cutting the dough.)

4 cups broth and water
1 cup chopped cooked ham
3 medium potatoes, diced

Heat to boiling.

Pot pie dough:
1 small egg, slightly beaten
⅛ tsp. salt
1 tbsp. water

Mix.

approximately ¾ cup flour

Add to make a stiff dough. Knead several times and roll out *as thin as possible* on floured surface. Cut into l-inch squares. Drop into rapidly boiling broth. Cover and simmer 20 min.

Minced parsley to garnish

Sprinkle over top if desired.

Variation: Use beef or chicken meat and broth instead of ham.

Yield: 6 servings

Ham (or Hot Dogs) and Scalloped Potatoes

2 tbsp. margarine **¼ cup flour** **2 cups milk**	Make white sauce. (See procedure on page 338.)

. . . .

4 or 5 med. potatoes, sliced or
   shredded
¼ to ½ lb. ham pieces (or about 6
   hot dogs sliced in rings)
¼ cup minced onion
1 tbsp. minced green pepper
   (optional)
1 cup cheese, cubed
1 tsp. salt
¼ tsp. black pepper
	Layer in greased 2-qt. casserole dish. Pour white sauce over all.

. . . .

Bake at 350 degrees for 1 to 1 ¼ hours.

Yield: 6 servings

. . . .

Hamburger Macaroni Casserole

1 lb. hamburger **⅓ cup minced onion** **⅓ cup chopped green pepper**	Sauté in skillet and drain.

. . . .

½ cup macaroni	Cook and drain.

. . . .

1 cup diced potatoes **½ cup diced carrots** **½ cup peas**	Cook until almost tender.

. . . .

1½ cups canned tomatoes, **chopped** **1 tbsp. sugar** **1 tsp. salt** **1 tbsp. Worcestershire sauce** **½ cup grated cheese**	Have ready.

. . . .

Combine all ingredients in 2-qt. greased casserole dish except cheese. Bake at 350 degrees for 30 minutes. Sprinkle with cheese and bake 5 minutes more.

Yield: 6 to 8 servings

. . . .

Hamburger (or Chicken) and Noodles

¾ lb. hamburger (or 1½ cups cooked cubed chicken)
⅓ cup chopped onion

Brown in skillet and drain. (Do not brown if using chicken.)

. . . .

6 oz. medium-cut noodles (scant 2 cups)

Cook until tender and drain.

. . . .

1 cup canned corn, or frozen corn-thawed
1 (10-oz.) can cream of chicken soup or tomato soup
1 tsp. salt
½ tsp. MSG (optional)

Combine all ingredients and pour into greased 2-qt. casserole dish.

. . . .

1½ cups bread crumbs
2 tbsp. melted butter

Mix and sprinkle over the top.

. . . .

Bake at 350 degrees for 30 minutes.

Lillian Shickel

. . . .

Hamburger Pie

1 lb. hamburger
1 med. onion, chopped

Brown in skillet and drain.

. . . .

2½ cups canned green beans, drained
1 (10-oz.) can tomato soup, or 1¼ cups thick tomato juice
1 tbsp. A-1 sauce (or other seasoning as desired)
1 tsp. salt
1 tbsp. sugar
¼ tsp. MSG (optional)

Combine with hamburger and pour into a 2-qt. casserole dish.

. . . .

3 cups leftover mashed potatoes (or instant)
1 egg

Beat together and spoon in mounds over meat mixture.

. . . .

1 cup grated cheese

Sprinkle over mounds of potatoes.

. . . .

Bake at 350 degrees for 30 minutes.

. . . .

Hamburger-Potato Crockpot Dinner

(Tossing the potatoes in cream of tartar water prevents having them turn dark from the slow heating.)

1 lb. hamburger	Brown in skillet and drain. Set aside.
1 cup water **½ tsp. cream of tartar**	Combine.
6 med. potatoes, thinly sliced	Toss in water. Drain.
1 onion, chopped **¼ cup flour** **½ tsp. salt** **¼ tsp. black pepper** **1 cup grated cheddar cheese** ** (reserve half)**	Layer all ingredients with hamburger and potatoes in greased crockpot.
2 tbsp. butter or margarine	Dot over top.
1 (10-oz.) can cream of mushroom ** soup**	Pour over all.

Cover and cook on low 7 to 9 hours, or on high 3 to 4 hours. Sprinkle reserved cheese over top 30 minutes before serving.

Yield: 6 to 8 servings   *Evelyn Basinger*

Easy Hamburger or Ham Quiche

1 unbaked 9″ deep-dish pie crust	Have ready.
½ lb. hamburger (or 1 cup cooked ** diced ham)**	Brown hamburger in skillet. Drain.
1 cup grated Swiss cheese, or 1 (10- ** oz.) can cheddar cheese soup*** **⅓ cup finely chopped green onion**	Add, and sprinkle mixture in pie crust.
½ cup milk **3 eggs** **⅓ cup mayonnaise** **½ tsp. salt** **⅛ tsp. black pepper** **1 tbsp. cornstarch**	Combine in blender container. Process until smooth. Pour over mixture in crust.

(*If using cheese soup, blend with milk mixture.) Bake at 350 degrees for 35 to 40 minutes until knife inserted in center comes out clean.

Haystacks

2 tbsp. margarine **1¼ cups rice**	Fry dry rice in margarine in pan until lightly browned.
3 cups hot water **1 tsp. salt**	Add, and heat to boiling. Cover tightly and simmer 20 minutes.
1 lb. hamburger **1 small chopped onion** **2 tbsp. chopped green pepper**	Sauté in skillet until lightly browned. Drain.
1 (1¾-oz.) env. taco seasoning mix	Add. May add a little water to make mixture slightly juicy. Spoon over rice to serve.
Toppings: **chopped lettuce** **chopped mushrooms** **sliced tomatoes** **bean sprouts** **chopped green peppers** **crushed corn chips**	Use any or all toppings as desired.
1 (10-oz.) can cheddar cheese soup, **or 2 cups your own cheese sauce**	Heat until hot through and spoon over top.

Yield: 6 servings

Cheryl Heatwol

Lasagna*

1 lb. hamburger **½ cup chopped onion**	Brown in skillet and drain.
3 cups tomato juice **2 tbsp. brown sugar** **1 tbsp. vinegar** **1½ tsp. salt** **2 tsp. leaf oregano or 1 tsp. ground** **oregano** **1 tsp. ground marjoram** **½ tsp. garlic powder**	Add, cover and simmer for 20 minutes.
2 tbsp. cornstarch **⅓ cup water**	Dissolve and add to sauce, stirring until thickened.
8 oz. noodles—use either lasagna **noodles or regular wide noodles**	Cook with 1 tbsp. oil for 12 minutes. Drain.

1½ cups cottage cheese (12 oz.)   Have ready.
2 cups shredded Swiss cheese
   (may use half Velveeta)
1 tbsp. parsley flakes (optional)
⅓ cup Parmesan cheese

In 9 × 13 greased baking dish, layer noodles, meat sauce, cottage and Swiss cheeses, and parsley flakes. Sprinkle Parmesan cheese over the top. Bake at 350 degrees for 35 to 40 minutes.

Yield: 8 servings

Pat Hertzler

*For Easy Lasagna that can also be baked in a conventional oven, see recipe on page 415 in the microwave section.

Meatballs and Spaghetti

Sauce:
1 (12-oz.) can tomato paste   Combine in heavy saucepan. Cover and simmer
3 cups water   20 minutes, stirring occasionally.
1 beef bouillon cube, dissolve in
   part of water
2 tbsp. dry minced onion
1 tbsp. grated Parmesan cheese
1 tbsp. sugar
1 tsp. Italian herb seasoning
½ tsp. salt
½ tsp. garlic powder
⅛ tsp. black pepper

1 (4-oz.) can sliced mushrooms,   Add to sauce.
   drained (optional)

Meatballs:
1 lb. hamburger   Mix together thoroughly and form into 16
¾ cup soft bread crumbs   meatballs. Fry in 1 tbsp. margarine in skillet
½ cup of the above sauce   until browned. Drain off fat. Pour sauce over
¼ cup grated Parmesan cheese   balls, cover, and simmer 20 to 25 minutes. Serve
1 tsp. seasoned salt   over spaghetti.
¾ tsp. garlic powder

Cook ½ lb. very thin spaghetti until tender. See directions for cooking on page 274.

Yield: 4 to 6 servings

Donna Shank

Meatballs and Rice

1 lb. hamburger ¼ cup chopped onion ½ cup bread crumbs 1 egg, slightly beaten 1 tsp. salt 1 tbsp. barbecue sauce, or other seasoning ⅛ tsp. garlic powder ¼ tsp. MSG (optional)	Mix thoroughly and shape into small balls about the size of a small walnut (about 24). Fry in skillet until browned on all sides.

. . . .

1 (10-oz.) can cream of mushroom soup or cream of celery soup ½ soup can of water 2 tbsp. chopped parsley	Combine, and pour over meat balls in skillet. Cover and simmer 20 minutes, stirring occasionally.

. . . .

Serve over cooked rice. (Cook 1 ½ cups rice.)

Yield: 6 servings

. . . .

Manicotti

(Even though this recipe takes some time to make, it is delicious and will serve 25 people. It makes 3 dishes and is ideal to freeze ahead for later use—eat one dish and freeze two!)

Sauce:

¼ cup oil 2 cups chopped onions 2 garlic cloves, minced	Sauté until tender. Drain off oil, and reserve for browning hamburger.

. . . .

1 qt. tomato juice 2 qts. home canned tomatoes ¼ cup chopped parsley 2 tbsp. sugar 1 tbsp. salt 1 tbsp. oregano leaves 2 tsp. basil leaves ½ tsp. black pepper	Add. Simmer 1 hour, stirring occasionally. May add up to 2 cups water if sauce becomes too thick.

. . . .

Filling:

¼ cup oil including amount reserved from sauce 3 lbs. hamburger 2 cups chopped onions 2 garlic cloves, minced	Sauté in oil about 20 minutes. Then drain off grease.

. . . .

2 eggs, lightly beaten 1 tbsp. salt 2 tsp. oregano leaves 1 tsp. basil leaves 8 oz. mozzarella cheese, coarsely grated (2 cups)	Mix in and set aside.

Manicotti Shells:

6 qts. water **2 tbsp. oil** **1 tbsp. salt**	Heat to boiling.

1 lb. manicotti shells (approx. 28)	Add to water, several at a time, and cook each batch 6 to 8 minutes until tender. Handle carefully, as they will break if crowded too much. Remove cooked shells and drain on a towel.

2 cups Parmesan cheese **1 lb. sliced mozzarella cheese**	Have ready.

Carefully pack each shell with filling. Arrange shells in three 9 × 13 bake dishes. Cover with sauce and sprinkle with Parmesan cheese. Lay sliced mozzarella cheese over the top. Cover with foil and bake at 375 degrees for about 40 minutes. Uncover and bake 15 minutes more.

Yield: 25 servings   *Evelyn S. Heatwole*

'More' Casserole

1 lb. ground beef **1 cup chopped onions**	Brown in skillet and drain.

1 (8-oz.) pkg. noodles, cooked
1 pint frozen peas
1 (12-oz.) can corn
1 (8-oz.) can water chestnuts,
  chopped
1 (8-oz.) can sliced mushrooms,
  drained
3 or 4 cups shredded cheddar
  cheese (reserve 1 cup)
	Mix together with meat. Pour into a 2½-qt. casserole.

1 (10-oz.) can cream of celery soup **1¼ cups milk** **3 tsp. chili powder** **2 tsp. salt** **¼ tsp. black pepper** **¼ tsp. garlic powder**	Mix well, and pour over mixture in dish.

Sprinkle reserved cheese over the top. Cover lightly with foil. Bake at 350 degrees for approximately 40 minutes or until bubbly.

Yield: 12 to 14 servings   *Annie Weaver*

Meat Pie

2 cups cooked cubed meat* **2½ cups broth or bouillon** **2 cups diced potatoes** **1 cup peas** **½ cup diced carrots** **¼ cup chopped onion** **¼ cup chopped celery**	Cook together until almost tender.

. . . .

3 tbsp. cornstarch dissolved in ⅓ **cup water** **1 tsp. Worcestershire sauce** **1½ tsp. salt** **¼ tsp. MSG (optional)**	Add, stirring until thickened. Pour in 2-qt. casserole dish. Top with little biscuits or rich pie crust.

. . . .

(*Meat may be canned beef chunks, or leftover chunks of roast. Or use 2 cups diced cooked chicken.)

. . . .

Biscuits:

1 cup flour **2 tsp. baking powder** **¼ tsp. cream of tartar** **½ tsp. salt** **1 tbsp. sugar** **¼ cup shortening**	Mix together until crumbly.

. . . .

1 egg, slightly beaten **⅓ cup milk**	Combine and stir in with fork just until moistened throughout.

. . . .

Knead several times, roll out, and cut with little insert to doughnut cutter, or other small cutter. Arrange over top of meat mixture. Bake at 375 degrees for about 20 minutes until biscuits are lightly browned. (⅓ cup grated cheese may be added to flour mixture before adding liquids for cheese biscuits.)

. . . .

Optional Rich Pie Crust:

1½ cups flour **¼ tsp. salt** **½ cup shortening** **2 tbsp. butter**	Mix together until crumbly.

. . . .

3 tbsp. ice water	Toss in with fork just until moistened.

. . . .

Press into ball. Roll out on waxed paper. Cut design in top to let out steam and to decorate. Place on top of pie and crimp edges. Bake at 400 degrees for about 20 minutes.

Yield: 6 servings

. . . .

Navajo Tacos

(Nancy brought this recipe from a Navajo Indian reservation in Kayenta, Arizona, where she taught school for several years. The base for the tacos is frybread. If you wish to reduce calories, you may use rice for the base instead. The Indians do not use measuring cups, but measure everything by so many 'handfuls.' Nancy measured the handfuls of flour the Indian lady measured out for the bread and found it to be 4 cups! If there is any frybread left over, the Indians love to eat it at another meal spread with honey.)

Frybread:

4 cups flour **3 tsp. baking powder** **½ tsp. salt**	Sift together into a large bowl.
½ cup milk **1¼ cups lukewarm water**	Combine and stir into mixture. Knead several times until smooth. Cover and let set for 20 minutes.

Heat at least 1 inch of oil in electric skillet or wok to 400 degrees. Divide dough into 8 balls. Grease your hands with shortening. Flatten a ball between your hands pulling and stretching into a pancake 5 or 6 inches in diameter. Or use a rolling pin to roll into a pancake. Lay pancake in hot oil. Turn when bottom is lightly browned. When other side is lightly browned, remove from oil and drain on paper towels to remove grease. (Place newspaper under paper towels to help absorb grease.) Continue with next ball until all are fried.

Taco Sauce:

½ lb. hamburger **1 small chopped onion** **2 tbsp. chopped green pepper**	Sauté in skillet until lightly browned. Drain.
1 (16-oz.) can kidney beans, undrained **2 (12-oz.) cans tomato sauce** **½ to 1 (1¾-oz.) env. taco seasoning mix (according to taste)***	Add.
3 tbsp. cornstarch **¼ cup water**	Dissolve and add, cooking and stirring just until thickened.

Toppings:

shredded lettuce **chopped onion** **chopped tomato** **sprouts** **shredded carrots** **grated cheese**	Put frybread on plate. Spread with sauce. Add any or all of the toppings as desired. It will look like a haystack!

*If you do not care for a spicy Mexican flavor, you may use spaghetti sauce in place of the tomato sauce and taco seasoning mix.

Nancy Ryan

Yield: 8 servings

Okra-Hamburger Skillet

½ lb. hamburger	Sauté in skillet until no pink color remains. Drain.
1 pint sliced okra	Add, and fry about 5 minutes longer, stirring frequently.
1 pt. tomatoes (canned or fresh), cut in chunks **1 tbsp. sugar** **1 tsp. salt** **1 tbsp. Worcestershire sauce**	Add, and cook on low for 10 to 15 minutes.

Yield: 4 servings   *Marie Shank*

Oven-Baked Beef Stew

2 lbs. stewing beef, cut in 1-inch cubes **3 tbsp. oil**	Brown meat in oil in skillet until dark brown on all sides.
1 qt. canned tomatoes, undrained and chopped **1 large onion, chopped** **2 cups beef broth or bouillon** **3 tbsp. minute tapioca** **1 garlic clove, minced**	Add, and bring to a boil. Pour into large casserole dish. Cover and bake in 350-degree oven for 1 ½ to 2 hours until meat is tender.
4 med. potatoes, quartered **4 med. carrots, cut in strips** **2 cups shredded cabbage** **½ cup sliced celery** **¼ cup chopped green pepper**	Add, and continue to bake for 1 hour longer or until vegetables are tender.
2½ tsp. salt **1 tbsp. sugar** **¼ tsp. black pepper**	Add seasonings 15 minutes before baking time is completed.

(If desired, meat may be cooked on top of the stove ahead, or use leftover chunks of roast. Then add remaining ingredients and bake for 1 hour and 15 minutes.)

Yield: 8 to 10 servings

Pinwheel-Vegetable Casserole

(This is an attractive way to serve vegetables to guests. Use it with any of the following vegetables: peas, frozen mixed vegetables, green beans and onions, or lima beans.)

Pinwheels:
Cut crusts from 4 slices bread. Then flatten bread *slightly* with palm of hand so it doesn't break when rolling it up. Spread with 5 oz. cheese spread. (Use pimiento cheese spread or

Cheez Whiz or Velveeta cheese—softened to room temperature and mixed with 1 tbsp. milk.) Roll up like jelly roll. Wrap in plastic wrap and place in refrigerator while preparing vegetables.

Creamed Vegetables:

1 qt. vegetables (your choice)	Cook until almost tender with small amount of water. After cooking, add to or pour off liquid so ½ cup remains.
½ cup rich milk or cream **2 tbsp. flour**	Shake in batter shaker until smooth. Then pour over vegetables, cooking and stirring just until thickened.
1 tsp. salt **1 tsp. sugar** **1 tbsp. butter** **1 cup diced cooked ham**	Stir in until thoroughly mixed. Pour in greased 2-qt. casserole dish.

Top with pinwheels made by slicing cheese rolls into ¼ to ½-inch thick slices. Arrange over top of casserole. Bake at 375 degrees just until bubbly and pinwheels are browned.

Yield: 6 servings

Plantation Casserole

2 cups chopped cooked chicken **1 pt. corn** **1½ cups peas, lightly cooked and drained** **½ cup diced cheese** **⅓ cup evaporated milk** **¼ cup chopped onion** **1 tbsp. Worcestershire sauce** **salt and pepper to taste**	Combine all ingredients and pour into a greased 8 × 12 bake dish. Bake at 350 degrees for 15 minutes, or until bubbly at edges. Remove from oven and pour biscuit dough over top.

Biscuit Dough:

1 cup Bisquick **¼ cup cornmeal** **1 tbsp. sugar** **½ tsp. salt**	Mix in bowl.
1 egg, beaten lightly **⅔ cup evaporated milk**	Combine, and stir in just until moistened through.

Pour over top of hot casserole, leaving center uncovered. Bake about 15 minutes more until golden brown.

Variation: Use diced ham in place of chicken and 20 oz. of mixed vegetables in place of corn and peas.

Yield: 6 to 8 servings

Pizza Pie

Topping:
½ lb. hamburger
1 small onion, chopped
Brown in skillet. Drain.

. . . .

2 cups tomato juice
½ tsp. ground oregano
¼ tsp. ground marjoram
¼ tsp. garlic powder
1 tsp. chili powder
2 tbsp. sugar
½ tsp. salt
Add, and simmer for 10 minutes.

. . . .

2 tbsp. cornstarch
⅓ cup water
Dissolve, then add, stirring until thickened.
Spread over dough.

. . . .

3 cups grated, or 8 slices cheese
  (use Swiss, mozzarella, cheddar,
  or other)
Have ready.

. . . .

Dough:
1 pk. dry yeast
⅓ cup warm water
1 tbsp. sugar
Stir together until dissolved. Set aside.

. . . .

1 egg, beaten lightly
¼ cup tomato juice
3 tbsp. melted shortening
1 tsp. salt
Combine and add to yeast mixture.

. . . .

2 cups flour
Add gradually. Knead until smooth.

. . . .

Grease, cover, and let rise in warm place until double (about 1 hour.). Roll out and fit into an 11 × 15 greased jelly roll pan. Spread topping mixture over dough. May sprinkle with additional leaf oregano if desired. Bake at 375 degrees about 15 minutes. Remove from oven and sprinkle grated cheese, or lay slices of cheese over the top. Return to oven 5 minutes more.

Yield: 8 servings

. . . .

Optional Pizza Crusts

Cornmeal Crust:
1¾ cups cornmeal
2 cups flour
3 tsp. baking powder
2 tsp. sugar
1 tsp. salt
Mix together in bowl.

. . . .

1 cup milk
½ cup vegetable oil
Combine and stir into flour mixture. Press into 11 × 15 pan.

Quick Biscuit Dough:

2½ cups flour **½ tsp. salt** **3 tsp. baking powder** **1 tsp. baking soda** **1 tbsp. sugar** **5 tbsp. margarine**	Mix together until crumbly.

1 egg, beaten lightly **1 cup thick sour milk or buttermilk**	Combine, then stir into flour mixture only until mixed.

Knead several times and roll to fit, or press into an 11 × 15 pan.

Pizza Parlor Dough:

1 pk. dry yeast **1 cup warm water** **1 tsp. sugar** **1 tsp. salt** **2 tbsp. vegetable oil**	Mix together until dissolved.

2½ cups flour (may use half whole **wheat if desired)**	Gradually add, kneading until smooth.

Cover and let rise 15 minutes. Divide into 2 balls and stretch into 2 regular-sized pizza pans

Mary Ann Heatwole

Crazy Crust Pizza

1 cup flour **1 tsp. salt** **1 tsp. ground oregano** **⅛ tsp. black pepper**	Combine in bowl.

2 eggs, beaten **⅔ cup milk**	Combine and stir into flour mixture. Pour batter into greased pizza pan.

1 lb. hamburger	Brown and drain.

⅓ cup chopped onions	Sprinkle over dough.

mushrooms, if desired	Sprinkle over dough.

1 cup pizza sauce **¾ tsp. basil** **¼ tsp. garlic powder** **1 tbsp. sugar** **1½ cups grated mozzarella cheese,** **or Velveeta cheese slices**	Have ready.

Bake at 375 degrees for 20 to 25 minutes. Remove from oven and spread on sauce. Sprinkle with seasonings and lay cheese slices on top. Return to oven 5 more minutes or until cheese melts.

Sauerkraut and Dumplings

4 wieners **½ tbsp. margarine**	Slice into ½-inch pieces and brown in skillet

1 pt. sauerkraut, undrained **1 tbsp. brown sugar**	Add and heat to boiling.

Dumplings: **1 cup flour** **½ tsp. salt** **2 tsp. baking powder**	Sift together.

1 egg, beaten slightly **⅓ cup milk**	Combine, and stir in quickly just until smooth. Drop by spoonfuls onto boiling sauerkraut.

Cover tightly at once and simmer until done, about 18 minutes. Do not remove cover until done! **Variation:** Shape ½ lb. sausage into little balls and brown on all sides in skillet in place of wieners.

Yield: 6 servings

Sausage and Cabbage Dinner

¾ lb. hot sausage	Brown in skillet and drain well. Remove from skillet and set aside.

4 cups shredded cabbage **2 tbsp. margarine** **¼ cup chopped onion**	Sauté in skillet until tender and lightly browned (7 to 10 minutes), stirring frequently. Keep covered between stirrings.

⅓ lb. noodles (2 cups)	Cook separately. Drain.

1 tbsp. Worcestershire sauce **1 tsp. salt** **½ tsp. MSG (optional)** **¼ tsp. garlic powder**	Add, and combine with cabbage and sausage, mixing well. Serve immediately.

Yield: 6 servings

Sausage (or Chicken) and Noodle Casserole

1 lb. pork sausage (or 2 cups chopped cooked chicken) 2 tbsp. chopped green peppers	Sauté in skillet and drain. (Do not sauté if using chicken.)
8 oz. noodles (3 cups)	Cook until tender and drain.
1 (10-oz.) can cream of chicken soup ¼ cup milk 1 tsp. salt ¼ tsp. MSG (optional) 1 cup grated cheese	Mix together and combine with sausage and noodles
cornflake crumbs to garnish	Have ready.

Pour into 2-qt. casserole dish. Sprinkle crumbs over top. Bake at 350 degrees for 30 to 35 minutes. **Variation:** Add 2 cups peas.

Yield: 6 to 8 servings

Marie Shank
Mae Shank

Sausage-Potato Quiche

3 tbsp. vegetable oil 3 cups shredded raw potato	Mix, and press over bottom and up sides of 9-inch deep-dish pie plate for crust. Bake at 400 degrees for 15 minutes or until just beginning to brown.
1 cup sausage, browned and drained 1 cup grated cheddar cheese ½ cup chopped onions	Sprinkle over hot crust.
2 eggs, beaten 1 cup evaporated milk or rich milk 1 tsp. salt ¼ tsp. MSG (optional)	Combine and pour over mixture.
1 tbsp. parsley flakes	Sprinkle over top.

Return to oven and bake at 400 degrees for 35 minutes more, or until knife inserted in center comes out clean. Cool 5 minutes, then serve.

Variation: Use 1 cup chopped cooked chicken in place of sausage.

Fannie S. Heatwole
Esther H. Wenger

Sausage-Rice Casserole

2 lbs. pork sausage	Brown in skillet, stirring to crumble. Drain.
1 med. onion, chopped **1 med. green pepper, chopped** **1 cup chopped celery** **1 cup rice (uncooked)** **½ cup slivered almonds, toasted** **1 (0.375-oz.) env. instant chicken** **noodle soup mix**	Add, mixing well. Pour in greased 9 × 13 bake dish.
2½ cups water	Pour over top.

Cover and bake at 350 degrees for 1 ¼ hours.

Yield: 8 servings   *Wanda Good*

Mock Spaghetti (Low Cal.)

1 lb. hamburger	Brown in skillet and drain.
1 qt. tomato juice	Add.
1 tbsp. minced onion **1 tbsp. parsley flakes** **1½ tsp. salt** **2 tsp. green pepper flakes** **1 tsp. sugar substitute** **¾ tsp. Italian seasoning** **½ tsp. instant minced garlic**	Combine and add. Cook 10 minutes.
1 tbsp. cornstarch dissolved in 3 **tbsp. water**	Stir in just until thickened. Turn off heat.
1 small head cabbage, shredded	Cook until tender and drain.

Serve meat sauce over cabbage. Sprinkle with Parmesan cheese.

Yield: 4 to 6 servings   *Alice Trissel*

Spaghetti Pie

6 oz. thin spaghetti	Cook until tender and drain.
2 tbsp. butter **⅓ cup Parmesan cheese** **2 eggs, slightly beaten**	Add, mixing well. Spread in 8 × 12 bake dish to form crust.
1 lb. hamburger **½ cup chopped onion** **¼ cup chopped green pepper**	Sauté in skillet until lightly browned. Drain.
½ tsp. salt **1 tbsp. sugar** **½ tsp. garlic salt** **¾ tsp. oregano** **2 cups whole tomatoes**	Add to hamburger, mixing well.
1 cup cottage cheese	Spread over unbaked spaghetti crust. Then spread hamburger mixture on next.
¾ cup shredded cheddar cheese	Sprinkle over top.
pepperoni slices (optional)	Lay over cheese if desired.

Bake at 350 degrees for 30 to 35 minutes.

Yield: 6 servings   *Sue Shank*

Supper-in-a-Dish

1 lb. hamburger or sausage, **browned and drained** **sliced raw potatoes** **sliced carrots** **peas** **chopped onion** **chopped celery** **chopped green pepper** **salt and pepper to taste**	Layer in bake dish according to your taste.
1 (10-oz.) can cream of chicken soup **or mushroom soup** **¼ cup milk**	Mix and pour over the top. Bake at 350 degrees for 1 ¼ hours.
⅔ cup grated cheese	Sprinkle on top and return to oven until melted.

(May cook in the crockpot on high for 4 hours.)

Impossible Taco Pie

1 lb. ground beef **⅓ cup chopped onion** **¼ cup chopped green pepper**	Sauté in skillet, and drain.
½ to 1 (1.5-oz.) env. taco seasoning **mix**	Add, mixing well. Spread in 8 × 8-inch baking dish.
1½ cups milk **1 cup Bisquick** **3 eggs**	Beat together until smooth—i5 seconds in blender, or 1 minute with hand beater. Pour over mixture in dish. Bake at 350 degrees for 25 minutes.
2 tomatoes, chopped **¾ cup shredded cheese**	Sprinkle over top. Bake 10 minutes more.

Tater Tot Casserole

¾ lb. hamburger **½ cup chopped onion**	Brown in skillet and drain.
1 cup cooked rice or ½ cup instant **rice** **1 (10-oz.) can cream of chicken soup** **½ soup can of water**	Mix in and spread in greased 8-inch square bake dish.
1 lb. Tater Tots	Layer over top.

Bake at 350 degrees for approximately 45 minutes. (**Variations:** May also add 1 qt. canned green beans—drained, with rice. Or mix in 1 pkg. mixed vegetables, cooked. May use cheddar cheese soup instead of chicken soup.)

Yield: 6 to 8 servings

Easy Turkey-Ham Quiche

6 slices buttered bread	Remove crusts from bread. Cut slices in half and line sides and bottom of 9-inch deep-dish pie plate—buttered side down.
4 strips bacon	Fry until crisp, drain, and crumble.
⅓ cup chopped onion **2 tbsp. chopped green pepper**	Sauté in bacon grease until tender. Drain.
1 cup shredded cheddar cheese **1 cup shredded Swiss cheese** **2 tbsp. flour**	Mix.
1 cup finely diced turkey ham	Combine with bacon, onion mixture, and cheese and sprinkle over bread in dish.

| 3 eggs, beaten
1½ cups milk
½ tsp. salt
¼ tsp. MSG | Mix, and pour over mixture in dish. |

Bake at 375 degrees for 35 to 40 minutes until filling is set. Cut in wedges to serve.

Yield: 6 servings

Texas Hash

¾ to 1 lb. hamburger ¼ cup chopped green pepper 1 med. onion, chopped	Sauté in skillet. Drain.
1 cup tomato juice ¾ cup water ½ cup rice (uncooked) 1 tsp. chili powder 1½ tsp. salt 2 tbsp. sugar 2 tsp. vinegar	Add.
grated cheese to garnish	Have ready.

May be simmered on top of the stove for 20 minutes. However, it is best to place in a casserole dish and bake at 350 degrees, covered, for 45 minutes. Sprinkle cheese over the top before serving.

Yield: 4 to 6 servings

Wild Rice-Hamburger Supreme

1 (6-oz.) pkg. long-grained wild rice	Cook according to package directions.
1 lb. hamburger 1 med. onion, chopped	Brown in skillet and drain.

1 (4-oz.) can mushroom pieces,
    drained
½ tsp. salt
½ tsp. celery salt
¼ tsp. black pepper
1 (10-oz.) can cream of mushroom
    soup
½ cup milk
	Combine with hamburger and rice, mixing well.
	Pour in greased 2-qt. casserole dish.

Bake at 350 degrees for approximately 35 minutes.

Yield: 6 servings

Zucchini-Hamburger Casserole

6 cups zucchini, cut in cubes	Cook in boiling water for 5 minutes. Drain.
1 lb. hamburger **½ cup chopped onions**	Brown in skillet and drain.
½ cup saltine cracker crumbs **1½ tsp. salt** **black pepper to taste**	Add to hamburger.
¼ cup butter or margarine **½ cup flour** **2 cups milk**	Make white sauce. (See procedure on page 338.)
1 cup grated cheese	Add to white sauce.

Place half of zucchini in greased 2-qt. casserole dish. Layer with half of hamburger and half of cheese sauce. Repeat layers. Bake at 350 degrees for 35 to 40 minutes.

Yield: 6 servings

Gladys Harman

Zucchini Lasagna (Low Cal.)

1 lb. hamburger **1 small onion, chopped**	Brown in skillet and drain.
1 (15-oz.) tomato sauce **½ tsp. garlic powder** **1 tsp. basil leaves** **1 tsp. ground oregano** **1 tsp. salt** **1 tbsp. sugar**	Add, and simmer uncovered for 10 to 20 minutes.
1½ cups dry cottage cheese **¼ cup grated Romano cheese** **1 egg, lightly beaten**	Combine and have ready.
1½ medium-sized zucchini, peeled **and cut into ¼-inch slices** **¼ cup flour** **1 cup shredded mozzarella cheese** **another ¼ cup grated Romano** **cheese**	Have ready.

Spray a 9 × 9 bake dish with low-calorie nonstick spray. Layer half of zucchini, flour, cottage cheese mixture, meat sauce, and mozzarella in dish. Repeat layers. Sprinkle Romano cheese over top. Bake at 350 degrees for 45 minutes. Let stand 15 minutes before serving.

Yield: 9 servings

Alice Trissel

Zucchini Pie

1 tbsp. fat 1 lb. hamburger ½ cup chopped onion 2 cups chopped raw zucchini (peeled or unpeeled)	Brown in skillet and drain. Spread in an 8-inch-square baking dish.
1 cup shredded cheddar cheese (reserve half) ½ tsp. salt ⅛ tsp. black pepper	Sprinkle over mixture.
1¼ cups milk ¾ cup Bisquick 3 eggs	Combine in mixer bowl or blender, and beat just until smooth. Pour over mixture in dish. Bake at 375 degrees for 25 minutes.
2 tomatoes, chopped (reserved cheese)	Sprinkle over top. Bake 8 to 10 minutes more.

Let set 5 minutes before serving.

Yield: 6 servings

Zucchini Pizza

Crust:

4 cups grated raw zucchini 1 cup mozzarella cheese, shredded (reserve half) 1 cup cheddar cheese, shredded (reserve half) 2 eggs, lightly beaten 3 tbsp. biscuit mix (Bisquick) 1 tsp. salt	Mix together thoroughly and press into a greased 11 × 15 jelly roll pan. Bake in 400-degree oven for 15 to 20 minutes until set.

Topping:

½ to 1 lb. ground beef 1 onion, chopped	Brown in skillet and drain.
1¾ cups pizza sauce*	Stir in. Spread over baked crust.
(reserved cheeses)	Sprinkle over top.

Bake at 375 degrees for 15 minutes more, or until cheese melts. (*You may use commercial sauce or make your own by mixing: 1 (12-oz.) can tomato sauce, ¼ tsp. garlic powder, 1 tsp. dried oregano, ¼ tsp. salt, ⅛ tsp. black pepper, and 2 tsp. sugar.)

VEGETABLE AND MISCELLANEOUS DISHES

Delightful Green Beans

3 or 4 slices bacon	Fry until crisp. Drain and crumble.
1 egg	Beat slightly in saucepan.
3 tbsp. sugar **1 tbsp. vinegar** **1 or 2 tbsp. margarine or bacon grease**	Add. Heat, stirring constantly until thickened.
1 qt. green beans, cooked or canned	Heat thoroughly.

Pour sauce over beans. Sprinkle with crumbled bacon.

Yield: 4 to 6 servings

Dorothy Slabaugh Grove

Favorite Green Beans

¼ cup butter or margarine **¼ cup chopped onions** **¼ cup chopped green pepper**	Sauté in skillet until tender.
1 qt. cooked or canned green beans, drained **½ tsp. salt**	Add and heat to boiling. Remove from heat.
⅔ cup cubed Velveeta cheese	Add, and cover just until slightly melted.

Yield: 4 to 6 servings

Barbara Bowman
Sandy Sherman

Saucy Green Beans

2 tbsp. oil or bacon drippings **½ cup chopped onion**	Sauté in skillet until tender.
1 qt. canned green beans, drained **1 tsp. prepared mustard** **1 tbsp. Worcestershire sauce** **1 tsp. sugar** **1 tsp. seasoned salt**	Add, and cook 4 or 5 minutes. May add a little bean liquid if needed, but beans are better cooked almost dry.
crumbled bacon or chopped cooked ham (optional)	Sprinkle over beans if desired.

Green Beans Supreme

1 med. onion, finely diced **2 tbsp. butter or margarine**	Sauté in skillet until tender.
2 tbsp. flour **1 tsp. salt** **¼ tsp. black pepper**	Blend in, stirring constantly until bubbly.
1 cup commercial sour cream	Stir in until thickened. Remove from heat.
2 (10-oz.) pkg. frozen green beans, **cooked and drained, or 1 qt.** **canned green beans, drained**	Add, mixing well. Pour into a 9-inch-square bake dish.
1 cup shredded cheddar or sharp **cheese**	Sprinkle over top.

Bake at 350 degrees 20 to 25 minutes until bubbly.

Yield: 4 to 6 servings

Annie Weaver

Baked Beans

2½ cups navy or pinto beans **5 cups water**	Soak overnight. Cook in the same water the next morning until almost tender (approx. 1 hour). Drain, reserve liquid.
3 strips bacon or several slices salt **pork**	Fry until browned.
1 cup tomato juice **1 medium onion, chopped** **¼ cup catsup** **¼ cup sorghum molasses** **¼ cup brown sugar** **½ tsp. dry mustard** **1½ tsp. salt** **¼ tsp. black pepper** **1 tsp. chili powder**	Combine with beans and bacon. Pour into 2-qt. casserole, adding enough reserve bean liquid to cover beans and have ½ inch standing above beans in dish.

Bake covered at 300 degrees for 3 hours. Then uncover and bake an additional hour. Add additional bean liquid if needed during baking. At end of baking time, beans should be very moist and coated with syrupy liquid. (May be cooked in Crockpot on low for 8 hours. Do not add extra liquid in Crockpot.)

Yield: 6 servings

Beans and Rice

4 slices bacon or ½ lb. hamburger
⅓ cup green pepper, chopped
1 med. onion, chopped

Sauté in skillet. Drain.

. . . .

1 cup tomatoes or juice
½ tsp. salt
1 tbsp. sugar
¼ tsp. black pepper
¼ tsp. oregano
1½ tsp. chili powder
1 tbsp. parlsey, chopped
1 (16-oz.) can kidney beans, or 2
  cups cooked beans

Add, simmer 10 minutes. Serve over cooked rice.

. . . .

Cook 1 ½ cups rice.

Yield: 6 servings

. . . .

Crockpot Baked Beans

2½ cups (1 lb.) dry pinto, or kidney
  beans
4 cups water

Cook in Crockpot on low overnight.

. . . .

1½ cups tomato sauce
1 large onion, chopped
⅓ cup green pepper, chopped
1 garlic clove, minced
3 tbsp. sorghum molasses
2 tsp. chili powder
1 tsp. dry mustard
2 tsp. salt
2 slices bacon, fried and crumbled
  (optional)

The next morning: add, and cook on low for approximately 6 hours or until tender. (May be baked in 300 degree oven if desired.)

. . . .

Yield: 6 servings

. . . .

Refried Beans

2½ cups (1 lb.) pinto beans
1 med. onion, chopped
5 cups water

Soak beans overnight.

. . . .

3 tbsp. shortening or bacon
  drippings

The next morning: Add, and cook in same water about 1 ½ hours until tender.

. . . .

1¼ tsp. salt
⅛ tsp. black pepper
dash garlic salt

Add, mixing well. Mash beans with potato masher.

| ½ cup grated cheese (optional) | Stir in. |
| 2 to 4 tbsp. fat (bacon drippings is good) | Heat in skillet and fry beans until hot and cheese is melted. |

Yield: 6 servings

Harvard Beets

2 or 3 cups diced cooked or canned beets	Heat with juice until hot through.
½ tsp. salt 2 or 3 tbsp. sugar 1 tbsp. butter	Add.
1 tbsp. cornstarch 1 or 2 tbsp. vinegar	Combine, stirring until dissolved. Then add, stirring until thickened.

Yield: 4 to 6 servings

Baked Broccoli

1 pt. chopped broccoli, fresh or frozen-thawed*	Cook 5 minutes in boiling water. Drain.
1 med. onion, chopped ¼ cup margarine	Sauté in skillet until tender and add.
1 cup minute rice or 1½ cups cooked rice 1 (10-oz.) can cream of chicken or mushroom soup ¼ cup milk ⅔ cup Velveeta cheese, cubed 1 tsp. salt	Mix in. Pour in greased 2-qt. casserole dish.
⅔ cup cornflake crumbs	Sprinkle over top, or sprinkle with paprika.

(*Not necessary to parboil if using frozen broccoli.) Bake at 350 degrees for 45 minutes.

Yield: 4 to 6 servings.

Mae Shank
Pam Weaver

Broccoli Pie

2 cups chopped broccoli, fresh or frozen-thawed*	Cook 5 minutes in boiling water. Drain. Arrange in 8-inch square bake dish.
⅓ cup finely chopped onion ⅓ cup finely chopped green pepper ¾ cup shredded cheese	Sprinkle over broccoli.
3 eggs, beaten 1½ cups milk ¾ cup Bisquick 1 tsp. salt	Beat together, and pour over top. Bake at 375 degrees for 35 to 40 minutes.

(*Not necessary to parboil, if using frozen broccoli.)

Yield: 6 servings

Sour Cream Party Broccoli

4 cups broccoli, fresh or frozen, cut into flowerets	Cook in boiling water until tender, about 10 minutes. Drain well.
2 tbsp. butter 2 tbsp. minced onion	Sauté in saucepan.
1½ cups commercial sour cream 2 tsp. sugar 1 tsp. white vinegar ¼ tsp. paprika ½ tsp. salt dash black pepper	Add, stirring well. Pour sauce over broccoli in heated serving dish.
½ cup broken cashew nuts	Sprinkle over top.

Yield: 4 to 6 servings

Annie Weaver

Baked Cabbage

1 med.-size head cabbage, cut in wedges ¾ inch thick	Cook in boiling water 10 minutes. Drain and place in greased 2-qt. casserole dish or 8 × 12 baking dish.
1 cup chopped corned beef, ham, or crumbled bacon	Sprinkle over top.
⅓ cup margarine ⅓ cup flour 2 cups milk 1 tsp. salt ⅛ tsp. black pepper	Make white sauce. (See procedure on page 338.) Pour over mixture in dish.

½ to 1 cup grated cheese	Sprinkle over top.

Bake at 350 degrees for 30 to 35 minutes.

Yield: 6 servings

Baked Cabbage Supreme

1 med.-size head cabbage, shredded (2 or 3 lbs.)	Cook until almost tender, about 8 minutes. Drain.
⅓ cup melted margarine ⅓ lb. Waverly wafer crumbs (crush 13 triple crackers)	Mix thoroughly. Set aside.
3 tbsp. margarine ⅓ cup flour 2 cups milk 1 tsp. salt	Make white sauce. (See procedure on page 338.) Mix with cabbage and put in 8 × 12 bake dish. Top with crumbs.

Bake at 335 degrees for about 45 minutes until browned. May also be topped with grated cheese instead of crumbs if desired. Add cheese 5 minutes before casserole is done so cheese can melt.

Yield: 6 servings

Elizabeth Yoder

Easy Cabbage Casserole

1 med.-size head cabbage, cut in wedges	Parboil 10 minutes. Drain and place in greased 8 × 12 bake dish.
1 (10-oz.) can cheddar cheese soup ½ soup can milk ½ tsp. salt	Mix, and pour over cabbage.
¼ cup bacon bits or crumbled bacon	Sprinkle over top.
1 (2.8-oz.) can French-fried onion rings.	

Bake at 350 degrees for about 30 minutes. Remove from oven and sprinkle with onion rings. Bake 5 to 10 minutes more.

Yield: 6 servings

Stuffed Cabbage (or Cabbage Rolls)

1 large head cabbage	Cut bottom core from cabbage. Place in boiling water to cover, without lid, and cook until leaves can be separated easily. Remove from water to cool.

2 eggs, beaten **1½ lbs. ground beef** **1 small onion, minced** **¾ cup tomato sauce** **½ cup uncooked rice** **1 tsp. salt** **⅛ tsp. black pepper**	Mix together thoroughly. Roll about 1 tbsp. mixture in each cabbage leaf. (Amount depends on leaf size.) Fold over sides, and beginning at stalk end, roll to leaf end. Fasten with toothpick if necessary. Shred small leaves and place in heavy pot. Arrange rolls seam side down over top.

1 small onion, minced **1 tbsp. margarine**	Sauté in saucepan until translucent.

2 (8-oz.) cans tomato sauce **3½ cups canned tomatoes** **juice of 2 lemons (about ⅓ cup)** **¾ cup brown sugar** **1 tsp. salt** **½ cup white raisins (optional)**	Add, and simmer several minutes.

Pour over cabbage rolls in pot. Bake, covered, at 375 degrees for 2 hours. Then reduce heat to 325 degrees and bake, uncovered, another 30 to 45 minutes until glazed. (Some cooks place the head of cabbage in the freezer overnight before making rolls to wilt it. This eliminates the preliminary cooking.)

Yield: 12 to 16 servings

Carolyn H. Reed

Orange-Spiced Carrots

8 med. size-carrots (about 1 lb.)	Cook until tender in small amount of water. Drain—save liquid for soup

¼ cup orange juice, or 1 rounded **tsp. orange-flavored breakfast** **drink powder** **2 tsp. cornstarch** **1 tbsp. sugar** **½ tsp. salt** **¼ tsp. ground ginger** **dash nutmeg**	Combine, then add, stirring until slightly thickened.

1 tbsp. margarine	Stir in.

Yield: 4 to 5 servings

Baked Carrots

4 cups carrots, cut in rings	Cook until tender, 15 to 20 minutes. Drain. Pour into 1 ½-qt. casserole dish.
3 tbsp. margarine **1 med. onion, chopped**	Sauté until tender.
⅓ cup flour **1¾ cups milk** **1 tsp. salt** **1 tsp. sugar** **¼ tsp. dry mustard**	Slowly add flour, then milk and seasoning, making white sauce.
⅔ cup grated cheddar cheese	Combine with carrots in dish. Pour white sauce over mixture.
1½ cups soft bread crumbs **3 tbsp. melted butter**	Mix and sprinkle over top.

Bake at 350 degrees for 25 to 30 minutes. (**Variation:** May use 1 can cream of celery soup in place of the white sauce. Omit mustard. May reserve half of cheese and sprinkle over top in place of bread crumbs.)

Yield: 6 servings

Sweet and Sour Carrots

2 to 3 lbs. carrots, sliced in rings	Cook until tender, 15 to 20 minutes. Drain.
1 (10-oz.) can tomato soup **1 cup sugar** **½ cup vegetable oil** **1 tsp. salt** **⅛ tsp. black pepper** **2 tsp. Worcestershire sauce** **¼ cup chopped green pepper** **⅓ cup chopped onion** **½ tsp. dry mustard** **¼ cup vinegar**	Combine in saucepan. Cook 10 minutes. Pour over carrots and let marinate 4 hours. Serve hot or cold.

Yield: 6 to 8 servings   *Karen Blosser*

Cauliflower (or Vegetables) and Cheese Sauce

1 large head cauliflower, whole	Cook in boiling water just until tender, 20 to 30 minutes. Drain.

3 tbsp. margarine **3 tbsp. flour** **1½ cups milk**	Make white sauce. (See procedure on page 338.)

¾ cup chopped Velveeta cheese **½ tsp. salt**	Add, stirring until melted.

Place head of cauliflower in warm dish. Pour sauce over top. (This recipe may be used with other vegetables such as broccoli, brussel sprouts, etc.)

Yield: 4 servings

Celery Supreme

4 or 5 cups diced celery **½ cup chopped green pepper** **½ cup water**	Combine, and cook 10 minutes. Drain.

1 (2-oz.) jar pimientos **¾ tsp. salt** **1 (10-oz.) can cream of celery or** **cream of mushroom soup** **1 (8-oz.) can sliced water chestnuts,** **drained**	Combine with celery and pour in greased 1½-qt. casserole dish.

¼ cup melted butter **1½ cups soft bread crumbs**	Mix and sprinkle over the top.

Bake at 350 degrees for 25 to 30 minutes or until bubbly through.

Yield: 6 to 8 servings

Chow Mein Noodles

(These taste so fresh, we like them better than the commercial ones.)

Cook desired amount of fine noodles or thin spaghetti in salted water until tender, about 10 to 12 minutes. (If using spaghetti, break into 3-inch lengths before cooking.) Drain immediately, and quickly rinse well with cold water. Drain thoroughly. Spread in a thin layer on paper towels on tray and chill thoroughly in refrigerator. Fry in deep hot fat (375 degrees) until lightly browned. Fry only ⅓ of a cup at a time. CAUTION: If there is too much moisture and you try to do too many at once, you may cause the fat to boil over. If noodles bunch together while frying, separate with a fork. Drain on paper towels. Sprinkle with salt. (See tips for deep fat frying on page 50.)

Baked Corn

2 cups fresh or canned corn **3 tbsp. melted margarine**	Place in greased 1 ½-qt. casserole dish.
1 tsp. salt **2 tsp. sugar** **1 tbsp. flour**	Mix, then stir in.
2 eggs, lightly beaten **1 cup milk**	Combine, then pour over mixture in dish.
½ cup grated cheese	Have ready.

Bake at 350 degrees for 30 to 35 minutes. Sprinkle with cheese, and bake 5 minutes more until cheese is melted and corn is firm.

Yield: 4 to 6 servings

Eggplant Casserole

¼ cup margarine **1 large onion, chopped** **1 green or red sweet pepper,** **chopped** **½ cup rice (uncooked)**	Sauté in skillet until lightly browned.
1 large eggplant, peeled and cubed	Parboil until almost tender, about 5 minutes. Drain.
1 cup beef broth or bouillon **1 tsp. salt** **¼ tsp. black pepper** **1 cup grated cheese (reserve half)**	Combine with onion mixture and egg-plant. Pour in greased 2-qt. casserole dish.

Cover and bake at 350 degrees for 45 minutes. Sprinkle with reserved cheese, and bake, un-covered, 15 minutes more.

Yield: 6 servings

Italian Tomato Sauce

(Janet said many Italians eat pasta every day for lunch. To test for doneness when cooking pasta, they remove a piece and bite into it. If no white remains, they consider it done.)

1 tbsp. vegetable oil 1 garlic clove, chopped 1 small onion, chopped	Sauté in skillet.

3 cups tomato juice or canned tomatoes, chopped 1 tbsp. olive oil ½ tbsp. sugar 1 tsp. salt basil to taste dash of black pepper	Add. Cook until thickened (15 to 20 minutes).

Serve over spaghetti or other pasta.

Janet Blosser

Baked Macaroni and Cheese

1½ cups macaroni	Cook in boiling water 10 minutes. Drain. Pour into greased 8-inch-square bake dish.

3 tbsp. fine saltine cracker crumbs 1 cup cubed cheddar cheese	Mix in.

1 tsp. salt ¼ tsp. black pepper	Sprinkle over mixture.

2 cups milk 1 small egg, beaten	Mix and pour over all.

¼ cup melted butter or margarine	Pour over top.

Bake at 350 degrees for 45 minutes.

Yield: 6 servings

Easy Bake Macaroni

1½ cups macaroni (uncooked) 2 tbsp. melted butter 1 tsp. salt pepper to taste	Stir together. Pour into greased 1 ½ or 2-qt. casserole dish.

1¼ cups cubed Velveeta cheese	Mix in.

4 cups milk   Pour over all.

Bake at 235 degrees for 3 hours. Remove from oven and let set 10 minutes before serving. This casserole needs long, slow cooking for best results. It is nice to put in the oven while at church.

Louise Heatwole

Noodles

3 egg yolks, slightly beaten   Combine.
3 tbsp. water
½ tsp. salt

approximately 1½ cups flour   Gradually add flour to make a stiff dough. Knead a few times until smooth.

Roll into a large circle *as thin as possible* on floured surface. Let dry for 1 to 2 hours. Do not allow dough to get too dry that it becomes brittle. It should be slightly moist. Fold up dough in layers. Cut into narrow strips. Drop in boiling broth and cook 10 to 15 minutes. Any extra should be dried thoroughly before storing.

Yield: 6 cups noodles   *Brownie Burkholder*

Cheesy Onions Supreme

1 (16-oz.) bag frozen small white   Cook in salt water about 5 minutes and drain.
    onions
¼ tsp. salt

2 tbsp. margarine   Make white sauce. (See procedure on page 338.)
3 tbsp. flour
1½ cups milk
salt and pepper to taste

4 or 5 slices American cheese   Have ready.
2 or 3 tbsp. saltine cracker crumbs

Layer half of onions, cheese, and white sauce in greased 1½-qt. casserole dish. Repeat layers. Top with crumbs. Bake at 350 degrees for 30 to 40 minutes.

Yield: 5 to 6 servings   *Ruth Heatwole*

Creamed Onions

Cook quartered medium-size onions in water until tender, about 15 to 25 minutes, depending on age. Add salt, butter, and cream batter to thicken liquid.

. . . .

Onion Rings

3 or 4 onions	Cut into rings ⅓ of an inch thick

. . . .

½ cup flour	Beat together until smooth. Dip onion rings,
¼ tsp. salt	then fry in hot fat (375 degrees) until browned,
½ tsp. baking powder	about 2 minutes. Drain on paper towel.
1 egg, slightly beaten	
2 tbsp. oil	
¼ cup milk	

. . . .

Stuffed Pepper Skillet

6 med. green peppers	Cut off tops, cut in half, take out seeds and membrane.

. . . .

1 lb. lean hamburger	Mix together thoroughly and stuff peppers.
1½ cups cooked rice	Stand peppers up around edge of skillet.
1 med. onion, finely chopped	
⅓ cup tomato juice	
1 tbsp. Worcestershire sauce	
1 tsp. salt	
1 tsp. sugar	
¼ cup water	

. . . .

4 cups carrots, cut in ¼-inch rings	Pile in center of the skillet. Sprinkle with salt
¾ tsp. salt	and dot with butter.
1 tbsp. butter	

. . . .

2 tbsp. light corn syrup	Have ready.

. . . .

Pour ½ cup water in skillet, cover, and simmer for 45 minutes. Drizzle corn syrup over carrots and serve.

Yield: 6 servings

. . . .

Gardener's Pizza

Crust:

1¼ cups flour	Sift together into bowl.
¾ cup enriched cornmeal	
1 tsp. baking powder	
1 tsp. salt	

⅔ cup milk **¼ cup vegetable oil**	Combine and stir in until mixture forms a ball.

Place on greased 14-inch round pizza pan. Let stand 5 minutes, then press dough into pan with back of large spoon. Shape edge to form rim. Bake at 400 degrees for 15 minutes. Remove from oven.

Topping:

2½ cups pizza sauce	Spread over crust.

1 med. green pepper, cut into thin rings **1 med. onion, thinly sliced** **1 med. zucchini, thinly sliced** **2 cups shredded mozzarella cheese** **¼ cup grated Parmesan cheese**	Arrange over top.

Return to oven and continue baking at 400 degrees for 15 to 20 minutes longer until golden brown.

Yield: 6 servings   *Jewel Shenk*

Baked Mashed Potatoes

(This is a versatile dish that can be refrigerated ahead, and then baked later. It can also be taken to a potluck meal in a Crockpot.)

6 cups mashed potatoes **8 oz. cream cheese** **¼ cup melted margarine** **1 tsp. salt** **¼ cup finely chopped onion, or ¼ tsp. onion powder** **½ tsp. garlic salt** **1 cup dairy sour cream**	Beat together until well blended. (If needed, add a little milk.) Pour into a greased 2-qt. casserole dish.

Bake at 350 degrees for 45 to 55 minutes. If potatoes are freshly mashed and are hot, this dish can be served without baking, or baking time may be reduced considerably.

Yield: 8 servings   *Carol Wyant*

Browned or Fried Potatoes and Onion

For browned potatoes, cook whole small potatoes until almost tender. Drain, sprinkle with a litte flour and salt, and fry in butter in skillet until browned on all sides. For fried potatoes and onions, grate raw potatoes or slice thin, cover, and fry in fat in skillet with chopped onions until tender—about 20 minutes, turning occasionally. Add salt when almost done.

Cheese Potato Balls

Peel, boil, and mash potatoes with salt and enough milk to make smooth and creamy, but a little stiffer than for serving. Cool slightly for easier handling. With hands, roll a heaping tablespoon of potato around a cube of American cheese. Then roll balls in crushed cornflake crumbs. Spoon a little melted butter over the top. Place in baking pan and bake at 350 degrees until browned. These can be made ahead and heated about 20 to 25 minutes just before serving. Serve at once. (Two small balls make a more attractive serving than one large one.)

. . . .

Cottage Potatoes

5 large potatoes, cooked and diced or grated	Mix well and pour into a greased 2 or 2½-qt. casserole dish.
1 cup grated cheddar cheese	
1 med. onion, chopped	
2 tbsp. chopped parsley	
½ cup fresh bread crumbs	
1 tsp. salt	
¼ tsp. black pepper	

. . . .

1½ cups milk	Heat together until margarine is melted. Pour over mixture.
⅓ cup margarine	

. . . .

½ cup cornflake crumbs	Sprinkle over the top.

. . . .

Bake at 350 degrees for 35 to 40 minutes.

Yield: 8 servings

. . . .

Creamed Potatoes and Turnips

Cook together half white potatoes and half young turnips until tender. Add cream batter to thicken liquid. Add salt and a little butter.

. . . .

Crispy Potatoes

(Potatoes the size of small walnuts are ideal for this recipe.)

Cook enough potatoes for a dishfull (5 or 6 med. or 18 very small) in boiling salted water (1 tsp. salt) for 15 minutes, or until almost tender. Drain. Roll 2 cups cornflakes into fine crumbs. Mix with ½ tsp. salt and 1 tsp. paprika. Coat potatoes with melted butter (about 2 tbsp.), and roll in crumbs. Place single layer in shallow bake dish and bake at 350 degrees for 25 to 30 minutes. These can be prepared ahead and covered with plastic wrap. Then bake at the last minute for guests.

French-Fried Potatoes
(See directions for deep-fat frying on page 50.)

Peel potatoes and cut into long narrow strips—about ¼-inch wide. Pat off excess moisture with a towel to prevent boil-over when frying. Heat fat to 375 degrees. Fill basket ¼ full, letting it down into the hot fat slowly. If fat threatens to boil over, lift basket up and down a few times until moisture has dissipated. Fry until crisp and golden brown—approximately 5 to 8 minutes. Drain on paper towels. Place towels over newspaper to help absorb grease. Sprinkle with salt and serve immediately.

. . . .

Baked 'French-Fried' Potatoes

Prepare 1 large potato for each person. Peel and cut into thin strips and place in a bowl. Pour 1 tbsp. vegetable oil for each potato over strips, tossing to coat well. Spread out in a single layer on cookie sheet. Broil in a 425-degree oven for 10 minutes until lightly browned. Reduce heat to 350 degrees and broil another 20 to 30 minutes until potatoes are tender throughout, turning with spatula occasionally. Sprinkle with salt and serve immediately.

. . . .

Diet Stuffed Potatoes (Low Cal.)

Prick 2 potatoes with a fork to let out steam, and bake in 375-degree oven for 50 minutes to 1 hour until soft. Cut in half lengthwise. Scoop out potato from each half, being careful not to break skins. Place potato in mixing bowl.

. . . .

½ cup lowfat cottage cheese
1 bouillon cube dissolved in ¼ cup
   boiling water
1 tbsp. fresh onion, minced
2 tbsp. chopped fresh parsley
¼ tsp. salt
dash black pepper

Add, beating until smooth. Spoon back into potato skins. Place on baking sheet. Bake at 350 degrees for 10 to 15 minutes until lightly browned.

. . . .

Yield: 4 servings

. . . .

Scalloped Potatoes

Put layers of sliced raw potatoes and finely chopped onion in greased casserole dish. Blend ½ cup milk into 1 (10-oz.) can cream of chicken (or mushroom) soup. Pour over potatoes. Dot with butter and sprinkle with paprika. Bake at 350 degrees for at least 1 hour. Two tbsp. chopped green pepper may also be added, and ⅔ cup grated cheese, if desired. Potatoes may be cooked on top of the stove first. Then slice or shred into dish. Baking time should be cut to about 30 minutes.

. . . .

Old-Fashioned Scalloped Potatoes

6 med. potatoes   Peel and slice ⅛-inch thick.

¼ cup flour   Mix and have ready.
1½ tsp. salt
¼ tsp. black pepper
¼ tsp. MSG

½ to 1 cup shredded sharp cheese   Have ready.
2½ cups hot milk
2 tbsp. butter

In greased 2-qt. casserole dish, layer ⅓ potatoes, and sprinkle with ⅓ of flour mixture and cheese. Repeat with two more layers. Pour hot milk over mixture. Dot with butter and bake at 350 degrees for 1 hour. (Or make a white sauce of ¼ cup margarine, ¼ cup flour, and 3 cups milk. You may also sauté ¼ cup chopped onion and 3 tbsp. chopped green pepper in the margarine before adding flour if desired. Pour over layers of potatoes and cheese in place of flour mixture.)

Yield: 8 servings

Scalloped Potatoes Supreme

(This dish can be frozen ahead before baking for a busy day. Or prepare a day ahead and refrigerate until time to bake—excellent to prepare on Saturday night to bake for Sunday dinner.)

7 cups cooked shredded potatoes   Combine in greased 2-qt. casserole dish.
⅓ cup chopped onion
1½ to 2 cups shredded cheddar
cheese (reserve half)

1 (10-oz.) can cream of chicken soup   Mix together thoroughly and pour over potato
¾ cup milk   mixture.
1 cup (8-oz.) commercial sour cream
¼ cup margarine, melted
½ tsp. salt
black pepper to taste

Top with reserved cheese. Bake at 350 degrees for 1 hour.

Variation: Omit soup and add 2 beaten eggs and ¼ cup dry bread crumbs instead. Or omit sour cream and increase milk to 1¾ cups instead.

Yield: 8 servings

Edith Branner
Louise Heatwole

How to Cook Rice

Place 1 cup rice, 2 ½ cups water, 1 tbsp. butter or margarine, and 1 tsp. salt in saucepan. Bring to a good rolling boil. Stir thoroughly over the bottom of pan to loosen any grains that may be sticking. Then cover with a tight-fitting lid and simmer for 20 minutes. Do not lift lid at all during this time. After 20 minutes, turn off burner. Keep covered until ready to serve. Then stir briskly to fluff rice before placing it in serving dish. Do not let sit long, however, or it will get sticky. (1 cup raw rice makes approximately 3 cups cooked rice.)

Easy Oven-Cooked Rice

2 cups rice
4 cups hot water
1 tsp. salt
2 tbsp. butter

Mix all ingredients together in greased 2 qt. casserole dish.

Bake, covered, in 350-degree oven for 1 hour. (**Variation:** Add 1 env. onion soup mix to mixture before baking.)

Yield: 8 servings

Browned Rice

1½ cups rice (uncooked)
3 tbsp. margarine

Fry (dry) rice in margarine in skillet until golden brown. Pour into greased 1 ½ -qt. casserole dish.

¼ tsp. garlic powder
½ tsp. sage
½ tsp. chicken bouillon (or dissolve
 1 cube in hot water)
½ tsp. salt
½ cup chopped canned tomatoes

Mix in.

3 cups boiling water

Pour over top. Do not stir.

Cover and bake at 350 degrees for 1 hour, or at 250 degrees for 2 ¼ hours. Serve with chicken.

Yield: 6 servings   *Evie King*

Rice Casserole

1½ cups rice (uncooked)
2 cups chicken broth or bouillon
1 cup hot water
2 tbsp. finely chopped celery
2 tbsp. finely chopped onion
2 tbsp. finely chopped green pepper
2 tbsp. butter or margarine, melted
1 tsp. salt
¼ tsp. garlic powder
⅛ tsp. black pepper

Combine in greased 1 ½ or 2-qt. casserole dish, stirring well.

Cover and bake at 350 degrees for 1 hour.

Yield: 6 servings

Baked Salsify

2 cups cooked or canned salsify,
   sliced in ⅛ to ¼-inch rings
2 cups saltine cracker crumbs

Mix in greased 8-inch-square bake dish.

1 tsp. salt
¼ tsp. pepper

Sprinkle over salsify.

2 cups milk, including a small
   amount of the liquid from salsify
4 eggs, beaten

Combine and pour over mixture.

3 tbsp. butter or margarine

Dot over top.

2 tbsp. chopped parsley

Sprinkle over all.

Bake at 350 degrees for approximately 45 minutes until lightly browned on top.

Yield: 8 servings

Tasty Sauerkraut

(Elva says sometimes she just simmers the kraut on top of the stove. If using bacon strips with this method, fry first and then crumble into the other ingredients.)

1 (2 lb.) bag sauerkraut (about 3
   cups)
¼ cup brown sugar
½ cup water
dash Tabasco sauce
¼ cup bacon drippings—melted, or
   4 strips bacon*

Combine all ingredients in a 1 ½-qt. casserole dish. Bake, covered, at 325 degrees for 1 hour.

(*If using bacon instead of drippings, lay strips of bacon over the top of casserole. Uncover for the last 10 to 15 minutes so bacon will brown.)

Elva Holloway

Yield: 4 to 6 servings

Hot Slaw

1 tbsp. butter	Melt in saucepan.
3 or 4 cups shredded cabbage ¾ cup water	Add. Cover and cook slowly for 10 minutes.
½ cup water 1 tbsp. flour	Combine in batter shaker and shake until smooth. Add, stirring until thickened.
1 tsp. salt 2 tbsp. sugar 1 tbsp. vinegar	Mix in thoroughly.

Yield: 4 servings

Frances Harman

Favorite Soybeans

3 cups green soybeans	Cook until tender in water to nearly cover, for 1 to 1 ½ hrs. Or pressure-cook 1 ½ minutes in ½ cup water.
¼ to ⅓ lb. hamburger	Brown and drain. Then add.
½ cup tomato juice 1 tsp. salt 2 tsp. sugar ½ tsp. chili powder	Add, and heat just to boiling again.

Yield: 4 to 5 servings

Fried Squash or Eggplant

1 or 2 tender squash or 1 eggplant	Cut into ¼-inch slices.
1 slightly beaten egg	Dip slices in.
1½ cups fine saltine cracker crumbs	Press slices in crumbs.
3 tbsp. butter or margarine	Melt in skillet and fry slices until browned on each side and tender.
salt	Sprinkle over slices while frying.

Delicious Spinach

2 lbs. fresh spinach, or 1 (18-oz.) pkg. frozen spinach, chopped	Cook 5 to 10 minutes until tender. Do not overcook. Drain *well*.
½ cup commercial sour cream **½ tsp. salt** **1 tsp. sugar** **½ tbsp. imitation bacon bits** **½ tbsp. dried onion flakes**	Add, and heat just to boiling point again. Do not cook. Serve immediately.

Yield: 4 to 6 servings

Savory Spinach

2 lbs. fresh spinach, or 1 (18 oz.) pkg. frozen spinach	Cook 5 to 10 minutes until tender. Drain *well*.
½ cup milk **1 tbsp. flour**	Shake in batter shaker until smooth. Stir into spinach until thickened.
5 slices bacon	Fry until crisp. Drain, crumble, and add.
½ tsp. rosemary, crumbled **¼ tsp. nutmeg** **½ tsp. salt** **1 chicken bouillon cube, mashed well**	Stir in until blended.

Yield: 4 to 6 servings

Spinach or Broccoli Casserole

2 (10-oz.) pkgs. frozen chopped spinach or broccoli	Cook 5 to 10 minutes until tender. Drain well.
2 eggs, beaten **2 onions, chopped** **1 (10-oz.) can cream of mushroom soup** **¾ cup mayonnaise** **½ tsp. salt** **1 cup grated sharp cheese**	Mix in and pour into greased 8 × 12 baking dish.
1½ cups soft bread crumbs **3 tbsp. butter, melted**	Mix together and sprinkle over top.

Bake at 350 degrees for 40 to 45 minutes.

Yield: 8 servings   *Kathryn Heatwole*

Butternut Squash Casserole

3 cups cooked, mashed butternut squash
½ cup sugar
½ cup brown sugar
¼ cup margarine, melted
1 (8-oz.) can crushed pineapple, undrained
1 tsp. ground cinnamon
1 tsp. vanilla
⅛ tsp. ground nutmeg

Combine thoroughly and pour into greased 2-qt. casserole dish.

....

⅓ cup chopped peanuts

Sprinkle over top.

....

Bake at 325 degrees for 40 to 45 minutes.

Yield: 6 servings

....

Squash-Onion Casserole

3 cups cooked cubed squash
½ cup chopped onion
1 cup bread crumbs
½ cup milk
3 tbsp. melted butter
2 eggs, beaten
1 tsp. Italian seasoning
salt and pepper to taste

Mix together thoroughly and pour into 2-qt. greased casserole dish.

....

3 slices bacon, crisply fried and crumbled
1 cup grated cheese

Sprinkle over top.

....

Bake at 350 degrees for 45 to 55 minutes.

Yield: 6 servings

....

Vegetable Spaghetti Squash

Boil whole vegetable spaghetti squash in water for 30 minutes. Cut open and scoop out center. Eat with spaghetti sauce, or with butter and melted cheese. Or cut in half. Place cut sides down in bake dish. Bake at 350 degrees for 1 hour.

The Wetsel Seed Company

....

Candied Sweet Potatoes

6 med. sweet potatoes	Peel, cut in chunks, and cook until tender. Arrange in greased 2-qt. casserole dish.
½ cup brown sugar **½ tsp. salt** **1 tbsp. cornstarch** **1 cup crushed pineapple, undrained** **½ cup orange soda pop, or orange juice** **¼ cup margarine, melted**	Combine in saucepan. Cook until thickened, stirring constantly. Pour over potatoes in dish.

Bake at 350 degrees for 20 to 25 minutes.

Yield: 6 servings   *Harriet Steiner*

Orange-Glazed Sweet Potatoes

1 cup water	Heat in skillet until boiling.
1 (3-oz.) pkg. orange-flavored gelatin	Add, stirring until dissolved.
½ cup brown sugar **½ tsp. salt** **¼ cup butter or margarine**	Mix in thoroughly.
2 (16-oz.) cans sweet potatoes, drained, or 6 med. home-cooked sweet potatoes	Add.
¼ tsp. allspice	Sprinkle over potatoes, and simmer for 5 minutes.
¼ cup water **1 tbsp. cornstarch**	Dissolve and stir in until thickened. Spoon over potatoes to glaze.

Yield: 6 servings

Sweet Potato Bake

6 med. sweet potatoes, cooked and mashed (3 or 4 cups) **½ cup milk, or ¼ cup milk and ¼ cup orange juice** **2 eggs** **1 tsp. vanilla** **½ cup sugar** **½ tsp. salt** **3 tbsp. butter, melted** **½ tsp. nutmeg**	Beat together just until well blended. Pour in 2-qt. casserole dish.

Pecan Topping:
⅓ cup butter
¾ cup brown sugar
½ cup flour
¾ cup chopped pecans

Mix until crumbly and sprinkle over top.

Bake at 350 degrees until hot through, about 45 minutes if potatoes were cold when put in dish, or 25 minutes if they were hot. (Optional Topping: Instead of pecan topping, sprinkle 2 cups miniature marshmallows over casserole about 5 minutes before oven time is up.)

Vegetable Casserole

1 (10-oz.) pkg. frozen lima beans
1 (20-oz.) bag frozen broccoli and cauliflower

Cook 10 minutes with lid slightly tilted. Drain. Arrange in greased 2-qt. casserole dish.

1 (8-oz.) jar Cheez Whiz, or 1⅓ cups finely diced Velveeta cheese
1 (10-oz.) can cream of mushroom soup

Blend together for sauce. Pour over vegetables. Bake at 350 degrees for 35 minutes.

onion rings to garnish

Sprinkle over top. Bake 5 minutes more.

Yield: 6 to 8 servings

Elizabeth Yoder

Zucchini-Vegetable Pot (Low Cal.)

2 cups diced zucchini
2 stems celery, chopped
¼ cup green pepper, chopped
1 large onion, chopped
2 large tomatoes, peeled and chopped
¼ cup uncooked rice

Combine in large cooking pot and cook until tender, about 20 minutes.

1 tsp. salt
1 tbsp. sugar or artificial sweetener
¼ tsp. garlic salt
⅛ tsp. sage
⅛ tsp. nutmeg
⅛ tsp. black pepper
1 tsp. Worcestershire sauce

Add seasoning, cook 5 minutes more.

(May also add ½ lb. browned and drained hamburger if desired.)

Yield: 6 servings

Baked Zucchini Squash

6 cups raw, cubed zucchini squash **½ cup chopped onions**	Cook 5 minutes and drain. Have ready.
7 oz. pkg. seasoned stuffing (such **as Pepperidge) (reserve half)**	Pour half in greased 2-qt. casserole dish.
1 (10-oz.) can cream of chicken soup **1 cup commercial sour cream*** **1 cup grated carrots** **1½ tsp. salt**	Combine, then mix with squash, and pour over stuffing.
¼ cup melted margarine	Mix with reserved stuffing and sprinkle over top.

Bake at 350 degrees for 35 minutes or until done. (*May substitute ¼ cup milk mixed with 2 tbsp. mayonnaise, if desired.)

Yield: 6 to 8 servings

Grace Campbell

Favorite Zucchini Casserole

2½ cups peeled and shredded raw **zucchini squash** **1½ cups dry bread crumbs** **1 env. golden onion soup mix** **1 tsp. salt** **1 tsp. crushed basil leaves** **4 eggs, lightly beaten** **⅓ cup milk** **1 cup shredded Swiss cheese** **(reserve half)** **2 tbsp. grated Parmesan cheese** **(reserve half)**	Combine all ingredients and pour into greased 8-inch square bake dish. Sprinkle reserved cheese over top.

Bake at 350 degrees for 40 to 45 minutes.

Yield: 6 servings

MISCELLANEOUS

Homemade Herb-Seasoned Bread Cubes

Use your own bread scraps, and cut into small cubes. Spread out on a baking tray. Spray with small amount of vegetable shortening and sprinkle with desired herbs—use oregano, thyme, garlic powder, celery salt, onion salt, or Italian seasoning, etc. Allow to dry thoroughly. May be put in a 250-degree oven for about ½ hour, but do not brown. Approximately 4½ cups of cubes equal an 8-oz. bag of stuffing. Make a big batch and store for instant use. Will keep indefinitely on pantry shelf, if thoroughly dried.

Cream Batter (for Vegetables)

It is best to cook vegetables in a small amount of water so there is only about ½ cup liquid remaining on them when vegetables are tender. (Use more or less batter for varying amounts of liquid.) For ½ cup liquid on vegetables, combine ½ cup cream or rich milk and 2 tbsp. flour in batter shaker. Shake until smooth. Stir into vegetables, cooking just until thickened. Add salt and a little butter. Remove from heat and serve.

. . . .

Blender Hollandaise Sauce

(Good on eggs, fish, and vegetables, especially asparagus)

All ingredients should be at room temperature. Melt ½ cup butter over low heat until it begins to foam. In blender container, place 2 tbsp. lemon juice, 3 egg yolks, and ½ tsp. salt. Blend at high speed for 30 seconds. Mixture will be thick and foamy. Remove the little insert cap in blender lid, turn blender to high speed, and *slowly* add butter in thin stream until all is added and mixture is thick and smooth. (If sauce would not thicken, turn blender on high, and *slowly* pour sauce back into blender in thin stream blending on high speed until thickened.) Serve sauce at once, or place container in pan of very warm, but not hot, water for up to 1 hour until ready to serve. Keep covered to prevent film from forming over the top. Yield: ¾ cup

. . . .

Mock Hollandaise Sauce

¼ cup mayonnaise or salad
 dressing
¼ cup dairy sour cream
1 tsp. sugar
1 tsp. lemon juice
½ tsp. prepared mustard

Combine and heat over low heat just until hot.

. . . .

Yield: ½ cup

. . . .

Salt Substitute

2 tbsp. onion powder
1 tbsp. garlic powder
1 tbsp. paprika
1 tbsp. dry mustard
1 tsp. thyme
½ tsp. white or black pepper
½ tsp. celery seeds

Mix thoroughly.

. . . .

Yield: ⅓ cup

. . . .

White Sauce

(This basic sauce or variations may be used in place of canned soups.)

¼ to ⅓ cup* butter or margarine	Melt in saucepan.
¼ to ⅓ cup* flour	Stir in until smooth and bubbly.
2 cups milk	Slowly add, stirring constantly until thickened and smooth. (Pan may be removed from heat just while adding milk to help avoid lumps. Then return to heat until smooth and bubbly.)

(*This amount makes a medium to medium-thick sauce. For thin sauce, use 3 tbsp. each of flour and fat with the 2 cups of milk.)

Optional Mixing Method:
It is easier to make sauce without lumps by this optional method even though taste may be slightly more bland since cooking fat and flour together brings out additional flavor.

1¼ cups milk	Heat in saucepan.
¾ cup milk ¼ to ⅓ cup flour	Combine in batter shaker and shake until smooth. Stir into hot milk until thickened. Remove from heat.
2 or 3 tbsp. butter or margarine	Add for flavor. (Less fat may be used if desired for lower calorie sauce.)

Variations: Celery sauce—sauté ½ cup finely chopped celery and 1 tbsp. minced onion in fat before adding flour. **Cheese sauce**—add ½ to ¾ cup grated cheese and ¼ tsp. dry mustard. Stir until melted. **Chicken sauce**—add 1 cup chicken broth or bouillon in place of 1 cup of the milk. Add ¼ tsp. poultry seasoning and a little chopped cooked chicken if desired. **Mushroom sauce**—sauté ⅓ cup chopped mushrooms and 1 tbsp. minced onion in fat before adding flour. **Tomato sauce**—use tomato juice in place of milk. Sprinkle in a little onion and garlic salt, oregano, and sugar.

Sour Cream Dressing for Baked Potatoes

1 cup mayonnaise 1 cup commercial sour cream 1 tbsp. parsley flakes 1¼ tsp. dill weed 1 tsp. seasoned salt ½ tsp. (or more) onion powder	Blend together thoroughly.

Yield: 2 cups

CHAPTER SEVEN

MEATS, POULTRY, & SEAFOOD

MEATS, POULTRY, AND SEAFOOD

MEAT

Since I grew up on a farm, meat was always an important part of the majority of meals at my home. With the strenuous field work, the philosophy seemed to prevail that you always needed some meat to stick to your ribs! Each year we butchered a beef, five or six hogs, numerous chickens, and some turkeys. Besides this, we had fish and occasionally butchered a sheep. This was for a family of 12 children plus many guests and extra farmhands for harvest seasons. I often wonder how many persons were fed at our table in a year's time!

For the majority of families today, meat is still the favorite main dish for the principal meal of the day. Nutritionists report however, that Americans as a whole consume too much meat for their physical well-being. So it is good to see people using more discretion in this area of their diet.

Meat is considered the most complete source of protein and also contains many other vitamins and minerals. However, it can easily be supplemented with other protein-rich foods. Milk, cheese, eggs, and beans can contribute to an economical and yet well-balanced diet with plenty of protein.

For those on the farm who raise and butcher their own animals, good-quality meat is often taken for granted. But those who buy meat soon learn the advantage of being knowledgeable about it.

For many people the highest portion of the food dollar is spent on meat. It is important to buy wisely and to cook and serve meat to the best advantage.

For the best-quality meat, young animals are confined closely in feedlots and placed on special feed to fatten them at least the last several weeks before slaughter. With exercise at a minimum, the muscles become weaker and tender. The lean meat becomes marbleized with flecks of fat. The fat separates the strands of meat, and when cooked, it melts throughout the meat, making it much more juicy, tender, and flavorful. Animals that have been active right before slaughter and have not been fattened will have tougher muscles and the meat will not be nearly as tender. The meat is also much tougher in older animals and in wild animals such as deer that have been active up to slaughtering time.

Immediately after an animal is slaughtered, the flesh is limp. However, the muscles soon tense and become rigid and hard. This condition is known as rigor. It takes from one to three days in beef until rigor disappears and muscles begin to weaken. If meat were processed during this time, it would be tough regardless of the quality. Therefore, the carcass needs to be held in a very cool place until rigor disappears and for a while longer to age. (This, of course, does not apply to small animals such as rabbits, squirrels, and poultry.)

In the aging process the muscles weaken and become much more soft and tender. Beef is usually aged for at least one week. It is important that the temperature is kept consistently cold and air around meat is fairly humid to avoid drying out the meat.

Pork is a more tender meat, and therefore is not aged as other large meat. Rigor in pork occurs sooner after slaughter and disappears fast. The eating quality of pork also does not usually change much with the animal's age.

Most meat sold in the United States is government inspected and graded. Meat is graded according to various standards, including quality, age of the animal, the marblization of fat throughout, and tenderness. Meat is stamped with purple coloring which is not harmful if eaten.

USDA Prime grade is placed on meat that has been bred from the best stock and has been fed and raised specifically to produce the highest-quality meat. Prime meats are, of course, the most expensive. The USDA Choice grade is the most popular in grocery stores and is slightly inferior in quality to the prime. USDA Good grade has considerable less marbling and meat will not be as tender and juicy. There are also Standard, Utility, and several other grades which are usually from older animals. This meat will be tougher and dry. It will not be marbleized and the fat will be more yellow. The nutritional value of older meats is essentially the same as that of younger animals; however, the eating quality is definitely not as good.

Steaks, chops, and prime roasts are popular because they are flavorful and easy to prepare. However, they are the most expensive choices. Chucks, shoulder cuts, and shanks are less expensive and are excellent to roast. Meat that comes from muscles the animal uses least will be the most tender. Connective tissue will be more tough. This is helpful to know when cooking it. The tougher, cheaper cuts of meat can usually be made tender by the proper cooking methods, but will take a little more time to cook. The grade you decide to buy will probably depend on your budget and whether you are serving guests, making stew, or something between.

Hamburger and sausage are usually less expensive. With the multitudes of ways we can prepare them, they are indispensable standbys. Be sure to buy the leaner mixes of these meats, however. Fat deteriorates and becomes rancid quickly and no cook likes to fry out a cupful of grease from one package of meat! Even if it was cheaper, you paid for grease that isn't good for your health or your pocketbook!

Always compare prices of meats with what you are getting—not just price per pound. A large bone and a big slab of fat on the side of the meat is a lot of waste. In poultry the more mature birds have much more meat per bone structure than small young ones, which makes them a much better buy. Usually the heavier the weight, the more meat there will be in comparison to bone.

Meat is always more expensive when extra cutting or deboning is involved.

Learn to do as much of this as possible yourself, so you can save paying the meat cutter to do it.

Don't forget about variety meats such as heart, tongue, liver, and brains. These meats have hardly any waste—with no bones or fat—and are very nutritious. They are usually much less expensive and add good variety to the menu.

Watch for freshness of meats, especially on sale items that may be marked down because they are too old. Fresh meat is firm and bright in color and should not have an off odor.

Meat should not be kept in the refrigerator too long after purchasing it. If you will not be cooking it promptly, store in the freezer. Chops, roasts, and whole poultry should keep for several days, but smaller cuts of meat, hamburger, sausage, cut-up poultry, and variety meats should be used within a day or two. This, of course, can vary with how fresh the meat was when purchased.

Cooked meat should be cooled promptly and refrigerated. Even then it should be used within four days. Otherwise, wrap tightly and freeze.

Choose the method for cooking that is best suited for the grade and cut of meat. An important general rule to observe with cooking meats is to use low to moderate heat. Low heat reduces the amount of shrinkage and keeps the juice and flavor in the meat. However, meat should never be cooked below 275 degrees (325 degrees for pork) to insure an internal temperature high enough to destroy bacteria. Pork needs to be cooked to a higher internal temperature than other meats because of the danger of trichinosis. Cook fresh pork to an internal temperature of at least 165 to 170 degrees to avoid this danger—until no pink color remains.

Meat should be thawed when put on to cook. A frozen roast does not cook evenly. The outside usually becomes overcooked while the center is still tough! It is best to thaw meats slowly, preferably in the refrigerator. Thawing meats with heat causes a loss of natural juices and flavor.

Tender meats are more flavorful if cooked by one of the dry heat methods (without water). These include broiling, frying, barbecuing, and roasting—uncovered. Tougher meats are best cooked by one of the moist heat methods, including boiling, braising, pressure cooking, and roasting—covered, with a small amount of water added.

Barbecuing is usually done over an open charcoal grill outdoors. Meat is cooked four to five inches above a bed of hot coals. Prior to cooking, meat may be marinated for several hours for more tenderness. Meat is basted frequently with barbecue sauce while being cooked. Meat juices dripping on the hot coals causes smoking which gives the meat a good flavor. The usual meats for barbecuing include hamburger, hot dogs, chicken, steaks, and chops.

Boiling is simply cooking meat in water on top of the stove—first heated to boiling, then reduced to low. Meat is actually simmered rather than boiled until tender. This method can be used for tongue, heart, corned beef, and stew meat. Stew meat should be browned thoroughly before adding water to give extra flavor. Do not brown the other meats. Dry-cured country hams are usually best boiled. Other hams are usually better roasted in the oven.

Braising is sometimes called pot-roasting or stewing. Meat is first browned thoroughly in fat in heavy cooker. (Do not underbrown. This gives good flavor.) Then seasoning and a small amount of water are added and meat is steamed until tender. Cooker must be tightly covered and meat should be turned occasionally to keep it moist. Add additional water if needed. Temperature should be just high enough to keep it simmering. Long, slow cooking results in more tender meat. This method is used for most any of the grades of meat, especially the less tender ones. (Meat can also be browned thoroughly on top of the stove as described for good flavor, and then placed in the oven for the remainder of the cooking time.)

Broiling is suitable for tender steaks and chops. Meat should be ¾ to 1-inch thick. Trim excess fat from meat and score fat around the edge to prevent curling. Grease the broiler rack to prevent sticking and line the broiler pan with foil or add one inch of water for easy cleanup. Preheat broiler and place meat approximately 3 inches from the heat. Broil until meat is browned. Use tongs to turn so you do not pierce meat and allow juices to escape. Broil until browned on other side. Season and serve immediately.

Frying (pan-frying) or sautéing is done in a skillet on top of the stove. Fat is heated slightly in the skillet and meat added and fried on each side until browned and tender. Skillet is usually not covered, but may be partially covered if needed to attain desired amount of tenderness and to prevent spattering. Meats good for frying include hamburger, sausage, liver, brains, bacon, also sliced raw ham and any other tender sliced meats and fish.

Pressure cooking can be used for the same cuts of meat that require braising or cooking in water. Meat can be cooked in ⅓ to ½ the time in the pressure cooker. Pressure cooking is excellent for heart and tongue from large animals and for stew meat that has been thoroughly browned. When pressure-cooked, roasts, steaks, and chops will not be as flavorful and pressuring is not recommended. However, when time is a problem, it can be used for these meats as well. It is often used for tough meat that will not become tender by other methods.

Roasting can be either by *dry heat* or *moist heat* or a combination of the two. **To roast by dry heat**, meat is placed in the oven in open pan uncovered. Fat side of the meat should be placed up, and if meat does not have fat on one side, strips of bacon or fat should be laid over the top to prevent drying out. No water is added and a low temperature should be used, usually 325 degrees. A cooking thermometer may be used to eliminate guesswork as to doneness. For dry roasting, meats must be tender and may include beef, veal, lamb, and fresh or cured pork.

When **roasting by moist heat**, meat is either partially or tightly covered to keep it from drying out. Meat that is partially covered may be basted occasionally to keep meat moist. It is very beneficial again, to use low temperature especially with tougher meats. Roasts that are cooked long and slow will be much more tender and juicy than with higher heat. Most any cuts of beef, veal, lamb, pork, and poultry can be roasted. I much prefer the moist heat method to the dry heat method because of the danger of drying the meat out. If covered too tightly, however, meat will be steamed as in braising on top of the stove instead of roasted. It depends on what results you prefer. A partial covering is excellent for large or medium cuts. This keeps moisture in and yet allows the roasting process which gives the meat the good flavor. A tight cover is best for smaller cuts or sliced meats. Oven cooking bags are frequently used to keep in moisture. Several holes should be pierced in the top, however, to let out steam.

Time and temperature for cooking meats can only be approximate at best since there are so many factors involved. These include the length of aging, the temperature of the meat when placed on to cook, the shape and thickness of the cut of meat, the amount of bone and fat, variation in oven temperature, and, of course, the tenderness of the meat. Meat thermometers aid in eliminating guess-work on larger cuts of meat. A meat thermometer should be inserted into the deepest portion of the meat, but away from fat or bone. If roast is covered with foil, simply stick thermometer through the foil.

Cooking time can also be affected by various procedures to help tenderize the meat. Meat can be marinated for several hours, or overnight for larger cuts, to enhance flavor and improve tenderness. Tougher roasts are sometimes marinated a couple of days. Meat is soaked in a liquid with seasoning and an acid such as vinegar or lemon juice. When marinating meat, use glass or ceramic container and turn meat occasionally, spooning marinade over it. Use approximately ½ cup marinade per pound of meat. If marinating overnight or longer, meat must be kept in refrigerator. Spoon marinade over the meat when cooking it.

A little plain vinegar sprinkled over any meat before cooking it acts as a tenderizer. Sprinkle 1 or 2 tbsp. on all roasts, steaks, chops, etc., right before cooking. This does not affect the taste.

Another method for tenderizing meat such as steaks is to pound it with a tenderizing hammer on a wooden cutting board. Sprinkle flour on both sides of meat and pound until flour is absorbed. This breaks down the tough fibers of the meat. This process can also be done at the meat shop by a machine that partially cuts the tissues on both sides. This is called **cubed meat**.

There are also commercial tenderizers containing a tenderizing agent as well as salt and seasoning which can be sprinkled on thin cuts of meat.

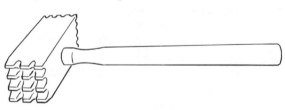

Meat Cuts and How to Cook Them

BEEF CHART

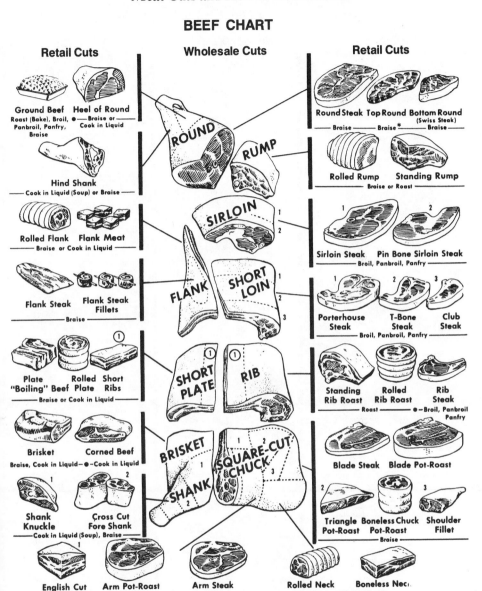

Retail Cuts   **Wholesale Cuts**   **Retail Cuts**

Ground Beef   Heel of Round
Roast (Bake), Broil,   ●—Braise or—
Panfry, Panfry,   Cook in Liquid
Braise

ROUND   RUMP

Round Steak   Top Round   Bottom Round
(Swiss Steak)
— Braise —   — Braise* —   — Braise —

Hind Shank
— Cook in Liquid (Soup) or Braise —

Rolled Rump   Standing Rump
— Braise or Roast —

Rolled Flank   Flank Meat
— Braise or Cook in Liquid —

SIRLOIN

Sirloin Steak   Pin Bone Sirloin Steak
— Broil, Panbroil, Panfry —

Flank Steak   Flank Steak
Fillets
— Braise —

FLANK   SHORT LOIN

Porterhouse   T-Bone   Club
Steak   Steak   Steak
— Broil, Panbroil, Panfry —

Plate   Rolled   Short
"Boiling" Beef   Plate   Ribs
— Braise or Cook in Liquid —

SHORT PLATE   RIB

Standing   Rolled   Rib
Rib Roast   Rib Roast   Steak
— Roast —   ●—Broil, Panbroil
Panfry

Brisket   Corned Beef
Braise, Cook in Liquid—●—Cook in Liquid

BRISKET   SQUARE-CUT CHUCK

Blade Steak   Blade Pot-Roast

Shank   Cross Cut
Knuckle   Fore Shank
— Cook in Liquid (Soup), Braise —

SHANK

Triangle   Boneless Chuck   Shoulder
Pot-Roast   Pot-Roast   Fillet
— Braise —

English Cut   Arm Pot-Roast   Arm Steak
— Braise —

Rolled Neck   Boneless Neck
— Braise or Cook in Liquid —

*Prime and choice grades may be
broiled, panbroiled or panfried

NATIONAL LIVESTOCK AND MEAT BOARD

Meat Cuts and How to Cook Them
LAMB CHART

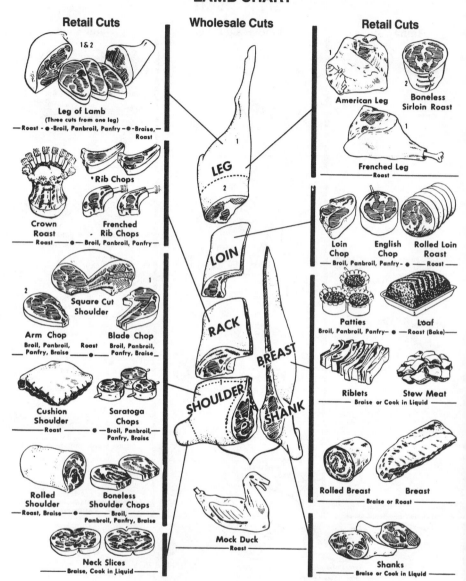

Retail Cuts   **Wholesale Cuts**   **Retail Cuts**

1 & 2

Leg of Lamb
(Three cuts from one leg)
—Roast - ●-Broil, Panbroil, Panfry –●-Braise,—
Roast

American Leg   **Boneless Sirloin Roast**

Frenched Leg
— Roast —

LEG

*Rib Chops

Crown Roast   **Frenched - Rib Chops**
— Roast —— ●—Broil, Panbroil, Panfry—

Loin Chop   **English Chop**   **Rolled Loin Roast**
— Broil, Panbroil, Panfry- ● —— Roast —

LOIN

Square Cut Shoulder

Arm Chop   **Blade Chop**
Broil, Panbroil,   Roast   Broil, Panbroil,
Panfry, Braise ____ ● ____ Panfry, Braise_

RACK

Patties   **Loaf**
Broil, Panbroil, Panfry– ●   —Roast (Bake)—

BREAST

Cushion Shoulder   **Saratoga Chops**
— Roast —   ●—Broil, Panbroil,—
Panfry, Braise

SHOULDER   **SHANK**

Riblets   **Stew Meat**
— Braise or Cook in Liquid —

Rolled Shoulder   **Boneless Shoulder Chops**
—Roast, Braise— ●—— Broil,
Panbroil, Panfry, Braise

Rolled Breast   **Breast**
— Braise or Roast —

Mock Duck
— Roast —

Neck Slices
—Braise, Cook in Liquid—

Shanks
— Braise or Cook in Liquid —

NATIONAL LIVESTOCK AND MEAT BOARD

Meat Cuts and How to Cook Them
PORK CHART

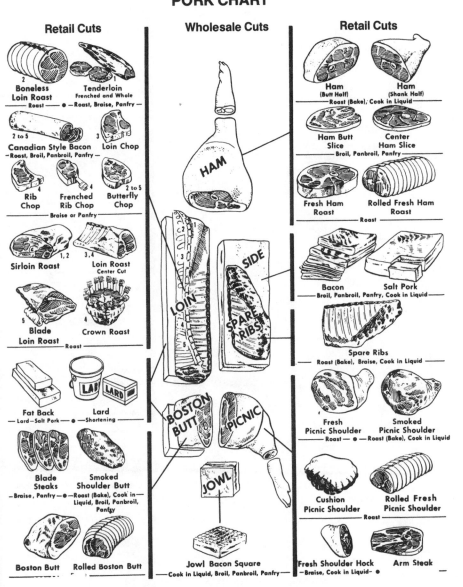

Retail Cuts

2 Boneless Loin Roast
— Roast — ● —

1 Tenderloin
Frenched and Whole
— Roast, Braise, Panfry —

2 to 5 Canadian Style Bacon
— Roast, Broil, Panbroil, Panfry —

3 Loin Chop

4 Rib Chop

4 Frenched Rib Chop

2 to 5 Butterfly Chop
— Braise or Panfry —

1, 2 Sirloin Roast

3, 4 Loin Roast
Center Cut

5 Blade Loin Roast

4 Crown Roast
— Roast —

Fat Back
— Lard — Salt Pork — ● —

Lard
— Shortening —

Blade Steaks
— Braise, Panfry — ● —

Smoked Shoulder Butt
— Roast (Bake), Cook in Liquid, Broil, Panbroil, Panfry —

Boston Butt

Rolled Boston Butt

Wholesale Cuts

HAM

LOIN

SIDE

SPARE RIBS

BOSTON BUTT

PICNIC

JOWL

Retail Cuts

Ham (Butt Half)

Ham (Shank Half)
— Roast (Bake), Cook in Liquid —

Ham Butt Slice

Center Ham Slice
— Broil, Panbroil, Panfry —

Fresh Ham Roast

Rolled Fresh Ham Roast
— Roast —

Bacon

Salt Pork
— Broil, Panbroil, Panfry, Cook in Liquid —

Spare Ribs
— Roast (Bake), Braise, Cook in Liquid —

Fresh Picnic Shoulder

Smoked Picnic Shoulder
— Roast — ● — Roast (Bake), Cook in Liquid —

Cushion Picnic Shoulder

Rolled Fresh Picnic Shoulder
— Roast —

Fresh Shoulder Hock
— Braise, Cook in Liquid — ●

Arm Steak

Jowl Bacon Square
— Cook in Liquid, Broil, Panbroil, Panfry —

NATIONAL LIVESTOCK AND MEAT BOARD

Meat Cuts and How to Cook Them
VEAL CHART

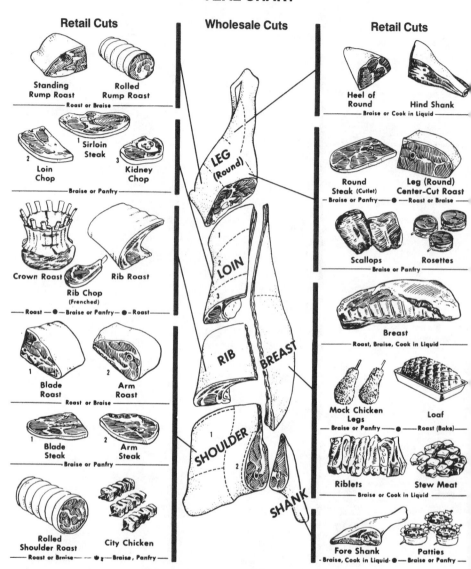

Retail Cuts

Standing Rump Roast | Rolled Rump Roast
— Roast or Braise —

¹ Sirloin Steak
2 Loin Chop | 3 Kidney Chop
— Braise or Panfry —

Crown Roast | Rib Roast
Rib Chop (Frenched)
— Roast — ● — Braise or Panfry — ● — Roast —

1 Blade Roast | 2 Arm Roast
— Roast or Braise —

1 Blade Steak | 2 Arm Steak
— Braise or Panfry —

Rolled Shoulder Roast | City Chicken
— Roast or Braise — — ♥₂ — Braise, Panfry —

Wholesale Cuts

LEG (Round)
LOIN
RIB
BREAST
SHOULDER
SHANK

Retail Cuts

Heel of Round | Hind Shank
— Braise or Cook in Liquid —

Round Steak (Cutlet) | Leg (Round) Center-Cut Roast
— Braise or Panfry — ● — Roast or Braise —

Scallops | Rosettes
— Braise or Panfry —

Breast
— Roast, Braise, Cook in Liquid —

Mock Chicken Legs | Loaf
— Braise or Panfry — ● — Roast (Bake) —

Riblets | Stew Meat
— Braise or Cook in Liquid —

Fore Shank | Patties
- Braise, Cook in Liquid- ● — Braise or Panfry —

NATIONAL LIVESTOCK AND MEAT BOARD

Wild Meats

Since my husband is not a hunter, and I have not had that much experience with wild meat, I am indebted to Minnie Carr for this information about wild meats. Minnie's husband and three sons have been avid hunters for many years and she said she learned these tips through much experience.

If deer or other large animal is chased a long distance before killing it, meat will be tough even if the animal is young. Still hunting is much better. Do not haul an animal around on the hood of a vehicle to display your prize! Engine heat ruins the meat.

Immediately after the kill, the animal should be bled. Cut the jugular vein at the base of the neck, slightly to the left of center. It is best to have animal on a slope with its head at the lowest point so blood will flow freely. Minnie's husband takes the animal to a clean-running creek as soon as possible after the kill, removes the entrails, and washes out the blood thoroughly. He skins it the same evening. Leaving skin on a dead animal overnight causes a bad taste.

It is best to let the carcass hang for several days in a cold meat locker before processing. When processing, remove every bit of fat you possibly can, because the fat becomes rancid, especially in the freezer, and gives the meat a bad taste. It is also good to remove as many bones as possible for best flavor. Freezing or canning the meat before using it helps remove the wild taste and tenderizes it. Canning is best. Meat may be cubed and canned the same as beef chunks.

Frozen meat should be thawed and soaked or marinated before cooking. Soak roast overnight in a cool place in vinegar and salt water to cover. Use 1 cup vinegar and ½ cup salt per gallon of water. The vinegar tenderizes the meat, and the salt draws out the blood. Minnie soaks the steaks in salt water for a couple of hours, using 2 tbsp. salt to 1 ½ qts. water rather than the vinegar-salt solution. The steaks should be naturally tender. If preparing a roast, such as fresh leg of venison, marinate for several days in a cool place in the All-purpose Marinade on page 365, or in vinegar and salt water. This helps remove the wild taste.

After soaking, prepare meat from large animals as you would beef, and small animals as you would poultry. She said meat should not be smothered with garlic and onions—a little is good, but many people use too much! A little herb seasoning is also excellent. Meat is good prepared with cream of mushroom soup thinned with half milk. Do not use open roasting; always cover. Cooking bags are excellent for keeping the moisture in the meat. Or cover with a lid, or wrap in foil. Bake at 325 degrees until tender. A small amount of water may be added if needed. Pressure cooker and Crockpot methods are also good. (Dress wild turkey according to the directions for poultry that follow.)

POULTRY

The whole process of catching a live chicken or other poultry and preparing it for the table has been a challenge to ambitious country girls, and some of the more aggressive type have had quite a bit of experience.

I was always glad if my husband was around when it was time to kill a chicken. However, husbands aren't always around when such jobs need to be done! So I found it advantageous to be able to manage the job myself when necessary. Where there is a will, there is a way! Following is the method I used and am passing on to my daughters. (If I were a chicken, I think I would prefer this route over the mass production method of being hauled many miles perhaps to a slaughtering plant to hang in a long waiting line for my turn!)

First, prepare a chopping block. Drive two nails with heads into a large chunk of wood. Nails should be only slightly more than an inch apart, depending on the size of the chicken's neck—just so the head won't slip through. Have a good *sharp* hatchet ready and a small cardboard box about the size of the chicken with a lid attached. Then, go catch the chicken.

It helps tremendously to have a chicken catcher to catch the chicken. This is nothing more than a long heavy wire with the end bent into a hook so you can reach into the hardest-to-get-to corner of the chicken house where the chickens are all bound to crowd when you are trying to catch them. You can just slip it around a leg without scaring the whole flock stiff, and pull it right into your hands.

Hold onto the feet of the chicken tightly with your left hand and place its head between the nails on the chopping block, stretching it gently just enough to hold its head and neck in place on the block. Now this part is amazing to me (and I just verified it today with a friend who has had a lot of experience and she agreed that it is true). The chicken will squawk as loud as possible all the way from the chicken house until you hold it snugly against the block of wood. Then it usually calms down, closes its eyes, and lies quite still for a few seconds, totally oblivious as to what is about to take place! While it is still, work fast because the spell is bound not to last long. With the hatchet in your right hand, give *one* mighty (and I mean mighty) whack! And whatever you do, don't miss your aim! (If you don't have a good swing, don't attempt it. You don't want the chicken jumping up and running off half killed!) If you do it right, the chicken won't have a clue as to what happened!

Do not let go of the headless chicken at this point. It would go flopping all over the place, bruising itself. Instead, quickly stuff it in the box and hold the lid down tightly against the chicken until it quits flopping. The box must be the size of the chicken or it will flop around in the box. If you have a cinder block handy, you can stick the chicken down in one of the openings of it, with its feet protruding. When all is quiet, proceed to scald and pluck the chicken.

Water for scalding should be 145 to 150 degrees, slightly hotter for older and tougher birds. Swish chicken around in bucket of water enough to cover well for 45 to 60 seconds, depending on its size and age. Make certain water gets to all areas, including under the wings. Pluck several tail feathers to test if scalding is sufficient. Do not overscald as this damages the skin causing it to tear and making it difficult to clean. Scald just until feathers will pull out satisfactorily. Then remove all feathers.

If necessary, chicken may be singed to remove any hair. To singe, move chicken quickly over a lighted candle or low gas flame just long enough to singe off hair. Be careful not to heat the meat. You can also pour a little rubbing alcohol in a can lid, light it with a match, and use this for singeing. (Old-timers used to light a newspaper and quickly swish it around over the chicken, but this left a black residue on the chicken from the newsprint that was difficult to remove.)

Remove the feet and lower legs by cutting in part way at knee joint and bending backward sharply to break joint. Then finish cutting off. In large birds, pull out leg tendons with a pair of pliers. Wash thoroughly, scrapping off any dark yellow outer skin and pinfeathers. These can usually be popped out with the back of a knife. (Pinfeathers are undeveloped feathers that look like stubs just breaking through the skin.)

Drawing the Bird: Remove craw (or crop) and windpipe first. The two tubes protruding at the neck are the gullet (which leads to the craw) and the windpipe.

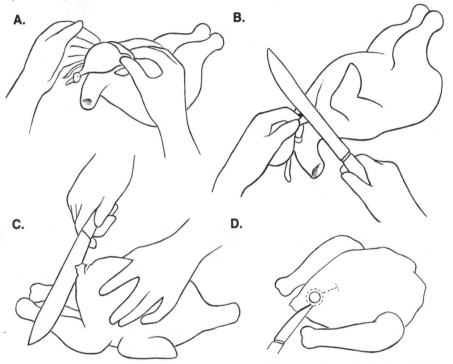

A. Tie a knot at the top end of the gullet. This keeps the contents from spilling out. (By the way, do not feed the chicken a big last meal before slaughtering or the craw will be stuffed with food. Simply give a drink of water the night before.)

B. Work craw loose and pull it out as far as you can, being careful not to tear it. Cut it loose down as far inside chicken as you can reach with a knife. (Some tie a knot at this end of gullet also before cutting it loose, but if craw is nearly empty, this is usually unnecessary.) Pull out windpipe also.

C. Cut out the oil sac just above the tail by cutting in from both ends.

D. Make an incision between the tip of the breastbone and the vent, being careful not to cut into the entrails. Carefully cut around the vent to loosen it completely.

E.　　　　　　　　　　　　　　　　　　　　**F.**

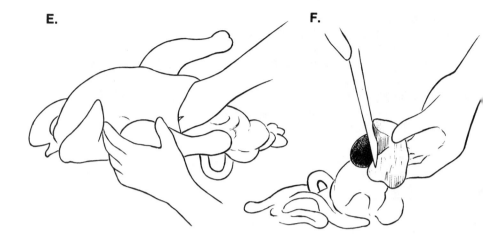

E. Reach into the cavity and locate the gizzard which is firm and rather round. Grasp it firmly and pull steadily and most of the insides will come out with it. Reach back in and remove any remaining parts such as kidneys and the lungs which may be slightly embedded between the ribs. These are red and spongy. Be sure any remaining portion of the other end of the windpipe and gullet came along out with other viscera. Flush out cavity thoroughly with water.

F. Remove giblets (liver, heart, and gizzard) from other entrails. Grasp both lobes of the liver and hold it up so weight of intestines will pull down enough to allow you to easily cut the gall bladder (green sac) loose. Be careful not to puncture this as it contains a bitter fluid which would contaminate whatever it touched. Cut any membrane, veins, and arteries from end of heart. Cut a shallow slit along the indented curve of the gizzard just through muscle on both sides. Do not pierce inner sac which contains food, but peel it loose with fingers and discard.

Chicken may be either roasted whole or cut up if desired. Procedures for cutting a chicken are basically the same for a turkey or other fowl. Turkeys are a little harder to handle since they are larger, but method is the same.

Cutting up a Bird: To cut through joints easily, always cut in part way at joint, and then bend portions backward sharply to break joint and expose bones. You can then easily see where to sever between the bones.

A. Cut off wings first.

B. Then remove legs and thighs. C. Cut legs and thighs apart if desired.

D. Separate the breast and back by cutting down through joints of the A-shaped bones joining them.

E. Separate upper and lower part of back just back of the rib section.

F. Divide breast in two pieces by cutting flesh loose along one side of breastbone at tail end of piece. Then break breastbone at wishbone area by bending both sections backward. Sever completely with knife.

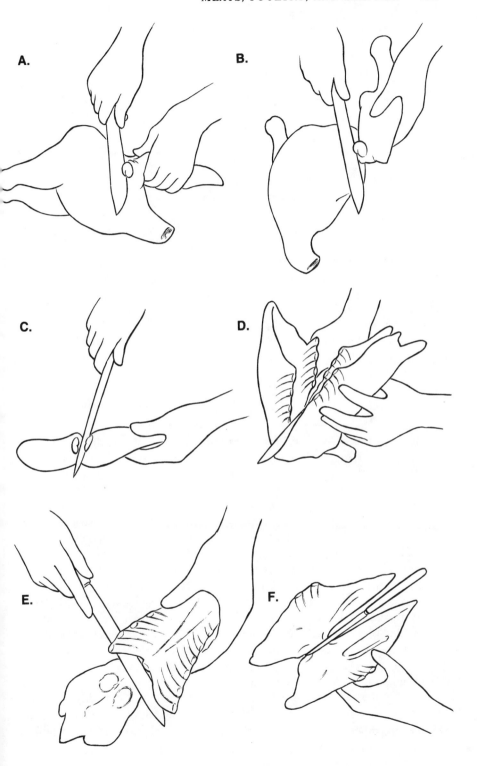

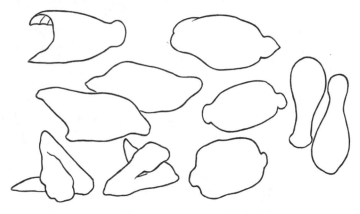

You will end up with 10 pieces of chicken. The back and neck pieces, of course, are not suitable for serving, but can be cooked along with other pieces and then deboned for other uses. Meat may be added to the gravy. Wings may or may not be included. Chickens are no longer cut this way commercially, since merchants have figured out a way to include most of the bony pieces in with the good ones. They can then sell breasts or legs with backs and ribs included at a much higher price per pound.

Chicken will have a better flavor and will be more tender if it is chilled from 4 hours to overnight, after slaughtering before cooking. Turkey should be chilled at least overnight.

FISH

There is a creek on our farm where our daughters enjoyed fishing in their growing-up years, especially when friends came to visit and went with them. They would come back to the house with anything from tiny sun perch to suckers a foot long or more. Occasionally they caught their hook on a large turtle, but were never able to land any. One day, however, the mail carrier spied a huge one crossing the lane heading for the creek. He hurried in to ask if he could have it for turtle soup. We gladly told him to help himself! We received a free lesson on butchering a turtle in the process. I didn't inquire about his recipe, however. Somehow, I haven't developed a craving for turtle soup to this day!

On another occasion when some friends were fishing with the girls, they all came dashing back to the house with a huge eel! The thing looked so much like a grossly overstuffed snake that I had a hard time believing it wasn't poisonous. They couldn't bear to pitch out such an unusual catch, so we searched a number of places and finally learned from the encyclopedia that it was supposed to be good to eat! So I cleaned and soaked it, breaded it with cornmeal, and fried it like a fish. And, lo and behold, it really did have a delicious flavor!

Back to the suckers. They seem to have a somewhat oily or muddy taste, but we found that soaking them in the refrigerator overnight in vinegar and salt water (3 tbsp. vinegar and 1 tbsp. salt per qt. of water) improved the flavor considerably.

Cleaning Fish

1. Lay fish on cutting board. Grasp fish firmly by the head or tail and scrape off scales with a knife. For quick removal, scrape in the opposite direction from

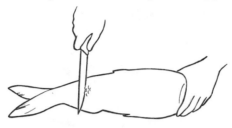

which scales lay. The tail is so small and slippery to hold onto that some prefer holding onto the head and working back up from the tail. Others hold onto the tail with a pair of pliers or a cloth, and work from that direction. If you clean a lot of fish, an inexpensive little fish scaler is a handy device for quickly scaling them. Be careful to do a thorough job of scaling, especially near the base of the fins and near the head.

2. Then cut a slit in the fish's belly from the head to the vent (anal opening). Do not cut deep—only through the flesh. Use your hand to clean out the insides. Cut out small vent area of flesh. Flush inside area well with water.

3. Cut all around the head into the backbone just beyond the gills, including the fins above the collarbone. Then break the backbone at the head by bending it sharply over edge of cutting board. Finish cutting off head and cut off tail.

4. Do not cut remaining fins with knife or shears since base of fin bone would not be removed with this method. Instead, cut into flesh on each side to the base of the fins and pull out fins. Base will come out easily with fin.

5. Wash fish thoroughly in cold running water, making sure any remaining viscera, blood, and scales are removed.

If the fish is small, it is now ready to fry or cook as desired. If it is large, however, you may wish to cut it into steaks, or simply cut it into two flat portions. Cut steaks one-inch thick.

If fish is large, some people like to fillet it for easy eating without the bones. This takes a little practice to be able to do a good job without cutting away a lot of the flesh with the bone. It is unnecessary to remove head and tail before filleting the fish. This gives you something to hold onto if needed and will be thrown out with the bones.

First, cut into flesh at head to free the end of the fillet. Then begin cutting along the backbone, keeping knife firmly against bones as you carefully cut away flesh from bones. Cut loose at tail, and repeat for the other side.

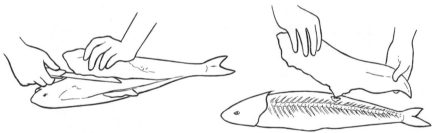

There are fish (such as catfish) that do not have scales. We used to catch these in the creek at my home on the farm when I was growing up. We found it was easiest simply to skin them.

First, cut the skin loose around the head. Then remove fins and cut off the tail. Lay fish on a board and drive a skinny nail down through the middle of the fish right back of the head to hold it securely to the board. With a pair of pliers, grasp skin at the head and pull it off.

Canning Fish

A friend told me that catfish are delicious canned. She said they skin and clean them as described. Then soak in salt water for 1 hour (use ½ cup salt to 1 gal. water). Drain and pack tightly in cans leaving 1 inch head space. Do not add more salt or liquid. Tighten lids and process at 10 lbs. pressure: pts. 90 minutes and qts. 100 minutes. She said they taste like salmon, and the bones are soft and edible after being pressure-cooked. I told a relative about this, and she gave me a sample can of suckers that she had canned by the same method. I did not tell my family, but prepared them for supper one evening. No one realized we were not eating salmon!

STOCK FOR SOUP

Soup stock or broth is obtained by stewing meat and bones for several hours to extract flavor and nutrients into a rich broth. If bones are totally clean of meat and no meat is added, broth will not be good. You must have some meat on the bones or add fragments of meat to obtain good broth.

Trim as much fat as you can from meat and bones. Large bones should be cracked so water can reach the bone marrow. Bones can either be raw or cooked.

The conventional method is to cover meat and bones with water and cook slowly for 2 or more hours. (Old-timers used to cook stock all day on the back of the cookstove. The long, slow cooking time enhances the flavor.) After first ½ to 1 hour, use a dipper to remove any scum that has collected on top. Many cooks add some vegetables after the first hour. (I prefer to cook vegetables separately later and add the desired amount of broth to them at that point.) Vegetables usually added are potatoes, onions, a garlic clove, carrots, celery, and seasoning of bay leaf, peppercorns, marjoram, or whatever you prefer. Stock should be cooked another hour after adding vegetables.

After cooking, remove vegetables. Any meat should be picked from the bones and placed with vegetables or returned to broth. Stock can be strained or simply poured into jars to use later. When chilled, the fat will collect in a hard cake at the top of the jar and should be removed before using. If using stock before it cools, fat should be skimmed off with a dipper. It is much easier to chill stock and lift off the hardened cake of fat from the top. This stock is excellent to use for vegetable soup, to cook noodles or rice, or for any recipe calling for broth or bouillon.

Because of the long cooking time for making stock, many persons feel it isn't worth the effort and they pitch out the bones and scraps. Here is where your pressure cooker can again come to the rescue! It takes little effort to put scraps of meat and bones in the pressure cooker, add water to come up at least ⅓ way on the bones, and cook at 10 lbs. pressure for 30 minutes. Small tender bones take even less time. This can be done while you are preparing other food, or while cleaning up after a meal. Drain off broth, pick meat from bones and return to broth, and you have the makings for a delicious and nutritious pot of soup.

Bones from cooked poultry do not need to be cooked nearly as long. Simply add 2 or more cups of water to bones, depending on amount, and pressure-cook for 10 to 15 minutes, or cook in saucepan for about 1 hour. Drain off broth, rinse with a little more water, and add this to broth.

Clarifying Stock: If you prefer clear stock, it can be clarified with egg white and shell. First skim off fat, then strain. Beat together 1 egg white and 1 tbsp. water for each quart of broth. Crumble some of the clean eggshell, and add shell and beaten white to broth. Heat broth, stirring until it boils. Boil slowly for 2 minutes. Turn off heat and let sit 20 minutes. Then strain out egg and shell through a fine strainer. Stock should be clear when cooled.

GRAVY

Mashed potatoes and gravy has been a favorite among farm families for many generations. Many youngsters (and oldsters!) didn't stop with mashed potatoes and gravy. They would lay a thick slice of homemade bread beside the potatoes and ladle good thick gravy over it as well.

At a banquet of persons from a wide range of vocations and backgrounds, I overheard one gentleman chuckle as he was dishing a generous amount of gravy onto his plate and then looked to see if anyone else was indulging. "This is the way you can tell the city boys from the country boys," he said. "Just look around and see who is having gravy bread!" In past years the country boys got plenty of exercise to work off the extra calories, but with all the modern machinery we have today to save manual labor, many people need to avoid foods laden with excessive calories. So gravy bread is becoming more unheard of all the time. Potatoes are more nutritious, however, and I believe there are few people who don't enjoy mashed potatoes and gravy at least occasionally!

There are several types of gravy and methods for making it. To make "brown gravy" heat flour and fat together in skillet until browned. Then slowly add milk, stirring constantly until thickened.

Gravy made from rich broth and drippings left in the pan from beef, pork roast, or chicken is called "pan gravy" or "meat gravy." Fragments of meat or cooked sliced giblets added to the gravy enhance it.

Other meats may also be used for gravy. Even though plain ham broth is usually not considered good for gravy, browned crumbled sausage with ham broth added makes delicious gravy. You can also make gravy by sautéing hamburger, or sausage, or chipped all-meat bologna in a small amount of fat until very brown and the pan is covered with a rich brown coating from the meat. (The secret to a good rich flavor is to brown the meat *very* well. Use approximately ½ to 1 cup meat for 2 cups of gravy. Then add water, stirring and scraping to loosen all the brown coating from the pan. Thicken with a batter made of milk and flour. If additional flavor or color is needed, bouillon cubes or bottled gravy coloring may be added. A little MSG will greatly enhance the flavor of any gravy made from meat or broth.

Some cooks make chicken giblet gravy by simply cooking the giblets in water on top of the stove until tender and then adding thickening. However, you cannot obtain nearly as much good rich flavor by boiling any kind of meat in water. I prefer baking chicken in oven with giblets tucked underneath so they don't dry out, and then adding water to the drippings and sliced giblets to make gravy. The brown drippings are the secret to a richer flavor in giblet gravy.

When making gravy with broth and drippings from a roast or chicken, again be sure to scrape loose all browned particles from the roasting pan. These are full of rich flavor. Soak in a little water if necessary to soften. The amount of water you can add to the broth for good gravy, of course, depends on the richness of the broth. If broth is very rich, you can add at least half water or more. Do not dilute too much, however. It takes good rich broth to make rich-tasting gravy. If the broth is weak, and you need a larger amount of gravy, some bouillon may be added to stretch it.

The basic procedure for making meat or pan gravy in most recipes is to remove the meat from the pan. Skim off fat and pour off any broth into another container. Return several tablespoons of fat to the pan, stir in flour, and heat until smooth and browned. Then gradually add reserved broth and water or milk until of desired consistency, stirring briskly to avoid lumps.

It is much easier to make smooth gravy if you pour the skimmed broth into a separate pan to make the gravy. Then combine milk and flour in a batter shaker or any glass jar with a tight-fitting lid. Milk should be put into shaker first, then flour, to avoid lumps. Shake until smooth. Slowly pour into boiling broth, stirring briskly just until thickened and smooth. Season and remove from heat. With this method you should not have to worry about lumpy gravy! You also do not need to include the fat, helping to reduce calories in the gravy. Some cooks include a small amount of fat for flavor.

Be sure to taste gravy made from broth before adding additional salt. Sometimes broth is salty enough from the meat that it does not need more salt.

Meat or Pan Gravy

Method 1. Make the same as brown gravy (next page), using fat from the meat. Heat in roasting pan. Add water to broth to make 2 cups liquid in place of milk, or use half milk for a creamy gravy.

Method 2. Skim off fat from broth. If broth is chilled, fat will collect on top and harden. It can then be removed easily.

1¼ cups rich broth and water	Heat in saucepan.
¾ cup milk **¼ cup flour**	Shake in batter shaker until smooth. Then slowly pour into boiling broth, stirring vigorously just until thickened and smooth.
½ tsp. salt or salt to taste **¼ tsp. MSG (optional)**	Add.

Brown Gravy

¼ cup fat **⅓ cup flour**	Heat in skillet until well browned, stirring constantly.
2 cups milk	Slowly add, stirring vigorously to avoid lumps. (Skillet may be removed from heat while milk is added to help avoid lumps. Then return to heat until smooth and bubbly.)
½ tsp. salt or salt to taste **¼ tsp. MSG (optional)** **bouillon, if desired**	Add.

Sausage Gravy

1¼ cups rich ham broth and water **½ to 1 cup browned crumbled** **sausage, drained**	Heat in saucepan.
¾ cup milk **¼ cup flour**	Shake in batter shaker until smooth. Then slowly pour into boiling broth, stirring vigorously just until thickened and smooth.
½ tsp. salt or salt to taste **¼ tsp. MSG (optional)**	Add.

Approximate Amount of Meat Needed per Serving

Boneless meats (such as roasts)	¼ to ⅓ lb.
Meat with some bone (roasts)	⅓ to ½ lb.
Bony cuts (such as ribs)	¾ to 1 lb.
Ham (with bone—precooked weight)	½ to ¾ lb.
Ham (boneless—precooked weight)	⅓ lb.
Ham (boneless—cooked weight)	⅛ to ¼ lb.
Chicken	½ to ¾ lb.
Turkey (small)	¾ lb. or more
Turkey (over 15 lbs. weight)	½ lb. or more

The amount of meat needed can vary considerably, depending on how thick you slice it. Some cooks cut slices twice as thick as others. Since persons usually take one medium-sized slice no matter how thick it is, this could almost double the amount needed. Thinner slicing is recommended. Those desiring more can take a second piece.

There is also a lot of difference in the amount of bone and cartilage in roasts. Take special note of this before cooking to determine whether the number of servings will be slightly more or less than average.

With poultry there are always a lot of small pieces of meat that aren't the nicest for serving, so the amount can vary with how concerned you may be about having enough larger pieces for serving. The small pieces are excellent to freeze and have on hand for casseroles and other dishes.

APPROXIMATE TIMETABLE FOR ROASTING MEATS
(Roasts without bone take about 10 minutes per lb. longer to cook than with bone.)

Kind and cut of meat	Internal temperature	Ready to cook weight	Approximate roasting time at 325 degrees
BEEF:			
Standing ribs (with bone)	170 degrees	6 to 8 lbs.	3 to 4½ hrs.
Rolled rib (without bone)	170 degrees	4 to 6 lbs.	3 to 4 hrs.
Rolled rump	170 degrees	5 lbs.	3 to 3¼ hrs.
Sirloin tip	170 degrees	3 lbs.	2 to 2¼ hrs.
Shoulder and chuck roasts	170 degrees	5 lbs.	3½ to 4 hrs.
VEAL:			
Leg	175 degrees	5 to 8 lbs.	2½ to 3½ hrs.
Loin	175 degrees	5 lbs.	3 hrs.
Rolled shoulder	175 degrees	3 to 5 lbs.	3 to 3½ hrs.
LAMB:			
Leg	180 degrees	6 to 7 lbs.	3¼ to 4 hrs.
Loin	180 degrees	3 to 6 lbs.	2¼ to 3¼ hrs.
Rolled shoulder	180 degrees	3 to 5 lbs.	2½ to 3 hrs.
Rib crown	180 degrees	5 lbs.	3¾ hrs.
PORK, FRESH:			
Loin	180 to 185 degrees	3 to 5 lbs.	3 to 4 hrs.
Shoulder	180 to 185 degrees	5 to 8 lbs.	3½ to 5 hrs.
Ham, whole	180 to 185 degrees	10 to 14 lbs.	5½ to 6 hrs.
Spareribs	180 to 185 degrees	3 lbs.	2 hrs.
PORK, CURED:			
Raw:			
Ham, whole	160 degrees	12 to 16 lbs.	3½ to 4½ hrs.
Ham, half	160 degrees	6 lbs.	2½ hrs.
Picnic shoulder	170 degrees	6 lbs.	3½ hrs.
Fully cooked:			
Ham, whole	135 degrees	12 to 16 lbs.	2 to 3 hrs.
Ham, half	135 degrees	6 lbs.	about 1½ hrs.
POULTRY:			
Chicken	180 to 185 degrees	3 to 5 lbs.	2½ to 3 hrs.
Turkey	180 to 185 degrees	8 to 10 lbs.	4 to 5 hrs.
Turkey	180 to 185 degrees	10 to 16 lbs.	5 to 6 hrs.
Turkey	180 to 185 degrees	18 to 25 lbs.	6½ to 7½ hrs.
Duck	180 to 185 degrees	4 to 6 lbs.	1½ to 2 hrs.

I like to turn the temperature to 425 degrees for the first hour for large turkeys, ¾ of an hour for smaller ones. Then reduce the total baking time given here by approximately 1 hour. This has the effect of browning meat in a skillet prior to baking. The whole bird is quickly heated to cooking temperature. With a low beginning temperature, it takes a long time for the center portion to become hot enough to actually start cooking. (If bird is stuffed, add 5 minutes per lb. to cooking time.)

TIPS FOR MEATS, POULTRY, AND SEAFOOD

• Meat added to a moderatly hot skillet will not stick nearly as much as when placed in a cold skillet and then heated. (Caution: Do not overheat an empty Teflon skillet as this could permanently damage the finish.)

• Drain freshly cooked bacon on paper towel placed on top of waxed paper. The drippings won't soak through and the paper towel can be folded inside the waxed paper and used later to grease casserole dishes and cake pans.

• Place bacon in cold skillet when frying to help prevent shrinkage. Try dipping bacon in milk and rolling it in flour before frying to improve flavor. It doesn't seem to shrink as much and seems to go a little further.

• To cook a quantity of bacon quickly for crumbled bacon, stack the number of slices needed. Snip with kitchen shears into ¼ to 1-inch pieces. Then toss and fry until browned.

• An easy way to fry bacon for a large group of people is to do it in the oven. Lay slices of bacon on a wire rack placed on a tray. Bake in 400-degree oven until browned, about 10 to 15 minutes. It does not need to be turned.

• To clean meat out of food grinder, run a slice of bread through after grinding the meat.

• Allow roasts to stand a little while after removing from the oven for nicer carving.

• When broth is not as richly flavored as desired, add 1 or more bouillon cubes. Soak first in a little hot water and mash with the back of a spoon to dissolve before adding to broth.

• Gravy thickened with flour will thin considerably if heated too hot or too long, especially when reheating. Turn off heat as soon as it has thickened, or has reheated sufficiently.

• Flour that has been browned for making gravy has less thickening power than unbrowned flour.

• Individual meat loaves can be made in muffin tins. They will bake in approximately half the time it takes for a large one. These can be frozen if desired for serving individually later on.

• When making a very large meat loaf, use a meat thermometer to be certain the loaf is baked to the center. It should be done at 170 degrees.

• Try baking meat loaf in a ring mold for guests. Fill center with vegetables, potatoes, or rice.

• For quick hamburgers on a picnic, you can prepare and fry them at home. Wrap tightly in foil. When you get a fire made at your picnic site, lay the foil-wrapped burgers on the coals and you will have hot juicy burgers in short order.

• When using a meat press or a meat baller to make hamburger patties, line with plastic wrap to keep the meat from sticking. You can quickly lift meat out with the wrap. Mixture may also be shaped into a roll. Then chill thoroughly and slice with a sharp knife into patties. Or use an ice-cream scoop to measure uniform portions of hamburger for patties.

• The membrane or skin on the outside of liver can be removed much more easily if liver is partially frozen first. This makes slicing much easier also, since it will hold its shape.

• Brush broiler rack lightly with oil and pour 1 cup water into the drip pan for easy cleanup afterward. This will prevent having burned on drippings.

• Meat for broiling should be at room temperature before beginning to broil it. Slash edges of meat before broiling to avoid curling.

•Never pierce meat when browning it, as this lets the juices escape. Use tongs or spatula to turn it over.

•When roasting meat, start with a cold oven and roast. The meat will shrink less and be more juicy.

•If roast or other meat turned out tough and no one enjoys eating it, run it through the food grinder. Use in soup or add to casseroles or meat loaf.

•Always slice meats across the grain of the meat fibers for much easier eating.

•There is no need to remove the bones from cans of salmon. After processing, they are edible and are in fact good for you!

•Fish keep much better in freezer if frozen in a block of ice. Place fish in a quart or ½ gallon cardboard milk carton or similar container. Fill with water, and then freeze. Oysters also keep much better if frozen in liquid. If they don't have enough liquid of their own, add water to cover.

•If you do not wish to place giblets in roasting pan when roasting turkey or chicken, they may be placed in a deep casserole dish alongside of roasting pan in oven. Cover with water and a lid, and they will cook with the same heat while bird is roasting.

•Allow poultry to cool about 20 minutes after removing from oven before carving. It will be much easier to slice.

•Broth from an older roasting hen is much richer and more flavorful than from a young fryer. This is also true of other meats such as beef.

•A broiler-fryer chicken usually yields about 3 cups cooked chopped meat. A four-pound stewing chicken about 4 cups.

•When deboning cooked chicken or turkey after a meal, do not waste the bones. Place in pressure cooker, add 1 or 2 cups water, and cook at 10 lbs. pressure for about 10 to 15 minutes. You will be surprised at all the extra good rich broth this makes. Drain into a bowl, rinse bones thoroughly with a little additional water, and pour in with broth. This can be done while you are cleaning up after the meal. It is delicious for cooking with noodles or rice.

•Do not throw away globs of fat or fat-coated skin when cutting up chicken. Place in skillet and fry slowly, partially covered to prevent splattering, until fat is rendered from tissue and until it ceases to pop and spatter—about 10 to 15 minutes, depending on quantity. Cool and use as part of the fat in corn bread, biscuits, and the like. Substitute this for ⅓ to ½ of the other fat called for in recipe. Baked goods would be too greasy if all chicken fat were used, but using about half the amount makes really flaky biscuits. (If you have a cholesterol problem, remember that animal fats are high in cholesterol. You may wish to save grease for soap instead!)

MEATS, POULTRY, AND SEAFOOD RECIPES

SAUCES AND SEASONINGS

All-Purpose Barbecue Sauce

(This is a good sauce to use on roast beef or roast pork sandwiches. It is also excellent to use for barbecuing beef chunks or pork chunks. Spread cooked meat chunks in a roasting pan, pour sauce over them, and roast, uncovered, at 350 degrees for 30 to 45 minutes, basting occasionally with the sauce.)

½ cup vegetable oil* ¾ cup chopped onion	Cook in saucepan until tender.

. . . .

¾ cup tomato catsup ¾ cup water ½ tsp. chili powder 3 tbsp. sugar 3 tbsp. Worcestershire sauce 2 tbsp. lemon juice 1 tsp. salt ½ tsp. black pepper	Add, and simmer for 15 minutes.

. . . .

Yield: 3 cups   *Monta-sue Clark*

(*May use ¼ cup oil and ¼ cup water if desired. If sauce isn't as thick as you like, dissolve 1 or 2 tbsp. cornstarch in a small amount of water and add at end of cooking time.)

. . . .

Oven Barbecue Sauce

1 cup catsup 1 tbsp. Worcestershire sauce 2 or 3 dashes Tabasco sauce 1 cup water ¼ cup vinegar 2 tbsp. brown sugar 1 tsp. salt 1 tsp. celery seed	Combine in saucepan. Heat to boiling and simmer 30 minutes.

. . . .

Delicious over chicken wings or spareribs.

Yield: enough for 4 lbs. meat

For chicken wings: Fry wings until browned on each side. Cover with sauce and bake at 300 degrees for 2 hours. (This is an excellent party item.)
For spareribs: Cook ribs until tender. Then cover with sauce and bake at 300 degrees for 2 hours.

Barbara Bowman

. . . .

Coating Mix for Chicken or Fish

1½ cups dry bread crumbs

Process a small amount at a time in blender until fine.

....

1 tsp. salt
1 tsp. paprika
1 tsp. celery salt
1 tsp. onion salt
¼ tsp. garlic powder
1 tsp. MSG (optional)
½ tsp. dry mustard
2 tbsp. vegetable oil

Add, and stir together with fork until well blended. Store at room temperature in covered container.

....

Pour mix in saucer and press both sides of chicken or fish in mix to coat. Lay in bake dish, skin side up. Bake chicken partially covered at 350 degrees for 1 to 2 hours until tender. Bake fish 30 to 50 minutes depending on size.

....

Basic Marinade for Meat

2 tbsp. vinegar
¼ cup olive or salad oil
½ tsp. salt
1 tsp. sugar
⅛ tsp. black pepper
1 garlic clove, crushed (optional)

Mix thoroughly, and spoon over meat.

....

Marinate meat at least 2 hours for flavor. To tenderize, place in refrigerator at least overnight, or up to 2 or 3 days.

Yield: enough for 1 lb. meat

....

All-Purpose Marinade

1½ tbsp. salt
2 tsp. sugar
¼ cup vinegar
1 med. onion, chopped
1 tsp. paprika
1 tsp. chili powder or black pepper
½ tsp. celery salt
½ tsp. garlic salt

Mix together thoroughly.

....

Rub mixture into meat and let stand several hours, or overnight, for larger roasts. Brush off marinade before browning meat, and reserve. Add to water and return to meat for cooking. It gives excellent flavor to the gravy. May also be used for fish fillets, steaks, and chicken, using lemon juice instead of vinegar. Use a little less salt for fish. When using for chicken, add 1 tbsp. soy sauce.

Minnie Carr

....

Steak Marinade

1½ cups vegetable oil
¾ cup soy sauce
¼ cup Worcestershire sauce
2 tsp. dry mustard
1 tsp. black pepper
½ cup vinegar
1½ tsp. parsley flakes
2 garlic cloves, minced
⅓ cup lemon juice

Mix thoroughly and spoon over meat.

Especially good on top round or flank steaks to barbecue on the grill. Marinate at least 2 hours to 1 day ahead.

Alice Trissel

Meat Seasoning

(Add flavor to food with a minimum amount of salt. Sprinkle on meats, poultry, and fish before broiling or baking.)

1½ tsp. grated lemon rind
2 tsp. dried parsley flakes
½ tsp. dried oregano or basil
  leaves, crushed
½ tsp. garlic powder
½ tsp. dried marjoram leaves,
  crushed
¼ tsp. ground allspice
¼ tsp. black pepper

Mix thoroughly and sprinkle on meat.

Mustard Sauce for Ham or Meat Loaf

3 egg yolks, slightly beaten
½ cup tomato juice
2 tbsp. prepared mustard
¼ cup margarine
½ cup brown sugar

Combine in saucepan. Cook until thickened, stirring constantly.

Serve hot with ham or meat loaf.

Polska Apple Glaze (for Baked Ham)

1 cup applesauce
¼ cup honey
¼ cup light brown sugar
1 tsp. prepared mustard

Combine all ingredients and spread over ham for the last 30 minutes of baking time.

Donna Lou Heatwole

Raisin Sauce for Ham

½ cup brown sugar
1 tsp. dry mustard
2 tbsp. cornstarch

Mix together.

....

2 tbsp. vinegar
2 tbsp. lemon juice
1½ cups water
½ cup raisins

Add. Cook, stirring constantly until thickened.

....

Serve over slices of boiled ham.

Yield: 2 cups   *Shirley Heatwole*

....

BEEF

Barbecued Hamburgers

1½ lbs. hamburger
1 cup bread crumbs
¼ cup chopped onion
½ cup milk or water
1 egg, slightly beaten
1 tsp. salt
¼ tsp. garlic salt
¼ tsp. celery salt
⅛ tsp. black pepper

Mix into 6 or 8 patties, and fry in skillet until browned on both sides.

....

Sauce:
1 cup tomato juice
¼ cup catsup
½ cup chopped onion
2 tbsp. brown sugar
1 tbsp. vinegar
¼ tsp. salt
1 tsp. dry mustard
dash Tabasco sauce
2 tbsp. Worcestershire sauce

Combine thoroughly in saucepan. Heat until boiling. Simmer 5 min.

....

½ cup water
1½ tbsp. cornstarch

Dissolve and stir in until thickened. Pour over hamburgers in skillet.

....

Bake at 350 degrees for 40 minutes. Serve in buns. Yield 6 to 8 servings

....

Juicy Hamburgers

1½ lbs. ground beef
¾ cup quick oatmeal
¼ cup chopped onion
1 tsp. sugar
¼ tsp. black pepper
1 tsp. salt
¼ tsp. MSG
½ cup tomato juice
few drops liquid smoke

Mix well. Shape into patties and fry on both sides until done.

Yield: 6 to 8 servings

Meat Loaf

1½ lbs. hamburger
¼ cup chopped onion (or 1 tbsp. onion flakes)
¼ cup oatmeal
2 tbsp. cornmeal
1 cup bread crumbs
1½ tsp. salt
1 tbsp. sugar
1 egg, slightly beaten
½ cup tomato juice
½ cup water
1 tbsp. barbecue sauce
⅛ tsp. liquid smoke
1 tbsp. vinegar

Mix all ingredients thoroughly. Pour into 9 × 5 bake dish.

Spoon a little additional tomato juice over the top to garnish or make the following topping.

Optional Topping:
¼ cup catsup
3 tbsp. brown sugar
2 tsp. prepared mustard
2 drops liquid smoke

Mix thoroughly and spread over top.

Bake at 350 degrees for approximately 1 hour.

Yield: 6 to 8 servings

Country Meat Loaf

1½ lbs. hamburger
2 to 4 tbsp. chopped onion
1 tsp. salt
⅛ tsp. garlic powder (see next page)

Mix thoroughly.

¼ tsp. poultry seasoning, or ½ tsp.
   sage
⅛ tsp. dry mustard
⅛ tsp. black pepper
2 tsp. Worcestershire sauce

. . . .

3 slices bread, cubed   Soak together.
1 cup warm milk

. . . .

2 eggs   Add to milk mixture and beat until blended.
                                Combine with meat mixture. Pour in 9 × 5
                                bake dish.

. . . .

Sauce:

2 or 3 tbsp. brown sugar   Mix thoroughly and spread over meat mixture.
¼ cup catsup
2 tbsp. water
⅛ tsp. nutmeg
½ tsp. dry mustard

. . . .

Bake at 350 degrees for 45 minutes to 1 hour.

Yield: 6 servings   *Sharon Shank Menefee*

. . . .

Poor Man's Steak

1½ lbs. hamburger   Mix together thoroughly and press into ½ to
¾ cup cracker crumbs   ¾-inch thickness in tray or on cookie sheet.
¾ cup water   Chill overnight. Cut in 4-inch squares. Coat
1 chopped onion   with flour. Brown on both sides in skillet. Place
1 tsp. salt   in bake dish.
¼ tsp. black pepper

. . . .

1 (10-oz.) can cream of mushroom   Combine and pour over meat.
   soup
½ cup milk

. . . .

Bake at 350 degrees for 1 hour.

Yield: 6 servings

. . . .

Cubed, Round, or Sirloin Steak

Fry steak in fat until well browned on both sides. Place in bake dish. Add ½ inch water
with 1 tbsp. vinegar added. Sprinkle with salt, MSG, and onion flakes. Pour 1 (10-oz.) can
cream of mushroom soup over the top. Cover and bake at 350 degrees for 2 to 2½ hours.

Variation: Add water to almost cover steak and omit soup. After baking, dissolve 2 tbsp.
cornstarch in a little water and stir into broth to thicken. Spoon over steak.

. . . .

Porcupine Balls

1 lb. hamburger 1½ cups bread crumbs 1 egg, beaten 1 cup milk 1 med. onion, chopped ½ tsp. chili powder 1 tsp. salt ¼ cup uncooked rice	Mix together thoroughly. Shape into 8 balls. Place rack in pressure cooker and pour ⅓ cup water in bottom. Place balls on rack.
1½ cups tomato juice	Gently pour over balls.
2 tsp. sugar	Sprinkle over juice.

Cook at 10 lbs. pressure for 15 minutes. (Or simmer in skillet with tight-fitting lid for 45 minutes.)

Yield: 8 servings

Roast Beef

3 to 4 lb. chuck roast	Cut a large piece of foil and place in roasting pan. Place roast on foil.
1 tbsp. vinegar	Sprinkle over roast.
1 (10-oz.) can cream of mushroom soup	Pour over roast.
1 env. onion soup mix 2 tsp. salt pepper to taste	Sprinkle over top. Then fold foil, tightly sealing all edges.

Roast at 350 degrees for 1 hour. Then reduce heat to 325 degrees and roast 2 hours longer, or until meat is tender.

Yield: 8 to 10 servings   *Carolyn H. Reed*

Crockpot 'Roast' Beef

A handy way to cook a roast, especially when you need to be away for several hours, is in the Crockpot. Before cooking, brown roast thoroughly on all sides in a little fat in a skillet. This adds to the flavor.

Place roast in Crockpot, and add about ½ cup water. Sprinkle with 1 tbsp. vinegar and 1 tsp. salt. Cover and cook a 4 or 5-pound roast on high for about 3½ to 4 hours. For easy slicing, let roast remain in broth to partially cool.

Barbecued Chuck Roast

4 to 5 lb. chuck roast	Cover and roast beef 2 hours at 350 degrees. Pour off fat and broth.
1 (8-oz.) can tomato sauce **½ cup A-l steak sauce** **2 tbsp. vinegar** **½ cup brown sugar**	Mix and pour over roast. Bake 1 hour longer or until tender.

Any left over is great sliced cold for sandwiches. (Save broth for gravy or other use.)

Yield: 10 to 12 servings   *Lois Kiser*

Lean Beef Salami

(Be sure to use Tender Quick meat cure for this recipe—not tenderizer. It may be found with butcher supplies.)

6 lbs. hamburger **3 tbsp. mustard seeds** **3 tbsp. cracked black pepper** **1 tsp. onion powder** **2 tbsp. liquid smoke** **6 tbsp. Tender Quick meat cure**	Mix together thoroughly. Form into 3 or 4 rolls 2 ½ or 3 inches in diameter, or of desired size, depending on whether you want larger or smaller size slices. Wrap tightly in foil and refrigerate for 24 hours.

Punch a row of several holes in the foil on the bottom side of the rolls. (This allows grease to escape.) Place on rack over broiler pan. Put about 4 cups of water in pan to catch drips. Bake at 325 degrees for 60 to 90 minutes, depending on how large you made the rolls. Leave in foil. Cool and chill in refrigerator tightly covered for 24 hours before slicing. (Salami freezes well. May be frozen in rolls, or slice and freeze slices on tray first. After frozen, place in plastic bag. You can then remove any amount individually for lunches.)

Dorothy Slabaugh Grove

Salisbury Steak

1½ lbs. hamburger **¾ cup quick oatmeal** **¼ cup chopped onion** **1 tsp. salt** **½ tsp. MSG (optional)** **1 egg, slightly beaten** **½ cup tomato juice**	Mix thoroughly. Shape into pieces like steak. Fry until brown on both sides.
1 (10-oz.) can cream of mushroom soup **¼ cup water**	Mix, and pour over meat.

Bake at 350 degrees for 1 hour.

Yield: 6 to 8 servings

PORK

How to Boil a Country (Cured) Ham

Trim off rind,* excessive fat, and any mold. Scrub any areas that did not have rind on to remove any curing mixture. If you don't care for very salty meat, soak overnight in cold water to cover. Discard soaking water. Place in large kettle, and cover with water, adding ¼ cup vinegar. Heat to boiling, reduce heat, and simmer 20 minutes per lb. If using meat thermometer, heat to 150 to 160 degrees. Remove kettle from heat, and allow ham to cool in broth. When cool, refrigerate until chilled for easier slicing.

(*Some cooks prefer to cook ham with rind on, and remove it after cooking. If you do this, be sure to scrub it well with warm water to remove all meat cure and any mold.)

How to Bake a Ham

Western hams are best baked. I prefer removing the rind and excessive fat. Leave enough fat to seal in the meat so it doesn't dry out during baking. Place ham on broiler pan or tray (tray must have an edge) with fat side up. Do not add water. Bake at 325 degrees about 20 minutes per lb. for a whole ham, or about 25 minutes per lb. for a half ham. Many cooks do not cover meat. I prefer laying foil loosely over top to hold in part of moisture.

If using a meat thermometer, insert it into thickest part of meat, but away from fat or bone. It may be inserted through the foil. A fresh ham (or pork roast) should be baked to 180 to 185 degrees. A cured ham should be baked to 160 degrees.

Fully Cooked Hams: These may be eaten without additional cooking, but will have much better flavor if baked some additional time. Bake a whole ham about 10 minutes per lb., and a half ham 14 minutes per lb. or to 135 degrees on meat thermometer.

Glaze for Ham: Hams may be glazed if desired for a little additional flavor and to make them attractive for serving hot. Remove from oven ½ hour before end of baking time. If cooked with rind on, remove it. If desired, you may score the fat in a diamond pattern and insert a whole clove in each diamond. Or simply spread on glaze.

Various glazes may be used. Mix ¾ cup brown sugar and ¾ cup undrained crushed pineapple for glaze. Or mix together ¾ cup brown sugar, 1 tbsp. cornstarch, ¼ cup vinegar, 1 tsp. dry mustard, and ½ cup water. Cook until slightly thickened and spoon over ham. Return to oven for the remaining half hour, and roast uncovered until done. If you desire to glaze a boiled ham, simply add glaze after cooking, and bake for ½ hour.

How to Carve a Ham

Ham should be cooled at least 15 minutes for carving. It is easiest to carve when almost cold. First, cut several slices from edge where bone is nearest surface. Then turn ham, setting it on this cut area. Cut all the slices you can of desired thickness from the center section, cutting from the top down to the bone. Turn ham over and cut remaining section as illustrated. All small pieces can be placed in containers to freeze for recipes calling for chopped cooked ham.

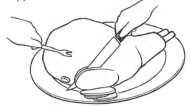

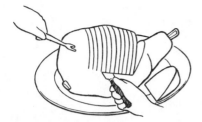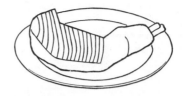

Do not discard the bone! It makes delicious bean soup. See index for recipe. If you have a kitchen saw, it is handiest to have it cut in several pieces so it will fit in the soup pot. If you don't have a saw, snitch one from the toolbox. Scrub it well, and use it! One bone usually makes three nice sections for three pots of soup. These can be frozen until used.

Ham Loaf

1½ lbs. cured ham, ground 1 lb. fresh ground pork 1 cup soft bread crumbs 2 eggs, slightly beaten 1 cup milk or tomato juice 2 tbsp. minced onion 1¼ tsp. salt ½ tsp. MSG (optional) ⅛ tsp. black pepper	Mix all ingredients thoroughly and place in a 9 × 5 loaf pan. Bake at 350 degrees for 45 minutes, then add glaze.

Glaze:

¾ cup brown sugar 1 tsp. dry mustard 1 tbsp. cornstarch ¼ cup vinegar ½ cup water	Combine in saucepan. Cook just until slightly thickened. After 45 minutes, spoon glaze over ham loaf. Continue to bake another 15 minutes.

Yield: 8 to 10 servings

Scalloped Ham

1½ cups cooked ground ham 2 cups saltine cracker crumbs	Mix in greased loaf pan or 1 ½-qt. bake dish.
2 eggs, beaten 2½ cups milk (may use ½ cup ham broth in place of ½ cup milk) 1 tsp. salt ¼ tsp. MSG (optional)	Combine and pour over mixture in dish.
1 tbsp. butter or margarine	Dot over top.
⅛ tsp. black pepper if desired	Sprinkle over top.

Bake at 350 degrees for 45 minutes.

Yield: 5 servings

Ham (or Chicken) Rolls

2 cups flour **3 tsp. baking powder** **½ tsp. salt**	Sift together.
⅓ cup margarine	Cut in until crumbly.
¾ cup milk	Stir in just until moistened. Press into ball. Roll out into rectangle ⅓ to ½-inch thick.
1½ cups ground cooked ham* **1 tbsp. prepared mustard*** **2 tbsp. soft margarine** **¼ tsp. MSG (optional)**	Mix together and spread over dough. Roll up like jelly roll. Cut into 1 ¼ inch thick slices. Place in greased 8-inch-square bake dish.
¼ cup ham (or chicken) broth	Spoon over top.

Bake at 375 degrees for 15 to 20 minutes. Serve plain or with cheese sauce. (*For chicken rolls, use chopped cooked chicken in place of ham, and mayonnaise in place of mustard. Make gravy with chicken broth instead of cheese sauce.)

Cheese Sauce:

3 tbsp. margarine **6 tbsp. flour** **1 tsp. salt** **2 cups milk**	Make white sauce. (See procedure on page 338.)
1 to 1½ cups grated yellow cheese	Stir in until melted.

Spoon sauce over rolls to serve.

Yield: 6 to 8 servings

Crockpot Pork Chops

½ cup flour **1 tsp. salt** **1½ tsp. dry mustard** **½ tsp. garlic powder**	Mix together thoroughly.
6 to 8 lean pork chops	Coat with flour mixture.
2 tbsp. oil	Fry in oil in skillet until well browned on both sides. Place in Crockpot.
½ tsp. MSG	Sprinkle over chops.
1 (10-oz.) can chicken and rice soup	Pour over chops.

Cover and cook on low for 8 hours, or on high for 4 hours.

Yield: 6 to 8 servings

Pork Chops

6 pork chops	Fry in fat in skillet until well browned on both sides.
1 med. onion, sliced	Top each chop with slice of onion.
½ cup water	Pour in skillet.
¼ cup catsup **2 tsp. Worcestershire sauce** **2 tsp., vinegar** **¼ tsp. MSG (optional)** **salt and pepper to taste** **1 (10-oz.) can cream of mushroom** **soup**	Mix thoroughly, and pour evenly over the the top.

Cover skillet and bake in 350 degree oven for 2 hours or until tender.

Yield: 6 servings

Oven Barbecued Spareribs

4 lbs. pork ribs	Add water to ¾ cover ribs, cover, and cook until tender—about 1 ½ hours. Or pressure-cook for 30 to 45 minutes. Drain and place in a shallow baking pan.
1 cup tomato juice **3 tbsp. vinegar** **⅓ cup brown sugar** **3 tbsp. Worcestershire sauce** **1 med. onion, minced** **1 tsp. dry mustard** **1 tsp. paprika** **½ tsp. chili powder** **½ cup catsup** **1 tsp. salt**	Combine in saucepan. Cook 5 minutes, stirring constantly. If sauce isn't as thick as desired, add 1 or 2 tbsp. cornstarch dissolved in a little water, and cook just until thickened.
1 tbsp. lemon juice	Add, and cool. Spoon over ribs, cover and chill overnight or 24 hours.

Uncover and bake at 350 degrees for 30 to 45 minutes basting several times with sauce. (May use bottled commercial barbecue sauce [such as Open Pit] if desired instead of making the sauce. Do not marinate. Pour sauce generously over cooked ribs in baking pan and bake as above.)

Yield: 4 to 5 servings *Janet Smith*

POULTRY

Chicken Barbecue Sauce

½ cup cooking oil
¾ cup vinegar
1½ tbsp. salt
¼ cup water
3 tbsp. sugar
1 tbsp. Worcestershire sauce
2 tsp. poultry seasoning
¼ tsp. black pepper

Combine in saucepan and heat to boiling. Let sit to cool.

Brush generously over chicken while cooking on outdoor grill. It usually takes about 3 hours to barbecue young chicken halves.

Harriet Steiner

Variation: Reduce poultry seasoning to 1 tsp. and add 1 tsp. garlic salt.

Yield: enough for 5 or 6 chicken halves   *Margaret Brubaker*

Oven Barbecued Chicken

8 to 10 serving pieces of chicken

Fry in fat in skillet until browned on both sides. Arrange in 9 × 13 bake dish.

⅓ cup chopped onions
3 tbsp. margarine

Sauté in skillet until tender

¾ cup catsup
⅓ cup vinegar
3 tbsp. brown sugar
½ cup water
2 tsp. prepared mustard
1 tbsp. Worcestershire sauce
¼ tsp. salt
⅛ tsp. black pepper

Combine in saucepan. Simmer 15 minutes. Pour over chicken in dish.

Bake at 350 degrees for 1½ hours, basting occasionally.

Yield: 4 to 5 servings

Buttermilk Baked Chicken

¼ cup butter

Melt in 9 × 13 bake dish.

1 young chicken, cut in serving
    pieces
1 cup thick sour milk or buttermilk
1 to 1½ cups cornflake crumbs

Dip chicken in milk, then in crumbs. Place in dish, skin side down.

. . . .

½ tsp. thyme	Sprinkle over chicken. (May vary seasonings
½ tsp. paprika	according to taste.)
½ tsp. MSG	
½ tsp. salt	
¼ tsp. garlic salt	

. . . .

Cover loosely with foil and bake 1 to 1½ hours, depending on tenderness of chicken. Remove foil, turn pieces of chicken over and bake, uncovered 20 minutes longer.

Yield: 4 to 6 servings

. . . .

Company Baked Chicken

12 to 15 serving pieces chicken	Arrange in a 9 × 13 or larger baking pan or dish.

. . . .

1 (16-oz.) can jellied cranberry sauce	Mix together thoroughly. Pour over pieces of chicken in dish
1 (8-oz.) bottle Russian lite salad dressing	
1 env. onion soup mix (such as Lipton's)	

. . . .

Cover loosely and bake at 400 degrees for 50 to 60 minutes. Uncover for last half of baking time.

Yield: 6 to 8 servings   *Grace Campbell*

. . . .

Company Stuffed Chicken

Use 12 deboned chicken breasts, or 16 thighs and legs, or a mixture. Remove skin from pieces of chicken.

. . . .

1 (2.5-oz.) pkg. chipped beef or dried beef	Line 9 × 13 or larger bake dish with beef.

. . . .

8 to 12 slices bacon	Partially fry bacon to eliminate part of grease, if desired—do not fry crisp. Place ½ or 1 strip bacon over top of each piece of chicken.

. . . .

1 (10-oz.) can cream of mushroom soup	Mix thoroughly, and spoon over chicken.
1 cup (8-oz.) commercial sour cream	

. . . .

Bake at 275 degrees for 3 hours, uncovered.

Yield: 12 servings   *Mae Shank*
                                                                                Ruth Weaver

. . . .

Crockpot Chicken

Place pieces of chicken in Crockpot as desired. Add ½ cup water in bottom of pot. Then pour bottled barbecue sauce over chicken as desired. Other seasonings may be added if desired, such as seasoned salt, and MSG. Or add water to come up ¾ of the way on chicken, add no season at all, and use chicken in recipes calling for cooked chicken. Cook all day on low setting, while at work.

Frances Justice
Elizabeth Yoder

Chicken Delight

1 med. onion, chopped ¼ cup margarine	Sauté in skillet.
2 cups chopped cooked chicken	Add. Cook and stir several minutes.
1 (10-oz.) can cream of chicken soup, or mushroom soup ½ soup can of water ½ tsp. salt ¼ tsp. MSG	Add and simmer 10 minutes. Serve over cooked rice.

Cook 1½ cups rice. Top with Chinese noodles.

Variation: Serve over corn bread.

Yield: 6 servings

Easy Baked Chicken

Press skin side of pieces of chicken in coating mix (such as Shake and Bake). Place in bake dish, coated side up. Sprinkle with salt, MSG, celery salt, paprika, and a little garlic powder. Dot with margarine. Cover loosely with foil and bake at 350 degrees for 1½ to 2 hours.

Variation: Omit coating mix, but sprinkle with other seasonings. Then combine 1 can mushroom soup with 1 cup cream or evaporated milk. Pour over top of chicken. Sprinkle with parsley flakes. Bake as above except do not cover.

Sweet and Sour Chicken

1 (8-oz.) can crushed pineapple	Drain and reserve juice. Set aside.
2 lbs. chicken breasts, deboned and cut into slivers 2 tbsp. butter or margarine	Sauté in butter until no longer pink.
½ cup chicken bouillon 2 large carrots, sliced	Add. Cover and cook until tender.
¼ cup brown sugar 2 tbsp. cornstarch ¼ cup vinegar 2 tsp. soy sauce	Mix together with reserved pineapple juice and stir in, cooking just until thickened.

| 1 med. onion sliced into rings*
 ½ cup green pepper strips*
 1 (8-oz.) can water chestnuts, thinly sliced | Add along with pineapple. Serve over rice. |

Cook 1 ½ cups rice. (*A smaller amount of onion and green pepper strips may be cooked with carrot mixture if preferred.)

Yield: 6 to 8 servings   *Patty Showalter*

Moist'n Crispy Onion Chicken

| 1 (2½ to 3½-lb.) young chicken, cut in parts
 ½ cup Hellmann's real mayonnaise | Brush chicken on all sides with mayonnaise. |
| 1 env. Lipton onion soup mix
 ¾ cup dry bread crumbs | Combine in plastic bag and shake until blended. Then place 1 piece of chicken at a time into bag and shake until coated. |

Place chicken on rack in broiler pan. Bake in 400-degree oven for 40 to 45 minutes or until golden brown and tender. (I prefer using a slightly lower temperature and then leaving the chicken in longer. To retain moisture you may wish to cover it loosely for the first half of baking time and uncover for second half.)

Yield: 4 servings   *Recipe courtesy Hellmann's real mayonnaise*

Vietnamese Chicken

(Gloria says do not use fork to test for doneness of chicken—it lets too many juices escape. Test with 1 prick of toothpick.)

3 or 4 garlic cloves 4 new green onions 2 tbsp. sugar 1 tsp. salt ½ tsp. black pepper	Combine and crush together.
18 pieces chicken—drumsticks and thighs	Rub seasoning mixture over chicken. Let set 1 to 2 hours. Then scrap off and reserve.
2 tbsp. oil	Heat in skillet and fry chicken over low heat until browned on both sides.
1 or more cups water.	Add along with reserved scrapings.

Cover and cook until tender, approximately 1 ½ hours. Serve with cooked rice.

Yield: 9 or more servings   *Gloria Tram Dak*

How to Roast a Turkey

I like to roast a turkey ahead of serving time so I don't have a lot of last-minute carving and handling of the carcass to do at a time I usually have a lot of guests. It can be done a day ahead and refrigerated until time to serve, or it can be frozen for several months if wrapped tightly. It also carves much easier when it is at least partially cooled.(I do not like to stuff a turkey with dressing since the dressing is always soggy. I much prefer baking the dressing in a bake dish separately so it is puffy and light. There is also extra danger of spoilage with a stuffed turkey that may not be cooked quite sufficiently with all that stuffing inside, or may not be cooled properly.)

I like to get a large turkey—20 to 25 lbs.—because they are a much better buy. There is much more meat per bone structure on larger birds. Also, it freezes so well, and while you are going to the trouble to roast it, you will have enough for several meals with almost the same effort.

Thaw a frozen turkey before roasting. A 20 to 25 lb. turkey will take 3 to 4 days to thaw in the refrigerator. If quicker thawing is needed, it may be placed in a heavy paper bag to prevent outside of turkey from becoming too warm, and thaw at 70-degree-or-less (not any warmer than this) room temperature. Close bag and place in sink or on a tray to catch any thawing liquid. It will take close to 24 hours to thaw with this method. Smaller turkeys (12 to 15 lbs.) should thaw in 2 to 2½ days in the refrigerator.

Rinse turkey well inside and out with cold water. Remove any pinfeathers, excessive globs of fat, and dark yellow outer skin. Remove giblets and neck, and cook separately in water either in the oven alongside of turkey, or on top of the stove. Simmer, covered, about 1½ to 2 hours, a little longer in the oven. Add liver during the last half hour of cooking.

Place turkey in roaster, or on broiler pan or tray if you don't have a roaster large enough. Tray must have an edge of at least 2 inches to catch the broth that accumulates during baking. I like to tie the legs with a string at the end of the drumsticks to hold them close to the sides of the turkey. Melt ¼ cup butter or margarine and pour over turkey. Sprinkle with 1 tbsp. vinegar and 1 tbsp. salt. Some liquid smoke may also be brushed over it if desired. Cover with a lid or with a large sheet of foil. Do not let foil edges hang over edge of pan. The dripping of grease and moisture onto heating element during baking could cause a fire. Tuck foil inside edge of pan. Do not add water; the turkey will accumulate its own broth.

Bake at 425 degrees for 1 hour. (The higher beginning temperature quickly brings all the meat to a cooking temperature, and saves about 1 hour of roasting time on a large bird.) Then reduce heat to 325 degrees and roast 3½ to 4½ hours longer, or until done. You may wish to baste the turkey occasionally with some of the accumulated broth in the pan during the last half of baking time. A good way to test for doneness is to wiggle the leg in the joint slightly. If it is loose, turkey is done—do not pull so hard that you disjoint it, especially if you wish to serve turkey whole! If serving immediately, allow to cool 15 to 20 minutes for easier carving. (See roasting chart on page 361.)

If serving later, loosen foil so steam can escape but so turkey won't dry out. Cool until almost cold (do not chill) before carving. As you carve, arrange meat in packages of the desired size, putting some light and some dark meat in each package. Accumulate all small pieces in separate containers to freeze for casseroles. Place broth in the same number of containers as you have meat, so you will have broth to use for gravy each time you serve turkey. It is good to pour a little broth over meat in each container also. I like to wrap each portion of sliced meat in plastic wrap, sealing tightly, and then place in a plastic bag also. Freeze immediately.

To use, place packages of meat and broth in refrigerator overnight to thaw. Carefully lay meat in a large skillet or electric skillet, so pieces don't get broken apart. Pour at least part of the broth over turkey (all of it, unless you wish to save part of it for gravy), adding a little water if needed so you have at least 1 cup of liquid. Sprinkle each piece of turkey with a little salt and MSG. Heat on medium until hot through. Dissolve 1 ½ tbsp. cornstarch in ¼ cup water.

Holding up one side of skillet so broth all runs to one side, pour in cornstarch mixture. Then tilt skillet back and forth a time or two so mixture is distributed throughout meat again, heating just until thickened slightly. Carefully lift out pieces of meat with spatula, and spoon a little of the thickened broth over it to keep it nice and moist on plate. Happy eating!

Overnight Roast Turkey: Prepare turkey as described. Bake at 425 degrees for 1 hour. Then reduce heat to 275 degrees and roast 8 hours, or until tender.

. . . . : . . . .

Carving a Turkey

For easier carving, turkey should be cooled 20 minutes if carving at the table. You will need a very sharp knife and a two-tined fork to hold the hot meat while carving.

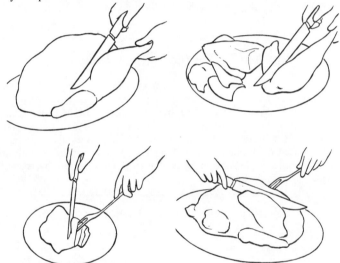

Remove leg and thigh portions first. Pull leg away from the body to expose joint, and cut between bones. Then cut thighs and drumsticks apart at joint between them. Slice meat from both pieces as shown in sketches.

Remove wings. Wings may be divided at second joint if large. Carve the breast by slicing meat across the grain parallel to the breastbone. Distribute light and dark meat on serving plate in attractive manner.

After the meal, remove all the small pieces of meat from the carcass. Place in containers to use for cassroles and other dishes calling for chopped cooked turkey or chicken.

. . . .

Oven Barbecued Turkey

Make one recipe of Barbecue Sauce used for Oven Barbecued Spare Ribs on page 375.

. . . .

Roast a 20 to 25 lb. turkey at 425 degrees for 1 hour. Then spoon sauce over turkey. Reduce oven temperature to 325 and roast 3½ to 4½ hours longer, or until done. Baste frequently with sauce during last half of roasting time. Turkey may be cut up before roasting. It is easier to baste entire amount when cut. If cut, roast at 425 degrees for ¾ hour, then at 325 for approximately 3 hours longer.

. . . .

Turkey Breast

Pour melted butter over turkey breast. Then rub with salt, vinegar, and liquid smoke. Cover and roast at 425 degrees for ¾ hour. Then reduce temperature to 325 and roast 3 hours more or until tender. Turkey breast may also be pressure-cooked the same as beef heart for 1½ hours, or cooked all day in the Crockpot, adding ½ to 1 cup water and salt.

. . . .

Smoked Turkey (or Chicken) Deluxe

(Very tender and delicious!)

Soak turkey for 2 or 3 days in a cool place in a brine made with Morton's Tenderquick meat cure. Use 1 cup cure to 7 cups water for brine, making enough to cover turkey. After soaking, remove turkey and rub well with liquid smoke. Roast as usual except that roasting time should be shortened—probably about 1 hour on a large turkey because brine tenderizes it. Cut-up roasting chicken may be soaked in brine in refrigerator overnight or up to 2 days. Rub with liquid smoke and bake.

. . . .

SEAFOOD
Crabmeat Casserole

2 cups crabmeat (canned or fresh) **2 cups soft bread crumbs** **1 (10-oz.) can cream of mushroom** ** soup** **⅓ cup mayonnaise** **1 med. onion, chopped** **⅓ cup celery, finely chopped** **½ tsp. salt** **¼ tsp. MSG (optional)**	Mix in a greased 9 × 13 baking dish.
3 eggs, beaten **1½ cups milk**	Combine and pour over mixture in dish.
⅔ cup grated cheddar cheese	Sprinkle over top

Bake at 350 degrees for approximately 1 hour.

Yield: serves 8 to 10.

Baked Stuffed Fish

(Minnie said she got this recipe from a Greek man who operated a restaurant in Wyoming. Select a large fish weighing from 5 to 8 lbs. Striped bass are good; so are cutthroat trout, rock bass, or any fish with firm flesh. Split fish, but do not cut through. Spread open to stuff.)

2 to 4 tbsp. vegetable oil **½ cup chopped celery** **½ cup chopped onions** **½ cup finely chopped green pepper** **½ cup raw chopped bacon**	Fry in skillet until golden brown.
2 cups canned tomatoes, or 4 or 5 ** fresh peeled tomatoes, cut in** ** chunks**	Add, and cook vigorously until thickened. Set aside.
2 eggs, slightly beaten **2 cups bread cubes** **1 tbsp. minced onion** **½ tsp. salt** **½ tsp. thyme** **¼ tsp. black pepper** **½ cup milk** **1 (6½-oz.) can crabmeat***	Mix together thoroughly and stuff into cavity of fish. Fold over and secure the open edge with skewers. Spoon sauce over fish.

Bake at 350 degrees for 45 to 60 minutes, until flaky. Make cuts every 2 inches in fish for serving to mark portions. (*May substitute other seafood such as oysters or shrimp.)

Yield: an 8 lb. fish will serve 10 people   *Minnie Carr*

Fried Fish

Fresh fish may be quickly and easily fried in a little fat in a skillet. Dredge both sides of fish in cornmeal or in coating mix (see page 365). Heat skillet until moderately hot, add 2 or more tbsp. fat, and fry fish until tender and browned on both sides (approximately 7 minutes on each side). Sprinkle lightly with salt while frying. Serve immediately.

Fried Oysters

Drain oysters in strainer. Check for any pieces of shell, etc. Dip oysters in slightly beaten egg, then roll in crumbs. (For crumbs, combine 1 cup saltine cracker crumbs to 2 tbsp. each cornmeal and flour.) Fry in hot shortening or oil in skillet until browned on both sides. Sprinkle with salt and a little MSG while frying. Serve piping hot.

Scalloped Oysters

½ cup margarine, melted 1½ cups saltine cracker crumbs	Mix together and reserve half.
1 pt. oysters, chopped	Mix with half of crumbs.
4 eggs, beaten 2 tsp. Worcestershire sauce ¼ cup green pepper, finely chopped ¼ cup onion, finely chopped 2 tbsp. parsley, chopped 1 tsp. salt ¼ tsp. MSG (optional) ¼ tsp. black pepper	Add, mixing well. Pour in greased 2-qt. casserole dish. Sprinkle reserved half of crumbs over the top.

Bake at 350 degrees for approximately 40 minutes.

Yield: 4 to 6 servings

Scalloped Corn and Oysters

1½ cups oysters with liquid 1 cup cream-style corn 3 eggs, slightly beaten 1 cup saltine crackers, crumbled ½ tsp. salt ¼ tsp. MSG (optional) ¼ tsp. celery salt black pepper to taste	Mix all ingredients and pour into a greased 1½ qt. casserole dish.
½ cup cracker crumbs 2 tbsp. melted butter	Combine and sprinkle over top.

Bake at 350 degrees for 50 to 60 minutes.

Yield: 5 servings

Oyster Dressing

5 cups dried cubed bread **1 pt. oysters, drained**	Combine in greased 8-inch-square bake dish.
½ tsp. salt **½ tsp. Italian seasoning** **¼ tsp. MSG (optional)** **¼ tsp. celery salt**	Sprinkle over mixture in dish.
4 or 5 large eggs, beaten **2½ cups milk**	Combine and pour over all.
1 or 2 tbsp. butter	Dot over top.

Bake at 350 degrees approximately 50 minutes.

Yield: 6 servings

Scalloped Salmon

1½ cups flaked salmon, undrained **¾ cup saltine cracker crumbs** **2 tbsp. cornmeal** **1 tsp. salt** **¼ tsp. MSG (optional)** **¼ tsp. black pepper**	Combine in greased 1 ½-qt. bake dish.
2 eggs, beaten **1¼ cups milk**	Combine and pour over mixture.
2 tbsp. margarine	Dot over top.

Bake at 350 degrees for 45 minutes.

Yield: 4 to 5 servings

Salmon-Spinach Strata

6 slices bread	Trim crust from 3 slices and reserve. Line bottom of 2-qt. casserole dish with other 3 slices and trimmings.
2 cups grated cheddar sharp cheese, (reserve ½ cup) **1 (16-oz.) can salmon, drained (reserve liquid)** **1 (10-oz.) pkg. frozen chopped spinach**	Sprinkle bread with ¾ cup cheese, then layer with salmon and spinach. Then add another ¾ cup cheese.

Cut the 3 reserved slices of bread in half diagonally, making triangles. Layer triangles, overlapping over top of cheese.

4 eggs, beaten **2 cups milk** **1 tbsp. finely chopped onion** **¾ tsp. salt** **⅛ tsp. black pepper** **¼ tsp. dry mustard**	Combine with reserved salmon liquid and pour over bread triangles in dish. Cover and refrigerate at least 1 hour.

Bake at 350 degrees for 1 hour, or until knife inserted in center comes out clean. Sprinkle reserved ½ cup cheese over top and bake 5 minutes more. Let stand 5 to 10 minutes before serving.

Yield: 6 servings　　　　　　　　　　　　　　　　　　　　　　　Lora Heatwole

Shrimp

1 cup butter	Melt in skillet.
¼ cup lemon juice **1 tsp. Worcestershire sauce** **1 tsp. soy sauce** **1 tsp. parsley flakes** **¾ tsp. salt** **¼ tsp. black pepper** **¼ tsp. garlic powder** **¼ tsp MSG (optional)**	Add. Heat to boiling.
2 lbs. large shrimp, peeled and deveined	Add. Cook over medium heat, stirring occasionally, for 5 to 7 minutes.

Serve immediately.

Yield: 5 to 6 servings　　　　　　　　　　　　　　　*Dorothy Shank Showalter*

Seafood Spaghetti Pie

6 oz. spaghetti	Cook and drain.
1 egg, beaten ⅔ cup grated Parmesan cheese (reserve half) ¼ tsp. garlic powder	Add, reserving half of the cheese. Toss to coat spaghetti well. Press mixture over bottom and up sides of a greased 9″ pie plate.
3 additional eggs, beaten 1 (4½-oz.) can tiny shrimp, drained 1 (4½-oz.) can crabmeat, drained and flaked 1 cup evaporated skimmed milk (reserved cheese) 3 tbsp. chopped green onion ½ tsp. dried dillweed	Combine well, and pour mixture in spaghetti-lined plate.
paprika	Sprinkle over top.

Cut out a circle of foil to cover edges of pie. Bake at 350 degrees for 35 to 40 minutes or until knife inserted just off center comes out clean—center will be moist. Let stand 5 minutes before serving.

Yield: 6 servings   *Donna Lou Heatwole*

Tuna (or Chicken) Salad Bake

¾ cup diced celery ⅓ cup chopped onion 2 tbsp. margarine	Sauté in skillet until tender.
1 (10-oz.) can cream of chicken soup 2 tbsp. mayonnaise or salad dressing ½ tsp. salt ¼ tsp MSG 3 hard-cooked eggs, chopped 1 (6½-oz. or 9-oz.) can tuna, drained, or 1½ cups chopped cooked chicken	Mix in, and pour into an 8-inch-square bake dish.
½ to 1 cup crushed potato chips, or other crumbs	Sprinkle over top.

Bake at 350 degrees for 35 to 40 minutes.

Yield: 4 to 6 servings

Tuna Bake Special

⅔ cup chopped onion ½ cup chopped green pepper 2 tbsp. vegetable oil	Sauté in skillet until tender. (Reserve 2 tbsp. for topping.)
1 cup thick tomato juice 2 tbsp. brown sugar 2 tbsp. lemon juice 2 tsp. soy sauce	Add, and simmer several minutes.
1 (9-oz.) can tuna	Add, and heat to boiling again. Pour into 2-qt. casserole dish. Top with little biscuits.
Biscuits: 1½ cups flour 2 tsp. baking powder ½ tsp. salt	Sift together.
¼ cup shortening	Cut in.
1 small egg approximately ¼ cup milk	Break egg in cup. Add milk to make ½ cup. Stir in the 2 tbsp. reserved onion mixture. Add all at once to dry ingredients , stirring only until moistened.

Shape into a ball. Knead several times. Roll out to ½-inch thickness on surface sprinkled with sesame seeds. Cut into little biscuits (a tomato paste can makes an excellent cutter). Arrange over top of casserole with seed side up. Bake at 375 degrees for 15 to 20 minutes.

Yield: 6 servings

VARIETY MEATS AND WILD MEATS

Beef (Veal or Pork) Brains

Soak brains in several changes of cold water for approximately 30 minutes to remove excess blood, or until water remains clear. Peel off outer membrane, dipping the brains in water repeatedly to help loosen it. Then soak brains in fresh water in the refrigerator for an hour, or overnight to whiten them. Drain off water, dip in flour to coat both sides, and fry in fat in moderately hot skillet until lightly browned on both sides. Sprinkle with salt while frying. Serve immediately.

Beef Heart

Trim any fat from end of medium-sized beef heart. Place in pressure saucepan, add ½ cup water, and sprinkle 1 tbsp. vinegar and 1 tsp. salt over heart. Close lid and process at 10 lbs. pressure for 1 to 1½ hours depending on size. Remove from heat and let heart soak in broth until cool enough to slice. Turn over occasionally so entire meat soaks in liquid.

Then slice and place back in saucepan, sprinkling each piece with a little MSG and a little more salt. Pour at least 1 cup broth over meat, and heat. Dissolve 1½ tbsp. cornstarch in a small amount of water and stir in to thicken. Spoon thickened gravy over meat to serve.

(If you will not be serving the entire heart at once, slice only what is to be served, and place remainder in narrow container in refrigerator with broth poured over it to keep it fresh and moist until ready to use. Then slice and heat as above.)

. . . .

Liver (Fried)

Slice beef or pork liver in ¼-inch-thick slices. (It will slice much more easily if half frozen first.) Press both sides of slices in cornmeal to coat. Heat fat in skillet to medium hot and add liver. Add chopped onion if desired. Sprinkle on salt, and fry on both sides just until browned and tender. Serve immediately.

(If liver isn't tender, before cooking run half-frozen pieces through the food grinder. Add chopped onion, salt, and a beaten egg if desired. Or simply drop mounds of ground liver in heated skillet. Sprinkle with dried minced onion and salt, and fry until browned on both sides. My family prefers this method.)

Do not overcook liver—this will make it tougher, rather than more tender! Chicken livers may be rinsed in a strainer and poured into fat in moderately hot skillet. Sprinkle with flour and salt, partially cover, and fry until browned on both sides. Serve immediately.

. . . .

Liverburgers

1 lb. liver **2 cups diced raw potatoes** **¾ cup chopped onions**	Run through food grinder twice.

. . . .

1½ tsp. salt **⅛ tsp. black pepper**	Add.

. . . .

2 tbsp. oil or margarine	Heat in skillet. Drop in liver mixture in mounds and fry quickly on both sides. Remove from pan.

. . . .

Gravy: **2 tbsp. flour** **¼ cup tomato juice**	Slowly add to drippings in pan, stirring constantly until smooth.

. . . .

1¾ cup milk	Stir in until boiling. Add liverburgers, cover, and simmer 15 minutes.

. . . .

Yield: 4 servings   *Anna Mae Weaver*

. . . .

Barbecued Hot Dogs

12 hot dogs	Arrange in 8 × 12 bake dish.
¼ cup chopped onions **1 tbsp. margarine**	Sauté in saucepan.
1½ cups tomato juice **2 tbsp. brown sugar** **1 tbsp. vinegar** **1 tbsp. Worcestershire sauce** **1 tsp. salt** **½ tsp. prepared mustard** **½ tsp. celery salt**	Add, and heat to boiling.
2 tbsp. corn starch dissolved in ¼ **cup water**	Stir in until thickened. Pour over hot dogs in bake dish.

Cover, and bake at 350 degrees for 45 minutes. Serve in buns.

Yield: 12 servings

Corn Dogs

½ cup flour **⅓ cup cornmeal** **1 tbsp. sugar** **1 tsp. dry mustard** **1 tsp. baking powder** **½ tsp. salt**	Sift together.
1 egg, beaten **½ cup milk** **1 tbsp. oil**	Combine and stir in until well mixed.
1 lb. hot dogs	Dip in batter, coating well.

Fry in deep hot fat (360 to 375 degrees) about 2 minutes until golden brown.

Yield: approximately 8 servings

Hot Dog Boats

Slit hot dogs ¾ of the way through lengthwise and fill with long narrow slices of cheese. Use biscuit mix to make biscuit dough. Roll out and cut into rectangles slightly longer than hot dogs. Lay a hot dog, cheese side up, on each rectangle. Bring up sides and pinch ends tightly to form boats. Place in bake dish and bake at 375 degrees for 15 to 20 minutes until lightly browned.

Variation: For **Pigs in a Blanket,** roll biscuit dough into a large circle ¼-inch thick. Cut like a pie into wedges. Spread dough lightly with melted butter and prepared mustard. Place a cheese-filled hot dog on wide end of each wedge. Roll up and place on greased baking pan with point underneath to hold in place. Bake as for Boats.

Fried Pheasant

Roll or coat pheasant in flour. Sprinkle with salt, black pepper, and oregano. Fry in hot fat in skillet until thoroughly browned on both sides. Add a small amount of water, cover tightly, and steam until tender. (Pheasant is often prepared like chicken and takes about the same amount of cooking time, depending on the tenderness of the bird.)

Quail with All-Game Dressing

4 quail	Wash, drain and pat dry. Set aside.
¼ cup butter, melted **⅓ cup onion, finely chopped** **⅓ cup celery, finely chopped**	Sauté in skillet until tender, but not browned.
1 cup dry bread crumbs **¼ tsp. poultry seasoning** **¼ tsp. dried savory**	Add, tossing lightly until mixed.
¼ cup beef broth **1 small egg, beaten**	Combine and add, tossing lightly until well moistened.
another ¼ cup melted butter **salt and pepper to taste**	Have ready.

Lightly spoon stuffing into cavity of each bird. Place birds breast side up in a greased baking pan. Brush with melted butter, and sprinkle with salt and pepper. Roast, uncovered at 350 degrees for 45 to 60 minutes, or until tender. Baste often with the melted butter.

Yield: 4 servings

Minnie Carr

Squirrel

Pressure-cook squirrel for ½ hour until tender. Then sprinkle with salt, black pepper, and seasoned salt, and fry in hot fat in skillet until browned on each side.

Miriam Haarer

Roast of Venison

Marinate roast overnight in salt and vinegar water to cover. (Use 1 cup vinegar and ½ cup salt to 1 gal. water.) Drain. Place in roasting pan. Combine 1 (10-oz.) can cream of mushroom soup and 1 soup can of milk, and pour over roast. Add chopped onion and chopped green pepper if desired. Cover tightly and roast at 325 degrees until tender. See time chart according to the size of roast. Time should be the same as for beef.

Minnie Carr

Venison Bologna

(This is an excellent recipe that can also be used with ground beef. Miriam says her family likes it so well that they often save out only the steaks, and grind the remaining meat for bologna. To make the cloth bags, you can use the better portions of clean worn-out bed sheets, or other cotton fabric. They can be made various sizes, depending on the size slices of bologna you prefer. A good size is to cut out a 12 × 12 or 12 × 14-inch piece of fabric, fold it in half, and sew down the one side and across the one end. This will give you a bag about 6 inches wide, and will give a slice of bologna at least 3 inches in diameter. Make any length that will fit into the kettle you use for boiling it.)

25 lbs. ground venison 5 lbs. pork sausage 1½ lbs. brown sugar ¼ cup salt 1 pt. Morton's Tenderquick meat 　cure ½ cup liquid smoke 4 tsp. saltpeter 2 tsp. mace 2 tsp. ground cloves 8 tsp. black pepper garlic to taste (optional)	Mix all ingredients together thoroughly. Cover tightly, and let stand in cool place for 3 days.

Heat water sufficient to cover the sticks of bologna in a large kettle to boiling. Add bags of bologna, cover and boil 1 hour, or until done. Sticks will float when done. Overcooking will dry meat out. Drain, cool, and chill for 1 or 2 days to cure meat out before freezing. You may wish to cut sticks in half before freezing so you don't need to thaw too large an amount at one time. It is best not to slice it before freezing. After thawing, slice and use like any bologna.

Miriam Haarer

Venison Stroganoff

2 lbs. tender raw venison	Cut in 1 or 2-inch cubes and place in a flat dish.
1 tsp. vegetable oil 1 tsp. black pepper juice of 1 lemon	Sprinkle over meat. Let marinate at least 10 minutes.
¼ cup butter 1 large onion, chopped	Heat in skillet, add meat, and fry over med.-high heat until browned.
1 (4 or 6-oz.) can sliced mushrooms	Add and fry until heated.
2 cups commercial sour cream 1 (10-oz.) can tomato puree 1 tbsp. flour 1 tsp. salt	Combine, then pour over mixture in skillet. Cover and simmer over low heat for 10 minutes.

Yield: 4 to 6 servings

Minnie Carr

CHAPTER EIGHT.

MICROWAVE COOKING

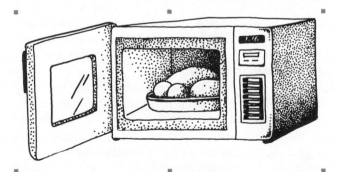

MICROWAVE COOKING

I am grateful to Jerry and Diane Horst for sharing with me much of the information included in this chapter. Jerry is part owner and manager of Appliances, Unlimited, in Harrisonburg, Virginia. He informed me of many of the questions their customers were asking as they learned to operate their microwave ovens, and also furnished other materials from which I gained information for this chapter. I attended their microwave cooking classes and most of the recipes, unless otherwise indicated, are favorite ones they have used in their classes or in their publication, *The Wave Line*.

Microwave cooking is an alternate process of introducing heat to food. Instead of cooking the food from heated air as in a conventional oven, the microwave oven cooks food with ultra-high-frequency microwaves emitted from a magnetron. These electromagnetic waves of energy, similar to light waves and radio waves, penetrate the food, causing the food molecules to vibrate at an ultra-high speed. As food molecules vibrate against each other, this friction creates heat which cooks the food. The microwaves strike the food from all sides. Since heat is created both on the surface of the food and inside the food itself, food cooks much faster than in a conventional oven.

Microwaves penetrate food to a depth of about ¾ to 1 ½ inches. Therefore, small food items cook very quickly. However, larger foods are cooked by conduction of heat to deeper areas, since microwaves lose approximately half their power every ¾ of an inch. Heat produced on outer layer of food is conducted to center of food. These foods continue to cook for a time after they are removed from the oven if they stand a while. This is called "standing time." The length of time food continues to cook depends on the density of the food and the heat buildup in the food. It is important to be aware of this, especially with larger, more dense foods. These foods need to be taken out of the oven before they are done or they may be overcooked after standing time.

Microwaves pass through the container and are absorbed by the food. The oven, the air in the oven, and the container do not get hot from the cooking process. The only heat in the container is conducted from the heated food to the container. You can test whether food is heated by feeling the container on the bottom. If it is heated, you can be sure the food inside is hot.

Be sure to follow the directions in the instruction manual that came with your specific oven. The information given here is very basic and is not intended to replace manufacturer's directions.

Microwaves reflect off metal. You should not use metal containers or those with any metal trim (such as china with metal trim, lead crystal, or foil-lined paper) in your microwave. This could damage your oven. Melamine dishes also should not be used because they contain metallic substances. This could cause them to crack during cooking. Technically, foil and TV trays should not be used in the microwave since foil is a metal. However, with care some foil can be used to an advantage and other foil items such as TV trays because of convenience may be used with caution. When using foil, it must be at least one inch away from the edge of the oven to prevent arcing. You should also have three times the amount of food exposed as foil. Do not have a pointed or crinkled area of foil protruding which could cause arcing.

Foil TV trays may be used in the microwave if height of the edge of the tray is less than ¾ of an inch. Food will take twice as long to cook, however, since the foil shields the microwaves from reaching the food on entire bottom surface. It is much quicker to transfer food from foil TV tray to a plate to heat. Foil is excellent to use for shielding areas of large food to avoid overheating. This blocks the microwaves and keeps them from reaching the area. For example, the end of the drumsticks on poultry should be shielded with foil to avoid overcooking until the center of the bird is done. Small pieces of foil can also be cut to shield the corners of a square dish when baking a cake, brownies, and the like.

Utensils made from glass, glass ceramics, paper, and most plastics can be used. There are a few glass ceramics which are not microwave safe and may be damaged if used in the microwave. You can test them by the following method:

Utensil Test. Place a glass measuring cup of water next to the empty dish to be tested in your microwave oven. Heat on high for 1 minute and 30 seconds. Then check the tested dish. If it is cool and the water in the cup is hot, the dish is safe to use. If the dish is warm, it should only be used for short-term cooking or heating. If dish is hot and the water in the cup is cool, do not use in the microwave at all! The dish is obviously absorbing the microwaves.

You can use many bake dishes you already have and do not need to go out and purchase special microwave dishes. Round dishes cook a little more evenly than square or rectangular ones. The corners in square dishes tend to become hotter than other parts of the dish and may overcook.

Casseroles cook faster in a ring mold since microwaves can enter food from center as well as all sides. You can make a regular round bake dish into a ring dish simply by inverting a microwave-safe juice glass or custard cup in the center of the dish. Then pour food around it.

Most paper products may be used safely. Paper products can be used for heating and serving food and to absorb moisture and spatters during cooking. Use white paper products rather than colored ones. Do not use paper towels or napkins containing nylon or other synthetic fibers since they could melt or become hot enough to ignite. Newspaper can also ignite from the ink used in printing and should never be placed in a microwave oven. Vegetables packed in cardboard boxes or plastic bags may be safely cooked in the containers if you puncture the box or bag to allow steam to escape.

Choose the type of covering which will give the desired cooking results for various foods. Use plastic wrap to retain moisture on vegetables and leftovers. Use paper towels for bacon to absorb grease and spatters. For muffins and breads, you may wish to use paper towels to avoid sogginess. If they tend to be too dry, sprinkle with a little water and partially cover with plastic wrap to retain moisture.

Best results are obtained with some foods, especially casseroles, if they are covered for the first part of the cooking time, and then left uncovered for the last portion of time. You can also partially cover containers to obtain desired results. Waxed paper forms a loose cover similar to partial covering and may be used to hold in heat and prevent spatters.

When completely covering food, always be sure to leave a little opening at one corner or edge to allow steam to escape.

Most plasticware is safe to use in the microwave for heating food only. Overheating or cooking food in a plastic container could cause the container to warp or melt from the heat transmitted to the container from the food itself. It is best not to use plastics for long-term cooking, and to use plastics labeled "dishwasher safe." Regular Tupperware is not recommended for microwave use. Only the "Ultra line" of Tupperware is considered microwave safe. Regular Tupperware can be easily warped or melted by overheated food. Some brands of plastic wrap are also too thin to hold up from the heat of the food and may shrink or melt. Usually packages are labeled "microwave safe" if heavy enough to use.

The majority of foods need to be stirred or turned during cooking time to obtain even cooking results. This is especially important with larger quantities or pieces of food.

Water, fat, and sugar attract microwave energy, so foods containing these ingredients will tend to cook faster.

Most foods do not brown in the microwave since they cook too fast to brown. An exception is larger cuts of meat having high fat content. The fat attracts more microwave energy and becomes very hot during cooking. With the longer cooking time, browning will occur. A **browning skillet** can be purchased to use for smaller cuts of meat, eggs, cheese, and sandwiches to obtain browning if desired.

Various sauces, liquid browning agents, and spices can be used to give a browned appearance or good eye appeal. You can use soy sauce, barbecue sauce, or Worcestershire sauce mixed with a little water on meats. For a nice effect on poultry, brush with melted butter and sprinkle with paprika.

Casseroles can be topped with crumbs, grated cheese, crushed corn chips, or potato chips. Or use crumbled bacon or crumbled french-fried onion rings. These should be added after the last stirring.

Cupcakes, muffins, or sweet breads can be sprinkled with spices, nuts, or a mixture of cinnamon and sugar, or coconut. Sprinkle on food immediately after microwaving.

To obtain more even cooking, it is important to arrange food so that thicker or larger parts are placed near the outside edge of the dish with thinner areas or smaller particles to the center. Corners and sides of dish receive more energy than the center.

Frozen items *should be defrosted* before cooking in the microwave. If not defrosted first, cooking will be uneven, especially with larger items. You can quickly defrost food on the defrost setting of your microwave before cooking.

For faster cooking of casseroles, choose a larger more shallow dish rather than a deep narrow one holding the same amount. A shallow dish exposes more food surface to microwave energy and will cook in less time.

Do not overcook foods. When in doubt about the amount of time needed, use the lesser amount and then test food. You can always put it back in the oven a little longer, but you cannot correct overdoneness!

Many microwaves are equipped with an **automatic temperature probe** which is a useful feature. It is especially helpful for things like warming soup and beverages, to heat water an exact temperature for dissolving yeast, and for cooking meats to the exact temperature you wish. Insert the probe into the food or liquid, set the temperature desired, and the oven will automatically turn off when correct temperature is reached. The probe can also be set to hold food at a certain temperature for any amount of time you may desire. Follow exact directions for probe which came with your specific oven.

To **adapt conventional recipes** to use in the microwave, remember that most foods cook 3 to 4 times faster in the microwave. If a recipe requires 1 hour to cook, reduce cooking time to 15 to 20 minutes on full power. Check food in 15 minutes and then add a few additional minutes if needed. If using a lower power level, allow extra time accordingly. It is helpful when adapting recipes to find a microwave recipe that is similar to the one you are using, and use it as a guide. Mark any necessary changes on the recipe for future use. The amouunt of liquid should be reduced when converting conventional recipes since the short cooking time does not cook nearly as much liquid out of food. A general rule is to use ¼ the amount of liquid called for—if recipe calls for 1 cup liquid, use ¼ cup.

Use a little less seasoning in the microwave since flavor is not lost in the shorter cooking process. It also takes less leavening for baked goods. Cakes, muffins, and the like will rise more in the microwave.

When doubling a recipe or the amount of food being cooked in the microwave, remember to increase cooking time. For a double recipe, cooking time should be just slightly less than two times as long. Two potatoes take slightly less than twice as long to cook as one. Three potatoes take slightly less than three times as long as one. Larger amounts of food need to be stirred more often to obtain even cooking. Foods do not need to be stirred as often when using a lower power level. If you are cooking something which you do not wish to stir, switch to a lower power level (between 50 percent and 80 percent) as soon as food reaches the cooking point.

Always keep in mind when heating foods that it makes a big difference whether food is refrigerator-cold or at room temperature. Adjust the amount of microwave time accordingly.

TIPS FOR HEATING LEFTOVERS

•When heating single plates of food for a meal, heat only one plate at a time. Cover each plate with plastic wrap to retain heat and moisture.

•Arrange food with thickest portions and hard-to-heat foods at outside edge of plate. Place smaller, quicker-heating foods and foods with high sugar or fat content in center of plate for more even heating.

•For faster heating, spread dense foods like mashed potatoes out somewhat rather than heaping them up in a thick pile.

•Add sauce or gravy to dry meats to provide moisture, or cover well with plastic wrap.

•When heating several small cups or dishes at one time, arrange in a circle near the center of the oven leaving center spot open, for more even heating. Place single plates or dishes in the center of the oven.

•Stir soups, sauces, or dips before heating to incorporate air.

•When reheating pizza, place paper towel on plate under pizza to keep crust from becoming soggy. Cover top with waxed paper or partially cover with plastic wrap.

DO'S AND DON'TS

•Do not heat eggs in the shell in the microwave oven. Always prick the yolk of an egg before heating to avoid a heat buildup and explosion.

•Foods with a skin such as potatoes, tomatoes, or hot dogs should be pierced before heating to allow steam to escape.

•Remove any metal fasteners from bread bags or other food before heating. You can cut a strip of plastic from the end of the bag to use as a tie.

•Never turn on an empty oven. This could damage the magnetron. Something needs to absorb the microwave energy.

•Cook pies on glass plates. Always cook crust before adding filling.

•When defrosting frozen foods, loosen lids of plastic boxes and pierce corner of cardboard boxes or plastic bags. Remove all metal bag closures.

•Arrange small food items in a circle such as several potatoes, or custard cups. When cooking single items, always place in center of oven.

•Watch milk-based liquids through oven door. They will boil over if heated too long.

•Use salt sparingly and add after vegetables are cooked.

•If food appears to be cooking too fast, switch to a lower power level.

•Do not dust cake pans with flour or use spray shortening. Grease with solid shortening and sprinkle with sugar or something granular.

•Remove muffins or cupcakes from containers immediately after cooking to avoid sogginess.

•For easy oven cleaning, place 1 cup water in microwave, heat, and let set in oven for several minutes to steam spatters. They will then wipe off easily.

•If food cannot be stirred, use lower power level and longer cooking time.

•Do not attempt to melt paraffin in the microwave. It is transparent to microwave energy and will not melt.

• Keep oven interior clean for better reflection of microwaves and more even cooking. Grease or food buildup inside oven can be a fire hazard since it will heat whenever oven is on. If fire should occur in oven, stop power immediately and leave door closed so it will snuff itself out.

• As a safety precaution, unplug microwave during a severe thunderstorm to prevent possible lightning damage.

• Do not use thin plastics such as cottage cheese containers for microwave cooking. They are too thin and deteriorate quickly from the heat of the food.

· USES FOR YOUR MICROWAVE OVEN

Baby Food: To warm baby's bottle or to heat baby food in jars, remove metal lid from jar and heat 15 to 20 seconds. Place home-prepared baby food in ice cube trays and freeze. Heat cubes in microwave to serve as needed. (**Caution:** Always shake bottle or stir food well to avoid any hot or cold spots. And always test on wrist after shaking to be certain it is not overheated.)

Bacon: To separate slices of cold bacon easily, heat the entire package on high for about 20 seconds.

Breads: Use to freshen breads or rolls, or to defrost bread. To defrost a 1½-lb. loaf of bakery bread, place in oven in wrapper on high 45 to 75 seconds or until bread is not icy, but is still cool. Let stand 5 minutes to complete defrosting.

Breads: Use to dry bread when you need croutons or to make dry bread crumbs. One qt. of cubes will dry in 6 to 7 minutes in an 8 × 12-inch glass baking dish if stirred occasionally.

Brown Sugar: To soften hard brown sugar, place in a glass dish, add a slice of white bread or an apple wedge, or sprinkle *lightly* with water and cover. One cup of brown sugar will soften in approximately 30 to 45 seconds. (Do not melt sugar). Let stand 5 minutes to complete softening.

Butter or Margarine: Use to soften or melt butter or margarine. To soften ½ cup, microwave at 30 percent power approximately 20 to 40 seconds. To melt ½ cup, microwave on high 45 to 75 seconds. (Different brands vary in melting temperature.)

Chicken: Use to partially cook chicken pieces for barbecuing on the grill. This can save a lot of time on the grill when you are in a hurry.

Chocolate: Use to melt chocolate. For a 1-oz. square, microwave at 50 percent power for 2½ to 3 minutes, depending on whether it is cut in smaller pieces or left whole.

Cookies: Use to freshen stale cookies in seconds right on the serving plate. Cover with plastic wrap.

Coconut: To toast coconut, spread 1 cup angel flake coconut on a large plate and microwave on high 3 to 3½ minutes, stirring occasionally until lightly browned.

Compress: For a warm compress, place a dampened washcloth in microwave on high for 15 to 30 seconds, or until warm to the touch.

Craft Projects: May use to dry decoupage or dough-clay projects. (Caution: Do not overdry! This could damage magnetron.)

Cream Cheese: Use to soften cream cheese or cheese spread. To soften an 8-oz. package of cheese, microwave at 50 percent power for 1 to 1½ minutes.

Defrost Frozen Food: Use to defrost half a package of frozen food such as hot dogs. Shield half of package with foil which reflects energy and leave other half exposed. Microwave at 50 percent power for 1½ to 2½ minutes or until unshielded side is cool and soft to the touch. Remove defrosted portion and return frozen portion to freezer immediately.

Drying Celery Leaves, Herbs, and Tea Leaves: Place ½ cup leaves between paper towels and heat about 2 minutes or until dry or crumbly. Amount of time will vary with different leaves and herbs. (Watch carefully so they do not overdry and ignite. This could damage oven. It is best not to do less than ½ cup at a time because of this.)

Eggs: Use to hard-cook eggs to be chopped and added to salads or casseroles. Crack one egg into small, lightly greased bowl or custard cup. Prick yolk and cover with plastic wrap. Microwave at 50 percent power for 1¾ to 2 minutes or until white is set and yolk is almost set. Let stand covered 1 minute to complete cooking.

Flowers: Use to dry flowers. See page 402 for flower drying chart.

Fruits: Use to soften dry fruits (prunes, raisins, etc.) which are too dry and hard. Sprinkle 1 cup fruit with 1 tbsp. water. Cover and microwave on high for 30 to 60 seconds. Stir once. Let stand covered for several minutes.

Gelatin: For easy preparation of flavored gelatin, fill a 2-cup glass measure to the 1-cup level with water. Heat on high for 1½ minutes or until hot. Stir in 1 (3-oz.) pkg. flavored gelatin until thoroughly dissolved. Then add ice cubes until mixture reaches the 2-cup level. Stir to melt and cool.

Honey: Use to melt crystallized honey. Remove lid and set jar of honey in microwave. Heat on high 1 to 3 minutes, stirring occasionally until clear.

Ice Cream: Use to soften hard ice cream for serving. Microwave ½ gallon ice cream on high for 1 minute.

Ironing: For easy ironing of linens, tablecloths, and napkins sprinkle lightly with water. Place in plastic bag, close end loosely, and microwave on high for 1 minute or until warm to the touch. Iron immediately.

Lemons and Oranges: Use to heat lemons and oranges before juicing to obtain more juice. Microwave on high for 20 to 30 seconds or until slightly warm.

Noodles: Use to warm chow mein noodles. Microwave 1 cup noodles at a time on high for 1 to 1½ minutes.

Pancakes, etc.: Use to reheat leftover pancakes, waffles, or cooked French toast that have been refrigerated or frozen. Heat two refrigerated pancakes on high for 30 seconds. If frozen, heat 1 minute.

Peanuts: To roast raw peanuts, first shell and skin the peanuts. (Skins slip off easily if the raw peanuts are placed in the freezer for several hours.) Place 2 cups peanuts in 10 × 6-inch glass dish. Dot with butter or margarine and microwave on high for 7 minutes, stirring after each minute. Remove from oven, sprinkle with salt, and cool before eating.

Pecans and Walnuts: To shell pecans or walnuts easier with less breakage, place about 2 cups nuts and 1 cup water in a covered glass dish. Heat 1 to 2 minutes. Drain off water, cool nuts, and then crack them.

Peel—Lemon and Orange: To dry lemon or orange peel, sprinkle 2 tbsp. grated peel in single layer on plate and microwave on high for 2 to 4 minutes until dry to touch. Use fork to toss twice during drying. Let stand several hours until brittle. Store in airtight container up to 2 months. (½ tsp. dried peel equals 1 tsp. grated peel.)

Pie and Ice Cream: Use to heat pie for serving à la mode. Heat 1 serving for 20 to 30 seconds on high, then add ice cream.

Potato Chips etc.: To freshen soggy potato chips, pretzels, or crackers, heat on high for 30 seconds to 1 minute. Let stand 2 minutes.

Raisins: To rejuvenate raisins, place ½ cup raisins and 1 tsp. water in 1-cup glass measure. Cover with plastic wrap and microwave on high 15 to 20 seconds. Stir, let stand 1 minute.

Soap: To make liquid hand soap, use one 3½-oz. bar of soap with moisturizing cream, or this amount of small pieces of soap. Shred soap. Place in large bowl and add 3 cups water. Microwave on high for 5 to 6 minutes, or until soap is dissolved, stirring occasionally. Let stand until cool. It will thicken as it cools. Use in soap dispenser.

Squash: To cut acorn squash easily, pierce skin of uncut squash with a fork. Microwave on high 1 or 2 minutes. It will soften enough for easy cutting into halves, quarters, or slices.

Tomatoes: To peel tomatoes easily, microwave 30 to 45 seconds. Skin should easily slip off. (Tomatoes should be vine ripened.)

DRYING FLOWERS IN THE MICROWAVE OVEN

As in any craft, it is important to follow the directions carefully and accurately.

Brightly colored flowers dry best. Flowers, such as roses, carnations, violets, and zinneas work well with this process. For flower drying, you will need silica gel which is available in most hobby shops and, of course, fresh flowers.

For best results, flowers should be only partially opened. Avoid using flowers with thick centers. Use the chart as a guide for drying other flowers.

FLOWER DRYING CHART

Flower Type	Heating Time on Full Power	Minimum Amount of Standing Time***
*Carnation	2½ to 3 min.	5 to 10 min.
Daffodil	1½ to 2 min.	5 to 10 min.
Pansy—1st drying	45 sec.	5 min.
2nd drying	1 to 1½ min.	10 min.
Rose	1½ min.	2 to 5 min.
Sunflower	1¾ min.	1½ days**
Violet	1½ to 2 min.	5 to 10 min.
Zinnia	2 to 2½ min.	5 to 10 min.

*For best results dry three carnations at one time.
**Sunflowers should stand covered with a plastic bag during standing time.
***You may wish to increase the standing time for some flowers.

General Instructions for Drying Flowers

1. Partially fill a large glass or jar with silica gel. Place a flower stem-down into the silica gel. Slowly fill the remaining portion of the jar with gel. Be careful to place the silica gel between all petals of each flower. Use a toothpick to separate the petals. Cover the flower completely with silica gel.

2. Place the jar in the microwave oven. Place 1 cup of water in the rear left corner of the microwave. Heat in microwave on full power for 1 to 3 minutes, depending upon the general size of the flower. Longer heating times are required for larger flowers. Check the chart for specific times.

3. Use a separate jar for each flower. Silica gel may be reused only after it is completely cooled. Remove the flower from the jar when it is cooled. See the chart for the recommended amount of standing time.

The above chart and directions for drying flowers are reprinted by permission of the copyright holder, Amana Refrigeration, Inc., Amana, IA 52204.

4. After the standing time, slowly pour the silica gel from the jar. Carefully remove the flower. Gently brush any excess grains of gel from the petals or stem. Allow the silica gel to cool before reusing.

5. Flower wire may be used to support the stems. Artifical coloring may be added to the flowers when the flowers are completely dry, if desired. Leaves should be dried separately and then added to the stems.

MICROWAVE HEATING CHART

(Times given are for 700-watt ovens. Increase time slightly for 650-watt ovens. Times will also vary according to volume, density, and thickness of food, and whether food is refrigerator-cold or at room temperature.)

POWER EQUIVALENTS
High . . . . .100% power
Medium-High . . . . .80 to 90% power
Medium . . . . .60 to 70% power
Medium-Low . . . . .40 to 50% power
Defrost . . . . .30% power

CONVERTING STANDARD RECIPES
•Reduce time ¼ to ⅓ of the regular amount of time.
•Decrease salt and seasonings.
•Salt after cooking.
•Cut foods into small uniform pieces.
•Add 1 tbsp. oil to cakes.
•Reduce liquids in vegetables and casseroles.

DEGREES FOR PROBE
Baby foods . . . . .130 degrees
Beverages . . . . .150 to 180 degrees
Cup of soup . . . . .150 degrees
Hot chocolate . . . . .150 degrees
Liquid for yeast . . . . .110 degrees
Soups, stews, and casseroles . . . . .140 to 150 degrees
Canned ham (at medium power) . . . . .130 degrees
Beef (at medium power) . . . . .170 degrees

Item	Time	Power
BEVERAGES		
1 (8-oz.) cup water	1½ min.	High
1 (8-oz.) cup milk	1½ to 2 min.	Medium
BREADS AND CAKES		
6 dinner rolls	3 to 5 min.	Defrost
1 doughnut	10 seconds	High
1 ham and cheese sandwich	30 to 45 seconds	High
6 muffins	5 to 6 min.	Medium
1 waffle	45 seconds	Medium
2 waffles	1½ min.	Medium
1 cupcake	15 seconds	High
1 (2½″ square) coffee cake	15 to 20 seconds	High

Item	Time	Power
MEATS		
1 hot dog	30 seconds	High
1 hot dog in bun (both frozen)	50 seconds	High
1 hamburger patty (frozen)	1½ to 3 min.	High
1 hamburger patty (thawed)	1 min.	High
4 hamburger patties	3½ to 4 min.	High
1 slice bacon	50 seconds	High
4 slices bacon	3½ to 4 min.	High
1 fresh pork sausage patty	2 to 4 min.	High
canned ham	8 to 10 min. per lb.	Medium
ham slice (8-oz.)	2½ to 3½ min.	High
4 pork chops	15 to 20 min.	Medium
whole chicken (to thaw)	10 min. per lb.	Defrost
whole chicken (to cook)	6 to 7 min. per lb.	High*
(8 oz.) fish sticks (to thaw)	3½ min.	Defrost
(8 oz.) fish sticks (to cook)	2 to 3½ min.	High
fish fillet (to thaw)	2½ min.	Defrost
fish fill (to cook)	1 to 2 min.	High
TO SOFTEN		
¼ cup butter	¾ to 1 min.	Defrost
3 oz. cream cheese	½ to 1 min.	Defrost
1 oz. square chocolate	2 to 3 min.	Medium
1 cup chocolate chips	1½ to 2 min.	High
VEGETABLES		
1 baked potato	4 to 5 min.	High
2 baked potatoes	7 to 8 min.	High
4 baked potatoes	10 to 12 min.	High
2 ears fresh corn on cob	3 to 4 min.	High
4 ears fresh corn on cob	8½ to 10 min.	High
16 oz. canned vegetables	3 to 4 min.	Medium-High
10 oz. pkg. frozen vegetables (or 1 pint)	7 to 9 min.	High**
MISCELLANEOUS		
1 jar baby food (not meat)	½ to 1½ min.	Medium
10-oz. condensed canned soup	4 to 6 min.	Medium-High
10-oz. ready-to-eat soup	3 to 6 min.	Medium-High
1 slice fruit pie	20 to 30 seconds	High
1 slice pizza	30 to 45 seconds	High
11-oz. TV dinner	5 to 7 min.	Medium-High
2 scrambled eggs (with 2 tbsp. milk—stir once)	1¼ to 1½ min.	High

*Chicken will be more tender if power level is reduced for the last ⅓ of cooking time. Reduce to 50 percent for a whole chicken, or to 70 percent for pieces. Increase cooking time slightly.

**Vegetables may be cooked quickly on high. However, some vegetables such as limas, carrots, and frozen vegetables will be more tender if heated to boiling on high, then reduce to 50 percent power for 5 additional minutes, stirring at least once. Let stand 10 minutes. Peas, broccoli, cabbage, and cauliflower may be cooked on high with excellent results if stirred at least once. Salt is usually added after cooking. If added before cooking, it should be dissolved in water first before adding. Use about 2 tbsp. water for 1 pint vegetables for cooking.

MICROWAVE RECIPES

BEVERAGES

Hot Butterscotch Milk

1 large cup milk	Heat on high 1½ minutes.
1 to 2 tbsp. butterscotch chips	Stir in until melted.
1 large marshmallow	Place on top and serve.

Yield: 1 serving

Mulled Cider

1 qt. apple cider **¼ cup brown sugar** **1 stick whole cinnamon** **3 whole cloves**	Combine and microwave on high for 6 minutes. Or use probe and heat to 140 degrees. Strain and serve hot.
orange slices to garnish	Insert on rim of cup.

Yield: 4 to 5 servings

MUFFINS

Big Batch Bran Muffins

5 cups flour **3 cups sugar** **5 tsp. baking soda** **1 tsp. salt**	Sift together.
1 (15-oz.) box raisin bran cereal **(approx. 6 cups)**	Stir in.
4 eggs, beaten **1 qt. buttermilk** **1 cup vegetable oil**	Combine, and stir in just until moistened. May store in refrigerator for up to 6 weeks in covered container.

To use, spoon into paper-lined muffin pans or custard cups, filling cups only ½ full. Microwave on high:

6 muffins—1 min. 10 sec. to 1 min. 20 sec.
4 muffins—40 to 50 seconds
2 muffins—23 to 30 seconds

Yield: entire amount makes approximately 7 dozen muffins

Honey Butter

Put ½ cup butter in small mixer bowl. Microwave at 30 percent power for 20 to 40 second until softened, stirring once. Do not melt. Add ⅓ cup honey and beat with electric mix until well blended. Delicious spread on any quick breads, toast, pancakes, and waffles. R frigerate any unused portion.

. . . .

MEATS
Easy Barbecue Sauce

(Use on any meat to barbecue. To speed up the outdoor grill, partially cook chops, ribs, or chicken in microwave. Then finish cooking on the grill.)

½ cup catsup ½ cup finely chopped onion 3 tbsp. brown sugar ½ tsp. salt ¼ tsp. black pepper ½ tsp. dry mustard 2 tsp. Worcestershire sauce 3 tbsp. vinegar	Combine in glass measuring cup. Microwave o high for approximately 2 minutes, stirring occa sionally until thoroughly heated.

. . . .

Oven-Fried Chicken

2 to 2½ lb. chicken, cut up	Have ready.

. . . .

1 env. seasoned coating mix (or about ½ cup) ½ tsp. salt ¼ tsp. black pepper	Mix, then coat chicken on all sides. Arrange pieces in an 8 × 12-inch baking dish. Cover wit waxed paper.

. . . .

Microwave on high for 18 to 21 minutes until chicken is tender. Or microwave on high f 9 minutes, then reduce power to 70 percent and microwave for 12 to 17 minutes longe

. . . .

Easy Chicken

Chicken should be completely thawed before cooking is started. Choose a bake dish larg enough so pieces of chicken do not need to be overlapped. Arrange pieces of chicken wit thicker, larger pieces toward outside of dish where they will microwave faster. If an oblon dish is used, rearrange pieces during cooking so corner or outside pieces are exchanged wit center pieces for more even cooking. Most microwave recipes do not suggest this, bu chicken will be more moist and tender if power level is reduced for the last ⅓ of cookin time. For whole chickens reduce to 50 percent power, and for chicken pieces reduce to 7 percent power. Increase cooking time slightly.

. . . .

2 whole skinned chicken breasts, cut in half (approx. 2 lbs. of breast)	Place in glass dish.

2 tbsp. melted butter	Drizzle over chicken.
1 small sliced onion	Arrange on top of pieces and cover with plastic wrap. Microwave on high for 8 minutes. Rearrange pieces.
1 (10-oz.) can cream of chicken soup	Spoon over chicken.
thyme **paprika** **garlic powder** **MSG**	Sprinkle over chicken. Cover and microwave on high for 2 minutes more. Turn dish, reduce power level to 70 percent and cook 8 more minutes or until done.

Variation: Use golden mushroom soup mixed with ¼ cup sour cream in place of chicken soup.

Yield: 4 servings

Baked Fish Fillets

1½ lbs. fish fillets, thawed	Arrange in bake dish.
3 tbsp. vegetable oil **3 tbsp. lemon juice** **2 tbsp. grated onion** **2 tbsp. Worcestershire sauce** **½ tsp. salt** **¼ tsp MSG (optional)** **⅛ tsp. black pepper**	Mix together thoroughly and spoon over fish. Marinate for 30 minutes turning once. Spoon marinade over fish again.
1 cup crushed cereal or fine bread crumbs	Press pieces of fish in crumbs and arrange in greased shallow bake dish with thicker edges of fish toward outside of dish. Do not overlap pieces.

Microwave on high for 7 to 8 minutes or until fish flakes easily. Let stand 3 minutes before serving.

Yield: 4 servings

Italian Meat Loaf

1½ lbs. lean ground beef 1 (8-oz.) can tomato sauce (reserve half) 1 tsp. oregano (reserve half) ½ cup seasoned bread crumbs (such as Pepperidge Farm) 1 tsp. salt ⅛ tsp. black pepper 1 egg, lightly beaten	Mix together thoroughly, using only half of tomato sauce and half of oregano, reserving other half. On waxed paper, pat into a rectangle ½-inch thick.

1½ cups mozzarella cheese, shredded	Sprinkle over mixture.

2 tbsp. grated Parmesan cheese	Have ready.

Roll up by starting at short side. Lift paper until meat begins to roll tightly. Peel back paper. Seal edges of meat and place in loaf dish. Microwave on High for 5 minutes, rotating dish once. Drain off grease. Reduce power to 50 percent, and microwave 7 to 9 minutes more, or until almost done. Drain again. Combine reserved tomato sauce and oregano, and pour over meat loaf. Sprinkle with Parmesan cheese. Microwave on high for 2 minutes longer to heat sauce. Cover loosely with foil, and let stand 5 minutes before serving.

Yield: 6 servings

Lois Wenger

Pork Chops

4 pork chops	Arrange in bake dish.

unseasoned meat tenderizer	Sprinkle over chops and marinate according to container directions.

2 tbsp. soy sauce 1 (10-oz.) can cream of mushroom soup	Combine and spread over top.

Cover with waxed paper and microwave on high for 20 to 35 minutes. Let stand 2 minutes before serving.

Yield: 4 servings

Carolyn Reed

Sweet and Sour Pork

(If meat isn't very tender, reduce power level for last ⅓ of time, and increase cooking time slightly until done.)

1½ lbs. boneless pork loin, cubed	Place in 1½-qt. casserole dish. Cover and microwave on high for 3 to 4 minutes or until meat is tender, stirring once.

1 (20-oz.) can crushed pineapple	Drain and reserve juice.
½ cup water **¼ cup brown sugar** **3 tbsp. vinegar** **2 tbsp. cornstarch** **1 tbsp. soy sauce** **½ tsp. salt**	Combine with reserved pineapple juice in glass measure. Microwave on high for 3 to 5 minutes until thickened, stirring once or twice. Pour over meat. Add pineapple. Microwave on high for 2 to 3 minutes until thoroughly heated.

Yield: 4 servings

Tuna Tetrazzini

4 oz. spaghetti, broken and cooked **1 (10-oz.) can cream of mushroom soup** **½ cup milk** **1 (6½ or 7-oz.) can tuna, drained** **1 (4-oz.) can sliced mushrooms, drained** **⅓ cup minced onion** **1 cup shredded cheddar cheese (reserve half)**	Combine all ingredients in greased 1 ½-qt. casserole dish, reserving half of cheese. Microwave on high for 5 to 6 minutes, or to 150 degrees on probe, stirring once.
(reserved cheese)	Sprinkle over top. Microwave 30 seconds more, or until cheese melts.

Yield: 6 servings   *Lois Wenger*

MAIN DISHES

Baked Beans

4 slices bacon, diced **½ cup chopped onion**	Place in 2-qt. casserole and microwave on high for 4 to 5 minutes. Drain off fat.
1 (28-oz.) can pork and beans **2 tbsp. brown sugar** **1 tbsp. Worcestershire sauce** **1 tsp. prepared mustard** **¼ tsp. chili powder**	Blend together with bacon mixture. Cover and microwave on high for 8 to 10 minutes, stirring twice.

Yield: 5 to 6 servings

Beef and Noodle Casserole

1 lb. ground beef	Crumble into 2-qt. casserole dish.
1 small onion, chopped	Add. Microwave, uncovered 5 to 6 minutes. Drain off fat. Crumble meat again.
¼ tsp. garlic powder **½ tsp. salt** **⅛ tsp. black pepper** **½ tsp. MSG (optional)** **1 tsp. prepared mustard** **1 tbsp. parsley flakes** **1 (4-oz.) can mushroom pieces,** **drained** **1 (10-oz.) can cream of mushroom** **soup** **4 cups uncooked noodles** **2½ cups water**	Add, mixing well. Microwave, covered, 12 to 14 mins. until noodles are tender, stirring 2 or 3 times.
½ cup sour cream	Stir in and microwave, covered, 2 minutes longer or until heated through.

Yield: 6 to 8 servings

Breakfast Sausage Cheese Casserole

3 tbsp. butter	Microwave on high in 9 × 13 dish until melted, 30 seconds. Spread over dish.
12 slices bread, broken into pieces	Layer in butter in dish.
1 lb. brown and serve sauage (May use 1 lb. bulk sausage, browned and drained)	Cut in ½-inch pieces and arrange over bread.
8 eggs, beaten **2½ cups milk**	Combine and pour over mixture in dish.
2 cups grated cheddar cheese	Sprinkle over top.
1 (10-oz.) can cream of mushroom soup	Spread over cheese. Mix lightly. Cover and refrigerate overnight.

Cover with waxed paper and microwave at 80 percent power for 22 to 25 minutes or until knife inserted in center comes out clean. May need to shield corners of dish.

Yield: 6 to 8 servings

Quick Broccoli Casserole

2 (10-oz.) pkgs. chopped broccoli	Place in 2-qt. casserole. Cover and microwave on high for 8 minutes, stirring once.
1 (8-oz.) jar Cheese Whiz, or 1 cup cubed processed cheese **1 (10-oz.) can cream of celery soup** **1 cup minute rice, uncooked** **½ tsp. salt**	Mix in well. Cover and microwave on high for 5 minutes. Let stand several minutes before serving.

Yield: 6 to 8 servings

Broccoli Casserole

1 (10-oz.) pkg. frozen broccoli spears	Microwave in plastic bag on high for 3 minutes. Open bag, and stir. Cook 3 minutes more until tender. Set aside.
2 tbsp. butter	In l-qt. casserole, microwave on high 20 to 25 seconds until melted.
2 tbsp. flour	Stir in.
1 cup milk	Slowly add. Cover and microwave at 70 percent power for 4 to 5 minutes or until thickened, stirring once.
salt and pepper to taste **½ cup shredded cheddar cheese**	Add seasoning. Then add broccoli and cheese.
¼ cup bread crumbs	Sprinkle over top. Microwave at 70 percent power 2 minutes more.

Yield: 2 to 4 servings

Cheese Pie

(Lois says, "Served with orange slices, coffee cake, and milk, this recipe is great for brunch, lunch, or a light supper.")

9 or 10 slices bacon	Microwave between 2 or 3 paper towels for 5 to 6 minutes, or until crisp. Crumble into a 9-inch glass pie plate.
1 cup shredded cheese, (Swiss, cheddar, or mozzarella) **¼ cup minced onion**	Sprinkle over bacon.
4 eggs **1 (13-oz.) can evaporated milk** **¾ tsp. salt** **¼ tsp. sugar** **⅛ tsp. black pepper**	Beat together with rotary beater until blended, and pour over mixture in dish. Microwave 9 minutes, stirring every 3 minutes. Let stand 10 minutes before serving.

Yield: 6 servings

Lois Wenger

Chicken and Broccoli Casserole

2 (10-oz.) pkgs. frozen broccoli	Pierce several holes in plastic bags and microwave both pkgs. together on high for 3 minutes or until stalks separate. Arrange in 2-qt. casserole dish with spears toward center.
1 (10-oz.) can cream of chicken soup **¼ cup sour cream** **1 tbsp. lemon juice** **½ tsp. garlic powder** **1 tsp. soy sauce** **¼ tsp MSG (optional)**	Mix thoroughly and spread half of mixture over broccoli. Reserve half
2 or 3 cups diced cooked chicken	Layer over top. Then spread reserved soup mixture over chicken.
¼ cup grated Parmesan cheese **¼ cup bread crumbs**	Sprinkle over top.

Cover and microwave at 80 percent power for 12 to 14 minutes or until heated through. Turn dish once during cooking. Serve over cooked rice—cook 2 cups rice.

Yield: 6 to 8 servings

Curried Chicken and Broccoli

1 (10-oz.) pkg. frozen broccoli **flowerets, cooked and salted**	Layer in bottom of a 9-inch round baking dish.
2 whole chicken breasts, cooked **and sliced**	Arrange over broccoli.
1 (10-oz.) can cream of chicken soup **or mushroom soup** **½ cup mayonnaise** **1 tbsp. lemon juice** **½ tsp. curry powder**	Mix, then pour over mixture in dish.
1 cup shredded cheddar cheese	Sprinkle over top.

Microwave, covered, at 70 percent power for 8 to 10 minutes, until hot and bubbly. Let stand 5 minutes before serving.

Yield: 4 servings

Lois Wenger

Scalloped Corn

2 cups creamed corn **8 oz. fresh mushrooms, sliced** **1 cup saltine cracker crumbs** **(reserve half)** *(see next page)*	Mix all ingredients in greased 1 ½-qt. casserole dish.

¼ cup milk
1 egg, beaten
½ tsp. salt
¼ tsp. black pepper
1 tsp. sugar

. . . .

1 tbsp. butter	Dot over top.

. . . .

(reserved cracker crumbs)	Sprinkle over all.

. . . .

Microwave on high for 9 minutes, turning dish once.

Yield: 4 to 6 servings   *Barbara Ryan*

. . . .

Green Bean and Bacon Casserole

4 slices bacon	Microwave on high for 2 to 3 minutes. Remove bacon, crumble, and set aside.

. . . .

¼ cup bread crumbs	Stir into bacon drippings. Microwave on high for 2 minutes, stirring once. Drain and set aside.

. . . .

1 (10-oz.) pkg. frozen green beans, cooked and drained, or 2 cups canned green beans **⅓ cup cream of mushroom soup, undiluted**	Combine with bacon in 1-qt. casserole dish, mixing well. Top with bread crumbs. Microwave on high for 4 to 5 minutes, or until hot through.

. . . .

Yield: 4 servings

. . . .

Hamburger and Macaroni

1 lb. hamburger	Crumble in a 2-qt. casserole dish.

. . . .

½ cup onion, finely chopped	Stir in. Microwave on high for 4 to 5 minutes, stirring once. Drain off fat.

. . . .

1 (8-oz.) can tomato sauce **1½ cups water** **1 cup uncooked macaroni** **½ cup catsup** **1 tbsp. brown sugar** **1 tsp. salt** **¼ tsp. black pepper** **¼ tsp. chili powder** **¼ tsp. MSG (optional)**	Stir in. Microwave at 30 percent power for 25 to 30 minutes or until macaroni is tender, stirring occasionally. Let stand, covered, for 5 minutes before serving.

. . . .

Yield: 4 to 5 servings

. . . .

Hamburger Broccoli (or Spinach) Casserole

1 lb. ground beef	Crumble into a 2½-qt. casserole dish, cover, and microwave on high for 4 to 5 minutes stirring to break up chunks. Drain
1 (10-oz.) pkg. frozen broccoli (or spinach, chopped)	Puncture pkg. and microwave on high for 3 to 4 minutes. Drain, and add to meat.
1 (10-oz.) can cream of mushroom soup **½ cup cottage cheese** **½ cup Velveeta cheese, cubed** **1 (4-oz.) can sliced mushrooms (opt.)** **¼ tsp. black pepper**	Add to mixture in dish.
1½ cups medium noodles, cooked **1 (2.8-oz.) can French-fried onions (optional) (reserve half)**	Add, reserving half of onions. Microwave on high for 5 to 7 minutes until heated through, or to 150 degrees on probe.
(reserved onions)	Sprinkle over top. Microwave 1 minute more.

Yield: 6 to 8 servings

Lois Wenger

Pizza Surprise

1 lb. lean ground beef	Crumble in 2½-qt. casserole dish.
1 small onion, chopped	Add, and microwave, covered with waxed paper, on high for 5 to 6 minutes, stirring to break pieces. Drain.
8 oz. uncooked noodles **1 (32-oz.) jar pizza sauce** **2 cups water** **1 (3-oz.) pkg. sliced pepperoni, chopped** **1 (4-oz.) can mushroom pieces, drained** **¾ tsp. Italian seasoning**	Mix in. Cover, and microwave on high for 18 to 20 minutes or until noodles are tender, and liquid is absorbed, stirring once.
1 cup mozzarella cheese, shredded	Sprinkle over top. Microwave, uncovered, on high for 1 to 2 minutes until melted.

Yield: 8 to 10 servings

Lois Wenger

Easy Lasagna

½ lb. ground beef	Crumble in 2-qt. casserole dish. Microwave on high for 2 to 3 minutes, stirring occasionally. Drain.
1 (32-oz.) jar spaghetti sauce **¼ cup water**	Stir in.
1½ cups cottage cheese **1 egg, slightly beaten** **¼ tsp. black pepper**	Combine and have ready.
8 lasagna noodles (8-oz.), uncooked **½ lb. sliced mozzarella cheese, or 2 cups grated cheese** **additional seasoning as desired—oregano, garlic powder, onion powder, crushed dried basil leaves, etc.** **½ cup grated Parmesan cheese**	Have ready. Make a layer in dish of half of sauce, then half of noodles, and cottage cheese mixture, and half of mozzarella cheese. Sprinkle with desired seasoning. Repeat layers with other half of ingredients and seasoning.

Cover and microwave on high for 8 minutes turning dish 3 or 4 times. Reduce power to 50 percent and cook for 30 to 32 minutes longer until noodles are tender. Top with Parmesan cheese. Let stand 15 minutes, covered, before serving. (Note: This dish may be baked in a conventional oven at 350 degrees for 50 minutes if desired. Prepare according to this recipe, except brown hamburger in skillet and drain, before adding it to the mixture.)

Yield: 6 servings   *Karen Blosser*

Baked Potatoes

Scrub potatoes well, prick twice with a fork so that some steam can escape. Place a paper towel on a plate to absorb excess moisture, and place potatoes on towel, at least 1 inch apart. Turn over halfway through cooking time for more even cooking. After cooking, wrap in foil to keep hot. Let stand 5 to 10 minutes before serving. Cooking time for medium-sized potatoes:

1 potato—4 to 5 minutes
2 potatoes—7 to 8 minutes
3 potatoes—8 to 10 minutes
4 potatoes—l0 to 12 minutes

Twice Baked: After standing time, slice top from each potato and scoop out center. Set shells aside, and mash potatoes with butter and milk. Season mixture as desired. You may add onion powder, chives, cheese, or crumbled bacon. Or mix ¼ cup dairy sour cream, 2½ tbsp. milk, 1 tbsp. grated Parmesan cheese, and salt to taste for each 2 potatoes. Spoon mixture back into shells. Sprinkle with paprika, and microwave on high for 1 to 2 minutes until heated through again.

Golden Potatoes and Onions

1 bouillon cube 1 cup hot water	Dissolve.
4 med. potatoes, peeled and shredded ¼ cup minced onion	Add. Microwave on high, covered, for 10 minutes, stirring occasionally just until tender.
½ cup shredded American cheese	Sprinkle over top. Microwave for 30 seconds more to melt cheese.
parsley to garnish	Sprinkle over top.

Yield: 4 servings   *Dorothy Shank Showalter*

Golden Mashed Potatoes

(This is an excellent way to use leftover mashed potatoes. Prepare this dish with the leftover potatoes at the end of the meal. Cover and place in refrigerator until ready to use. Then dish is ready to heat at a moment's notice for another meal!)

Place half of a medium-sized bowl of mashed potatoes in a greased casserole dish. Cover with a layer of cheese slices, or grated cheese. Then add other half of potatoes and dot generously with butter or margarine. If desired, sprinkle buttery popcorn seasoned salt over the top for additional color and flavor. Microwave, covered, with waxed paper, for 4 to 10 minutes at 80 percent power until hot through.

Lois Wenger

Quick Company Potatoes

1 (24-oz.) pkg. frozen hash brown potatoes with onion and green pepper, thawed 1 (10-oz.) can cream of potato soup 1 (10-oz.) can cream of celery soup 1 cup commercial sour cream ½ tsp. salt ¼ tsp. black pepper	Combine all ingredients in 10-inch square or round bake dish. Cover and microwave at 50 percent power for 15 minutes. Stir.
paprika	Sprinkle over top. Microwave at 50 percent power for 20 minutes more.

Cover and let stand 5 minutes before serving.

Variation: In place of potato soup and sour cream, use 4 oz. softened cream cheese and ½ cup finely chopped onion. Do not omit celery soup. Sprinkle ½ cup grated cheddar cheese over the top.

Yield: 6 to 8 servings

Ham and Potato Casserole

2 cups cubed potatoes 1 cup sliced carrots ¾ cup chopped celery ½ cup water	Combine in 2-qt. casserole dish. Cover and microwave on high for 7 to 8 minutes until crisp tender, stirring once. Drain and set aside.
1 cup cubed ham 2 tbsp. chopped green pepper 2 tbsp. chopped onion 3 tbsp. butter or margarine	Microwave on high for 3 to 4 minutes until tender, stirring once. Combine with potato mixture mixing well.
¼ cup butter	Microwave on high for 55 seconds or until melted.
3 tbsp. flour	Add, stirring until smooth.
1½ cups milk	Gradually add, stirring well. Microwave on high for 3 to 5 minutes until thickened and bubbly stirring at 1 minute intervals.
½ cup shredded cheddar cheese ½ tsp. salt ⅛ tsp. black pepper	Add, stirring until cheese melts. Pour over ham mixture.
4 round buttery crackers, crushed	Sprinkle over top.

Microwave at 70 percent power for 8 to 9 minutes, turning once.

Yield: 6 servings   *Wanda Good*

Cheesy Tuna Bake (Lower Cal.)

1 cup skim milk ½ tsp. salt 2 tbsp. cornstarch	Combine in small bowl. Cover and microwave for 2 to 3 minutes until thickened, stirring once.
¼ cup shredded cheddar cheese substitute	Mix in well.
1 (10-oz.) pkg. frozen cauliflower ¼ cup chopped green pepper	Place in 1½-qt. casserole dish. Microwave, covered, on high for 6 minutes until tender, stirring once or twice.
1 (6½-oz.) can water-packed tuna, drained	Flake and arrange over top.
¼ tsp. MSG (optional)	Sprinkle over tuna. Cover with sauce.

Cover and microwave on high for 2 to 2½ minutes more until heated through.

Yield: 4 servings

Tuna and Macaroni Casserole (Lower Cal.)

2 stems celery, finely chopped	Place in 1 ½-qt. cassrole dish. Cover and microwave on high for 2 ½ to 3 minutes until tender.
1½ cups skim milk 2 tbsp. cornstarch ½ tsp. salt ¼ tsp. black pepper	Stir in. Cook, covered for 2 to 3 minutes or until thickened, stirring twice.
1 (6½-oz.) can water-packed tuna, · drained 2 cups cooked macaroni	Add, mixing well.
2 tbsp. grated Romano cheese paprika	Sprinkle over mixture.
5 ripe olives, sliced	Arrange over top. Cover and cook on high for 1 to 2 minutes until hot through..

Yield: 4 to 6 servings

Tuna Spaghetti Supper (Lower Cal.)

1 (6½-oz.) can water-packed tuna, drained 1 (8-oz.) can tomato sauce ¼ cup finely chopped onion ½ cup water 1 tsp. instant chicken bouillon ½ tsp. crushed leaf oregano ⅛ tsp. garlic powder ¼ tsp. salt ¼ tsp. MSG (optional)	Combine in 1 ½-qt. casserole dish. Cover and microwave on high for 3 to 4 minutes until heated through.
2 cups cooked spaghetti	Stir in.
2 tbsp. Romano cheese	Sprinkle over top.

Cover and microwave for 1 to 2 minutes, or until heated through.

Yield: 4 servings

Shepherds Pie

1 lb. ground beef	Crumble into a 2-qt. casserole dish.
1 med. onion, chopped	Add. Microwave on high 4 to 6 minutes. Crumble meat again and drain.

1 (10-oz.) pkg. frozen peas and carrots or cut green beans	Microwave in package on high for 5 to 6 minutes until tender-crisp.
1 (10-oz.) can tomato soup **1 tsp. Worcestershire sauce** **½ tsp. salt** **¼ tsp. crushed basil leaves** **⅛ tsp. black pepper**	Stir into meat mixture. Spread evenly in dish. Sprinkle vegetables over mixture.
3 cups hot mashed potatoes	Spoon in mounds over vegetables. Microwave 5 to 6 minutes or until hot through.
1 cup shredded cheddar cheese	Sprinkle over top.

Microwave 2 to 3 minutes, or until cheese melts. Let stand 3 minutes before serving.

Yield: 4 to 6 servings

MISCELLANEOUS

Scrambled Egg

Grease small dish or custard cup. Break egg in dish. Add 1 tbsp. milk and mix with fork until blended. Cover with waxed paper and microwave on high 40 to 50 seconds. Season to taste. (Grated cheese, or crumbled bacon may be added before cooking if desired.)

Egg Salad

To hard-cook egg for egg salad, break egg in greased custard cup. Stir yolk lightly with fork. Cover loosely with plastic wrap and microwave on high for 1 ½ minutes. Let stand 2 minutes. Then mash with fork. Stir in 1 tbsp. mayonnaise, 1 tsp. finely chopped pickle relish, and salt and pepper to taste.

Basic White Sauce (Medium)

¼ cup butter or margarine	Microwave butter in a 4-cup measure on high for 40 to 50 seconds until melted.
¼ cup flour **½ tsp. salt**	Stir in until smooth.
2 cups milk	Slowly add, stirring vigorously until blended.

Microwave 5 to 6 minutes until thickened, stirring every minute. (For cheese sauce, add ⅔ cup grated sharp cheese and ¼ tsp. dry mustard after sauce has thickened. Microwave 1 minute longer, and stir until cheese is melted.)

Yield: 2 cups

SOUPS AND STEW

Chicken Noodle Soup

½ cup chopped onion
½ cup finely chopped celery
1 cup frozen corn, thawed
¼ cup water

Combine in 2 ½-qt. casserole dish. Microwave on high for 4 to 5 minutes, or until tender.

. . . .

1½ cups cooked chopped chicken
2 cups cooked noodles
3 cups water
2 tsp. instant chicken bouillon
1 tsp. salt
¼ tsp. MSG (optional)
⅛ tsp. black pepper
1 tbsp. parsley flakes

Mix in thoroughly. Cover and microwave on high for 5 to 7 minutes or until heated through.

. . . .

Yield: 6 to 8 servings

. . . .

Chili Stew

1 lb. ground beef, crumbled
1 large onion, chopped
1 garlic clove, crushed

Combine in 2 ½-qt. casserole dish. Microwave on high for 6 to 7 minutes, stirring once. Drain off fat.

. . . .

1 (16-oz.) can kidney beans
1 cup canned tomatoes
1 (12-oz.) can tomato sauce
1 tsp. salt
2 tsp. sugar
1 to 2 tsp. chili powder

Stir in. Cover and microwave on high for 6 to 7 minutes again. Stir and reduce power to 50 percent. Cook, covered, for 35 to 40 minutes, stirring occasionally.

. . . .

Dumplings:
2 cups buttermilk biscuit mix
⅔ cup milk

Combine just until moistened throughout. Drop by tablespoonfuls around edge of stew forming about 10 dumplings.

. . . .

Microwave, covered, for 4 ½ to 6 minutes or until dumplings are cooked.

Yield: Yield: 6 servings

. . . .

French Onion Soup

3 onions, thinly sliced
3 tbsp. butter or margarine

Arrange in 2 ½-qt. casserole dish. Cover and microwave on high for 10 minutes stirring occasionally

. . . .

4 cups beef broth or bouillon
1 tsp. Worcestershire sauce
½ tsp. salt

Stir in. Cover and cook on high for 5 minutes. Ladle into bowls.

| 5 or 6 slices French bread, toasted
grated Parmesan cheese | Sprinkle cheese on toast and float in soup.
Microwave on high for 30 seconds. |

Yield: 5 or 6 servings

DESSERTS

Apple Crisp

1 qt. apple pie filling	Spread in 8 or 9-inch-square or round dish.
3/4 cup quick oatmeal 1/2 cup brown sugar 1/2 cup flour 1/4 cup margarine	Mix together until crumbly. Spread over pie filling.
cinnamon	Sprinkle over top.

Microwave, uncovered, on high for 10 minutes, turning dish once. Serve warm with milk or ice cream. **Variation:** Use peach or cherry filling instead of apple.

Yield: 6 servings

Apple Delight (Low Cal.)

2 slices bread	Toast.
1 large apple	Microwave on high for 2 minutes. Then slice and arrange on toast.
cinnamon artificial sweetener	Sprinkle over apple slices.
2 slices Monterey Jack cheese	Lay on top. Microwave on high for 1 1/2 minutes or until cheese is melted.

Yield: 2 servings

Baked Bananas

¼ cup orange juice 1 tbsp. butter ½ tsp. grated orange peel ½ tsp. ground cinnamon ¼ tsp. ground clove ¼ tsp. ground nutmeg	Combine in 1 ½ qt. casserole. Microwave on high for 2 to 3 minutes or until bubbly, stirring twice.
4 bananas, peeled and sliced	Stir in. Microwave on high for 1 minute. Serve warm.

Variation: Cut bananas in half lengthwise. Sprinkle with flaked coconut and chocolate chips. Or sprinkle with lemon juice and brown sugar. Microwave for 1 to 2 minutes. Bananas may be baked at 350 degrees in a conventional oven for about 15 minutes if desired.

Yield: 4 servings

Blueberry Crunch

½ cup butter or margarine ¾ cup quick oatmeal 1 cup brown sugar 1 cup flour	Mix together until crumbly. Press half of crumbs in an 8-inch-square dish. Reserve other half.
1 cup sugar 2 tbsp. cornstarch 1 cup water	Microwave on high for 2 to 4 minutes, stirring several times, until thick and clear.
3 cups fresh or frozen blueberries ½ tsp. vanilla ¼ tsp. lemon flavoring	Stir in, and pour over crumbs in dish.
(reserved crumbs)	Sprinkle over top.

Microwave on high for 8 to 10 minutes. Let set 10 minutes before serving. Serve with milk or ice cream.

Yield: 6 servings   *Lois Wenger*

Toasted Pecan Pudding

½ cup margarine	Microwave on high for 45 seconds until melted.
1 cup flour 1½ cups flaked coconut ½ to 1 cup chopped pecans ¼ cup brown sugar	Mix in until crumbly. Brown half of crumbs at a time in flat dish for 6 to 7 minutes, stirring frequently to brown evenly. Cool.

Pudding:

2 (3½-oz.) pkgs. instant vanilla pudding **3 cups milk**	Beat together on low for 2 minutes. Chill 5 minutes until set.
1 (9-oz.) container Cool Whip	Fold in.

Spread half of crumbs in bottom of 8 × 12 dish. Spread pudding over crumbs. Sprinkle remaining crumbs over the top. Chill and serve the same day made.

Yield: 8 servings

CAKES AND COOKIES

Black Forest Cake

1 (18-oz.) chocolate cake mix **2 eggs** **½ cup water**	Mix until well blended.
1 (20-oz.) can cherry pie filling **1 tsp. almond flavoring**	Stir in. Divide batter between 2 waxed paper-lined 8 or 9″ glass baking dishes.

Microwave 1 layer at a time at 60 percent power for 6 minutes. Turn dish. Microwave on high for 3 minutes. Let stand 5 minutes. Then remove cake from dish to cool. Bake second layer the same way. Dust with powdered sugar to serve.

Brownies

2 eggs **1 cup sugar** **½ tsp. salt** **1 tsp. vanilla**	Beat together in small bowl for 1 minute at medium speed of electric mixer until light.
½ cup margarine, melted **¾ cup flour** **⅓ cup cocoa powder**	Blend in on low speed.
⅔ cup chopped nuts	Stir in. Spread evenly in 8-inch-square dish.

Microwave on high for 6 to 7 minutes rotating dish ¼ turn every 2 minutes. When done top should spring back when lightly touched, but will still be moist.

Rhoda Wenger

Caramel Apple Squares

½ cup butter or margarine	Microwave on high for 45 seconds to melt.
1½ cups flour ¼ cup sugar 1 egg yolk	Blend in. Press in bottom of 8 × 12 bake dish. Microwave on high for 5 to 6 minutes, turning dish once.
30 caramels (such as Kraft's) 2 tbsp. water	Place in another dish and microwave on high for 2 to 2½ minutes, stirring twice..
6 med. apples, peeled and sliced	Arrange on baked crust.
1 tbsp. lemon juice	Drizzle juice and caramel mixture over apples.
Topping: 1 cup flour ⅓ cup brown sugar ½ cup butter ½ tsp. ground cinnamon	Mix together until crumbly. Sprinkle over apples. Microwave on high for 10 to 12 minutes. Cool. Cut into bars.

Chocolate No-Bake Cookies

2 cups sugar ½ cup milk 3 tbsp. margarine 2 tbsp. cocoa powder pinch of salt	Mix together in bowl. Microwave on high for 2 minutes, and stir well. Microwave until mixture comes to *full* rolling boil (important for stiffness of cookie). Continue to cook on high for 2 minutes.
½ cup peanut butter 3 cups quick oatmeal 2 tsp. vanilla	Stir in until well mixed. Drop mixture by spoonfuls onto tray or waxed paper to cool and harden.

Yield: 3 to 4 dozen

Crunchy Butterscotch Bars

1 cup butterscotch chips ½ cup sugar ½ cup light corn syrup ½ cup peanut butter	Combine in bowl. Microwave on high for 1 to 1½ minutes until softened enough to stir smooth.
5 cups cornflakes cereal	Stir in. Press into buttered 8-inch square bake dish.
⅔ cup chocolate chips	In glass measure, microwave on high for about 1 minute until melted enough to spread over cereal. Cool, and cut into bars.

Chocolate Toffee Bars

11 graham crackers	Arrange to cover bottom of 8 × 12 dish.
½ cup margarine **½ cup brown sugar**	Microwave on high for 2 minutes. Stir well.
½ cup powdered sugar **1 tbsp. cornstarch** **¼ tsp. salt** **1 cup angel flake coconut** **⅔ cup chopped nuts**	Blend in. Spread over crackers.
1 cup chocolate chips	Sprinkle over the top.

Microwave on high for 2 to 2½ minutes. Let stand several minutes for chocolate to soften. Then spread over bars. Cool before cutting.

Rhoda Wenger

Fruit Squares

1 cup flour **¼ cup sugar** **½ cup butter or margarine**	Mix together until crumbly. Pat in 8 inch-square bake dish. Microwave on high for 5 minutes.
½ cup angel flake coconut **½ cup chopped dates or raisins** **½ cup chopped nuts**	Sprinkle evenly over crust.
2 eggs **¾ cup brown sugar** **2 tbsp. flour** **1 tsp. baking powder** **1 tsp. vanilla** **⅛ tsp. salt**	Beat together and spread over fruit. Microwave on high for 6 minutes. Cut into squares when cool.

German Chocolate Upside-Down Cake

½ cup brown sugar ⅓ cup butter or margarine	Combine in bowl. Microwave on high for ½ minute until melted. Stir until smooth. Line an 8 or 9-inch round bake dish with waxed paper. Spread mixture over paper.
½ cup chopped pecans ½ cup angel flake coconut	Sprinkle over mixture.
2 tbsp. milk	Drizzle over top.
8 or 9 oz. chocolate cake mix (single layer mix)	Prepare according to pkg. directions. Pour over coconut.

Microwave at 50 percent power for 6 ½ to 8 minutes. Let stand, covered for 10 minutes. Invert onto plate. Carefully peel off waxed paper. Cover to cool.

Oatmeal Chocolate Chip Bars

½ cup butter or margarine	Microwave on high for 45 seconds until melted.
⅔ cup brown sugar	Blend in.
2 cups quick oatmeal ½ cup chopped nuts ½ cup angel flake coconut 1 tsp. vanilla	Stir in until well mixed. Spread in a greased 8-inch-square dish. Put dish on an inverted saucer in oven. Microwave on high for 3 to 6 minutes until bubbly all over, turning dish several times. Cool 2 minutes.
½ cup chocolate chips	Sprinkle over top of hot bars.
¼ cup peanut butter	Dot small chunks over top. When soft, spread to frost, leaving marbled effect.

Cut into bars while still slightly warm.

Peanut Butter Bars

1 cup butter or margarine 1 cup peanut butter	Microwave on high for 1 ½ to 2 ½ minutes or until melted. Stir until smooth..
2 cups graham cracker crumbs ½ cup chopped peanuts 2 to 2½ cups powdered sugar	Mix in thoroughly until stiff. Press in buttered 8 × 12-inch dish.
1 cup chocolate chips 2 tbsp. butter	Microwave on high for about 1 ½ to 2 minutes until melted enough to blend smooth. Spread over bars. Cool before cutting.

Pineapple Upside-Down Cake

¼ cup butter or margarine ⅓ cup brown sugar	Microwave in 9-inch square bake dish on high ½ to 1 minute or until melted.
4 or 5 pineapple slices	Drain and reserve juice. Arrange in dish.
4 or 5 maraschino cherries	Place in center of each slice.
¼ cup chopped pecans (optional)	Sprinkle over top.
8 or 9 oz. yellow cake mix (1 layer mix) ½ cup pineapple juice (reserved from slices) 1 egg	Mix thoroughly. Pour over mixture in dish. Microwave on high for 8 ½ minutes. Let stand for 3 min. Invert on plate.

Pumpkin Bars

¼ cup butter	Microwave on high for 30 seconds to melt.
¾ cup brown sugar	Blend in.
2 eggs	Add, one at a time, beating after each addition.
1 cup flour ½ tsp. baking powder ½ tsp. baking soda ½ tsp. salt 1 tsp. pumpkin pie spice* 1 cup canned pumpkin 1 tsp. vanilla	Add sifted dry ingredients alternately with pumpkin and vanilla.
¼ cup chopped nuts ¼ cup chopped raisins	Stir in.

Lightly grease bottom only of 9-inch-square bake dish. Spread batter in dish. Place dish on inverted saucer in oven. Microwave at 50 percent power for 6 minutes. Increase power to high and microwave for 5 to 6 minutes until very little unbaked batter appears through bottom of dish. Let stand 5 to 10 minutes. Cool before frosting.

Cream Cheese Frosting: 3 oz. cream cheese 2 tbsp. margarine	Microwave together on high for 10 to 20 seconds to soften. Stir well.
1½ cups powdered sugar or more	Beat in until smooth and of good spreading consistency. Spread on cake. Cut into bars when set.

(*If you do not have pumpkin pie spice, use ½ tsp. cinnamon, ¼ tsp. nutmeg, and ¼ tsp. ginger instead.)

SNACKS AND CANDY

Caramel Apples

6 small apples **6 wooden skewers**	Wash and dry apples thoroughly. Insert skewer into stem end of each apple.
25 (7 oz.) candy caramels (such as Kraft's) **1 tbsp. water**	Microwave in small bowl on high for 4 to 8 minutes until melted. Stir.
2 tsp. milk	Stir in until smooth. Dip apples in caramel turning to coat all over.
¾ cup finely chopped peanuts	Immediately roll apples in nuts. Set on blossom end on waxed paper to cool. Refrigerate when cold.

Caramel Popcorn

1 cup brown sugar **½ cup margarine** **¼ cup light corn syrup** **½ tsp. salt**	Combine in a 1-qt. measuring pitcher. Microwave on high for 2 minutes after mixture reaches the boiling point. Remove from oven.
½ tsp. baking soda	Stir in.
3 to 4 qts. popped corn	Place in large glass bowl. Pour syrup over corn, stirring until evenly coated. Do not cover.

Microwave on high for 1 ½ minutes, and stir. Cook 45 seconds more and stir; then another 45 seconds more and stir. Spread on tray or waxed paper to cool.

Coconut Candy Special

½ cup butter or margarine	Microwave in 8 × 12-inch bake dish on high for about 1 minute until melted.
2 cups graham cracker crumbs **¼ cup sugar**	Stir in until well mixed. Press evenly in bottom of dish.
2 cups angel flake coconut **1 (14-oz.) can sweetened condensed milk**	Combine and spread over crust. Microwave, uncovered, at 50 percent power for 9 to 11 minutes until heated through, turning dish once.
1¾ cup chocolate chips	Microwave on high for 2 to 3 minutes just until melted. Spread over candy.

Cut into bars when cool.

Fruity Popcorn Treat

2 qts. popped corn 1 cup peanuts 1 cup sunflower seeds 1 cup shredded coconut	Combine in large glass bowl. Set aside.
½ cup sugar ¼ cup margarine 1 tsp. ground cinnamon 1 tsp. salt ½ cup honey	Combine in 1-qt. glass measure. Microwave on high for 2 minutes until boiling, stirring once. Stir well, and microwave at 30 percent power for 5 minutes. Pour over popcorn mixture. Microwave at 30 percent power for 5 minutes more, stirring once.
1 cup raisins 1 cup dried apricots or peaches, chopped	Stir in.

Yield: 3 ½ qts.

Gloria Snider

Marshmallow Cream Fudge

(Never fails)

½ cup butter or margarine	Slice into 9-inch-square bake dish. Microwave on high for 1 minute or until melted.
2 cups sugar ⅔ cup evaporated milk (5-oz.)	Blend in until well mixed. Microwave at 80 percent power for 8 to 10 minutes, stirring frequently.
1¾ cups chocolate chips 1 tsp. vanilla 1 (7-oz.) jar marshmallow creme ¾ cup chopped nuts	Stir in until smooth. Chill until firm. Cut into small squares.

Rice Krispies Bars

6 tbsp. margarine	In mixing bowl, microwave on high for 45 to 60 seconds until melted.
1 (10-oz.) pkg. miniature marshmallows (6 cups) ⅓ cup peanut butter	Add. Microwave on high 1 ½ to 2 minutes until melted, stirring once. Stir until smooth.
6 cups Rice Krispies cereal 1 cup salted peanuts	Add, stirring until well coated. Press mixture in buttered 8 × 12 bake dish.
1 cup chocolate chips ¼ cup peanut butter 1 tbsp. butter	Combine in small bowl. Microwave at 50 percent power for 2 ½ to 4 minutes until soft enough to blend smoothly. Spread over bars. Cool before cutting.

Italian TV Mix

2 cups peanuts **2 cups chow mein noodles** **2 cups Corn Chex** **2 cup pretzels**	Mix in large glass bowl. Set aside. (Combination of ingredients may be varied according to taste—use 8 cups.)
¼ cup butter **2 tbsp. dry spaghetti sauce mix**	Combine in glass measuring cup. Microwave on high for 45 seconds. Pour over mixture in bowl and toss until evenly mixed. Microwave at 30 percent power for 7 to 8 minutes until toasted & heated through, stirring twice.
2 tbsp. Parmesan cheese **1 tsp. Italian herb seasoning**	Sprinkle over mixture. Cool. Store in airtight container.

Yield: 8 cups

Gloria Snider

Party Mix

3 cups Cheerios cereal **3 cups Rice Chex cereal** **2 cups thin pretzel sticks** **1 cup peanuts or mixed nuts**	Combine in large bowl.
½ cup vegetable oil **1 tbsp. Worcestershire sauce** **1 tsp. garlic salt** **2 tsp. seasoned salt** **dash Tabasco sauce**	Blend together thoroughly, then pour over mixture in bowl, stirring to coat evenly. Microwave on high for 8 to 10 minutes or until cereal is hot and crisp, stirring twice.

Yield: 2 ¼ qts.

Peanut Brittle

1 cup sugar **½ cup light corn syrup**	Blend together in a 1 ½-qt. casserole. Microwave on high 4 minutes, stirring once.
1 cup salted peanuts	Stir in, and microwave on high 3 to 5 minutes until mixture is light brown. (Do not overcook.)
1 tsp. butter **1 tsp. vanilla**	Blend in thoroughly. Microwave on high for 1 to 2 minutes.
1 tsp. baking soda	Add, stirring gently until light and foamy. Pour onto greased cookie sheet, or foil. Cool, then break into pieces.

Yield: about 1 lb.

Rocky Road Candy

2 cups chocolate chips **2 cups butterscotch chips** **1 cup peanut butter**	Combine in large glass bowl and microwave at 70 percent power, uncovered for 5 minutes. Stir until melted.
1 (10-oz.) pkg. miniature marshmallows **1 cup salted peanuts**	Fold in. Spread in buttered 9 × 13 dish. Refrigerate until set.

Lois Wenger

Some-Mores

Spread a 3-inch square of graham cracker with peanut butter, and place a 3-inch square of candy bar or chocolate chips on next. Add a large marshmallow. Microwave on high for 15 to 20 seconds, or until marshmallow puffs up. (Fun to watch through glass oven door!) Add second graham cracker after cooking.

Stuffed Mushrooms

8 oz. fresh mushrooms	Wash thoroughly. Remove and chop stems.
2 tbsp. butter or margarine **¼ cup finely chopped celery** **¼ cup finely chopped onion**	Combine with chopped stems and microwave on high for 2 to 3 minutes, or until tender crisp, stirring once.
¼ cup dry bread crumbs **1 tsp. Worcestershire sauce** **1 tsp. parsley flakes** **¼ tsp. salt** **⅛ tsp. oregano** **⅛ tsp. MSG (optional)**	Stir in until well mixed. Pile in caps and arrange on a paper towel on a plate. Place larger caps to outside of plate. Microwave on high for 1 ½ to 3 minutes until thoroughly heated, rotating plate once or twice.

Yield: 6 to 8 servings

JAM AND JELLY

Grape Jelly

1 (6-oz.) can frozen grape juice	In large bowl, microwave on high for 1 minute.
1 (1¾-oz.) pkg. powdered fruit pectin (such as Sure-jel)	Stir in thoroughly.
2 cups hot water	Add. Microwave, covered, on high for 6 to 8 minutes until mixture boils, stirring twice.
3¾ cups sugar	Stir in. Microwave, covered, on high for 4 to 6 minutes until mixture comes to a boil, stirring twice.

Microwave on high for 1 minute at full boil. Skim off foam. Pour into sterilized jars and seal.

Yield: 4 cups

Strawberry Jam

1 (20-oz.) pkg. frozen strawberries	In large bowl, microwave on high for 2 minutes, stirring once.
1 (1¾-oz.) pkg. powdered fruit pectin (such as Sure-jel).	Stir in gradually. Microwave on high for 2½ to 3 minutes until strawberries begin to boil, stirring once.
2½ cups sugar **1 tbsp. lemon juice**	Stir in. Microwave on high for 4 to 5 minutes until mixture comes to a boil, stirring every 2 minutes. Microwave 1 minute more on high. Let stand 2 minutes. Skim and pour into jelly glasses. Seal.

Yield: 3½ cups

PASTRY & PIES ·

PASTRY AND PIES

Pie (along with ice cream) reportedly ranks as the favorite dessert in the United States. First choice is apple and then cherry. But, unfortunately, making good pies is an art that has plagued many beginners and some others to the point of despair and even to concluding that "pies are something I simply cannot make!" This certainly need not be the case. Most failures are the result of a lack of knowledge and too little practice!

A good pie must have a good crust, and the crust, of course, gives the most problem. There is an art to making a flaky tender crust, but like any other worthwhile accomplishment in life, a few failures should not cause one to conclude that a good job is impossible. One of my philosophies of life is that we are usually able to accomplish about what we make up our minds we can do! The secret is in the determination. Just think. If you take a little extra time right now and keep at it faithfully until you master the art, you will be able to make delicious pies for the remainder of your life!

Those who have never made a pie crust will be amazed at how well it can be done the very first time by just following these simple directions. So let's get down to a few basics.

Two important items are the kind of flour and the kind of fat you use. Different brands of flour and fat can give quite different baking results. Flours are milled for various uses. Choose a softly milled, all-purpose flour for pies. Bread flour is a stronger, high-protein flour with high gluten content and does not do nearly as well for pies and cakes. If you do choose to use bread flour for pies, you will need to use extra fat to have the same amount of flakiness. If you are a beginner and have no idea which brands are for what, ask someone you know who is experienced and does a good job. (I personally prefer Robin Hood for bread, Gold Medal or White Fawn for all-purpose use, and Softasilk for delicate cakes. I use all-purpose for many cakes. Unfortunately, some flours may be labeled all-purpose that are actually harder wheat flours.) There are so many brands on the market and every community seems to have different brand names, so the surest way is to ask an experienced cook in your area who has already tried out different kinds and can tell you the best brand.

434

Don't hesitate to ask helpful information of others. People usually feel flattered that you trusted their judgment or thought they made something extra special and will gladly share information with you. Where would any of us be if others had not shared with us! (Only occasionally is there a family secret, or for commercial purposes individuals are not free to give information, but I've found this to be the exception. Be tactful if in doubt.)

Lard and butter are greasy fats and it is easiest to obtain a flaky crust using one or the other, preferably lard. However, many people cannot tolerate animal fat. Fortunately, hydrogenated shortening is also excellent for pie crusts. There are also combinations of shortening and lard, and many people have excellent results using margarine. If you use margarine, it is important to use a good grade (not necessarily an expensive brand). You need to use a little more in proportion to the amount of flour than when using lard (approximately 2 tbsp. more per 1 cup fat called for in the recipe.) Some of the cheap poorly refined brands of margarine do not give the best baking results. They may work fine for purposes other than baking, but I believe this is the source of much frustration to many uninformed cooks. If you prefer using margarine, experiment a little, or you may wish to check with a friend.

Glass or dull metal pie pans give the best results with pastry. This is just the opposite of most baking where the shiny aluminum pans give best results. The reason is that you want pie crusts to turn out crisp and lightly browned, while most other baked goods are better when soft and moist. The shiny pans reflect heat and keep the contents light, and the glass or dull pans absorb it causing browning. This helps to avoid having soggy crusts.

While learning it is better not to make too large a batch of dough at once. After a little practice you can multiply the recipe and store extra crusts in the freezer for later use. An amount for a two-crust pie or two single-crust pies works easily.

I prefer making only the bottom crust for fruit pies and then top them with crumbs instead of using a top crust. They do not juice over in the oven nearly as quickly. Also, I usually keep a supply of crusts and crumbs on hand in the freezer, so if I need a pie on short notice, I can produce one quickly. You can have your own home-canned pie filling on hand or use commercial brands already prepared. Your own home-canned or frozen fruit is probably much better You simply take a crust from the freezer, open a can of prepared pie filling to fill it, sprinkle crumbs on top, place it in the oven for about 25 minutes, and you have a nice warm pie to be served with ice cream for guests!

The correct proportions of flour, water, and fat are of prime importance. Too much fat will make a greasy dough that will tend to cling together before you add the water. It will be difficult to roll out and will probably fall apart when you try to put it in the pie plate. If too much water is added, the dough will become soggy and sticky and will take up too much flour as you roll it out. This will cause it to become tough. The amount of water may vary slightly with brands of flour. Water should be ice cold for good mixing results. If too much flour is added, the crust will be tough.

The dough must also be mixed correctly. The flakiness in pastry is obtained by the proper amount of mixing. The tiny particles of fat throughout the dough cause it to flake apart. Overmixing the dough when combining flour and fat causes the fat areas to dissolve and makes for less flakiness. Mix only until the texture resembles coarse crumbs about the size of peas. The tenderness of the crust depends a lot on how much the dough is worked when mixing in the liquid and rolling out the crust. Working the dough excessively develops the gluten structure in the flour and toughens the dough. This is why you should not add flour after mixing in the liquid. For best results ingredients for making pastry should be cold. This is just the opposite of most baking where ingredients should be room temperature.

Procedure for Making Pastry

Sift flour and salt into mixing bowl. Work the fat into the flour using a pastry blender or two knives, scissor-fashion, or use your hands. (I prefer using my hands.) Again, do not overmix. Work only until you have uniform crumbs about the size of peas. Heat from your hands with prolonged working of the dough can soften fat too much and toughen dough.

Sprinkle the cold water over the crumbs while stirring with a fork so that no portion gets too damp, but that all of it will be damp enough to cling together. The amount of water varies with brands of flour. (When you decide on the brand of flour and fat you prefer, it is helpful to note exact amounts right on your recipe so you can quickly achieve perfect results in the future without guesswork.)

Quickly gather the dough together with your hands, cleaning the sides of the bowl and press it into a firm ball. Then break in two individual portions for each single crust—a slightly larger ball for the bottom crust if you are making a two-crust pie. (Many people like to wrap each individual ball in plastic wrap at this point and refrigerate at least 30 minutes until chilled for easier handling. Also, chilled dough shrinks less when baked.) I usually go ahead and roll it out immediately. Experiment a time or two to see which works best for you.

Roll dough out on lightly floured countertop, or pastry board or cloth, or on waxed paper or plastic wrap. The waxed paper method is easiest for beginners because excess flour need not be rolled into the dough to keep it from sticking to the surface. You can also mark the size of the pan on the paper. Sprinkle a few drops of water on the counter first and then lay paper on top. This keeps paper from slipping as you roll. Flatten ball of dough with hand, smoothing the edges. Put a few sprinkles of flour on top or another sheet of waxed paper or plastic wrap, and roll from center to outside edge with quick, light strokes in all directions forming as near perfect a circle as possible about 1/8 inch thick. Be sure to lift rolling pin slightly near the edge each time to keep pastry the same thickness and to keep edge from splitting. Do not roll back and forth on pastry. Repair any cracks or torn places by pressing together. If needed, you can dampen your finger with a little water, moisten edge to be repaired, and overlap slightly, but use water sparingly! If pastry sticks to surface while rolling, loosen gently with knife and lightly flour area. Do not gather back into ball to reroll. Rerolled dough is always tougher.

To transfer to pie plate carefully fold dough in half, and place with fold in center of plate. Then unfold other half to other side of plate. (With waxed paper method, peel off top waxed paper. Lift two center edges of paper with dough hanging down on each side and transfer to plate. Place center of dough in center

of plate and unfold other half of dough. Underneath paper will be on top. Carefully peel off paper.) Gently ease into plate, being careful not to pull or stretch dough—this will cause shrinkage during baking. Press gently against bottom and sides to remove air bubbles under crust.

Use a pair of kitchen scissors or a sharp knife to trim edge that overhangs about 1/4 inch from rim of pie plate for double-crust pie, or 1/2 inch from rim for single-crust pie. Complete procedure according to the type pie you are making.

For a one-crust pie in which filling and crust are baked together, fold overhanging pastry back and under slightly at rim, building it up to keep pie filling from running over. The finished edge should extend over the edge of the pie plate slightly to help prevent shrinkage during baking. To form fluted edge, firmly place left index finger inside of the rim, and with right thumb and index finger on the outside, pinch pastry at that point into a V or rounded shape, repeating all around the edge. (Do not prick this type crust, or filling will seep through the holes.) Fill and bake according to directions for filling.

For a one-crust pie to be baked and filled afterward, flute the edge as described. Then with sharp fork make deep pricks close together all over bottom and sides and especially around the bottom curve of the crust to let air bubbles escape. Bake in hot oven at 400 degrees for about 10 to 12 minutes until lightly browned. Until experienced you may want to peek in oven after five minutes to check if there are bubbles. If so, prick them with fork or pick, and finish baking. (If you have trouble with shrinkage, it helps considerably to chill these crusts at least 10 minutes in refrigerator before baking. Be cautious with glass plates, however. You may wish to make this type pie in metal pans.)

For a two-crust pie, roll out the top crust the same as the bottom. With a sharp knife or miniature cookie cutter make small holes or slits near the center of the crust. This will allow steam to escape during baking. Otherwise, the top crust will puff up, leaving a hollow space underneath. (Here is your chance to be creative and to make a seasonal design or whatever you like. You may want to cut dough into ¼-inch strips and make a latice top. Or you can make pastry cutouts with large cookie cutters. Bake these separately on tray alongside pie for about 10 minutes. Lay on hot pie as soon as you remove it from the oven. If they are large, it is best to half bake them separately. Then use spatula to transfer them to top of pie to finish baking so they conform to shape of pie.)

Place desired filling in crust. Moisten the edge of the rim of bottom crust with fingers slightly dampened with water. Carefully place top crust over filling. Trim off excess dough leaving 1/2-inch rim. Fold the extra edge of the top under the edge of the bottom crust. Press around edge of plate to seal together. Flute edge as described for one-crust pie. Bake according to directions for filling.

There are several methods for making **tart crusts**. Dough may be formed into rolls as large in diameter as needed to fit tart pans. Chill well, then slice off circles of dough. Press into pans. Prick well and bake at 400 degrees for approximately 10 to 12 minutes.

For larger tarts to be served as individual pies, cut 6-inch circles of dough.

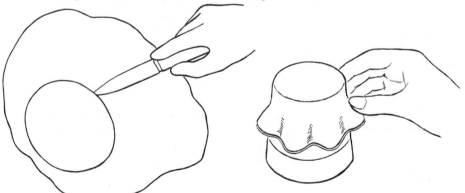

Also, cut the same size circles of foil. Place foil over an inverted cup of the size desired and place dough on top. This gives a base for forming the dough. Prick dough with fork. Then shape both foil and dough forming cups with scalloped edges to take up excess fullness. Carefully lift both foil and dough onto a baking sheet, still in inverted position. Bake at 400 degrees for 12 to 15 minutes. Cool and remove foil. Fill as desired.

Some cooks form dough over inverted muffin tins to bake. However, the foil seems to give nicer results.

How to Make Meringue

To make a nice high meringue on a 9-inch pie use 3 egg whites, 1 tsp. warm water (helps increase volume), 1/4 tsp. cream of tartar (stabilizes whites and helps them hold their shape), and 6 tbsp. sugar. If you do not have cream of tartar, use 1 tsp. lemon juice instead. The addition of 2 tsp. cornstarch along with the sugar helps to prevent weeping and makes a delicate meringue

Eggs separate best when cold, but it is *very* important to have them warmed to room temperature when beating to ensure good volume. Place egg whites in mixer bowl, and swish the bowl around in a larger bowl of rather warm water if you are in a hurry. Be careful not to get a single speck of yolk in with the whites as this will decrease volume immensely. Also, the bowl and beaters must be thoroughly clean and free of grease. Egg whites will not beat into volume at all with greasy or soiled utensils. As mentioned elsewhere, you can beat the yolks with the same beater you use for the whites, but you cannot beat the whites with a beater you first used for the yolks without washing it.

Add warm water and beat at highest speed until frothy. Sprinkle in cream of tartar. Then reduce speed slightly and gradually sprinkle in sugar and cornstarch. Quickly return to highest speed and beat until sugar is dissolved and *very* stiff glossy peaks are formed. Underbeating causes brownish droplets of liquid to form on baked meringue and causes it to shrink after it is baked. It also will seep liquid (weep) when baked pie is chilled. Overbeating makes it dry out and hard to spread smoothly and seal to edges. It can also cause meringue to break down in volume as it bakes since cells are stretched beyond their capacity to expand. To test whether sugar is dissolved, rub a little between your fingers to feel whether it is grainy.

Pile meringue on pie going around edges first, being careful to completely "seal" the meringue onto the crust edge. This helps prevent shrinkage and pulling away during baking. Pile a little higher in center and swirl to make attractive. Bake at 325 to 350 degrees for approximately 12 to 15 minutes until golden brown. (Too hot an oven reduces height of meringue.) Remove from oven and cool on rack at room temperature away from draft. Cooling meringue too fast causes it to pull away from edges and shrink. To slice easily, dip knife in hot water or grease knife.
To Garnish: Before baking, sprinkle graham cracker crumbs or flaked coconut over top of meringue for attractive effect.

Cream Pies

There are numerous recipes for cream pies, so I have done quite a bit of experimenting to find the advantages and disadvantages of various ones. The basic recipe seems to be much the same. The difference is mostly in what you use as a thickening agent.

Many people use cornstarch for a nice light custard. However, the custard tends to water or weep considerably, often causing a soggy crust especially after a day or two. To avoid this problem you can add one envelope of unflavored gelatin

441 PASTRY AND PIES

(softened in 1/4 cup cold water) to the hot custard after the custard is thickened and as soon as you remove it from the stove. Stir thoroughly to dissolve. This works well for pies which you make one day to be eaten the following day, as it gives the gelatin time to chill and set up firmly. If you will be eating the pie the same day, especially while it is slightly warm, this method does not help because the gelatin has not set up and actually thins the custard slightly.

You may also use Clearjel. This does not water and holds up well. However, it is sensitive to precise cooking time when used in custards and can be frustrating to the inexperienced.

The use of flour for thickening makes a heavier custard. However, the custard waters little and holds up well. If you use flour, you will need to use at least 1½ times the amount of cornstarch called for. You also need to cook the custard a little longer before adding the egg yolks to allow it to thicken completely. I've concluded that for the easiest all-around best effect, a combination of flour and cornstarch proves most satisfactory. This makes a nice custard that holds up well with a minimum amount of watering. (Be aware that the meringue can also water if not made properly. If you are trying to correct this problem, note carefully whether the source is the custard or the meringue.)

The custard is best made in a double boiler. If you do not have a double boiler, you can use a saucepan, but you will obtain a nicer, smoother custard in a double boiler without the problem of scorching. If you do use a saucepan, it helps to use a spatula or pancake turner for stirring so you can keep the entire bottom surface of the pan cleared almost constantly to prevent sticking Stir briskly, especially in the thickening process, to avoid lumps. Custards tend to get a little thicker when made in a saucepan than in a double boiler, and thicken quickly. You may wish to reduce amount of thickener slightly if making in a saucepan. Do not cook as long.

Cream pies are usually topped with meringue made from the whites of the eggs used in the custard. If you prefer a whipped cream topping, you can freeze the whites to use later on, or you can add them to the custard. To use in the custard, beat whites like meringue—except use 2 tbsp. sugar per 3 egg whites instead of the 6 tbsp. called for in meringue. Then fold the hot custard into the whites, slowly at first, stirring briskly, and then more quickly until well blended. This makes a nice fluffy filling.

If you do not use meringue, cover hot custard in pie shell with plastic wrap to cool to prevent a film from forming over the top. Chill pie well and top with whipped cream just before serving.

TIPS FOR PASTRY AND PIES

•If you have problems with the crust browning too much on the edge before the center of the pie is done, cut a 1 1/2-inch wide circle of foil, or cut the center out of a foil pan, and lay on top of edge while baking. (Save to use again.) Remove foil about 10 minutes before pie is done so edge will brown slightly.

•To measure sizes for top and bottom crusts when rolling out dough, hold inverted pie plate over rolled dough.

•If unfilled crusts insist on shrinking while being baked in spite of all you've done, the oven temperature probably was not hot enough. The oven needs to be hot enough to set the crust quickly before it shrinks, usually 400 degrees. Thermostats on ovens vary considerably, so pay close attention to this until you learn at what temperature on your oven you get the correct results, then mark this on your recipe.

•A friend told me of a little trick she uses to obtain a flaky pie crust. First, mix together the flour and salt (and any other dry ingredients the recipe may call for). Then reserve the same amount of this dry mixture as the liquid called for in the recipe. Cut shortening into remaining dry mixture. Combine reserved dry mixture with the liquid first, making sort of a batter. Then add this batter to the flour and shortening mixture, tossing until moist. [Evelyn Kratz]

•Crumb crusts do not need to be baked before filling, but if using unbaked they should be chilled first to set the melted margarine. Otherwise, the filling will immediately begin to soak into the crust. They will be crisper if baked a short time. Cool filling before pouring into crust.

•When making a crumb crust, save some of the crumbs or make a few additional crumbs to sprinkle on top of the pie to garnish.

•Pie tape can be purchased to moisten and place around top edge of pie plate if you have a lot of trouble with pies running over in the oven. However, it is best not to fill them too full, to build the edge up a little, and seal them well. The tape also helps to keep crust edges from getting too brown.

•When you are in a hurry, instant puddings make quick cream pies. However, you should never try to bake a meringue on an instant pie filling. Use whipped topping or whipped cream for the topping, or garnish with nuts, crumbs, coconut, or chocolate curls. (To make curls easily, warm the bar of chocolate slightly and it will shave off beautifully with a sharp knife.)

•Use glass pie plates for custard pies or fruit pies when the crust and filling are baked together. Metal pans reflect heat and for this type pie often the bottom crust is still soggy when the remainder of the pie is done. (Many people complain of problems with soggy crusts on pumpkin custard pies.) The use of a glass pie plate instead of a metal pan should eliminate the problem. It also helps to place the pie on the lower rack in the oven nearer the heating element. Do not let a custard pie stand before baking. Place in oven immediately after pouring filling into crust so liquid does not soak into crust.

•If you like a shiny top crust on pies, brush lightly with slightly beaten egg whites. (Caution: Do not let excessive egg white settle in low places on top of pie.) For a special touch, sprinkle the top with granulated sugar or cinnamon and sugar.

•When making a custard pie that calls for only the egg yolks, or if you use whipped cream on top instead of meringue, freeze the whites to use for angel food cake, or icings, or whatever. Label container with the quantity. Egg whites freeze very well.

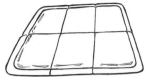

•To help avoid having the crust become soggy with raw fruit filling, the bottom of the crust may be brushed with a little slightly beaten egg white before filling it. (Some cooks bake this about 5 minutes before filling to set the egg white; others do not.) Or sprinkle a thin layer of sugar over the crust before filling it.

•If you wish to top cream pies with whipped cream instead of meringue, you will need to chill them well before adding the whipped cream. Lay a piece of plastic wrap over the top of the hot pie to keep a film from forming on custard as it cools.

•Do not freeze cream or custard pies. The filling will separate when thawing and crust will become soggy. Fruit pies may be frozen, however, if desired. Bake before freezing to prevent soggy crusts.

•Use a pizza cutter for quick cutting of strips for a lattice pie top.

•If you have a crust that you know is not rich enough after it is in the pie pan, melt a tablespoon or more of butter and brush over the crust before baking. This is helpful if you had scraps that needed to be rerolled and have too much flour worked into them.

•Do not place pies against the edge of the oven when baking as edges will tend to burn. Leave a little space around each pie for even baking and browning.

•For an easy topping on pumpkin pies, arrange a layer of miniature marshmallows in bottom of shell, then pour in filling and bake. Marshmallows will rise to the top.

•At my home we usually made what we called **apple butter rolls** from leftover pastry that wasn't quite large enough for an additional crust. (Sometimes we made extra just for this purpose!) Roll dough in rectangle and spread with apple butter.

Cut into desired sizes and fold in each edge of roll, overlapping in center. Bake along with pies about 15 to 20 minutes until golden brown. Delicious eaten warm. We sometimes broke them into a cereal bowl and poured milk over them. Eat immediately before they get soggy. My daughters loved to cut out leftover scraps of dough with small cookie cutters and sprinkle them with sugar and cinnamon. They always ate them before they had a chance to cool!

•To avoid sogginess in crust of a pie containing a raw fruit filling or a cold liquid filling, increase oven temperature for the first 10 minutes of baking to quickly set the crust (400 to 425 degrees). Then turn it back to a moderate temperature for the remainder of baking time (around 350 degrees). When beginning with a hotter temperature, reduce the total baking time slightly.

•When making lemon meringue pie or lemon cream pie, always add lemon juice or rind immediately *after* custard has thickened. The addition of acid such as lemon juice or vinegar reduces firmness of custard and may also cause curdling if added before custard thickens. Many cooks use water as a base for lemon pies to prevent this problem when they could use milk for more nutrition. Then simply add a little more thickener, and add the lemon *after* custard has fully thickened.

PASTRY AND PIES RECIPES

PASTRY

Basic Pastry

3 cups flour **1 tsp. salt**	Sift together.
1 cup shortening*	Cut in until crumbly.
6 tbsp. ice water	Sprinkle in, tossing with fork just until mixture is moistened. Form into a ball. Roll out as desired.

Bake at 400 degrees about 10 to 12 minutes. (*If using margarine, increase to 1 ¼ cups.)

Yield: 3 single crusts

Never-fail Pastry

3 cups flour **1 tsp. salt**	Sift together.
1 cup shortening	Cut in until crumbly.
1 egg, slightly beaten **2 tsp. vinegar** **4 to 5 tbsp. ice water**	Combine, then sprinkle in, tossing with fork just until mixture is moistened. Form into ball and roll out as desired.

Bake at 400 degrees approximately 10 to 12 minutes.

Yield: 3 single crusts

Easy Pastry

3 cups flour **1 tsp. salt**	Sift together.
1 cup shortening	Cut in until crumbly.
3 tbsp. milk **3 tbsp. water** **2 tbsp. vegetable oil**	Combine, then sprinkle in, tossing with fork just until mixture is moistened. Form into ball. Roll out as desired.

Yield: 3 single crusts

Darlene Logan

Pie Crust Mix

6 cups all-purpose flour
½ tsp. salt
½ tsp. baking powder

Sift together.

2 cups of a good solid shortening
(such as Crisco)

Cut in until crumbly.

Store in tightly covered container in cool place. To Use: For 1 pie crust, use 1 slightly rounded cup of mix and 2 tbsp. cold water. Total amount makes 6 crusts and takes ¾ cup water.

Gladys and Brownie Driver

Mix-in-Pan Crust

1½ cups flour
½ tsp. salt
½ cup oil
2 tbsp. milk
1 tbsp. sugar

Measure all ingredients into pie pan and toss together with fork in pan. Press into shape in pan with hand.

Bake at 400 degrees approximately 10 to 12 minutes.

Crumbs for Topping Pies

(Crumbs are excellent for topping fruit pies. I like to keep a supply in the freezer for instant use.)

3 cups flour
1 cup brown sugar
¾ cup margarine

Mix together until crumbly. Store in tightly covered container in cool place.

Variation: Use half flour and half oatmeal for oatmeal crumbs. Also add 1 tsp. cinnamon if desired. Use about 1 cup crumbs for each pie.

Yield: enough for 4 to 5 pies

Chocolate Crumb Crust

1½ cups chocolate cookie crumbs
6 tbsp. melted margarine

Mix well. Press in 9" plate and chill.

Chocolate Coconut Crust

1 (1-oz.) square unsweetened
   chocolate, melted
2 tbsp. milk

Combine.

2 cups angel flake coconut
½ cup powdered sugar

Stir in. Press into 9″ plate and chill.

Chocolate Crunch Crust

⅓ cup margarine
¾ cup chocolate bits

Stir over low heat just until melted.

3 cups oven-toasted Rice Krispies
   cereal

Stir in until coated. Press in lightly greased 9″
pie plate and chill.

Cocoa Crumb Crust

1½ cups vanilla wafer crumbs
¼ cup cocoa powder
⅓ cup powdered sugar
6 tbsp. melted margarine

Mix thoroughly and press in 9″ plate. Bake at
350 degrees for 8 minutes. Cool.

Coconut Crust

2 cups angel flake coconut
2 tbsp. sugar
1 tbsp. flour
2 tbsp. melted margarine

Combine thoroughly and press in 9″ plate. Bake
at 350 degrees for 8 to 10 minutes. Cool.

Coconut Pastry Crust

1¼ cups flour
½ cup angel flake coconut
3 tbsp. brown sugar
½ cup melted margarine

Mix together thoroughly. Press into 9″ plate.
Bake at 400 degrees for 8 to 10 minutes. Cool.

Cornflake Crumb Crust

1⅓ cups cornflake crumbs (takes 3
   cups cornflakes)
2 tbsp. sugar
¼ cup melted margarine

Mix together thoroughly. Press into 9″ plate.
May use as is, or bake at 375 degrees for 5 to 7
minutes.

Will hold up slightly better and has crisper taste when baked.

Cream Cheese Tart Crust

2¼ cups flour
¼ tsp. salt

Sift together.

. . . .

1 cup margarine
6 oz. cream cheese

Cream together, then cut into flour mixture until crumbly.

. . . .

Shape into two 2-inch rolls, wrap in plastic wrap, and chill in refrigerator for several hours or overnight. Slice into 36 portions and fit into 2″ muffin tins.

. . . .

Crunchy Crust

¾ cup flour
½ cup quick oatmeal
½ cup chopped nuts
2 tbsp. sugar
¼ tsp. salt
½ cup melted butter

Mix together thoroughly. Press into 9″ plate. Bake at 375 degrees for about 12 minutes. Cool.

. . . .

Gingersnap Crust

1½ cups crushed gingersnaps
6 tbsp. melted margarine

Mix together thoroughly. Press into 9″ plate. Chill.

. . . .

Graham Cracker Crust

1½ cups graham cracker crumbs
  (about 18 single crackers)
2 tbsp. sugar
⅓ cup melted margarine
1 tsp. ground cinnamon (optional)

Mix together thoroughly. Press into 9″ plate. Chill as is, or bake at 350 degees for 8 minutes for crisper, firmer crust.

. . . .

Oatmeal Pastry Crust

1 cup quick oatmeal
⅓ cup flour
⅓ cup brown sugar
½ tsp. salt

Mix thoroughly.

. . . .

⅓ cup shortening

Cut in until crumbly.

. . . .

Press firmly into 9″ plate. Bake at 375 degrees for 12 to 15 minutes. Cool.

. . . .

Spiced Nut Crust

1 cup flour
½ cup finely chopped nuts
¼ cup brown sugar
½ tsp. ground cinnamon
½ cup melted margarine

Mix together thoroughly. Press into 9″ plate.

10 to 12 pecan halves (optional)

If desired, press pecan halves onto rim of crust. Bake at 350 degrees for 8 to 10 minutes.

PIES

Apple Pie

Peel and slice 4 to 6 apples (my family prefers Stayman, or Grimes). Add 1 cup water and ½ to ¾ cup sugar, depending on the sweetness of the apples. Bring to boil in saucepan. Cook just a couple of minutes until softened, but *not* until mushy. Dissolve 3 tbsp. Clearjel or cornstarch in ⅓ cup water and add, stirring just until thickened. Remove from heat and stir in ½ tsp. cinnamon, ¼ tsp. allspice, ¼ tsp. vanilla, and 1 tbsp. margarine. Pour into unbaked 9″ pie crust, top with crumbs (see recipe on page 445), and bake at 350 degrees approximately 25 minutes until browned. Best served warm with ice cream.
For a special treat: Mix 3 or 4 tsp. cinnamon into 1 qt. of slightly softened vanilla ice cream. Return to freezer until firm. Serve a scoop of cinnamon ice cream on warm apple pie slices.

Bavarian Apple Tarts

1 cup flour
⅓ cup sugar
½ cup butter or margarine

Mix together until crumbly. Press on bottom and up ½ inch onto sides of an 8 × 12 bake dish.

8 oz. cream cheese, softened
¼ cup sugar
1 egg
½ tsp. vanilla

Beat together and spread over pastry.

4 cups, peeled and thinly sliced apples
⅓ cup sugar
½ tsp. ground cinnamon

Combine and spread over mixture.

⅓ cup chopped nuts

Sprinkle over apples.

Bake at 425 degrees for 10 minutes. Then reduce heat to 375 degrees and bake 25 minutes more. Cool 5 minutes, then cut around edge of pan with knife to loosen. Cut in squares. Serve warm or cold.

Apple Macaroon Pie

9″ unbaked pie crust	Have ready.
4 cups thinly sliced peeled apples	Arrange in pie crust.
⅔ cup sugar **1½ tbsp. flour** **⅛ tsp. salt** **1 tsp. cinnamon** **⅛ tsp. allspice**	Mix, then sprinkle over apples in crust. Bake at 350 degrees for 20 minutes.
1 egg, lightly beaten **¼ cup sugar** **1 tbsp. flour** **3 tbsp. melted margarine** **1 cup flaked coconut**	Combine and pour over hot mixture in crust. Return to oven and bake 30 minutes longer.

Blueberry Cake Pie

9″ unbaked pie crust	Have ready
2 cups blueberries, fresh or frozen—thawed **½ to ¾ cup sugar—lesser amt. if berries are sweetened** **¼ cup water** **1½ tbsp. Clearjel or cornstarch** **½ tsp. lemon flavoring**	Combine in saucepan. Cook until thickened, stirring constantly. Set aside.
Cake Part: **¼ cup shortening** **⅔ cup sugar**	Cream together thoroughly.
1 egg **1 tsp. vanilla**	Add, beating until fluffy.
1 cup flour **1 tsp. baking powder** **½ tsp. salt** **½ cup milk**	Add sifted dry ingredients alternately with milk.

Pour blueberry mixture into pie crust. Drop cake batter by spoon as evenly as possible over mixture. Bake at 350 degrees for approximately 40 minutes. Do not overbake. Delicious served warm with ice cream.

Fresh Berry Pie

(Use blueberries, blackberries, raspberries, etc.)

9″ unbaked pie crust	Have ready.

4 cups fresh berries **1 cup sugar** **1 cup water** **1 tsp. lemon juice** **3 tbsp. Clearjel or cornstarch**	Combine in saucepan, and cook just until thickened, stirring constantly. Pour into pie shell and top with crumbs. (Recipe for crumbs on page 445.)

Bake at 350 degrees for approximately 25 minutes. Delicious served warm with ice cream.

Caramel Pie

9″ baked pie crust	Have ready.

⅔ cup brown sugar **¼ cup cream**	Caramelize in heavy pan until medium brown in color—not too dark.

3 egg yolks, slightly beaten **¼ tsp. salt** **⅓ cup flour—shake in batter shaker** **with part of milk until smooth** **2 cups milk**	Combine and stir into mixture. Cook and stir constantly until thickened. Pour into baked crust.

Make meringue of the 3 egg whites, 6 tbsp. sugar, and ¼ tsp. cream of tartar. Spread over top of filling sealing to edges of crust. Bake at 325 degrees for 12 to 15 minutes until golden brown. Cool and chill.

Kathryn Heatwole

Cherry Pie

(My family prefers the Bing cherries for pies. If using red sour cherrries increase amount of sugar slightly.)

9″ unbaked pie crust	Have ready.

2 to 3 cups canned cherries **undrained** **⅓ to ½ cup sugar** **¼ tsp. salt** **few drops red color**	Combine in saucepan and heat to boiling.

½ cup water **3 tbsp. Clearjel or cornstarch** **(add 1 tbsp. light corn syrup if using** **cornstarch)**	Dissolve and stir in. Cook just until thickened, stirring constantly. Remove from heat.

½ tsp. almond flavoring 1 tbsp. margarine	Stir in. Pour in crust. Add crumbs (recipe on page 445) for topping or make a lattice of pastry strips.

Bake at 350 degrees for 25 minutes or until browned. Delicious served warm with ice cream. Filling may also be cooled and poured into a baked crust. Top with whipped cream or ice cream to serve.

Luscious Cherry Cheese Pie

(You may also use blueberry, raspberry, or strawberry filling. Or use a mixture of strawberries and rhubarb for filling.)

9″ graham cracker crust	Have ready.
8 oz. cream cheese, softened 2 tbsp. milk ½ cup sugar or powdered sugar*	Beat together until smooth.
2 cups Cool Whip	Fold in. Pour into crust.
2 cups cherry pie filling (or other fruit)	Pour over top. Chill at least 3 hours or overnight.

(*Powdered sugar gives a little stiffer consistency to pie than the granulated sugar.)

Jane Burkholder
Lillian Shickel

Chocolate Chiffon Pie

9″ graham cracker or regular baked crust	Have ready.
1 env. unflavored gelatin ¼ cup cold water	Soak until softened.
3 egg yolks, slightly beaten 1 cup water ⅔ cup sugar 3 tbsp. cocoa powder 1 tbsp. margarine ⅛ tsp. salt	Combine in saucepan. Cook, stirring constantly until mixture comes to a full rolling boil. Remove from heat, and stir in softened gelatin until dissolved. Place pan in cold water to cool mixture.
1 tsp. vanilla	Add.
3 egg whites ¼ tsp. cream of tartar ⅓ cup sugar	Make meringue. Fold into cold chocolate mixture. Pour into crust and chill for at least 2 hours.
whipped cream chocolate curls	Top each piece to garnish.

Chocolate-Bottom Cake Pie

9″ unbaked pie crust	Have ready.
½ cup sugar **3 tbsp. cocoa powder** **⅛ tsp. salt** **½ cup water** **½ tsp. vanilla**	Combine in saucepan. Heat until sugar is dissolved and mixture is smooth, stirring constantly. Remove from heat. Set aside.
Cake Part: **¼ cup vegetable oil** **⅔ cup sugar**	Cream together.
1 egg **½ tsp. vanilla**	Add, beating until fluffy.
1 cup flour **1 tsp. baking powder** **¼ tsp. salt** **½ cup milk**	Add sifted dry ingredients alternately with milk.

Pour chocolate mixture into crust. Drop cake batter by spoon as evenly as possible over mixture. Bake at 350 degrees for approximately 40 minutes. Do not overbake. Best served warm.

Super Chocolate Pie

9″ graham cracker crust	Have ready.
8 oz. milk chocolate candy bar (with or without almonds) **18 large marshmallows, or 1⅔ cups miniature marshmallows** **½ cup milk**	Heat in double boiler, or over low heat in saucepan until melted and smooth, stirring constantly. Cool thoroughly.
1 cup whipping cream, or 2 cups Cool Whip	Whip cream and fold into mixture. Pour into crust and chill until set.
chocolate curls or whipped cream	Garnish as desired to serve.

Variation: Omit chocolate bar and fold ⅔ cup chocolate chips into marshmallow-whipped cream mixture for chocolate chip-marshmallow pie.

Elizabeth Yoder
Pam Weaver

Chocolate Pecan Pie

two 9″ unbaked pie crusts	Have ready.
4 eggs, beaten **¾ cup sugar** **¼ cup brown sugar** **1 tbsp. flour** **½ cup butter, melted** **1 cup light corn syrup** **1 tsp. vanilla** **1 cup chocolate chips** **1 cup coarsely broken pecans**	Mix thoroughly and pour into 2 pie crusts. Bake at 350 degrees for 40 to 45 minutes.

Carolyn Reed

Cranberry-Apple Pie

9″ unbaked pie crust	Have ready.
1¼ cups sugar **¼ cup flour** **¼ tsp. salt**	Combine thoroughly in saucepan.
2 cups fresh cranberries **¼ cup maple, or maple-flavored, syrup**	Stir in. Heat to boiling, stirring constantly. Cover and cook 5 minutes, stirring occasionally.
5 large baking apples, peeled and sliced	Add, continuing to cook until apples are tender—3 to 5 minutes more. Remove from heat.
½ cup chopped walnuts	Add. Pour into pie crust.
1 cup crumbs for topping (see recipe on page 445)	Sprinkle over top.

Bake at 375 degrees for approximately 30 minutes. Serve warm with vanilla ice cream.

Cream Pie (Basic)

9″ baked pie crust	Have ready.
1¾ cups milk	Heat in double boiler to boiling.
½ cup sugar **¼ tsp. salt** **2 tbsp. cornstarch** **3 tbsp. flour**	Combine in small bowl or pitcher.
another ½ cup milk	Stir in until smooth. Then stir paste into hot milk. Cook, stirring constantly until thickened. Cover and cook 5 minutes more, stirring occasionally.
3 egg yolks, slightly beaten	Stir small amount of hot mixture into yolks first, then stir into hot custard. Cook 2 minutes longer, stirring constantly. Remove from heat.
1 tbsp. butter or margarine **1 tsp. vanilla**	Stir in. (See variations following.) Pour into baked crust.

Top with meringue made with the whites of the eggs used in the custard. See page 440 for directions. Or cool and top with whipped cream before serving.

Almond Cream Pie: Toast ¾ cup blanched slivered almonds in 350-degree oven approximately 12 minutes until slightly browned. Stir ½ cup into the filling after removing it from heat. Also add ¼ tsp. almond flavoring to custard. Top chilled pie with whipped cream and sprinkle remaining almonds over the top.

Banana Cream Pie: Slice two bananas over the bottom of pie crust before pouring in custard. Also, add ½ tsp. banana flavoring to the custard. Either top pie with meringue, or use whipped cream instead, and garnish with banana slices on top. (Dip banana slices in a mixture of half lemon juice and half water, and drain on paper towel first to help prevent darkening.)

Butterscotch Cream Pie: Use ¾ cup dark brown sugar in place of white sugar in custard.

Chocolate Cream Pie: Add 3 tbsp. cocoa powder to the sugar-flour mixture before stirring it into the hot milk (or add a 1-oz. square unsweetened chocolate to cold milk in double boiler). Increase sugar to ¾ cup. Either top with meringue or whipped cream. If using whipped cream, sprinkle with chocolate curls.

Coconut Cream Pie: Add ⅔ cup angel flake coconut and ½ tsp. coconut flavoring to custard after you remove it from the heat. Sprinkle another ⅓ cup coconut over meringue before baking.

Peanut Butter Cream Pie: Mix together ¾ cup powdered sugar and ½ cup peanut butter until crumbly. Sprinkle ⅔ of crumbs in pie shell before pouring in custard. Sprinkle remaining ⅓ on top of meringue before baking. If you use whipped cream instead of meringue, sprinkle remaining crumbs on top of whipped cream.

Raisin Cream Pie: Use half brown sugar in place of all granulated sugar in custard. Then add ½ cup chopped raisins, ½ tsp. lemon flavoring, and ½ tsp. allspice to custard before filling pie. Top with meringue.

Quick Coconut Pie

(Makes its own crust!)

2 cups milk **4 eggs** **¼ cup soft margarine** **1 tsp. vanilla** **¼ tsp. salt** **¾ cup sugar** **½ cup flour** **1 tsp. baking powder**	Combine in blender container or mixing bowl. Blend or beat at high speed for 1 minute or until well mixed.
1 cup angel flake coconut	Add, and pour into a greased 9″ deep-dish pie plate.
⅛ tsp. nutmeg	Sprinkle over the top.

Bake at 325 degrees for about 55 minutes until knife inserted in the center comes out clean.

Coconut Chiffon Pie

9″ baked pie crust	Have ready.
½ cup sugar **¼ cup flour** **¼ tsp. salt** **1 env. unflavored gelatin (1 tbsp.)**	Mix in saucepan.
1¾ cups milk	Stir in. Heat to a good rolling boil, stirring constantly. Remove from heat and sit pan in cold water to cool thoroughly.
½ tsp. vanilla **¼ tsp. coconut flavoring** **¼ tsp. almond flavoring**	Stir in.
3 egg whites **¼ tsp. cream of tartar** **½ cup sugar**	Make meringue.
½ cup whipping cream	Whip.
¾ cup fresh grated coconut, or **frozen coconut—thawed**	Fold together with gelatin mixture, meringue, and whipped cream. Pour in crust.
¼ cup additional coconut	Sprinkle over top and chill.

Dorothy Shank Showalter

Super Fresh (or Frozen) Fruit Pie

(This is my favorite fruit pie. The filling is excellent for using as the fruit topping for the Cherry Delight on page 195 in place of regular pie filling. Use peaches, strawberries, raspberries, or blueberries.)

9″ graham cracker or regular baked crust	Have ready.
½ to 1 cup sugar—use lesser amount if using already sweetened frozen fruit **3 tbsp. Clearjel or cornstarch** **2 tbsp. light corn syrup (if using cornstarch)** **1 cup water**	Combine in saucepan. Cook until thick and clear, stirring constantly. Remove from heat.
3 tbsp. flavored gelatin—use flavor to match fruit you are using	Stir in until dissolved. Cool until just before it begins to congeal.
3 cups fresh fruit, or frozen fruit— half thawed	Stir in. Pour in baked pie crust. Chill until set.
whipped cream	Top with whipped cream to serve.

(If using strawberries, add several drops red color to sugar mixture.)

Fannie B. Heatwole, my mother
Harriet Steiner

Grape Pie

9″ unbaked pie crust	Have ready.
3 cups Concord grapes	Pop grapes out of skins by pressing with your fingers into saucepan. Reserve skins.
1 cup sugar	Add, and heat to boiling. Boil 2 minutes. Press through sieve to remove seeds. Place strained pulp back in saucepan.
1 tbsp. lemon juice	Add juice and reserved skins and heat to boiling again.
3 tbsp. Clearjel, or cornstarch **¼ cup water**	Dissolve, then stir in. Cook, stirring constantly until thickened. Remove from heat.
1 tbsp. butter	Add. Pour into crust.

Cover with top crust, lattice, or crumbs. (Recipe for crumbs on page 445.) Bake on lower rack in oven at 350 degrees for 45 to 50 minutes.

Grasshopper Pie

24 creme-filled Oreo chocolate cookies, crushed fine
¼ cup margarine, melted

Mix thoroughly. Press in 9″ pie plate. Reserve ½ cup crumbs for topping.

. . . .

1½ cups marshmallow creme
¼ cup milk
several drops peppermint extract
several drops green color

Blend together thoroughly.

. . . .

1½ cups whipping cream

Whip and fold into marshmallow mixture. Pour into crust. Sprinkle with reserved crumbs. Freeze until firm.

. . . .

Remove from freezer 15 minutes before serving to soften.

. . . .

Green Tomato Pie

(The greener the tomatoes, the better, Alice says!)

9″ unbaked pie crust

Have ready.

. . . .

4 cups green tomatoes (if large, squeeze out the seeds before slicing)

Peel and thinly slice.

. . . .

1 tbsp. lemon juice
1 tsp. grated lemon rind
½ cup raisins or green seedless grapes, sliced in half

Add.

. . . .

1¼ cups sugar
3 tbsp. flour
¼ tsp. salt
2 to 3 tsp. ground cinnamon

Combine, then add. Pour in pie crust. (May be topped with a top crust, a lattice top, or with crumbs—recipe for crumbs on page 445.)

. . . .

Bake at 400 degrees for 12 minutes. Then reduce heat to 375 degrees and bake 30 minutes more.

Alice Trissel

Ice Cream Pie

2 (1-oz.) squares unsweetened chocolate
2 tbsp. butter

Stir together over low heat just until melted.

⅔ cup powdered sugar
2 tbsp. hot water

Add, mixing thoroughly.

1½ cups angel flake coconut

Stir in until well coated. Spray a 9″ pie plate with vegetable spray and press mixture firmly onto bottom and sides of plate. Chill until firm.

1 qt. vanilla ice cream, softened

Spread into crust. Freeze until firm.

Drizzle with chocolate syrup, or sprinkle with chocolate curls to serve. Remove from freezer 10 to 15 minutes before serving to soften.

Krispy Ice Cream Pie

½ cup clear corn syrup
½ cup peanut butter

Mix together thoroughly.

3 cups Rice Krispies cereal

Stir in until well coated. Press evenly in a 9″ pie plate. Chill in freezer 5 to 10 minutes.

1 qt. vanilla ice cream, softened

Spread into crust. Freeze until firm.

Remove from freezer 15 minutes before serving to soften. Top with fresh or frozen fruit or pie filling. Or pour a little chocolate syrup over each piece and sprinkle with chopped peanuts.

Japanese Fruit Pie

9″ unbaked pie crust

Have ready.

2 eggs, beaten
⅓ cup margarine, melted
1 cup sugar
1 tsp. vanilla
1 tbsp. vinegar

Beat together until smooth.

½ cup chopped pecans
½ cup coconut
½ cup raisins

Stir in. Pour in crust and bake at 350 degrees for approximately 40 minutes.

Ina Heatwole
Carolyn Shank

Lemon Cream Pie

9″ baked pie crust	Have ready.
½ cup flour **1 cup sugar** **¼ tsp. salt**	Mix together in top of double boiler.
3 egg yolks, slightly beaten **2¼ cups milk**	Combine and stir in gradually until smooth. Cook, stirring constantly until very thick, approximately 7 minutes. Remove from heat.
2 tsp. grated rind and the juice of 1 large lemon **1 tbsp. butter**	Stir in. Pour into baked crust.
3 egg whites **¼ tsp. cream of tartar** **6 tbsp. sugar**	Make meringue. See page 440 for directions. Spread over pie and bake as directed.

(Do not add lemon juice and rind until mixture has thickened. This would cause the custard to curdle.)

Old-Fashioned Lemon Meringue Pie

9″ baked pie crust	Have ready.
1¼ cups sugar **6 tbsp. cornstarch** **¼ tsp. salt** **1½ cups water**	Combine in saucepan. Cook until thick and clear, stirring constantly.
3 egg yolks **⅓ cup lemon juice**	Beat together. Add small amount of hot mixture to yolks first. Then stir into custard and cook until mixture comes to a full boil again. Remove from heat.
2 tsp. grated lemon rind **1 tbsp. butter**	Stir in. Cover while making meringue.
3 egg whites **¼ tsp. cream of tartar** **6 tbsp. sugar**	Make meringue. See directions on page 440. Stir ¼ cup meringue into warm custard. Pour into crust. Pile remaining meringue on top.

Bake at 325 degrees approximately 15 minutes until lightly browned.

Oatmeal Pie

9″ unbaked pie crust	Have ready.

3 eggs, well beaten **½ cup sugar** **½ cup brown sugar** **2 tbsp. margarine, melted** **½ cup light corn syrup** **½ cup water** **1 tsp. vanilla** **½ tsp. salt** **⅔ cup angel flake coconut** **⅔ cup quick oatmeal** **½ cup pecans, coarsely chopped**	Mix together in order listed. Pour into crust.

Bake at 375 degrees for 10 minutes. Then reduce heat to 325 degrees and bake 35 minutes more.

Pauline Blosser

Fresh Peach Pie

9″ unbaked pie crust	Have ready.

3 cups fresh sliced peaches	Spread in crust.

1 egg, beaten **⅓ cup melted margarine** **1 cup sugar** **⅓ cup flour** **½ tsp. nutmeg**	Mix together thoroughly. Pour over peaches in crust. (May add crumbs on top if desired, or bake plain. See recipe for crumbs on page 445.) Bake at 350 degrees for approximately 45 minutes until lightly browned.

(May use canned peaches if desired, but decrease sugar to ½ cup.)

Pat Hertzler

Peach (or Strawberry) Torte Pie

3 egg whites **1 tsp. vanilla** **dash of salt**	Beat together until foamy.

¾ cup sugar	Gradually add, beating into very stiff peaks.

1 cup walnuts, chopped **½ cup saltine cracker crumbs** **1 tsp. baking powder**	Fold in. Spread in a well-greased 9″ pie plate, pushing meringue higher around the edge. Bake at 300 degrees for 40 minutes, or until dry on the outside. Cool completely.

2 to 3 cups sliced fresh peaches (or **strawberries)***	Arrange in crust.

Whipped cream   Garnish over top.
Additional fruit, if desired

(*Sprinkle with a small amount of sugar if desired. Crust is sweet enough that it doesn't require much. May also use frozen or canned fruit, well drained.)

Donna Lou Heatwole

Frozen Peanut Butter Pie

9″ graham cracker crust	Have ready.
4 oz. cream cheese, softened ¼ cup milk	Beat together until fluffy.
⅔ cup sugar ½ cup peanut butter	Add, beating until smooth.
3 cups Cool Whip	Fold in. Pour into crust.
¼ cup chopped salted peanuts	Sprinkle over top.

Freeze until firm. Remove from freezer 15 minutes before serving to soften.

Pecan Pie

9″ unbaked pie crust	Have ready.
3 eggs, beaten ¾ cup light corn syrup ¼ cup sugar ½ cup brown sugar 3 tbsp. margarine, melted 1 tsp. vanilla ¼ tsp. salt	Mix together thoroughly. Pour into crust.
¾ to 1 cup coarsely chopped pecans	Sprinkle over top.

Bake at 350 degrees for 40 to 45 minutes.

Cream Cheese Pecan Pie

9″ unbaked pie crust	Have ready.
8 oz. cream cheese, softened **1 egg, beaten** **½ cup sugar** **¼ tsp. salt** **1 tsp. vanilla**	Beat together until blended and spread in crust.
1¼ cups coarsely chopped pecans	Sprinkle evenly over cheese layer.
3 eggs, beaten **1 cup light corn syrup** **¼ cup sugar** **1 tsp. vanilla**	Beat together until smooth. Pour over pecan layer. Place on lower rack in oven and bake at 375 degrees for 40 to 45 minutes until center is firm.

Cool and serve with whipped cream.

Alice Trissel

Pecan Tarts

Pastry:

1 cup margarine **6 oz. cream cheese, softened**	Cream together.
2¼ cups flour **¼ tsp. salt**	Mix in until crumbly. Shape into two 2-inch rolls. Wrap in plastic wrap and chill in refrigerator several hours or overnight. Then slice into 36 portions and fit into 2″ tart or muffin tins.

Filling:

2 eggs, slightly beaten **1 cup brown sugar** **½ cup light corn syrup** **2 tbsp. margarine, melted** **¼ tsp. salt** **½ tsp. vanilla**	Mix together well. Pour in tart shells.
1½ cups coarsely chopped pecans	Sprinkle over top of tarts.

Bake at 350 degrees for approximately 20 minutes.

Yield: 36 tarts

Ruby Petersheim

Pumpkin Chiffon Pie

9″ baked pie crust	Have ready.
1 env. unflavored gelatin (1 tbsp.) **½ cup milk** **1¼ cups canned pumpkin** **3 egg yolks** **¾ cup brown sugar** **½ tsp. salt** **½ tsp. ground cinnamon** **¼ tsp. ground nutmeg** **¼ tsp. ground ginger**	Combine in saucepan. Cook, stirring constantly, until mixture comes to a good boil. Remove from heat and place pan in cold water to cool. Cool thoroughly.
3 egg whites	Beat into soft peaks.
⅓ cup sugar	Gradually add, beating into stiff peaks. Fold into pumpkin mixture. Pour into crust. Chill until set.

Serve with whipped cream.

Old-Fashioned Pumpkin Pie

9″ unbaked pie crust	Have ready.
1 cup canned pumpkin **1 egg yolk** **⅔ cup sugar** **⅛ tsp. salt** **½ tsp. ground cinnamon** **¼ tsp. ground cloves** **1 tbsp. cornstarch** **1 tsp. vanilla** **1½ cups milk**	Mix together thoroughly.
1 egg white, stiffly beaten	Fold in. Pour in crust.
nutmeg	Sprinkle over top.

Bake at 350 degrees for 45 minutes until center is set.

Mary Shank, my mother-in-law

Frozen Pumpkin Pie or Pumpkin Squares

(Filling may be spread in two 9" crumb crusts or in a 9 × 13 bake dish. Delicious with cornflake, gingersnap, or graham cracker crumb crusts.)

½ cup brown sugar ¼ tsp. salt 1 tsp. ground cinnamon ¼ tsp. ground ginger ¼ tsp. ground cloves 1½ cups canned pumpkin, chilled ½ gal. vanilla ice cream, softened	Combine in chilled bowl. Beat together with heavy-duty electric mixer or heavy spoon until well blended. (Work fast; if ice cream melts too much it gets icy when refrozen.) Pour into prepared crusts.
½ cup chopped walnuts or pecans	Sprinkle over top. Freeze until firm.

Remove from freezer 20 minutes before serving to soften.

Pumpkin Pie Special

9" unbaked pie crust	Have ready.
¼ cup margarine 1 cup sugar	Cream together thoroughly.
2 eggs, beaten	Add, beating well.
1 cup canned pumpkin 1 cup flaked coconut ½ tsp. ground cinnamon ½ tsp. ground nutmeg ¼ tsp. salt	Add, blending well. Pour into crust.

Bake at 425 degrees for 10 minutes. Then reduce to 350 degrees for 35 minutes more.

Marie Shank

Raspberry Chiffon Pie

(Cook 3 cups raspberries in ⅔ cup water for 3 to 5 minutes or until soft. Press through sieve or strainer to remove seeds and to obtain raspberry pulp.)

9" graham cracker crust	Have ready.
1 env. unflavored gelatin (1 tbsp.) ¼ cup cold water	Soak until softened.
1 cup raspberry pulp 3 egg yolks, slightly beaten ⅔ cup sugar	Heat in saucepan to a full rolling boil, stirring constantly. Remove from heat. Stir in gelatin until dissolved. Place pan in cold water to cool completely.

| 3 egg whites
¼ tsp. cream of tartar
⅓ cup sugar | Beat egg whites as for meringue. See method on page 440. |
| ½ cup whipping cream | Whip. Fold all 3 mixtures together. |

Pour in crust. Chill at least 2 hours. Garnish with whole raspberries to serve.

Raspberry Dream Pie (Frozen)

9″ graham cracker pie shell	Have ready.
2 egg whites ⅛ tsp. salt	Beat into soft peaks
¾ cup sugar	Gradually add, beating into stiff peaks.
1½ cups frozen raspberries, half thawed and drained 2 tsp. lemon juice	Add, and continue beating at highest speed until mixture is thick and light colored—at least 6 to 8 minutes.
½ cup whipping cream ½ tsp. vanilla	Whip, and fold into mixture. Pour into crust and freeze at least several hours.

Remove from freezer 15 minutes before serving to soften. **Variation:** Use strawberries instead of raspberries.

Strawberry Dream Pie (Lower Cal.)

9″ graham cracker crust	Have ready.
1 cup lowfat cottage cheese 1 tbsp. lemon juice	Process in blender until smooth.
¼ cup sugar ½ tsp. vanilla dash of nutmeg	Beat in until smooth.
¾ cup crushed strawberries	Stir in.
2 cups Cool Whip ¼ cup powdered sugar	Combine and fold in.
¼ cup sliced strawberries	Fold in. Pour into crust. Chill several hours or overnight.

Garnish with additional berries to serve.

Dorothy Suter Showalter

Rhubarb Pie

9" unbaked pie crust	Have ready.
5 cups rhubarb, cut in ½-inch pieces **1 (3-oz.) pkg. strawberry-flavored** **gelatin** **1 egg, slightly beaten** **1⅓ cups sugar** **2½ tbsp. minute tapioca**	Combine thoroughly. Pour in crust. Cover with top crust, lattice top, or crumbs (see recipe for crumbs on page 445). Bake at 400 degrees for 10 minutes. Then reduce to 350 degrees and bake for 30 to 40 minutes more.

Shoofly Pie

9" unbaked pie crust	Have ready.
1 cup flour **⅔ cup brown sugar** **2 tbsp. margarine**	Mix together until crumbly. Reserve ½ cup crumbs.
½ cup dark corn syrup **½ cup sorghum molasses** **1 egg** **¼ tsp. salt** **¾ cup hot water**	Blend into remaining crumbs until well mixed.
1 tsp. baking soda **another ¼ cup hot water**	Add. Pour into crust. Top with reserved crumbs.

Bake at 400 degrees for 10 minutes. Then reduce to 325 degrees and bake 30 minutes more until center doesn't shake. **Variation:** Add 1 cup angel flake coconut to crumb mixture.

Rhoda Longenecker

Squash Pie

9" unbaked pie crust	Have ready.
2 eggs, beaten **1 cup evaporated milk** **1 cup sugar** **1½ cups cooked squash** **½ tsp. salt** **1 tsp. ground cinnamon** **½ tsp. ground nutmeg** **1 tsp. vanilla**	Blend together thoroughly. Pour in crust. Bake at 400 degrees for 10 minutes. Then reduce to 350 degrees and bake 40 minutes more.

Bertha H. Shank

Optional Praline Topping for Squash or Pumpkin Pies:
Before serving, combine 2 tbsp. melted butter, ½ cup dark brown sugar, and ⅓ cup chopped pecans. Sprinkle over pie and place under broiler in oven for about 1 minute. Watch carefully; do not burn.

CHAPTER TEN.

SALADS, SANDWICHES, & SOUPS

SALADS, SANDWICHES, AND SOUPS

Salads: When we mention salad, our thoughts usually visualize the tossed variety of lettuce or other greens with miscellaneous chopped raw vegetables added. However, salads can vary from a hearty main course dish with meat included to a fancy fruit salad, sometimes frozen and served as a dessert. Therefore, salads are served at almost any point in the meal from first to last course.

Salads are an especially great complement to a soup-and-sandwich lunch, or to a casserole meal. They can often round out a full-course dinner with whatever may be lacking nutritionally in the remainder of the menu. You may choose a raw vegetable salad, or a fruit salad may be just what is needed.

Many people love to make a meal out of a salad, especially in hot weather when no one feels like cooking. Salads can be as varied as your appetite, and are great for the calorie-conscious, unless loaded down with calorie-laden dressings.

Be creative with salads. This is a good place to use leftover pieces of meat, or miscellaneous raw vegetables collecting in the refrigerator. Also, those peaches or other fruit that no one is eating can be dressed up in a delicious gelatin mold that will not be detected as leftover! Add some sliced bananas, a few miniature marshmallows, and several drops of peppermint flavor, or some crushed pineapple.

About Gelatin

Gelatin will not dissolve in cold water. Water needs to be heated to at least 120 degrees to melt it. Plain gelatin powder *must* first be allowed to soften in cold water before adding it to hot water. If put directly into hot water, the powder will clump together and will not dissolve properly. (It may also be softened in cold milk. However, it takes at least twice as long to soften in milk.) If gelatin powder is first mixed with sugar, which separates the granules, it can be added directly to hot water. Add ¼ cup sugar to 1 tbsp. plain gelatin powder. The flavored gelatins you can buy (such as Jell-O) are simply mixtures of mostly sugar, plain gelatin, and flavoring. Therefore, they can be added directly to hot water without first soaking in cold water.

Plain gelatin is usually softened in about ¼ cup cold water for each 1 tbsp. gelatin. The water can then be heated to at least 120 degrees, or hotter water can be added to it. Temperature of total mixture must reach at least this point, however. Be sure to dissolve gelatin *thoroughly* before chilling. Stir until liquid is clear.

One tablespoon (or 1 envelope) of plain gelatin will jell 2 cups of liquid or 1 ½ cups of solids—vegetables and fruits added.

Several factors may affect the strength of a jell. An extra amount of sugar, or any acid such as lemon juice or vinegar added to gelatin, tends to weaken the jell. You may need to increase the amount of gelatin used when adding these ingredients. Stirring after gelatin begins to set also weakens the jell. Gelatin cooled slowly forms a slightly stiffer jell than when ice cubes are added. Gelatin chills more quickly in the refrigerator in a metal container than in a glass or ceramic one.

There are several fresh fruits containing proteinase enzymes which will not jell and cannot be used in gelatin molds. These include raw pineapple, kiwi, fresh figs, and papaya. Cooked or canned pineapple will jell, however. When using fresh or frozen pineapple or pineapple juice, boil 2 minutes before adding to the dissolved gelatin.

Gelatin that melts at a warm temperature can be placed in refrigerator and will usually rejell satisfactorily. Also, if you intended to chill gelatin to the "just-beginning-to-jell" stage and it accidentally became too firm, place the bowl of gelatin in a few inches of warm water to melt it slightly. Beat with wire whip or egg beater until smooth and of desired consistency. Beater may also be dipped in hot water.

To unmold gelatin easily, set mold in container of warm water for about 5 seconds (not so hot that it melts too much). Tilt or shake to loosen and invert plate over mold. Holding firmly, turn both over. Shake gently to release gelatin. If it doesn't slide out, lift one edge of mold and carefully slip a narrow knife along the side to let a little air into the top. It should come right out.

Soup: Another great way to use up leftover vegetables is to make soup, especially on a cold evening when you need something hot to warm you up.

Many kinds of soup are best made with good rich broth, with or without meat added. The leftover fragments and broth from a roast make excellent soup. (If you do not have rich broth, bouillon cubes will help to add flavor.) The meat can be roast beef, browned hamburger, roast pork, or chicken.

Creamed soups are also quite popular and can be complemented with a sandwich to balance out the menu.

Sandwiches: Sandwiches range from the hoagie type, which practically make a meal in themselves, to dainty party fare served as a refreshment.

IDEAS FOR SANDWICHES

(See ideas for fancy sandwiches in the party section. The addition of MSG is optional in all fillings.)

•Ham Salad Filling: Combine 1 cup ground or finely chopped cooked ham with ½ tsp. prepared mustard, 1 tbsp. well-drained chopped pickle relish, ¼ cup mayonnaise, and ⅛ tsp. MSG.

•Deviled Ham Filling: Combine 2 (4½-oz.) cans deviled ham with ¼ cup chopped pimiento-stuffed olives, ¼ cup mayonnaise, and ⅛ tsp. MSG.

•Egg Salad Filling: Combine 4 finely chopped hard-cooked eggs with 1 tsp. prepared mustard, 2 tbsp. chopped ripe olives or grated cheese, ¼ tsp. salt, 3 tbsp. mayonnaise, and 1 tsp. sugar.

•Chicken, Salmon, or Tuna Salad Filling: Combine 1 cup finely chopped meat (chicken, salmon, or tuna), ¼ cup finely chopped celery, 3 tbsp. mayonnaise, 1 tsp. lemon juice, ¼ tsp. salt, and ⅛ tsp. MSG. (Chicken may be run through the food grinder.)

•Olive-Cream Cheese Sandwiches: Spread English muffin halves with cream cheese and arrange a solid layer of sliced olives in cream cheese.

•Apple-Cream Cheese Sandwiches: Slice an apple, toss slices in a mixture of ½ tbsp. lemon juice and ½ tbsp. water to prevent darkening, if desired. Drain. Mix 4 oz. cream cheese with 1 ½ tbsp. honey. Spread on 4 slices plain or toasted pumpernickel or raisin bread. Place apple slices on cheese. Add second slice of bread to each sandwich.

•Peanut Butter Combinations for Sandwiches:
—Spread bread with peanut butter, dip banana slices in mixture of half lemon juice and half water to retard darkening (not necessary if eating immediately), and arrange a solid layer of banana slices in peanut butter.
—Spread bread with peanut butter and arrange slices of sweet pickle in peanut butter.
—Spread bread with peanut butter, drizzle with honey, and sprinkle with raisins or sunflower seeds.
—Spread bread with peanut butter and add grated carrots and raisins or shredded cabbage.
—A mixture of peanut butter and mayonnaise is also good. Some crumbled bacon may be added.
—Use your imagination. Other combinations are also delicious, including fruits and jellies.

•Date Filling: Combine ½ cup grated cheddar cheese, 1 tbsp. honey, and ½ cup chopped dates. Mix with milk, cream, or mayonnaise.

•Beef Tongue Sandwiches: Cook and cool tongue. Run through food grinder. Add 2 medium-sized finely chopped sweet pickles and 1 large sweet apple. Add salt to taste and ¼ tsp. MSG.

•Do not freeze sandwiches spread with mayonnaise. It will make the bread soggy when thawed. Use butter, margarine, or mustard when freezing.

•Use a thin cheese spread on bread instead of butter for a delicious change.

•It is easier to spread frozen bread for sandwiches.

•For sandwiches in a lunch box, wrap lettuce and tomato in separate package to be added at mealtime—to prevent the sandwich from becoming soggy.

•Celery leaves make a delicious addition to tomato sandwiches.

•Slice meat thinly for sandwiches. Several thin slices are better than one thick slice.

•Place condiments or pickle between meat instead of next to bread to avoid sogginess.

•For a bacon-lettuce-and-tomato sandwich, try using imitation bacon bits instead of bacon.

•**Flavored Butter.** To perk up a sandwich, add seasonings to the butter to suit your taste. Try one or more of horseradish, mustard, curry powder, onion or garlic powder, celery salt, chives, or parsley.

•**Honey Butter:** Beat together 1 cup butter, ½ cup honey, and 2 tbsp. cream until well blended. Refrigerate until used.

•A variety of flavors may be added to most any kind of cooked ground meat sandwiches such as: diced onions, dash of garlic, alfalfa sprouts, pickles, grated carrots, finely diced celery, lettuce and chopped cabbage, as well as spices, seasonings, or herbs, parsley, dill, chives, Worcestershire sauce, and sage.

TIPS FOR SALADS AND SOUPS

•Use a minimum amount of dressing for a tossed salad to avoid undue wilting. Do not add dressing until just before serving. (Greens may be cut ahead and placed in airtight container in refrigerator.)

•If salad contains mushrooms, add a little lemon juice to salad dressing to help keep them white.

•If oil is added to lettuce before adding the vinegar dressing for lettuce salad, it will not wilt nearly as quickly. Use 1 tbsp. oil for 1 medium-size head of lettuce and toss lightly, but thoroughly. Lettuce should be as dry as possible so oil will stick.

•For improved flavor in vegetable or tossed salads, marinate any of the hard ingredients (such as carrots, broccoli flowerets, celery, and radishes) in the salad dressing at least one-half hour ahead of serving time. Add ingredients that will deteriorate quickly right before serving.

•For crisper salads, dry greens completely until absolutely water-free and chill thoroughly. To help dry large batches quickly, place in absorbent cloth bag and spin in washing machine for a short time.

•It is easiest to wash homegrown lettuce and other greens by quickly holding each leaf under a slowly running water faucet. This rinses away all the dirt and bugs or other creepy little critters that have a way of clinging onto leaves when doused up and down in water quantity fashion. It may take slightly more water, but this is better than having a little worm come wiggling out of the salad on someone's plate!

•To peel tomatoes easily, dip tomato in boiling water for ½ to 1 minute, then rinse in cold water. Skins should slip off easily. (Tomatoes should be vine-ripened.)

•If you mind the acid in raw tomatoes, sprinkle a small amount of sugar over each slice before eating it. This counteracts the acid and helps to prevent acid sores in the mouth.

•Do not sit tomatoes in the sun to finish ripening. This softens the tomatoes rather than ripening them. If you need a green tomato to ripen in a hurry, place it in a brown paper bag. The tomato gives off a natural gas that speeds up the ripening process.

•To prolong the life of cucumbers, peppers, zucchini, and other fresh vegetables in refrigerator, wrap in paper towel to absorb moisture and place in a plastic bag with a few holes punched in it for air.

•When cutting broccoli flowerets, cut only through stems, and pull bud section apart. This prevents cutting buds into fine pieces.

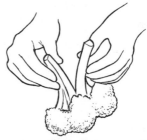

•To minimize splitting of carrots when cutting carrot sticks, begin cutting at small end of carrot. For delicious sweet flavor, soak carrot sticks in water with a little artificial sweetener added for 1 hour (2-grain saccharin to 2 cups of water).

•To quickly shred cabbage or carrots for cole slaw or salad, half fill blender container with ice water. Add chunks of the vegetable to fill container, and process on and off several times until shredded. Drain in strainer. Catch water to use over if second turn is needed, since you can't do a large amount at one time.

•Use a potato peeler to peel a long continuous strip from a nice red ripe tomato. Wind strip round and round into a tomato rose to garnish salads.

•To make fringed cucumber slices, trim ends of cucumber, but do not peel. Pull sharp fork prongs firmly down length of cucumber on each side all around making indentations the entire length of cucumber. Then slice thinly and chill.

•Cucumbers need plenty of moisture during the growing season to develop properly. They become bitter if weather is dry and hot. This bitterness begins at the stem end of the cucumber. If problem isn't too severe, you can usually eliminate it by simply cutting off an extra half inch or so at the stem end. Then rub the two cut areas together in a circular motion drawing out a foamy liquid. Rinse off foam and sample the next slice to see if bitterness has been removed. Discard small cut end. If problem is severe, it probably cannot be removed.

•If you like **bread croutons** on your salads, you can make your own. Butter slices of bread, stack and slice through the whole stack with electric knife, making strips. Cut strips into cubes. Sprinkle with garlic salt and Parmesan cheese. Place in 300-degree oven until dry and barely beginning to toast. Do not brown.

•Vinegar becomes much darker and stronger with age. The amount used should be reduced when it has aged. When using less, just add water to dilute vinegar so you will have the same amount of liquid called for in recipe. (I buy vinegar ahead so it will have time to increase in strength and will go much further.)

•Salad dressing usually contains more vinegar than mayonnaise. This is helpful to know when adding vinegar to dressings.

•When making a molded salad, spray mold with vegetable spray or rinse with cold water before adding salad for easier removal of salad when molded. Also rinse salad plate with cold water before turning out salad. If salad is off-centered on plate, you will then be able to shake it over to center.

•For individual gelatin salads or frozen desserts or salads, use paper baking cups set in muffin tins for molding. When molded, paper can be torn off, leaving an attractive mold.

•To prevent spattering when grinding cranberries for salad, half freeze cranberries before grinding.

•To remove jellied cranberry sauce easily from tin cans, remove one end of can, then turn can over dish and open other end. Use loosened lid to push sauce out of opposite end of can.

•Instant potato flakes make an excellent thickening for stews and soups.

•Use bouillon cubes for extra flavor when adding liquid to homemade or canned soups.

•When adding whole spices such as bay leaf or garlic buds to soup, put in an aluminum tea-ball caddy and place in soup. Remove when finished cooking and you will not have pieces of unwanted spice throughout the soup.

•In making **tomato soup,** the acid in tomatoes can cause the milk to curdle when poured into the tomato base. To prevent this, add a little baking soda to the tomatoes before adding milk. If you prefer not to use soda, it helps to add the tomatoes to the milk rather than the milk to the tomatoes, to have both milk and tomatoes hot when they are combined, and to thicken either the tomatoes or milk before they are combined.

•For a special touch, there are numerous ways to garnish soup before serving. Choose a garnish that best suits the soup: snipped parsley or chives, croutons, shredded cheese, toasted slivered almonds, crumbled bacon or chipped ham, crushed corn chips, or a dab of sour cream.

SALADS, SANDWICHES, AND SOUPS RECIPES

FRUIT SALADS

Ambrosia Salad

1 (11-oz.) can mandarin oranges, drained **1 cup pineapple chunks, drained** **1 cup flaked coconut** **1½ cups miniature marshmallows** **1 cup dairy sour cream*** **1 cup sliced white grapes (optional)**	Mix all ingredients together and chill several hours or overnight.

....

1 sliced banana (optional)	Add just before serving.

....

(*Or whip 1 env. Dream Whip and add ¼ tsp. lemon flavoring.)

Yield: 6 to 8 servings

....

Angel Salad

1 tbsp. butter or margarine	Melt over bottom of saucepan.

....

½ cup pineapple juice **2 tbsp. vinegar** **2 tbsp. sugar** **⅛ tsp. salt** **1 tbsp. cornstarch** **2 egg yolks, or 1 whole egg**	Add. Heat, stirring constantly until thickened. Remove from heat and cool thoroughly. Chill.

....

1 cup whipping cream	Whip cream and blend in.

....

1 lb. white grapes, sliced **4 cups miniature marshmallows** **1 cup crushed pineapple, drained**	Mix in.

....

Yield: 12 servings   *Fannie B. Heatwole, my mother*

....

Apple Salad

2 or 3 unpeeled Red Delicious apples, diced ¼ cup finely chopped celery ¼ cup raisins 1 diced banana ¼ cup chopped dried papaya (optional) ¼ cup flaked coconut ¼ cup peanuts or walnuts	Mix together in bowl.

Dressing:

⅓ cup sugar 1½ tbsp. cornstarch ⅛ tsp. salt ½ cup water* ¼ tsp. lemon flavoring*	Combine in saucepan. Cook until thickened, stirring constantly. Cool thoroughly and pour over fruit.

(*May use ½ cup pineapple juice instead of water, and omit lemon flavoring.)

Optional Dressing:

⅓ cup Cool Whip 1 tbsp. mayonnaise 2 tbsp. peanut butter 1 tbsp. sugar	Mix until smooth. Pour over fruit.

Yield: 4 to 5 servings

Apple Gelatin Salad

2 large Red Delicious apples, diced, unpeeled ⅓ cup sugar	Mix and let sit 5 minutes.
¼ cup raisins ½ to 1 stem celery, diced 1 banana, diced	Add.
1 pineapple-(or lemon) flavored gelatin	Mix according to pkg. directions. Cool until just beginning to jell. Pour over mixture. Chill until firm.
½ cup chopped English walnuts	Sprinkle over top.

Yield: 6 servings

Old-Fashioned Apple Salad

3 unpeeled Red Delicious apples,
   diced
1 banana, diced
¼ cup raisins
¼ cup peanuts

Mix together.

. . . .

Dressing:
3 tbsp. peanut butter
¼ cup sugar
1 or 2 tbsp. mayonnaise
2 tbsp. cream, or frozen orange
   juice, to mix

Mix together until smooth. Stir into fruit mixture. Serve immediately.

. . . .

Optional Dressing:
Take double the amount of the recipe of fruit for this dressing.

. . . .

½ cup sugar
2 tbsp. flour
⅛ tsp. salt

Mix in saucepan.

. . . .

1 egg, slightly beaten
¾ cup water

Add, and cook, stirring constantly until thickened. Cool thoroughly.

. . . .

2 tsp. vinegar
¼ tsp. prepared mustard (optional)

Add.

. . . .

2 cups Cool Whip

Fold in.

. . . .

Apple Dapple Salad (Lower Cal.)

4 unpeeled Red Delicious apples,
   diced
2 cups finely shredded cabbage
½ cup chopped celery
½ cup raisins
½ cup sunflower seeds

Mix in bowl.

. . . .

Yogurt Dressing:
½ cup plain yogurt
¼ to ½ cup peanut butter*
1 or 2 tbsp. sugar

Blend together until smooth. Mix into fruit.

. . . .

*Variation: Omit peanut butter for plain yogurt dressing. Plain yogurt dressing is delicious on other fruits such as blueberries or strawberries.

. . . .

Apricot Salad

1 (3-oz.) pkg. apricot-flavored gelatin 1 (3-oz.) pkg. orange-flavored gelatin 2 cups boiling water	Combine, stirring until dissolved.
1½ cups miniature marshmallows	Stir in until mostly dissolved.
1 (16-oz.) can apricots, chopped 1 (16-oz.) can crushed pineapple	Drain fruits. Reserve 1 cup juice for topping. Add water and ice to remaining juice to make 2 cups. Stir into gelatin. Chill until just beginning to jell. Stir in fruits. Pour into a 9 × 13 dish and chill until firm.
Topping: ½ cup sugar 1½ tbsp. cornstarch (1 cup reserved juice) 1 egg, slightly beaten	Combine in saucepan. Cook just until thickened, stirring constantly. Remove from heat. Cool and chill.
2 cups Cool Whip	Fold in. Spread over gelatin mixture in dish.
coconut or nuts to garnish	Sprinkle over top.

Yield: 12 to 15 servings

Avocado Salad Mold

1 tbsp. unflavored gelatin ¼ cup cold water	Soak until softened.
1 cup crushed pineapple	Drain, reserving ½ cup juice. Heat reserved juice and stir in softened gelatin until dissolved.
1 tbsp. lemon juice	Add. Cool mixture.
3 oz. cream cheese, softened 2 tbsp. milk dash of salt	Beat together until smooth, and blend in.
½ cup mayonnaise	Stir in.
1 med. avocado, peeled and cubed	Add avocado and pineapple.
½ cup whipping cream	Whip, and fold into mixture. Pour into mold and chill until firm.

Yield: 6 servings

Alice Trissel

Blueberry Salad

1 (6-oz.) pkg. black-cherry flavored gelatin (or grape flavored) **2 cups boiling water**	Stir together until dissolved.
1½ cups cold water and ice	Add, stirring to cool.
1 cup crushed pineapple, undrained **2 cups blueberries, drained, or pie filling**	Add. Pour in 9 × 13 dish. Chill until set.
Topping: **8 oz. cream cheese, softened** **1 cup sour cream, or Cool Whip** **½ cup sugar** **1 tsp. vanilla**	Beat together until smooth. Spread over salad.
½ cup chopped pecans	Sprinkle over top.

Yield: 8 to 10 servings

Jeanette Shank Key
Annie Weaver

Molded Blueberry Salad

2 cups blueberries, canned or frozen—thawed	Drain and reserve juice.
1 (3-oz.) pkg. raspberry flavored gelatin	Dissolve according to pkg. directions using reserved juice and water to make 1 cup. Pour half of mixture into a 6-cup mold. Chill until firm.
1 cup whipping cream	Whip until stiff.
¼ cup sugar (or to taste)	Add, and fold together with remaining gelatin and blueberries. Pour over chilled mixture in mold. Chill until firm. Unmold to serve.

Yield: 6 to 8 servings

Donna Lou Heatwole

Bing Cherry Salad

2 cups Bing cherries	Drain, reserving ¼ cup juice.
8 oz. cream cheese, softened	Add to reserved juice and beat until smooth.
1 (16-oz.) can pineapple chunks, drained **1 cup miniature marshmallows**	Add, along with cherries to cheese mixture.
1 cup Cool Whip **¼ cup sugar**	Fold in. Chill several hours before serving.

Yield: 8 to 10 servings

Cherry Salad

1 (20-oz.) can crushed pineapple, drained (reserve juice)	Add water to reserved juice to make 2 cups. Heat to boiling.
1 (6-oz.) pkg. cherry-flavored gelatin	Add to hot liquid, stirring to dissolve. Add 6 large ice cubes to cool. Chill until just beginning to congeal.
1 (21-oz.) can cherry pie filling **2 bananas, sliced** **1 cup Cool Whip**	Fold in, along with pineapple until blended. Pour in large glass dish.
1½ additional cups Cool Whip	Spread over mixture.
½ cup chopped nuts	Sprinkle over top.

Yield: 12 servings   *Barbara Bowman*

Cinnamon Apple Salad

1 (3-oz.) pkg. cherry or strawberry-flavored gelatin **1 cup boiling water** **¼ cup red hot cinnamon candies**	Stir together until dissolved.
1 cup cold water and ice	Add, stirring to cool. Chill until just beginning to congeal.
1½ cups peeled apples, cubed **½ cup finely chopped celery** **½ cup chopped nuts**	Fold in. Chill until set.
a few additional nuts to garnish	Sprinkle over top.

Yield: 6 to 8 servings

Cottage Cheese Salad

1 (16-oz.) container cottage cheese **1 (3-oz.) pkg. orange-flavored gelatin**	Mix together (dry gelatin and cheese).
1 (16-oz.) can mandarin oranges, drained **1 (9-oz.) container Cool Whip**	Fold in. Chill.

Variations: Use banana-pineapple gelatin and crushed pineapple, or strawberry gelatin and strawberries, instead of orange gelatin and mandarin oranges. Or for **Pistachio Salad,** use 1 pkg. instant pistachio pudding instead of gelatin, and pineapple instead of oranges.

Yield: 8 servings   *Frances Justice*

Fluffy Salad

1 env. Dream Whip	Whip according to pkg. directions.
8 oz. cream cheese, softened	Cut in chunks and add to Dream Whip, beating until blended.
1 (20-oz.) can crushed pineapple, drained **1 cup angel flake coconut** **3 cups colored miniature marshmallows**	Stir in. Chill several hours or overnight.

Yield: 6 to 8 servings

Cranberry Fluff

2 cups raw cranberries, ground in food grinder* **¾ cup sugar**	Combine. Cover and chill 2 or 3 hours.
2 cups diced apples **½ cup seedless white grapes, chopped** **3 cups miniature marshmallows** **½ cup chopped walnuts** **¼ tsp. salt**	Add.
1 cup whipping cream	Whip, and fold in.

(*Half freeze berries before grinding to avoid spattering.)
Variation: Omit apples and grapes, and add 1 (8-oz.) can crushed pineapple, drained.

Yield: 12 servings   *Lillian Shickel*

Cranberry Salad

½ lb. raw cranberries* 3 apples, peeled and quartered	Run through food grinder.
½ to 1 stem celery, finely chopped 1 cup crushed pineapple, undrained 1½ cups sugar	Add.
1 (3-oz.) pkg. strawberry-flavored gelatin 1 cup boiling water	Stir together until dissolved. Add 4 large ice cubes to cool. When cool, pour over fruit. Chill until set.
½ cup chopped walnuts	Sprinkle over top.

(*Half freeze berries before grinding to avoid spattering.)

Yield: 6 servings

Cranberry Sauce

½ lb. cranberries, half frozen	Grind in food grinder.
1 cup crushed pineapple	Drain, and heat liquid to dissolve gelatin.
1 (3-oz.) pkg. raspberry-flavored gelatin	Stir into hot liquid until dissolved.
⅓ cup frozen orange juice concentrate, or add 2 or 3 tbsp. Tang and ⅓ cup water 1 cup sugar	Blend in. Then cool thoroughly.
2 cups applesauce	Add, with cranberries and pineapple. Pour into large glass dish and chill until set.
½ cup chopped walnuts	Sprinkle over top.

Yield: 10 servings

Dessert Salad

2 oranges, sectioned and cut in chunks 1 cup pineapple chunks, drained 1 cup white seedless grapes, cut in halves 1 cup chopped dates 2 bananas, diced	Combine in bowl.
1 cup Cool Whip or whipped cream ½ cup salad dressing 3 tbsp. sugar	Mix, then fold into fruit. Chill and serve on lettuce.

¾ cup chopped pecans | Sprinkle over top.

maraschino cherry halves | Top each serving.

Yield: 8 servings

Frozen Fruit Salad

1 pt. frozen strawberries, half
   thawed | Drain 2 tbsp. liquid from strawberries.

8 oz. cream cheese, softened
⅔ cup sugar | Add to liquid and beat until smooth.

2 large bananas, diced
1 (20-oz.) can crushed pineapple,
   drained | Add, along with strawberries.

1 pkg. Dream Whip | Whip according to pkg. directions and fold in.

Pour into an 8-inch-square dish, or into 9 cupcake papers for individual salads. Cover with plastic wrap and freeze. May be kept for several weeks in freezer. Remove 30 minutes before serving to thaw partially. Cut into squares if frozen in dish.

Yield: 9 servings

Luscious Fruit Salad

2 cups miniature marshmallows
1 cup crushed pineapple, drained
   (reserve juice)
1 cup mandarin oranges, drained
1 cup peaches, diced
1 cup white grapes, sliced
2 bananas, sliced—sprinkle with
   small amount of sugar to retard
   darkening | Combine.

Dressing:
½ cup sugar
2 tbsp. cornstarch
reserved pineapple juice plus
   enough water to make 1 cup | Combine in saucepan. Cook just until thickened, stirring constantly. Remove from heat.

½ tsp. vanilla | Add. Cool and chill thoroughly. Pour over fruit.

Yield: 10 servings

Fruit Delight (Low Cal.)

3 cups unpeeled Red Delicious apples	Dice.
2 tbsp. lemon juice	Sprinkle over apples to retard darkening.
2 cups sliced fresh strawberries **1 (16-oz.) can pineapple chunks, partially drained** **1 (11-oz.) can mandarin oranges, drained and sliced** **artificial sweetener to taste**	Add, tossing lightly. Add desired amount of juice drained from pineapple.

Yield: 8 servings

Ginger Ale Salad

3 env. unflavored gelatin (3 tbsp.) **¼ cup cold water**	Soak until softened.
2 cups boiling water	Add, stirring until dissolved.
¾ cup sugar **juice of 2 lemons** **few drops green food color**	Add. Cool until tepid.
2 cups ice cold ginger ale	Add. Chill until mixture just begins to congeal.
1 (16 or 20-oz.) can pineapple tidbits, drained (reserve juice) **1 (16-oz.) can seedless white grapes, drained**	Mix in. Pour into ring mold. Chill until set. Unmold to serve.
Ginger Ale Salad Dressing: **2 eggs** **½ cup sugar** **2 tbsp. flour**	Beat together in saucepan.
¾ cup (reserved pineapple juice)	Mix in well. Cook until thickened, stirring constantly. Remove from heat.
1½ tbsp. butter	Stir in until melted. Chill thoroughly.
1 cup whipping cream	Whip, and fold into mixture. Serve in center of ring mold.

Yield: 10 to 12 servings   *Mary Ethel Lahman Heatwole*

Honeydew Salad

3 to 4 cups honeydew melon balls	Chill thoroughly, and spoon into dessert goblets.
1 cup commercial sour cream **2 tbsp. apricot preserves** **¼ cup flaked coconut** **¼ cup chopped pecans or walnuts**	Blend together thoroughly and spoon over melon.

Yield: 4 servings

Jell-O Sauce

1 env. unflavored gelatin **¼ cup cold water**	Soak until softened.
1 (3-oz.) pkg. strawberry Jell-O **1 cup boiling water**	Add to softened gelatin and stir until dissolved.
few drops red color **3 or 4 large ice cubes**	Add, stirring to cool.
1 qt. applesauce **3 drops oil of cinnamon, or ¼ cup** **red cinnamon candies***	Stir in. Chill until set.

(*If using candies, dissolve in boiling water with gelatin.) May garnish with sliced bananas to serve, if desired.

Yield: 8 servings

Pear Salad

1 qt. pears, drained and crushed **slightly**	Heat juice just to boiling.
1 (3-oz.) pkg. lime-flavored gelatin	Add, stirring until dissolved.
8 oz. cream cheese, softened	Beat in until blended. Chill until just beginning to congeal.
1 cup whipping cream	Whip.
2 tbsp. sugar	Add to cream.

Combine pears, gelatin mixture, and cream. Pour in pretty glass dish. May be garnished with chopped nuts if desired.

Yield: 8 to 10 servings

Molded Pineapple Salad

1 (20-oz.) can crushed pineapple, undrained	Heat in saucepan, just to boiling.
1 (3-oz.) pkg. strawberry or lime-flavored gelatin	Add, stirring until dissolved.
4 large ice cubes	Stir in to cool. Chill until just beginning to congeal.
1 pkg. Dream Whip	Whip according to pkg. directions.
1 (3-oz.) pkg. cream cheese, softened (or larger pkg. if desired)	Blend in.
⅓ cup sugar **¼ tsp. salt**	Add, then fold into gelatin mixture. Pour into l-qt. mold and chill until set.

Variation: May add 3 or 4 drops peppermint flavor if using lime gelatin for mint mist salad.

Yield: 8 servings   *Kathryn Heatwole*

Pineapple Salad

2 (3-oz.) pkgs. lemon, or orange-pineapple-flavored gelatin **2 cups boiling water**	Stir together until dissolved.
6 large ice cubes	Stir in to cool mixture. Chill until just beginning to congeal.
1 (20-oz.) can crushed pineapple, drained (reserve juice) **2 cups miniature marshmallows** **3 bananas, diced**	Fold in, and pour in 9 × 13 dish. Chill until set.
Topping: **¾ cup sugar** **3 tbsp. flour**	Mix in saucepan.
add water to reserved pineapple juice to make 1¾ cups **1 egg, beaten**	Add. Cook just until thickened, stirring constantly. Remove from heat. Sit pan in cold water to cool. Chill.
1 cup whipping cream	Whip, and fold into custard. Spread over salad.
½ cup shredded cheddar cheese (optional)	Sprinkle over top.

Variation: omit marshmallows and add 3 apples, peeled and diced.

Yield: 12 to 15 servings   *Eileen Shenk*

Strawberry Pretzel Salad

2⅔ cups crushed pretzel sticks (8-oz. pkg.) ¾ cup margarine, melted 3 tbsp. sugar	Mix together. Pat ⅔ mixture in 9 X 13 bake dish. Reserve ⅓ crumbs. Bake at 350 degrees for 10 minutes. (Bake reserved crumbs in separate pan.) Cool.
8 oz. cream cheese, softened 1 cup sugar	Blend together.
2 cups Cool Whip	Mix in until blended. Spread over crust and chill.
6 oz. pineapple juice	Add water to make 3 cups and heat to boiling.
1 (6-oz.) pkg. strawberry-flavored gelatin	Add, stirring until dissolved.
2 (10-oz.) pkgs. frozen strawberries, or 3 cups	Add, mixing well. Chill 30 minutes. Pour over mixture. Chill 4 hours.

Sprinkle reserved crumbs over the top. Serve the same day or the following day. Pretzels get soggy after second day.

Yield: 12 servings

Fannie Beachy
Carolyn Reed

Summertime Refresher (Low Cal.)

2 cups watermelon balls 2 cups sliced fresh strawberries 1 cup seedless white grapes, halved 2 cups sliced fresh peaches	Place in bowl.
2 tbsp. lime juice artificial sweetener to taste	Combine and lightly toss through fruits. Serve in dessert goblets. Garnish with mint leaf.

Yield: 8 servings

Strawberry Gelatin Salad

2 (3-oz.) pkgs. strawberry- flavored gelatin 1½ cups boiling water	Stir together until dissolved.
1 pt. (16 oz.) sliced frozen strawberries	Add. (Berries will thaw in mixture and help to chill it quickly.)
1 (20-oz.) can crushed pineapple, undrained 2 large bananas, diced	Add. Pour in 9 × 13 dish, or large pretty glass dish. Stir mixture once just as it begins to congeal so fruit doesn't sit on top.
1 cup commercial sour cream or 2 cups Cool Whip	Spread over salad.
½ cup chopped pecans	Sprinkle over top.

Yield: 10 to 12 servings   *Linda Shenk*

Three-Layer Christmas Salad

1 (3-oz.) pkg. lime-flavored gelatin 1 (3-oz.) pkg. lemon-flavored gelatin 1 (3-oz.) pkg. strawberry-flavored gelatin	Dissolve each pkg. gelatin separately in 1 cup hot water each.
1. 1 (8-oz.) can crushed pineapple, drained 2 tbsp. lemon juice	Add lemon juice to pineapple juice and enough water to make 1 cup. Add to lime gelatin and chill until cold. Add pineapple and pour into an 8 × 12 inch dish. Chill until firm.
2. 8 oz. cream cheese, softened ⅓ cup mayonnaise	Chill lemon gelatin until just beginning to congeal. Whip until light and fluffy, Blend cheese and mayonnaise together and fold into gelatin. Pour over first layer and chill until firm.
3. 2 bananas	Slice over lemon layer. Add 3 large ice cubes or 1 cup cold water to strawberry gelatin and pour over bananas. Chill until firm.

May be cut in squares and served on lettuce leaf.

Yield: 8 servings

Waldorf Salad

diced apples **pineapple chunks** **halved white grapes** **diced bananas** **chopped celery** **blueberries** **coarsely chopped nuts** **miniature marshmallows**	Combine about 5 or 6 cups of fruits as desired in bowl.

Dressing:

8 oz. cream cheese, softened **3 tbsp. mayonnaise** **3 tbsp. sugar**	Blend until smooth. Gently stir into fruit mixture. Chill.

Optional Dressing:

1 cup Cool Whip **¼ cup mayonnaise** **3 tbsp. sugar** **1 tsp. lemon juice**	Blend together and gently stir into fruit mixture. Chill.

Yield: 8 servings

Frozen Waldorf Salad

1 (20-oz.) can crushed pineapple	Drain and reserve juice.
¾ cup sugar **2 tbsp. cornstarch** **¼ tsp. salt**	Combine in saucepan.
2 eggs, lightly beaten **2 tbsp. lemon juice** **¾ cup reserved pineapple juice**	Add. Cook just until thickened, stirring constantly. Cool thoroughly.
½ cup diced celery **⅓ cup raisins** **1 diced banana** **3 unpeeled Red Delicious apples,** **diced** **½ cup chopped nuts**	Add, along with pineapple.
1½ cups whipping cream	Whip, and fold in. Pour in 8 × 12 dish and freeze.

To serve, cut in squares and place on lettuce-lined plates. Garnish with a dab of salad dressing inserted with slices of unpeeled red apples.

Yield: 8 to 10 servings

VEGETABLE SALADS
Alfalfa Sprouts
(Buy seeds for sprouting at your health food store. Sprouts are delicious in salads or on mayonnaise bread.)

Put at least 2 cups *lukewarm* (not hot) water into a 3-or 4-qt. jar. Add ¼ cup alfalfa seeds. Cover jar with gauze or several thicknesses of nylon net fastened with a rubber band. Soak seeds overnight or at least several hours. Then pour off water and gently rinse seeds with fresh lukewarm water each morning and each evening. (Water may be poured off and added right through gauze without removing it.) Jar may sit on cupboard, but do not place in sunlight. Some people put it inside a dark cupboard, but I like to have it in sight so I don't forget to rinse the seeds. It takes from 3 to 5 days for sprouts to become full grown. I like to sit them where they receive more light the last day to develop some green in the leaves. As soon as they are full grown, refrigerate in covered container. They will become musty, if left too long.

. . . .

Bean Sprouts
(Use the little green mung beans for sprouting. These can usually be purchased at a health food store.)

Follow method used for alfalfa sprouts, using ⅓ cup beans for a 3 or 4 qt. jar. Carefully rinse beans 3 times a day instead of the 2 times for alfalfa sprouts. Allow 3 or 4 days to develop about 1 ½-inch-long sprouts. The small green hulls may be left on sprouts to eat. Or to remove them, swish in water, skimming off the hulls as they rise to the surface. Sprouts are good eaten raw in sandwiches or salad. Or cook in chow mein, or stir-fry with onions. Recipe is on page 558.

. . . .

Bean Salad

2 cups canned green beans **2 cups canned wax beans** **1 (16-oz.) can kidney beans**	Drain and place in bowl.

. . . .

½ cup chopped onion **½ cup chopped green pepper** **1 stem celery, finely chopped**	Add.

. . . .

½ cup vegetable oil **½ cup sugar** **⅓ cup vinegar** **1 tsp. salt**	Combine thoroughly and pour over beans, tossing well. Chill overnight. Toss again before serving.

. . . .

Yield: 10 to 12 servings

. . . .

Favorite Broccoli Salad

2 bunches broccoli (or use half cauliflower)	Separate into small flowerets.

8 strips bacon, fried and crumbled ⅓ cup chopped onion 1 cup chopped tomato 2 hard-cooked eggs, chopped	Add.

1 cup salad dressing or mayonnaise ⅓ cup sugar 2 tbsp. vinegar	Mix until smooth. Pour over broccoli mixture.

Salad may be prepared ahead several hours, if dressing is not poured over broccoli mixture until right before serving.

Variation: Omit tomato and eggs, and add ⅔ cup raisins. Then sprinkle 3 tbsp. chopped peanuts over top to garnish.

Yield: 6 to 8 servings

Doris Heatwole

Sweet and Sour Brussel Sprouts

2 (10-oz.) pkgs. frozen brussel sprouts	Cook just until barely tender and drain. Dunk in cold water to cool.

¼ cup vegetable oil ¼ cup vinegar ¼ cup sugar ½ tsp. salt ¼ tsp. dry mustard 2 tsp. parsley flakes ⅓ cup finely chopped onion	Mix together until smooth. Pour over cooled sprouts. Refrigerate several hours or overnight to marinate.

1 or 2 tomatoes, cut in wedges	Add just before serving.

Yield: 6 to 8 servings

Fannie Heatwole

Cabbage Salad

1 (3-oz.) pkg. lime-flavored gelatin 1 cup boiling water 4 large marshmallows	Stir together until dissolved.

1 cup crushed pineapple ¾ cup cottage cheese	Add. Cool until just beginning to congeal.

1 cup whippng cream, whipped ¾ cup shredded cabbage ½ cup mayonnaise	Fold in. Pour in pretty glass dish. Chill until firm.

Yield: 6 to 8 servings

Phyllis Weaver

Carrot Salad

1 (3-oz.) pkg. orange-flavored gelatin 1 cup boiling water	Stir together until dissolved.
1 cup crushed pineapple, drained	Add juice from pineapple and 2 ice cubes to cool.
1 cup grated carrots ¼ tsp. salt ¼ cup sugar	Add, along with pineapple. Pour in pretty glass dish and chill until set.

Yield: 6 to 8 servings

Sweet and Sour Carrot Salad

6 cups carrots, sliced into ⅛ to ¼-inch rings	Cook until tender, but not mushy. Cool.
1 cup chopped celery ½ cup chopped green pepper 1 large onion, cut in rings	Add.
¾ cup sugar ⅓ cup vinegar ½ cup vegetable oil 1 tbsp. Worcestershire sauce ½ tsp. dry mustard 1 (10-oz.) can tomato soup, or 1 cup thick tomato juice	Mix together until smooth. Pour over mixture. Marinate in refrigerator overnight. Serve cold.

Will keep 2 or 3 weeks in refrigerator. **Variation:** Cook 1 (10-oz.) pkg. frozen lima beans separately from carrots. Cool, and add to mixture.

Yield: 12 servings

Fannie S. Heatwole
Ina Heatwole

Coleslaw with Poppy Seed Dressing

1 med. head cabbage	Chill and shred finely.
⅓ cup vinegar ½ tsp. salt 1 tsp. dry mustard 1 tsp. garlic powder 1½ tsp. poppy seeds 1 tsp. onion salt ⅔ cup sugar	Mix together well.

1 cup vegetable oil	Slowly add, beating until stiff. Pour over cabbage just before serving.

(Cabbage may be shredded ahead and chilled, but do not add dressing until just before serving.)

Yield: 6 servings   *Harriet Steiner*

Seafoam Coleslaw

1 (3-oz.) pkg. lime-flavored gelatin **¾ tsp. salt** **1 cup boiling water**	Stir together until dissolved.
¾ cup ice water	Add.
½ cup mayonnaise **1 tbsp. vinegar** **1 tbsp. grated onion** **¾ tsp. celery seed**	Add, beating slightly to blend well. Chill until just beginning to congeal.
2 cups finely shredded cabbage	Fold in. Pour in 3-cup mold and chill until set.

(May be poured in 6 individual molds, if desired.)

Yield: 5 or 6 servings   *Dorothy Shank Showalter*

Corn Salad

2 (12-oz.) cans vacuum-packed **shoe peg corn (or regular packed,** **drained)** **2 tomatoes, chopped** **1 cup green pepper, chopped** **½ cup purple onion, chopped** **1 small unpeeled cucumber,** **chopped**	Combine in bowl.
½ cup commercial sour cream **¼ cup mayonnaise** **2 tbsp. vinegar** **2 tbsp. sugar** **1 tsp. salt** **½ tsp. celery seed** **½ tsp. dry mustard** **⅛ tsp. black pepper**	Mix thoroughly and pour over vegetables in bowl. Toss gently. Cover and chill 1 hour.

Yield: 6 to 8 servings   *Joyce Showalter*

Old-Fashioned Cucumber Salad

1 large cucumber, peeled and thinly sliced ¼ cup chopped green pepper ¼ cup chopped onion	Combine in dish.

. . . .

½ cup water 2 tbsp. vinegar 1 tsp. salt 1 or 2 tbsp. sugar, if desired	Pour over mixture. Refrigerate a short time before eating, or make ahead for the next meal.

. . . .

Yield: 2 servings   *Fannie S. Heatwole*

. . . .

German Slaw

(This slaw will keep several weeks in the refrigerator, or may be frozen in tightly covered containers. It is delicious eaten as slaw and also when added to cold pork roast or pork barbecue sandwiches.)

1 med. head cabbage, finely shredded 1 whole green pepper, finely chopped 1 med. onion, finely chopped 1 carrot, grated	Mix in bowl.

. . . .

¾ cup vinegar ¾ cup vegetable oil 1½ cups sugar 1 tsp. salt 1 tsp. celery seed	Combine in saucepan. Heat to a good rolling boil. Remove from heat and pour over cabbage mixture immediately. Cover tightly. Let stand to cool. Then refrigerate.

. . . .

Chill at least 1 hour before serving. Chopped raw tomatoes or canned tomatoes may also be added after cooling if desired.

Yield: approximately 1 to 1 ½ qts.   *Lois Hess*

. . . .

Greek Salad

1 med. head romaine lettuce	Tear into small pieces. (Lettuce should be dry.)

. . . .

1 med. onion, sliced 2 medium tomatoes, cut in wedges 1 cucumber, peeled and thinly sliced 1 small green pepper, chopped	Add.

¼ cup olive oil ¼ cup vegetable oil ¼ cup wine vinegar ½ tsp. salt ¾ tsp. oregano ⅛ tsp. garlic powder	Measure into a jar. Cover tightly and shake well. Add to vegetables, tossing to coat.
1 cup feta cheese, cut into ½- inch cubes, or 1 cup large-curd cottage cheese	Add, and gently toss.
sliced radishes, chopped parsley, black olive slices, or anchovy fillets	Arrange over top to garnish. Serve immediately.

Yield: 8 to 10 servings   *Ruth Heatwole*

Lettuce Salad (or Other Greens)

(This is a good basic salad recipe that may be used with greens other than lettuce. Use chopped spinach, dandelion, endive, kale, or watercress.)

1 large head lettuce	Chop or tear into small pieces.
2 or 3 hard-cooked eggs, diced 6 slices bacon, fried and crumbled, or bacon bits	Add.
2 tbsp. flour 2 tbsp. sugar ½ tsp. salt	Mix together in saucepan.
1 egg yolk 1 cup milk	Slowly add, stirring vigorously to avoid lumps. Cook until thickened, stirring constantly. Cool to lukewarm.
1 tbsp. vinegar 1 tbsp. prepared mustard	Add, mixing well. Add to lettuce mixture, tossing to coat. Serve immediately.

Yield: 8 servings   *Joyce Brunk*

Lettuce and Cauliflower Salad

1 head lettuce, chopped
1 head cauliflower, broken into
    flowerets
1 small onion, chopped
8 slices bacon, fried and crumbled
    (reserve ¼ cup)

Layer in bowl in order listed.

2 cups salad dressing
1 tbsp. sugar

Mix and spread over mixture.

¼ cup Parmesan cheese

Sprinkle cheese and reserved bacon over top.
Refrigerate overnight.

Toss together just before serving.

Yield: 8 to 10 servings   *Mae Shank*

Seven Layer Lettuce Salad

1 small head lettuce, broken in
    pieces
½ cup celery, finely chopped
¾ cup frozen peas, thawed
½ cup onion, finely chopped
¼ cup green pepper, finely chopped
3 hard-cooked eggs, diced

Layer in 8-inch-square dish in order listed.

1 cup Miracle Whip (or other) salad
    dressing
1 tbsp. sugar
2 tbsp. cream

Combine and spread over mixture.

⅔ cup grated cheddar cheese, or ¼
    cup grated Parmesan cheese
Crumbled bacon

Sprinkle over top.

Refrigerate several hours or overnight before serving.

Yield: 8 to 10 servings   *Mary Ann Heatwole*

Potato Salad

5 cups potatoes finely chopped, and
    cooked
1 tsp. salt
2 tbsp. sugar

Mix well while warm so seasoning soaks into
potatoes. Refrigerate until cold.

6 hard-cooked eggs, diced
1 carrot, grated
3 stems celery, finely chopped
1 onion, chopped

Add to cold potatoes.

2 cups salad dressing **1 cup sugar** **2 tbsp. prepared mustard** **¼ cup vinegar**	Mix thoroughly, then stir into potato mixture until well blended.

(Salad keeps well for a week. However, it usually needs a little more sugar and maybe other seasoning after the first day, Ruby says.)

Yield: 10 to 12 servings   *Ruby Petersheim*

Easy Potato Salad

2 lb. or about 6 med. potatoes	Cook until tender and dice.
¾ tsp. salt	Sprinkle over warm potatoes so it soaks in.
3 to 6 hard-cooked eggs, diced **2 to 4 tbsp. chopped onion**	Add.
2 cups or more of basic cooked **dressing on page 500.**	Add while potatoes are warm for better penetration of flavor.

Yield: 8 servings   *Jeanne Heatwole*
Mary Ann Heatwole

Potato or Macaroni Salad for a Group

(Recipe serves approximately 40 persons. Small recipe given in brackets serves 12.)

7½ lbs. (18 to 20 med.) potatoes [6
   med. potatoes,] or
1½ lbs. (about 5 cups) macaroni
   [1½ cups]
	Cook and dice potatoes, or cook and drain macaroni. Cool.

2½ tsp. salt [1 tsp.] **8 hard-cooked eggs, diced [3]** **1½ cups chopped celery [½ cup]** **¾ cup chopped onion [¼ cup]**	Add.
2¼ cups mayonnaise [¾ cup] **⅓ cup prepared mustard [2 tbsp.]** **¾ cup vinegar [¼ cup]** **1 cup sugar [⅓ cup]**	Mix together thoroughly and then stir into potato mixture until well mixed.

Yield: 1 ½ gallons (amount in brackets yields ½ gallon)   *Fannie S. Heatwole*

Rabbit Salad

1 cup grated carrots 1 cup chopped celery 1 cup chopped unpeeled Red Delicious apples ½ cup raisins	Mix in bowl.
⅔ cup mayonnaise or salad dressing ½ tsp. salt 3 tbsp. sugar	Combine thoroughly and stir into mixture in bowl.
½ cup chopped nuts	Sprinkle over top.

Yield: 6 servings   *Margaret Brubaker*

Sauerkraut Salad

1 qt. sauerkraut, drained	Rinse with cold water and drain well.
1 cup chopped green pepper 1 cup chopped celery 1 cup chopped onion 2 tbsp. chopped sweet red pepper, or pimiento	Add.
¾ cup sugar ½ cup vegetable oil ⅓ cup vinegar	Mix together until smooth. Pour over mixture and refrigerate overnight.

(This is also excellent to use as a relish for hot dogs.)

Yield: 10 servings   *Alice Trissel*

Spinach Salad

2 lbs. fresh spinach	Chop or break into bite-size pieces. Drain well and dry thoroughly.
1 med. onion, finely chopped 4 hard-cooked eggs, diced 6 slices bacon, fried and crumbled ½ lb. fresh mushrooms, sliced (optional)	Add.

¾ cup vegetable oil	Process in blender until smooth. Pour over
⅔ cup sugar	spinach mixture and toss to coat.
½ cup catsup	
¼ cup vinegar	
2 tsp. Worcestershire sauce	

| croutons | Sprinkle over top to garnish. Serve immediately. |

Yield: 8 to 10 servings

Tomato and Cucumber Salad

(Delicious served with green beans)

4 med. tomatoes, diced	Combine in bowl.
2 med. cucumbers, peeled and thinly sliced	
2 large onions, sliced and separated into rings	

¼ cup oil	Combine in jar and shake until thoroughly
2 tbsp. vinegar	mixed. Pour over mixture in bowl. Marinate 2
2 tbsp. sugar	hours before serving.
1 tsp. salt	
½ tsp. black pepper	
2 tsp. minced fresh parsley	

Yield: 6 servings   *Dorothy Shank Showalter*

Crunchy Vegetable Salad

| 1 small head cauliflower | Break into small flowerets. |
| 1 large head broccoli | |

3 carrots sliced in thin rings	Add.
2 small zucchini, halved and sliced in thin half-rings	
1 onion, finely chopped	
⅓ cup chopped celery	

⅔ cup mayonnaise or salad dressing	Combine thoroughly and add. Chill several hours before serving.
⅓ cup vegetable oil	
3 tbsp. vinegar	
⅓ cup sugar	
1 tsp. salt	

Yield: 8 to 10 servings.

MISCELLANEOUS SALADS
Chicken Salad

2 cups diced cooked chicken
½ cup finely chopped celery
½ cup mayonnaise or salad
    dressing
½ tsp. salt
¼ tsp. MSG (optional)
1 tbsp. vinegar
2 tsp. sugar
2 hard-cooked eggs, diced
¼ cup minced green pepper, or
    chopped sweet pickle

Mix all ingredients together thoroughly and chill. May add 1 or 2 tbsp. of cream if needed to thin slightly.

Yield: 5 to 6 servings

Chicken Salad Mold (or Pressed Chicken)

3 cups finely chopped cooked
    chicken
salt to taste
½ tsp. poultry seasoning
⅛ tsp. pepper

Combine and put in an 8 ½ × 4 ½-inch dish.

¼ cup cold water
1 env. (1 tbsp.) plain gelatin

Soak until softened.

2 cups hot water
1 chicken bouillon cube
⅛ tsp. MSG (optional)

Add to gelatin and stir until dissolved. Cool, then pour over mixture in dish.

Chill until firm. Slice to serve. May be garnished with mayonnaise if desired. (For an attractive mold, keep light and dark chicken meat separate when chopping it. Place a layer of dark meat in dish first, then a layer of light on top. Add seasoning to hot water mixture. After cooling, pour in dish carefully so you don't disturb layered effect.)

Yield: 8 servings   *Lois Good*

Favorite Club Salad

1½ cups diced cooked chicken, or
    use ¾ cup chicken and ¾ cup
    tuna
1 cup shredded carrots
½ cup chopped celery
2 tbsp. diced onion
½ cup salad dressing
1 tbsp. milk or cream
2 tsp. sugar (see next page)

Mix all ingredients together thoroughly. Serve immediately.

¼ tsp. dry mustard
2 cups shoestring potatoes or
  potato sticks

. . . .

Salad can be made ahead by combining all ingredients except potato sticks. They should be added just before serving to avoid sogginess.

Yield: 6 servings   *Erma Moyers*

. . . .

Ham-a-Roni Salad

1 cup macaroni	Cook until tender and drain. Hold under cold running water to cool. Chill.

. . . .

1 cup diced cooked ham ½ cup chopped celery ¼ cup chopped green pepper ¼ cup chopped onion 1 cup grated carrots	Add.

. . . .

½ cup mayonnaise or salad dressing 1½ tbsp. barbecue sauce 2 tbsp. catsup 1 tsp. prepared mustard ½ tsp. salt ¼ cup sugar	Mix together thoroughly, and add.

. . . .

Yield: 6 servings

. . . .

Macaroni-Tuna Salad

1 cup macaroni	Cook until tender and drain. Hold under cold running water to cool. Chill.

. . . .

1 (6½ oz.) can tuna, flaked ½ med. onion, minced 1 cup frozen peas, thawed 1 or 2 tomatoes, diced ½ cup celery, finely diced ½ cup cheese, shredded	Add.

. . . .

½ cup salad dressing 2 tbsp. vinegar 1 tsp. salt ¼ tsp. MSG (optional) 2 or 3 tbsp. sugar ½ cup evaporated milk	Combine thoroughly and stir in until well mixed. Chill until served.

. . . .

Yield: 8 servings

. . . .

Taco Salad

1 lb. hamburger, browned and drained	Cool, but do not chill.

1 med. head lettuce, shredded **1 (16-oz.) can kidney beans, drained** **1 cup shredded cheddar cheese** **3 or 4 tomatoes, cut in chunks** **1 (6-oz.) pkg. taco or corn chips, crushed lightly** **1 med. onion, chopped** **1 (8-oz.) bottle or 1½ cups French dressing**	Add, mixing together thoroughly. Serve immediately.

Yield: makes a meal for 6   *Bertha H. Shank*

SALAD DRESSINGS
Basic Salad Dressing (Cold)

(This dressing is good on lettuce, or other greens, on coleslaw or cucumber salad—cucumber slices and tomato chunks, etc.)

2 tbsp. sugar **¼ tsp. salt** **1 tbsp. vinegar** **3 tbsp. salad dressing**	Mix together until smooth.

Basic Salad Dressing (Cooked)

(Also called Half and Half Dressing. Good on lettuce or other greens, or on potato salad and coleslaw.)

1 tbsp. cornstarch **¾ cup sugar** **½ tsp. salt**	Mix in top container of double boiler.
1 cup water **1½ tbsp. vinegar**	Add gradually.
3 eggs, beaten lightly	Add. Cook over boiling water, stirring constantly until thickened. Remove from heat.
2 tbsp. butter or margarine	Add. Cool thoroughly.
2 cups Miracle Whip (or other) salad dressing **½ to 1 tsp. prepared mustard**	Blend in.

Store in refrigerator. Keeps for weeks.

Yield: 1 qt.

Jeanne Heatwole
Mary Ann Heatwole

Buttermilk Dressing

(Tastes similar to Hidden Valley dressing)

1 cup buttermilk
1 cup mayonnaise
¼ tsp. onion salt
¼ tsp. garlic salt
¼ tsp. celery salt
¼ tsp. MSG (optional)
⅛ tsp. black pepper
½ tsp. crushed parsley flakes

Combine all ingredients in jar and shake well.

Delicious on tossed salads, taco salads, or on baked potatoes.

Darlene Logan
Julia Witmer

Celery Seed or Poppy Seed Dressing

½ cup sugar
1 tsp. dry mustard
1 tsp. salt

Mix.

1 tbsp. grated onion
¼ cup white vinegar

Add.

1 cup vegetable oil
1½ tsp. celery seeds or poppy
    seeds

Stir in.

Good on fresh fruit or grapefruit sections, or on greens.

Harriet Steiner

French Dressing

¾ cup vegetable oil
¼ cup vinegar
½ cup sugar
½ cup catsup
¾ tsp. paprika
¾ tsp. celery seed
¾ tsp. salt
¾ tsp. grated onion

Place in blender container in order listed.
Process until smooth.

Variation: For creamy dressing, add ¼ cup heavy cream or evaporated milk.

Wanda Good

Basic French Dressing

¾ cup vegetable oil
3 tbsp. vinegar
1 tsp. salt
¼ cup sugar
1 tbsp. lemon juice
¼ tsp. black pepper
¼ tsp. paprika

Combine in jar, and shake until smooth. Or process in blender until smooth.

Add any of the following for delightful flavor change:
—1 garlic clove, finely minced, or ⅛ tsp. garlic powder
—a few drops onion juice, or Tabasco sauce; or 1 ½ tsp. Worcestershire sauce, ½ tsp. dry mustard, and another ½ tsp. paprika
— ¼ cup chili sauce or catsup and 1 tbsp. finely chopped green pepper
— ⅛ tsp. curry powder
—for thicker dressing, just before serving add 1 tbsp. mayonnaise
—for creamy dressing, just before serving add 2 tbsp. heavy cream, or sour cream, or mayonnaise

Favorite Lettuce Dressing

¾ cup vegetable oil
¼ cup vinegar
2 tbsp. sugar
1 tsp. onion, grated
1½ tsp. Worcestershire sauce
½ tsp. salt
¼ tsp. chili powder
¼ tsp. garlic powder

Combine all ingredients in jar and shake well. Chill. Pour over chopped lettuce or lettuce wedges and sprinkle with chopped hard-cooked eggs.

Blender Mayonnaise

(We think this is better than commericial mayonnaise. It has a cheesy taste. Try it!)

2 eggs
1 tsp. salt
1¼ tsp. dry mustard
½ tsp. paprika
1 tsp. sugar

Place in blender container. Process at highest speed until thoroughly mixed.

2 tbsp. lemon juice

Add, continuing to blend at high speed. Remove little insert cap in lid.

2 cups vegetable oil
2 tbsp. vinegar

Slowly pour in half of oil while continuing to blend at highest speed. (If added too quickly mayonnaise will curdle.) Slowly add vinegar and then remainder of oil until smooth and creamy.

This recipe makes delicious **deviled eggs**. Add enough mayonnaise to mashed egg yolks to moisten well. Then fill whites.

Yield: 2 ¼ cups

Salad Dressing
(Similar to Miracle Whip salad dressing)

1 cup water ¾ cup flour	Process in blender just until smooth. Pour into saucepan.
½ cup white vinegar	Add. Cook just until thickened, stirring constantly.
1 egg, plus water to make ⅔ cup ¾ cup vegetable oil ½ cup sugar 2 tsp. salt ½ tsp. dry mustard 1 tbsp. lemon juice ¼ tsp. paprika (optional) ¼ tsp. garlic salt (optional)	Combine in blender container and process until smooth. Add hot mixture, and continue to blend until smooth again.

Yield: 3¼ cups

Russian Dressing

1 cup mayonnaise ⅓ cup catsup 2 tsp. lemon juice 2 tsp. sugar 2 tbsp. finely chopped onion (optional)	Mix all ingredients together thoroughly. Cover and chill.

Yield: 1½ cups   *Phyllis Martin Basye*

Thousand Island Dressing

½ cup sugar 2 tbsp. flour	Mix in saucepan.
1 cup water ½ cup vinegar 2 eggs, slightly beaten 1 tsp. prepared mustard ½ tsp. salt	Slowly add, stirring until smooth. Cook just until thickened, stirring constantly. Remove from heat. Cool thoroughly.
1 cup salad dressing ½ cup catsup or chili sauce 1 minced onion (optional) ¼ cup chopped green pepper (optional)	Add, mixing well. Will keep in refrigerator for a long time.

Yield: approximately 1 qt.

Tossed Salad Dressing

1 cup vegetable oil
½ cup vinegar
½ cup sugar
½ cup catsup
1 tsp. salt
1 tsp. prepared mustard
½ tsp. celery seed
3 tbsp. grated onion, or 1 tbsp. dry
   onion flakes

Combine all ingredients in blender container and process until smooth, or shake in jar until dissolved.

· ·

(The addition of ½ tsp. raw egg white helps to keep vinegar and oil from separating as much.)

Yield: 2 ½ cups   *Gladys Harman*

· ·

Yogurt Dressing (Low Cal.)

½ cup plain yogurt
2 tsp. lemon juice
1 tbsp. vegetable oil
½ tsp. salt
½ tsp. paprika
¼ tsp. minced garlic
dash liquid hot red pepper
   seasoning

Combine in jar and shake vigorously. Store in refrigerator. Shake again before serving.

· ·

Delicious on sliced cucumbers or tomatoes.

· ·

SANDWICHES

Chicken Burgers

2 slices white bread	Tear into small pieces in bowl.
1 (6-oz.) can chunk-style chicken, drained and flaked **1 egg, slightly beaten** **1 med. carrot, finely grated** **1 tbsp. onion, finely grated** **½ tsp. salt** **¼ tsp. MSG (optional)**	Add, mixing well. Shape into two 3-inch patties.
1 tbsp. oil	Heat in skillet and fry burgers until browned on each side—8 to 10 minutes.

Yield: 2 servings   *Dorothy Shank Showalter*

Chili Burgers

1 lb. hamburger	Brown and drain.
1 (11 ½-oz.) can chili beef soup	Add and heat. Spoon into 6 buns.
6 slices American cheese	Lay a slice on top of mixture in each bun. Heat in 350-degree oven, or microwave, until cheese melts.

Yield: 6 burgers   *Carolyn Reed*

Egg-Cheese Sandwich Filling

½ tsp. vinegar **2 tsp. onion, grated** **½ tsp. prepared mustard** **¼ tsp. salt** **1 tsp. sugar** **3 tbsp. mayonnaise or salad dressing**	Mix together thoroughly.
3 hard-cooked eggs, chopped* **1 cup grated American cheese**	Stir in. Fill sandwiches or buns.

(*May omit cheese and use 6 eggs instead of 3.)

Yield: 4 buns

Fishburgers

1 (16-oz.) can salmon, or mackerel, or tuna	Drain. Reserve liquid. Flake fish into bowl.
½ cup onion, chopped 2 tbsp. fat or oil	Sauté in skillet until tender. Add to fish.
½ cup dry bread crumbs 2 eggs, beaten ½ cup reserved liquid from fish ½ tsp. salt ½ tsp. mustard ¼ tsp. MSG (optional)	Mix in. Shape into cakes, and fry in fat in skillet until browned on each side. Place in buns to serve, if desired.

Yield: 6 servings

Ham Buns

8 Pepperidge Farm or other rolls	Have ready.
½ cup soft butter or margarine 2 tsp. prepared mustard 1 tbsp. poppy seeds 2 tsp. Worcestershire sauce 1 small onion, grated	Mix together and spread inside rolls.
5 or 6 oz. sliced ham	Place in rolls.
1 cup Swiss or other cheese, grated	Arrange over ham.

Place in shallow pan and cover with foil. Heat in 350-oven for 15 to 20 minutes until hot.

Yield: approximately 8 buns

Ham Dogs

½ cup salad dressing ½ cup chili sauce 1 tsp. sugar	Combine thoroughly.
2 cups chopped cooked ham 2 cups shredded sharp or cheddar cheese 2 hard-cooked eggs, diced ¼ cup chopped onion 2 tbsp. chopped green pepper (opt.)	Stir in until well mixed.
8 hot dog or hamburger buns	Spread mixture in buns.

Wrap each in foil. Heat in 400-degree oven for 10 minutes.

Yield: 8 buns   *Wanda Good*

Hot Deviled Ham Sandwich

12 slices white bread or 6 hamburger buns **salad dressing**	Spread bread with salad dressing
12 slices cheese (reserve half)	Make 6 sandwiches, adding a slice of cheese to each.
1 (4½-oz.) can deviled ham **¼ cup chopped pickle relish**	Mix and add to sandwiches.
6 tomato slices	Add next, and top with reserved slices of cheese. Cover with remaining bread.

Brush with melted margarine and grill on both sides until lightly browned. **Variation:** Use fried bacon slices instead of ham.

Yield: 6 servings

Hamburger Buns

1 lb. hamburger **½ cup onion, chopped**	Sauté in skillet. Drain
½ cup chopped relish (optional) **½ cup catsup** **½ tsp. salt** **¼ tsp. black pepper** **1 tsp. sugar** **1 cup mozzarella cheese, shredded** **few drops liquid smoke (optional)**	Add. Fill 8 to 10 buns. Wrap in foil, or place in foil-covered pan. Heat in 350-degree oven until warmed through, approximately 15 minutes.

Yield: 8 to 10 buns

Hoagies

Place in hoagie buns: ham, salami, cheese (Swiss or American), chopped lettuce, onion, and sliced tomato. Make dressing by combining: 2 parts oil, 1 part vinegar, salt, pepper, and sugar to taste. Pour over contents in buns. Do not make too damp, but moisten well. Sprinkle with leaf oregano.

Gladys Harman

Pizza Burgers

1 lb. ground beef
⅔ cup tomato paste
¼ cup chopped onion
⅓ cup Parmesan cheese
1 tsp. oregano
1 tsp. salt
1 tsp. sugar
dash black pepper

Combine all ingredients. Shape into 6 patties. Fry on barbecue grill or in skillet on stove until browned on both sides. Place in 6 hamburger buns.

. . . .

6 slices mozzarella cheese

Insert on top of patty in each bun. (Heat from meat will soften cheese.)

. . . .

Yield: 6 burgers

. . . .

Barbecued Pork Buns

(This is a good way to use up leftover pork roast.)

3 cups chopped roast pork
⅔ cup catsup
⅔ cup water
½ tsp. salt
¼ tsp. black pepper
¼ tsp. paprika
¼ tsp. MSG (optional)
2 to 4 tbsp. prepared mustard
1 large onion, chopped

Combine all ingredients in saucepan. Simmer for 10 minutes.

. . . .

1 tbsp. cornstarch
¼ cup water

Dissolve and stir in, cooking just until thickened. Serve in 12 hamburger buns.

. . . .

Yield: 12 buns

. . . .

Barbecued Turkey Buns

(A good way to use up leftover turkey)

1 tbsp. Worcestershire sauce
¾ cup catsup
2 tbsp. finely chopped onion
½ tsp. salt
¼ tsp. black pepper
1 tbsp. brown sugar
1 tbsp. vinegar

Combine in saucepan. Stir until boiling. Cover and simmer 15 minutes.

. . . .

1½ cups cooked diced turkey
½ tbsp. cornstarch dissolved in ¼ cup water

Add. Cook and stir until thickened. Spoon into 6 large buns.

. . . .

Yield: 6 buns

. . . .

Sloppy Joes

1 lb. hamburger ¼ cup chopped onion	Sauté in skillet. Drain.
1 tbsp. Worcestershire sauce 2 tbsp. brown sugar 1 tbsp. vinegar 1 tsp. prepared mustard 1 cup tomato juice, or ½ cup catsup 1 tsp. salt	Add, and simmer 15 minutes to ½ hour. Serve in 6 to 8 hamburger buns. (If mixture is too juicy, sift in a small amount of flour while stirring vigorously.)

Yield: 6 to 8 buns

Spamburgers

1 (12-oz.) can Spam 1 cup cheese 1 med. onion 1 tbsp. pickle relish	Run through food grinder.
3 tbsp. catsup 3 tbsp. milk ½ tsp. salt 1½ tbsp. mayonnaise	Add, mixing well. Spread on 10 or 12 hamburger buns. Wrap individually in foil. Bake at 250 degrees for 30 minutes.

Yield: 10 to 12 buns

Miriam Haarer

Tuna Burgers

1 (6½-oz.) can tuna, drained and flaked 3 hard-cooked eggs, diced ⅓ cup mayonnaise 1 tsp. prepared mustard ½ tsp. Worcestershire sauce 1 tsp. sugar 2 tbsp. minced sweet pickle 2 tbsp. minced onion 2 tbsp. minced green pepper ½ cup shredded cheese ¼ tsp. salt ¼ tsp. MSG (optional)	Mix all ingredients together thoroughly. Fill 6 hamburger buns. Place in foil-covered pan or wrap each bun in foil. Heat in 250-degree oven for 30 minutes, or until cheese melts.

Variation: Mix 1 can tuna with 1 (10-oz.) can cream of mushroom soup and 2 tsbp. minced pickles. Fill buns. May heat at 375 degrees for 12 minutes if desired.

Yield: 6 burgers

Broiled Turkey Buns

6 hamburger buns **margarine**	Spread margarine on bottom half of buns.
2 cups chopped cooked turkey **½ cup finely chopped celery** **⅓ cup mayonnaise or salad** **dressing** **1 tbsp. chopped onion** **2 tsp. lemon juice** **¼ tsp. MSG (optional)** **salt and pepper to taste**	Mix together thoroughly, and spread mixture over margarine on buns. Place in pan and broil about 4 inches from heat for about 3 minutes.
6 slices cheese, or 1 cup grated **cheese**	Add, and broil another minute or until cheese is bubbly.

Top halves of buns may be placed in oven underneath the halves being broiled to heat at the same time. Add tops to serve.

Yield: 6 buns

SOUPS

Bean Soup with Ham Bone

1 lb. navy or pinto beans **5½ cups water**	Combine in large saucepan. Heat to boiling. Turn burner off, keep tightly covered, and let sit 1 hour.
1 ham bone wih some meat on it* **½ cup chopped onion** **½ cup chopped celery** **½ cup chopped carrots**	Add. Heat to boiling again, and simmer for 1 ½ to 2 hours until tender.
1½ tsp. salt **¼ tsp. black pepper** **¼ tsp. oregano or other seasoning** **several drops liquid smoke (opt.)** **2 chicken bouillon cubes, crushed**	Add all seasonings about 10 minutes before end of cooking time, stirring well.

Remove bone, trim off meat, and add to soup. (*May use ¼ lb. bacon ends instead of hambone.)

Yield: 10 to 12 servings

Nine Bean Soup Mix

1 lb. dried great northern beans **1 lb. dried black beans** **1 lb. dried pinto beans** **1 lb. dried kidney beans** (see next page)	Mix together thoroughly in large bowl. Divide into 9 portions, 2 cups each, and put in plastic bags or jars.

1 lb. dried navy beans or baby lima
   beans
1 lb. barley pearls
1 lb. dried lentils
1 lb. dried split peas
1 lb. dried black-eyed peas

(For a unique hostess gift, place one portion of the soup mix in a decorative basket with a tin of canned ham, an onion wrapped in mesh and tied with ribbon, 2 cans of tomatoes, a box of chili powder, and the soup recipe!)

Nine Bean Soup

2 cups Nine Bean Soup Mix **5 cups water**	Combine in large saucepan or Dutch oven. Soak overnight.
1 lb. ham, diced **1 large onion, chopped** **1 qt. canned tomatoes, chopped**	Add, and heat to boiling. Reduce heat and simmer until tender, approximately 2 hours.
1 tbsp. sugar **1 tsp. chili powder** **1 tsp. salt** **¼ tsp. MSG (optional)**	Add, about 10 minutes before end of cooking time.

Yield: 10 to 12 servings   *Carolyn H. Reed*

Brunswick Stew

3 squirrels* **3 qts. water**	Heat in large saucepan to boiling. Simmer gently 1 ½ to 2 hours until tender. Skim surface occasionally. Remove meat from bones and return to broth.
¼ lb. diced smoked bacon (raw) **2 cups diced potatoes** **1 tsp. black pepper** **½ tsp. cayenne pepper** **1 cup chopped onion** **1 qt. canned tomatoes** **2 cups lima beans, fresh or frozen**	Add. Heat to boiling again, and simmer for 1 hour.
2 cups corn **2 tsp. salt**	Add, and cook 10 minutes more.

(*May use 1 fat hen instead of squirrels. Serve with corn bread and coleslaw.)

Yield: 8 to 10 servings   *Minnie Carr*

Old-Fashioned Beef Stew

2 lbs. beef stew meat, cut in 1-inch cubes ⅓ cup flour 2 tbsp. fat	Coat meat with flour and fry in fat until very dark brown on all sides.
6 cups water	Add, and heat to boiling. Cover and simmer for 1 ½ to 2 hours.until tender.*
4 med. potatoes, cubed 3 carrots, sliced 1 cup cabbage, shredded 1 med. onion, chopped ½ cup celery, chopped ⅓ cup green pepper, chopped 1 bay leaf	Add. Heat to boiling again, and simmer 30 minutes more until tender. Add more water if needed.
2 beef bouillon cubes 2 tsp. salt ¼ tsp. MSG (optional) other seasoning if desired	Remove bay leaf, and add.
2 tbsp. cornstarch dissolved in ¼ cup water	Add, stirring until thickened.

(*Instead of simmering, meat may be pressure-cooked at 10 lbs. pressure for 25 to 30 minutes. Reduce amount of water to 3 cups.)

Yield: 8 servings

Old-Fashioned Chicken and Dumpling Soup

(Cooks of the past simmered their soups on the back of the cookstove for hours to bring out a good rich flavor. This soup is typical of that era.)

1 (2½ to 3 lb.) fryer 6 cups cold water 6 chicken bouillon cubes 6 peppercorns 3 whole cloves	Cut up chicken, and simmer 1 ½ hours until tender. Remove, debone, and chop chicken. Skim broth, and strain out spices. Return meat to broth.
1 (10-oz.) can cream of chicken soup 1 (10-oz.) can cream of mushroom soup 1 cup water or rich broth 1 cup diced potatoes 1 cup chopped celery ½ cup chopped onion 1½ cups chopped carrots 1 cup frozen peas 1 bay leaf 1 tsp. seasoned salt ½ tsp MSG (optional)	Add and simmer for 2 or 3 hours longer.

Dumplings:
2 cups flour   Sift together into bowl.
1 tsp. salt
4 tsp. baking powder

....

1 egg, beaten   Combine and stir in quickly just until smooth.
2 tbsp. melted butter
⅔ cup milk

....

Drop by spoon evenly around over boiling soup. Cover tightly and simmer 18 minutes until done, *without* peeping!

Yield: 12 servings   *Dorothy Shank Showalter*

....

Chicken Corn Soup

3 med. potatoes, diced*   Cook together until tender, about 20 minutes.
1 small onion, chopped
½ stem celery, chopped

....

1 to 1½ cups chopped cooked   Add, and heat to a good rolling boil.
  chicken
1 cup corn
½ tsp. poultry seasoning
⅛ tsp. garlic powder
1¼ tsp. salt
¼ tsp. MSG (optional)
½ tbsp. chopped parsley, or a few
  dried snipped chives

....

(*May substitute ⅓ lb. (2 cups) noodles. Cook noddles 10 to 12 minutes.)

Yield: 6 to 8 servings

....

Chicken and Noodle Soup

⅓ lb. (2 cups) noodles   Cook until tender, about 12 minutes.
4 cups rich chicken broth and
  water—bouillon may be added if
  needed

....

1 to 2 cups cooked diced chicken   Add, and heat to boiling again.
1 tsp. salt*
¼ tsp. MSG (optional)

....

(*If broth is salty, omit part of salt. Additional water may be added for a thinner soup, if desired. Canned beef chunks or leftover roast may also be used with water added in place of broth and chicken.)

Yield: 6 servings

....

Chicken and Rice Soup

4 cups rich chicken broth and water—bouillon may be added if needed 1 cup rice ¼ cup chopped celery (optional) ¼ cup chopped onion (optional)	Heat to boiling. Stir thoroughly. Cover tightly and simmer for 20 minutes.

. . . .

1 to 2 cups cooked diced chicken 1 tsp. salt* ¼ tsp. MSG (optional)	Add, and heat to boiling again.

. . . .

(*If broth is salty, omit part of salt. Additional water may be added for a thinner soup if desired. Canned beef chunks or leftover roast may also be used with water added in place of the broth and chicken.)

. . . .

Chili Con Carne

(This recipe is large, but part of soup may be frozen for later use. Eileen says her mother always made a large pot of the soup to treat the Christmas carolers at their little country church after an evening of caroling in the cold Indiana weather.)

1 lb. dried kidney beans* 5 cups water	Soak overnight and cook 1 ½ to 2 hours until tender in 6-qt. pot.

. . . .

1½ lbs. hamburger 1 large onion, chopped 1 or 2 stems celery, chopped (opt.) 1 large garlic clove, minced, or ¼ tsp. garlic powder 2 tbsp. green pepper, chopped (opt.)	Sauté in skillet until hamburger is slightly browned.

. . . .

1 to 1½ qts. tomato juice 1 pt. canned tomatoes, chopped 3 tsp. salt 3 tbsp. brown sugar 1 tbsp. chili powder ½ tsp. celery seed ⅛ tsp. black pepper ¼ tsp. dried crushed red peppers (optional) ⅛ tsp. oregano (optional) ⅛ tsp. sage (optional)	Add to hamburger mixture, stirring well. Then add beans and simmer several minutes longer.

. . . .

(*Or 3 (16-oz.) cans kidney beans)

Yield: approximately 5 quarts   *Eileen Shenk*

. . . .

Weight Watcher's Chili (Low Cal.)

½ lb. hamburger	Sauté in skillet and drain.
1 cup green beans ½ cup chopped celery ¼ cup chopped green pepper 2 cups tomato juice sliced mushrooms, if desired	Add, and simmer ½ hour.
1 tsp. chili powder 1 tsp. artificial sweetener ½ tsp. salt	Add, stirring well.

Yield: 2 to 3 servings   *Alice Trissel*

Clam Chowder

5 slices bacon	Fry until crisp. Drain and crumble. Set aside.
1½ cups diced potatoes ½ cup chopped onions ½ cup water 1 tbsp. bacon grease	Cook until tender, about 15 minutes.
1 (7½-oz.) can clams, undrained 1½ cups evaporated milk 1 cup milk ¾ tsp. salt ¼ tsp. MSG (optional) (half of bacon)	Stir in. Cook 5 minutes longer.
2 tbsp. flour another ½ cup milk	Shake in batter shaker until smooth. Then stir in just until thickened.
parsley (other half of bacon)	Sprinkle over top to garnish.

Yield: 4 to 5 servings

Corn Chowder

3 med. potatoes, diced 1 stem celery, chopped 1 large onion, chopped	Add water to almost cover and cook until tender, about 15 minutes.
2 cups corn (may use 1 cream-style and 1 whole grain) 1 (12-oz.) can evaporated milk 2 tbsp. margarine ¾ tsp. salt ¼ tsp. black pepper	Add, and heat to boiling again.
2 tbsp. cornstarch dissolved in ¼ cup water	Add, stirring until thickened.
3 strips bacon, fried and crumbled	Sprinkle over top.

Yield: 4 to 5 servings

Lois Kiser

Cream of Celery Soup

1½ to 2 cups finely diced celery 1 cup water 1 chicken bouillon cube	Combine in saucepan and cook until tender. Puree in blender if desired. Add part of milk if needed to puree.
2 cups milk ½ tsp. salt ½ tsp. onion salt ⅛ tsp celery salt	Add, and heat to almost boiling.
1 cup milk 2 tbsp. flour	Shake in batter shaker until smooth. Add. Cook and stir just until thickened.
celery seed	Sprinkle over top to garnish.

Yield: 4 to 6 servings

Cream of Mushroom Soup

1½ cups finely chopped fresh mushrooms 3 tbsp. butter or margarine	Sauté in skillet until lightly browned.
1 cup water 1 chicken or beef bouillon cube	Add and simmer 5 to 10 minutes until tender.
2 cups rich milk ¾ tsp. salt ½ tsp. onion salt	Add, and heat to almost boiling.

1 cup milk **2 tbsp. flour**	Shake in batter shaker until smooth. Add. Cook and stir just until thickened.
minced parsley	Sprinkle over top to garnish.

Yield: 4 to 6 servings

Ham Soup

2 med. potatoes, diced **1 small onion, chopped** **1 cup fine-cut noodles**	Cook in about 1 cup water until tender and water is mostly cooked away.
1 cup chopped cooked ham **½ tsp. salt** **¼ tsp. MSG (optional)**	Add, and cook several minutes more.
3 cups milk*	Add, and heat to almost boiling again.
½ cup milk **2 tbsp. flour**	Shake in batter shaker until smooth. Add. Cook and stir just until thickened.
1 tbsp. butter	Add to garnish.

(*A little ham broth may be substituted for part of milk, if desired, for more of a ham flavor.)

Yield: 4 to 5 servings

Hamburger Bean-Pot Soup

1 cup dried pinto beans **3 cups water**	Heat to boiling. Turn off heat. Let stand 1 hour tightly covered. Then simmer 20 minutes.
2 cups canned tomatoes **1 cup celery, diced** **1 carrot, cubed** **1 potato, diced** **¼ cup uncooked rice** **⅓ cup onion, chopped** **½ lb. hamburger, browned and** **drained**	Add, and simmer 1 hour.
1½ tsp. salt **¼ tsp. black pepper** **1 beef bouillon cube**	Add about 10 minutes before end of cooking time.

Yield: 3 qts.   *Lillian Kiser*

Delicious Hamburger Soup

1 lb. hamburger 1 cup chopped onion 1 tbsp. oil	Sauté in skillet until lightly browned. Drain.
2 cups tomato juice 2 cups diced potatoes 1 cup diced carrots ½ cup chopped celery ¼ cup chopped green pepper	Add, and cook until tender, about 25 minutes.
1½ tsp. salt 1 tsp. seasoned salt 1½ tbsp. sugar ⅛ tsp. black pepper	Add.
1 cup milk ⅓ cup flour	Shake in batter shaker until smooth. Add, stirring until mixture boils.
3 additional cups milk	Add, and heat to almost boiling, stirring frequently.

Yield: approximately 1 gal.   *Margaret Brubaker*

(Freeze extra soup for later use. Soup is also good canned, but omit milk and flour if canning, until you open can to serve.)

Lentil Soup

(Harriet brought this recipe home from a trip to Africa.)

2 cups dried lentils 7 cups water 2 slices uncooked bacon (or ham bone or bouillon) ½ cup chopped carrots 1 med. onion, chopped ½ cup chopped celery 3 tbsp. minced parsley 1 garlic clove, crushed	Heat to boiling in large saucepan. Simmer for 1½ hours.
2 cups canned tomatoes 2 tbsp. vinegar 2 tbsp. sugar ½ tsp. oregano 2 tsp. salt ¼ tsp. black pepper	Add, and simmer 30 minutes more.

Yield: 8 servings   *Harriet Steiner*

Minestrone

(Do not substitute other sausage. The Italian sausage gives the soup a delicious flavor. Soup is just as tasty left over as fresh!)

1 lb. Italian sweet sausage (mild—in casing) **1 tbsp. vegetable oil**	Slice sausage in ½-inch rings and brown in oil.
1 cup diced onion **1 cup sliced carrots**	Add and cook 5 minutes more.
3 beef bouillon cubes dissolved in 1½ cups hot water **2 small raw zucchini, sliced, or 1 (16-oz.) can sliced zucchini** **2 cups canned tomatoes, chopped** **2 cups finely shredded cabbage** **1 tsp. crushed basil leaves** **¼ tsp. oregano** **¼ tsp. garlic powder**	Add, and heat to boiling. Cover and simmer 1 hour.
2 cups cooked great northern beans, or 1 (16-oz.) can, undrained **1 tbsp. sugar** **1 tsp. salt** **¼ tsp. black pepper** **¼ tsp. MSG (optional)**	Add, and cook 20 minutes more.
chopped parsley	Garnish to serve.

Yield: 3 qts.   *Dorothy Shank Showalter*

Potato Rivel Soup

3 med. potatoes, diced **1 small onion, chopped** **1½ cups water**	Cook until almost tender.
1 small egg **approx. ½ cup flour** **¼ tsp. salt**	To make rivels, mix with a fork into little stringy lumps. Add, cover, and cook 7 minutes more.
4 cups milk **1 tbsp. butter** **½ tsp. to ¾ tsp. salt** **⅛ tsp. celery seed**	Add, and heat to boiling point. If soup isn't as thick as you like, add 1 or 2 tbsp. flour mixed with a little additional milk before adding.
parsley, chives, or crumbled bacon	Garnish over top.

Yield: 4 to 6 servings

Potato Soup

3 med. potatoes, diced ¼ cup chopped onion, or 2 tsp. dried onion flakes ¼ cup chopped celery (optional)	Cook in small amount of water so water is mostly cooked away until tender— ¾ to 1 cup.
2 cups milk	Add, and heat to almost boiling.
another ½ cup milk 2 tbsp. flour	Shake in batter shaker until smooth. Add and heat, stirring constantly just until slightly thickened.
½ tsp. salt 1 tsp. margarine	Add.
dried snipped chives crumbled bacon	Sprinkle over top to garnish.

Yield: 3 servings

Onion Soup

⅔ cup green onions, including part of the tops, sliced thin ½ cup celery, finely diced ¼ cup butter	Sauté in large saucepan until tender, but not browned.
¼ cup flour	Blend in.
4 cups milk 1 cup chicken broth or bouillon	Gradually stir in. Cook until thickened, stirring constantly.
½ cup sharp cheese, shredded 1½ tsp. salt ⅛ tsp. black pepper ¼ tsp. MSG	Stir in until blended.

Serve with toast squares.

Yield: 4 to 6 servings   *Dorothy Showalter*

Salmon or Oyster Soup (or Salsify Soup)

1 (15-oz.) can salmon, or 1 pint oysters	Heat to boiling in its own liquid.
½ tsp. salt ¼ tsp. MSG (optional) 3 cups milk	Add, and heat to almost boiling.

another ½ cup milk 2 tbsp. flour	Shake in batter shaker until smooth. Add. Heat, stirring constantly just until slightly thickened.
2 tsp. butter	Add and serve with crackers.

Variation: Instead of salmon or oysters, use 1½ cups salsify, cut into rings, cooked and drained.

Yield: 4 to 5 servings

Tomato Soup

3 tbsp. butter or margarine 2 tbsp. finely chopped onion	Sauté until lightly browned.
3 tbsp. flour	Slowly add until blended.
2 cups drained cooked tomatoes or thick tomato juice ¼ tsp. baking soda 1 tsp. salt 2 tsp. sugar dash black pepper, if desired	Add, and heat to good rolling boil.
3 cups milk	Add, and heat to almost boiling—do not boil. Serve with crackers.

Yield: 5 servings

Tuna-Potato Soup

4 med. potatoes, diced 1 small onion, finely chopped 1 stem celery, chopped	Cook in small amount of water until tender—about 1 cup.
1 (6½-oz.) can tuna, drained ½ tsp. salt ¼ tsp. MSG (optional) 1½ cups milk	Add and heat to boiling.
another ½ cup milk 1½ tbsp. flour	Shake in batter shaker just until smooth, then add. Heat, stirring constantly just until slightly thickened.

Dot with butter and serve.

Yield: 5 servings

Vegetable Soup

3 or 4 cups cooked cubed beef and broth, or 1½ to 2 lbs. hamburger, browned and drained 4 med. potatoes, cubed 3 med. carrots, sliced 1 chopped onion ½ cup chopped celery ¼ cup chopped green pepper 2 cups shredded cabbage 2 cups peas or green beans	Combine in large saucepan, and cook until tender, 25 to 30 minutes.

. . . .

½ cup rice or macaroni	Cook separately until tender, then add.

. . . .

1 cup canned tomatoes or juice 1½ tsp. salt 1 tbsp. sugar ½ tsp. MSG (optional) 2 tsp. Worcestershire sauce 1 tsp. chili powder or other seasoning	Add, and heat to boiling again.

. . . .

3 tbsp. cornstarch ½ cup water	Dissolve and add, stirring until thickened.

. . . .

Yield: 10 to 12 servings

. . . .

Weight Watcher's Vegetable Soup (Low Cal.)

3 carrots, sliced 3 stems celery, chopped 2 cups canned tomatoes 1 small head cabbage, shredded 1 med. onion, chopped 2 med. potatoes, diced 6 cups water 6 bouillon cubes—chicken or beef	Combine in large saucepan and heat to boiling. Then simmer 25 to 30 minutes until tender, stirring occasionally. Add additional water if needed.

. . . .

add seasoning as desired—salt, chili powder, oregano, a little thyme	Add, stirring well.

. . . .

Yield: 5 servings   *Alice Trissel*

. . . .

ENTERTAINING; QUANTITY COOKING, & PARTY FOODS

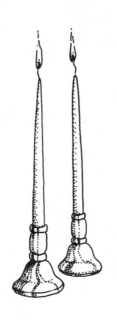

ENTERTAINING, QUANTITY COOKING, AND PARTY FOODS

Having guests over for something to eat is a wonderful way to show hospitality. Beginners, however, are often inclined to cringe at the thought of having guests for a meal. They fear their food may not taste as good as someone else's or that something will flop. This is unfortunate. Most cooks would agree that food often tastes better when someone else has prepared it, and we all like a change sometimes from our own cooking. We feel honored that someone desired our company, and the last intent is to scrutinize the food. The most important thing is not the food, but having a good time socializing together.

It is important, therefore, that the hostess is not in a stew about the food. We would all rather have a good time together over a casserole meal than to feel we caused a terrible burden on our hostess who felt obligated to sweat it out with an elaborate dinner!

The secret here again as with many other situations is to plan ahead. If you are inexperienced at entertaining, invite a smaller group until you gain confidence. Plan foods that you already have prepared successfully and know how they will turn out. Do not experiment with guests! Plan things that can be prepared in advance until you develop confidence. A roast that needs to be carved at the last minute, potatoes that need to be mashed, a tossed salad, and a perishable dessert can make an impossible amount of last-minute work at the time guests may begin to arrive. If meat and potatoes are in the oven, a gelatin salad is in the refrigerator, and a frozen or other dessert is waiting in the freezer or refrigerator, you can concentrate on a vegetable dish and a few last-minute details, ready to greet your guests with confidence.

If you find several menus that work exceptionally well for entertaining, there is no harm in using the same ones often with different guests. No one will know except your family that you served the same thing the last three times you entertained! The chances are that it is a meal your family enjoys having repeated anyway. It builds confidence to prepare something you've had practice with and you know works out well. If you do this, however, it helps to keep a little notebook of who you entertained and what you served, so that you do not repeat the exact same menu when they are guests again!

Quantity Cooking

The amount of food it takes to feed a group of people can vary considerably. It is helpful to keep a few variables in mind, so you know whether to increase or decrease average amounts slightly. It may depend on whether you are feeding farm folks or city folks, young people or older ones. Even seasons of the year can make a difference. When it is very hot, food doesn't go as fast, but a terrific amount of cold drink may be consumed. Hot drinks are much in demand in cold weather. Snacks go over big with young people and groups including a lot of children. The time of day can also make a difference. If you're serving working guests much later in the day than their regular mealtime, they can feel half-starved! Or if you're serving an early meal when out-of-town guests have been snacking and haven't had a chance to work up an appetite, they may eat less than you expect.

For entertaining large groups it is often easier to figure amounts in foods when dishing out servings on individual plates than it is when serving buffet or family-style. You can figure ½-cup (or whatever size desired) servings per person and then serve in these exact portions. (Don't figure ½-cup servings and then dish out 1 cup amounts, however!) One-half cup does make a nice serving of many foods. Since there are 16 cups in a gallon, each gallon should give 32 servings. All you need to do is multiply this amount times your number of guests and you will have a good idea of the total amount needed.

Buffet meals usually have a way of balancing out. For those who take double portions, there are usually about as many who take half portions. It is good to allow some extra, however.

Ham is one of the easiest meats to serve to large groups. However, some cooks put twice the amount of ham in a sandwich than others do. So it is important to decide on an amount and then portion it out accordingly. One to 1 ½ pounds of thinly sliced ham divided between 20 small buns or 10 sandwiches (with 2 slices of bread) is a nice proportion. Somehow, it tastes better to use several thin slices of meat rather than one thick slice.

When making casseroles or any other dishes for a group, simply figure the number of people one dish serves and multiply by the number needed. Figuring approximate amounts for groups is not nearly as difficult as many people think.

It is always helpful to know whether your group likes to fill up on potatoes or on ice cream. Or whether they indulge in potato chips or coffee. If you've planned a reasonable amount, don't worry if one item runs low. Guests may fill up on something else! Amounts needed, of course, will also vary with the number of items on the menu. The more items guests have to choose from, the less they usually take of each.

APPROXIMATE AMOUNTS FOR 100 PEOPLE

*Punch	9	gals. (1½ cups each person)
*Coffee	3	lbs. (1½ cups each person)
Cream	3	qts.
Sugar	2	lbs.
Rolls	200	(2 each)
Butter	1½ to 2	lbs.
Roast beef	35 to 40	lbs.
Roast pork	35 to 40	lbs.
Meat loaf	25	lbs.
Ham	35	lbs. (sliced on plates)
Oysters	16 to 18	qts.
Soup	6	gals. (about 1 cup each)
Hamburger	35	lbs.
Baked beans	4	gals.
Roast turkey	4 18-lb.	turkeys
Vegetables	4	10-lb. cans
Potatoes	35	lbs.
Scalloped potatoes	4 to 4½	gals.
Cabbage (for coleslaw)	25	lbs.
Potato salad	3½ to 4	gals.
**Relish plate: 2 large heads cauliflower	2	pts. dip

      2 large heads broccoli
      1 lb. carrots
      1 lb. radishes
      2 bunches celery

Pickles	2	qts.
Cheese balls	3	1-lb. balls
Crackers	2	lbs.
Potato chips	5	lbs.
Fruit cocktail	3	gals.
Pies	17	
Cakes	7	
Mints	3	lbs.
Nuts	3	lbs.
Ice cream	3 to 4	gals.

(When buying commercial ice cream in individually wrapped bricks, there are usually 32 bricks per gallon.)

    *In moderate weather beverages are usually figured at 1 ½ cups per person. About half the group usually want a refill and the other half does not. In hot weather, figure at least 2 cups or more of cold beverage per person. Instead of mixing far too much, it is a good idea to have extra ingredients on hand, ready to open and mix quickly if needed.

    **Relish plates often go further than people think. If you are excluding one or more items of the amount given, however, be sure to increase the other amounts, since the total amount here is for 100 guests. It is intended to be included with a light meal or with other refreshments. If you are serving only refreshments and the relish plate is the principal item, increase amounts slightly.

Party Ideas

There are so many ideas for party foods we sometimes don't know where to begin. Occasions vary from serving a light refreshment at the end of a meeting to inviting guests for an open house or party where food is the principal feature.

Here again, the type of group you are having will influence the type of entrées you select for the occasion. Possibilities range from meats, cheese, and vegetables, to fruits and sweets. It is always a good idea to include something for the calorie-conscious. With the ever popular fruit and vegetable trays, this is not difficult. Where a larger amount of food is planned for, a variety is certainly best.

There is no end to the variety and ideas for fancy sandwiches or hors d'oeuvres with all kinds of spreads and salad-type mixtures. No attempt is made to go into these in detail, but ideas are given in the recipes that follow. Use your own creative skill to come up with originals that befit the occasion.

Some ideas for spreads for bread cutouts or party crackers may include:
—Cream cheese with chopped pickle.
—Minced egg with anchovies and mayonnaise.
—Cream cheese and horseradish.
—Cream cheese and anchovy paste with minced onion.
—Cream cheese with deviled ham and minced onion.
—Caviar mixed with cream cheese with a dash of Worcestershire sauce.
—Cream cheese with a dash of Worcestershire sauce and chives.

For dainty **ribbon sandwiches,** use 4 slices bread—2 white and 2 brown. Alternate slices of light and dark bread. Spread 1 slice with pimiento cheese, 1 slice with cream cheese tinted green with a few snipped chives added, and 1 slice with ham salad tinted pink. Top with fourth slice. Chill and slice crosswise into 4 attractive sandwiches. (Use other fillings as desired.)

To make **pinwheel sandwiches,** buy a loaf of unsliced bread, or bake your own. Moist bread is best. Slice lengthwise. With rolling pin, lightly roll over slice to flatten just slightly. This prevents cracking when rolling up. Do not use pressure. You don't want the bread to be matted! Spread with desired filling (chicken salad is good). Place a row of olives along one end. (These will form an attractive center for pinwheels.) Roll up like a jelly roll, wrap in plastic wrap, and chill thoroughly. Slice to serve.

See other ideas for sandwich fillings beginning on page 469 in the Salads, Sandwiches, and Soups chapter, and on page 540 in this chapter.

Use mini-cutters to cut fancy shapes of sliced cheese to decorate items. Slices of olive and pieces of hard-cooked egg, or grated hard-cooked egg yolks, make nice garnishes. Egg yolks may be grated and mixed with mayonnaise and seasoning. Then put in cake decorator and pipe on flowerettes or other designs for garnish. Soft cheese mixtures may also be used in a cake decorator for garnishes. Raisins, tinted coconut, or tinted sugar may be used on sweet items. All kinds of icings, piped on whipped cream, cinnamon candies, and other commercial sprinkles may be used on confections or cakes.

If time isn't a problem, there are many ways to cut fancy vegetable items from carrots, radishes, cucumbers, and tomatoes. A large green pepper half with the edge notched makes a nice container for dip. Whole pineapple and watermelon rinds also make unique containers for fruits and dips. Apples with holes cut in the center make creative candle holders to use along with other fruit as a centerpiece.

Many recipes elsewhere in this book may be used for party items. Small party-size cream puffs may be filled with different mixtures from ham or chicken salad to puddings or ice cream. Ice cream filled puffs are delicious topped with chocolate icing or chocolate sauce.

There are multitudes of ideas with cakes—sheet cake cut in squares and decorated, or small squares or triangles of cake dipped in coating icing and decorated. Small cupcakes lend themselves to many ideas. Even the mini-tart pans are excellent for mini-cakes that can be decorated to suit any occasion. Mini-cupcake papers are available to fit them. The same pans, of course, can be used with various pie fillings for delicious tarts. Decorate with whipped cream, nuts, or cherries, depending on the flavor of the filling.

If you have teenagers over for an evening, a taffy pull is great fun. Or let them help make soft pretzels. They will have great sport rolling out the thin strips of dough and shaping it into all kinds of creations! Be sure to have coarse salt to sprinkle over the dough before baking. Pizza parties are always popular.

Young people also love to make doughnuts out of refrigerator biscuits for on-the-spot refreshments. They can poke a hole in the center before frying in hot fat. Have an assortment of coatings or toppings ready for them to garnish their own such as powdered sugar, cinnamon, coating icing; and coconut, chocolate, and butterscotch sauce, jellies, and the like. These doughnuts are much better eaten while still warm. Baked bananas also make a nice refreshment for teenagers to help prepare.

Other party foods may include:

—Muffin cups or toast cups with a variety of fillings.

—Stuffed mushrooms, stuffed miniature peppers.

—Vegetable trays and fruit trays with dips of many kinds:

For **fruit trays,** use canned or fresh pineapple chunks, apple wedges, orange or tangerine segments, mandarin oranges, banana slices, kiwi slices. Use strawberries, nectarines, cherries, grapes, peaches, and melons in season. You can use raisins, dried apple slices and dried banana chips, dates stuffed with nuts or cream cheese. Melon balls or fruit mixtures may also be served chilled or half frozen in clear plastic cups. Small fruits may be served on cocktail picks.

For **vegetable trays,** use celery, carrots, bell pepper strips, broccoli flowerets, cauliflower flowerets, radishes, cucumber slices, kohlrabi wedges, and the like.

—All kinds of cheeses, cubed or cut with small cookie cutters, may be served with crackers served in basket with print napkin, or on toothpicks, with an olive slice attached. Or serve cheese balls. See index for recipes.

—Finger gelatin.

—Fruit pizza.

—Caramel apples or frozen bananas.
—Party mix of cereal and nuts.
—Popcorn in many flavors, both sweet or salty.
—Petite cherry cheesecakes. (See index for recipe).
—Monkey bread, or pluckit bread or sweet rolls.
—All kinds of cookies and candies including homemade mints.
—Ice cream served in many ways and with many toppings, including crushed fruits; or homemade popsicles, or ice cream sandwiches. (See ideas for flavored ice creams in tip section on page 191.)

PARTY FOODS RECIPES

APPETIZERS

Marinated Broccoli

3 large heads broccoli	Break into flowerets. (Do not use stems. save these for another dish.)
1 cup cider vinegar	Combine thoroughly, and pour over broccoli.
1 tbsp. sugar	Refrigerate 6 hours, stirring once or twice.
1 tbsp. dill weed*	Drain before serving.
1 tbsp. MSG	
1 tsp. salt	
1 tsp. black pepper	
1 tsp. garlic salt	
1½ cups vegetable oil	

(*Recipe uses dill weed, not dill seed! May add cherry tomatoes or part cauliflower.)

Yield: 20 servings   *Doris Trumbo*

Party Chicken Wings

Remove tips from chicken wings and discard. Cut main portion of wing in two pieces at joint, making two little mini-drumsticks. Press in coating mix (recipe on page 365), and bake 1 hour at 325 degrees. Or fry until browned on each side, dip in barbecue sauce (recipe on page 364), and bake 2 hours at 300 degrees, or 1 hour at 325.

Chicken Nuggets

3 or 4 large chicken breasts	Remove skin, debone, and cut into small chunks.
½ cup buttermilk **1 tsp. lemon juice**	Combine and spoon over chicken. Put in refrigerator for 3 or 4 hours to marinate.
¾ cup flour **1 tsp. baking powder** **½ tsp. salt** **1 tsp. garlic salt** **1 tsp. celery salt** **1 tsp. black pepper**	Mix thoroughly. Lift chicken pieces from milk mixture allowing excess to drain off. Coat with flour mixture.

Fry in deep fat (365 degrees) for about 5 minutes until golden brown. Fry about 6 or 8 chunks at a time. Serve as main dish, snacks, or appetizers. (May also be fried in fat in skillet, but results are not quite as good.)

Cheese Fondue

½ tsp. dry mustard **¼ tsp. paprika** **dash cayenne pepper**	Mix.
⅔ cup cream **2 tsp. Worcestershire sauce**	Stir in. Heat over low heat until hot.
1 lb. processed sharp American **cheese, grated**	Add, stirring constantly until melted. Keep warm to serve.

Use to coat:

toast	ham cubes
crackers	turkey breast cubes
broccoli	chicken breast cubes
cauliflower	bacon (fried crisp)

Barbecued Franks

1 lb. skinless frankfurters (8 to 10)	Cut each into 6 equal portions. Place in cold skillet. Heat and fry until lightly browned, stirring frequently.
¾ cup bottled barbecue sauce **1 tbsp. prepared mustard** **1 tsp. sugar** **dash Tabasco sauce**	Combine thoroughly, and pour over franks in skillet. Stir and heat until well coated.

Serve with toothpicks.

Yield: 48 to 60 pieces

Ham Ball Appetizers

1 egg, slightly beaten 2 tbsp. milk ¼ tsp. MSG (optional) ½ cup fine dry bread crumbs 3 cups ham—run through the food grinder (about 1 lb.)	Combine thoroughly. Shape into l-inch balls.
2 tbsp. vegetable oil	Heat in skillet and fry balls until browned. Remove from skillet.
1 cup pineapple juice 2 tbsp. cornstarch 2 tbsp. vinegar 2 tbsp. sugar 2 tbsp. soy sauce 1 beef bouillon cube	Combine thoroughly and stir into drippings in skillet. Cook, stirring constantly until thickened. Return meatballs to mixture in skillet and simmer 5 minutes until thoroughly heated.

Serve in chafing dish over warmer with toothpicks.

Yield: 4 or 5 dozen balls

Ham Puffs

Make 1 recipe cream puff dough (recipe on page 215) omitting the saccharin. Drop dough by rounded teaspoonfuls onto greased baking sheet. Bake at 375 degrees 20 to 25 minutes until golden brown and beads of moisture disappear. Cool away from draft. Make filling as follows:

2 cups chopped or ground-up ham, or 3 (4½-oz.) cans deviled ham ⅓ cup commercial sour cream 2 or 3 tsp. horseradish (optional), or 1 tsp. prepared mustard ¼ tsp. MSG (optional) ¼ tsp. black pepper ¾ tsp. onion salt	Mix together thoroughly. Cut cooled puffs and fill with slightly rounded teaspoonful of ham mixture.

Yield: 5 or 6 dozen puffs

Surprise Hamburger Muffin Cups

¾ lb. hamburger ¼ cup chopped onion	Sauté in skillet. Drain.
⅓ cup barbecue sauce 1 tbsp. brown sugar	Add.
1 can refrigerator biscuits (10)	Place each biscuit into a muffin cup and press over bottom and up sides forming a cup. Spoon meat mixture into each.
¾ cup shredded cheddar cheese	Sprinkle over the tops. Bake at 350 degrees for 12 to 15 minutes.

Yield: 10 cups

Hot Dog Treats

Cut hot dogs into 3 pieces. Wrap in biscuit dough. May add grated cheese to biscuit dough, or slit hot dog pieces and put small amount of cheese inside. Bake 10 to 14 minutes until lightly browned. (Best to use cheddar cheese rather than a soft cheese which would melt too much.)

Meatballs Deluxe

1½ lbs. ground beef 1 cup dry oatmeal 1 (4-oz.) can water chestnuts, drained and chopped 1 egg, beaten ½ cup milk 1 tbsp. soy sauce ½ tsp. chili powder 1 tbsp. MSG (optional) ½ tsp. salt ½ tsp. onion powder ¼ tsp. garlic powder	Mix together thoroughly. Form into small balls.
1 tbsp. margarine	Heat in skillet and fry balls until browned. Drain.

Sauce:

1 cup crushed pineapple, undrained ¾ cup brown sugar 2 tbsp. cornstarch 1 beef bouillon cube ¼ cup vinegar (see next page)	Combine in saucepan. Cook until thickened, stirring constantly. Pour over meatballs in skillet and simmer, covered, for 25 minutes.

¼ cup chopped green pepper
1½ cups water
2 tbsp. soy sauce

. . . .

Serve with toothpicks. (Balls may be made larger and served as main course anytime.)

Yield: about 75 small party balls   *Ruth Heatwole*

. . . .

Mushroom Rolls

½ to ¾ lb. fresh mushrooms, finely chopped 3 tbsp. butter	Sauté until lightly browned.
3 tbsp. flour	Blend in.
1 cup light cream or rich milk	Slowly add, stirring constantly until thickened.
1 tsp. lemon juice 1 tsp. Worcestershire sauce 2 tsp. minced chives ½ tsp. salt ¼ tsp. MSG (optional)	Add. Cool filling slightly before spreading on bread.
1 loaf white bread	Trim off crusts. Roll each slice lightly with rolling pin to flatten slightly. Spread with filling. Roll up and pinch ends.

Wrap in plastic wrap and freeze. When ready to serve, defrost and cut into little pinwheels, or simply cut in half and toast in 375-degree oven until lightly browned. Serve warm.

. . . .

Stuffed Mushrooms

Wipe mushrooms clean. Remove stem. Fill with stuffing of softened cream cheese mixed with dry onion soup mix to taste. Heat under broiler just until bubbly.

. . . .

Elegant Party Loaf

Cut 1 loaf of homemade bread into 4 slices horizontally. Crusts may be trimmed off if desired. (I prefer leaving crusts on.) Spread with butter. Place 1 slice on serving plate and spread with chicken salad. Top with second slice and spread with egg salad. Top with third slice and spread with ham salad. Cover with fourth slice. Soften an 8-oz. pkg. of cream cheese and beat in 2 tbsp. milk until smooth. Frost top and sides of loaf with cream cheese. Garnish with a hard-cooked egg sliced to make a flowerette. Add celery leaves or parsley for leaves. Slice to serve.

Chicken Salad:

1 cup chopped cooked chicken	Mix together thoroughly. (Chicken, celery, and
¼ cup mayonnaise	pickle may be run through food grinder, instead
¼ cup finely diced celery	of chopping.)
1 sweet pickle, finely chopped	
½ tsp. salt	
1 tbsp. cream	

Egg Salad:

3 or 4 chopped hard-cooked eggs	Mix together thoroughly.
¼ cup mayonnaise	
½ tsp. salt	
½ tbsp. chopped parsley (optional)	
2 tsp. vinegar	
1 tsp. sugar	
1 tbsp. cream	

Ham Salad:

1 cup chopped ham	Mix together thoroughly.
¼ cup mayonnaise	
¼ tsp. dry mustard	
¼ cup finely diced celery	
1 sweet pickle, finely chopped	
¼ tsp. MSG (optional)	
¼ tsp. salt	
1 tbsp. cream	

Yield: 12 to 16 slices

Pizza Snacks

saltine crackers	Spread crackers with cheese spread. Add a dab
your favorite cheese spread	of chili sauce, and a slice of frankfurter. Bake in
chili sauce	350-degree oven for 5 to 10 minutes until
frankfurters or Vienna sausages, sliced in rings	bubbly, or heat in the microwave.

Sausage Bites

Cut Vienna sausages in half. Pull apart canned refrigerator biscuits in half and roll around sausages, pressing ends firmly. Fry in deep fat (375 degrees) until golden brown. Drain on paper towel and dip in catsup or mustard.

. . . .

Sausage Cheese Balls

1 lb. sausage—hot or mild (raw) **1 cup grated sharp cheese** **3 cups Bisquick** **1 med. onion, finely chopped** **½ cup water**	Mix together thoroughly and shape into small balls. Place on ungreased baking sheet and bake at 350 degrees for 15 to 20 minutes. Drain on paper towel to absorb grease. Serve hot.

. . . .

These balls may be frozen and reheated. Allow to thaw at room temperature before reheating.

Yield: approximately 50

. . . .

Saucy Sausage Squares

4 (8-oz.) containers refrigerated crescent rolls, or make your own biscuit dough and roll out to ¼-inch thickness to fit pans	Line bottom of two 9 × 13 pans with dough from 2 pkgs. of rolls.

. . . .

1 lb. mild sausage **1 lb. hot sausage**	Sauté in skillet. Drain well.

. . . .

3 eggs, lightly beaten	Mix with sausage and spread over dough in pans.

. . . .

2 cups Swiss or cheddar cheese, grated **½ tsp. garlic powder** **2 tsp. minced or dry parsley** **1 tsp. salt** **black pepper to taste**	Sprinkle over sausage. Cover with dough from 2 remaining pkgs. of rolls.

. . . .

another egg, lightly beaten	Brush over top of dough.

. . . .

Bake in 350-degree oven for 30 to 35 minutes. Cut into little squares. Serve warm or at room temperature. May be frozen and reheated if desired.

Yield: 48 or more

. . . .

Spinach Balls

1 (20-oz.) bag frozen spinach	Cook until tender, 5 to 10 minutes. Drain *well* and squeeze to remove moisture.
3 cups herb-seasoned stuffing mix 1 finely chopped onion ¾ cup melted margarine 6 eggs, beaten ½ cup grated Parmesan cheese 1 tsp. black pepper 1½ tsp. garlic salt ½ tsp. thyme	Add, mixing well. Shape into little balls the size of a walnut. Place on lightly greased baking sheet. Bake at 350 degrees for 12 to 15 minutes.

To freeze, place on tray and freeze until firm. Then store in plastic bags. To serve, thaw slightly, and bake at 325 degrees for 20 to 25 minutes.

Yield: 6 to 7 dozen balls

Toast Cups

Remove crusts from thin-sliced sandwich bread. Spread both sides of bread lightly with butter. Press in muffin cups. Toast in 350-degree oven until lightly browned. Fill with any kind of sandwich filling.

Turkey Muffin Cups

¼ cup finely chopped celery ¼ cup chopped onion 3 tbsp. chopped green pepper 1 tbsp. margarine	Sauté in skillet until tender.
2 cups chopped cooked turkey 2 tbsp. mayonnaise ½ tsp. salt ¼ tsp. MSG (optional) ½ cup chopped almonds (optional)	Add, mixing thoroughly.
1 can refrigerator biscuits (10)	Place each biscuit in a greased muffin cup. Press to cover bottom and sides. Spoon turkey mixture evenly into cups.
⅔ cup shredded cheddar cheese	Sprinkle over tops.

Bake at 350 degrees for 15 to 20 minutes until biscuits are lightly browned.

Yield: 10 cups

Party Vegetable Bowl

Mix together a large bowl of broccoli and cauliflower flowerets, sliced raw mushrooms, green pepper slices, and sliced onion (if desired). Pour 1 (8-oz.) bottle Italian dressing over all and marinate overnight. Add black olives and cherry tomatoes to serve. Place cocktail picks beside bowl.

Carolyn Reed

. . . .

DIPS

Bacon and Cottage Cheese Dip

2 cups cottage cheese 2 tbsp. milk 3 tbsp. mayonnaise 1 tsp. lemon juice 1 tsp. onion salt ¼ tsp. garlic powder	Combine and process in blender until smooth.

. . . .

8 slices bacon, fried and crumbled	Stir in. Cover and chill.

. . . .

Delicious with vegetables or chips.

. . . .

California Dip

2 cups (16-oz.) commercial sour cream 1 env. Lipton onion soup mix	Stir together in bowl.

. . . .

Delicious plain, or add other seasonings as desired: crumbled bleu cheese, bacon bits, or finely diced ham.

. . . .

Cheese Dip

2 (8-oz.) pkgs. cream cheese,
    softened
1 (12-oz.) bottle chili sauce (such as
    Heinz)
dried minced garlic to taste
	Beat all ingredients together until smooth.

. . . .

Dip with potato chips or vegetables.

. . . .

Cottage Cheese Dip (Low Cal.)
(Also delicious as a topping for baked potatoes)

2 cups lowfat cottage cheese ½ tsp. lemon juice ¼ tsp. onion powder ¼ tsp. garlic powder	Process in blender until smooth.

Variations: May add ½ pkg. onion soup mix instead of powders. Or add dry parsley or chives, paprika, or Tabasco sauce, if desired. Serve with chips or raw vegetables.

Curry Dip

2 cups mayonnaise ½ cup commercial sour cream 2 to 3 tsp. curry powder 4 tsp. sugar 2 tsp. lemon juice ½ tsp. salt ½ tsp. garlic powder ¼ tsp. tumeric	Mix together until smooth.

Excellent dip for raw vegetables.

Carolyn Shank

Deviled Ham Dip

1 (4½-oz.) can deviled ham 1 cup commercial sour cream 1 tsp. prepared mustard 1 tbsp. finely minced onion ½ tsp. celery salt	Stir together thoroughly. Cover and chill.

Serve with raw vegetables.

Deviled Ham and Cheese Dip

2 cups cottage cheese or 8 oz. cream cheese, softened 1 or 2 tbsp. horseradish 2 tbsp. mayonnaise 1 tbsp. grated onion ¼ tsp. salt ¼ tsp. MSG (optional)	Combine in blender and process until smooth.

1 (4½-oz.) can deviled ham	Stir in. Chill.

Fresh Fruit Dip

8 oz. cream cheese, softened
1 (7-oz.) jar marshmallow creme
1 tbsp. orange juice (optional)
1 tsp. grated orange rind (optional)

Beat together until blended.

Serve with fresh fruit.

Mary Ethel Lahman Heatwole
Carolyn H. Reed

Onion Dip

1 cup mayonnaise or salad dressing
1 cup commercial sour cream
½ cup finely chopped green onion,
    or 1 tbsp. dry minced onion
1½ tsp. Worcestershire sauce
¼ tsp. MSG (optional)
⅛ tsp. garlic powder

Mix together thoroughly. Chill.

Serve with potato chips or vegetables.

Peanut Butter Fruit Dip

1 cup marshmallow creme
¼ cup orange juice

Beat together until fluffy.

½ cup peanut butter
¼ cup mayonnaise or salad
    dressing
1 tsp. lemon juice

Blend together, then fold in.

Delicious served with apple wedges, banana chunks, etc.

Jewel Shenk

Vegetable Dip

1 (8-oz.) can Jerusalem artichokes,
    or 1 (8-oz.) can water chestnuts,
    chopped
1 cup mayonnaise
1 cup commercial sour cream
1 (10-oz.) pkg. frozen spinach,
    drained
1 (1.4-oz.) pkg. dry vegetable soup
    mix (such as Knorrs)

Mix thoroughly. Serve with vegetables, or on crackers or toast cutouts.

Yield: 3 cups

Dorothy Logan
Tillie Yoder

SANDWICH SPREADS

(See recipes for other sandwich fillings which may also be used for party sandwiches, on pages 469 and 527.)

Chipped Beef Spread

2 (8-oz.) pkgs. cream cheese, softened
1 (2.5-oz.) pkg. chipped beef, or dried beef, finely chopped
1 (3-oz.) jar olives, chopped
¼ cup onions, finely chopped
3 to 4 tbsp. mayonnaise
1 tbsp. prepared horseradish

Mix together thoroughly. Chill overnight so flavors can soak into cheese.

Serve with crackers or small bread squares.

Pam Weaver

Cheese Spread

8 oz. cream cheese, softened
½ cup mayonnaise
1 (8-oz.) can crushed pineapple, drained
½ cup finely chopped nuts (optional)
several drops food coloring

Mix together thoroughly.

Serve on fancy crackers or in party sandwiches.

Yield: 1 ¾ cups

Blue Cheese Spread

8 oz. cottage cheese
2 oz. Danish blue cheese

Process in blender until smooth.

Yield: 1 ¼ cups

Pineapple Cheese Spread

8 oz. cottage cheese
½ cup well-drained crushed pineapple
2 tsp. sugar
¼ tsp. vanilla

Process in blender until smooth.

Yield: 1 ¼ cups

Cucumber Spread

8 oz. cream cheese, softened	Beat until creamy.
1 med. cucumber, finely chopped 1 small onion, finely chopped 2 drops hot pepper sauce dash of salt a little mayonnaise to mix	(Cucumber and onion may be chopped in blender.) Stir together with enough mayonnaise to make of desired spreading consistency.

Spread on thinly sliced bread.

Annie Weaver

Egg Salad Spread

4 hard-cooked eggs, chopped 3 tbsp. finely chopped celery 3 tbsp. finely chopped onion 2 tbsp. chopped pimiento ¼ cup mayonnaise ¼ tsp. salt 1 tsp. sugar	Mix together thoroughly.

Spread on rounds or triangles of bread. Garnish with olive slices. Bread may be toasted on one side if desired. Spread on untoasted side.

Ham Spread

3 tbsp. mayonnaise or salad dressing ½ tsp. prepared mustard	Combine.
1 cup ground cooked ham ½ cup shredded Swiss cheese	Mix in.

Trim crusts from 16 to 20 slices of raisin bread. Spread with softened butter or margarine. Spread half of slices with ham mixture. Top with remaining bread. Cut sandwiches into 3-inch fingers. Seal tightly with plastic wrap until served. Makes 24 to 30. Or spread on crackers or fancy bread cutouts as desired.

Mary Ethel Lahman Heatwole

Ribbon Sandwiches

Use 3 or 4 slices of bread, alternating dark and white bread.
1. Spread slices of bread with butter or cream cheese, and jam or salad spread. Press together, forming a stack of alternate dark and white slices.
2. Wrap in plastic wrap and refrigerate for an hour or more for easier handling.
3. Gently press down on stack and trim crusts from all 4 sides using a sharp knife and a sawing motion. Cut into slices ⅓ of an inch thick.
4. Each ribbon slice may be cut into thirds, halves, or triangles.

Tuna Spread

8 oz. cream cheese, softened **1 (6½-oz.) can tuna** **1 or 2 tbsp. finely chopped onion**	Mix together thoroughly.

....

Variation: Use chunk ham, such as Hormel, instead of tuna.

Evelyn Borntrager

. . . .

MISCELLANEOUS

Stuffed Celery Sticks

½ cup shredded Swiss cheese **½ cup finely chopped or ground- up** **ham** **⅓ cup mayonnaise or salad** **dressing** **½ tsp. prepared mustard**	Mix together thoroughly.

....

7 med. stems celery	Cut each in half. Dry centers and fill with about 1 tbsp. of filling each. Cover and chill 1 hour.

....

Yield: 14 appetizers

....

Cheese Filled Celery

1 cup creamed cottage cheese **⅓ cup crumbled blue cheese** **⅓ cup chopped walnuts** **½ tsp. Worcestershire sauce**	Mix together thoroughly.

....

8 stems celery	Chill and fill with mixture.

....

Cucumber Tidbits

2 med. cucumbers	Peel and cut into ¼ -inch slices.

....

1 (3-oz.) pkg. cream cheese, **softened** **⅛ tsp. salt** **½ tsp. sugar** **mayonnaise**	Mix together well with just enough mayonnaise to make a good spreading consistency. Spread on both sides of each cucumber slice.

....

¼ cup finely chopped parsley	Press sides of slices in parsley to coat. Arrange on serving plate. Cover with plastic wrap and chill at least 1 hour.

....

Party Carrots

Add finely grated carrot to cheese ball ingredients. Shape into little carrots. Slip parsley sprig in end of each carrot for the top.

Chocolate Fondue

1 cup light cream **1½ cups sugar** **4 (1-oz.) squares unsweetened** **chocolate** **¼ cup butter**	Heat in fondue pot on high, stirring constantly, until chocolate is melted. Reduce heat to medium and cook several minutes until thickened, stirring constantly.
1 tsp. vanilla	Add, turn heat to low just to keep warm for serving.

Delicious served with:

cherries	pineapple chunks
strawberries	little cake squares
banana chunks	lady fingers
apple slices	mini-doughnuts or doughnut holes
	nuts

Frosted Fruit

(Frost grapes or cherries for pretty party pleasers)

Wash and *dry* fruit. Add 2 tsp. cold water to 1 egg white and beat until frothy. Then let stand about 10 minutes. Dip each fruit in egg white, and let excess drip off. Put about 1 cup sugar in a shallow dish. Hold fruit over dish and (using a teaspoon), sprinkle fruit with sugar. Place on wire rack to dry. The fruit should dry until the sugar forms a candylike crust. Refrigerate until ready to serve.

Party Popcorn

(With the popular craving for many flavors of popcorn, this is sure to hit the spot with teenagers. Choose any flavor gelatin that strikes your fancy!)

3 or 4 qts. popped corn	Have ready.
⅓ cup butter	Melt in saucepan.
2 cups miniature marshmallows	Add, stirring constantly over low heat until melted. Pour over popped corn, stirring to mix well.
1 (3 oz.) pkg. flavored gelatin (your **choice of flavor)**	Sprinkle dry gelatin over corn mixture, stirring to coat evenly.

Party Strawberries

(Delicious and pretty!)

1 (3-oz.) pkg. strawberry-flavored gelatin (dry) 8 oz. cream cheese, softened 1 cup finely chopped coconut (put flaked coconut in the blender to chop fine) 1 cup finely chopped pecans	Mix together thoroughly. Refrigerate mixture for 2 or 3 hours. Roll into shape of strawberries,
red tinted sugar	Roll strawberries in sugar to coat.

Insert tea leaves for stems (plastic work best). These freeze well. Thaw slightly to serve.

Ruth Weaver

Stuffed Dates

Stuff pitted dates with whole almonds or walnut pieces. Or stuff with peanut butter or cream cheese. Roll in powdered sugar or in very fine shredded coconut.

Sugarcoated Pecans

1 egg white 1 tbsp. water	Whip together just until frothy.
1 lb. pecan halves	Dip pecans in mixture.
1 cup sugar ¾ tsp. salt ½ tsp. cinnamon, if desired	Combine, and then dip pecans in this mixture also. Place on greased baking sheet and bake at 250 degrees for 1 hour. Stir every 15 minutes.

Mae Shank

CHAPTER TWELVE

QUICK~FIX SECTION

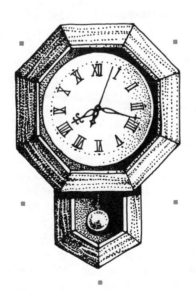

QUICK-FIX SECTION

This chapter is a deviation from traditional Mennonite-style cookery. Mennonites of the past have been known to make practically everything from scratch, not even considering the thought of buying food in tin cans unless there was a dire emergency! Mennonites, along with most others, however, are finding themselves caught in the dilemma of not having nearly enough time to do all the things they would like to do. In order to save time, they are also resorting to canned and packaged products much more often to speed up the cooking process.

Even though most of us would agree that the homemade is better and cheaper, sometimes we do have to consider which is more important at the moment—the time or the money. If you are working out on the job all day and need to hurry home in the evening and have a hearty meal ready for your family as quickly as possible, you probably need all the help you can get with quick-fix ideas. And some of the ideas given in this book for saving small things may take time that you positively do not have. So you need to evaluate your own situation. However, many persons tend to be wasteful. Often it takes little extra time to salvage many things people quickly dump out!

In writing this book, I checked with a number of young brides about some of their cooking problems. A major frustration seems to be, "How can I quickly fix a good supper when I get home from work?"

Since many more homemakers are also working away from home, this chapter is intended to give ideas to make it a pleasure rather than a headache to feed your family with a minimum amount of time. Although many quick-fix methods call for opening containers of prepared foods, this certainly does not always need to be the case.

One of the most important secrets for efficiency in this area is to plan ahead! It takes only a small amount of time to plan your menu for the evening meal. You can do it the evening before, when you are relaxed before going to bed. Take a package of hamburger (or whatever you decide on) out of the freezer and place in the refrigerator to thaw overnight and the next day. Or you can be haunted all day long in your spare moments on the job thinking, "What in the world am I going to have for supper tonight!" Then you can rush home, get a piece of bone-hard meat out of the freezer and attempt to thaw it in hot water (or in the microwave if you have one), while in your frustrated state you are trying to decide, "What can I ever come up with to serve with it!" You may even quickly start something only to discover that you do not have all the ingredients on hand to complete it. How much easier it is to plan ahead and save in many ways.

Meat and many other foods taste better when thawed slowly. You also take advantage of the frozen item releasing its cold in the refrigerator where it is utilized rather than in the kitchen which you may be heating in cold weather. If you have a large roast or other large item, you may want to thaw it overnight in the sink if the weather isn't too warm. It may take several days to thaw in the refrigerator, but this is a safer method as far as any potential spoilage is concerned. If thawing in the sink, it helps to place the frozen food in a heavy paper bag to prevent the exterior part from getting too warm until center is thawed.

Some cooks have found menu cards to be the perfect solution to a very busy schedule. Large menu cards can be made out for a whole week of basic meals suited to your family's tastes and needs. It is easier at one sitting to fit together foods that complement each other, and to include the variety you would like for the week. You will notice if you haven't included that liver or fish or whatever else is needed that may be forgotten with haphazard planning.

Enough cards may be made to last for a month or two and placed in a file. Each week you can choose a card of menus for the week and make a grocery list accordingly. The grocery list may even be included for the week on the menu card. This system may take extra effort to get started, but it will save an unbelievable amount of time and effort in the weeks to come! Some highly organized persons prefer to plan two weeks, or even a month ahead, making only one major shopping trip for the month. A few perishable things, such as milk, may be picked up as you have need for them.

Menu cards can be used over again each month with whatever slight changes you may wish to make. A lot of variety can be added with specific menu items during the various weeks, such as using tomato soup instead of mushroom soup in the green bean casserole on page 557 for an entirely different taste change. Or the quick stroganoff on page 570 may be served over rice one week, and over toast or pancakes, or in crepes, another week. Creamed chicken may be served over noodles, rice, or corn bread. Salads may be varied extensively with the seasons and what is available. You will probably think up many other ideas as you go along.

A tremendous amount of time and energy can be saved by occasionally setting aside a bake day. While the ingredients and utensils are all out, the oven is hot, and the kitchen is a mess, make the most of it! You can reuse many of the same utensils without washing them between batches. While one item is baking, you can be mixing something else to have ready when the other is done. This saves reheating the oven. I seldom make a single recipe for cookies, and often double recipes for casseroles, cakes, breads, rolls, and other baked goods. It takes such little extra time to measure twice the ingredients, and often two items can be baked together with the same heat. The savings in time, oven heat, and dishwashing with this method is considerable.

(Caution: Do not overcrowd things in the oven for best results. Cakes especially need plenty of room for a good flow of air around the pans. If your oven is small, you will need to take this into consideration.)

To alleviate the problem of tying up containers in the freezer, line bake dishes or pans with foil before baking. Freeze, and then turn out of container and place foil containing food in a plastic bag and return to freezer. To use, peel off foil and return contents to original container to thaw and heat.

Two friends of mine who are busy schoolteachers tell me they reserve one Saturday a month to cook and bake the whole day. They then divide the food into desired portions and freeze it. Each evening before they retire, they remove from the freezer whatever they choose for the following evening meal and place it in the refrigerator. They often add a salad or raw fruit or something else to go with it, but they seldom spend more than 10 or 15 minutes in the evening to have a delicious meal all completed. They feel this works great for their situation!

Recipes can also be doubled or tripled for homemade soups, stews, chili, and other long-cooking items. The extra can be frozen for a quick meal later on. It takes almost no more time to sauté two pounds of hamburger at once than it does to do one pound alone. Bake at least double the amount of chicken you need for a meal. Debone the extra and freeze it for use in the many casseroles and other dishes that call for cooked diced chicken. Baked chicken is much more flavorful than boiled chicken, and you can do enough for several meals with the same oven heat.

You can also cook a large pot of dry beans with almost the same amount of heat as a small pan and have the extra for several different recipes containing beans. Whenever you find the time to prepare mashed potatoes, make at least a double batch and use the extra for potato cakes or a casserole in a day or two. Potatoes can also be cooked and then grated to make into potato cakes. Freeze in layers between plastic wrap so you can remove just what you need for breakfast or any meal. Fry in margarine in a skillet until browned on both sides.

Use your imagination for make-ahead items that will freeze well and thaw quickly, especially if you are cooking only for two or prefer individualized portions of a variety of foods. Bake individual meat loaves in muffin tins. Freeze, then place in plastic bags and return to the freezer so you can easily remove one or all.

Make individual pies in small foil-lined pans. Freeze, then remove foil-lined pie from pan so you will have the pan to use. Store in plastic bags in freezer. Thaw and reheat to serve. Leftovers can be utilized in this way also. Instead of dumping out leftovers, freeze serving-size portions in small plastic bags. When you accumulate enough for a meal, each person can choose their preference from the assortment for delicious homemade "TV dinners."

Double recipes for crumbs or toppings or other partial ingredients for recipes that you make often. If you serve something like apple crisp fairly often, double the recipe for the crumb topping and place half of it in the freezer. It takes almost no more time to mix up a double batch than a single one. The next time you wish to serve it, all you need to do is open up a can of pie filling, sprinkle the crumbs from the freezer over it (they hardly even need thawing), and bake while you are getting the remainder of the meal on the table. This dish can be microwaved for ten minutes. Serve warm with ice cream for a dessert guests will enjoy. The list of possibilities could go on, so watch for similar ideas, depending on the recipes your family enjoys.

Another time-saver is to have ready-mixes on hand which can be whipped up in short order. These can be prepared on your day off and can save a lot of time in measuring small amounts of ingredients at the last minute. Some of these are included in this chapter and others may be located in other chapters through the index. The Ready Hamburger Mix, Spaghetti Seasoning Mix, Sloppy Joe Mix, biscuit mix, and cake mix are examples.

The **Crockpot** and your oven timer are two helpful devices when you are away for the day. Many casseroles and meats can be put in the Crockpot on low for a full 8 hours or slightly longer. One of my sisters uses this method for cooking chicken for recipes calling for cooked chicken. She places a whole chicken or chicken parts in the Crockpot, adds water to about ¾ cover, and lets it cook all day while she is at work. In the evening, a pot of succulent chicken and broth is ready for use in many different ways.

Usually recipes that take about 60 minutes to cook or bake can be cooked in the Crockpot on high in about 4 hours or on low for approximately 8 hours. Recipes taking a couple of hours in the oven, will take approximately 6 to 8 hours on high, or 12 to 14 hours on low. For meats it is better to turn the Crockpot on high until the meat is cooking and then turn it on low for the remainder of the time. If you have a large quantity of food in at once, it will probably take the high setting to keep it cooking. Use less liquid on food cooked in the Crockpot, since little liquid is cooked away with the low temperature. In fact, it seems to generate some of its own liquid.

Some busy cooks have found they can put frozen meat in the oven in the morning and set the timer. It will thaw during the early part of the day and then the timer will turn the heat on to bake it the last few hours before mealtime. This would take some discretion since a large roast probably would not thaw entirely in a closed oven, and in hot weather a small amount of meat may become too warm until baking time. A smaller roast would probably work well. Some potatoes could be scrubbed and placed in a separate casserole dish to bake beside it.

This method works well with a frozen casserole which thaws slowly. In fact, you may find with a large casserole that you can remove it from the freezer and place it in the refrigerator overnight to begin thawing. Then place it in the oven the next morning with the timer set to come on about one-half hour before mealtime. You will need to keep in mind that there are many variables to consider with casseroles and how long they take to thaw and bake. The density of the food is significant and also how thick the contents are in the dish. A small deep dish filled to the top will take much longer to bake than a large flat dish with the same amount of food spread out and maybe only half full. Food keeps better in the freezer in a more consolidated form, however, so probably a compromise between the two extremes is best.

Make-ahead refrigerator casseroles can also give you a break in the evening when you come home tired and would like to sit down and prop your feet up a little while instead of preparing supper. The make-ahead chicken casserole on page 281 (which can also be made with dried beef or ham) and the egg soufflé on page 260, made with ham, sausage, or bacon, are examples. Prepare casseroles in the morning and refrigerate them during the day. Simply pop them in the oven when you get home. Then sit down and rest your weary bones while supper is baking!

Keep an emergency shelf stocked with a few basics for that unexpected company which is sure to pop in sooner or later. Have a few menus in mind for these quick-fix meals and always keep enough ingredients on hand for one or more of them. When you use these supplies for one reason or another, replace them immediately so you aren't caught with a feeling of exasperation about what to serve.

Storing foods so you can quickly find what you are looking for saves a tremendous amount of time. Keep shelves organized, always putting the oldest in the front so stock is kept fresh. A friend showed me how she organized her refrigerator and freezer to save her lots of time. She labeled the ends of shoe-size boxes to fit her needs. She puts all supplies for packing lunches (meats, spreads, etc.) in one box, items for soup in another, and condiments and jellies for table setting in another, so all she needs to do is pull out a box and everything is at hand. It only takes one trip also to return it to the refrigerator or freezer. You won't believe what a nifty idea this is until you try it! Use categories to fit your needs. Boxes may be lined with plastic shelf paper so they can be easily kept clean.

It is also important to keep a good shopping list so that you are not stranded without an ingredient needed in the middle of food preparation. A quick trip to the grocery store wastes time and gas! While you are preparing meals or baking and notice an item is running low, write it on your list immediately so you won't forget. This can save much unnecessary frustration.

Don't let those extra few winks of sleep which you are tempted to feel you need in the morning spoil your day! Just 15 or 20 minutes of preparation time in the morning before you leave for the day can make a world of difference in the evening when you are tired and less organized. You will probably be much less tired by bedtime with considerably less stress than if you had gotten the extra sleep. You may even be able to go to bed 20 minutes earlier!

Good management and planning ahead can make an unbelievable difference on your schedule as well as on your morale and peace of mind. You can look forward to mealtime, rather than being plagued by it—and just think of all the time you have saved in the process!

And here is one last little secret which a friend told me to be sure to include, and which I have tried several times myself. Even though we may usually do a good job of planning ahead, we all need the liberty to goof off once in a while. This is for one of those days that is sure to come along occasionally. You are so engrossed in some project that you are totally unaware of the time. All of a sudden you realize it is mealtime, the family is about to appear, and not one thing is prepared! Your first impulse is to quickly get the leftovers on the stove so they will be heating while you set the table. (This is really the sensible way—but sometimes we have to use our ingenuity and do otherwise!) Instead, quickly grab the plates and silverware out of the cupboard and have the table at least partly set before anyone appears. You won't believe what a calming effect the presence of those few dishes will have on raving appetites! It will only take about one minute longer than the other way, and everyone remains happy!

TIPS FOR QUICK-FIXES

•Instead of rolling out biscuits and cutting them with a biscuit cutter, make drop biscuits by simply adding additional liquid to the ingredients. Add approximately ⅓ more liquid than the amount for regular biscuits. Then drop the dough from a spoon onto a greased baking sheet as for cookies. If you prefer the cut-out biscuits, roll out the dough and cut it with a knife into squares or triangles instead of with a biscuit cutter.

•Make quick doughnuts by poking a hole in the middle of canned refrigerator biscuits. Fry in hot fat and dust with powdered sugar. Best eaten while still warm.

•A short-cut method for making doughnuts is to roll out the dough to ½-inch thickness. Then cut into strips ¾ inch wide by 3 inches long. Place strips on greased baking sheets. Brush tops with vegetable oil. Let rise until double and fry in deep fat. Roll in powdered sugar. This saves a lot of cutting time, plus the extra time it takes to handle the doughnut holes.

•When cutting a loaf of bread into cubes for dressing or croutons, lay a stack of at least 6 slices on the cutting board. Use an electric knife to quickly cut down through the whole stack in rows in both directions making cubes of desired size. If bread is about half frozen, a sharp bread knife will work just as well.

•A vegetable peeler (often called potato peeler) not only speeds up the process of peeling many vegetables, but does a quick job with fruits such as apples and pears as well.

•When chopping long-stemmed foods such as celery and rhubarb, use the cutting board. Hold a large stack of stems together with one hand and with the knife in the other, cut down through the whole stack at once. Some cooks use this method for stringless green beans also. If beans have strings, they should be broken, however, so that any remaining strings may be discovered and removed.

•Cucumbers and some other vegetables are more attractive in salads with the peeling left on. The peeling also contains vitamins that are often wasted. New potatoes can be shredded and fried, or prepared other ways, with the peeling left on. Apples left unpeeled are more attractive in an apple salad.

•For a quick coating of meats for frying, put flour mixture in a paper or plastic bag. Put in several pieces at a time and shake until coated. Doughnuts may also be coated this way with powdered sugar.

•Add a can of cream of mushroom soup thinned with half a soup can of water to roasts, steaks, chops, or meatballs before cooking. Beside enhancing the flavor, the meat is surrounded with ready-made gravy to put on the table just as soon as cooking time is completed.

•To save the time it takes to make white sauce, use a 10-oz. can of creamed soup for casseroles or vegetables when time is limited.

•To shorten baking time on casseroles, quickly heat the milk or other liquid in the recipe on top of the stove while you assemble the remaining ingredients. Casserole will then already be hot when placed in the oven and baking time is considerably less. This works especially well for dressing, scalloped potatoes, and the like.

•For a good quick pot of noodle soup for the entire family, add 1 envelope of chicken noodle soup (such as Lipton) to 4 to 6 oz. of fine-cut noodles and cook together for approximately 12 minutes. The flavor in the soup mix will enhance the whole pot of soup. A little chopped chicken or broth, or a chicken bouillon cube, may also be added if desired.

•If your family likes to sprinkle sugar and cinnamon on food such as toast or applesauce, keep a mixture of it in a salt-shaker and place on the table with other condiments.

•Dust cakes with powdered sugar instead of frosting them. If you prefer frosting, a sheet cake can be frosted much more quickly than a layer cake. A broiled topping is also excellent for a quick finish on sheet cakes. Make bar cookies instead of drop or rolled cookies to save time.

•An extra long cord or a cordless telephone is almost an indispensable item for the kitchen area. It is amazing what you can accomplish while talking on the telephone! Peel the potatoes ahead for dinner, shell the peas or any other chore that can be done ahead when you receive a lengthy call. If I'm planning to make pudding or other items that need a long amount of stirring time on the stove, I save calls that aren't urgent and make them during that time. If your telephone isn't in the kitchen area, place projects near the phone that you can work at, such as shelling pecans or sewing on missing buttons, while you are chatting on the phone.

•And one other thing that I feel saves an incredible amount of time is to follow the old adage, "A place for everything and everything in its place." Then whenever you need something, you can locate it immediately. A tremendous amount of time can be wasted frantically searching through piles of clutter or unorganized cupboards to find something you need at a moment's notice. Besides saving much time and frustration, a tidy, organized household is a real morale booster to most any homemaker!

QUICK-FIX RECIPES

(Check microwave section for other quick-fix recipes)

BEVERAGES AND BREADS

Floats

Put 1 or 2 scoops vanilla ice cream in tall glass. Fill with ginger ale or root beer, or other soda.

Easy Lemonade

1 cup bottled lemon juice
  (reconstituted)
1 cup sugar
4 whole-grain saccharin, dissolved
  in a little water

Mix with enough water and ice to make 1 gal.

Quick Orange Refresher

¾ cup orange breakfast drink
  powder
⅓ cup bottled lemon juice
1½ cups sugar
⅛ tsp. salt

Mix with enough water and ice to make 1 gal.

Summer Refreshers (Low Cal.)

Pour equal amounts of grape juice and club soda over ice in tall glasses. Or mix chilled apple juice half and half with 7-Up.

. . . .

Parmesan Biscuits

1 (8-oz.) container refrigerator buttermilk biscuits **1½ tbsp. butter or margarine, melted**	Separate biscuits. Brush tops and sides of each biscuit with the butter.
¼ cup grated Parmesan cheese **¼ tsp. garlic salt** **¼ tsp. onion salt** **1 tsp. dried parsley flakes**	Combine. Dip buttered sides of biscuits into mixture. Place in pan and bake at 375 degrees for 10 to 12 minutes.

Yield: 10 biscuits

. . . .

Cheese-Bacon Crescent Rolls

½ cup shredded cheddar cheese **3 slices bacon, browned and crumbled** **1 tbsp. bacon drippings**	Combine.
1 can refrigerator crescent dinner rolls (8 rolls)	Unroll dough. Spread each triangle with cheese mixture. Roll up as directed on package. Place on greased baking pan.
1 tbsp. milk **caraway or sesame seeds**	Spread over top with milk and sprinkle with seeds.

Bake at 375 degrees for 10 to 12 minutes. Serve warm.

Yield: 8 rolls

. . . .

Quick Monkey Bread

3 cans (10 each) refrigerator biscuits	Cut each biscuit into 4 pieces and place in bowl.
½ cup butter, melted	Pour over biscuits, tossing to coat.
1 cup brown sugar **1 tbsp. ground cinnamon** **½ cup chopped nuts**	Combine and sprinkle over pieces, gently mixing just until coated. Pour in greased bundt pan.

Bake at 350 degrees for 25 to 30 minutes. Cool 5 minutes, then invert on plate.

. . . .

Quicky Sticky Buns

2 (1 lb.) loaves frozen bread dough, thawed*	Pull or cut into small balls, about the size of a large walnut. Place in a layer in a greased 9 × 13 pan.

½ cup melted margarine **1 large (5-oz.) box regular butterscotch pudding (not instant)** **1 cup brown sugar** **2 tbsp. milk** **1 tsp. ground cinnamon (optional)** **¾ cup chopped nuts (optional)**	Mix together thoroughly. Pour evenly over dough balls, and let rise until double.

Bake at 350 degrees for 15 to 20 minutes until done. (*You may use 32 frozen dough balls in place of loaves. For overnight rising, place frozen balls in greased pan, and pour pudding mixture over them. Lay a piece of foil over pan to keep in enough cold so they don't rise too much until morning. Leave on countertop overnight. Depending on the temperature of the kitchen, they will probably be just right to bake for breakfast. If not doubled in bulk, let rise until double before baking.)

Susan Offerdahl

Upside-Down Caramel Rolls

2 tbsp. melted butter	Brush in 12 large muffin cups or an 8 × 12 baking pan.

½ cup caramel sundae sauce **¼ cup light corn syrup**	Combine and spoon evenly in pan.

⅔ cup chopped walnuts	Sprinkle over syrup in pan.

2 containers refrigerated dinner butterflake rolls (6 large or 12 small rolls each can)	Place 2 small or 1 large roll in syrup in each cup or in pan.

Bake at 375 degrees for 12 minutes. Let stand 2 minutes. Then invert on plate. Serve warm.

Yield: 12 rolls

Toasted Onion Sticks (with Onion Butter)

Mix together ½ lb. butter or margarine and 1 env. dry onion soup mix to make onion butter. Spread generously on slices of bread and cut each slice into 4 or 5 strips. Place on baking sheet and bake at 375 degrees for approximately 10 minutes or until golden brown. (Onion butter may be refrigerated and used later. It is delicious on baked potatoes and on toast.)

Spicy Flowerettes

1 can (10) refrigerator biscuits	Cut through each biscuit from outside edge ¾ of the way to center 5 times. (This forms 5 petals.)
3 tbsp. butter or margarine, melted **⅓ cup sugar** **½ tsp. cinnamon** **¼ tsp nutmeg**	Dip each biscuit in butter, then in sugar-spice mixture. Place on ungreased cookie sheet.
10 maraschino cherry halves, **drained**	Garnish with cherry halves in center of each biscuit.

Bake at 350 degrees for 12 to 14 minutes until golden brown. Serve warm.

Yield: 10 flowerettes

Melt-in-Your-Mouth Pancakes or Waffles

1 egg, beaten **½ cup vegetable oil** **1 cup club soda**	Combine.
2 cups Bisquick	Add, stirring only until moistened.

Fry in waffle iron for waffles, or on griddle for pancakes.

Yield: approximately 12

Quick-Mix Yeast Rolls

1 pkg. dry yeast **¾ cup warm water** **2 tsp. sugar**	Stir together until dissolved. Let sit until foamy.
2½ cups Bisquick	Add, stirring vigorously.

Turn dough out on floured surface and knead until smooth, approximately 20 times. Shape as desired into crescents, or rolls, etc. Place on greased baking sheet. Cover with damp cloth. Let rise until double, about 1 hour. Bake at 375 degrees for 12 to 15 minutes. Brush with butter while hot.

Yield: 16 rolls

Quick Apple Butter

9 cups applesauce **4½ cups sugar** **½ cup vinegar** **½ cup red hot cinnamon candies** **1 tsp. ground cinnamon**	Combine all ingredients in saucepan. Heat to boiling, and cook 20 minutes, stirring constantly. (If not as thick as desired, add a little cornstarch or Clearjel dissolved in water to thicken.)

Yield: 6 pts.

MAIN COURSE

Breakfast Pizza

1 (8-oz.) container crescent rolls	Spread dough in greased 9 × 13 pan.
½ lb. hot sausage **½ cup chopped onion**	Sauté in skillet. Drain and sprinkle over dough.
1 cup shredded cheddar cheese **2 tbsp. green pepper, minced**	Sprinkle over sausage.
4 eggs, lightly beaten **½ tsp. salt** **½ tsp. oregano** **⅛ tsp. black pepper** **¾ cup milk**	Combine until well blended. Pour over mixture in pan.
1 cup shredded mozzarella cheese	Sprinkle over top.

Bake at 350 degrees for 25 minutes.

Yield: 6 servings

Quick and Easy Baked Beans

4 strips bacon, diced **1 small chopped onion**	Sauté together until half cooked. Drain.
2 (16-oz.) cans pork and beans **3 tbsp. sorghum molasses** **⅓ cup catsup** **1 tsp. prepared mustard** **a few drops liquid smoke (optional)**	Mix together with bacon mixture. Pour in 1½-qt. casserole dish. Cover and bake at 350 degrees for 45 minutes.

Yield: 6 servings

Hearty Pork and Beans Casserole

1 (28-oz.) can pork and beans
4 or 5 hot dogs sliced in rings

Heat in saucepan. Then pour in greased 2-qt. casserole dish.

. . . .

1 (8 or 10-oz.) pkg. corn bread mix

Mix according to pkg. directions and pour over the top.

. . . .

Bake at 350 degrees 25 to 30 minutes until corn bread is done.

Yield: 6 servings   *Elizabeth Yoder*

. . . .

Baked Green Beans

1 qt. canned green beans, drained
1 (2.5-oz) can French-fried onion
** rings (reserve half)**

Combine with half of rings and pour into greased 2-qt. casserole dish.

. . . .

seasoned salt (such as Lawry's)

Sprinkle over beans.

. . . .

1 (10-oz.) can cream of mushroom
** soup**

Combine and pour over top.

. . . .

¼ cup milk

. . . .

Bake at 350 degrees for 20 minutes. Sprinkle reserved onion rings over top of casserole and bake 15 minutes more.

Variations: Browned hamburger may be added for a heartier dish. Or use tomato soup instead of mushroom soup.

Yield: 4 to 6 servings   *Elizabeth Yoder*

. . . .

Dilly Green Beans (Low Cal.)

1 lb. fresh green beans, cut
1 beef bouillon cube
½ tsp. dill seed
½ tsp. dill weed
½ cup water or less

Cook together until beans are tender crisp, 12 to 15 minutes. (It is best to cook all water off, just until beans are cooked dry.)

. . . .

Yield: 3 to 4 servings   *Dorothy Rowe*

. . . .

Stir-Fried Bean Sprouts

(See page 488 for directions for sprouting beans.)

2 tbsp. oil	Heat in wok or skillet until very hot.
1 lb. bean sprouts **2 green onions, cut in 1½-inch lengths** **1½ tsp. salt** **dash soy sauce**	Add, and stir-fry approximately 3 minutes.

Serve with rice. (Cook 1 cup rice.)

Yield: 4 servings   *More-with-Less Cookbook*

Beef-Macaroni Skillet

1 lb. ground beef **1 med. onion, chopped**	Sauté in skillet. Drain.
3 cups tomato juice **1 tbsp. Worcestershire sauce** **1 tbsp. vinegar** **1 tbsp. brown sugar** **1 tsp. salt** **⅛ tsp. black pepper** **1 tsp. dry mustard** **1 cup uncooked macaroni**	Add. Cover and cook until macaroni is tender, about 20 minutes, stirring occasionally.
⅔ cup grated cheese	Sprinkle over top just before serving.

Yield: 6 servings   *Marj Heatwole*

Busy Day Casserole

1 lb. ground beef **1 med. onion, chopped**	Sauté in skillet. Drain.
1 (10-oz.) can cream of mushroom soup **1 (10-oz.) can vegetable soup** **1 (5-oz.) can chow mein noodles (reserve ⅓)**	Combine with ⅔ of noodles and meat mixture and pour in 2-qt. casserole dish.

Bake at 350 degrees for 25 minutes. Sprinkle remaining ⅓ of noodles over top of casserole and bake an additional 10 minutes. (May be mixed ahead or frozen.)

Yield: 6 servings   *Katherine Nauman*

Beef and Vegetable Lunch (Low Cal.)

½ lb. ground beef
1 onion, chopped
½ cup green pepper, chopped

Sauté in non-stick skillet to save calories. Drain.

3 cups shredded cabbage (approx.
    ½ head)
2 cups canned tomatoes
1 (4-oz.) can mushrooms, drained

Add. Cover and simmer until tender, about 15 to 20 minutes, stirring occasionally.

seasoning to taste—salt, chili
    powder, or Worcestershire
    sauce, a dash of sugar and MSG

Stir in.

1 tbsp. grated Parmesan cheese

Sprinkle over top.

Yield: 2 to 3 servings

Skillet Cabbage

1 tbsp. vegetable oil

Pour in skillet.

3 cups finely shredded cabbage
1 cup finely chopped celery
1 small green pepper, chopped
1 small onion, chopped
½ tsp. salt
dash black pepper
½ cup chipped ham or crumbled
    sausage (optional)

Add. Cover, and cook 7 to 10 minutes until of desired tenderness, stirring occasionally. May add 2 tbsp. water if needed. Serve immediately.

Variation: For flavor change, add 2 tsp. soy sauce.

Yield: 4 servings   *Nancy Heatwole*

Super Chicken Breasts (Low Cal.)

Marinate skinless, boneless chicken breasts in oil-free Italian dressing for 1 to 2 hours. Cook on grill or broil in oven for 5 to 10 minutes on each side. Serve immediately.
Carolyn Reed

Fried Chicken Breasts

(Fast, easy, and delicious!)

If breasts are large, slice into thirds, leaving one edge intact with first cut and opposite edge intact with second cut, making one long thin piece. If breast is small, make only one cut to double the size, rather than to triple it. Open piece out flat. Coat with beaten egg and salted fine bread crumbs. Squeeze a little lemon juice over the top. Fry in a small amount of fat in a skillet until browned on each side. **Variation:** Instead of cutting, breasts may be pounded out flat with a steak hammer.

Janet Blosser

Chicken-etti

(Use small amount of water for cooking spaghetti so most of water is cooked away until spaghetti is tender—approximately 1 ¼ cups.)

4 oz. spaghetti **¼ cup chopped onion** **2 tbsp. chopped green pepper**	Cook until tender, about 12 minutes.

1 chicken bouillon cube dissolved in
  ½ cup hot water or ½ cup broth
1 (10-oz.) can cream of mushroom
  soup
2 cups diced cooked chicken
¼ tsp. salt
⅛ tsp. celery salt
⅛ tsp. black pepper
⅛ tsp MSG (optional)
	Add, and cook 1 minute.

1 cup grated American cheese	Add, and stir until melted.

Yield: 4 to 5 servings

Dorothy Slabaugh Grove

Impossible Chicken Pie

½ cup small-curd cottage cheese	Spread in greased 9″ deep-dish pie plate.
2 cups chopped cooked chicken 1 (6-oz.) can tomato paste 1 tsp. crushed oregano leaves ½ tsp. crushed basil leaves 1 cup shredded mozzarella cheese (reserve half)	Mix together with half of cheese and spread over cheese in plate.
1 cup milk 2 eggs ⅔ cup Bisquick 1 tsp. salt ¼ tsp. black pepper	Combine in blender container. Process 15 seconds, or beat 1 minute with beater. Pour over mixture in plate.

Bake at 350 degrees for about 30 minutes until knife inserted in center comes out clean. Remove from oven and sprinkle with reserved cheese. Let stand 5 minutes before serving.

Yield: 6 servings

Impossible Chicken and Broccoli Pie

1 (10-oz.) pkg. frozen chopped
    broccoli—thawed, rinsed, and
    drained well
1½ cups chopped cooked chicken
⅔ cup chopped onion
1½ cups shredded cheddar cheese
    (reserve half)
	Mix together with half of cheese in greased 10-inch pie plate.

1⅓ cups milk 3 eggs ¾ cup Bisquick ¾ tsp. salt ¼ tsp. black pepper	Combine in blender container. Process 15 seconds, or beat 1 minute with beater. Pour over mixture in plate.

Bake at 375 degrees for 25 to 35 minutes until knife inserted in center comes out clean. Top with reserved cheese and bake several minutes longer just until cheese melts. Cool 5 minutes.

Yield: 6 to 8 servings

Curried Chicken-Rice Skillet

¼ cup cooking oil	Heat in skillet.
3 whole chicken breasts, split (about 3 lbs.) ¾ tsp. salt	Add. Cook 7 minutes, turning once, until browned. Push chicken to one side of skillet.
½ cup chopped onion 1 garlic clove, minced 1 cup green pepper strips ¼ lb. fresh mushrooms, sliced	In other side of skillet, sauté about 5 minutes until tender.
2 (10-oz.) cans condensed chicken broth and water enough to make 3¼ cups 1½ cups uncooked rice 1 tsp. curry powder ¼ tsp. salt	Stir into vegetables. Rearrange chicken over the top. Cover, and simmer 15 minutes, stirring occasionally.
1 (6-oz.) pkg. frozen sugar peas (pods), thawed 1 med. tomato, sliced	Add. Cover and cook 2 minutes more. Serve immediately.

Yield: 6 servings

Wanda Good

Stir-Fried Chicken and Pineapple

1 large chicken breast	Skin, debone, and cut in cubes.
1 tbsp. cornstarch 1 tsp. salt 1 tsp. soy sauce ½ tsp. vinegar	Combine, and dredge over chicken. Let stand to marinate for 15 minutes.
choppped onions chopped celery sliced water chestnuts, drained sliced carrots sugar peas French-cut green beans	Stir-fry any vegetables to suit your family's taste and size—approx. 6 cups. Fry until tender. Remove from skillet and stir-fry chicken until no pink color remains—about 3 minutes. Then return vegetables to skillet with meat.
1 cup crushed pineapple, undrained	Pour over top of all, heating just until hot and bubbly throughout.

Serve over hot cooked rice. (Cook 2 cups rice)

Yield: 6 to 8 servings

Cheryl Heatwole

Chicken and Stuffing Special

1 (6-oz.) pkg. Chicken Flavor Stuffing Mix (reserve flavor packet)	Place crumbs from mix in 2-qt. casserole dish.
1 cup water **¼ cup margarine**	Combine in saucepan with reserved flavor packet and heat to boiling. Pour over crumbs in dish and mix well.
2 cups chopped cooked chicken	Mix in.
1 can cream of chicken soup **¼ cup milk**	Combine and mix in.
parsley to garnish	Sprinkle over top.

Bake at 350 degrees for 35 minutes.

Yield: 6 servings   *Ruby Petersheim*

Chicken and Vegetable Stir-Fry (Low Cal.)

2 lbs. chicken breasts	Skin, remove bones, and cut in cubes.
vegetable spray	Coat bottom of wok or skillet. Heat to 325 degrees, and add chicken.
1 tsp. paprika **½ tsp. salt** **¼ tsp. black pepper** **¼ tsp. MSG (optional)** **⅛ tsp. garlic powder**	Add, and stir-fry with chicken for 4 to 6 minutes.
1 large onion, chopped **1 green pepper, chopped** **½ cup celery, chopped** **½ cup carrots, sliced** **½ cup chicken broth or bouillon**	Add, cover and cook 1 ½ minutes.
2 large tomatoes, cut in chunks	Add, and cook 2 to 3 minutes more.
an additional ½ cup chicken broth or bouillon **2 tbsp. cornstarch** **3 tbsp. soy sauce**	Combine, and stir in. Heat just until thickened.

May be served over cooked rice. (Cook 1 ½ to 2 cups rice.)

Yield: 8 servings   *Mary Ann Heatwole*

Quick Chili con Carne

2 tbsp. vegetable oil 1 lb. ground beef 1 med. onion, chopped 1 med. green pepper, chopped 2 garlic cloves, minced	Sauté in skillet until slightly browned. Drain.

1 (16-oz.) can tomato sauce ¼ tsp. cayenne pepper 2 tsp. chili powder ¾ tsp. crushed oregano leaves 1 tsp. salt	Add. Cover and simmer 20 minutes, stirring occasionally. Add small amount of water if mixture becomes too thick.

2 (16-oz.) cans kidney beans, drained	Stir in. Heat several minutes more.

Yield: 6 servings

Dressing Balls

1 (11-oz.) bag dried bread croutons (unseasoned—10 cups)	Empty into bowl.

3 eggs 2¼ cups milk 1 tsp. poultry seasoning 1 tsp. salt ⅓ cup celery ¼ cup onion	Measure into blender container. Process until well blended. Pour over bread cubes. Soak 10 minutes. Then shape into 15 balls (⅓ cup each). Place in greased 8 × 12 dish and bake at 350 degrees for 18 minutes.

(For a nice main-course dish to take to a potluck meal, place sliced turkey in bake dish. Make gravy from turkey broth and pour over turkey to keep it moist. Bake dressing balls on tray. Immediately after baking, use pancake turner to transfer to dish. Place in a layer all over the turkey. Pop in oven a few minutes at destination to reheat.)

Yield: 7 to 8 servings   *Louise Heatwole*

Creamed Dried Beef

¼ cup margarine 1 med. onion, chopped ¼ lb. mushrooms, sliced (optional)	Sauté in skillet for 3 minutes.

¼ cup flour	Blend in until smooth.

1¾ cups milk	Slowly add, stirring constantly until thickened.

3 or 4 oz. dried beef, chopped   Stir in and simmer for 1 minute uncovered.
¼ tsp. MSG
¼ tsp. salt

Serve over hot toast, corn bread, or noodles.

Yield: 4 servings

Favorite Enchiladas Casserole

1 lb. hamburger   Sauté in skillet. Drain.
1 med. onion, chopped

1 (10-oz.) can enchiladas sauce   Add, mixing thoroughly. Pour in 2 qt. casserole
  (mild)   dish.
1 (16-oz.) can kidney beans, drained
2 cups frozen corn, thawed

½ cup grated cheddar cheese   Sprinkle over top.
1 cup crushed corn chips

Bake at 350 degrees for 40 to 45 minutes.

Yield: 6 servings

Green Bean Stroganoff

1 qt. canned green beans   Combine and heat to boiling.
1 cup chipped ham (optional)

1 (10-oz.) can cream of mushroom   Combine in small pan and heat to boiling but
  soup   do not cook. Drain beans and pour sauce over
¼ cup tomato catsup   them.
¼ tsp. salt
½ tsp. garlic salt
1 tsp. sugar
½ cup commercial sour cream

Yield: 4 to 6 servings

Ham and Potato Skillet

3 tbsp. oil or margarine	Spread in skillet.
3 cups shredded raw potatoes **½ cup chopped onions** **2 tbsp. chopped green pepper**	Add, and cook 20 minutes until tender, stirring occasionally.
1 cup cooked chopped ham **1 tsp. salt** **black pepper to taste**	Add, and cook 1 minute more.

Yield: 4 servings

Hamburger Pie

2 lbs. hamburger **1 cup chopped onion**	Sauté in skillet. Drain.
2 (10-oz.) cans tomato soup **2 tsp. salt** **½ tsp. black pepper** **½ tsp. celery seed**	Add. Heat until hot through. Pour into an 8-inch-square bake dish.
2 cups Bisquick	Measure into bowl.
1 egg, slightly beaten **1 cup milk** **3 tbsp. vegetable oil**	Combine, and stir in, just until mixed. Pour evenly over top of meat mixture in dish.

Bake at 375 degrees for 20 minutes.

Yield: 8 servings

Carolyn Reed

Hamburger Stroganoff

2 tbsp. corn oil **1 lb. hamburger (ground round)** **½ cup chopped onions**	Sauté in skillet until lightly browned. Drain.
8 oz. uncooked noodles (3 cups)	Layer over mixture.
3 cups tomato juice **½ cup water** **1 tsp. salt** **⅛ tsp. black pepper** **1 tsp. celery salt** **2 tbsp. Worcestershire sauce**	Mix together, then pour over noodles. Do not stir. Bring to a boil, turn heat to low, and simmer 30 minutes, or until noodles are tender.
½ cup sour cream	Stir in, and heat just to boiling again.

Yield: 6 servings

Kathryn Forrester

Super Hamburgers

Make hamburger patties seasoned as desired and fry until browned on both sides. Mix 1 (10-oz.) can cream of mushroom soup with half a soup can of milk. Pour over burgers, cover, and simmer 20 minutes. Makes a delicious gravy to serve over mashed potatoes.

Dorothy S. Grove

Hearty Supper Omelet

For a good quick supper (or breakfast) fry several cups shredded raw potatoes with chopped onion in margarine in skillet until tender, about 20 minutes. Add salt and pepper to taste. Beat 3 or 4 eggs and pour over potatoes. Fry over low heat until lightly browned underneath. Turn and fry other side. (Chopped ham, crumbled bacon, or grated cheese may be added if desired. Sprinkle over potatoes just before adding eggs. Cooked, leftover potatoes may be used instead of raw potatoes.)

Hot Dogs in a Blanket

Slit 10 hot dogs ¾ of the way through lengthwise. Place strips of cheese in slit. Unroll 1 can of 10 crescent refrigerator rolls, and starting at large end, wrap each hot dog in a roll. Place on baking sheet with tip underneath to hold it in place. Bake at 375 degrees until lightly browned, approximately 20 minutes.

Janet Heatwole

Quick Lasagna

1½ lbs. ground beef	Brown in skillet and drain.
2 (12-oz.) cans tomato sauce 1 env. onion soup mix 1 cup water	Add, and simmer 15 minutes.
8 oz. broad noodles, cooked 2 cups mozzarella cheese, shredded	Have ready.

Layer meat, noodles, and cheese in 2-qt. casserole dish ending with cheese on top. Bake at 400 degrees for 15 minutes until cheese is bubbly.

Yield: 6 to 8 servings

Pam Weaver

Luncheon Special

2 cups med. white sauce 2 cups canned green beans, drained 1 (12-oz.) can luncheon meat, diced 1 tbsp. chopped pimiento salt and pepper to taste 1 cup shredded cheddar cheese	Combine all ingredients in saucepan. Cook over low heat until cheese is melted and mixture is hot through. Serve over toast.

Quick Individual Pizzas

Place canned refrigerator biscuits on greased baking sheet. Flatten out the center of each biscuit with the bottom of a juice glass, leaving a little rim around outside edge of each. Place a spoonful of pizza sauce in center, and add meat and cheese on top as desired. Sliced hot dogs, or Vienna sausages, or browned hamburger or sausage may be added as desired.

. . . .

Creamy Rich Potatoes

8 servings instant mashed potatoes or 8 med. potatoes, cooked and mashed 8 oz. cream cheese 1 cup commercial sour cream ¼ tsp. garlic powder 2 tbsp. dried onion flakes	Mix together thoroughly and pour in greased 2-qt. casserole dish.
4 tbsp. melted butter	Pour over potatoes.
paprika	Sprinkle over top.

Bake at 350 degrees for 35 to 40 minutes. **Variation:** Omit sour cream and add 2 lightly beaten eggs.

Yield: 8 servings

Elizabeth Yoder

. . . .

Quick Baked Mashed Potatoes (or Potato Cakes)

Beat together leftover mashed potatoes, 1 egg, and grated yellow cheese as desired. May also add minced dried onion flakes and a little garlic powder, if desired. Place in greased casserole dish. Dot with butter and more cheese. Bake at 350 degrees for 45 minutes. Or shape into cakes, flour, and fry in skillet until browned on each side.

. . . .

Quick Scalloped Potatoes

¼ cup margarine	Melt in saucepan.
2 (10-oz.) cans cream of mushroom soup or chicken soup 8 oz. cream cheese, softened ⅔ cup milk	Add, blending well over low heat until warm.
½ tsp. salt ¼ tsp. black pepper 1 (32-oz.) pkg. frozen hash brown potatoes	Add, mixing well. Spoon into a 2½-qt casserole dish. Cover and bake at 350 degrees for 45 minutes.

1 cup shredded sharp cheddar cheese	Sprinkle over top. Bake, uncovered, 5 minutes more until cheese is melted.

Variation: Use 2 cups sour cream instead of cream cheese. Omit milk and use only 1 can of soup. Do not heat ingredients, but simply mix together and bake as directed.

Yield: 8 servings   *Carolyn H. Reed*

Quick Quiche

1 tbsp. margarine **1 small onion, chopped**	Sauté until tender. Sprinkle in greased deep-dish 9″ pie plate or 9″-square bake dish.
4 strips bacon, fried and crumbled **1 cup grated sharp cheese**	Sprinkle over onion.
1½ cups milk **3 eggs** **½ cup Bisquick** **½ tsp. salt** **½ tsp. dry mustard**	Combine in bowl or in blender container. Beat or process until well blended. Pour over mixture in dish.
1 (4-oz.) can sliced mushrooms, drained (optional)	Arrange over top.

Bake at 375 degrees for approximately 35 minutes or until knife inserted in center comes out clean. Let stand 5 minutes before cutting into wedges or squares. (For quicker quiche, use ¼ cup bacon bits and 2 tbsp. instant minced onion instead of bacon and onion. Melt the margarine and add to milk mixture.)

Yield: 6 servings

Quick Spam Dinner

2 tbsp. margarine **1 (12-oz.) can Spam, diced**	Sauté in skillet until hot through.
1 pt. cream-style corn (frozen— thawed, or canned) **6 eggs, beaten** **½ tsp. salt** **1 tsp. sugar**	Combine, then pour into mixture in skillet. Cook and stir gently with spatula or rubber scraper just until mixture is set. Serve immediately.

Yield: 6 servings

Quick Spinach Souffle

1 (18-oz.) pkg. frozen chopped spinach	Cook about 5 minutes and drain *well*.
½ cup commercial sour cream ½ tsp. salt pepper to taste	Mix in well. Pour in 1 ½-qt. bake dish.
¾ cup shredded cheese ¼ cup dry bread crumbs	Mix and sprinkle over the top.
2 tbsp. butter	Dot over top.

Place under broiler for approximately 2 minutes until top is bubbly and lightly browned.

Variation: Add 1 env. onion soup mix to spinach. May omit cheese and crumbs. Bake 20 minutes until hot instead of broiling.

Yield: 4 servings

Jewel Shenk

Quick Stroganoff

1 lb. hamburger 1 med. onion	Sauté in skillet. Drain.
1 (10-oz.) can cream of mushroom soup ½ tsp. Lowry's seasoned salt	Add, and heat to boiling. May add a little milk if desired.
½ cup commercial sour cream	Add, and heat just to the boiling point again. Do not cook.

Serve over rice, toast, pancakes, or in crepes. (Or use tuna instead of hamburger and serve over noodles.)

Yield: 4 to 6 servings

Elizabeth Yoder

Quick Tuna and Macaroni Dinner

1 (7-oz.) pkg. macaroni and cheese dinner (such as Kraft)	Cook according to pkg. directions.
1 (6½-oz.) can tuna 1 (10-oz.) pkg. peas	Add, and heat thoroughly.

May be served immediately, or bake at 375 degrees for 20 minutes.

Yield: 6 to 8 servings

Frances Justice

Quick Tuna Skillet

2 tbsp. chopped onion 1 tbsp. margarine	Sauté in skillet until tender.

1⅓ cups water
1½ cups minute rice
1 (10-oz.) can cream of mushroom
  soup
1 (6½-oz.) can tuna, drained and
  flaked
2 cups cooked or canned green
  beans drained
2 tbsp. chopped pimiento
	Stir in. Cover and simmer 5 minutes or until liquid is absorbed.

1 tsp. salt 1 tbsp. Worcestershire sauce ¼ tsp. MSG (optional)	Add.

Yield: 6 servings

Quick Tuna Supper

1 pt. peas, cooked and drained 1 (10-oz.) can cream of mushroom soup or chicken soup 1 (6½-oz.) can tuna	Combine in saucepan. Heat just until bubbly. Serve over toast or baked potato.

Variation: Melt a slice of cheese over toast or potato before adding tuna.

Yield: 4 to 5 servings

Evelyn Basinger
Carolyn Reed

Ten-Minute Tuna

8 oz. med..noodles (3 cups)	Cook and drain.
1 (10-oz.) can cream of celery soup ¾ cup milk 1 (6½-oz.) can tuna, drained and flaked 1 cup cooked peas 2 tbsp. diced pimiento	While noodles are cooking, combine in saucepan and heat to boiling.
salt and pepper to taste	Add, and serve over the cooked noodles.

May be garnished with lemon slices.

Jewel Shenk

Stove Top Meat Casserole

1 lb. hamburger (or use 2 cups chopped roast or other meat) 1 med. onion, chopped ¼ cup chopped green pepper	Sauté in skillet (if using hamburger), and drain.
2 cups canned tomatoes 1 cup water or more	Add, and heat to boiling.
¾ cup uncooked rice	Add, cover, and cook slowly about 20 min. or until rice is done.
1 tsp. chili powder 1 tsp. salt 1 tbsp. sugar pepper to taste	Stir in.
½ to 1 cup grated cheese	Sprinkle over top. Cover until melted. Serve.

Yield: 6 servings

Tuna Potato Patties

1 (6½-oz.) can tuna, drained and lightly flaked 1 tbsp. lemon juice	Toss lightly with fork.
4 servings instant mashed potatoes mixed according to pkg. directions, or 2 cups your own mashed potatoes (do not add salt to potatoes) 1 tsp. dried parsley flakes 1 tbsp. instant minced onion 1 egg, beaten 1 tsp. seasoned salt ¼ tsp. black pepper	Mix in. Shape into 8 patties.
¼ cup flour	Coat patties with flour.
3 tbsp. oil or shortening	Heat in skillet, and fry patties until brown on both sides.
1 (8-oz.) can tomato sauce with cheese	Heat and spoon over patties to serve.

Yield: 4 servings

Wanda Good

Turkey (or Chicken) Shortcake

1 (10-oz.) can cream of chicken soup **¼ cup milk**	Blend together.

....

1 cup leftover diced turkey (or **chicken)** **½ cup cooked peas** **1 tbsp. chopped pimiento** **salt to taste** **¼ tsp. MSG**	Add. Heat until bubbly, stirring often.

....

Serve over toast, corn bread, waffles, or hot biscuits.

Yield: 4 servings

....

Vegetables with Cheese Sauce

Cook 2 or more cups of vegetables (lima beans, brussel sprouts, a head of cauliflower or broccoli or cabbage) until tender. Add salt and a little black pepper if desired. Mix ¼ cup milk with 1 (10-oz.) can cheese soup and pour over vegetables. Heat until bubbly. (Or place cooked vegetables in cassserole dish. Pour soup and seasoning over the top. Bake at 350 degrees for 35 to 40 minutes until bubbly through. Top with French-fried onion rings, halfway through baking time.)

....

Vegetable Skillet Souffle

4 eggs, beaten **½ cup milk** **1 tbsp. instant minced onion (or** **sauté 1 small chopped onion in** **the butter called for)** **½ tsp. garlic salt** **¼ tsp. black pepper**	Combine.

....

1 cup cooked vegetables (chopped **broccoli, asparagus, or spinach)** **½ cup pitted ripe olives (opt.)** **½ cup grated cheese (reserve half)**	Stir in, including half of cheese.

....

1 tbsp. butter or margarine	Melt in 8-inch skillet. Pour in egg mixture. Top with reserved cheese.

....

Cover and cook over low heat for 15 minutes. Cut into wedges to serve.

Yield: 4 to 6 servings   *Jewel Shenk*

....

Vegetable Stir-Fry

Heat small amount of oil in wok or large skillet over medium-high heat. Add coarsely grated potatoes. Sauté briefly, then add sliced onion, zucchini, sugar peas (pods), tomatoes, carrots, cabbage, celery (most any vegetable combination you have on hand). When tender crisp, add 1 recipe of Spaghetti Seasoning or Chili Seasoning Mix. Or for a heartier dish, add 1 recipe Ready Hamburger Mix (recipes on pages 575 to 577) and any leftover pieces of meat you may have on hand. This makes a very quick one-dish meal that is delicious, and amounts can be adjusted to fit any number of servings needed.

Gloria Snider

. . . .

Vegetable Tomato Soup (Low Cal.)

1 (20-oz.) pkg. frozen mixed vegetables
may also add chopped onion, green pepper, or other vegetables, if desired
1½ to 2 cups water

Cook vegetables in water until tender—about 15 to 20 minutes.

. . . .

3 cups tomato juice, or V-8 juice
2 beef bouillon cubes dissolved in a little of the juice
salt and other seasoning to taste such as chili powder

Add, and heat to boiling again. (May thicken slightly with 2 tbsp. cornstarch dissolved in ¼ cup water, if desired.)

. . . .

Yield: 4 to 6 servings

. . . .

Zucchini Stir-Fry—Mexican-Style

¼ cup margarine or oil

Melt in skillet.

. . . .

4 cups thinly sliced zucchini, unpeeled
1 cup carrots, coarsely shredded
1 cup chopped onion
½ cup finely diced celery
⅓ cup chopped green pepper

Add. Cover and cook 4 to 5 minutes, stirring occasionally.

. . . .

2 med. tomatoes, cubed (optional)

Add.

. . . .

⅓ cup taco sauce (mild)
2 tsp. prepared mustard
½ tsp. garlic salt
¼ tsp. dried basil
dash black pepper

Combine and add. Cook 5 minutes more.

. . . .

salt to taste
1 cup shredded sharp cheese

Sprinkle over top. Cover just until cheese is melted. Then serve.

. . . .

Yield: 4 to 6 servings

Dorothy Shank Showalter

. . . .

Ten-Minute Zucchini Stir-Fry

Cut young zucchini in small cubes. Add chopped green pepper and sliced onions as desired. Stir-fry in small amount of oil in skillet until tender, approximately 10 minutes. Sprinkle with salt and serve.

Ruth Heatwole

MIXES

Chili Seasoning Mix

1 tbsp. flour
2 tbsp. instant minced onion
1½ tsp. chili powder
1 tsp. seasoned salt
½ tsp. crushed red pepper
½ tsp. instant minced garlic
½ tsp. sugar
½ tsp. ground cumin

Combine in a small bottle. Label. Cover tightly and store in cool dry place. Use within 6 months.

This mixture may also be added to hot popped corn.

Gloria Snider

Quick Chili, Using Mix

1 lb. hamburger

Brown in skillet and drain.

2 (16-oz.) cans or 4 cups cooked kidney beans
2 (16-oz.) cans or 1 qt. canned tomatoes
1 recipe of Chili Seasoning Mix

Add, and heat thoroughly.

Yield: 4 to 6 servings

Sloppy Joe Seasoning Mix

1 tbsp. instant minced onion
1 tsp. green pepper flakes
1 tsp. salt
1 tsp. cornstarch
½ tsp. instant minced garlic
¼ tsp. dry mustard
¼ tsp. celery seed
¼ tsp. chili powder

Combine in small seasoning bottle. Label. May be stored in cool dry place for 6 months.

Yield: about 3 tbsp.

Gloria Snider

Quick Sloppy Joes, Using Mix

1 lb. hamburger	Brown in skillet and drain.

1 cup tomato sauce **½ cup water** **1 recipe Sloppy Joe Seasoning Mix**	Add. Heat to boiling, then reduce heat and simmer 10 minutes, stirring occasionally. Serve in buns.

Yield: 6 buns

Ready Hamburger Mix

4 lbs. hamburger **1 large onion, chopped**	Sauté and drain.

2 tsp. salt **½ tsp. black pepper** **½ tsp. ground oregano** **½ tsp. chili powder** **¼ tsp. garlic salt**	Add. Cool. Spoon into pint freezer containers. Cover tightly and label. Use within 3 months.

Use in taco salad, as spaghetti sauce, for lasagna, chili, or vegetable stir-fry, or most any recipe calling for browned hamburger.

Yield: about 4 pts.   *Gloria Snider*

Spaghetti Seasoning Mix

1 tbsp. instant minced onion
1 tbsp. parsley flakes
1 tbsp. cornstarch
2 tsp. green pepper flakes
1½ tsp. salt
1 tsp. sugar
¾ tsp. Italian seasoning (oregano
   basil, rosemary, thyme, sage,
   marjoram)
¼ tsp. instant minced garlic
	Combine in small seasoning bottle. Label. May store in cool dry place for 6 months.

May use to make TV mix, vegetable stir-fry, spaghetti, lasagna, pizza sauce, etc.

Yield: ⅓ cup   *Gloria Snider*

Quick Spaghetti Sauce, Using Mix

1 lb. hamburger	Brown in skillet and drain.
1 (6-oz.) can tomato sauce **1 (6-oz.) can tomato paste** **2¾ cups tomato juice or water** **1 recipe Spaghetti Seasoning Mix**	Add, and simmer 30 minutes.

Serve with cooked spaghetti.

Yield: 4 to 6 servings

Taco Seasoning Mix

2 tsp. instant minced onion **1 tsp. salt** **1 tsp. chili powder** **½ tsp. cornstarch** **½ tsp. crushed dried red pepper** **½ tsp. instant minced garlic** **½ tsp. ground cumin** **¼ tsp. dried oregano**	Combine in small bottle. Label. May store in cool dry place for 6 months

Variation: When time is limited, simply mix 2 tsp. chili powder, and a little salt, red or black pepper, onion, and garlic powder.

Gloria Snider

Quick Taco Filling, Using Mix

1 lb. hamburger	Brown in skillet and drain.
½ cup water **1 recipe Taco Seasoning Mix**	Add, and simmer 10 minutes. Stir occasionally.

SALADS

Carrot Salad

3 cups shredded carrots **1 (20-oz.) can pineapple chunks,** **drained** **1 cup miniature marshmallows** **½ cup raisins** **½ cup finely chopped celery**	Toss together in bowl.
⅔ cup Miracle Whip salad dressing **2 tsp. sugar**	Combine, and add. Serve in lettuce-lined dish.

Yield: 6 to 8 servings

Quick Salad Dressing

(For potato salad or greens)

½ cup Miracle Whip salad dressing   Mix together thoroughly.
1 tsp. prepared mustard
1 tbsp. sugar

. . . .

Jeanne Heatwole

. . . .

Quick Fruit Salad

1 qt. canned peaches, diced   Drain any juice from fruit.
1 pt. frozen strawberries, *half*
    thawed
1 (20-oz.) can crushed pineapple or
    pineapple chunks
2 bananas, sliced

. . . .

1 (3½-oz.) pkg. instant vanilla   Add to fruit juice and beat slowly until
    pudding*   dissolved and beginning to thicken. Combine
2 tbsp. orange breakfast drink   with fruit and chill thoroughly.
    powder (optional)

. . . .

(*I prefer the Royal or Kroger brand pudding for fruit salad dressing. Some other brands of pudding give a milky appearance which is excellent for milk pudding, but is not very attractive in a fruit salad dressing.)
Optional Fruit Mixture: Mix 1 (16-oz.) can fruit cocktail, 1 (16-oz.) can pineapple tidbits, 2 sliced bananas, 2 cups miniature marshmallows, and ¼ cup flaked coconut.

. . . .

Quick Topping for Jell-O Fruit Salads

1 (3½-oz.) pkg. instant lemon   Mix according to pkg. directions. Chill 5
    pudding   minutes.
1 cup milk

. . . .

1 cup Cool Whip   Fold in. Spread over top of salad.

. . . .

If desired, maraschino cherry halves, grated cheese, or chopped nuts may be arranged over top to garnish.

. . . .

Quick Peach Salad

Place large lettuce leaves on individual salad plates. Top each with a peach half. Fill each cavity with a tbsp. of cottage cheese and top with a maraschino cherry half.

. . . .

Lazy-Day Salad

1 (20-oz.) can crushed pineapple
 (undrained)
1 (16-oz.) can fruit cocktail, drained
1 (16-oz.) can mandarin oranges,
 drained
1 pkg. instant vanilla pudding mix
 (dry)
9 oz. Cool Whip

Mix all ingredients together well and chill.

Yield: 6 to 8 servings   *Carolyn Shank*

Quick Pear Salad

Stuff pear halves with cream cheese mixed with a little pear juice. Place on lettuce leaf and sprinkle with chopped walnuts. Or mix a little milk and chopped green pepper with cheese instead of pear juice. Top with a little dab of salad dressing.

Pistachio (or Watergate) Salad

1 (3½-oz.) pkg. instant pistachio
 pudding (dry)
1 (20-oz.) can crushed pineapple,
 undrained

Mix together thoroughly. Chill 5 minutes.

1 (9-oz.) container Cool Whip
2 cups colored miniature
 marshmallows
½ cup flaked coconut (optional)

Fold in. Pour in pretty dish.

⅔ cup chopped nuts

Sprinkle over top.

Yield: 8 to 10 servings   *Mary Ann Heatwole*

Tuna Salad

1 (7-oz.) can tuna (packed in water)
3 tbsp. mayonnaise
2 tbsp. chopped zucchini relish
½ tsp. salt
pepper to taste

Mix together and serve on crackers or in a sandwich, or as desired.

Yield: 3 to 4 servings   *Pauline Carr*

DESSERTS
Skillet Baked Apples

(The variety of apples and how ripe they are make a considerable difference in the amount of cooking time needed. Do not cook until mushy, just until tender.)

1 cup water 3 tbsp. red hot cinnamon candies ¾ cup brown sugar	Heat in skillet until candies are mostly dissolved.
6 apples, pared and quartered	Add, cover, and simmer just until tender, approximately 3 to 8 minutes.
2½ tbsp. Clearjel or cornstarch dissolved in ¼ cup cold water	Add to apple mixture in skillet, stirring until thickened.
⅓ cup chopped pecans (optional)	Sprinkle over apples. Cool and chill.
whipped cream or topping	Garnish to serve.

Quick Apple Butter Rolls

Mix up biscuit dough from Bisquick. Roll out like pie dough. Spread generously with apple butter. Cut in rectangles. Fold in each side, lapping over in the middle. Place on greased baking sheet. Bake at 350 degrees for approximately 20 minutes until golden brown. Delicious served warm with milk.

Martha Heatwole

Banana Pudding Special

8 oz. cream cheese, softened ½ cup milk	Beat together until smooth.
1 (3½-oz.) pkg. instant vanilla pudding another 1¾ cups milk	Add, beating at low speed for 1 minute.
24 vanilla wafers 2 large bananas, sliced	Have ready.

Layer ⅓ of pudding mixture in bottom of pretty glass dish. Then layer half of wafers and bananas. Repeat layers, and add third layer of pudding on top. Sprinkle with several additional crushed wafers. Keep chilled until served.

Yield: 6 to 8 servings

Banana Pudding Supreme

2 cups graham cracker crumbs ⅓ cup melted margarine 3 tbsp. sugar ½ tsp. ground cinnamon	Mix thoroughly. Press in 9 × 13 dish.

1 (5½-oz.) pkg. instant banana pudding	Mix according to pkg. directions except use 2 ½ cups milk instead of the 3 called for. Spread over crumbs.
1 (20-oz.) can crushed pineapple, drained **2 or 3 bananas, sliced**	Layer over pudding.
3 cups Cool Whip	Layer over next.
maraschino cherries or coarsely chopped nuts to garnish	Arrange over top. Chill until served.

Yield: 8 to 10 servings

Busy-Day Lemon Cheesecake

2 cups graham cracker crumbs **3 tbsp. sugar** **¼ cup margarine, melted**	Mix, and reserve ½ cup crumbs. Press remaining crumbs in bottom of 8-inch square dish.
8 oz. cream cheese, softened **½ cup milk**	Beat together until smooth.
another 1½ cups milk **1 (3½-oz.) pkg. instant lemon pudding**	Add, beating slowly, just until well mixed— about 1 minute. Do not overbeat. Pour into crust.

Sprinkle reserved crumbs over the top. Chill at least 1 hour before serving.

Variation: Fold 2 cups Cool Whip, with ½ tsp. lemon flavoring added, into pudding mixture before pouring into crust. This makes a nice, light cheesecake.

Yield: 6 to 9 servings

Quick Cheesecake

graham crackers	Layer whole crackers in bottom of 9-inch square dish.
8 oz. cream cheese, softened **1 (15-oz.) can sweetened condensed milk** **⅓ cup lemon juice** **1 tsp. vanilla**	Process in blender until smooth. Pour over crackers and chill.
1 (21-oz.) can pie filling (cherry, blueberry, or strawberry)	Spread over mixture. Chill.

Yield: 6 servings   *Evelyn Borntrager*

Cherry Crisp

1 (21-oz.) can cherry pie filling, or 2 cups your own filling	Spread in greased 8-inch square bake dish.
1 cup water	Pour over cherries.
1 (8 oz.) white or yellow cake mix, or half of an 18 oz. mix	Sprinkle over next.
½ cup chopped nuts	Sprinkle over mix.
¼ cup margarine, melted	Pour over top.

Bake at 350 degrees approximately 15 minutes. Serve warm with milk or ice cream.

Yield: 6 servings   *Lillian Shickel*

Cranberry Crunch

| 2 (16-oz.) cans whole cranberry sauce | Spread in an 8-inch-square baking dish. |
| 1 cup quick oatmeal
½ cup flour
½ cup brown sugar
⅓ cup margarine | Mix together until crumbly. Spread over sauce. |

Bake at 350 degrees for approximately 15 minutes. Serve warm with vanilla ice cream.

Yield: 6 servings   *Bertha Shank*

Quick-Mix Pumpkin Dessert

1 (16-oz.) can pumpkin ½ cup milk 1 (3½-oz.) pkg. instant vanilla pudding (dry) 1 tsp. ground cinnamon ¼ tsp. ground cloves ¼ tsp. nutmeg	Beat together slowly until well blended. Chill 5 minutes.
1 (9-oz.) container Cool Whip 3 cups miniature marshmallows	Fold in. Pour in 9 × 13 dish.
½ cup chopped nuts	Sprinkle over top. Chill several hours or overnight.

Yield: 12 servings

Fruit Pudding

2 (3½-oz.) pkgs. buttered pecan instant pudding **3 cups milk**	Beat together on low speed for 2 minutes. Chill 5 minutes.
1 (9-oz.) container Cool Whip	Fold in. Spread half of mixture in pretty glass dish.
1 (8-oz.) can crushed pineapple, well drained **2 bananas, sliced**	Layer over pudding. Then spread remaining pudding over top.

Garnish with graham cracker crumbs and maraschino cherries.

Yield: 8 to 10 servings

Fruit Cobbler

2 (21-oz.) cans pie filling (apple, cherry, or blueberry)	Pour into 2 ½-qt. casserole dish.
1 can (10) refrigerator biscuits	Cut biscuits into fourths and layer over top of fruit.
1 or 2 tbsp. sugar **cinnamon**	Sprinkle over top.

Bake at 350 degrees for 15 to 20 minutes, or until biscuits are lightly browned. Serve warm with milk.

Yield: 6 to 8 servings

Quick Pineapple Dessert

Top chilled canned pineapple slices with sherbet. Sprinkle generously with angel flake coconut.

Fresh Strawberries and Cream

2 cups sliced fresh strawberries **3 tbsp. sugar**	Mix. Let stand 10 minutes.
2 cups miniature marshmallows **1 cup commercial sour cream**	Combine thoroughly. Fold into strawberries. Refrigerate at least 1 hour before serving.

Very attractive served in dessert goblets, topped with a whole strawberry.

Yield: 6 servings

Strawberry Pudding Delight

1½ cups graham cracker crumbs **2 tbsp. sugar** **¼ cup melted margarine**	Mix. Sprinkle half of crumbs in bottom of glass dish. Reserve other half.
1 (3½-oz.) pkg. instant vanilla **pudding** **1½ cups milk**	Beat together at low speed for 2 minutes.
1½ cups sliced frozen strawberries, **half thawed and drained***	Blend into pudding, and pour over crumbs in dish. Sprinkle reserved crumbs over top.

This is also attractive served in dessert goblets. Sprinkle half of crumbs in bottom of 6 goblets and other half on top. (*May use fresh berries if desired. Slice and sprinkle ⅓ cup sugar over berries. Let stand 10 minutes. Then drain and fold into pudding.)

Yield: 6 servings

COOKIES, CAKES, AND PIES

Quick and Easy Brownies

1½ cups flour **2 cups sugar** **½ cup cocoa powder** **½ tsp. salt** **1 cup vegetable oil** **4 eggs** **2 tsp. vanilla** **½ cup chopped walnuts**	Measure all ingredients in mixing bowl in order listed. Beat at medium speed of electric mixer for 3 minutes. Pour into greased 9 × 13 pan and bake at 350 degrees for 30 minutes.

May be frosted with Quick Chocolate Frosting on page 141, if desired.

Grace Campbell

Quick Chocolate Cherry Upside-Down Cake

1 (21-oz.) can cherry pie filling	Spread in well-greased 9 × 13 pan.
18 oz. German chocolate cake mix	Mix according to pkg. directions. Pour batter over cherries.

Bake at 350 degrees for 30 to 35 minutes. Cool in pan 5 minutes, then turn out to finish cooling. Serve warm with whipped cream.

Quick-Mix Dump Cake

1 (16-oz.) can crushed pineapple undrained
1 (21-oz.) can cherry pie filling
1 (18-oz.) yellow or white cake mix (sprinkle on dry)
1 cup chopped nuts

Layer in a greased 9 × 13 bake dish in order listed.

. . . .

½ cup margarine, melted

Pour over top.

. . . .

Bake at 350 degrees for 40 to 50 minutes. Serve warm with vanilla ice cream or whipped cream.

Carolyn Reed

. . . .

Granola Bars

(A handy snack or breakfast bar)

2 eggs, beaten
2 cups brown sugar
1 cup oil
1 tsp. vanilla
1 tsp. salt
4 cups quick oatmeal

Mix together thoroughly.

. . . .

1 cup flaked coconut
1 cup raisins
¾ cup peanut butter
1 cup sunflower seeds
1 cup chopped dates
1 cup chocolate chips
½ cup chopped nuts

Add any 3 or 4, or all these ingredients. Mix well and press in ungreased 11 × 15 pan. Bake at 375 degrees for about 12 minutes. Do not overbake.

. . . .

Cool 5 minutes. Then cut into bars and remove from pan to finish cooling.

Dorothy S. Grove

. . . .

Easy Chocolate Chip Cookies

18 oz. white cake mix
½ cup oil
2 eggs
2 tbsp. warm water
¾ cup tiny chocolate chips

Beat together until blended. Drop from spoon onto greased baking sheet.

. . . .

Bake at 350 degrees for 10 to 12 minutes.

Yield: approximately 3 dozen

. . . .

Quick Cream Cheese Cookies

8 oz. cream cheese, softened
1 egg
½ tsp. vanilla
¼ cup margarine, softened

Cream together until smooth.

. . . .

18 oz. yellow or chocolate cake mix   Add, beating only until well mixed.

. . . .

Drop onto greased cookie sheet. Bake at 375 degrees for 8 to 10 minutes.

Yield: approximately 3 dozen

. . . .

Lemon Whippersnaps

18 oz. lemon cake mix
2 cups Cool Whip *
1 egg, beaten

Mix together. Drop from spoon into powdered sugar and roll to coat.

. . . .

Place on greased cookie sheet. Bake at 350 degrees approximately 10 minutes. Do not overbake. (*If using whipped topping that isn't quite as stiff, you may need to add ¼ cup or more flour so cookies hold their shape well.)

Yield: approximately 3 dozen   *Joyce Bowman*

. . . .

Rosie's Cookie Bars

2 tbsp. margarine   Melt in 8-inch-square pan.

. . . .

2 cups graham cracker crumbs
1 cup chocolate chips
½ cup angel flake coconut
½ cup chopped pecans

Sprinkle in layers in pan in order listed.

. . . .

1 (14-oz.) can sweetened
   condensed milk

Pour over all.

. . . .

Bake at 350 degrees for approximately 30 minutes. Cut into bars when cooled. (For drop cookies, stir all ingredients together until well mixed, and drop by spoon onto greased baking sheet. Bake at 350 degrees for 10 to 12 minutes.)

Yield 2 or 3 dozen   *Rosie Weaver*

. . . .

Instant Pie

Crumble graham crackers into dessert goblets. Pour prepared instant pudding over crumbs. Top with Cool Whip. Crushed fresh fruit may also be added on top of Cool Whip, or add prepared pie filling if desired.

. . . .

Dream Pie

9″ graham cracker pie crust	Have ready.
2 env. Dream Whip **1 cup cold milk** **1 tsp. vanilla**	Whip according to pkg. directions in large mixer bowl.
1¾ additional cups milk **2 (3½-oz.) pkgs. instant Jell-O** **pudding (any flavor desired)**	Blend in slowly. Then beat at highest speed for 2 minutes, scraping bowl occasionally. Pour into pie shell.

Chill at least 4 hours. Garnish as desired with chocolate curls, banana slices, chopped nuts, or other garnish to match flavor of filling.

Quick Peanut Butter Pie

9″ graham cracker pie crust	Have ready.
¾ cup powdered sugar **½ cup peanut butter**	Mix together until crumbly. Spread ⅔ crumbs in pie crust. Reserve ⅓.
1 (3½-oz.) pkg. instant vanilla **pudding**	Mix according to pkg. directions. Pour over crumbs. Chill.
Cool Whip	Top each piece with Cool Whip and sprinkle with reserved crumbs to serve.

Quick Pumpkin Pie

9″ graham cracker pie crust	Have ready.
1 (3½-oz.) pkg. instant vanilla **pudding** **¼ tsp. salt** **1 tsp. ground cinnamon** **¼ tsp. cloves** **¼ tsp. nutmeg** **1 cup canned pumpkin** **⅔ cup milk**	Beat together at low speed for 2 minutes. Chill 5 minutes.
1 env. Dream Whip	Whip according to pkg. directions and fold into mixture. Pour into pie crust. Chill thoroughly.

May be topped with additional Dream Whip to serve. Or, top with chopped nuts, toasted coconut or ice cream.

Instant Strawberry Pie

9″ graham cracker or regular crust	Have ready.
1¼ cups sugar **⅓ cup Redisol or instant Clearjel**	Mix together *thoroughly*.
2 cups crushed strawberries (if not juicy, add a little water to make glaze of desired consistency)	Sift sugar mixture slowly into berries while stirring vigorously to avoid lumps (May use electric mixer if desired.)
2 cups whole strawberries, cut in half	Pour half of glaze mixture into crust, then add berries. Pour remaining glaze over top. Chill at least ½ hr.
Whipped cream to garnish	Pile on top.

Ella Ruth

Variation: if desired you may add ½ of a small pk. (1 tsp.) strawberry Kool-Aid to 1 cup water and add this to the 2 cups of crushed berries.

Vera Showalter

Instant Strawberry Ice Cream

(Place blender container in freezer until thoroughly chilled.)

½ cup whipping cream **2 eggs** **⅓ to ½ cup sugar**	Combine in chilled blender container. Process on high for several seconds.
3 cups whole frozen strawberries (Do not thaw berries—add right from the freezer.)	Drop in one at a time through center insert on lid while processing at high speed. Blend until smooth, stopping when necessary to scrap mixture down.

Spoon into dishes and serve immediately.

Yield: 4 servings

Hot Fudge Sauce

1 (14-oz.) can sweetened condensed milk **1½ (1-oz. squares) unsweetened chocolate** **¼ cup water**	Combine in saucepan. Stir over medium heat until boiling. Simmer several minutes until smooth and thickened, stirring constantly. Remove from heat.
1 tsp. vanilla	Add.

Delicious served on ice cream or cake.

Susan Offerdahl

CANNING, FREEZING, & PRESERVING

CANNING, FREEZING, AND PRESERVING

One of the many blessings of summertime is the abundance of fresh fruits and vegetables. Nothing quite replaces having your own garden just out the back door for top-quality fresh vegetables throughout the whole summer. Gardening is a wonderful way to exercise and have something to show for it at the same time!

After you have gone to a lot of effort to produce a garden full of food, it is important to know how to process it for winter usage. Even if you don't have a garden, many times prime quality food can be purchased in bulk from markets or farms during peak season to process for your own use. It doesn't take much experience to soon prove the difference in quality in fresh home frozen or canned versus the store-bought variety!

When I think back to the hundreds of jars of food my mother used to put up for the winter, I'm sure young cooks of today would think it was enough to open a country store!

She had a large copper boiler that held about 14 qts. at one time. It was oval-shaped and would fit over two burners on the stove at once.

One of our relatives owned a peach orchard. When the peaches were ripened just right, my parents would go to the orchard early in the morning and come back with at least 7 bushels of peaches to can that day! They would call my grandparents to come to help peel.

My job was to wash the peaches, then wash jars, and finally to pack peaches in the jars. My hand seemed to be smaller than anyone else's and would fit down into the jar. I was kept busy the whole day rotating from the one job to the other. I couldn't wait for the time to come when I would be "big enough" to be trusted with helping to peel the peaches. It was important to be able to peel almost razor thin, so you wouldn't waste any of the peach! By evening we would have well over 100 quarts of peaches. Mother made preserves out of any that were extra ripe.

When we had several bushels of beans to can at once, or at butchering time when there was a lot of meat to can, we would make a fire under the big iron kettle in the washhouse and use it for canning. My father had made a wooden rack to fit in the bottom of the kettle to set the jars on. It would hold about 25 quarts at one time. We would keep the water boiling for 3 or 4 hours, depending on what we were canning.

Once in a while I almost wish for that iron kettle again, even though the pressure canning of today has many advantages!

Canning

There are three basic methods for canning: (1) by steam processing in a pressure canner, (2) by boiling in a hot-water bath, or (3) by the open-kettle method.

The USDA (United States Department of Agriculture) now recommends that all low acid foods be pressure-canned to kill all harmful bacteria and enzymes. To kill the spores that cause botulism food poisoning, low acid foods need to be brought to a temperature of 240 degrees. This can be done only in a pressure cooker. Low acid foods include most vegetables and meats.

If you will be doing a lot of canning, you will certainly want to invest in a pressure canner. Even though they are expensive, they last for many years. Besides being a safer method for canning many foods, a pressure canner saves much processing time as well. For example, the savings in energy for processing green beans for 25 minutes in the pressure canner compared to boiling them for 3 hours in a hot water bath is significant, to say nothing about the extra heat in the kitchen on a hot summer day.

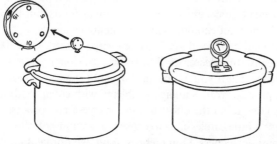

Pressure canners come with two different types of gauges. Some people prefer the *dial gauge* with a needle indicator that registers the amount of pressure. This takes close watching to maintain the correct amount of pressure since pressure can fluctuate to either extreme without hearing anything. The type with a *weighted gauge* which is set on the vent pipe allows excess steam to escape which causes a jiggling noise. If jiggling is persistent, pressure is above set level. If it is infrequent, the canner is not hot enough. The advantage of this type is that you can hear it function. Some people mind the noise. With excessive jiggling or escaping steam, you may have more problems with loss of liquid in jars. So there are advantages with either type. (I prefer the weighted gauge because of being able to hear it. However, I make extra effort to maintain consistent pressure without too much escaping steam to avoid loss of liquid in the jars.)

The **hot water bath or boiling water bath method** of canning is recommended for acid foods. By this method, jars are placed in a large canner or kettle with water enough to cover the jars. They are then processed by boiling. The USDA recommends this method for processing fruits, tomatoes, rhubarb, sauerkraut, and foods with vinegar added, such as pickles.

Since many people in the past did not have access to pressure canners, they canned most foods by the hot water method. This is the way most of our ancestors did for years, and they seemed to get by. It is important to be careful, however, and not take unnecessary risks.

Check jars carefully when opening them. Anything obviously not properly sealed or spoiled should be discarded immediately. If there is any question whatsoever about the contents, boil the food for 15 minutes before tasting it. The same precautions should be taken with commercially canned foods as well. If there is any bulging of the lid or metal can, spurting of liquid when opening, off color, or mold, food may be dangerous.

The **open kettle method** for canning is not recommended anymore except for jellies and some pickles. By this method food is cooked in an open kettle and placed boiling hot in sterilized jars. Clean jars may be sterilized by pouring some of the boiling liquid into the jar. Swish it around and pour back into the kettle to boil again. Do this several times until the jar is thoroughly heated and rinsed with boiling liquid. Then fill with boiling food. Place the lids on the hot jars immediately and tighten so they will seal without processing. (Jars may also be sterilized by boiling in water for 15 minutes, or place clean jars upside down in 250-degree oven for 20 minutes.) Many people have used the open kettle method in the past for tomato juice, grape juice, and similar foods, but the danger is that food cannot be heated hot enough to kill all potential bacteria.

It is unfortunate that food needs to be overprocessed to be 100 percent sure of its safety, because this decreases flavor and nutritional value. I have found in my own experience that if you are particular about the way you handle food and in the canning process, your spoilage problems with either method will be rare. After you have gone to all the effort to raise, harvest, and process food, you certainly don't want a little carelessness to cause it to spoil. Food should be processed at the prime point of ripeness. Don't let ripe food deteriorate until it fits into your schedule to process it if you want a good finished product! Food should be clean and free of any dirt whatsoever. Utensils used in the canning process should also be thoroughly cleaned. Cut out any bruised or spoiled spots in the food. Do not let half-processed food stand overnight in a warm place because you're too tired to finish it. These conditions invite bacteria to multiply, and require overprocessing to avoid spoilage.

Regular canning jars or mason jars are recommended for all canning. The glass is tempered to withstand the heat of pressure canning. Many people also use a good grade of mayonnaise and peanut butter jars for canning. I find these usually work well for hot water bath canning, but when used for pressure canning, they may burst with the high heat. Thin glass jars should not be used for either method. Always check jars before using making certain they have a good rim and threads for tightening, and that they are the correct size for a good seal. Especially check around the top rim of all jars for any cracks and chips which would prevent a good seal.

Jars should be washed in hot soapy water. They do not need to be sterilized when used for hot water bath or pressure canning. They will be sterilized along with the food during processing.

The most popular and easiest to use lids for canning are the two-piece lids with a metal screw band and a flat metal lid with a rubberlike sealing compound around the edge (Fig. 1). The metal bands may be used over many times until they become rusty or corroded, but the sealing lid should only be used once.

Cold Pack and Hot Pack. Most fruits and meats are cold packed. Vegetables can be hot or cold packed. Cold pack simply means to place food in the cans cold or raw. Hot pack means to blanch or cook food and place in the cans hot. Care should be taken in handling glass jars so they do not crack or break due to sudden temperature change. Do not pour boiling liquid into a cool jar. Temper jar first by slowly pouring a small amount of hot liquid into jar, swish it around, add a little more and swish again. Do not place hot jars on a cold or wet surface, or in a draft.

Prepare only one canner load of food at a time so partially processed food stands for the minimum amount of time possible. A canning funnel is a big help for filling jars of many kinds of food (Fig. 2). Don't fill jars too full. Approximately ½ to 1 inch of space should be left between rim of jar and food level. This is called **"headspace."** If jars are filled too full, food may spew out during processing and could prevent obtaining a proper seal because of food lodging on rim of jar. If too much space is left, the food may turn dark on top or the jar may not seal properly because of excessive air in the jar. Juices and hot packed foods usually need only ½ inch of headspace. Starchy vegetables such as corn, peas, and lima beans need slightly more than other vegetables, even if hot packed, because of swelling. Most other foods should have 1 inch if cold packed, and ½ inch if hot packed. (For most foods, I simply fill jars right up to the neck which is actually a scant inch.)

After filling jars, check for any air bubbles throughout jar. Carefully run a table knife or narrow spatula between food and jar if needed to allow any air bubbles to escape. A sharp knife could damage interior of jar (Fig. 3).

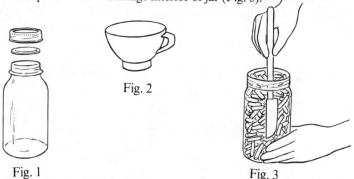

Fig. 2

Fig. 1   Fig. 3

Be sure to wipe rim of jars thoroughly after filling to remove any food on edge which would prevent a proper seal.

Place metal lids in very hot water for a few minutes before placing on jars. This softens rubber compound and helps to seat it tightly on the rim.

Tighten lids firmly with hands. Do not use jar wrench since air needs to escape during processing.

For **boiling water bath,** place jars on rack in canner. (If you only have a few jars, you can use a vegetable blancher or spaghetti cooker. It must have a rack in the bottom, however, to keep jars from touching bottom of cooker.) Add water to cover jars one or two inches over the top. It is best to add very hot water from faucet so food quickly reaches the boiling point. Slow cooking does not produce a top quality product. Do not begin to count processing time until water has come to a full rolling boil. Lower heat slightly, but *be certain water keeps boiling* gently and steadily the entire time. The longer the processing time, the less heat the canner will take, so temperature will need to be lowered several times during processing to prevent too rapid boiling which causes a lot of steam to escape. Jars should be removed from the boiling water as soon as processing time is completed.

For **pressure canning,** place jars on rack in cooker and add water to a depth of 2 or 3 inches depending on the length of processing time. Fasten cover in place but leave steam vent open allowing steam to escape for 7 to 10 minutes to drive all air from pressure cooker. This is necessary to avoid having air pressure as well as steam pressure which could give an incorrect pressure reading. Then close petcock or place gauge in place and bring pressure to the proper amount specified in canning directions which is 10 pounds for most foods (5 pounds for fruits only). Begin to count processing time when gauge reaches the correct amount of pressure. It is important to maintain a consistent pressure. To allow pressure to go too high could cause loss of liquid in jars or even breakage. Letting it go too low could prevent destroying bacteria and cause spoilage. The longer food cooks, the less heat it takes to maintain pressure, so heat will need to be lowered several times during processing.

As soon as processing time is up, remove cooker from heat and let stand until pressure is completely down. Do not try to hurry cooling process as this may cause loss of liquid in jars. Open petcock or remove gauge and if no steam escapes, remove lid. Lift edge of lid away from you first to prevent hot steam from escaping into your face or over your arms which could cause severe burns.

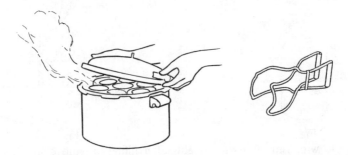

Use a can lifter to carefully remove hot jars from canner or pressure cooker. Do not allow a draft to blow over hot jars. Place jars on a towel or newspapers, not on a cold or wet surface. Allow air space around each jar. Do not tighten bands after processing. If liquid was lost in processing, do not open jars to add more. This would require reprocessing them. If sealed, food will keep, but top may become discolored.

Jars should seal while they cool. You can usually hear a snap or pinging sound as the vacuum seal is formed. Lids will be slightly concaved when sealed. To test the seal, lightly tap the lid with a spoon or your fingernail. A clear ringing sound indicates a seal unless food is touching the lid, in which case the sound will be dull, but not hollow or empty. Or press down on the center of the lid. If it is firm and does not move, the jar should be sealed.

Any unsealed jars will need to be reprocessed with new lids. Or you may wish to use the food immediately since overprocessed food is not as good. If you decide to reprocess it, check cans to make sure there are no nicks and check lids for any defective spots in sealing compound around the edge. Reprocess fruits for 15 minutes more if using boiling water bath method. Vegetables or meats need to be reprocessed the full amount of original time again.

After 10 hours, bands should be removed for reuse. If jars are stored without removing bands they may become corroded or rust on the jars and could be difficult to remove later.

Jars should be wiped clean before storing. If stored where it is slightly damp, any syrup or liquid residue left around top of jars may mold. (Wiping threads around top of jar with a cloth dipped in vinegar is especially effective in preventing mold.)

It is a good idea to mark the date on the lids of the jars before storing, so you can always use oldest food first. Canned food should maintain its excellent quality for at least a year, but gradually deteriorates with age in flavor, appearance, and quality. It may be stored at room temperature, but keeps best and longest if stored in a cool, dark, dry place, preferably between 45 and 60 degrees. Do not allow it to freeze since this could cause the seal or jars to break, and softens the texture of the food. Light increases oxidation and destroys certain vitamins. Jars may be placed in cardboard boxes, or covered with newspaper to protect from light if needed. If jars are stored where it is too damp, the metal lids may rust or corrode and this could eventually break the seal.

Freezing

Freezing is the simplest and quickest way to preserve foods. It keeps the fresh flavor, color, and nutritional value of food better than any other method.

The most common problem with freezers seems to be that we seldom have enough space for all the things we would like to put in them! Therefore, we usually need to decide what foods have the least undesirable canned taste or quality and save freezer space for those where the flavor and quality is significantly better when frozen. I usually can things like green beans, applesauce, and cherries, and save freezer space for strawberries, most other vegetables, and meats. If you have unlimited freezer space, most foods have better flavor preserved in the freezer.

There are advantages in having some things canned for quick opening in emergencies. I like to have some vegetable soup or stew, and some beef chunks, chicken, or bologna canned for quick heating when needed. It takes quite a bit of time to thaw and cook meat, and I find it advantageous to have a shelf stocked with at least a few extra items for those special times that always seem to come along!

Temperature in freezer should be kept at 0 degrees or slightly below. If there is a **power failure,** do not open freezer unless absolutely necessary since this allows a lot of the cold air to escape. A fully loaded freezer at 0 degrees will keep food frozen for a couple of days if unopened. A half-filled freezer may not stay frozen for more than one day. If power outage is prolonged, dry ice may be placed in the freezer to keep food frozen. If added promptly, 50 pounds of dry ice should keep a 20-foot freezer of frozen food below freezing for 3 or 4 days. If freezer is half loaded, it should last for 2 or 3 days. If food has partially thawed before discovering power outage, it may be refrozen if there are still ice crystals in the packages even though quality will not be as good. If food is still cold, but has totally thawed, it is best to use it. Or it may be refrozen after cooking. If food has been warm for any length of time, it should be discarded. If it has only been warm a short time, it may be cooked thoroughly and used.

Freezer should be defrosted regularly to avoid a frost buildup which hinders efficiency. Defrosting once a year usually works well, preferably in the spring before filling with summer produce. If you have a lot of changeover of food, it may need to be oftener—after ¼- to ½-inch frost buildup. This is a good chance to get it organized again. Sometimes it is surprising what you find in the bottom that you forgot was there!

Food should be packed tightly in airtight containers or packages to prevent **freezer burn.** Freezer burn occurs when dry air in freezer circulates over exposed surface of food, causing it to dry out and toughen. When packing food in plastic bags, press air out of unfilled portion of bag and fasten tightly so air can't get back in. It is good to double wrap packages and to double bag in plastic if plastic is thin, especially for items to be stored for a considerable length of time. Poorly packaged products do not keep nearly as well. When using rigid containers or boxes, allow approximately ½-inch headspace per pint for food packed dry and 1 inch for food packed in liquid. Food expands as it freezes and will push the lid off if filled too full.

Prepare small batches of food at a time, so processing can be completed before food stands long enough to deteriorate. Place containers in the freezer immediately as they are filled. Place in quick-freeze section or coldest part of freezer to freeze as rapidly as possible. Or place against the outside walls of the freezer.

Most fruits and meats are frozen raw, but may be frozen after cooking if desired. They do not keep as long in the freezer after cooking. Vegetables should be blanched before freezing to kill enzymes which could cause off color and flavor.

Foods are usually best thawed slowly in the refrigerator. Planning ahead makes it easy to simply place food in refrigerator either the night before for larger items, or a meal ahead for small packages.

Processing Fruits

Fruits should be ripe, but not bruised and mushy when processed. Hard green fruit will not have a good sweet flavor after processing. Sort through fruit and set aside any that is not ripe, allowing it to ripen before processing. Tree-ripened or vine-ripened fruit is much better flavored than fruit picked green and let stand to ripen. There is a big advantage in going directly to an orchard to purchase fruit rather than buying it at a grocery store. Orchards pick fruit to be shipped at a much greener stage so it will not ripen before there is plenty of time to sell it.

Cut out any bruised or defective spots in fruit. Some persons soak fruit to be canned in a salt-vinegar solution (2 tbsp. each to 1 gal. of water) as it is peeled to prevent browning. I do not use this method since the water will soak some of the juices out of the fruit. I prefer to do one canner at a time, working as quickly as possible to avoid undue browning. A quick rinsing of fruits such as apples and pears right after peeling retards browning and washes away any loose trimmings on fruit. Slight browning will cook away during processing. Fruits are usually cut into the desired form for serving before processing. This saves time when serving.

For canning, fruits are usually cold packed with a **sugar syrup** added. Many persons make a standard sugar syrup. Sugar and water are combined in saucepan and heated, stirring constantly until sugar is dissolved. Jar is first packed with fruit and then filled with syrup, leaving 1 inch headspace at the top. Syrup is made according to sweetness desired. Thin syrup may be used for small fruits that are naturally sweet. Medium syrup is used for most fruits like peaches, sweet cherries, and berries. Heavy syrup may be used for tart fruits such as rhubarb and sour cherries. Proportions are:

Thin syrup—use 1 cup sugar to 4 cups water
Medium syrup—use 2 cups sugar to 4 cups water
Heavy syrup—use 4 cups sugar to 4 cups water

It usually takes 1 to 1 ½ cups syrup for each quart jar of fruit. However, this can vary considerably, depending on how tightly fruit was packed in jar, and whether it was halved, chopped, sliced, or packed whole, either with or without seeds. Cherries that are seeded have a lot of their own juice and if packed tightly will have little room left for syrup. Plums canned whole with the seeds left in have lots of room between fruit for syrup. This results in having the most room for sugar syrup in jars with the least amount of fruit. For this reason, I prefer measuring the exact amount of sugar per quart for the number of jars I have ready to process into the saucepan. (I usually use ½ cup sugar per quart, a little less for sweet fruits, and slightly more for tart fruits.) Add enough water to dissolve the sugar well (approximately ½ cup water per jar or a little less for cherries, so you won't have syrup left over after jars are filled). Heat syrup, stirring constantly until sugar is dissolved. Using a measuring cup as a dipper, divide syrup evenly into each of the jars. Then finish filling with water. With this method, you can put an exact amount of sugar in each jar and will have no extra syrup left over.

Fruits are usually frozen with dry sugar sprinkled over layers of fruit as container is filled. The sugar helps preserve the quality and flavor of the fruit. Artificial sweetener could give an off flavor if added before freezing. Instead, add right before serving. If desired, ascorbic acid (purchased at drugstore) may be added to retard browning of fruits such as peaches. Follow directions on container for amount to use which is usually ¼ to ½ tsp. per quart. Non-browning agents may also be purchased at grocery stores. These are usually, a mixture of ascorbic aicd, sugar, and other filler, and will take a larger amount per quart. One tablespoon lemon juice per quart is sometimes used to prevent browning. However, this may alter the flavor undesirably in some fruits.

Some people pack fruit in a sugar syrup for freezing, but this prolongs thawing time tremendously and leaves a large amount of watery syrup on thawed fruit. I use this method only for fruits that are eaten in the slushy (half-thawed) stage. This method is tops for retaining flavor, however.

Again, foods, and especially fruits, are best thawed slowly in the refrigerator rather than at room temperature. Serve strawberries and melons half thawed.

Apples

Apples are usually canned as pie filling (see recipe on page 615) or as applesauce. If desired, apples may be quartered or sliced and sugar syrup may be added instead of thickening for pies. Leave 1 inch headspace. Tighten lids and process 25 minutes in boiling water bath.

Apple Cider

A mixture of several varieties of good ripe apples make the best cider. This should include the Delicious variety along with at least one that is a little more tart. Cider is usually best 2 or 3 days after pressing.

To Can: Fill jars with cold or hot cider, leaving ½ inch headspace. Tighten lids and process 15 minutes in boiling water bath.

To Freeze: Simply fill containers and freeze, leaving 1 inch headspace.

Applesauce

The consistency of applesauce is greatly affected by how ripe the apples are when processed. Do not process hard, green apples and expect to have good naturally sweet sauce. Sauce probably will be greenish in color, tart, and thick unless lots of water is added to thin it. If apples are very ripe, applesauce will be quite thin. I've found most local orchards pick apples at a stage that requires about 2 weeks ripening to have them at best stage for processing. If you purchase them at a grocery store, they may have already been there for 2 weeks. Apples should be ripe and mellow but still firm and sound, not soft and pithy.

The varieties which ripen in the early summer (such as Transparent) are very tart. They are not suitable for baking, but are used mainly for sauce. Summer rambos come a little later and are moderately sweet. These make good pies and sauce. The fall maturing apples are naturally sweet and my family prefers these over the tart varieties. They seem to take about half the amount of sugar to sweeten. Staymans are our favorite for baking and canning. Grimes is second choice. There are many good varieties and each household seems to have a favorite. Many people like the Golden Delicious variety for sauce.

There is no need to peel apples for sauce. This results in considerable waste of good apple being peeled away. Wash *thoroughly* to remove pesticides and soil. Then remove seeds, stem and blossom ends, and any bruised or defective spots. Cut into quarters or less for quicker cooking. Rinse to remove any particles of trimmings. Add a small amount of water for cooking. (I use a large kettle that holds about 3 or 4 gallons of apples and add about 3 cups or less of water.) Cook until soft and mushy, approximately 15 to 20 minutes. Stir occasionally, especially when beginning to cook, to prevent sticking. Immediately run through sieve or strainer. If sauce is thicker than you like, a little additional water may be added to thin it. Sugar will thin sauce slightly, however, so don't add too much. Sugar may be added while still in the kettle or add sugar to each container as you fill it.

To Can: Using funnel, dip sauce into canning jars, adding ½ cup sugar or less per quart. I fill jars ⅔ full, then add sugar, stirring with wooden spoon until dissolved. (Metal spoon may crack or chip jar.) Finish filling, leaving 1 inch headspace. Stir again. Tighten lids and process for 25 minutes in boiling water bath.

To Freeze: Fill containers, adding sugar as desired. Cool and freeze.

Apricots

Select firm, ripe fruit. Wash thoroughly. May be canned either peeled or unpeeled. If desired, may be blanched for easy peeling. See directions under peaches. Cut in half and remove pits.

To Can: Pack in jars and fill with sugar syrup (see page 597 for directions) leaving 1 inch headspace. Tighten lids and process 25 minutes in boiling water bath.

To Freeze: Peel, slice, and pack in containers, sprinkling sugar over layers of fruit as you fill. Freeze immediately.

Berries (Except Strawberries)

Select firm, ripe fruit. Wash thoroughly, picking over carefully to remove any bad berries or stems.

To Can: Pack in jars, fill with sugar syrup (see page 597 for directions) leaving 1 inch headspace. Tighten lids and process 20 minutes in boiling water bath.

To Freeze: Drain and pack in containers, sprinkling sugar over layers of fruit as you fill. (Blueberries may be frozen without sugar if desired.) Freeze immediately.

Cherries

Select firm ripe fruit. Wash thoroughly, removing any stems and defects. Remove seeds, using a cherry seeder, the rounded end of a paper clip, or squeeze gently just enough to pop seed out. Cherries may be canned with seeds left in if desired. Save any juice that escapes when seeding. (Reminder: Sour cherries take more sugar than sweet cherries.)

To Can: Pack in jars, fill with sugar syrup (see page 597 for directions), leaving 1 inch headspace. Use any cherry juice as part of water in sugar syrup. (Use less liquid in syrup than usual since there is little space left for syrup with seeded cherries.) Tighten lids and process 20 minutes in boiling water bath.

To Freeze: Pack in containers, sprinkling sugar over layers of fruit as you fill, including any juice from seeding. Freeze immediately.

Cranberries

Select firm, ripe fruit. Wash thoroughly, removing any stems and defects.
To Can: Boil 3 mins. in heavy sugar syrup (see page 597 for directions). Fill jars, leaving ½ inch headspace. Tighten lids and process 10 mins. in boiling water bath.
To Freeze: Drain and pack in containers, sprinkling sugar over layers of fruit as you fill. Or they may be frozen plain without sugar if desired. Freeze immediately.

Grape Juice (Concentrate)

To Can: Select ripe sound fruit. Remove grapes from stems and discard any defective ones. Wash thoroughly. Place in large cooker and add water to almost cover grapes. Bring just to boiling point and simmer slowly (boiling causes poor flavor) for 20 minutes. Drain overnight in cloth bag or fine strainer. Pour into jars, adding ¾ to 1 cup sugar per quart. Stir with wooden spoon to dissolve sugar. Tighten lids and process 15 minutes in boiling water bath. (This juice is double strength—dilute with half water when serving.)

Grape Juice (Quick)

To Can: Prepare grapes as in preceding recipe. Place 1 cup grapes and ½ cup sugar in each quart jar. Fill with hot water, leaving ½ inch headspace. Stir to dissolve sugar. Tighten lids and process 15 minutes in boiling water bath. (This juice is quick to process, but takes twice the number of jars since it is regular strength.) Strain into pitcher to serve.

Melons

To Freeze: Use a melon baller to cut balls or cut cubes from ripe watermelon or cantaloupe. Place in container, sprinkling sugar over layers of melon as you fill. Or pack containers with melon and fill with sugar syrup made by boiling together 1 cup sugar to 2 cups water for 3 minutes. Chill thoroughly before pouring over melon. Serve melon only half thawed, otherwise it will be watery.

Peaches

Select ripe firm fruit just beginning to soften. Wash thoroughly before peeling to remove fuzz and insecticides. Some varieties of peaches, if evenly ripened, work nicely when blanched for easy peeling. Other varieties and unevenly ripened ones do not. If suitable, dip wire basket of peaches in boiling water approximately 1 minute. Dunk in cold water immediately. Drain and halve to remove seeds. Peeling should slip off easily. If this method causes peaches to become ragged, peel thinly with knife instead. (I think it usually works best to use a knife.)
To Can: Pack halves into jars with pitted side down. Or they may be cut into chunks for mixed fruit or fruit cobbler. Simply cut a medium-sized half of peach twice in both directions and pop them in the can. (I prefer the chunks for con-

venience when opening them.) Fill with sugar syrup, leaving 1 inch headspace. (Use ½ cup sugar or slightly less per quart. See page 597 for directions.) Tighten lids and process 25 minutes in boiling water bath.

To Freeze: Slice into containers, sprinkling sugar over layers of fruit as you fill. Ascorbic acid may be added to sugar to retard browning if desired. (Some varieties of peaches freeze with much less browning than others. The Red Haven variety is especially good for freezing.)

Pears

Select firm ripe fruit which has turned yellow and is just beginning to soften. (Bartlett pears are best for canning. Kieffers will be good if well ripened and if gritty area around core is removed.) Halve and peel. Use melon baller for easy removal of core, and a vegetable peeler for easy peeling (often called a potato peeler). Scoop out any gritty portion around core. Rinse peeled pears quickly. Do not soak in water—this bleeds out juices. Pack pear halves the same as peaches, or cut into chunks for mixed fruit if desired. Fill with sugar syrup leaving 1 inch headspace. (Use ½ cup sugar or slightly less per quart. See page 597 for directions.) (If desired, ½ tsp. mint flavoring or a few drops peppermint oil, and a little green color may be added to syrup for minted pears.) Tighten lids and process for 25 minutes in boiling water bath.

Pineapple

Select ripe fruit and wash thoroughly. Peel first, or slice and peel each piece. Remove eyes and core. A sturdy doughnut cutter may be used if size is correct. It may be left in slices, cut into chunks, or run through coarse blade on food grinder for crushed pineapple. Simmer in sugar syrup (see page 597) for about 5 mins.

To Can: Fill jars leaving ½ inch headspace. Tighten lids and process 30 minutes in boiling water bath.

To Freeze: Cool, pour in containers, and freeze.

Plums

To Can: Select meaty rather than juicy plums for canning. Plums have better flavor if canned unpeeled with pits left in. Wash thoroughly and prick with fork so skins won't burst during processing. Pack into jars and fill with sugar syrup (see page 597 for directions) leaving 1 inch headspace. Tighten lids and process 25 minutes in boiling water bath.

Rhubarb

Pull stems when young and tender. Trim off each leaf and wash thoroughly. Cut into 1 inch lengths.

To Can: Pack into jars and fill with sugar syrup (see page 597 for directions), leaving 1 inch headspace. Tighten lids and process 10 mins. in boiling water bath.

To Freeze: Sprinkle sugar over layers of fruit as you fill container. Freeze immediately.

Strawberries

To Can: (Quality is not good canned.)

To Freeze: Process as promptly after picking as possible. Remove caps and wash thoroughly. Freeze whole or slice and sprinkle sugar over layers of fruit as you fill container. Sugar will penetrate much better if each berry is sliced at least once. (I prefer using ⅓ cup sugar per pint on strawberries.) Berries may be lightly crushed with potato masher if desired. Add sugar and stir just until mixed. Freeze immediately. (Strawberries are much better served only half thawed.)

Tomatoes

To Can: Select red-ripe firm tomatoes. Peel and remove cores and any defective spots. (For easy peeling, dip fruit in boiling water ½ to 1 minute. Then dunk in cold water. Skins should slip off easily.) Quarter, or cut into desired sizes and pack firmly into jars. Do not add liquid. Press firmly enough into jars so that some juice is extracted from tomatoes. Leave 1 inch headspace. Add ½ tsp. salt and 1 tsp. sugar per quart. Tighten lids and process 25 minutes in boiling water bath if tomatoes are acid. If they are mild, process 45 minutes. Acid may be added if desired. Add ½ tsp. citric acid per quart, or 2 tbsp. white distilled vinegar per quart. Vinegar may slightly alter flavor; acid won't.

Tomato Juice

To Can: Select red-ripe firm tomatoes. Remove cores and any defective spots and blemishes on peeling. It is not necessary to peel. Cut into chunks for quick cooking. Do not add water. Squish a few tomatoes in bottom of kettle to obtain enough juice to start cooking. Tomatoes will soon juice out in cooking process. Stir several times until boiling so tomatoes don't stick and burn. Cook just until soft, about 10 minutes. Run through sieve. (Or pour 1 quart at a time into blender and process on and off several times until pureed. Do not incorporate a lot of foam. Stir through strainer to remove seeds and small amount of peel. This makes nice thick juice.) Fill jars, adding ½ tsp. salt and 1 tsp. sugar per quart. Leave ½ inch headspace. Tighten lids and process 15 minutes in boiling bath.

Processing Vegetables

Vegetables should be harvested when just barely mature for best flavor and tenderness. They should then be processed promptly. It is best to pick them in the cooler part of the day when there isn't a lot of sun heat in the vegetables. They should be pared, cored, and cut up for preserving just as for serving immediately.

Most vegetables may be either packed hot or cold in jars for canning. Some vegetables seem to have better flavor when blanched first. There will be less shrinkage and a larger amount can be placed in each jar.

If you have freezer space, most vegetables are much better frozen. Green beans and beets are the two vegetables most often canned. Other vegetables are usually frozen, if possible.

Blanching: Vegetables should be blanched before freezing to kill enzymes which could cause off color and flavor. Don't try to blanch too many at one time. The quicker vegetables are cooked and cooled, the better they will be.

It works best to use a kettle or blancher large enough to hold 3 or 4 quarts of water with extra space for boil-up. Too large a container takes too long to heat and reheat. Use the largest burner on stove and heat water to a good rolling boil *before* adding any vegetables. Do only about 2 pints at one time so water will quickly come back to a boil again after vegetables are added.

Place vegetables into basket or strainer and lower into boiling water. As soon as water begins to boil again, it helps to stir slightly to distribute heat and to help prevent boiling over before entire amount is cooked evenly. I try to cook vegetables the minimum amount of time I feel it takes to be certain they will be boiling hot through to center. This will result in best flavor. Small vegetables like peas don't take long after they begin to boil, especially if they are stirred. Coarser vegetables like brussels sprouts or stems on broccoli take longer. Corn on the cob varies considerably because of the wide range of ear sizes with the different varieties and how well it is filled out. Therefore, time charts for blanching are quite variable. If water boils rapidly for a short time, this is usually sufficient. Count time after vegetables begin to boil, not when first placed in boiling water.

Cool vegetables as quickly as possible after blanching. Dunk strainer of vegetables in cold water immediately upon removal from heat. If you don't have two strainers, dump cooked vegetables into a colander for cooling, so second batch may be placed in strainer to keep process going. Swish around until heat has mostly dissipated, and then place in ice water. With larger vegetables like corn on the cob, use two cold water dunkings before placing in a final ice water bath to save ice. Save second pan of water to use for first dunking of next batch and so on. Drain well and fill containers, leaving ½ inch headspace.

Mark date on containers so you will always be sure to use oldest vegetables first. Place in freezer immediately for quick freezing. With this method, vegetables should taste almost garden fresh all year long!

Asparagus

Pick new tender stalks. Wash thoroughly. Starting at tip end, use dull knife to cut into 1-inch pieces so you can easily tell when you get to tough portion of stem. Discard tough end. Asparagus may also be processed in slightly less than jar lengths if desired.

To can (Raw Pack): Pack into jars. Add ½ tsp. salt per pint and fill with hot water, leaving 1 inch headspace.

(Hot Pack): Blanch in boiling water for 1 minute. Pack into jars. Add ½ tsp. salt per pint and fill with hot water leaving ½ inch headspace.

Tighten lids and process at 10 pounds pressure: quarts 30 minutes, and pints 25 minutes.

To Freeze: Blanch in boiling water for 1 minute. Cool quickly and drain. Pack in containers and freeze immediately.

Beans (Green or Wax)

Pick beans when young and tender. If some are tough, shell these out and discard shells. Add the kernels to beans to be processed. Remove ends, any strings, and defective spots. Break into 1 to 1 ½-inch pieces. Wash thoroughly and drain.

To Can (Raw Pack): Pack into jars. Add 1 tsp. salt per quart and fill with hot water leaving 1 inch headspace.

(Hot Pack): Blanch in boiling water for 1 to 2 minutes. Pack in jars. Add 1 tsp. salt per quart and fill with hot water leaving 1 inch headspace.

Tighten lids and process at 10 lb. pressure: quarts 25 mins., pints 20 mins.

To Freeze: Blanch in boiling water for 1 to 2 minutes. Cool quickly. Drain, pack in containers, and freeze immediately.

Beans (Lima)

Pick beans when just barely mature. Shell. Wash thoroughly and drain.

To Can (Raw Pack): Pack loosely in jars. Add ½ tsp. salt per pint and fill with hot water leaving 1 inch headspace.

(Hot Pack): Blanch in boiling water 1 to 1 ½ minutes. Pack loosely into jars. Add ½ tsp. salt per pint and fill with hot water leaving 1 inch headspace. (Quality and flavor are poor when canned.)

Tighten lids and process at 10 lbs. pressure: quarts 50 mins.; pints 40 mins.

To Freeze: Blanch in boiling water for 1 to 1 ½ minutes. Cool quickly. (Pick out any overripe beans that are turning yellowish. Put these all in one container so they can be cooked together when serving. They will need to be cooked slightly longer than tender green ones.) Drain and freeze immediately.

Beets

Harvest beets while young and tender. Cut off tops leaving 1 inch of stem and also leave root attached. This helps to prevent having nutrients cook away in water to be discarded. Wash thoroughly. Cover with hot water and cook until tender enough that skins slip off, approximately 15 to 25 minutes, depending on size. Dunk in cold water to cool enough to handle. Cut off remaining tops and roots. Cut into cubes, slices, or quarters. If quite small, they may be left whole.

To Can: Pack into jars. Add ½ tsp. salt per pint and fill with hot water leaving ½ inch headspace. Tighten lids and process at 10 pounds pressure: quarts 40 minutes, and pints 30 minutes.

To Freeze: Cool beets thoroughly. Trim and cut as desired. Pack in containers and freeze immediately.

Brussels Sprouts

Cut when heads are mature, but dark green and compact. Trim, removing any coarse outer leaves and stem. Wash thoroughly.

To Can: Blanch in boiling water for 2 to 3 minutes. Pack in jars. Add ½ tsp. salt per pint and fill with hot water leaving ½ inch headspace. Process at 10 pounds pressure: quarts 55 minutes, and pints 45 minutes.

To Freeze: Blanch in boiling water for 2 to 3 minutes. Cool quickly and drain. Pack in containers and freeze immediately.

Broccoli

Cut heads while compact, dark green, and tender before any buds begin to flower. Trim off any woody stem and large leaves. Leave on tender stems. Wash thoroughly. Cut into flowerets. Cut just through stem and then pull bud section apart to avoid cutting buds into fine pieces (quality not good canned).

To Freeze: Blanch in boiling water for 1½ to 2 minutes. Cool quickly and drain. Pack in containers or in plastic bags and freeze immediately.

Cabbage

Cut heads when solid, but before they begin to burst. Discard any coarse dark outer leaves. Wash thoroughly. Cut into medium shreds.

To Can: Blanch in boiling water for 1 to 1½ minutes. Pack into jars. Add ½ tsp. salt per pint and fill with hot water leaving ½ inch headspace. Tighten lids and process at 10 pounds pressure: quarts 55 minutes, and pints 45 minutes.

To Freeze: Blanch in boiling water for 1 to 1½ minutes. Cool quickly and drain. Pack in containers and freeze immediately. (May be frozen in wedges if desired. Blanch wedges 2 minutes.)

Carrots

Pull carrots as soon as full grown so they will be tender and sweet. Trim and peel. Wash thoroughly. Cut into ¼ inch slices or into strips.

To Can (Raw Pack): Pack into jars. Add ½ tsp. salt per pint and fill with hot water, leaving 1 inch headspace.

(Hot Pack): Blanch in boiling water for 1½ to 2 minutes. Pack into jars. Add ½ tsp. salt per pint and fill with hot water, leaving ½ inch headspace.

Tighten lids and process at 10 lbs. pressure: quarts 30 mins.; pints 25 mins.

To Freeze: Blanch in boiling water for 1½ to 2 minutes. Cool quickly and drain. Pack in containers and freeze immediately. (Carrots may also be shredded raw for use in carrot salad or carrot cake. Pack tightly in containers and freeze with no other treatment.)

Cauliflower

Cut heads when firm and mature, but still compact and white. Trim off any leaves. Wash thoroughly. Break into flowerets. If needed, soak in a brine of 1 tbsp. salt to 1 quart of water for 20 minutes to remove small insects. Rinse and drain.

To Can: Blanch in boiling water for 2 to 2½ minutes. Pack into jars. Add ½ tsp. salt per pint and fill with hot water leaving ½ inch headspace. Tighten lids and process at 10 pounds pressure: quarts 40 minutes, and pints 30 minutes.

To Freeze: Blanch in boiling water for 2 to 2½ minutes. Cool quickly and drain. Pack in containers and freeze immediately.

Corn

Pick corn when barely mature, while still tender and juicy, preferably early in the morning while still cool. Process as promptly as possible after picking for good quality. Trim off end of cob and also any damaged places. Pull off all silk that comes easily with your hand. Then brush with a dry vegetable brush to remove remaining silk. Brush diagonally across ears so silk doesn't become embedded in rows of corn. Wash under very slowly running water, brushing again to wash. Blanch in boiling water for 2½ to 3½ minutes. Cool quickly in cold water and drain. Use very sharp knife for cutting corn from cob.

For *whole kernel corn,* cut kernels from the cob at about ⅔ the depth of the kernel. Hearts are not added to corn. (Scrape hearts from cobs into separate container and use, since hearts are too good to waste.)

For *cream-style corn,* cut corn from the cob at about the center of the kernel or deeper. Scrape cobs to remove the hearts of the kernels, adding them to corn. (Some people use a corn cutter for quick creaming of corn, but this makes corn very juicy. I prefer cutting it with a knife, cream-style.)

To Can: Pack into jars. Add ½ tsp. salt per pint and fill with hot water leaving 1 inch headspace. Tighten lids and process at 10 pounds pressure: quarts 85 minutes, and pints 55 minutes.

To Freeze: Blanch in boiling water for 2½ to 3½ minutes and cool quickly. Cut off corn as described above. Pack in containers and freeze immediately. (Corn may be frozen on the cob, but quality is not very good. It becomes quite watery when cooked for serving.)

Greens

Harvest greens while young and tender. Check carefully for insects. Remove any tough stems and defective leaves. Wash thoroughly. Blanch in boiling water for 1½ to 2 minutes until wilted.

To Can: Pack into jars. Add ½ tsp. salt per pint and fill with hot water leaving ½ inch headspace. Tighten lids, process at 10 lbs. pressure; quarts 70 mins., pints 45 mins.

To Freeze: Blanch as described. Cool quickly and drain. Pack in containers and freeze immediately.

Okra

Pick pods while still young and tender. Trim off stem. Wash thoroughly. Okra may be blanched whole or slice in ¼ to ½-inch slices. If blanching whole do not cut into seed section when trimming. Blanch in boiling water for 1 minute for slices, or 1½ to 2 minutes for pods. (Water will become gooey with the liquid from the slices. Therefore, some flavor will be lost in the water, but you will be rid of much of the goo with this method!) Okra may be sliced after blanching.

To Can: Pack in jars. Add ½ tsp. salt per pint and fill with boiling water, leaving ½ inch headspace. Tighten lids and process at 10 pounds pressure: quarts 40 minutes, and pints 25 minutes.

To Freeze: Cool quickly and drain. Pack in containers and freeze immediately.

Peas (Green)

Pick pods when they are just barely mature, but well filled. (Depending on the season, sometimes pods do not fill out as well as other times.) Pick while still bright green. Shell and wash thoroughly.

To Can (Raw Pack): Pack loosely into pint jars. (Do not use quart jars because they will get too mushy if processed long enough for quarts.) Add ½ tsp. salt per pint and fill with hot water, leaving 1 inch headspace.

(Hot Pack): Blanch in boiling water for 1 minute. Pack into jars. Add ½ tsp. salt per pint and fill with hot water leaving 1 inch headspace.

Tighten lids and process at 10 pounds pressure: pints 40 minutes.

To Freeze: Blanch in boiling water for 1 minute. Cool quickly and drain. Pack in containers and freeze immediately.

Peas (Snow or Sugar)

To Freeze: Pick when just barely mature, while pods are still bright green, young and tender. Wash thoroughly and blanch in boiling water for 2 minutes. Cool quickly and drain. Pack in containers and freeze immediately.

Peppers (Green—Bell Peppers)

Pick peppers when mature and thick walled, but while still green and crisp. Cut in half, remove stem, seeds and white core. Wash thoroughly.

To Can: May slice in strips or rings. Blanch in boiling water for 2 to 3 minutes. Pack in jars. Add ½ tsp. salt per pint and fill with hot water, leaving ½ inch headspace. Tighten lids and process at 10 pounds pressure: pints 35 minutes.

To Freeze: It is not necessary to blanch peppers for freezing. Chop for ready use. May be put into a container, but are handiest when individually frozen. Spread out on a tray and freeze. Remove from tray when frozen, place in heavy plastic bag, and return to freezer. With this method you can quickly remove any amount you wish without thawing entire package.

Pimiento Peppers

Pick when red ripe, but firm. Cut in half, cut out stem, and remove seeds. Peel by roasting in oven or by boiling until tender. The roasting method results in better flavor. Place skin side up on tray in 400-degree oven (not too near broiler element) and broil for 3 to 6 minutes until slightly charred. Rinse in cold water and remove skins. Or place in boiling water for 10 to 12 minutes until skins are loosened. Rinse in cold water and remove skins. (Pimientos will have better flavor if frozen, but may be canned if desired.)

To Can: Pack in jars. Add 2 tsp. vinegar and ¼ tsp. salt per pint. Fill with hot water, leaving ½ inch headspace. Tighten lids and process at 10 pounds pressure: pints 35 minutes.

To Freeze: Cool and drain. Pack in containers and freeze immediately.

Potatoes (Irish)

To Can: Can new potatoes soon after harvesting. (Many people like to can the small potatoes from the harvest.) Scrape or peel. Be sure to remove eyes and any soil from eye areas. Wash thoroughly.

(Raw Pack): Pack into jars. Add ½ tsp. salt per pint and fill with hot water, leaving 1 inch headspace.
(Hot Pack): Boil potatoes 3 minutes. Pack in jars. Add ½ tsp. salt per pint and fill with hot water leaving ½ inch headspace.

Tighten lids and process at 10 pounds pressure: quarts and pints 40 mins.

Pumpkin

Harvest when color is good and stem will break loose easily. (I always preferred canning pumpkins soon after harvest while the shells were tender and easy to peel. After storing for a month or two, the shells become hard and dried out. However, I recently learned from the Wetsel Seed Company that the flavor improves and becomes sweeter if held for a month or more. You never get too old to learn!) Cut, remove pulp and seeds. Pare and cut into 1-inch cubes. Wash thoroughly. Add just enough water to prevent sticking and cook until tender—about 20 to 25 minutes. Run through sieve. If pumpkin shells are too tough to peel, you can cut them in half, and scoop out the seeds. Place cut side down in a flat bake dish, and bake in 350-degree oven until tender—about 1½ hrs. Then scoop out pumpkin into containers. (This is a much less efficient use of heat for cooking, however.)
To Can: Pour into jars hot, leaving 1 inch headspace. Add ½ tsp. salt per quart. Tighten lids and process at 10 lbs. pressure: quarts 80 mins.; pints 60 mins.
To Freeze: Cool. Pour into containers and freeze.

Salsify (or Oyster Plant)

Dig salsify when mature, but tender. Scrub thoroughly and peel or scrape. Cut into ¼-inch slices and blanch in boiling water for 2 minutes.
To Can: Pack in jars. Add ½ tsp. salt per pint and fill with hot water, leaving ½ inch headspace. Tighten lids, process at 10 lbs. pressure: qts. 40 mins.; pts. 30 mins.
To Freeze: Cool immediately in cold water. Drain, pack in containers, and freeze.

Sauerkraut

Harvest mature, solid heads of cabbage. Discard any coarse dark outer leaves. Wash thoroughly. Cut into fine shreds. Pack in a crock jar, sprinkling salt over layers of cabbage as you fill. Add approximately 2 tsp. salt per quart of cabbage. Use a potato masher to pack firmly enough to draw brine as you go. Lay a china plate on top held down with a clean stone, or a jar filled with water for weight, to keep cabbage covered with brine. Plate should be only slightly smaller than top of jar so all of cabbage is covered. Place jar in basement and let sour for one to four weeks, depending on how sour you like sauerkraut. (I leave it for only one week.) Ideal temperature for fermenting is 65 to 70 degrees. After fermentation process, drain off brine, and pack in jars. Add fresh water to fill jars leaving 1 inch headspace. Tighten lids and process 15 minutes in boiling water bath.

Soybeans (Green)

Pick beans before frost when stalks are just beginning to turn yellow, but pods are still green. Wash thoroughly and blanch beans in pods for 2 to 3 minutes, stirring several times. Rinse in cold water. Squeeze pods to pop out beans. Wash again. (Flavor is not good canned.)

To Freeze: Drain, pack in containers, and freeze immediately.

Squash

If canning squash that has been cooked and pureed, preparation and method is the same as for pumpkin. Process summer squash (such as zucchini and yellow or summer crookneck) at 10 lbs. pressure: quarts 30 minutes, pints 25 minutes. Process winter squash (such as acorn, butternut, and hubbard) at 10 lbs. pressure: quarts 90 minutes, and pints 60 minutes. Zucchini and yellow squash may be sliced and canned for soups or other uses. For slices, squash should be picked while young before seedy area is developed (about 8 inches in length). Slices may be cut in half or in fourths if desired. Pack tightly in jars. Add ¼ tsp. salt per pint. Fill with hot water, leaving 1 inch headspace. Process at 10 lbs. pressure: quarts 30 minutes, and pints 25 minutes.

To Freeze: More mature zucchini squash may be grated and frozen raw for use in breads and cakes. Peel before grating and remove seeds. Pack tightly in plastic bags in the exact amount needed for recipes.

Sweet Potatoes

To Can: Can sweet potatoes soon after harvest. Pare and wash thoroughly. Cut into medium-sized pieces. Cook 5 minutes. Pack in jars. Add ½ tsp. salt per pint and fill with hot water, leaving ½ inch headspace. Tighten lids and process at 10 pounds pressure: quarts 90 minutes, and pints 55 minutes.

APPROXIMATE YIELD PER BUSHEL OF FRUITS AND VEGETABLES

The yield per bushel from fruits and vegetables will vary considerably, depending on the size of the fruit and on how well the pods of vegetables such as peas are filled out.

With fruits such as peaches you will have better yield per bushel with smaller-sized fruit. Large fruit has more air space between the fruit in the basket than small fruit does. However, small fruit takes much longer to process, since you are probably peeling twice the number of individual fruits. Therefore, a medium size is usually preferable. Bruised and defective fruit will have a lot of waste, so buy wisely if purchasing it.

Approximate Yields of Fruits When Processed

	Weight per Bushel	Yield per Bushel
Apples	42 to 48 lbs.	16 to 20 quarts
Applesauce		15 to 18 quarts
Apricots	46 to 50 lbs.	20 to 24 quarts
Cherries	56 lbs.	24 to 28 quarts, unpitted
(depends on variety of cherries)		13 to 25 quarts, pitted
Grapes	44 to 50 lbs.	16 quarts, juice
Peaches	48 to 52 lbs.	18 to 24 quarts
Pears	48 to 50 lbs.	20 to 25 quarts
Plums	50 to 56 lbs.	28 to 32 quarts, unpitted
Strawberries	(24-quart crate)	(12 to 16 quarts per crate)
Tomatoes	50 to 60 lbs.	15 to 20 quarts
Tomato juice		12 to 16 quarts

Approximate Yields of Vegetables When Processed

	Weight per Bushel	Yield per Bushel
Beans, lima (in pod)	32 lbs.	12 to 16 pints
Beans, green or wax	28 to 30 lbs.	15 to 16 quarts
Beets	50 to 60 lbs.	16 to 22 quarts
Cabbage	(3 lb. head)	(makes 1 qt. sauerkraut)
Carrots	50 lbs.	32 to 40 pints
Corn (1 bushel = 50 to 60 ears)	35 to 40 lbs.	14 to 18 pints
Cucumber	48 to 50 lbs.	24 quarts pickle
Greens	18 to 20 lbs.	12 to 18 pints
Okra	26 lbs.	17 quarts
Peas (in pod)	28 to 30 lbs.	12 to 16 pints
Potatoes	50 to 60 lbs.	20 quarts
Squash—summer	40 to 44 lbs.	16 to 20 quarts
Sweet potatoes	50 to 55 lbs.	18 to 22 quarts

Processing Meats

(See information about meats in meat chapter beginning on page 340.)

For freezing, cut meat into suitable portions, then double wrap and seal tightly to prevent freezer burn. Meat is usually frozen raw, and most meats keep longer if frozen raw. However, it may also be cooked before freezing if desired.

The recommended length of storage time for meat varies with different authorities. Recommended time for pork is usually from 6 to 9 months. Beef is from 1 to 1½ years. Ground meats do not keep as long as larger cuts. To keep well, meats *must* be well wrapped and kept at a steady temperature of at least 0 degrees. (I prefer double wrapping food that will be stored for any length of time. Many things can be wrapped in plastic wrap and then inserted in a plastic bread bag.)

For canning, meat is usually packed cold, but may also be packed hot if desired. Avoid freezing or soaking raw meat in water before canning. This gives a poor quality product. (Exceptions are fish or some wild game which may be soaked in salt water prior to canning if desired.) If cleaning is needed, wipe with cloth. Trim off excess fat which becomes rancid sooner when meat is frozen. When canned, it may cause a strong flavor and may soften rubber sealing compound on lids. For cold pack, cut in 1-inch cubes and place in canning jars. Usually 2 pounds of raw boneless cubed meat will fill a 1-quart jar. Chicken with bones may take about 3 or 4 pounds to fill a 1-quart jar. Pack in jars, sprinkling with salt (1 tsp. per quart) as you fill jar. Leave 1 inch headspace. Do not add liquid when packing raw. If meat is hot-packed, add broth or water to fill, leaving 1 inch headspace. Tighten lids and process at 10 pounds pressure: quarts 90 minutes, and pints 75 minutes. (See page 356 for directions for canning fish.)

Timetable for Processing Fruits

	Boiling Water Bath (Minutes)		*Pressure Cooker (Minutes) (Pounds	
	Pints	Quarts	Pints/Quarts	Pressure)
Apples	20	25	15	5
Apple cider	—	15	—	-
Applesauce	25	25	15	5
Apricots	20	25	10	5
Berries (except strawberries)	15	20	8	5
Cherries	20	20	10	5
Cranberries	10	10	—	-
Fruit juices	15	15	—	-
Grapes	20	20	8	5
Peaches	20	25	10	5
Pears	20	25	10	5
Pineapple	30	30	10	5
Plums	20	25	10	5
Rhubarb	10	10	5	5
Tomatoes	35	45	15	5
Tomato juice	15	15	—	-

*Many books do not give processing time for pressure canning fruits because it is *very* easy to overprocess fruits in the pressure cooker. A few minutes extra in the cooker can damage quality considerably. (Peaches, for instance, will shrink excessively in the cans if overprocessed.) I've found it to be an easy and timesaving method, but I do use extra precaution not to overprocess. It saves heating up a whole canner of hot boiling water, since you use only 2 inches of water in the cooker. It also takes only a short time to attain the proper pressure and for it to recede after processing since you only use 5 pounds pressure for fruits.

Timetable for Processing Vegetables

	*Boiling Water Bath	Pressure Cooker (Minutes)		
		Pints	Quarts	Pounds Pressure
Asparagus	3 hrs.	25	30	10
Beans, limas	3 hrs.	40	50	10
Beans, string and wax	3 hrs.	20	25	10
Beans, dry	3½ hrs.	60	60	10
Beets	2 hrs.	30	40	10
Broccoli	2½ hrs.	30	40	10
Brussels sprouts	2 hrs.	45	55	10
Cabbage	2 hrs.	45	55	10
Carrots	2 hrs.	25	30	10
Cauliflower	2½ hrs.	30	40	10
Corn	3½ hrs.	55	85	10
Greens	3 hrs.	45	70	10
Okra	3 hrs.	25	40	10
Onions	3 hrs.	40	40	10

(continued)

	*Boiling Water Bath	Pressure Cooker (Minutes) Pints	Quarts	Pounds Pressure
Peas	3 hrs.	40	—	10
Peppers, green	2 hrs.	35	35	10
Peppers, pimiento	40 mins.	10	10	5
Potatoes, Irish	3 hrs.	40	40	10
Pumpkin	3 hrs.	65	80	10
Salsify	2½ hrs.	30	40	10
Sauerkraut	15 mins.	—	—	—
Soybeans	3½ hrs.	80	80	10
Squash, summer (pureed or sliced)	3 hrs.	25	30	10
Squash, winter (pureed)	3 hrs.	65	80	10
Sweet Potatoes	3 hrs.	55	90	10

Timetable for Processing Meats

Beef, lamb, pork, venison	3½ hrs.	75	90	10
Chicken	3½ hrs.	75	90	10
Fish	4 hrs.	90	100	10
Broth	2 hrs.	30	35	10

*WARNING: A pressure cooker is recommended for all low acid foods and meats as it gives a greater degree of safety. The processing time for boiling water bath for vegetables and meats given here is only in case you have no access to a pressure cooker. The USDA recommends all vegetables and meats should be boiled 15 minutes in an open vessel *before tasting or using,* to kill any potential poisonous enzymes or bacteria.

Timetable of Approximate Blanching Time for Freezing Vegetables

(Water should be boiling when vegetables are placed in water. Do not begin counting time until vegetables return to a boil.)

Asparagus	boil 1 minute
Beans, lima	boil 1 to 1½ minutes
Beans, green and wax	boil 1 to 2 minutes
Broccoli	boil 1½ to 2 minutes
Brussels sprouts (small)	boil 2 to 3 minutes
Cabbage, shredded	boil 1 to 1½ minutes
Carrots, sliced	boil 1½ to 2 minutes
Cauliflower, cut	boil 2 to 2½ minutes
Corn, on the cob	boil 2½ to 3½ minutes
Greens	boil 1½ to 2 minutes
Okra	boil 1 minute
Peas, green	boil 1 minute
Peas, sugar or snow	boil 2 minutes
Peppers	do not blanch
Soybeans, in pods	boil 2 to 3 minutes

Storing Vegetables

Cabbage. Cabbage will keep several weeks in the refrigerator if stored carefully. It is important to dry off head of cabbage as thoroughly as possible. Place in a plastic bag with a paper towel to absorb any additional moisture. Punch several air holes in the bag and store in refrigerator.

Carrots. Tops should be removed because they will feed on the carrot if not removed. Carrots should be washed before storing and dried off thoroughly. (I lay the carrots out on several thicknesses of newspaper and let them air dry overnight.) Then place in plastic bags with several air holes punched in the sides and store in refrigerator. They should keep for many weeks.

Onions: Cut tops from onions before storing and spread out in a dry place several days before storing, but *not* in the sun. When thoroughly dry, store in a cool dry place where air will circulate around them. Some people place them one by one in net bags or the legs of old panty hose, tying a knot between each onion. Hang these on nails on the ceiling joists in the cellar. Each time you need an onion, simply cut off one and the remainder are not disturbed.

Potatoes: As with storing any other vegetables, potatoes must be thoroughly dry to avoid rotting in storage. We've found a method for handling potatoes that seems to work quite well. Haul buckets or sacks of potatoes near an outside water hydrant. Using the wheelbarrow as a washtub, swish potatoes around in water until dirt is loosened. Transfer potatoes to an egg basket or wire basket. Use a garden hose to rinse basket of potatoes. After draining, pour out on newspapers spread in the garage. Let dry overnight. Pick out any cut potatoes to use promptly since these will soon spoil. Pack in bushel baskets and store in cellar.

Do not let temperature go below 45 degrees if you wish to use potatoes for chips. Chilled potatoes do not make good crisp chips. Potatoes may also develop black streaks inside if they become too chilled. Ideal temperature is between 45 and 50 degrees. Any long sprouts which develop during storage should be broken off. They take nourishment from the potato and potatoes will deteriorate rapidly if not removed. Any green portion on potatoes should be cut off and discarded when using. This is harmful to eat. It is caused by letting potatoes stand in the sun or in a place where there is too much light. Potatoes should be stored in a dark cool place. Potato stalks also need to be well hilled up with soil or mulch during the growing season to prevent exposure of potatoes to the sun before harvesting.

Tomatoes: You may be able to store green tomatoes a number of weeks in the fall until ripened. Just before frost gather in the green tomatoes and wrap individually in newspaper. Place in single layer in a box and store in cool dry place until ripened. After ripening, tomatoes should be refrigerated.

TIPS FOR CANNING, FREEZING, AND PRESERVING

• A freezer filled full of food does not take as much electricity to keep frozen as one half filled or less. This is because food retains cold much better than cold air which soon dissipates.

• If jars don't seal promptly or look like they might not seal, sometimes it helps to turn them upside down to finish cooling. I always mark these jars and use them first, however, just in case the seal may not be as tight.

• The use of iodized salt for making pickles may cause black or dark blotches on pickles. The minerals in hard water may also adversely affect the quality of pickles. It may cause the pickles to split inside during the soaking process for "Seven-Day Pickles." Splitting may also be caused by adverse weather conditions in the growing season. Pickles will have better flavor if not eaten for 6 weeks after canning.

• If you do not have a blancher, use 30-inch squares of nylon net as bags to blanch vegetables for freezing. Gather up corners and sides, and fasten with pipe cleaner, twister, or clothespin. Large strainers are also excellent for blanching.

• Store small plastic bags of vegetables together in a large heavy plastic bag to keep different kinds together and to keep them from getting lost in the freezer.

• Store nut meats in freezer to keep from getting old and rancid. They will keep indefinitely and do not need to be thawed to use.

• Grapes may be frozen individually for snacking. Place in single layer on jelly roll pan to freeze. When frozen, remove to plastic bags and return to freezer. Serve when just barely thawed.

• The amount of natural pectin in fruit may vary with the ripeness of the fruit. Overripe fruit contains less pectin. However, fruit that is too green will not contain pectin in the most usable form. It is best to use fruit that is just barely ripe unless you will be adding commercial powdered pectin such as Sure-jell. If jelly does not thicken properly with correct amount of cooking time, a little Clearjel or cornstarch dissolved in cold water may also be added to thicken it.

• Add ½ tsp. butter or margarine to boiling jelly to keep it clear. This also reduces foam and helps eliminate the need to skim jelly.

• If you don't care for chunks of strawberries in jam, process berries a few at a time in the blender. Don't overdo this—just process on and off a couple of times to chop thoroughly.

• Cook fruit or juice rapidly when making jelly. Slow cooking does not make nice jelly. Squeezing the bag of cooked fruit pulp when draining juice for jelly tends to make the juice cloudy.

• Use a clean tin can for melting paraffin to seal jelly jars, so you will not need to clean the paraffin out of a pan. Shape rim of can into spout with pliers to make easier pouring of hot paraffin. Pour a small amount of paraffin onto jelly in jar, then lay a clean string across the top. Add remaining paraffin. The string ends will make handles for easy removal later.

• Jellies and jams keep better frozen or sealed with canning lids. A paraffin-sealed jelly needs to be stored in a cool place and is quite susceptible to a poor seal unless you are very careful.

CANNING, FREEZING, AND PRESERVING RECIPES

Spiced Apple Rings

12 Delicious apples	Wash, remove cores, and peel. Cut at least ¼-inch thick into rings, half rings, or slices.
8 cups water **1 cup sugar** **3 tsp. red food coloring**	Heat to boiling.
1 tsp. whole allspice **1 tsp. mace** **1 tsp. whole cloves**	Tie in gauze bag and place in water. Add apple slices, and boil until tender but still firm. Remove pan from heat.

Weight apples down (may use a heavy plate) so they are covered with liquid, and let stand overnight. The next morning, pack into jars, leaving 1 inch headspace. Tighten lids and process in boiling water bath for 25 minutes.

Yield: 5 pints

Apple Pie Filling to Can

(Use any good cooking apple for canning. I prefer the Stayman or Grimes Golden varieties.)

9½ cups water **4½ cups sugar** **1 cup Clearjel or cornstarch** **1 tsp. salt** **2 tsp. ground cinnamon** **¼ tsp. ground nutmeg** **¼ tsp. ground allspice**	Combine in large saucepan. Cook until thickened, stirring constantly. Remove from heat.
3 tbsp. lemon juice (optional)	Add.
7 qts. apple slices	Slice apples directly into jars adding layers of syrup as you fill (otherwise there will be too many air pockets).

Leave at least 1 inch headspace. (If jars are filled too full, syrup will spew out during processing!) Tighten lids and process in boiling water bath for 25 minutes.

Yield: 7 qts.

Barbara Bowman

Fruit Pie Filling to Can

(This recipe is excellent for cherries, raspberries, blueberries, and the like. You may wish to can in pints rather than quarts, so you can use your own homecanned pie filling in place of a 21-oz. commercial can called for in many recipes. Home-canned usually has a much better flavor, especially if you use tree-ripened or vine-ripened fruit.)

9½ cups water **4½ cups sugar** **1 cup Clearjel or cornstarch**	Combine in large saucepan. Cook until thickened, stirring constantly.

Stir 7 qts. of fruit into syrup and ladle into jars, leaving at least 1 inch headspace. (If jars are filled too full, syrup will spew out during processing!) Tighten lids and process in boiling water bath for 25 minutes. (You may wish to add a little flavoring to fruit when opening the jars. Add 1 tsp. lemon juice per qt. to blueberries or raspberries, and 1 tsp. almond flavoring and several drops of red color to each qt. of cherries.)

Harriet Steiner

Dried Beans

(Can kidney beans for chili, or any other dried beans or peas for various other recipes that call for a can of beans or peas.)

Wash beans and soak overnight in cold water enough to cover 2 inches over beans. Cook in same water for 30 minutes. Drain, reserving liquid, and pack loosely into jars. Add ½ tsp. salt to each pint jar. Then fill jar to within 1 inch of top with reserved bean liquid. Add boiling water if you do not have enough bean liquid. Tighten lids and process at 10 lbs. pressure: pints 75 minutes and quarts 90 minutes.

Canned Hamburger Bologna

30 lbs. hamburger **¾ lb. Morton's Tenderquick meat cure**	Mix together well, and let stand in cool place for 24 hours.
½ cup sugar **2 tbsp. salt** **2 tsp. black pepper** **2 tsp. saltpeter** **2 tsp. garlic salt** **2½ tbsp. liquid smoke**	Mix in thoroughly. Pack in widemouthed jars. (You would not be able to remove the chunk of balony in narrow mouthed cans!)

Tighten lids and process at 10 lbs. pressure: pints 75 minutes and quarts 90 minutes. (May be sliced and eaten cold, or fried until brown on each side.)

Pork and Beans

4 cups navy beans	Soak overnight in water to cover 2 inches over top of beans. Cook 1 hour in the same water. Drain, reserving liquid.
½ lb. chopped salt pork, bacon, or ham **2 cups chopped onion** **½ cup brown sugar** **1½ cups catsup** **¼ cup molasses** **2 tbsp. prepared mustard** **4 tsp. salt** **½ tsp. cinnamon** **¼ tsp. black pepper**	Mix in thoroughly, adding 2 cups of the reserved bean liquid. Ladle into jars leaving 1 inch headspace.

Tighten lids and process at 10 lbs. pressure: pints 75 minutes and quarts 90 minutes.

Yield: approximately 8 pts.

Catsup

(Rapid boiling helps to retain color and flavor.)

1 peck tomatoes (2 gals.) (a little over 1 gal. juice)	Cook until tender and sieve. Then boil rapidly to ½ volume (approx. 2 or 3 hours).
6 small onions **3 red sweet peppers**	Process in blender with a little of the juice and add after the first hour of cooking.
2 tbsp. mixed pickling spice **1½ tbsp. celery seed**	Tie in cheesecloth bag and add with peppers.
3 cups sugar **1 cup vinegar** **1 tbsp. salt**	Add with peppers, and continue to cook until volume is reduced to half.
1½ tsp. black pepper **1½ tsp. tumeric** **2 tbsp. Clearjel or cornstarch dissolved in ¼ cup water**	Add, stirring constantly until slightly thickened.

Pour into jars and seal.

Yield: 8 pts.

Zola Showalter

Smooth Catsup

6 pts. tomato juice 4 cups sugar 2 cups vinegar 2 tsp. salt 1 tsp. dry mustard 1 tsp. ground cloves	Combine in large kettle.

. . . .

1 med. onion, finely chopped 1 tsp. celery seed	Tie in gauze bag and place in mixture so it can be removed after cooking. Cook for 1 hour.

. . . .

¼ cup Clearjel or cornstarch dissolved in ½ cup water	Add, stirring until thickened. Ladle into jars.

. . . .

Tighten lids, and process in boiling water bath for 10 minutes.

Yield: 7 pts.

Kathryn Heatwole

. . . .

Cole Slaw to Freeze

See recipe on page 492 for German Slaw which is excellent for freezing.

. . . .

Easy Frozen Corn

Shuck, silk, and wash corn. Then chill it (raw) thoroughly in ice water. Drain and cut off cob.

. . . .

15 cups corn ¾ cup sugar 1½ tbsp. salt 1 qt. ice water	Mix and put in containers.

. . . .

(For 1 pt. use the following portions: 1 ¼ tbsp. sugar, ¾ tsp. salt, and ½ cup ice water.)

Yield: 9 pts.

Elizabeth Yoder

. . . .

Mincemeat

(Use cold roast beef for the meat. You may include part pork roast or a little browned sausage.)

1½ gal. raw apples ½ gal. meat	Run through coarse blade on food grinder

. . . .

2 lbs. raisins	Cook in water to almost cover for 15 minutes.

. . . .

2 qts. canned cherries, undrained 2 qts. apple cider 2 tbsp. salt 4 cups sugar ½ cup vinegar (see next page)	Combine with meat and cooked raisins (including liquid), mixing thoroughly. Cook for 5 minutes, stirring constantly. Fill jars leaving 1 inch headspace.

1 tbsp. ground cinnamon
1 tbsp. ground cloves
1 tbsp. ground allspice

Process in boiling water bath for 1 hour.

Yield: approximately 12 qts.   *Kathryn Heatwole*

"Crushed Pineapple" from Zucchini Squash

(Some people really like this recipe and others definitely do not! I believe some brands of pineapple oil give a much better flavor than others. Use large zucchini. Peel and remove seeds. Cut into long strips. Use coarse blade on food grinder to grind it. Drain in colander and then measure 1 gallon.)

1 gal. ground zucchini squash	Have ready.
1 (46-oz.) can pineapple juice (unsweetened) **3 cups sugar**	Heat to boiling, stirring to dissolve sugar.
½ cup lemon juice (may use reconstituted bottled) **½ tsp. pineapple oil**	Add and mix well with squash. Dip into pint jars, leaving 1 inch headspace.

Process at 10 lbs. pressure for 30 minutes.

Yield: 11 pts.   *Alice Trissel*

Pizza (or Spaghetti) Sauce

3 gal. tomato chunks **3 med. onions, chopped** **1 bay leaf**	Cook together until tender, about 15 minutes. Then sieve.
¾ cup sugar **⅓ cup salt** **1 tbsp. paprika** **4 tsp. ground oregano** **1 tbsp. chili powder** **2 tbsp. garlic salt**	Mix in thoroughly, and heat to boiling.
3½ to 4 cups Clearjel or cornstarch **2 cups water or more**	Stir until dissolved, and add to mixture, stirring constantly until thickened.

Fill jars, leaving 1 inch headspace. Tighten lids and process in boiling water bath for 15 minutes.

Yield: approximately 25 pts.   *Dorothy Shank Showalter*

Sauerkraut (Made in Jars)

Shred amount of cabbage desired. Mix with salt, adding 1 tsp. salt per 1 lb. of cabbage which will fill a 1 pt. jar. Pack cabbage solidly in jar to within 1 inch of the top. If there is not enough cabbage juice in jar, add cold water to come to the top of the cabbage, leaving 1 inch headspace. Place lids on jars loosely. Let sit in basement for 1 week to sour. Clean off sealing edge of jar, screw lids tightly, and process in boiling water bath for 15 minutes. To develop flavor let canned sauerkraut stand 6 weeks before using.

Tomato Juice Cocktail

6 qt. tomato juice
1½ tbsp. salt
1 cup sugar
1 tsp. onion salt
1 tsp. celery salt
½ tsp. garlic salt
¼ tsp. black pepper

Mix thoroughly.

Pour into cans leaving ½ inch headspace. Tighten lids and process in boiling water bath for 15 minutes.

Yield: 6 qts.

Anna Mae Weaver

Tomato Soup

2¼ gals. tomatoes, cut in chunks
6 med. onions, chopped
6 stems celery, finely chopped
3 bay leaves

Cook together until tender (approx. 20 to 30 minutes). Discard bay leaves. Run mixture through a sieve.

1 cup sugar
2 tbsp. salt
1 tsp. black pepper
2 tbsp. butter or margarine

Stir in until dissolved.

½ cup Clearjel or cornstarch
¾ cup water

Dissolve and stir in. Cook, stirring constantly until thickened.

Fill jars, leaving 1 inch headspace. Tighten lids, and process in boiling water bath for 45 minutes.

Yield: 14 pts.

Wanda Good

Vegetable Juice Cocktail
(A good substitute for V-8 juice)

1¾ gals. tomato chunks
2 cups chopped onions
1 cup chopped carrots
2 cups chopped celery
2 cups shredded cabbage

Cook together in large kettle until tender, about 20 to 30 minutes. Run through sieve.

¾ cup sugar
4 tsp. salt
1 tbsp. celery seed
¼ tsp. garlic powder
⅛ tsp. cayenne pepper

Mix in thoroughly. Fill jars, leaving ½ inch headspace.

Tighten lids and process in boiling water bath for 35 minutes.

Yield: 7 qts.

Vegetable Soup

2 lbs. hamburger, browned and drained
1½ qts. water
1½ qts. chopped tomatoes, about 9 large
1½ qts. cubed potatoes, 6 med.
1 qt. finely shredded cabbage
1 qt. cut corn, uncooked, about 9 ears
1 qt. sliced carrots, 8 med.
2 cups diced celery
2 cups chopped onions
1 green pepper, chopped
1 qt. green beans, cut in ¾ inch pieces
2½ tbsp. salt
3 tbsp. sugar

Combine all ingredients in large kettle, and cook 5 minutes. Fill jars, leaving 1 inch headspace.

Tighten lids, and process at 10 lbs. pressure for 90 minutes. (Additional seasoning may be added when you open jars to serve.)

Yield: 7 qts.

Sliced Zucchini

Pick zucchini when young and tender before seedy area is developed. Do not peel. Slice in rings. If desired, rings may be cut into halves or fourths. Pack tightly in jars until ¾ full. Then add seasoning. For each pint of squash add:

1 tbsp. chopped green pepper	Place in each jar of squash. Then finish packing
1 tbsp. chopped onion	tightly with squash until filled up to the neck of
1 tsp. sugar	the jar.
½ tsp. salt	
⅛ tsp. basil	
⅛ tsp. leaf oregano	
a dash of garlic powder	

thick tomato juice to fill can	Fill can with juice leaving ¾ inch headspace.

Process at 10 pounds pressure for 35 minutes.

Beet Pickle

(Small beets are best, but larger beets may be cut in quarters or ⅜-inch slices if desired. Cook beets and prepare according to directions for canning beets on page 604.)

4 qts. beets	Pack in jars.

2½ cups vinegar	Combine in saucepan, and heat to boiling. Boil
2½ cups water	5 minutes.
2½ cups sugar	
½ tsp. salt	
2 tsp. whole allspice	
1 (3-inch) stick cinnamon	
½ tsp. whole clove	
1 tbsp. pickling spice (optional)	

Pour over beets in cans leaving 1 inch headspace. Tighten lids, and process in boiling water bath for 10 minutes.

Yield: 4 qts.

Evelyn Basinger
Margaret Adams

Old-Fashioned Cucumber Pickles

Pick cucumbers while still very small (2 or 3 inches long) and wash. Pack jars with cucumbers. Add a slice of onion on top of each jar. Fill jars with brine made by combining the following ingredients for *each* quart:

1½ cups hot water	Combine, stirring until dissolved. Fill jars leav-
½ cup strong vinegar*	ing 1 inch headspace.
1 tsp. salt	
5 whole-grain saccharin	

Tighten lids, and process in boiling water bath for 10 minutes. (*If vinegar is very light in color, use 1 cup vinegar and 1 cup water.)

Old-Fashioned Bread and Butter Pickles

(Use fresh cucumbers, about 3 to 5 inches long, for these pickles. Do not peel.)

1 gal. cucumbers **2 large onions**	Slice thinly.
½ cup salt **ice water to cover**	Stir to dissolve, and pour over cucumber mixture. Cover with heavy plate to hold down under water. Let stand 3 hours. Drain thoroughly and pack in jars.
8 cups vinegar **4 cups sugar** **4 tsp. mustard seed** **1 tsp. celery seed** **1 tsp. tumeric**	Mix together in saucepan. Heat to boiling and fill jars, leaving 1 inch headspace.

Process in boiling water bath for 10 minutes.

Barbara Bowman

Corn Relish

Cook 18 to 20 ears of corn in boiling water enough to cover (do in 2 or 3 batches) for 5 minutes. Cool in cold water. Cut from cob. Put scrapings in another container to use otherwise. Use only whole kernels in relish.

8 cups cut corn **2 cups water** **4 cups finely chopped celery** **2 cups red sweet pepper, chopped** **2 cups green pepper, chopped** **1 cup chopped onion** **2 cups sugar** **2 cups vinegar** **2 tsp. celery seed** **2 tbsp. salt**	Combine in large saucepan and cook 5 minutes.
½ cup water **½ cup flour** **2 tbsp. dry mustard** **1 tsp. tumeric**	Shake in batter shaker until smooth. Stir in. Cook and stir 5 minutes more. Fill jars, leaving 1 inch headspace.

Tighten lids and process in boiling water bath for 15 minutes.

Yield: 7 pts.

Alice Trissel

Dill Pickles (with Fresh Dill)

Wash cucumbers and let stand in cold water overnight. For crisper pickles, you may add 1 cup pickling lime to 1 gal. water to soak. Small cucumbers may be canned whole, or medium ones may be sliced. Pack in jars.

⅛ tsp. powdered alum **1 garlic clove (or 3 tbsp. chopped onion)** **2 sprigs fresh dill** **1 tsp. salt**	Add to each quart jar.
1 cup vinegar **3 cups water**	Heat to boiling and pour over cucumbers in jars, leaving 1 inch headspace.

Tighten lids, and process in boiling water bath for 10 minutes.

Dill Pickles (with Dill Seed)

Use small whole cucumbers, or slice in rings, and pack in jars raw.

1 tsp. salt **½ tsp. dill seed** **½ tsp. mustard seed** **2 whole grain saccharin**	Add to each qt.
onion slices	Put a slice on top of each jar.
vinegar **water**	Fill jars with a mixture of half vinegar and half water, leaving 1 inch headspace

Tighten lids and process in boiling water bath for 10 minutes.

Gladys and Brownie Driver

Amish Garlic Sweet Dill Pickles

Slice medium-sized pickles ¼ inch thick into jars. Place 1 garlic bud and 1 or 2 sprigs fresh green dill into each qt.

3 cups sugar **1 cup vinegar** **3 cups water** **2 tbsp. salt**	Combine in saucepan. Heat to boiling. Pour over cucumbers in jars, leaving 1 inch headspace.

Tighten lids. Process in boiling water bath for 8 to 10 minutes. Ready to eat after two weeks.

Dorothy Slaubaugh Grove

Lime Pickle

Slice 7 lbs. cucumbers crosswise into ¼ inch or less slices. Mix 1 cup pickling lime with 1 gal. water and soak cucumbers in glass jar or crock for 24 hours. (Do not use aluminum.) Stir occasionally. Then remove from lime water and rinse in 3 cool waters. Soak 3 more hours in ice water. Remove carefully to drain. Then make syrup:

. . . .

2 qts. vinegar
7 cups sugar
1 tbsp. salt
several drops green color

Combine in saucepan. Heat to boiling, and pour over cucumbers. Let stand 5 or 6 hours, or overnight.

. . . .

2 tbsp. mixed pickling spice

Place in cheesecloth bag, and add to cucumber and syrup mixture. Heat to boiling and simmer 30 minutes.

. . . .

Remove bag of spice. Pack sterilized jars with cucumbers. Fill with boiling syrup, leaving ½ inch headspace, and seal. May be processed in boiling water bath for 10 minutes, if desired.

. . . .

Seven-Day Sweet Pickles

First day: Wash 7 lbs, medium-sized cucumbers and cover with boiling water.
Second day: Drain. Cover with fresh boiling water.
Third day: Repeat second day.
Fourth day: Repeat second day.
Fifth day: Cut pickels into ¼-inch rings
Combine:

. . . .

1 qt. white vinegar
6 cups sugar
8 whole-grain saccharin
2 tbsp. salt
2 tbsp. mixed pickling spice (Tie
 loosely in cheesecloth or gauze
 bag.)

Bring to a full rolling boil. Pour over sliced pickles.

. . . .

Sixth day: Drain off syrup, heat it to boiling, and pour over pickles.
Seventh day: Pack pickles in jars, fill jars with syrup, leaving 1 inch headspace. Tighten lids and then process in boiling water bath for 10 minutes.

. . . .

Refrigerator Pickles

Wash 3 qt. jars and rinse inside with boiling water to sterilize them. Slice 1 med. onion into each jar, then fill with cucumbers sliced into ⅛ to ¼-inch thick slices. Make syrup.

. . . .

4 cups sugar
3 cups vinegar*
1 cup water
½ cup salt
1¼ tsp. tumeric
1¼ tsp. celery seed
1¼ tsp. mustard seed

Stir together until sugar is dissolved. (Do not heat, syrup is used cold.) Pour over cucumbers in jars to cover. Screw on lids.

. . . .

Refrigerate at least 5 days before using. (*If vinegar is mild, use 4 cups and omit water.) These pickle are delicious and will keep for as long as 10 months in the refrigerator!

Yield: 3 qts.

Dorothy Shank Showalter

Crisp Sweet Pickles

1. Scrub 4 gallons medium-sized cucumbers, and place in large crock with enough salt water to cover. Add 2 cups salt per gallon of water. Let stand 1 week.
2. Then pour off brine and rinse off pickles. Drain well. Add enough boiling water to cover and let stand overnight.
3. Drain. Cut in ¼-inch slices. Dissolve 3½ tbsp. alum in boiling water enough to cover pickles and let stand overnight again.
4. Drain. Make syrup:

. . . .

5 qts. sugar (a 10-lb. bag)
2 qts. white vinegar
2 tbsp. mustard seed
2 tbsp. broken stick cinnamon
2 tbsp. celery seed
2 tbsp. whole clove
several drops green color if desired

Combine in saucepan. Heat to boiling and pour over pickles.

. . . .

Let stand overnight. The next day, drain off syrup, heat to boiling, and pour over pickles again. Do this for two more days. On third day, pack pickles in jars, fill with syrup, leaving 1 inch headspace. Tighten lids and process in boiling water bath for 10 minutes.

Gladys Harman

Watermelon Rind Pickles

Save rind from one large watermelon, (about 6½ lbs.) Pickles will be most attractive with a small amount of pink melon left on rind. Peel rind, and cut in 1½-inch pieces.
Dissolve ½ cup salt in 2 qts. water. Pour over rind and soak overnight.
Drain, rinse with clear water, and drain again.
Cook rind in fresh water until tender and translucent. Drain well.
Make syrup:

. . . .

5 cups sugar	Combine in saucepan and boil for 2 minutes.
2 cups vinegar	Pour over rind. Let stand overnight.
¼ tsp. oil of cinnamon, or 2 (3-inch) sticks cinnamon, crushed	
¼ tsp. oil of cloves, or 24 whole cloves	
(It is best to tie spices loosely in a cheesecloth or gauze bag so they can be removed before canning pickles.)	

. . . .

Drain off syrup, heat it to boiling, and pour over rind again for two more days.
On the third day, pack rind in jars, and fill with syrup, leaving 1 inch headspace. Tighten lids and process in boiling water bath for 10 minutes.

Yield: approximately 7 pts.

Miriam Brubaker

. . . .

Zucchini Relish

12 cups thinly sliced or shredded zucchini	Mix together well and let stand overnight. The next morning rinse with cold water and drain well.
4 cups chopped onions	
4 cups finely shredded cabbage (optional)	
2 red sweet peppers, chopped	
2 green sweet peppers, chopped	
5 tbsp. salt	

. . . .

6 cups sugar	Combine in saucepan and cook until slightly thickened. Add vegetables and mix well. Fill jars, leaving ¾ inch headspace. Tighten lids.
2½ cups vinegar	
5 tbsp. cornstarch	
1 tbsp. dry mustard	
1½ tsp. celery seed	
1 tsp. tumeric	
½ tsp. nutmeg	
½ tsp. black pepper	

. . . .

Process at 5 lbs. pressure for 10 minutes. Or process in boiling water bath for 15 minutes.

Yield: 6 pts.

Barbara Bowman

. . . .

Old-Fashioned Apple Butter (Large Amount)

(This recipe is used to make apple butter for the Mennonite Central Committee relief sales in Virginia. I was privileged to help with the most recent apple butter boiling. Fourteen large kettles of apple butter were boiled the first day, each yielding approximately 30 gallons of apple butter! The same amount was boiled the following day, and it was all sold at the relief sale. Since they ran out of apple butter, they are planning to have 3 boilings for the next sale for a total of 42 kettles of apple butter! Eldon and Sue Brydge graciously shared the recipe with me. Use a 40-gallon copper kettle for boiling the apple butter. Peeled, cored, and quartered apples may be used, if desired. Apples will disintegrate during cooking. The sauce is used here to save a lot of time at the last minute.)

30 to 35 gals. applesauce or apple
  snitz
5 gals. apple cider
60 lbs. sugar
¼ cup salt
¼ cup ground cinnamon
1½ tbsp. ground allspice
2 tbsp. red color
1 (¼-oz.) bottle oil of cinnamon
¼ of a (¼-oz.) bottle oil of cloves

6:00 a.m.—Pour all of cider into kettle and enough applesauce to fill up to 4 inches below top of kettle. Make a fire under the kettle and keep fire hot enough to keep mixture boiling continuously and rapidly during the whole process. Slow cooking takes too long and does not produce top-quality apple butter. Stir mixture constantly with a wooden stirrer to keep it from scorching. Keep adding applesauce until 10:00, keeping kettle filled to 4 inches below top of kettle. Do not add more applesauce after 10:00.

11:00—Add the food coloring.

12:00—Add the sugar and ground spices, continuing to cook, stirring constantly. Mixture should be beginning to thicken when you add the sugar.

Add oil of cinnamon and cloves just before removing kettle from the fire. If boiled rapidly, apple butter will probably be finished at about 1:30 or 2:30. To test for doneness, dip several tablespoonfuls onto a plate. Tilt plate sideways, if no liquid runs out to the side of the plate, it is done. Pour in sterilized jars, and seal.

Yield: approximately 120 qts.   *Eldon and Sue Brydge*

Apple Butter (Oven Method)

1 gal. applesauce
6¾ cup brown sugar
1 cup apple cider, or vinegar
1 cup crushed pineapple (optional)
1 tsp. ground cinnamon
¼ tsp. ground allspice
¼ tsp. ground cloves

Mix together in bottom part of roaster or deep pan. Bake in 350-degree oven for approximately 3 hours, stirring occasionally until thickened. Pour in sterilized jars and seal.

May be cooked on top of the stove for approximately 1 ½ hours, if desired. Stir frequently.

Yield: about 5 pts.

Apple Butter (Small Amount)

2 qts. apple cider	Boil until reduced to 1 qt.
4 qts. apples*	Pare, core, and slice in thin pieces. Add, and cook slowly until mixture begins to thicken, stirring frequently.
3 cups sugar 1 cup brown sugar 1 tsp. ground cinnamon, or ¼ tsp. oil of cinnamon	Add, and continue to cook until of spreading consistency. (Use test given in large amount recipe.)

(*You may substitute applesauce in place of apples. Reduce sugar to 3 cups, since applesauce will already be sweetened.)

Yield: 5 to 6 pts. *Ella May Miller*

Grape Jelly Made from Juice

1 (6-oz.) can frozen grape juice concentrate 2½ cups water 1 (1¾-oz.) pkg. powdered fruit pectin (such as Sure-jell)	Combine in large saucepan. Heat to a good rolling boil.
3¾ cups sugar	Add all at once, and boil hard 1 minute, stirring constantly. Remove from heat.

Skim off foam. Ladle into jar, leaving ½ inch headspace. Seal with melted paraffin.

Yield: 4 ½ cups

Cider-Cinnamon Jelly

5 cups apple cider 7½ cups sugar 1 tsp. red food coloring ¼ tsp. oil of cinnamon	Combine in saucepan and heat to boiling. Boil 1 minute.
2 (1¾-oz.) pkgs. powdered fruit pectin (such as Sure-jell)	Add, and heat to boiling again, stirring constantly. Boil 3 to 5 minutes.

Pour into jars and seal.

Barbara Bowman

Blackberry or Raspberry Jelly

(Cook berries for about 5 minutes until tender. Mash through a strainer with the back of a spoon to remove seeds.)

5 cups berry pulp **1 (1¾-oz.) pkg. powdered fruit pectin (such as Sure-jell)**	Combine in large saucepan and heat to a full rolling boil, stirring constantly.
7 cups sugar	Add—all at once, Bring to full rolling boil again, stirring constantly. Boil hard 1 minute. Remove from heat.

Skim off foam. Ladle immediately into hot jars, leaving ¼ inch headspace. Tighten lids and process in boiling water bath for 10 minutes.

Yield: about 4 pts.

Orange Marmalade

(Choose thick-skinned fruit free of blemishes. Avoid fruit which has "waxtreated" or "color added" stamped on the skins. Wash thoroughly and trim off any scarred spots, and the stem area.)

4 large oranges **1 large lemon**	Cut in half and squeeze out juice. Discard seeds and woody membrane. Grind rinds and pulp through smallest blade of food grinder. Combine juice and rinds in saucepan.
2 qts. water	Add. Heat to boiling and simmer 5 minutes. Cover, and let stand overnight. The next morning, cook rapidly until peel is tender, about 1 hour.
5½ cups sugar	Add, stirring until dissolved. Cook rapidly to jellying point, about 30 minutes, stirring frequently. Pour into sterilized jars and seal.

Yield: about 4 pts.   *Ella May Miller*

Old-Fashioned Peach Butter

Peel, pit, and slice about 18 medium-sized ripe peaches. Cook until soft, adding only enough water to prevent sticking, a little over 1 cup. Press through a sieve.

4 cups sugar **1 tsp. lemon juice**	Add, and cook until thick, at least 30 to 45 minutes. Stir frequently to prevent scorching.
1 tsp. ground cinnamon **½ tsp. ground nutmeg**	Add. Pour into sterilized jars and seal.

May process in boiling water bath for 10 minutes.

Yield: 4 pts.

Peach Jam

6 cups crushed peaches 6 cups sugar 1 tbsp. lemon juice 2 cups crushed pineapple	Combine in saucepan. Cook 20 minutes.

1 (3-oz.) pkg. orange-flavored
   gelatin
1 (1¾-oz.) pkg. powdered fruit
   pectin (such as Sure-jell)
	Add, and cook 2 minutes.

Pour into jars and seal.

Red Beet Jelly

6 cups red beet juice
½ cup lemon juice (bottled
   reconstituted)
2 (1¾-oz.) pkgs. powdered fruit
   pectin (such as Sure-jell)
	Combine in saucepan. Boil 1 minute.

8 cups sugar 1 (3-oz.) pkg. red-raspberry- flavored gelatin	Add, and boil several minutes more, stirring constantly.

Pour into jars and seal.

Barbara Bowman

Strawberry Honey (or Ice Cream Topping)

1 cup cold water 1 (1¾-oz.) pkg. powdered fruit pectin (such as Sure-jell)	Mix in saucepan. Boil 1 minute. Remove from heat.
6½ cups sugar 3½ cups crushed fresh strawberries	Add, stirring well.

Let stand 24 hours. Fill jars, and store in the freezer.

Yield: about 5 pts.

Fannie B. Heatwole, my mother

Frozen Strawberry Jam (Uncooked)

4 cups crushed fresh strawberries	Pour in saucepan.
1 (1¾-oz.) pkg. powdered fruit pectin (such as Sure-jell)	Sift in, and stir thoroughly. Let set 30 minutes, stirring occasionally.
1 cup corn syrup **5½ cups sugar**	Add, mixing well. Warm very slightly just to dissolve sugar.
¼ cup lemon juice	Add.

Pour into jars and freeze.

Wanda Good

Strawberry Freezer Jam

2 cups crushed strawberries **4 cups sugar**	Combine thoroughly and let stand 10 minutes.
¾ cup water **1 (1¾-oz.) pkg. powdered fruit pectin (such as Sure-jell)**	Heat to boiling in saucepan. Boil 1 minute, stirring constantly. Remove from heat.

Immediately stir into fruit mixture. Continue stirring 3 minutes. Then ladle into jars leaving ½ inch headspace. Cover and let stand at room temperature 24 hours. Then store in freezer.

Yield: 4¾ cups

NON~FOOD RECIPES & MISCELLANEOUS TIPS

NON-FOOD RECIPES AND MISCELLANEOUS TIPS

Ideas for Leftovers

My parents taught us from little up not to waste things, especially food. There wasn't much tolerance for our likes and dislikes. If we didn't care for something, they thought we were just being *snousy* or too *persnickety* to eat it! (They did not speak Pennsylvania Dutch, but a few words were handed down from previous generations to describe various situations where an English word didn't seem quite to fit the occasion. Anyway, our parents didn't think it was right to pass up good food just because we were too choosy in our tastes. When we misbehaved, sometimes we would receive a *snelicks* (we called it) on top of the head. This was a quick snap of the second finger over the thumb. Language Professor Ernest G. Gehman tells me that *persnickety* is a correct word used commonly among the Dutch, but "snousy" was probably our family version of the Dutch word "schnausich." He said "snelicks" probably came from the Dutch word, "schneller," pronounced "schnella" and meaning a quick snap (the English word is fillip).

We were also required to eat every bit of the fat on any meat and every bit of skin on the chicken whether it turned out crispy or soft, so we wouldn't be guilty of wasting it. With people in the world starving to death, we dared not be wasteful with food!

I'm thankful that our parents taught us to be responsible and thrifty, and that we learned to enjoy foods we didn't think we liked simply because we were required to eat a small amount of them along with foods we enjoyed. I'm also thankful that we are much better informed today about good nutrition and the effects of various foods on our health. The fat still doesn't need to be discarded by the thrifty homemaker; it can be rendered for soap making. (See the index for the recipe.)

I also feel strongly that it is important not to waste food. Many times food is unintentionally wasted simply because persons are not aware of good ways to manage leftovers. So here are a few ideas. I'm sure you'll discover many others along the way.

Bananas: Don't waste extra ripe bananas. Freeze whole or sliced to eat as a snack while frozen. Or peel and either slice or mash and sprinkle with lemon juice to use in banana bread or milk shakes. Whole bananas can be frozen peeled or unpeeled. Freezing unpeeled prevents darkening, but banana should be thawed approximately 5 to 10 minutes for easier peeling before eating.

Bread: Leftover scraps of bread, stale bread, leftover biscuits, or corn bread are excellent for dressing, for seasoned bread cubes, for egg casseroles, and for bread crumbs. Let dry until hard. Accumulate in a bag in the freezer for use as needed. For seasoned bread cubes, see page 336. For fine bread crumbs to use for breading foods, place dried scraps in a plastic bag and use rolling pin to crush into fine crumbs.

Cake or Cookie Crumbs: These can be sprinkled over desserts to garnish them, or to liven up a bowl of cereal, or as a topping for ice cream.

Celery Leaves: These are excellent used fresh in soups and stews, or in tossed salad and lettuce salad. They may also be dried in the microwave, or spread out on a tray and placed in the attic or other warm place to dry for several days. When thoroughly dried, crush the leaves with your hand and place in tightly covered jars to store. Or chop them and store in the freezer. Use for soups, sauces, and the like.

Chicken (or Turkey): There are so many good things you can make with diced cooked chicken that I usually bake double what I think we will eat so I have plenty left over! Debone right after the meal, place in tightly covered containers, and freeze. It can be used for creamed chicken, chow mein, casseroles, or added to a pot of cooked noodles or rice along with chicken bouillon if you don't have broth. It is also handy for chicken salad, chicken rolls, and many other dishes. Leftover turkey can be substituted in most recipes calling for chicken. Don't throw away the bones! See page 357 for directions for recycling the bones.

Cooked Cereals: These can be reheated with a little additional water for another meal, or they can be added to meat loaf or hamburgers. Leftover mush or cream of wheat can be sliced cold, fried on each side in margarine in skillet, and served with syrup or apple butter.

Fruits: Drain the juice from leftover peaches or other fruit and thicken it on the stove with cornstarch or Clearjel. Chill and fold in fruit, a diced banana, and some orange breakfast drink powder. Swirl with whipped cream or topping for a delightful new dessert. Fruit can also be used for fruit cobbler. Or set the fruit in gelatin with a little mint or vanilla flavoring and a banana added to give it new appeal. Another way to perk up leftover fruit, especially in the summertime, is to place it in the freezer until half frozen. This is especially good with a combination of peaches (crushed slightly), crushed pineapple, and diced bananas with orange juice added. Use leftover fruit juice in gelatin in place of water. Many kinds of juices are delicious mixed with orange breakfast drink. Leftover strawberries that look wilty make delicious milk shakes. Add a little red color for looks. Peaches and berries also make delicious milk shakes.

Green Pepper: Portions of leftover green pepper can be chopped and frozen in a plastic bag to add to casseroles, soups, and stews.

Ham Broth: Use for sausage gravy, or as part of liquid when cooking dry beans. Or use as part of liquid for potato, lentil, or split pea soup.

Icings: Leftover icing can be placed in small tightly covered containers, or little dabs of powdered sugar icings may be wrapped in plastic wrap and fastened with a twist tie or rubber band. Store in freezer until you have enough for a sheet cake. Use it to ice cake rainbow fashion, or mix lighter colors for special shades. It is also handy for icing cupcakes or spreading between graham crackers to serve for snacks. Leftover white icing can be used in place of part of the sugar in custards or other dishes that you want to sweeten.

Liver: Run cooked liver through the food grinder. Mix with mayonnaise and other seasoning, such as onion, as desired. Serve on crackers or in celery sticks.

Macaroni: Break an egg into 1 or 2 cups of leftover macaroni, toss, and heat in margarine in skillet until egg is set and macaroni is heated through. Any leftover chipped ham or corned beef may be added. Macaroni may also be added to soup.

Meats: Leftover fragments from roasts can be chipped and used in stews and soups. Hamburger can also be used in soups or chili, in hash or pizza. *Ham* is another item which is certainly great to have stored in the freezer for casseroles. It can be ground up or chipped and added to scalloped potatoes, eggs, omelets, salads, and many other dishes. You can make a cream sauce using chipped ham, chicken bouillon, a little MSG, or gravy seasoning. Thicken with a little cornstarch and serve over toast or biscuits. Chipped ham or crumbled bacon is delicious in green beans, navy beans, and other vegetables. Crumbled *bacon* is excellent in scrambled eggs and salad. Leftover *hot dogs* or *sausages* can be sliced in rings and frozen until you collect enough for a meal. Then heat in skillet with barbecue sauce and serve with toothpicks for Sunday evening snack. They could also be added to scalloped potatoes instead. Leftover *roast,* or other meat that turned out tough, can be run through the food grinder and added to soups, stews, or casseroles. Leftover *meat loaf* makes excellent sandwich meat when sliced cold. Meat that is too dried out can also be salvaged in soups or casseroles. (On one occasion I unknowingly bought some dried beef that was too hard and dried out to suit anyone's taste. I tried to figure out how to salvage it, and decided to add it to some scalloped potatoes. The family enjoyed them so much they wanted me to buy more just for that purpose!)

Potatoes: Leftover mashed potatoes are another such versatile food that I usually make extra on purpose. Stir an egg and some minced onion or garlic powder, or both, into 2 or 3 cups of mashed potatoes, shape into cakes, and fry on both sides in margarine in skillet. Or place in casserole dish and bake for 40 to 45 minutes. Grated cheese can be added or sprinkled on top. Vegetable casseroles can be topped with mounds of mashed potatoes and grated cheese. For a quick supper, split hot dogs and mound with mashed potatoes with strips of cheese pressed into the hot dogs. Sprinkle with paprika and bake 30 to 40 minutes. Leftover boiled potatoes can be sliced and fried with onion or tossed in the skillet with an egg, or they can be used for potato salad or in potato soup or vegetable soup. Boiled potatoes can be grated, made into potato cakes, and frozen for a quick breakfast. Just fry frozen cakes in margarine in skillet until browned on each side.

Rice: Leftover rice can be reheated with a little water in tightly covered pan, or it can be added to vegetable soup. Make chicken and rice soup by adding chopped cooked chicken and chicken bouillon. Or add 1 egg, 1 tbsp. sugar, and 1 tbsp. flour to approximately 2 cups rice. Shape into cakes and fry on both sides in a little margarine in skillet. It can also be used to make "Glorified Rice" (see index).

Salads: Leftover chipped ham or other meats and vegetables (such as peas or green beans) can be tossed in a salad along with leftover grated bits of cheese. To salvage leftover tossed salad, rinse off dressing in a strainer and cook quickly. May be frozen to add to soups. Many people do not add dressing to a bowl of salad, but pass it in a pitcher at mealtime so salad will not wilt.

Sandwich Fillings: Finely chop up or grind leftover meat and add mayonnaise, mustard, or catsup to make a tasty sandwich spread.

Soup: There is no end to the leftovers that can be accumulated in the freezer for soups! Chopped-up meat fragments, all kinds of vegetables, snipped green onion tops, celery leaves, and the shredded outer leaves of cabbage can all be used. Leftover macaroni, rice, and noodles may be added as well. Broth for soup can be obtained by cooking bones after deboning meats. See page 357. (Young people often used to call this "Deuteronomy soup"—Deuteronomy meaning a collection of a little bit of everything! When I was in school, it was traditional at Eastern Mennonite College and High School to serve this soup on Friday or Saturday evening. The students always recognized bits and pieces of the meals they had been served earlier in the week! Ice cream topped off this meal, a special treat that wasn't often served. We have more delightful seasonings to perk up leftovers today that old-timers didn't have, and soup can be something to look forward to.)

Spaghetti Sauce: Add pinto or kidney beans, onions, and chili powder to leftover spaghetti sauce to make chili.

Tomato Paste: Leftover tomato paste spoils quickly. Spoon onto the dull side of foil in 1-tbsp. mounds and freeze. Then transfer to a plastic bag, label, and return to freezer. This gives premeasured amounts ready to add to any desired dish.

Whipped Cream: Leftover whipped cream can be frozen in a covered container, or place individual mounds of whipped cream on a cookie sheet and freeze until hardened. Use a spatula to loosen mounds, place in plastic bag, and return to freezer. To use, simply place frozen mounds on individual portions of dessert or pie and let thaw at least 15 minutes before serving. If frozen in container, place in refrigerator for a couple of hours to thaw.

Soap Making

Making soap is a fascinating and yet surprisingly easy process. To be able to turn old fats, which many people discard, into soap to be used to wash away grease is an amazing art!

Most of the homemade soap today is processed by the relatively simple cold soap method.

My mother used to make the old-fashioned boiled soap which is a more time-consuming procedure. She used this method so she could salvage the rinds of hams, all fatty tissues trimmed from meat, and most any fatty substance imaginable. Additional caustic soda or lye was added which literally ate up the tissues and meat rinds as we stirred the boiling mixture in a big iron kettle. Not many people today accumulate enough of these at one time to make it worth the effort of making boiled soap, so that process seems to be basically a thing of the past.

I well remember stirring the boiling soap with a smooth wooden stirrer until the hot liquid was light in color and all the rinds and particles were totally dissolved. We would then let the fire go out and leave it in the kettle overnight to cool. The next day when the soap had hardened enough to hold its shape, Mother would cut it out of the kettle in large blocks with a butcher knife. Underneath the thick layer of soap, there was always a layer of a thinner dark soapy lye mixture called "underlye" which had separated to the bottom of the kettle. After removing the soap, we would dip this underlye into a 5-gallon crock jar and save it to use to scrub the washhouse floor, the cement walks around the house, and the porch floor. A dipperful of this mixture in a bucket of hot water, along with some "elbow grease" and a broom, really made things clean!

Making cold soap seems to be increasing in popularity, however, as more people are finding that it is not difficult to make and is a good way to put to good use the fats that are often discarded.

In our local area this week we engaged in a churchwide soap-making effort to make soap for relief to send to needy countries around the world where soap is scarce. This is an interesting project.

The fat for making the soap was acquired from another church relief project. Several months ago Mennonite Central Committee's portable meat canner made its annual stop here in the Shenandoah Valley to can beef which was donated for relief by local farmers. This project has been going on for many years and involves Mennonite congregations all across the United States. In recent years our area has been putting up approximately 20,000 (28-oz.) cans of beef during the canner's stop here. Volunteers came in each day from the different congregations to help process the meat. All the fat that was trimmed from the meat, and the tallow collected from the broth, were saved to make soap. This fat was rendered and set aside for the soap being made this week.

Local people who are interested in the project also save fat throughout the year and bring it to add to the collection. A total of almost 9,000 pounds of fat was accumulated for this year's project. As with the meat canning, each day volunteers come from the different Mennonite churches in the area to help for the day. Yesterday, when I was at the farm where the project was in progress, 13 tubs of soap were being made at one time. As soon as one batch was finished, another was started, keeping the process going until all the 52 forms or molds were filled with soap. Each mold held 2 tubs of soap. The soap is cut out of the molds the following morning, and the molds are filled again each day until all the fat is made into soap. According to Byard and Nell Knicely who are in charge of the project, between 6 and 7 tons of soap will be made by the time the week is over to send for relief—mostly to foreign countries!

If you are discarding any sizable amount of fat, you may want to consider saving it for an MCC project, or to make soap for your own use. Fat can be collected in the refrigerator or in the freezer until you have enough to make it worthwhile to render. Any fatty tissues from any kind of meat, including globs of fat from chicken, can be "fried out" or "rendered" for soap making. This is simply the process of melting the fat out of the fatty meat tissues just the same way lard is made from pork fat.

Rendering Fat: Do not add water to the fat. Simply heat the fat in a skillet, stirring at first until enough fat is melted to keep tissues from sticking. Then cover skillet to prevent spattering, and heat, stirring occasionally, until fat is all melted out of the tissues and only the crisp "cracklings" remain. This will probably take about 10 to 15 minutes for a skillet of fat. Do not heat to the smoking point. Heat only until tissues are no longer spongy, but have become crisp. Let stand until cool enough to handle, then pour through a strainer to remove the cracklings. Store the grease in a cool place until you are ready to make soap. When rendered (or fried out) properly, grease usually keeps well in a cool basement.

Any grease that is collected when you sauté hamburger or other meat, and also the tallow that collects on top of broth, needs to be refrigerated until it is rendered or it will spoil because of the small amount of broth or meat particles that may be in it. A good method to use is to keep a tin can or carton in the refrigerator to add to regularly. When the container gets full, render it, and store it in the basement.

Cleaning Fat: Any fat or tallow from meat that was salted, or rancid or moldy fat, must be cleaned. Salt will cause the soap to separate. To clean the fat, add 1 quart water to 1 quart grease, and heat to the boiling point. Stir mixture, and simmer for several minutes. Let set in a cool place to solidify. The clean fat will collect in a cake on top of the container. Remove fat and discard water with any settlings.

. . . .

Homemade Soap (Cold Soap Method)

1. Prepare a box or mold for the soap. You may simply line a shallow cardboard box with plastic, plastic wrap, or freezer paper—waxed side out. Or you may use waxed milk cartons if desired. This makes a nice long bar that can be cut into 2 blocks. Blocks should not be over 4 inches square, so they can dry out properly.
2. Measure 5 cups of cold water into a stainless steel or a plastic container. (Do not use tin or aluminum.) Slowly add 1 (13-oz.) can caustic soda (Red Seal lye) to the water, stirring with a stainless steel or wooden spoon until lye is dissolved. Solution will become hot. Set aside until mixture is lukewarm. (Be very careful not to splash mixture on skin or on cupboards. Rinse any spatters well with water.)
3. Weigh 6 lbs. of fat into a large stainless steel kettle or saucepan. Heat just until fat is melted. The fat should then be cooled to lukewarm also.
4. When both fat and lye mixture are lukewarm, pour lye mixture very slowly (in a thin stream) into the liquid fat, stirring slowly and constantly to mix evenly throughout container. (Rapid pouring or rapid stirring causes mixture to separate.) Continue stirring until mixture just begins to thicken, and is about the consistency of thick cream or honey. This usually takes about 20 to 30 minutes. Immediately pour mixture into molds or containers to harden.
5. Let set approximately 24 hours until hard enough to hold its shape well when cut. Cut

into bars or cakes with a knife as desired. If using milk cartons, they can usually be torn off and bar can be cut into 2 or more cakes.

6. Lay out cakes of soap with air space between each cake to dry thoroughly and harden. The soap should air-dry from 2 to 6 weeks, depending on the size of the cakes, before storing. It is best to let soap cure about 3 months before using.

Yield: approximately 9 pounds soap

Nell Knicely
Ruth S. Hostetter

. . . .

Homemade soap is excellent when used in soft water. It does not work very satisfactorily in hard water, however. If using in hard water, a water softening compound will need to be added to the water before adding the soap. It may be finely grated for laundry use, or it may be coarsely chopped or grated, and then heated with a little water in a saucepan until mostly melted before pouring into washer. (My mother always felt there was nothing quite like good homemade soap and hot water to get things clean!)

. . . .

WAYS TO SAVE!

Many of the small things we do to save may sound insignificant, and some may wonder if it is worth the effort, but over a period of time they can add up to unbelievably big savings! The difference is often just a matter of thrifty habits that actually take little if any more time and that become a way of life.

The ideas given here are not new, but for the inexperienced it may be helpful to have some listed. You will probably think of many others along the way.

•Use stove burner to fit pan size. A small pan on a large burner wastes a lot of heat.

•Use a lid on pans whenever possible when heating water or food. The lid holds in heat and contents will heat much faster.

•Bake two items instead of one while oven is hot. Make entire oven meal instead of just baking one dish. Double recipes and freeze second batch of cookies, casserole, or whatever, for later use.

•Turn oven off a little while ahead of the time to remove food. There will still be enough heat to finish baking. Stove burners on electric stoves can be turned off ahead. There is no need to have a red hot burner when pan is removed from heat. Food will usually cook or fry for several more minutes after heat is turned off even when not on high heat. (This is not true with gas stove burners.)

•Whenever possible, cook stews and reheat foods on top of the stove instead of heating up the whole oven just to cook or warm a small item. Even leftover casseroles can be heated on top of the stove. Transfer food to skillet, add a little water to steam, cover, and heat.

•Resist temptation to check on food in the oven unnecessarily. Each time oven door is opened, a lot of heat escapes.

•Do not preheat oven way ahead of when you need it. It usually takes between 5 and 10 minutes to heat. Adjust racks before preheating to avoid holding door open when oven is hot. There is no need to preheat oven for foods such as roasts, most casseroles, and baked potatoes. When oven has been preheated, open and close door quickly when inserting food. Place food right by the oven door to keep time door is open to a minimum. If you are basting in the oven, do so quickly so a minimum amount of heat escapes. If it will take a while, quickly remove item from the oven, and place on top of the stove to baste. Then return to oven.

• Do not open the refrigerator door and stand there trying to decide what to have for supper while letting the cold out!

• Keep basic items in the same place in the refrigerator, so you won't have to search for the jelly or cheese, or whatever, each time you open the door, but will be able to locate items immediately.

• When clearing the table at mealtime, collect all refrigerator items next to the refrigerator. Then put them all in the refrigerator at one time instead of opening the door for each item. The same applies for getting them out.

• Do not place warm foods in the refrigerator. Let cool to room temperature, then refrigerate.

• If you do not have a frost-free refrigerator, it is important to defrost it regularly (when frost is over ¼-inch thick) to avoid a frost buildup. It takes more electricity to cool through a thick coat of frost and causes more wear on the motor of the refrigerator.

• Most principles for holding the door of a refrigerator open unnecessarily also apply to the freezer. Decide what you want before opening the door. Keep foods organized so you know where to find quickly what you want.

• A chest-type freezer will not let out nearly as much cold as an upright one when door is opened. Do not slam door closed as the air pressure with quick movement forces out much inside air.

• Keep a pitcher handy by the sink to save the water you draw off to get hot water. Use it to water houseplants, instead of letting it run down the drain. Houseplants don't like chlorinated water or water that is too cold. I keep a bucket in the laundry

room to collect water for this purpose. It gives the chlorine a chance to evaporate and the room temperature of the water will be just right for plants whenever you need it. Besides saving water, you will have healthier plants as well!

• Recycle *good* pieces of aluminum foil and bread bags. They can be run through the dishwater, clipped on a towel rod with a clothespin to dry, and used again for many purposes. (Place a rod on the back of the utility or pantry door just for this purpose. It is important to have a place allotted for specific items you wish to recycle. Many things are thrown out simply because there isn't a specific place to store them out of the way!) Don't waste time trying to clean badly soiled items, however.

• Learn to improvise. When we started housekeeping, I found I could stir flour through a strainer with a spoon to sift it. A tall smooth glass served as a rolling pin until we could afford one. Think up other ways to make do with what you have. You can prepare excellent meals without having a kitchen stocked with all the latest gadgets!

• Do not waste foods. Much of what is thrown away in the kitchen can be used. Before pitching something out, try to think of a way to recycle it! Small amounts of meat and vegetables can be added to salads or they can be frozen for soup. Keep a large plastic bag in the freezer into which you add small bags of ingredients for soup as available. This way the small bags will not get lost in the freezer. Whenever you collect a sizable amount, make soup.

• Cook anything that may be getting a little old in the refrigerator (not food that has spoiled!) just long enough to kill any beginning bacteria. Then add to another food such as a casserole or soup. (This is the way old-timers used to keep food from spoiling when they didn't have refrigerator space.) Fruit can be cooked a minute or two, and made into a gelatin salad, or may be added to other fruit.

• Stale crackers or cereal can be freshened in a turned-off oven after baking.

•Don't throw out crystallized honey or syrup. Place jar on a rack in a pan of water and heat until crystals are melted. Do not boil. Avoid storing honey in refrigerator which causes it to crystallize.

•Soften hardened brown sugar by placing a moistened sponge on a piece of waxed paper on top of sugar in an airtight container. Leave for 2 or 3 days. Remove and replace lid tightly. Sugar may also be heated in 200-degree oven, or in the microwave until softened—but do not melt.

•It is cheaper to make your own whipped butter than to buy it. Soften a stick of butter to room temperature, beat with electric mixer until creamy. Slowly add ½ cup vegetable oil or 2 tbsp. milk, beating until light and fluffy. Store covered in refrigerator.

•Learn to cut up poultry yourself instead of paying extra for cut-up packages. It is also easy to debone chicken breasts. Those already deboned are quite expensive.

•Packages of individual serving-size boxes of cereal usually cost two to three times as much per ounce as the same cereal in a larger box. Pre-sugared cereal also costs considerably more than unsweetened and often contains less nutrients and more calories. If large boxes of cereal usually get stale before you can use them, place half of box in a plastic bag and freeze when box is first opened.

•When appearance makes no difference, buy second grade or chopped cheaper grade of vegetables, fruits, olives, and the like. The quality should be the same; the only difference is that pieces can be used in the chopped grade while only perfect fruit can be used in the top grade.

•When purchasing fresh produce, specialize on items in season when they are cheaper. Learn to do without expensive off-season items until they are in season again. Besides the savings, you'll be hungrier for them and they'll be more of a treat!

•Onions often come in plastic mesh bags that can easily be made into handy pot scrubbers. An 8-inch square or a 6 × 8-inch rectangle of mesh is a nice size—whatever you have. Use at least 4 thicknesses of mesh, sewing it together with nylon fishing line. Stitch in and out straight through the middle of 2 or more thicknesses of the net first. (This gives extra fullness to the center.) Then lay this section onto the other 2 thicknesses and continue around the edge, stitching through all 4 thicknesses. Pull both ends of nylon thread together to draw mesh into a ball. Knot securely, and enjoy your free scrubber!

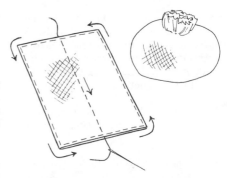

•Check the expiration date on perishable groceries before buying. Don't be stuck with old items at the price of fresh ones, especially if you don't intend to use them immediately.

•Mix leftover pickle juice with vegetable oil to make salad dressing.

•Food in pressurized cans (such as cheese) is very expensive. Buy in jars instead.

•Keep a good supply of basic stock foods on hand so you don't need to make extra trips to the grocery store. Keep a shopping list faithfully. As you are preparing meals and see an item running slightly low, put it on your shopping list immediately so you won't forget. Keep trips to the grocery store to a minimum. Plan at least a week in advance. Don't go grocery shopping when you are hungry to avoid impulse buying! Stick to your memorandum unless you find a better buy while shopping. Buy the cheaper economy size of things you use regularly. Freeze extra amount for later use. Don't buy something just because you have a coupon without checking other brands first to see which is cheaper.

•Buy enriched whole grain or restored cereals, breads, rice, and flour for more nutrition. Cost is usually about the same.

•Avoid buying heavily processed convenience foods that you can make much cheaper yourself. Many half-cooked and breaded convenience foods have lost much of their nutritional value in the processing, besides having many additives to preserve them.

•Watch newspaper ads for specials of the week to plan your menus around.

•In warm weather, keep an insulated cooler in the trunk of the car for placing cold or frozen items to keep them cold until you get home from grocery shopping. I always keep a plastic bottle of ice in the freezer that I pop in the cooler right before leaving. Simply return it to the freezer when you get home so it is ready for the next trip.

•Store foods properly so they won't dry out or absorb flavor from other foods. Leftovers should always be stored tightly covered in refrigerator. Perishable foods should be refrigerated as quickly as possible after purchase.

•An inexpensive rubber scraper is a necessity for removing entire amounts of batters and foods from bowls and pans. Keep several handy in a drawer. It is surprising how much more can be scraped out with a rubber scraper!

•Leftovers deteriorate more quickly than you think. Have a special place for them in plain sight that you check often so they don't get lost in the back of the refrigera-

tor. Yesterday's leftovers can often be added to today's casserole, salad, or sandwich. If it doesn't suit to use them soon, freeze for use later.

•Store small things in the freezer where they won't get lost. I like to keep small things in the freezer part of the refrigerator close at hand. I check this section fairly often, so I don't forget to use up the little dabs of this or that. (In checking the freezer section one time when my daughters were quite small, I spied a jar of something that looked a little like raisins. I didn't remember putting it there, so I opened it to inspect. To my absolute horror, it was a supply of dead flies! I could not believe my eyes, much less figure out what in the wide world was going on! I confronted the girls to see if they knew anything about it, and sure enough, they did. They had taken turns swatting them when I was out, for their little turtle who loved flies! They must have thought I would not approve! I had recently remarked that the turtle would need to get his fill of flies during the summer because there wouldn't be any over winter. They didn't want him to be without his favorite food, so they figured out a way to provide!)

•It saves much effort to keep stove and baking utensils clean as you go. You can easily wipe spills from drip pans or oven as you are doing the dishes before they are baked on. Keep a little metal scrubber by the sink to scour any little spots from bakeware routinely as they occur. You won't believe how much easier this method is over setting aside a big block of time to scour off accumulations that have been repeatedly baked on and are almost impossible to remove! Foods bake much nicer in shiny pans. You also have the satisfaction of clean shiny equipment continually. Appliances last *much* longer if they are well taken care of.

GARDENING TIPS

•Garden seeds can be kept well for a number of years by storing them in the freezer. If you simply store them in the garage, many of the seeds will not germinate the second year.

•Do not do any cultivating or even walk in your garden unless absolutely necessary when soil is wet. This causes soil to become very hard and difficult to work for the remainder of the season.

•Do not destroy broccoli stalks after main head is harvested. New flowerets will grow out all over the stalk for quite some time. Dust or spray stalks *after* each harvest, so you will not get any spray on new growth that is eaten. The hotter the weather gets, the more problem there will be with bugs on broccoli!

•Excess suckers should be pruned from tomato stalks for larger fruit. These can be rooted in water and planted for late tomatoes.

•Gardeners often complain of blight on green beans which often is not blight, but is a root and stem rot caused by a fungus. Just as soon as you notice browning beginning to occur, mix up liquid fertilizer such as Rapid Grow or Miracle Grow, and soak foliage of stalks as well as soil around stalks. It is good to treat again in two weeks. This is an effective cure if weather isn't too dry.

•A handful or two of lime mixed in the soil of each tomato hill helps blossom-end rot and black rot. Mix in 1 tsp. sulphur also to help blight. Cantaloupe, peas, and lima beans will produce better if a little extra lime is mixed in the soil in the row. Peas especially like a treatment of nitrate of soda when stalks are around 2 inches tall for a much larger yield. Use a hoe or garden plow to make a shallow row just on upper side of row of peas so the next rain will soak it into the roots. Sprinkle in a light application of the fertilizer. If there is plenty of rain, a second application two weeks later will help even more.

•It is important to have garden soil tested occasionally, so you know what is needed to improve the soil. This service is usually furnished free by county extension offices. Soils often lack lime. This hinders the growth of many vegetables. However, too much lime can also cause problems which are expensive to cure. So it is best to have a chemical analysis done.

•To save a Christmas poinsettia, store in a cool place 45 to 60 degrees after the leaves fall off. Water only enough to keep stems from shriveling. In April, cut stems back to about 4 to 6 inches above soil. Repot in equal parts of sand, peat moss, and garden soil. Water plant, and place in a spot where the nights are longer than the days—must not be in room where artificial light is on all evening.

MISCELLANEOUS TIPS

•Keep cookbook clean by slipping it into a clear plastic bag while using it. Besides keeping it from getting splattered, this helps to hold the page open.

•A standard canning jar will fit the base of most blenders. This is handy for blending small amounts. Use quart, pint, or even half pint jars for small amounts. It saves washing the large blender container as well as allowing you to screw on a regular jar lid and store any leftover food right in the jar in which it was blended. If stirring is needed while blending, simply lift the jar with blades and screw band still attached off the base and jolt jar a time or two with the palm of your hand to settle contents into blades again.

•When you are mixing a batter that calls for both sugar and flour, combine the two ingredients thoroughly first. Sugar keeps the flour separated and liquid can then be stirred in easily without lumps.

•If you do not have a microwave and need butter softened in a hurry for spreading, pour boiling water into a large bowl for several minutes to heat it. Pour water out and invert heated bowl over saucer of butter for a short time.

•Keep spices in alphabetical order on the shelf, so they can be located quickly.

•If you don't have the correct size baking tin needed, make one out of double thickness of aluminum foil. Press around any pan or pot the size you wish. Remove container, trim, and fold back top edge of foil slightly. Place on baking sheet for support in the oven.

•Place food to be rolled into crumbs in a heavy plastic bag to roll (graham crackers, cornflakes, dried bread cubes, and the like). This saves a mess on the countertop. Also, any amount left over may be stored right in the bag.

•A small squeeze bottle of corn oil is a time-saver when kept handy near your stove. (Corn oil keeps longer at room temperature without getting rancid than other vegetable oils.)

•Do not store honey in refrigerator. This will cause it to crystallize.

•Mark date on all containers of food you freeze, including packages from the grocery store, so the oldest foods may always be used first.

•When cooking with spices that need to be removed before serving (such as whole clove, bay leaves, or garlic buds), place in a tea-ball caddy and hang in kettle to cook. Remove when food is done.

•Grease lip of milk or cream pitcher with butter to prevent dripping or running back while pouring.

•When plastic wrap won't cling, moisten edge of bowl or rim of container with water and it will stick immediately.

•If mixing bowl or cutting board slips around on countertop while using, simply place on a damp dishcloth and it will stay put.

•For easier pouring, punch 2 holes (one on each side) in the lid of canned milk, fruit juices, or other liquid, so air can enter can. This prevents a "blub, blub" spasmodic flow.

•To loosen the top of a tight jar lid that won't seem to budge, hold lid area of jar under hot water a short while to expand the metal.

•To remove onion or garlic smell from hands, wash with baking soda and water, or lemon juice.

•Chew a few fresh parsley leaves to remove garlic odor from your breath.

•A cold stove burner is a handy place to sit a container of food either to cool or thaw more quickly. Air can circulate under the bottom of it. If placed on a solid countertop, this would hold in the heat or cold longer.

•To keep **iron cookware** from rusting, do not let stand in hot soapy water. Wash quickly and dry thoroughly. Then apply a small amount of unsalted vegetable oil to a piece of paper towel and rub over the inside surface. If a thorough scrubbing is needed, reseason after scouring by coating well with unsalted shortening. Then heat in a 300-degree oven for approximately 1 hour.

•For nonstick frying in iron cookware, heat just enough oil or fat in skillet to coat bottom of skillet lightly (about 1 tbsp.). Sprinkle a light coating of salt over oil. When skillet is medium hot, take a piece of paper towel and wipe out salty oil. Then place food in hot skillet and fry without additional fat. (The small amount of fat absorbed into the skillet prevents sticking!)

Do not use iron cookware for mixtures containing tomato juice. The acid in the tomatoes eats away the seasoning and causes rusting.

•If you prefer to cover the drip pans on the stove with foil instead of cleaning them, do not cover the open hole in the center of the pan. This open area provides ventilation needed to prevent a heat buildup which would greatly reduce the life of the heating element of the burner. (I prefer simply to wipe up spills immediately as they occur instead of allowing them to burn on repeatedly, making cleaning very difficult. They can be soaked in the dishwater and washed along with the dishes whenever a spill occurs. This takes very little effort and leaves you with a nice clean stove continually.)

•Do not boil water in aluminum pots as this will cause a darkened stain. If this happens, add 2 tsps. cream of tartar to 1 qt. water and boil until stain disappears. Or add several tbsp. vinegar to the pan of water and boil a few minutes to brighten.

•To remove lime deposits from a teakettle, boil a solution of equal parts of water and vinegar in kettle until accumulation is loosened.

•When adding salt or sugar to foods while beating them with an electric mixer, be careful not to let the granules get sucked into the air vents of the mixer motor. An appliance repairman told me he has seen many badly damaged motors full of salt and sugar. Small portable mixers are especially susceptible to this problem.

•Always clean off top of cans before opening them so any dirt will not drop into can of food. Clean the wheel of the can opener occasionally with a toothbrush and soapy water.

•Use drycleaning fluid to remove any glue residue left after removing labels and price tags from containers. (Dry cleaning fluid is excellent for removing many kinds of substances that soap and water won't budge.)

•Never pour greasy things down the sink drain. After cooling, the grease hardens in the pipes. This is a sure way to clog the drain!

•Use your hand or a small brush to occasionally clean the rubber baffle (the flexible flange-like collar that fits in the drain opening of the garbage disposal side of the sink) on the underneath side. This can become covered with gunk that will cause a foul odor if not cleaned that some cooks think is coming from the drain.

•Use mineral oil, not vegetable oil, to season wooden cutting boards. Vegetable oil eventually becomes rancid.

•Candles will burn longer and drip less if you place them in the freezer for a day just before lighting them. When candle won't fit holder, dip end of candle in boiling water to soften wax. Then insert with a little pressure into holder.

•Add a few drops of chlorine to the rinse water for dishes to sanitize them when someone is sick or has a bad cold.

•Do not buy chlorine bleach and cleaners containing bleach way ahead. The chlorine loses its potency and deteriorates in quality with age. This includes most automatic dishwasher compounds.

•Always dilute chlorine bleach with at least half water when using to clean bathroom furnishings and grouting. Even though it may appear to have done a beautiful job at first, the full-strength solution will damage the glaze or finish and eventually make it impossible to do a good cleaning job!

•Never mix chlorine bleach with cleaning solutions containing ammonia. This combination will give off a poisonous gas which is hazardous!

•To remove stickiness from plasticware, make a paste of baking soda and water and rub affected areas. This is especially effective on plastics used for salad dressings when hot soapy water won't remove the stickiness.

•To clean rubber dish drainer or mats, let soak in solution of 1 part chlorine bleach to 3 parts water. Then brush thoroughly in grooves and rinse well.

•Ammonia is excellent for cleaning greasy utensils. It helps to dissolve grease. Add a little to your dishwater if dishes are greasy.

•When you cannot remove the glass stopper from a bottle, pour small amount of vegetable oil around the edge. Place bottle in a warm place and let soak. Tap gently to loosen.

•When food is accidentally burned in a pan, pour 1 pt. hot water and 1 tsp. baking soda in the pan. Soak until cooled. Burned-on residue will remove more easily.

•To remove stains and to clean non-stick (Teflon) finish on pots and pans, simmer 15 to 20 minutes in a solution of 1 cup clorox and 3 cups water. Wash pan thoroughly with soap and water. Do not overheat these non-stick finishes which could cause permanent damage.

•For easy starting of charcoal fire for barbecuing, soak a brick in kerosene for a day or two and use in bottom of stack of charcoal.

•If you live in town, spray garbage bags with ammonia and you will not have to worry about dogs tearing them up before pickup!

•Car wax is excellent to use on dull kitchen appliances. Use as you would to wax your car.

•The recommended temperature setting for the refrigerator is 40 degrees. When cleaning refrigerator, wash out interior with a solution of 3 tbsp. baking soda to 1 qt. water to keep it fresh and to eliminate any odors.

•Pull out the refrigerator and vacuum the coil area of the back occasionally to prevent a dust buildup which could eventually damage the unit.

•To clean oven racks, lay down several thicknesses of newspaper. Put both racks on paper with the one pushed over slightly so both are exposed. Spray with oven cleaner. Turn over and spray the other sides. Cover with more newspaper to keep fumes inside. Leave 1 or 2 hours. Take outside, discard papers, and hose off. You may need to brush slightly. Or place racks in plastic garbage bag. Pour in 1 or 2 cups of ammonia and tightly close bag. Leave overnight. The next morning, hose off racks, and brush clean. This should be done outside or in a porcelain bathtub— not in a fiberglass tub.

•Another method for oven cleaning is to fill an empty air-wick bottle with ammonia, raise wick, and place in oven overnight. Oven should wipe out easily the next morning.

•Baking soda is a good cleaner for the glass on your oven door. It cleans well without scratching the glass.

•To clean steam iron, fill with equal parts of vinegar and water. Heat iron on low for 30 minutes. Pour out mixture and rinse several times thoroughly. Dry iron before using.

•Usually the right-hand rubber glove wears out first, leaving several left-handed ones. Just turn a left-hand glove inside out and use on the right hand. For easy turning, turn the hand section, then gather glove around top with hands, hold to your mouth, and blow in it to quickly flip fingers out!

•Here is an easy way to play detective if an appliance keeps blowing a fuse in the electrical box and you can't seem to locate the culprit. First, unplug everything from that circuit. Then screw a light bulb in the socket where the fuse was. Plug appliances back in one at a time. When faulty one is plugged in, bulb will become very bright. This saves blowing a lot of new fuses unnecessarily. This information was shared by Margaret Keller and was given to her by an electrician.

•If you need to pick up or handle something you don't wish to touch (like a mouse out of a trap!) slip your hand into a plastic bread bag first, using it as a glove to pick up the item. Then pull top of bag down over hand and item, turning bag wrong side out over item to be disposed of and your hand will not need to touch it. Discard bag with item in it!

•Mattress on bed should be turned every several months to avoid lumping and to extend wear considerably. If you always just flip it over, the same ends are repeatedly used at head end of the bed which gets more wear. To be sure of switching ends, as well as top-to-bottom rotation, mark mattress with a small number with ballpoint pen in each corner as illustrated, starting with #1 in top right-hand corner of bed. Always turn mattress so next consecutive number is in top right-hand corner of bed, going to #1 again after #4. This will give a complete rotation for best distribution of wear without trying to remember what you did last time!

•Never store a broom standing on its bristles. This ruins it! Either drill a small hole near the end of the handle and insert a piece of cord from which to hang it, or stand it on the end of the handle.

•To remove chewing gum from a child's hair, rub well with baby oil, and work the gum out. Then shampoo hair.

•Try rubbing alcohol or hair spray to remove ballpoint pen marks from garments. Remove as soon as possible after stain occurs.

•To avoid having a dingy dishcloth to wash eating utensils, always soak in water with a little chlorine added before laundering. I simply dump cloth and water in

washing machine, and the whole load of clothes gets sanitized. It is a good practice to include a little chlorine in most loads of laundry (unless fabric of certain garments does not permit). Since washcloths are used for all parts of the body, it is nice to have them sanitized for your face! (Caution: Be careful not to let any chlorine unknowingly drip onto countertop or washer top. If a colored garment comes in contact with it, you might have a white spot in the middle of something!)

•Add ½ cup ammonia to a washer load of heavily soiled work clothes to help remove soil.

•To keep shower curtains and liners clean, occasionally place them in the washer along with a few towels and run on warm cycle.

•White nylon has a tendency to yellow when hung in the sun to dry. Dry in the shade or indoors.

•It is good to hang white clothes outside on a sunny day when temperature is below freezing. Freezing and sunshine helps to whiten them. This is not good for colors, however, as they tend to fade.

•When placing white garments in storage, wrap in blue tissue paper and place in an airtight plastic bag to avoid yellowing. (Be certain garment is completely clean and dry before storing!)

•Glue a paper plate onto bottom of paint can before painting to catch any drips. Or place can in a paper bag with top rolled down. Saves moving a paper each time can is moved.

•To prevent plaster of paris from setting up too quickly with craft projects, mix with a solution of half water and half vinegar instead of all water.

•If thread insists on knotting when hand sewing, draw thread through a cake of wax (preferably beeswax) to eliminate the problem.

• Place new panty hose in the freezer for a day before wearing the first time. This sounds questionable, but it definitely does increase the life of the hose!

• Add just enough water to baking soda to make a stiff paste. Put on beestings to relieve the pain.

• Rub chigger bites with a slightly dampened aspirin tablet to relieve pain.

• An effective old-time remedy for superficial burns is to coat them with honey. If stickiness is too much of a problem, cover with a thin cloth.

• Another good thing to have around for treating superficial burns is an aloe vera plant. The plant is easy to grow. Simply pick off a stem when needed, break it open, squeeze out the jellylike substance, and apply it to the burn. It is not only soothing, but promotes healing as well. Severe burns should, of course, be treated by a physician.

• When shoestrings lose their plastic caps, trim end, dip in clear fingernail polish, shape into point, and let harden.

• Soda is good for removing odors from carpet. Sprinkle dry baking soda over area, brush it in, and let set for several hours. Then vacuum thoroughly.

• To remove grease spots from suede shoes, rub with a clean cloth dipped in glycerine.

• Soak new dark-colored cotton fabrics in salt water (for 1 hour to overnight) to set the color and help prevent fading. Use 2 or 3 tbsp. salt per ½ gal. water.

• If a grease spot remains on a garment made of part cotton and part synthetic fabric after laundering it, apply a coat of dry cornstarch to the spot and iron over it with a medium-hot iron so the grease soaks into the powder. Let set a short time, and then brush off cornstarch thoroughly.

• To hammer a short tack easily in a small corner, insert tack through slip of paper first, then hold paper while hammering tack. Saves bruised fingers!

• Do not use soap to wash windows, since it will leave a film. A mixture of 2 tbsp. vinegar and 2 tbsp. ammonia to 1 qt. water is excellent for window washing. If outside windows next to the drive are coated with dust and grit, squirt off thoroughly with the garden hose before washing. This makes washing them much easier and saves on window cleaning solution.

• Save the pieces of soap that are too small to use. When you acquire an accumulation, add a little water and heat on low heat until softened and a gooey mixture has accumulated. Press this into a cup or something to form a cake. When cool, but still soft, carefully remove and shape smoothly into a free bar of soap. Allow to dry thoroughly before using.

• Cut flowers will last longer if cut early in the morning before the sun shines on them. Place in warm water for an hour so they drink in plenty of water. Then place them in cold water in a dark place for a couple of hours. Add an aspirin in the vase. Do not place bouquet in the sun. Placing it in the refrigerator during the night while you sleep also prolongs its life.

• To help minimize odor of marigolds in a flower arrangement, add 1 tsp. sugar to water in vase.

• Cracks in flower vases may be sealed with melted paraffin.

• When watering houseplants, water should be at room temperature instead of directly out of the cold faucet. If water supply is chlorinated, draw a bucket of water and let it sit at least overnight to allow chlorine to evaporate. Plants don't like chlorine.

NON-FOOD RECIPES

Recipe for Life

1 cup good thoughts 1 cup kind deeds 1 cup consideration 3 cups forgiveness 2 cups well-beaten faults 3 cups sacrifice	Mix thoroughly with tears of joy and sorrow, and plenty of sympathy. Flavor with love and kindness.

. . . .

6 cups prayer   Blend in thoroughly.

. . . .

Bake well in the heat of human kindness and serve with a smile.

Twila Showalter

. . . .

Christmas Snow

(The lime used in this recipe must be fresh new lime. Old lime does not work. Use a glass or granite plate or tray. Mixture could damage metal. Make up a scene as desired. We cut little squares of cardboard and tack it onto pine-cones with a thumbtack to make the base for the pinecone trees. We included a mirror for a little lake. A miniature toy deer or bear always adds a delightful touch. Little rocks and small pebbles enhance the landscaping—use your imagination!)

1¼ cups agricultural lime 1¼ cups salt ¼ cup blueing	Add enough water to make a thick gravy, and pour over scenery on tray.

. . . .

Grows beautifully overnight.

. . . .

Clothes Stain Remover

(This is excellent for baby's and children's clothing, or for dingy synthetics.)

1 gal. hot water   Pour in plastic bucket.

. . . .

½ cup automatic dishwashing
   compound
½ cup bleach
½ cup ordinary detergent (do not
   use detergent containing
   ammonia)
	Add, stirring until completely dissolved. Add garment. Let soak for 30 minutes, or overnight. Then launder as usual.

. . . .

Eileen Heatwole

. . . .

Finger Paints for Children

2 cups water	Heat to boiling in saucepan.

½ cup cornstarch	Mix until smooth, then stir in, stirring
1 cup cold water	constantly until thickened.

Divide into desired portions and tint various colors.

Floating Mothballs

(This is a nice conversation piece. The addition of the acid and soda causes the water to effervesce. The mothballs will bob up and down in the water.)

mothballs	Place a handful of balls in a glass bowl or jar.

¾ cup water (tinted with food coloring as desired)	Add.
2 tbsp. citric acid*	
1 tsp. baking soda	

(*1 cup white vinegar may be substituted for the citric acid.)

Papier-Mâché

Cut newspaper into narrow strips. Soak 24 hours in water. Add enough thick laundry starch to hold it together. Shape as desired and allow to dry thoroughly.

Sore Throat Gargle

(This recipe originally came from a Harrisonburg throat specialist and is good. Use 2 or 3 times daily as a gargle or mouthwash.)

1 cup water	Mix. Store at room temperature.
½ tsp. salt	
1 tsp. baking soda	

Put 2 drops iodine in ½ glass of above solution just before using.

Variation: Dissolve ¼ tsp. salt and 1 tsp. vinegar in ½ cup warm water for an effective gargle.

Gladys and Brownie Driver

Old Time Mustard Plaster

(Several persons told me that this plaster 'really works wonders'! I faintly remember my own mother making plasters out of some kind of leaves for other problems, but she usually rubbed us well with Vicks when we had chest congestion, and applied warm cloths to keep the heat in. Margaret said her mother raised 12 children with these kinds of remedies, and her doctor said she was a really good "doctor." She always seemed to know what to do. Margaret agreed that in her home it was the same as in ours. We usually didn't think of going to the doctor unless we were afraid someone might die if we didn't!)

1.Sift together 1 tbsp. dry mustard and 4 tbsp. flour for a plaster for an adult; or 1 tbsp. dry mustard to 6 tbsp. flour for a child. (If you do not sift mixture, there could be lumps which may cause blistering.)
2. Gradually add just enough lukewarm water to make a paste that does not run. Then spread mixture ⅛-inch thick on an old piece of muslin, a little larger than the area to be covered. Cover mixture with second piece of muslin the same size so mustard mixture is enclosed inside.
3. Lay plaster pack on the chest and neck area where congestion is located. (Lay on the bare skin; skin should be dry.)
4. Check area frequently for redness of the skin. Remove plaster when skin is red, usually in about 10 to 20 minutes. Keep area covered with warm clothing or flannel during and after use of mustard plaster. The buildup of heat is really what helps to relieve the congestion.
5. After removing plaster, rub area lightly with Vaseline and cover well to keep warm. A warm turtleneck top is excellent for keeping in heat.
    Apply plaster two or three times a day until relief is obtained.

Margaret Keller
Alma Keyser
Ella Ruth

. . . .

Gelatin Treatment for Houseplants

(Unflavored gelatin is a source of organic nitrogen for houseplants.)

Soften 1 env. (1 tbsp.) unflavored gelatin in ½ cup cold water. Add 1 cup hot water, and stir to dissolve. Then add 2½ cups cold water to make 1 qt. of liquid. Water your houseplants with this mixture once a month. Prepare only as much as you plan to use at a time.

. . . .

Liquid Fertilizer for Houseplants

(This mixture is especially good for African violets.)

1 gal. warm water
1 tsp. baking powder
1 tsp. epsom salts
1 tsp. saltpeter
1 tsp. ammonia

Stir together until dissolved. Give a medium-sized plant ½ cup of mixture once a month.

. . . .

Liquid Snow

¼ cup water **¼ cup bluing** **¼ cup ammonia**	Mix and pour over wet rocks and scenery.
¼ cup salt	Sprinkle evenly over mixture.

Play Dough

1½ cups boiling water **½ cup salt** **food coloring as desired**	Mix, stirring to dissolve.
2 tbsp. alum **1 tbsp. vegetable oil**	Add.
2 cups flour	Pour liquid into bowl of flour and stir well. Knead until smooth.

Will keep for a long time if stored in a tightly closed plastic bag when not in use.

"Edible" Play Dough

(When your little ones want to help in the kitchen, let them roll out this dough and cut out miniature cookies to their heart's content! They will end up eating most of the delicious dough. It is a good way to get protein into a poor eater. NOTE: Use only in the kitchen. You would not want them to be eating dough full of germs from continued playroom usage.)

½ cup creamy peanut butter **¼ cup honey or syrup** **½ cup instant dry milk powder** **2 tbsp. powdered sugar (or more)**	Mix and knead into a pliable dough, adding more powdered sugar if necessary.

Roll out and cut with miniature cookie cutters. Use powdered sugar for "flour," for rolling. This can also be used for modeling, or can be pressed into a shallow pan as "candy."

Pre-wash Stain Treatment

½ cup household ammonia **½ cup dishwashing detergent** **½ cup water**	Mix together. Fill dispenser bottle with mixture. Spray spots and stains, and let soak at least 15 minutes before laundering.

Potting Soil

(This is a good all-purpose mixture for most houseplants.)

4 cups good garden soil
1 cup peat moss
1 cup black potting soil
1 cup sand
3 or 4 tbsp. fine granular fertilizer*

Mix thoroughly.

....

(*Some sensitive plants cannot take granular fertilizer. This may be omitted, and liquid fertilizer may be added to the water as needed.)

Mary S. Suter

....

Soap Bubbles

⅓ cup dishwashing detergent
1½ cups water
2 tsp. sugar
1 drop food coloring

Combine in bottle. Use ring-collared bottle cap for a wand to make bubbles.

....

Spray for Roses

2 tbsp. Rapid Grow fertilizer
1½ tbsp. Phaltan
1 tbsp. Isotox
1 gal. water

Mix together thoroughly. Use in garden sprayer.

....

Annie Weaver

....

Spring Flowers

Refrigerate flower bulbs (such as tulips, hyacinths, etc.) at 40 degrees for 2 months. Then place at room temperature and add water as needed. Stalks should bloom in about 1 month.

....

Sugar Starch (to Starch Crocheted Doilies)

(Generally, I prefer to use cooked starch for doilies, making it very stiff for the ruffle doilies. However, it has become difficult to purchase starch in this form. Since many people prefer instant starch for general use, the demand for the granules for preparing cooked starch has diminished. Instant starch is not stiff enough for doilies, however. I've also discovered that sugar starch holds its stiffness longer than homemade cooked starch which tends to weaken somewhat after several months.)

Sugar starch is simply a mixture of water and sugar. For flat doilies, use 3 parts sugar to 4 parts water, making just enough mixture to immerse the doily. For ruffle doilies use equal parts of sugar and water, or for a *very* stiff mixture, use 1½ parts sugar or more to 1 part water. (Caution: It is possible to have doilies so stiff that the threads may actually break if they are accidently bent sharply.)

Heat water and sugar mixture to a full rolling boil. Remove from heat and cool to lukewarm. Immerse doily until thoroughly saturated, then squeeze out excess liquid. Lay doily on a piece of plastic wrap or foil. This may be placed over a towel, or on the ironing board, to give a base for pinning the doily into shape for drying if desired. For ruffle doilies, the foil can be shaped to hold ruffles in place. Or use crumpled pieces of waxed paper or foil to shape raised areas.

The sugar starch may take as long as several days to dry completely. You may wish to do additional shaping after doily is partially dry for best results with the ruffle doilies.

Elva Lois Turner
Carolyn Showalter

. . . .

Window Cleaner

2 oz. rubbing alcohol
2 oz. ammonia
12 oz. water

Mix, pour in spray bottle, and use as you would any glass cleaner.

. . . .

Windshield Washer Cleaner

1 cup rubbing alcohol
¼ cup household detergent
1¼ cups water

Mix.

. . . .

REMOVING STAINS FROM FABRIC

(Always remove stains as promptly as possible after they occur. Stains are much more difficult to remove if dried on, or if run through a hot water cycle in the washing machine. Always test a hidden spot of a garment if there is any question about the fabric or mixture being used to clean it so you don't ruin the garment.)

Blood: Soak in cold water at least 30 minutes. Rub well with detergent and rinse. If stain remains, soak in a mixture of half ammonia and half warm water. Then work in detergent and launder. If you prick your finger when quilting and get a spot of blood on the quilt, touch spot with a little hydrogen peroxide to remove stain.

Candle Wax: Let wax harden, then scrape off all you can with a table knife (a sharp knife may damage the threads of the fabric). Place spot between two pieces of absorbent tissue or paper towel, and iron over it with a warm iron, changing tissue frequently until no more wax will melt onto the paper. Scrub spot well with dry-cleaning fluid and let dry. (Caution: Do not iron over red candle wax, since this may set the red stain. After scraping off wax, use commercial stain remover.)

Chewing Gum: First spray the gummed side of garment with a prewash stain-removal spray; then place it in the freezer. When gum is frozen solid, remove from freezer and immediately spray the gummed area from the underside of the garment. Gum should lift off easily. Some people work baby oil into the gummed area to clean the gum out, or use lighter fluid to remove it.

Chocolate and Cocoa: Soak in cool or lukewarm water. Rub detergent into spot and launder in very warm water. May also apply dry-cleaning fluid.

Coffee and Tea: Sponge with cold water and detergent. Then rinse and apply white vinegar, or ammonia to spot. May use dry-cleaning fluid if there was cream in the beverage.

Crayon: Scrape with a table knife. Wash in hottest water safe for fabric, with detergent and a strong baking soda solution. If crayon went through washer with full load of laundry, take clothes to the dry cleaners or run through coin operated dry cleaning machine.

Dingy Synthetic Clothes and Stained Baby Clothes: See recipe on page 650.

Dye: If you tinted a whole washer load of clothes by accidentally putting in an item that bled into the load, bleach the load of clothes immediately *while they are still wet.* Follow directions on container of bleach for amount. A stronger solution, of course, may be used on white items than on colored ones.

Fruit Juices and Soft Drinks: Sponge with cold water and soak with liquid detergent. Rinse and apply white vinegar. Or soak spot in lemon juice and sprinkle with salt (or dampen and sprinkle with cream of tartar) and lay in bright sunlight. May need to use bleach.

Grass: Treat spot with one of the following: pure alcohol, white vinegar, dry-cleaning fluid, or glycerine. Soak 30 minutes, then rub detergent in spot and launder in very warm water. Or dampen and rub well with homemade soap. Soak and launder in very warm water.

Grease, Oil, and Tar: Treat well with dry-cleaning fluid, using a paper towel to blot out stain. After removing as much as possible with this method, rub in detergent and wash in very warm water. Old-timers used to rub lard in the spot, then rub in detergent, and finally launder in hot water. Another effective method is to apply a waterless hand cleaner (purchased in automotive departments) to spot, soak well, then launder as usual.

Ink (Ballpoint Pen): Remove as soon as possible! Rub well with alcohol or hair spray. Rub in petroleum jelly. Then sponge with dry-cleaning fluid, rub in detergent, and launder.

Ink (Fountain Pen): Run cold water through stain immediately until water is clear. Rub in lemon juice and then detergent. Wash with bleach. If yellow stain remains, use commercial rust remover.

Iodine: Soak spot in solution of ⅓ ammonia and ⅔ water. Rinse thoroughly.

Mildew: Immediately treat with detergent. It is easiest to use bleach if fabric will allow it. Soak in 1 qt. warm water with ½ cup bleach and ¼ cup vinegar added. Spot may be soaked with lemon juice, sprinkled with salt, and placed in bright sunlight.

Milk, Cream, Mayonnaise: Sponge with cool or lukewarm water. Soak spot with dry-cleaning fluid. Rub in detergent and wash in very warm water.

Mustard: Work glycerine into stain and soak. Then launder. Or soak spot with undiluted detergent, and launder in very warm water. Sometimes stain may be removed by soaking in ginger ale.

Paint: Saturate spot with equal parts of turpentine and ammonia, or with dry-cleaning fluid. Soak well, then launder with detergent and very warm water.

Perspiration: To remove odors, soak in solution of 2 tbsp. baking soda or more to 2 cups water. Soak fresh stains in ammonia to remove stain and odor. Wash in very warm water.

Rust: Soak spot in lemon juice, sprinkle with salt, and place in bright sunlight—or use commercial rust remover. (If using commercial remover, handle with care. It is very poisonous and can also damage finish on washer and dryer.)

Scorch: Soak in white vinegar until removed. Or soak a pressing cloth in hydrogen peroxide and iron over spot. Or soak in a mixture of ¼ cup bleach to ¾ cup water. It may help to dampen spot and place in bright sunlight. Severe scorching cannot be removed because the fabric is damaged.

Miscellaneous: Here is one last tip for those stains that somehow defy every method you could think of that was supposed to work wonders! Take the stained item outside at night and lay it on an area of clean grass where the sun will hit it first thing in the morning. Let the dew settle on the garment (it is important that there is plenty of dew), and then go to bed and forget it. Depending on what the stain is, often the sun will "magically" take the stain right out before your unbelieving eyes! This seems to be nature's way of helping to solve our problems for us.

Stains on Carpet: (This method is excellent for liquid stains. I've removed a fresh iodine stain with it! For grease stains, use dry-cleaning fluid.)

1. Blot up every bit of liquid or stain possible. Work dry baking soda into stain if still wet. If stain is dry, make a thin paste of baking soda and water. Dab mixture into area well to coat yarns. Let this dry. Then vacuum well.

2. Wet area again with water. Mix 1 tsp. of an enzyme presoak powder (such as Axion or Biz) in 1 cup warm water and saturate stain. Lay foil over top and let set 30 minutes.

3. Blot dry with towels. Rinse area well with clear water—at least 3 times, blotting thoroughly after each rinse to remove all solution, stain, and water.

4. To draw any remaining moisture out of carpet, you may wish to make a pad of paper towels or use absorbent toweling. Cover towels with foil to keep moisture from damaging books, and weight down with a stack of books, changing towels occasionally until all moisture is absorbed.

EQUIVALENT MEASURES

Apples	1 lb.	3 cups or 3 medium apples
Bananas	1 lb.	3 large bananas or 1½ cups mashed

Beans:

kidney beans	1 lb.	2½ cups dried or 7 cups cooked
navy beans	1 lb.	2⅓ cups dried or 6 cups cooked
split peas	1 lb.	2 cups dried or 5 cups cooked
Butter or margarine	1 oz.	2 tablespoons
	¼ lb. stick	½ cup
	1 lb.	2 cups
Cabbage	3 lbs.	1 medium head
	1 lb.	4 cups shredded
Carrots	1 lb.	3 cups finely shredded

Cheese:

cheddar cheese	1 lb.	4 cups grated
cottage cheese	1 lb.	2 cups
cream cheese	3 oz. pkg.	6 tablespoons
cream cheese	8 oz. pkg.	1 cup
Chocolate chips	6 oz. pkg.	1 cup, scant
Chocolate chips	12 oz. pkg.	1⅞ cups
Chocolate syrup	1 lb. can	1⅔ cups
Coconut	3 oz.	1 cup shredded, lightly packed
Coconut	1 lb.	5 cups shredded, lightly packed
Coffee (grounds)	1 lb.	4½ cups grounds (makes 60 cups brewed coffee)
Cornmeal	1 lb.	3 cups

Crackers:

graham crackers	1 cup crumbs	12 single crackers
graham crackers	1 lb.	6 cups crumbs
saltines	1 cup crumbs	20 single crackers

Cream:

sour cream	8 oz.	1 cup
whipping cream	1 cup	2 cups whipped
Dates (pitted)	1 lb.	2½ cups chopped

Eggs:

4 or 5 large eggs	1 cup (or 6 medium eggs)	
8 whites	1 cup	
12 yolks	1 cup	

Flour:

cake flour	1 lb.	4½ cups
white all-purpose	1 lb.	4 cups
whole wheat flour	1 lb.	3½ cups
Gelatin, plain	1 envelope	1 tablespoon (will gel 2 cups liquid)
Flavored gelatin	1 3-oz. pkg	⅓ cup granules (will gel 2 cups liquid)
Herbs	1 tsp. dried	1 tbsp. fresh
Honey	1 lb.	1⅓ cups

Lemon:

juice	1 med. lemon	2 to 3 tablespoons
rind, grated	1 med. lemon	2 to 3 teaspoons
Marshmallows	1 large	10 miniature
(varies with brands)	10 large	1 cup miniature, lightly packed
	100 miniature	1 cup lightly packed

                                    1 lb. . . . . 8 cups miniature or about 75 to 80
                                                                          (large)
                                    10-oz. bag miniature . . . . 6 cups

Milk:
  evaporated . . . . 5 oz. can . . . . ⅔ cup
  evaporated . . . . 13 oz. can . . . . 1⅔ cups
  sweetened
    condensed . . . . 14 oz. can . . . . 1⅓ cups
Mustard, prepared . . . . 1 tablespoon . . . . 1 tsp. dry mustard
Nuts:
  almonds . . . . 1 lb. in shell . . . . 1¾ cups shelled
  pecans . . . . 1 lb. in shell . . . . 2¼ cups shelled
  peanuts . . . . 1 lb. in shell . . . . 2¼ cups shelled
  walnuts . . . . 1 lb. in shell . . . . 1⅔ cups shelled
  almonds . . . . 1 lb. shelled . . . . 3½ cups
  pecans . . . . 1 lb. shelled . . . . 4 cups
  peanuts . . . . 1 lb. shelled . . . . 3 cups
  walnuts . . . . 1 lb. shelled . . . . 4 cups
Oatmeal . . . . 1 lb. raw . . . . about 5 cups raw or 9 cups cooked
Onion . . . . 1 med. onion . . . . ½ cup chopped
Orange:
  juice . . . . 1 med. orange . . . . ⅓ to ½ cup
  rind, grated . . . . 1 med. orange . . . . 2 to 3 tablespoons
Pasta:
  macaroni, 1 lb. . . . . 4 cups raw . . . . 8 cups cooked
  noodles, 1 lb. . . . . 6 cups raw . . . . 9 cups cooked
  spaghetti, 1 lb. . . . . 4 cups raw . . . . 6 to 8 cups cooked
Peanut butter . . . . 1 lb. . . . . 2¼ cups
Peppers, green . . . . 1 large . . . . 1 cup diced
Popcorn . . . . 1 cup raw . . . . 5 quarts popped
Potatoes:
  sweet p., 1 lb. . . . . 3 medium . . . . 2 cups cooked and mashed
  white p., 1 lb. . . . . 3 medium . . . . 2 cups cooked and mashed
Raisins . . . . 1 lb. . . . . 2¾ cups
Rice . . . . 1 lb. . . . . 2 cups dried or 6 cups cooked
Rice, instant . . . . 1 cup . . . . 2 cups cooked
Saccharin . . . . ¼ grain . . . . 1 teaspoon sugar
Shortening . . . . 1 lb. . . . . 2 cups
Stuffing:
  herb-seasoned . . . . 8-oz. bag . . . . 4½ cups seasoned dried bread
                                                                          cubes
  croutons . . . . 11-oz. bag . . . . 10 cups (these are large cubes,
    (unseasoned)   and, therefore, make more cups)
Sugar:
  brown . . . . 1 lb. . . . . 2¼ cups
  confectioners . . . . 1 lb. . . . . 3½ cups sifted
  granulated . . . . 1 lb. . . . . 2 cups
Tomatoes . . . . 1 lb. . . . . 3 medium
Vegetable oil . . . . 1 lb. . . . . 2 cups
Vanilla wafers . . . . 24 wafers . . . . 1 cup crumbs
Whipped toppings . . . . 9 oz. container . . . . 3 cups
  (frozen)   12-oz. container . . . . 4 cups
Yeast, cake . . . . 2 oz. cake . . . . 3 pks. dry yeast
Yeast, dry . . . . 1 envelope (¼ oz.) . . . . 1 tablespoon

SUBSTITUTES FOR INGREDIENTS

Apple pie spice—for 1 tsp use: ½ tsp. cinnamon, ¼ tsp. nutmeg, ⅛ tsp. allspice, and ⅛ tsp. cardamon.

Baking powder—for 1 tsp. use: ⅓ tsp. baking soda and ½ tsp. cream of tartar.

Biscuit mix—for 1 cup: mix together 1 cup flour, 1 ½ tsp. baking powder, ½ tsp. salt, and 3 tbsp. shortening until crumbly.

Bouillon—for 1 cube use: 1 tsp. instant bouillon powder.

Brown sugar—for 1 cup use: 1 cup granulated sugar and 2 tbsp. dark corn syrup or molasses.

Butter—for 1 cup use: 1 cup plus 2 tbsp. margarine.

Buttermilk—for 1 cup use: 1 cup thick sour milk or 1 cup yogurt.

Cake flour—for 1 cup: place 2 tbsp. cornstarch in cup and fill with all-purpose flour.

Carob powder—for 1 oz. chocolate called for use: 3 tbsp. carob powder and 2 tbsp. water.

Chives—for 1 tbsp. finely chopped fresh chives use: 1 tsp. freeze-dried chives.

Chocolate—for a 1-oz-square use: 3 tbsp. cocoa and 1 tbsp. butter or margarine.

For a 6-oz. pkg. semisweet chocolate pieces melted: use 6 tbsp. unsweetened cocoa powder, ½ cup sugar, and ¼ cup shortening; or 2 (1-oz.) squares semisweet chocolate.

For a 4-oz. bar sweet cooking chocolate: use 3 tbsp. unsweetened cocoa powder, 4 ½ tbsp. sugar, and 3 tbsp. shortening.

Corn syrup—for 1 cup use: 1 cup granulated sugar and ¼ cup liquid; or 1 cup honey; or 1 cup molasses.

Cornstarch (for thickening)—for 1 tbsp. use: 1 ½ to 2 tbsp. flour; or 4 tsp. minute tapioca; or 1 tbsp. Clearjel.

Cream—for 1 cup cream in baking use: ¾ cup milk and ¼ cup butter; or 1 cup evaporated milk.

Egg—for 1 whole egg use: 2 egg yolks in custards; or 2 egg yolks plus 1 tbsp. water in cookies.

Garlic—for 1 garlic clove use: ¼ tsp. garlic salt (reduce salt by ⅛ tsp.); or ⅛ tsp. garlic powder.

Herbs—for 1 tbsp. fresh herbs use: 1 tsp. dried herbs; or ¼ tsp. powdered herbs.

Honey—for 1 cup honey use: 1 cup granulated sugar plus ¼ cup liquid; or use 1 cup corn syrup or molasses.

Jello-O—for 1 3-oz. pkg. flavored gelatin (or Jell-O) use: 1 tbsp. (1 env.) plain gelatin and 2 cups fruit juice.

Lemon—for 1 tsp. grated lemon peel use: ½ tsp. lemon extract.

Milk—for 1 cup whole milk use: ½ cup evaporated milk and ½ cup water; or use ⅓ cup nonfat dry milk powder, ¾ cup water, and 2 tbsp. fat.

Mushrooms—for 8 oz. fresh mushrooms use: 1 6-oz. can mushrooms, drained.

Mustard—for 1 tbsp. prepared mustard use: 1 tsp. dry mustard.

Onion—for 1 medium onion use: 2 tbsp. minced dried onion; or 1 tsp. onion powder; or 2 tsp. onion salt (reduce salt in recipe by 1 tsp.).

Pumpkin pie spice—for 1 tsp. use: ½ tsp. cinnamon, ¼ tsp. ginger, ⅛ tsp. allspice, and ⅛ tsp. nutmeg.

Powdered sugar—Combine 1 cup granulated sugar and 1 tbsp. cornstarch in blender. Process until powdery. Makes 1 ⅓ cups.

Self-rising flour—for 1 cup use: 1 cup all-purpose flour with 1 ½ tsp. baking powder and ½ tsp. salt added.

Shortening—for 1 cup use: 1 cup margarine; or ¾ cup chicken fat; or ⅞ cup butter; or ⅞ cup lard; or ⅞ cup oil; or ¾ cup bacon fat.

Sour cream (in baking)—for 1 cup use: ⅞ cup thick sour milk and 3 tbsp. margarine.

(Dairy sour cream)—use substitute most suited to food you are using it with: 1 cup plain yogurt; or 1 cup cottage cheese creamed in blender with 1 tbsp. lemon juice; or 1 tbsp. lemon juice (or vinegar) plus evaporated milk to make 1 cup; or 1 cup Cool Whip with ¼ tsp. lemon extract added for dessert topping; or ½ cup milk and 2 tbsp. mayonnaise in casseroles.

Sour milk—for 1 cup use: 1 cup yogurt; or place 1 tbsp. lemon juice (or vinegar) in cup, fill with milk and let stand 5 minutes.

(To substitute sour milk in place of sweet milk in a recipe) for 1 cup sweet milk called for use: 1 cup sour milk and ½ tsp. soda. Then decrease baking powder called for by 1 ½ tsp. (If recipe calls for 1 cup milk and 2 tsp. baking powder, use 1 cup sour milk, ½ tsp. soda, and ½ tsp. baking powder.)

Stuffing—for 8-oz. bag (herb-seasoned) use: 4 ½ cups your own seasoned small dried bread cubes. See index for recipe. For 11-oz. bag (unseasoned) croutons use: 10 cups larger dried cubes.

Sugar—for 1 cup use: 1 cup honey or corn syrup less ¼ cup other liquid called for in recipe.

Tapioca—for 2 tbsp. use: 3 tbsp. flour.

Tartar sauce—for ½ cup use: 6 tbsp. mayonnaise plus 2 tbsp. finely chopped sweet pickle relish.

Tomato catsup or chili sauce—for 1 cup use: 1 cup tomato sauce plus ¼ cup sugar and 2 tbsp. vinegar.

Tomato juice—for 1 cup use: ½ cup tomato sauce and ½ cup water.

Tomato paste—for 1 tbsp. use: 1 tbsp. tomato catsup.

Tomato puree—for 1 cup use: 2 tbsp. tomato paste plus water or tomato juice to make 1 cup.

Tomato sauce—for 1 cup use: 1 cup tomato puree; or place 2 tbsp. catsup or chili sauce in cup and fill with thick tomato juice.

Tomatoes (canned)—for 1 cup use: 1 ⅓ cups cut-up fresh tomatoes simmered 10 minutes.

Vinegar—for 1 tbsp. use: 1 tbsp. lemon juice.

Whipping cream—for 1 cup cream which makes 2 cups whipped cream use: 1 envelope whipped topping mix; or chill ⅔ cup evaporated milk well (both bowl and beaters) and whip; or use 2 cups Cool Whip.

Yogurt—for 1 cup use: 1 cup thick sour milk or buttermilk.

WEIGHTS AND MEASURES

a pinch or dash = slightly
   less than ⅛ tsp.
3 teaspoons = 1 tablespoon
2 tablespoons = 1 ounce
16 tablespoons = 1 cup
5 tablespoons + 1 teaspoon = ⅓ cup
12 tablespoons = ¾ cup
1 cup = 8 oz. liquid
2 cups = 1 pint

2 pints = 1 quart
4 quarts = 1 gallon
2 gallons = 1 peck
4 pecks = 1 bushel
8 gallons = 1 bushel
28 grams = 1 ounce
1 kilogram = 2.2 pounds
1 liter = Approximately 1
   qt. (1.06 qts.)
3.785 liters = 1 gallon
29.6 milliliters = 1 oz.
1 tablespoon = scant 15 milliliters
1 cup = 250 milliliters

COMMERCIAL CONTAINER SIZES

Weight	Contents or Can Size	Measure
3 ½-oz. can	coconut	1 ⅓ cups coconut, lightly packed
5 oz. can	evaporated milk	⅔ cup
6 oz. can	frozen juices and tomato paste	¾ cup
8 oz. can	fruits and vegetables	1 cup
10 oz. box	frozen vegetables	2 cups
10½ oz. can	No. 1 or picnic condensed soups	1¼ cups
13 oz. can	evaporated milk	1⅔ cups
14 oz. can	sweetened condensed milk	1⅓ cups
15½ oz. can	No. 300	1¾ cups
16 oz. can	chocolate syrup	1⅔ cups
16 oz. can	No. 303—fruits and vegetables	2 cups
20 oz. can	No. 2	2½ cups
20 oz. bag	frozen vegetables	4 cups
1 lb. 13 oz. can	No. 2½	3½ cups
46 oz. can	Juices and fruit drinks	5¾ cups
6 lb. 9 oz.	No. 10	12 cups

GENERAL INDEX

All recipes for microwave cooking are indicated by the code **(mic-w)** preceding the page number. The separate Canning, Freezing, and Preserving Index begins on page 679.

Abbreviations and ingredients, 17
Alfalfa sprouts, 488
Almond bark candy, 236
Almond cream pie, 454
Almond-lime punch, 30
Ambrosia salad, 473
Angel food cake, procedure for making, 96
Angel food cake recipe, 104
Angel salad, 473
Appetizers, 529-537
Apple butter rolls, 443
Apple butter rolls, quick, 580
Apple butter, quick, 556
   (see Canning section for other recipes
    for apple butter)
Apple cake, 104
Apple dapple cake, l05
Apple cookies, 159
Apple crisp, 192, **(mic-w)** 421
Apple dapple salad, 475
Apple delight, **(mic-w)** 421
Apple dumplings, 194
Apple gelatin salad, 474
Apple macaroon pie, 449
Apple pie, 448
Apple salads, 474, 475, 478
Apple strudel, 202
Apple tarts (Bavarian), 448
Apples
   baked, l92
   (skillet) baked, 580
   (candied) caramel, 230, **(mic-w)** 428
   delightful macaroon, 193
   stuffed, 231
Applesauce cake, 106
Applescotch dessert, 193
Apricot salad, 476
Asparagus (and ham) casserole, 289
Avocado salad mold, 476

Bacon, tips for cooking, 362
Bacon and cottage cheese dip, 537
Bacon quiche, 278
Banana cakes, l06, l07, l08
Banana chocolate chip cookies, 160
Banana cream pie, 454
Banana ice cream, 225
Banana fruit punch, 30
Banana milk shake, 41
Banana oatmeal bread, 79
Banana puddings, 580
Banana punch, 30
Banana tarts, 176
Bananas, baked, 231, **(mic-w)** 422
Bananas, frozen 231, 634
Barbecue sauce for chicken, 376
Barbecue sauces, 364, 375, 390, **(mic-w)** 406
Bean (nine) soup, 511
Bean salad, 488
Bean soup with ham bone, 510
Bean sprouts, directions for, 488
Bean sprouts, stir-fried, 558
Beans
   baked, 313, **(mic-w)** 409
   baked (crockpot), 313, 314

baked (quick), 556, 557
dry, how to cook, 274
green and bacon casserole, **(mic-w)** 413
green (baked), 557
green (delightful), 312
green (dilly), 557
green (favorite), 312
green (saucy), 312
green (stroganoff), 565
green (supreme), 313
refried, 314
Beans and rice, 314
Beef (see Meats)
   (see also Main Dishes for recipes
    containing)
Beef (chipped) spread, 540
Beef stew (old-fashioned), 512
Beets, harvard, 315
Beverages, 30-42, **(mic-w)** 405, 552
   —Information about, 26
   —Tips for, 29
   Almond-lime punch, 30
   Banana fruit punch, 30
   Banana punch, 30
   Banana shake, 41
   Breakfast-in-a-glass, 31
   Butterscotch milk (hot), 38, **(mic-w)** 405
   Chocolate milk, syrup for, 39
   Chocolate mix (hot), 38
   Chocolate shake, 42
   Christmas punch, 31
   Cider, mulled, **(mic-w)** 405
   Cider, spicy, 39
   Cocoa mix (hot), 38
   Coffee, procedure for making, 27
   Coffee punch, 31
   Cranberry punch (cold), 31
   Cranberry punch (hot), 38
   Dieter's delight, 32
   Easy punch, 32
   Eggnog, 32
   Eggnog liquid breakfast, 32
   Floats, 552
   Fruit cooler, zesty, 37
   Fruit slush mix, 32
   Fruity liquid breakfast, 32
   Fruity milk shake, 42
   Lemonade mint drink, 33
   Lemonade syrup, 33
   Lemonade, easy, 552
   Lime-light banana crush punch, 33
   Milk, butterscotch (hot), 38, **(mic-w)** 405
   Milk, chocolate (hot), 38
   Milk, chocolate syrup for, 39
   Milk, maple, 39
   Milk, orange drinks, 34
   Milk punch, strawberry, 35
   Milk punch, summer shower, 36
   Milk, spicy steamers, 40
   Milk shakes, 41-42
   Mocha drink (hot), 39
   Orange float, 34
   Orange jubilee, 34
   Orange milk shake, 41
   Orange punch, 34

Beverages (cont.)
Orange refresher, quick, 552
Peach drink, super, 36
Pudding shake, thick, 42
Rhubarb punch (cold), 34
Rhubarb punch (hot), 40
Russian tea, 40
Spiced tea mix, instant, 41
Spicy punch (hot), 40
Strawberry milk punch, 35
Strawberry shake, 42
Strawberry sparkle, 35
Summer refreshers, 553
Summer shower punch, 36
Tea, procedure for making, 27
    Concentrate for a group, 36
    Garden tea, 28
    Hot tea, 27
    Iced tea, 28
    Iced tea syrup, 36
    Instant spiced tea mix, 41
    Instant tea, 28
    Russian tea, 40
    Tea lemonade, 29
Wedding punch (pink), 37
Wedding reception punch, 37
Zesta fruit cooler, 37
Biscuits (see Breads)
Blackberry buckle, 195
Blackberry (fresh) pie, 450
Blue cheese spread, 540
Blueberry buckle, 195
Blueberry cheesecake dessert, 196
Blueberry coffee cake, 82
Blueberry (upside-down) cake, l33
Blueberry crunch, **(mic-w)** 422
Blueberry muffins, 75
Blueberry (cake) pie, 449
Blueberry (fresh) pie, 450
Blueberry salads, 477
Boston cream pie, 209
Bread croutons, 472
Bread cubes, homemade herb-seasoned, 336
Bread sticks, Italian, 232
Bread sticks, onion, 554
Breads, 53-88, **(mic-w)** 405, 553-555
    —Information about, 44
    —Procedure for making, 45
    —Tips for breads and sweet breads, 51
Banana oatmeal bread, 79
Batter bread, 54
Biscuits, procedure for making, 48
    Angel, 53
    Buttermilk, 69
    Mix, 68
    Parmesan, 553
    Sweet Potato, 69
Carrot-pineapple bread, 79
Cinnamon buns, easy, 62
Cinnamon rolls, procedure for making, 49
    (see also Sweet Breads), 48
Cinnamon rolls, from biscuit mix, 68
Cinnamon rolls, soft, 63
Cinnamon swirl bread, 54
Coffee cakes (see Coffee Cakes, 667)
Communion bread, 58
Corn bread, 70
Corn bread, Mexican, 70
Cranberry nut bread, 80
Cream cheese danish, 62
Crepes, basic, 72
Crepes, basic dessert, 71

Crepes, chicken filling for, 72
Crepes, taco, 71
Crescent rolls (refrigerator), 55
Dill bread, 56
Doughnuts
    procedure for making, 50
    baked, 64
    bakery, 64
    potato, 65
Dumplings, 73
French bread, 55
Hush puppies, 73
Lemon bubble ring, 66
Monkey, quick, 553
Muffins, procedure for making, 48
    Blueberry, 75
    Bran (big batch), **(mic-w)** 405
    Carrot-raisin, 75
    Cheese-stuffed pumpkin, 76
    French brunch puffs, 76
    Oatmeal, 77
    Raisin muffins (old-timey), 77
    Raisin bran (refrigerator), 78
    Sugary orange, 78
Oatmeal bread, 57
Onion sticks, toasted, 554
Pancakes, procedure for making, 48
    Basic, 85
    Buckwheat (old-fashioned), 86
    Corn cakes, 85
    Melt-in-your-mouth, 555
    Made from mix, 68
    Oatmeal, 85
    Whole wheat, 85
Pepperoni and cheese loaf, 57
Pita bread, 58
Pluck-it bread, 66
Pocket bread, 58
Pumpkin bread, 80
Quick breads, procedure for making, 48
Rolls, procedure for making, 48
    Angel flake, 53
    Crescent (cheese-bacon), 553
    Crescent (refrigerator), 55
    Quick-mix yeast, 555
    Top-notch dinner, 56
    Upside-down caramel, 554
Sour cream twists, 67
Spicy flowerettes, 555
Spoon bread, cheesy, 74
Spoon bread, southern, 74
Sticky buns, procedure for making, 49
Sticky buns, oatmeal-nut, 66
Sticky buns, quicky, 554
Strawberry bread, 80
Sweet breads, procedure for making, 48
Tea rings, procedure for making, 49
Unleavened bread, 58
Waffles, 86
Waffles, melt-in-your-mouth, 555
White bread, basic, 60
Whole wheat bread, basic, 60
Whole wheat orange bread, 61
Zucchini bread, 81
Breakfast-in-a-glass, 31
Broccoli casseroles, 289, 315, 332,
    (mic-w) 410-411; 561
Broccoli, marinated (party), 529
Broccoli pie, 316
Broccoli salad, 488
Broccoli (vegetable) salads, see 497, 537
Broccoli, sour cream party, 316

Brownies (see Cookies)
Brunswick stew, 511
Brussel sprouts, sweet and sour, 489
Burnt sugar syrup, 225
Busy day casserole, 558
Butter, flavored, 470
Butter, honey, 470, **(mic-w)** 406
Butter, onion, 554
Buttermilk biscuits, 69
Buttermilk coffee cake, 83
Buttermilk salad dressing, 501
Buttermilk sauce, 229
Butterscotch bars, **(mic-w)** 424
Butterscotch cream pie, 454
Butterscotch crunchies candy, 237
Butterscotch pudding, 211
Butterscotch sauce, 229
Butterscotch steamer, 38

Cabbage, baked, 316
Cabbage, baked supreme, 317
Cabbage casserole (easy), 317
Cabbage salad, 489
Cabbage, skillet, 559
Cabbage, stuffed (or rolls), 318
Cake Frostings (Icings) and Fillings, 141-146
—Information about, 95
—Testing for doneness, 187
—Tips for, 100
Boiled flour icing, 143
Broiled pineapple frosting, 144
Brown sugar (quick fluffy icing), 141
Caramel (quick) frosting, 141
Chocolate frosting (old-fashioned), 141
Chocolate frosting (quick), 141
Chocolate peanut butter frosting, 142
Coating icing, 142
Cocoa fluff, 142
Cocoa frosting, 142
Cream cheese frosting, 142
Decorating icing, 142
Fillings, information about 145
   Chocolate cream, 145
   Date, 146
   Fruit, 146
   Orange or lemon, 146
   Pineapple, 146
Maple cake topping, 143
Peanut butter frosting (creamy), 144
Pineapple frosting, broiled, 144
Powdered sugar frosting (quick), 144
Satiny beige icing, 144
Sour cream chocolate frosting, 144
White icing (quick fluffy), 143
White mountain frosting, 145
Cakes, 104-140; **(mic-w)** 423, 426-427; 584-585
—Information about, 92
—Quick checklist for failures with, 99
—Tips for, 100
Angel food, 104
   Procedure for making, 96
Apple, 104
Apple dapple, 105
Applesauce, 106
Banana, filled, 106
Banana nut, 107
Banana pudding, 108
Black cherry forest, 107
Black forest, **(mic-w)** 423
Black walnut coconut pound, 108
Cake mix, basic, 137
Cake roll, basic, 130

Cakes (cont.)
Cake roll, creamy chocolate, 131
Cake roll, pumpkin, 132
Carrot gold, 109
Chiffon, anniversary, 110
Chiffon, orange, 110
Chiffon, spicy, 110
Chiffon, walnut, 110
Chiffon, yellow, 110
Chocolate, basic, 109; from mix, 137
Chocolate brownie, 110
Chocolate cherry valentine torte, 111
Chocolate chip, 112, 137
Chocolate mayonnaise, 112
Chocolate marshmallow, 112
Chocolate zucchini, 136
Coconut cream, 114
Coconut, fresh, 113
Coconut pound cakes, 108, 127
Coconut, sour cream, 114
Coconut, special day, 113
Coffee cakes, (see Coffee cakes, 667)
Cupcakes, carrot-pineapple, 139
Cupcakes, little cream cakes, 138
Cupcakes, mini date, 139
Cupcakes, never fail, 139
Cupcakes, raisins and spice, 140
Cupcakes, yummy, 140
Dream, 115
Dump, quick-mix, 585
Fruit, applesauce, 116
Fruit, candied orange, 115
Fruit cocktail, 116
German chocolate, 118
German chocolate upside-down, **(mic-w)** 426
Gingerbread, glorified, 118
Gingerbread, soft, 117
Holiday, 117
Honey-pecan, 119
Hot milk sponge, 133
Hummingbird, 119
Imagination, 120
Jell-O, 120
Lady fingers or sponge drops, 121
Mix, basic, 137
Nameless, 121
Oatmeal, 122
Orange (candied) fruit, 115
Party, 123
Peanut butter, 122
Pecan crunch, 123
Pineapple delight, 124
Pineapple, sponge, 124
Pineapple, Swedish, 125
Pistachio, 125
Polka dot, 126
Poppy seed, 126
Pound, coconut, 108, 127
Pound, five-flavor, 127
Pound, lemon, 128
Pound, poppy seed, 128
Pound, sour cream, 128
Pound, torte, 128
Prune (or plum), 129
Pumpkin, 130
Quick-mix, 138
Rolls (see cake rolls)
Shoofly, 131
Southern special, 134
Spice, 137
Sponge, fluffy yellow, 132
Sponge, hot milk, 133

Strawberry, 134
Swedish pineapple, 125
Upside-down, blueberry, 133
Upside-down, chocolate cherry (quick), 584
Upside-down, chocolate nut, 135
Upside-down, German chocolate **(mic-w)** 426
Upside-down, pineapple, 137, **(mic-w)** 427
White, basic fluffy, 135
White, from mix, 138
Yellow, basic fluffy, 136
Yellow chiffon, 110
Yellow, from mix, 138
Yellow, sponge, 132
Zucchini, 81, 136
California dip, 537
Candied apples, 230, **(mic-w)** 428
Candy, 236-242, **(mic-w)** 429-431
—Information about, 184
—Testing for doneness, 187
—Tips for, 188
Almond bark, 236
Butterscotch crunchies, 237
Candy bars, 237
Candy cookies, 174
Candy wreaths, 174
Chocolate coconut bars, 237
Chocolate drops (or Easter eggs), 238
Church windows, 175
Coconut candy special, **(mic-w)** 428
Coconut, three-tier, 241
Fudge, fantastic, 238
Fudge, holiday rocky road, 238
Fudge, marshmallow cream, **(mic-w)** 429
Mints, party, 239
Peanut brittle, 240, **(mic-w)** 430
Peanut butter cereal squares, 239
Peanut butter chews, 239
Peanut butter drops, 238, 240
Peanut butter eggs, 240
Rice Krispies bars, **(mic-w)** 429
Rice Krispies marshmallow squares, 241
Rocky road, **(mic-w)** 431
Some-mores, **(mic-w)** 431
Taffy, 242
Toffee butter crunch, 242
Cannelloni, 279
Canning and Freezing Index (see page 679)
Caramel apple squares, **(mic-w)** 424
Caramel apples, 230, **(mic-w)** 428
Caramel custard, 210
Caramel frosting, 141
Caramel pie, 450
Caramel popcorn, 234, **(mic-w)** 428
Caramel rolls, upside-down, 554
Carrot pineapple bread, 79
Carrot gold cake, 109
Carrot raisin muffins, 75
Carrot salad, 490
Carrot salad, quick 577
Carrot (sweet and sour) salad, 490
Carrots (party), 543
Carrots, baked, 319
Carrots, orange-spiced, 318
Carrots, sweet and sour, 319
Casseroles (see Main Dishes and
    Vegetables)
Casseroles (create your own) chart, 275
Cauliflower and cheese sauce, 320
Cauliflower vegetable salads, 494, 497, 537
Celery (cream of) soup, 516
Celery seed dressing, 501
Celery sticks, stuffed, 542

Celery supreme, 320
Cereals, 88-90
—Information about, 51
—Tips for, 51
Granola, 88
Grape nuts, 89
Maple granola, 89
Oatmeal, how to cook, 90
Cheese, 255-257
—Information about, 246
—Tips for, 248
(see Eggs and Cheese Recipes for
    dishes containing)
Cheese ball, 255
Cheese ball, chipped beef, 255
Cheese ball, ham, 256
Cheese ball, holiday, 256
Cheese, cottage, 256
Cheese, cream, 257
Cheese, (mock) cream, 256
Cheese dip, 537
Cheese (cottage) dip, 538
Cheese fondue, 530
Cheese pie, **(mic-w)** 411
Cheese sauce, 320, 338
Cheese, soda, 257
Cheese spreads, 540
Cheese-stuffed pumpkin muffins, 76
Cheesecakes (see Desserts)
Cherry (black) forest cakes, 107, **(mic-w)** 423
Cherry (petite) cheesecakes, 212
Cherry cheese pie, 451
Cherry crisp, 582
Cherry delight dessert, 195
Cherry pie, 450
Cherry rolls, 196
Cherry salads, 478
Chicken (see Poultry; see also Main Dishes
    for recipes containing)
Chiffon cakes (see Cakes)
Chiffon pies (see Pies)
Chili burgers, 505
Chili casserole, 284
Chili con carne, 514
Chili con carne, quick, 564, 575
Chili, seasoning mix, 575
Chili stew, **(mic-w)** 420
Chili, weight watcher's, 515
Chocolate (tips for melting), 186
Chocolate angel delight, 214
Chocolate cakes, 109-112, 137
    (see also Cakes)
Chocolate chip cakes, 112, 137
Chocolate cake roll, 131
Chocolate cupcakes, 139, 140
Chocolate (upside-down) cakes, 135; **(mic-w)**
    426; 584
Chocolate cookies (see Cookies)
Chocolate coconut candy bars, 237
Chocolate drops, 238
Chocolate eclair cake dessert, 213
Chocolate eclairs, 215
Chocolate fondue, 543
Chocolate and cocoa frostings, 141-142, 209,
    213
Chocolate lush dessert, 219
Chocolate milk shake, 42
Chocolate mix (hot), 38
Chocolate pies (see Pies)
Chocolate puddings, 211, 214
Chocolate sauces, 229, 230, 588
Chocolate syrup, 39

Chow mein, 284
Chow mein casserole, 285
Chow mein noodles, 320
Christmas fruit cookies, 163
Christmas (ribbon) cookies, 162
Christmas punch, 31
Christmas (three-layer) salad, 486
Cider, spicy (hot), 39, **(mic-w)** 405
Cinnamon apple salad, 478
Cinnamon buns and rolls (see Breads)
Cinnamon pudding, 214
Cinnamon swirl bread, 54
Clam chowder, 515
Clarifying fat, procedure for, 50
Clarifying stock, procedure for, 357
Clothes stain remover, 650
Club salad (favorite), 498
Coating mix for chicken and fish, 365
Cobblers, fruit, 199
Cocoa mix (hot), 38
Coconut
—how to tint, 190
—how to toast, 190, **(mic-w)** 399
Coconut cakes, 113, 114, 132
Coconut pound cakes, 108, 127
Coconut candy special, **(mic-w)** 428
Coconut candy, three-tier, 241
Coconut-chip meringue squares, 150
Coconut cookies, 159, 164
Coconut cracker pudding, 216
Coconut lush dessert, 219
Coconut pie, chiffon, 455
Coconut pie, cream, 454
Coconut pie, quick, 455
Coffee, how to make, 27
Coffee cakes
Blueberry, 82
Buttermilk, 83
Fruit-filled, 82
Orange, 83
Pumpkin (optional recipe), 76
Raspberry, 84
Yummy any-cake, 84
Coffee punch, 31
Coleslaw, 490, 491
Commercial container sizes, 662
Cookies, 147-182; **(mic-w)** 423-427; 584-586
—Procedure for making, 97
—Quick checklist for failures with, 99
—Tips for, 100
Anise fruit-nut, 158
Apple, 159
Banana chocolate chip, 160
Banana tarts, 176
Boy friend, 160
Brownies, 147, **(mic-w)** 423
Brownies, chocolate chip blonde, 148
Brownies, mint, 147
Brownies, peanut butter, 148
Brownies, quick and easy, 584
Butterscotch bars, **(mic-w)** 424
Candy cookies, 174
Candy wreaths, 174
Caramel apple squares, **(mic-w)** 424
Cherry winks, 160
Chocolate animal, 177
Chocolate chip, easy, 585
Chocolate chip, pudding, 162
Chocolate crinkles, 162
Chocolate marshmallow, 161
Chocolate marshmallow bars (deluxe), 149
Chocolate no-bake, 174, **(mic-w)** 424

Cookies (cont.)
Chocolate toffee bars, **(mic-w)** 425
Chocolate whoopie pies, 176
Christmas fruit, 163
Christmas ribbon, 162
Church windows, 175
Coconut, 159, 164
Coconut delights, 164
Coconut-chip meringue squares, 150
Congo squares, 151
Cream cheese, quick, 586
Date bars (crispy), 150
Date drops (chewy), 166
Date pinwheels, 181
Date-filled, 178
Date-filled oatmeal pies, 178
Date-filled oatmeal squares, 152
Drop, basic, 159
Fruit squares, **(mic-w)** 425
Fruit-filled oatmeal squares, 151
Ginger snaps, 168
Gingerbread men, 179
Graham crackers, 177
Granola bars, chewy, 148
Granola bars, quick, 585
Hawaiian delights, 165
Holiday specials, 166
Jubilee jumbles, 167
Lemon bars, 151
Lemon whippersnaps, 586
Melting moments, 168
Meringue tea-party, 168
Molasses crinkles (old-fashioned), 168
Monster, 167
Nutritious no-bake, 175
Oatmeal (old-fashioned), 170
Oatmeal chip, 170
Oatmeal chocolate chip bars, **(mic-w)** 426
Oatmeal bars, 152
Peanut blossom, 172
Peanut butter bars, 153, **(mic-w)** 426
Peanut butter chip chocolate, 172
Peanut butter oatmeal (favorite), 171
Peanut butter quickies, 175
Peanut squares (favorite), 154
Pumpkin, 169
Pumpkin bars, 155, **(mic-w)** 427
Pumpkin-oatmeal, 170
Pumpkin whoopie pies, 180
Raggedy top bars, 154
Raisin, basic, 159
Raisin-filled, 178
Raisin-filled oatmeal squares, 152
Raisin pinwheels, 181
Rocky road fudge bars, 156
Rosie's cookie bars, 586
Russian tea cakes, 172
Spicy oatmeal cookie pies, 180
Spicy raisin bars, 155
Sugar, 182
Sugar (spicy), 181
Thumbprint, 173
Toffee-nut bars, 156
Turtles, 158
Whoopie pies, 176, 180
Zucchini bars, 157
Zucchini chocolate chip, 173
Corn, baked, 321, **(mic-w)** 412
Corn bread (see Breads)
Corn chowder, 516
Corn dogs, 390
Corn salad, 491

Cornmeal mush, old-fashioned, 87
Cornmeal pancakes, 85
Cottage cheese dip, 538
Cottage cheese salad, 479
Crabmeat casserole, 383
Cranberry-apple pie, 453
Cranberry crunch, 582
Cranberry dessert, frozen, 222
Cranberry fluff, 479
Cranberry nut bread, 80
Cranberry punch (cold), 31
Cranberry punch (hot), 38
Cranberry salad, 480
Cranberry sauce, 480
Cream (see Milk and Cream)
Cream batter for vegetables, 337
Cream cheese cookies, quick, 586
Cream cheese danish, 62
Cream cheese frosting, 142
Cream cheese pecan pie, 462
Cream pies (see Pies)
Cream puffs, 215
Crepes (see Breads)
Crockpot, information about, 549
Crockpot recipes
  "Roast" beef, 370
  Baked beans, 313, 314
  Chicken, 378
  Hamburger-potato dinner, 293
  Pork chops, 374
  Supper-in-a-dish, 307
Crumbs for topping pies, 445
Cucumber salads, 492, 497
Cucumber spread, 541
Cucumber tidbits (party), 542
Cupcakes (see Cakes)
Curry dip, 538
Custards and puddings (see Desserts)

Daily nutrition guide, 21
Danish dessert, 197
Date bars, crispy, 150
Date cakes (mini), 139
Date drops, chewy, 166
Date-filled cookies, 178
Date-filled oatmeal cookie pies, 178
Date-filled oatmeal squares, 152
Date filling for cakes, 146
Date pinwheels, 181
Date pudding favorite, 216
Date whipped cream pudding, 217
Dates, stuffed (party), 544
Deep fat frying, procedure for, 50
Definitions of food and cooking terms, 18
Dessert salad, 480
Desserts and Fruits, 192-228; (mic-w) 421-422; 580-584
  —Information about, 184
  —Tips for, 188
  Apple butter rolls, 443, 580
  Apple crisp, 192, (mic-w) 421
  Apple delight, (mic-w) 421
  Apple dumplings, 194
  Apple strudel, 202
  Apples, baked, 192, 580
  Apples, delightful macaroon, 193
  Applescotch dessert, 193
  Banana puddings, 580
  Bananas, baked, 231, (mic-w) 422
  Blueberry cheese cake, 196
  Blueberry crunch, (mic-w) 422
  Blueberry or blackberry buckle, 195

Desserts and Fruits (cont.)
  Boston cream pie, 209
  Cheesecakes
    Blueberry, 196
    Lemon, 212, 581
    Petite cherry, 212
    Quick, 581
    Weight watcher's, 212
  Cherry crisp, 582
  Cherry delight, 195
  Cherry rolls, 196
  Chocolate angel delight, 214
  Chocolate eclair cake, 213
  Chocolate eclairs, 215
  Chocolate lush, 219
  Coconut cracker pudding, 216
  Coconut lush, 219
  Cranberry crunch, 582
  Cranberry dessert, frozen, 222
  Cream puffs, 215
  Custard (see also Pudding)
  Custard, baked vanilla, 210
  Custard, caramel, 210
  Custard, soft, 216
  Danish dessert, 197
  Eclairs, chocolate, 215
  English trifle, 218
  Frozen desserts, 200, 222-228, 231, 236
  Fruit cobbler, 199, 583
  Fruit, curried, 197
  Fruit dessert, 204
  Fruit pizza, 198
  Fruit pudding, 583
  Fruit slush, frozen, 200
  Gelatin-pineapple, 202
  Graham cracker fluff, 218
  Grapefruit, broiled, 201
  Grapefruit, filled-Alaska, 201
  Ice cream, 225-228, 588
    (see also sherbet)
    —Procedure for making homemade, 185
    Banana, 225
    Basic homemade, 225
    Grapenut, 225
    Junket, 226
    Maple-nut, 225
    Orange pineapple, 226
    Peach, 225
    Raspberry, 225
    Refrigerator, 227, 228
    Soft, 226
    Strawberry, 225, 588
  Ice cream crunch dessert, 224
  Lemon lush, 219
  Melon and fruit wedges (surprise), 201
  Melon, frozen, 209
  Orange fluffs, 200, 220
  Orange tapioca delight, 207
  Oreo cookie lush, 219
  Oreo ice cream dessert, 222
  Peach crisp, 192
  Peach strudel, 202
  Peanut butter ice cream squares, 224
  Peanut butter lush, 219
  Pineapple dessert, quick, 583
  Pineapple, easy, 202
  Plum good dessert, 204
  Prunes, cooked, 203
  Puddings (see also Custard)
    Basic vanilla, 211
    Banana, 580
    Butterscotch 211

Desserts and Fruits (cont.)
    Chocolate, 211, 214
    Cinnamon, 214
    Coconut cracker, 216
    Date (favorite), 216
    Date, whipped cream, 217
    Fruit, 583
    Lush, 219
    Strawberry, 206, 584
    Tapioca (fluffy), 221
    Toasted pecan, 221, **(mic-w)** 422
  Pumpkin dessert, quick-mix, 582
  Pumpkin lush, 219
  Pumpkin squares, luscious, 220
  Pumpkin stack-ups, 223
  Raspberry dessert, 203
  Rhubarb dessert and tortes, 204, 205
  Rice, glorified, 218
  Sherbet, orange, 227
  Sherbet, pineapple, 227
  Sherbet, strawberry, 227
  Snow cream, 228
  Strawberries and cream (fresh), 583
  Strawberrioca, 206
  Strawberry dessert, 203, 222
  Strawberry puddings, 206, 584
  Strawberry-rhubarb compote, 206
  Strawberry shortcake, old-fashioned, 207
  Strawberry shortcake, sponge, 133
  Strawberry squares, frosty, 224
  Strawberry swirl, 208
  Tapioca fruit, pearl, 208
  Tapioca, orange delight, 207
  Tapioca pudding (fluffy), 221
  Watermelon magnifique, 208
Deviled eggs, 249, 502
Dieter's delight, 32
Dill bread, 56
Dips, 537-539
  Bacon and cottage cheese, 537
  California, 537
  Cheese, 537
  Cottage cheese, 538
  Curry, 538
  Fruit (fresh), 539
  Ham (deviled), 538
  Ham (deviled) and cheese, 538
  Onion, 539
  Peanut butter fruit, 539
  Vegetable, 539
Doughnuts (see Breads)
Dressing, 258
  Balls, 258, 564
  Cheesy, 259
  Oyster, 385
  Salsify, 258
Dump cake, quick-mix, 585
Dumplings, 73
Dumplings, apple, 194
Dumplings (and chicken) soup, 512
Dumplings (and sauerkraut), 304

Easter egg candy, 238
Eggnog, 32
Eggnog liquid breakfast, 32
Eggplant casserole, 321
Eggplant special, 286
Eggplant, fried, 331
Eggs and cheese
  —Information about, 244
  —How to freeze eggs, 245-246
  —Tips for, 248

Eggs
  deviled, 249, 502
  eggs in a hole, 250
  fried, 250
  golden rod, 250
  hard cooked, 246
  pickled, 250
  poached, 251
  scrambled, 251, **(mic-w)** 419
  soft cooked, 246
Eggs and Cheese recipes, 249-262; **(mic-w)** 419; 556, 564
  Breakfast casserole, **(mic-w)** 410
  Breakfast pizza, 556
  Brunch casserole, 259
  Cheese and bacon pie, 257
  Cheese grits soufflé, 258
  Cheese pie, **(mic-w)** 411
  Cheese-bacon crescent rolls, 553
  Cheeseburger strata, 280
  Dressing, 258, 259
  Dressing balls, 258, 564
  Egg salad, **(mic-w)** 419
  Egg-cheese sandwich filling, 505
  Egg salad sandwich spread, 541
  Egg soufflé, 260
  Eggs with cheese, 260
  French toast, 262
  Ham and egg casserole, 260
  Omelet, potato, 261
  Omelet, puffy breakfast, 261
  Omelet, zucchini, 261
  Quiche, quick, 262, 569
Enchiladas casserole, favorite, 565
Entertaining, information about, 524
Equivalent measures, 658-659

Fat, clarifying, 50
Fat, deep frying, 50
Fertilizer for houseplants (liquid), 652
Fillings (see Cake Frostings and Fillings)
Fillings (see Sandwich Fillings and Spreads)
Finger gelatin, 232
Finger paints, 651
Fish (see Seafood for recipes containing)
  —Information about, 354
  —Canning, procedure for, 356
  —Cleaning, procedure for, 355
Floats, 552
Fondue, cheese, 530
Fondue, chocolate, 543
Frankfurter casserole, 287
Franks, barbecued (party), 530
Freezing and Canning Index, (see page 679)
French bread, 55
French brunch puffs, 76
French dressing (basic and variations), 501-502
French toast, 262
Frosted fruit (party), 543
Frostings (see Cake Frostings)
Frozen desserts, 222-228, 231, 236
Fruit breads (see Breads)
Fruit cakes, 115, 116
Fruit cobblers, 199, 583
Fruit (filled) coffee cake, 82
Fruit, curried, 197
Fruit delight, 482
Fruit desserts, 192-209; **(mic-w)** 421-422; 580-584 (see also Desserts and Fruits)
Fruit dips (fresh), 539
Fruit fillings for cakes, 146

Fruit, frosted (party), 543
Fruit (filled) oatmeal squares, 151
Fruit pizza, 198
Fruit pudding, 583
Fruit salads, 481, 482
Fruit salad, quick, 578
Fruit shortcakes, 68, 133, 207
Fruit slush mix, 32
Fruit slush, frozen, 200
Fruit squares, **(mic-w)** 425
Fruit trays, 528
Fruity liquid breakfast, 32
Fruity milk shake, 42
Fruity popcorn treat, **(mic-w)** 429
Fudge candy, (see Candy)
Fudge sauces (hot), 229, 230, 588
Fudgesicles, 231

Gardening tips, 644
Gargle, sore throat, 651
Gelatin, information about, 468
Gelatin snacks, finger, 232
Gelatin treatment for houseplants, 652
German chocolate cake, 118, **(mic-w)** 426
German slaw, 492
Ginger ale salad, 482
Ginger snaps, 168
Gingerbread, 117, 118
Gingerbread men, 179
Gorp trail mix, 233
Graham cracker fluff, 218
Graham crackers, 177
Granola bars, 148, 585
Granola cereal, 88
Grape nut ice cream, 225
Grape nuts, 89
Grape pie, 456
Grapefruit, broiled, 201
Grapefruit, filled-Alaska, 201
Grasshopper pie, 457
Gravy, information about making, 358
    Brown, 360
    Meat or pan, 359
    Sausage, 360
    Tomato, 262
Greek salad, 492
Green beans, recipes for (see Beans)
Green tomato pie, 457
Greens, dressings for, 493, 500
    (for endive, dandelion, kale, spinach,
    and watercress)
Ground beef (see Main Dishes for recipes
    containing)

Ham (see Meats, see also Main Dishes for
    recipes containing)
Ham (deviled) dip, 538
Ham ball appetizers, 531
Ham puffs (party), 531
Ham soup, 517
Ham spread, 541
Ham-a-roni salad, 499
Hamburger (see Meats, see also Main
    Dishes for recipes containing)
Hamburger bean-pot soup, 517
Hamburger mix, ready, 576
Hamburger muffin cups (party), 532
Hamburger soup, 518
Haystacks, 294
Hoagies, 507
Hollandaise sauce, blender, 337
Hollandaise sauce, mock, 337
Honey butter, 470, **(mic-w)** 406

Honey pecan cake, 119
Honeydew salad, 483
Hot dog treats (party), 532
Hot dogs in a blanket, 567
Hush puppies, 73

Ice cream (see Desserts)
Ice cream, procedure for homemade, 185
Ice cream pie, 458
Icings (see Cake frostings)
Instant pie, 586
Iron cookware, tips about, 645-646
Italian bread sticks, 232
Italian TV mix, **(mic-w)** 430
Italian tomato sauce, 322

Jam and jelly (see also Canning and
        Freezing Index on page 679)
    Grape jelly, **(mic-w)** 432
    Strawberry jam, **(mic-w)** 432
Japanese fruit pie, 458
Jell-O cake, 120
Jell-O sauce, 483

Lady fingers, 121
Lamb (see Meats)
Lasagna, 294, **(mic-w)** 415
Lasagna, quick, 567
Lasagna, zucchini, 310
Leftovers, ideas for, 634
Lemon bars, 151
Lemon bubble ring, 66
Lemon cheesecakes, 212, 581
Lemon cream pie, 459
Lemon filling for cakes, 146
Lemon lush dessert, 219
Lemon pound cake, 128
Lemon whippersnaps, 586
Lemonade mint drink, 33
Lemonade syrup, 33
Lemonade, easy, 552
Lentil soup, 518
Lettuce and cauliflower salad, 494
Lettuce dressing (favorite), 502
Lettuce salad, 493
Lettuce salad (seven layer), 494
Life, recipe for, 650
Lime-light banana crush punch, 33
Liver, 389
Lower calorie cooking, tips for, 22

Macaroni (see also Main Dishes for recipes
    containing)
Macaroni and cheese, baked, 322
Macaroni salad (for a group), 495
Macaroni, easy bake, 322
Macaroni-tuna salad, 499
Main Dishes, 278-311; **(mic-w)** 409-419; 556-577
    (see also Seafood for Main Dishes
        containing)
    —Information about, 264
    —Tips for, 276
    Bacon quiche, 278
    Bean (green) and bacon, **(mic-w)** 413
    Beef'n bean casserole, 278
    Beef-macaroni skillet, 558
    Beef and noodle casserole, **(mic-w)** 410
    Beef stew, oven-baked, 300
    Beef and vegetable lunch, 559
    Beef-vegetable casserole, 279
    Busy day casserole, 558
    Cannelloni, 279
    Casseroles (create your own) chart, 275

Main Dishes (cont.)
Cheese pie, **(mic-w)** 411
Cheeseburger strata, 280
Chicken 'n biscuits (country), 280
Chicken and broccoli casserole, 281, **(mic-w)** 412
Chicken and broccoli pie, 561
Chicken casserole, favorite, 283
Chicken casserole (make-ahead), 281
Chicken delight, 378
Chicken-etti, 560
Chicken and noodle casseroles, 292, 305
Chicken pie, impossible, 561
Chicken and pineapple, stir-fried, 562
Chicken and rice casserole, 282, 283
Chicken and rice, curried, 282
Chicken-rice skillet (curried), 562
Chicken and stuffing special, 563
Chicken and vegetable stir-fry, 563
Chili casserole, 284
Chow mein, 284, 285
Dinner-in-a-package, 286
Dried beef casserole (make-ahead), 281
Eggplant special, 286
Enchiladas casserole, favorite, 565
Frankfurter casserole, 287
Ground beef oriental, 287
Ground beef stroganoff casserole, 288
Ham and asparagus casserole, 289
Ham and broccoli bake, 289
Ham casserole (quick-mix), 290
Ham and cheese bake, 288
Ham and potato casserole, **(mic-w)** 417
Ham and potato skillet, 566
Ham and scalloped potatoes, 291
Hamburger broccoli casserole, **(mic-w)** 414
Hamburger mix, ready, 576
Hamburger and macaroni, **(mic-w)** 413
Hamburger macaroni casserole, 291
Hamburger and noodles, 292
Hamburger or ham quiche (easy), 293
Hamburger pie, 292, 566
Hamburger-potato Crockpot dinner, 293
Hamburger spinach casserole, **(mic-w)** 414
Hamburger stroganoff, 566
Haystacks, 294
Hot dogs and scalloped potatoes, 291
Lasagna, 294; quick, 567
Lasagna, easy, **(mic-w)** 415
Luncheon special, 567
Manicotti, 296
Meat and rice, curried, 285
Meat casserole, stove top, 572
Meat pie, 68, 298
Meat pinwheels, 68
Meatballs and rice, 296
Meatballs and spaghetti, 295
Miscellaneous tips, 644
(More) casserole, 297
Okra-hamburger skillet, 300
Omelet, hearty supper, 567
Pinwheel-vegetable casserole, 300
Pizza pie, 302
Pizza, breakfast, 556
Pizza, crazy crust, 303
Pizzas, quick individual, 568
Pizza surprise, **(mic-w)** 414
Plantation casserole, 301
Pork and beans casserole, 557
Potpie (old-fashioned), 290
Sauerkraut and dumplings, 304
Sausage and cabbage dinner, 304

Main Dishes (cont.)
Sausage cheese casserole, **(mic-w)** 410
Sausage and noodle casserole, 305
Sausage-potato quiche, 305
Sausage-rice casserole, 306
Shepherds pie, **(mic-w)** 418
Spaghetti and meatballs, 295
Spaghetti, mock, 306
Spaghetti pie, 307
Spaghetti sauce, using mix, 577
Spaghetti seasoning mix, 576
Spam dinner, quick, 569
Stroganoff, 288, 565, 566, 570
Supper-in-a-dish, 307
Taco filling, using mix, 577
Taco pie (impossible), 308
Taco seasoning mix, 577
Tacos, Navajo, 299
Tater Tot casserole, 308
Texas hash, 309
Turkey casserole (favorite), 283
Turkey-ham quiche, 308
Wild rice-hamburger casserole, 309
Zucchini hamburger casserole, 310
Zucchini lasagna, 310
Zucchini pie, 311
Zucchini pizza, 311
Manicotti, 296
Maple cake topping, 143
Maple granola, 89
Maple milk, 39
Maple nut ice cream, 225
Marinades for meats, 365-366
Mayonnaise, blender, 502
Measures, equivalent, 658-659, 662
Meats, 364-392; **(mic-w)** 406-409
(see also Poultry and Fish)
(see also Main Dishes for recipes
   containing various meats)
—Information about, 340
—Information about wild meats, 349
—Approximate amounts needed per
   serving, 360
—Meat cut charts, 345-348
   (beef, lamb, pork, veal)
—Methods for cooking, 342
—Timetable for roasting, 361
—Tips for, 362
Bacon, tips for cooking, 362
Bacon quiche, 278
Barbecue sauces, 364, 375, 390, **(mic-w)** 406
Beef, roast, 370, 371
Brains (beef, veal, or pork), 388
Chicken (see Poultry)
Chuck roast, barbecued, 371
Corn dogs, 390
Dried beef, creamed, 564
Ham, how to boil or bake, 372
Ham, how to carve, 372
   Glazes for, 366, 372
   Raisin sauce for, 367
Ham buns, 506
Ham dogs, 506
Ham loaf, 373
Ham rolls, 374
Ham (deviled) sandwiches, 507
Ham, scalloped, 373
Ham spread, 541
Hamburger pie, 566
Hamburgers, 368, 507, 567
Hamburgers, barbecued, 367
Heart, beef, 388

Meats (cont.)
Hot dog boats, 390
Hot dog treats (party), 532
Hot dogs, barbecued, 390, 530
Hot dogs in a blanket, 567
Liver, fried, 389
Liverburgers, 389
Marinades for meats, 365-366
Meatballs deluxe (party or main dish), 532
Meat loaf, 368, **(mic-w)** 408
Mustard sauce for, 366
Pigs in a blanket, 390
Porcupine balls, 370
Pork buns (barbecued), 508
Pork chops, 375, **(mic-w)** 408
Pork chops, Crockpot, 374
Pork, sweet and sour, **(mic-w)** 408
Raisin sauce for ham, 367
Roast beef, 370, 371
Salami, lean beef, 371
Sauces and seasoning for meats, 364-366, 575-577
Sloppy Joes, 509, 576
Sloppy Joes, seasoning mix, 575
Spamburgers, 509
Spareribs, oven barbecued, 375
Squirrel, 391
Steak, cubed, round, or sirloin, 369
Steak, poor man's, 369
Steak, salisbury, 371
Turkey (see Poultry)
Venison bologna, 392
Venison, roast, 391
Venison stroganoff, 392
Melon, frozen, 209
Melon and fruit wedges (surprise), 201
Meringue, procedure for making, 440
Microwave cooking, 394-432
—Information about, 394
—Adapting conventional recipes, 397
—Do's and don'ts, 398
—Flower drying chart, 402
—Heating chart, 403
—Uses for, 399
—Utensil test, 395
—Tips for heating leftovers, 398
Microwave recipes, 405-432
Milk and Cream, 252-255
(see Beverages for milk beverages)
—Information about, 26, 246
—Tips about, 29, 248
—Tips for whipping cream, 248-249
Cream, mock sour, 253
Cream, mock whipped, 253
Cream, stabilized whipped, 254
Dieter's topping, 253
Dry milk powder, mixing, 252
Milk, whipped evaporated, 254
Pasteurize, how to, 252
Sweetened condensed, homemade, 252
Thick sour, making, 252
Yogurt, 254
Minestrone, 519
Mints, party, 239
Miscellaneous tips, 644
Mixes
Bean (nine) soup mix, 510
Biscuit mix, 68
Cake mix, 137
Chili seasoning, 575
Hamburger, ready, 576
Pancake mix, 68

Pie crust mix, 445
Sloppy Joe seasoning, 575
Spaghetti seasoning, 576
Mocha drink (hot), 39
Molasses crinkles, 168
Monkey bread, quick, 553
Mothballs, floating, 651
Muffins (see Breads)
Mush, old-fashioned cornmeal, 87
Mushroom (cream of) soup, 516
Mushroom rolls (party), 533
Mushrooms, stuffed, 533, **(mic-w)** 431
Mustard plaster (old-time), 652

Noodles (see also Main Dishes for recipes containing)
Noodles, 323
Noodles, chow mein, 320
Nuts, directions for toasting, 190

Oatmeal, 90
Oatmeal bread, 57
Oatmeal cake, 122
Oatmeal chocolate chip bars, **(mic-w)** 426
Oatmeal cookies, 152, 170-171
Oatmeal cookie bars, 152
Oatmeal cookie pies, 178, 180
Oatmeal muffins, 77
Oatmeal pancakes, 85
Oatmeal pie, 460
Oatmeal sticky buns, 66
Okra hamburger skillet, 300
Omelets, 261, 567
Onion butter, 554
Onion dip, 539
Onion rings, 324
Onion soup, **(mic-w)** 420; 520
Onion sticks, toasted, 554
Onions, cheesy supreme, 323
Onions, creamed, 324
Orange coffee cake, 83
Orange filling for cakes, 146
Orange float, 34
Orange fluff, 200, 220
Orange jubilee, 34
Orange milk shake, 41
Orange muffins, sugary, 78
Orange pineapple ice cream, 226
Orange punch, 34
Orange refresher (quick), 552
Orange sherbet, 227
Orange tapioca delight, 207
Oreo cookie lush, 219
Oreo ice cream dessert, 222
Oyster recipes, (see Seafood)

Paints, finger, 651
Pancake syrup, 87
Pancakes (see Breads)
Papier-mâché, 651
Parmesan biscuits, 553
Party food and ideas, information about, 524
Party food recipes, 527-544
Party loaf (elegant), 534
Party mix, 232, **(mic-w)** 430
Pasta, how to cook, 274
Pastry (see Pies)
Peach crisp, 192
Peach drink, 36
Peach ice cream, 225
Peach (fresh) pie, 456, 460
Peach salad, quick, 578

Peach strudel, 202
Peach torte pie, 460
Peanut brittle, 240, **(mic-w)** 430
Peanut butter cake, 122
Peanut butter candies (see Candies)
Peanut butter cookies (see Cookies)
Peanut butter frosting, 144
Peanut butter fruit dip, 539
Peanut butter ice cream squares, 224
Peanut butter lush dessert, 219
Peanut butter (cream) pies, 454, 587
Peanut butter (frozen) pie, 461
Peanut butter popcorn balls, 235
Peanut butter sauce, 230
Peanuts, roasted, 233, **(mic-w)** 400
Pear salad, 483
Pear salad, quick, 579
Pecan crunch cake, 123
Pecan pie, 461
Pecan (chocolate) pie, 453
Pecan (cream cheese) pie, 462
Pecan pudding, toasted, 221, **(mic-w)** 422
Pecan tarts, 462
Pecans, sugarcoated (party), 544
Peppernuts, 233
Pepperoni and cheese loaf, 57
Peppers (stuffed), raw, 234
Peppers (stuffed), skillet, 324
Pheasant, fried, 391
Pickled eggs, 250
Pies and Pastry, 444-466, 586-588
 —Information about, 434
 —Information about cream pies, 440
 —Procedure for making meringue, 440
 —Procedure for making pastry, 436
 —Tips for, 442
Apple, 448
Apple (bavarian) tarts, 448
Apple macaroon, 449
Blackberry, 450
Blueberry, 450
Blueberry cake, 449
Caramel, 450
Cherry, 450
Cherry cheese, 451
Chocolate (super), 452
Chocolate bottom cake, 452
Chocolate chiffon, 451
Chocolate pecan, 453
Coconut (quick), 455
Coconut chiffon, 455
Cranberry-apple, 453
Cream pies, information about, 440
  Almond, 454
  Banana, 454
  Basic, 454
  Butterscotch, 454
  Chocolate, 454
  Coconut, 454
  Lemon, 459
  Peanut butter, 454, 587
  Raisin, 454
Crumbs for topping, 445
Dream, 587
Fruit pies (fresh), 456
Grape, 456
Grasshopper, 457
Green tomato, 457
Ice cream, 458
Ice cream, krispy, 458
Instant pie, 586
Japanese fruit, 458

Lemon cream, 459
Lemon meringue (old-fashioned), 459
Oatmeal, 460
Pastry, procedure for making, 436
  Basic, 444
  Chocolate coconut crust, 446
  Chocolate crunch crust, 446
  Chocolate crumb crust, 445
  Cocoa crumb crust, 446
  Coconut crust, 446
  Coconut pastry crust, 446
  Cornflake crumb crust, 446
  Cream cheese tart crust, 447
  Crunchy crust, 447
  Easy, 444
  Gingersnap crust, 447
  Graham cracker crust, 447
  Mix, 445
  Mix-in-pan, 445
  Never-fail, 444
  Oatmeal pastry crust, 447
  Spiced nut crust, 448
Peach (fresh), 456, 460
Peach torte, 460
Peanut butter (frozen), 461
Peanut butter, cream, 454, 587
Pecan, 461
Pecan, chocolate, 453
Pecan, cream cheese, 462
Pecan tarts, 462
Pumpkin, chiffon, 463
Pumpkin (frozen), 464
Pumpkin (old-fashioned), 463
Pumpkin, quick, 587
Pumpkin (special), 464
Raspberry chiffon, 464
Raspberry (fresh), 450, 456
Raspberry dream (frozen), 465
Rhubarb, 466
Shoofly, 466
Squash, 466
Strawberry (fresh), 456
Strawberry dream, 465
Strawberry, instant, 588
Strawberry torte, 460
Pineapple cakes, 124-125
Pineapple cheese spread, 540
Pineapple dessert, 202
Pineapple dessert, quick, 583
Pineapple filling for cakes, 146
Pineapple frosting, broiled, 114
Pineapple salads, 484
Pineapple sherbet, 227
Pineapple topping, 230
Pineapple upside-down cakes, 137, **(mic-w)** 427
Pistachio cake, 125
Pistachio salad, 579
Pistachio cottage cheese salad, 479
Pizza, breakfast, 556
Pizza burgers, 508
Pizza, crazy crust, 303
Pizza, fruit, 198
Pizza, gardener's, 324
Pizza pie, 302
  Crusts for, 68, 302-303
Pizza, quick individual, 568
Pizza snacks (party), 534
Pizza surprise, **(mic-w)** 414
Pizza, zucchini, 311
Plaster, mustard, 652
Play dough, 653
Play dough, edible, 653

Plum cake, 129
Plum good dessert, 204
Ponhoss, old-fashioned, 88
Poor man's steak, 369
Popcorn, procedure for making, 187
   Balls, 234
   Balls, peanut butter, 235
   Caramel, 234, **(mic-w)** 428
   Fruity treat, **(mic-w)** 429
   Party, 543
Poppy seed cakes, 126, 128
Poppy seed dressing, 501
Popsicles, strawberry pudding, 236
Porcupine balls, 370
Pork (see Meats)
   (see also Main Dishes for
   recipes containing)
Potpie (old-fashioned), 290
Potato (cheese) balls, 326
Potato cakes, 568
Potato omelet, 261
Potato rivel soup, 519
Potato salads, 494, 495
Potato salad (for a group), 495
Potato soup, 520, 521
Potatoes, baked, 273, **(mic-w)** 415
   Toppings for baked potatoes, 253, 338, 501
Potatoes
   baked "French fried," 327
   baked (mashed), 325, **(mic-w)** 416; 568
   browned or fried, 325
   (quick) company, **(mic-w)** 416
   cottage, 326
   crispy, 326
   diet stuffed, 327
   French-fried, 327
   mashed, 273
   (golden), and onions, **(mic-w)** 416
   scalloped, 291, 327, 328
   scalloped (quick), 568
   scalloped supreme, 328
   and turnips, creamed, 326
Potting soil, 654
Poultry and wild fowl, 376-382;
   (mic-w) 406-407; 559-560
   (see also Main Dishes for recipes
      containing)
   —Procedure for processing, 349
   —How to cut up, 352
   —Amounts needed per serving, 360
   —Timetable for roasting, 361
   —Tips for, 362
   Chicken (buttermilk), baked, 376
   Chicken (company), baked, 377
   Chicken barbecue sauce, 376
   Chicken breasts (super), 559
   Chicken breasts, fried, 560
   Chicken burgers, 505
   Chicken, company stuffed, 377
   Chicken, Crockpot, 378
   Chicken, delight, 378
   Chicken, easy, 378, **(mic-w)** 406
   Chicken, moist 'n crispy onion, 379
   Chicken nuggets, 530
   Chicken, oven barbecued, 376
   Chicken, oven-fried, **(mic-w)** 406
   Chicken, pressed, 498
   Chicken rolls, 374
   Chicken salad, 498
   Chicken salad bake, 387
   Chicken salad mold, 498
   Chicken shortcake, 573

   Chicken, smoked, 382
   Chicken corn soup, 513
   Chicken and dumpling soup, 512
   Chicken and noodle soup, 513, **(mic-w)** 420
   Chicken and rice soup, 514
   Chicken, sweet and sour, 378
   Chicken, Vietnamese, 379
   Chicken wings (party), 529
   Coating mix for chicken, 365
   Pheasant, 391
   Quail, with all-game dressing, 391
   Turkey, how to carve, 381
   Turkey, how to roast, 380
   Turkey breast, 382
   Turkey buns (barbecued), 508
   Turkey buns (broiled), 510
   Turkey muffin cups (party), 536
   Turkey shortcake, 573
   Turkey, oven barbecued, 382
   Turkey, smoked, 382
Pound cakes, 127, 128
Pretzels, soft, 235
Prune cake, 129
Prunes, cooked, 203
Pudding milk shake, 42
Puddings and Custards (see Desserts)
Pumpkin bars, 155, **(mic-w)** 427
Pumpkin bread, 80
Pumpkin cake, 130
Pumpkin cake roll, 132
Pumpkin cookies, 169, 170
Pumpkin dessert, quick-mix, 582
Pumpkin lush dessert, 219
Pumpkin muffins, 76
Pumpkin pies, 463-464, 587
Pumpkin seeds, roasted, 235
Pumpkin squares (frozen), 464
Pumpkin squares, luscious, 220
Pumpkin stack-ups dessert, 223
Pumpkin whoopie pies, 180
Punch (see Beverages)

Quail, with all-game dressing, 391
Quantity cooking, amounts for l00, 526
Quantity cooking, information about, 524
Quiche
   Bacon, 278
   Hamburger or ham (easy), 293
   Quick, 262, 569
   Sausage-potato, 305
   Turkey-ham 308
Quick-Fix recipes, 552-588
   —Information about, 546
   —Tips for, 551

Rabbit salad, 496
Raisin bars, spicy, 155
Raisin-filled cookies, 159, 178
Raisin and spice cupcakes, 140
Raisin muffins, 77
Raisin, bran muffins, 78
Raisin-filled oatmeal squares, 152
Raisin cream pie, 454
Raisin pinwheels, 181
Raisin sauce for ham, 367
Raspberry (fresh) pie, 450, 456
Raspberry chiffon pie, 464
Raspberry coffee cake, 84
Raspberry dessert, 203
Raspberry dream pie (frozen), 465
Raspberry ice cream, 225
Refrigerator rolls, 55

Rhubarb desserts, 204-206
Rhubarb pie, 466
Rhubarb punch (cold), 34
Rhubarb punch (hot), 40
Rhubarb tortes, 204, 205
Ribbon sandwiches, 527, 541
Rice (see also Main Dishes for recipes
    containing)
Rice, how to cook, 329
Rice, browned, 329
Rice casserole, 330
Rice, easy oven-cooked, 329
Rice, glorified, 218
Rice Krispies bars, **(mic-w)** 429
Rice Krispies marshmallow squares, 241
Rice (wild)-hamburger casserole, 309
Rivel (potato) soup, 519
Rolls (see Breads)
Rolls, cake (see Cakes)
Roses, spray for, 654
Russian dressing, 503
Russian tea, 40
Russian tea cakes, 172

Salad Dressings, 500-504
    Basic (cold), 500
    Basic (cooked), 500
    Buttermilk, 501
    Celery seed, 501
    French, 501
    French, basic and variations, 502
    Lettuce (favorite), 502
    Mayonnaise, blender, 502
    Miracle whip substitute, 503
    Poppy seed, 501
    Quick salad dressing, 578
    Russian, 503
    Thousand island, 503
    Topping for fruit salads, quick, 578
    Tossed salad, 504
    Yogurt dressings, 475, 504
Salads, 473-500, 577-579
    —Information about, 468
    —Tips for, 471
    Ambrosia, 473
    Angel, 473
    Apple, 474
    Apple (old-fashioned), 475
    Apple dapple, 475
    Apple gelatin, 474
    Apricot, 476
    Avocado mold, 476
    Bean, 488
    Blueberry, 477
    Blueberry (molded), 477
    Broccoli, 488
    Broccoli (vegetable) salads, 497, 537
    Brussel sprouts, sweet and sour, 489
    Cabbage, 489
    Carrot, 490
    Carrot, quick, 577
    Carrot, sweet and sour, 490
    Cauliflower (vegetable) salads, 497, 537
    Cherry, 478
    Cherry, bing, 478
    Chicken, 498
    Chicken salad mold, 498
    Christmas (three-layer), 486
    Cinnamon apple, 478
    Club (favorite), 498
    Coleslaw, poppy seed, 490
    Coleslaw, seafoam, 491

Salads (cont.)
    Corn, 491
    Cottage cheese, 479
    Cranberry, 480
    Cranberry fluff, 479
    Cranberry sauce, 480
    Cucumber (old-fashioned), 492
    Dessert, 480
    Egg salad, **(mic-w)** 419
    Fluffy, 479
    Fruit (frozen), 481
    Fruit (luscious), 481
    Fruit delight, 482
    Fruit, quick, 578
        quick topping for, 578
    Gelatin, information about, 468
    German slaw, 492
    Ginger ale, 482
    Greek, 492
    Greens, dressing for, 493, 500
        (endive, dandelion, kale, spinach,
        watercress)
    Ham-a-roni, 499
    Honeydew, 483
    Jell-O sauce, 483
    Lazy-day, 579
    Lettuce, 493
    Lettuce and cauliflower, 494
    Lettuce, seven-layer, 494
    Macaroni (for a group), 495
    Macaroni-tuna, 499
    Peach, quick, 578
    Pear, 483
    Pear, quick, 579
    Pineapple, 484
    Pineapple (molded), 484
    Pistachio, 579
    Pistachio, cottage cheese, 479
    Potato, 494
    Potato (easy), 495
    Potato (for a group), 495
    Pressed chicken, 498
    Rabbit, 496
    Sauerkraut, 496
    Seven-layer lettuce, 494
    Slaw, German, 492
    Spinach, 496
    Sprouts, for in, 488
    Strawberry, 485, 486
    Summertime refresher, 485
    Taco, 500
    Tomato and cucumber, 497
    Tuna, 579
    Tuna-macaroni, 499
    Vegetable (crunchy), 497
    Vegetable trays, 528
    Waldorf, 487
    Waldorf (frozen), 487
    Watergate, 579
Salami, lean beef, 371
Salmon recipes (see Seafood)
Salsify soup, 520
Salsify, baked, 330
Salt substitute, 337
Sandwich Fillings and Spreads, 469-470,
        527, 534, 540-542
    Apple butter, quick, 556
    Beef (chipped) spread, 540
    Blue cheese spread, 540
    Cheese spread, 540
    Chicken salad, 534
    Cucumber spread, 541

Egg salad spreads, 534, 541
Ham salad, 534
Ham spread, 541
Party spreads, ideas for 527
Pineapple cheese spread, 540
Tuna spread, 542
Sandwiches and Buns, 505-510, 527, 541, 576
—Ideas for fillings, 469
Chicken burgers, 505
Chili burgers, 505
Egg-cheese filling, 505
Fishburgers, 506
Ham (deviled) hot, 507
Ham buns, 506
Ham dogs, 506
Hamburger buns, 507
(see also 367-368, 567)
Hoagies, 507
Party loaf (elegant), 534
Pinwheel, 527
Pizza burgers, 508
Pork buns (barbecued), 508
Ribbon, 527, 541
Sloppy Joes, 509, 576
Spamburgers, 509
Tuna burgers, 509
Turkey buns (barbecued), 508
Turkey buns (broiled), 510
Sauces and Toppings
Baked potato toppings, 253, 338, 501
Barbecue sauce, all-purpose, 364
Barbecue sauce, easy, **(mic-w)** 406
Barbecue sauce, oven, 364
Buttermilk sauce, 229
Butterscotch sauce, 229
Cheese sauces, 320, 338
Chocolate sauces, 229, 230
Fruit salad topping, 484
Fruit salad topping, quick, 578
Fudge sauce, quick, 588
Hollandaise sauce, 337
Italian tomato sauce, 322
Mustard sauce for meats, 366
Peanut butter sauce, 230
Pie (squash or pumpkin) topping, 466
Pineapple topping, 230
Raisin sauce for ham, 367
Sour cream toppings, 253, 338
Spaghetti sauce, quick, 577
White sauce and variations, 338
White sauce, **(mic-w)** 419
Whipped cream (mock) for fruits, 253
Sauerkraut and dumplings, 304
Sauerkraut salad, 496
Sauerkraut, tasty, 330
Sausage (see also Main Dishes for recipes containing)
Sausage bites (party), 535
Sausage cheese balls (party), 535
Sausage squares (party), 535
Save, ways to, 640
Scrapple, 87
Seafood, 383-388; **(mic-w)** 407, 409, 417-418; 570-572, 579
—Information about, 354
—Tips for, 363
Clam chowder, 515
Coating mix for fish, 365
Corn and oysters, scalloped, 384
Crabmeat casserole, 383
Fish, baked fillets, **(mic-w)** 407
Fish, baked stuffed, 383

Seafood (cont.)
Fish, fried, 384
Fishburgers, 506
Oyster dressing, 385
Oyster soup 520
Oysters, fried, 384
Oysters, scalloped, 384
Salmon, scalloped, 385
Salmon soup, 520
Salmon-spinach strata, 386
Seafood spaghetti pie, 387
Shrimp, 386
Tuna (cheesy) bake, **(mic-w)** 417
Tuna bake special, 388
Tuna burgers, 509
Tuna and macaroni casserole, **(mic-w)** 418
Tuna and macaroni dinner, quick, 570
Tuna macaroni salad, 499
Tuna potato patties, 572
Tuna potato soup, 521
Tuna salad, 579
Tuna salad bake, 387
Tuna sandwich spread, 542
Tuna skillet, quick, 571
Tuna spaghetti supper, **(mic-w)** 418
Tuna supper, quick, 571
Tuna, ten-minute, 571
Tuna tetrazzini, **(mic-w)** 409
Seasoning for meats, 366, 575
Shepherds pie, **(mic-w)** 418
Sherbet (see Desserts)
Shoofly cake, 131
Shoofly pie, 466
Shortcake, fruit, 68
Shortcake, strawberry, 133, 207
Shrimp, 386
Slaw, German, 492
Slaw, hot, 331
Sloppy Joe seasoning mix, 575
Sloppy Joes, 509
Sloppy Joes, using mix, 576
Snacks, 187, 230-236; **(mic-w)** 428-431; 542-544
—Information about, 184, 527-529
—Tips for, 188
Snow, Christmas, 650
Snow cream, 228
Snow, liquid, 653
Soap, information about making, 637
Soap bubbles, 654
Soap (cold) recipe, 639
Some-mores, **(mic-w)** 431
Soufflé, cheese grits, 258
Soufflé, egg, 260
Soufflé, spinach (quick), 570
Soufflé, vegetable skillet, 573
Soups and Stews, 510-522; **(mic-w)** 420
—Information about, 469
—Making stock for, 357
—Tips for, 472
Bean (nine), 511
Bean (nine) soup mix, 510
Bean, with ham bone, 510
Beef stew (old-fashioned), 512
Beef stew (oven baked), 300
Brunswick stew, 511
Celery, cream of, 516
Chicken, corn, 513
Chicken and dumpling (old fashioned), 512
Chicken and noodle, 513, **(mic-w)** 420
Chicken and rice, 514
Chili con carne, 514

Chili con carne, quick, 564
Chili, quick (using mix), 575
Chili seasoning mix, 575
Chili stew, **(mic-w)** 420
Chili, weight watcher's, 515
Clam chowder, 515
Corn chowder, 516
Ham, 517
Hamburger (delicious), 518
Hamburger bean-pot, 517
Lentil, 518
Minestrone, 519
Mushroom, cream of, 516
Onion, **(mic-w)** 420; 520
Oyster, 520
Potato, 520
Potato rivel, 519
Salmon, 520
Salsify, 520
Tomato, 521
Tuna-potato, 521
Vegetable, 522
Vegetable tomato soup, 574
Vegetable, weight watcher's, 522
Sour cream chocolate frosting, 144
Sour cream dressings, 253, 338
Sour cream pound cake, 128
Sour cream twists, 67
Soy nuts, 236
Soybeans, favorite, 331
Spaghetti (see also Main Dishes for recipes containing)
Spaghetti and meatballs, 295
Spaghetti (mock), 306
Spaghetti sauce, using mix, 577
Spaghetti seasoning mix, 576
Spaghetti pie, 307
Spamburgers, 509
Spice cake, 137
Spiced tea mix, instant, 41
Spicy flowerettes, 555
Spinach balls (party), 536
Spinach casserole, 332
Spinach, delicious, 332
Spinach salad, 496
Spinach, savory, 332
Spinach soufflé, quick, 570
Spoon bread (see Breads)
Spray for roses, 654
Spring flowers, 654
Sprouts, alfalfa and bean, 488
Squash (butternut) casserole, 333
Squash-onion casserole, 333
Squash, fried, 331
Squash pie, 466
Squash, vegetable spaghetti, 333
Squirrel, 391
Squirrel (brunswick stew), 511
Stain remover (for clothes), 650
Stain treatment, pre-wash, 653
Stains, removing, 655-657
Starch, sugar, 654
Steak (see Meats)
Steak marinade, 366
Stews (see Soups and Stews)
Sticky buns, oatmeal-nut, 66
Sticky buns, procedure for making, 49
Sticky buns, quicky, 554
Stock for soup, clarifying, 357
Stock for soup, how to make, 357
Storing vegetables, 264, 613
Strawberries and cream (fresh), 583

Strawberries (party), 544
Strawberrioca, 206
Strawberry angel dessert, 222
Strawberry bread, 80
Strawberry cake, 134
Strawberry dessert, 203
Strawberry gelatin salad, 486
Strawberry ice cream, 225, 588
Strawberry milk punch, 35
Strawberry milk shake, 42
Strawberry pies, 456, 460, 465, 588
(see also Pies)
Strawberry pretzel salad, 485
Strawberry puddings, 206, 584
Strawberry pudding popsicles, 236
Strawberry-rhubarb compote, 206
Strawberry sherbet, 227
Strawberry shortcake (old-fashioned), 207
Strawberry shortcake (sponge), 133
Strawberry sparkle punch, 35
Strawberry squares, frosty, 224
Strawberry swirl dessert, 208
Sustitutes for ingredients, 660-661
Sugar, how to tint, 190
Sugar cookies, 181, 182
Sugar starch for doilies, 654
Sweet breads (see Breads)
Sweet potato bake, 334
Sweet potatoes, candied, 334
Sweet potatoes, orange-glazed, 334
Syrup, burnt sugar, 225
Syrup, chocolate, 39
Syrup, pancake, 87

Taco filling (using mix), 577
Taco pie (impossible), 308
Taco salad, 500
Taco seasoning mix, 577
Tacos, Navajo, 299
Taffy, 242
Tapioca fruit, pearl, 208
Tapioca, orange delight, 207
Tapioca pudding, fluffy, 221
Tarts, apple (bavarian), 448
Tarts, banana, 176
Tarts, pecan, 462
Tater Tot casserole, 308
Tea (see Beverages)
Tea rings, procedure for making, 49
Texas hash, 309
Thousand island dressing, 503
Toast cups (party), 536
Tomato and cucumber salad, 497
Tomato soup, 521
Toppings (see Sauces and Toppings)
Tossed salad dressing, 504
Trail mix, gorp, 233
Tuna (see Seafood section for recipes containing)
Turkey (see Poultry)
Turnips and potatoes, creamed, 326

Unleavened bread, 58
Upside-down cakes (see Cakes)

Variety meats (see Meats)
Veal (see Meats)
Vegetables and Miscellaneous Dishes, 312-338; **(mic-w)** 409-419
(see also salads for vegetable salads)
—Information about, 264
—Chart for cooking, 268-272

Vegetables and Misc. Dishes (cont.)
—Cheese sauces for, 320, 573
—Cream batter for, 337
—Methods for cooking, 265-267, 274, **(mic-w)** 404
—Methods for storing, 264, 613
—Tips for, 276
Beans
baked, 313, **(mic-w)** 409
baked (Crockpot), 313, 314
baked (quick), 556, 557
dry, how to cook, 274
green (and bacon casserole), **(mic-w)** 413
green (baked), 557
green (delightful), 312
green (dilly), 557
green (favorite), 312
green (saucy), 312
green (stroganoff), 565
green (supreme), 313
refried, 314
Beans and rice, 314
Bean sprouts, stir-fried, 558
Beets, harvard, 315
Broccoli, baked, 315
Broccoli casseroles, 289, 332, **(mic-w)** 410-411
Broccoli, marinated (party), 529
Broccoli pie, 316
Broccoli, sour cream party, 316
Cabbage, baked, 316, 317
Cabbage casserole (easy), 317
Cabbage, skillet, 559
Cabbage, stuffed (or rolls), 318
Carrots, baked, 319
Carrots, orange-spiced, 318
Carrots, sweet and sour, 319
Cauliflower and cheese sauce, 320
Celery, stuffed (party), 542
Celery supreme, 320
Cheese sauce, vegetable with, 573, 320
Chow mein noodles, 320
Corn, baked, 321
Corn, scalloped, **(mic-w)** 412
Cucumber tidbits (party), 542
Eggplant casserole, 321
Eggplant, fried, 331
Gardener's pizza, 324
Green beans (see Beans, green)
Italian tomato sauce, 322
Macaroni and cheese, baked, 322
Macaroni, easy bake, 322
Noodles, 323
Onion rings, 324
Onions, cheesy supreme, 323
Onions, creamed, 324
Pastas, how to cook, 274
Peppers (stuffed) skillet, 324
Pinwheel-vegetable casserole, 300
Potato (cheese) balls, 326
Potato cakes, 568
Potatoes
baked, 273, **(mic-w)** 415
baked "french-fried," 327
baked (mashed), 325, **(mic-w)** 416; 568
toppings for, 253, 338, 501
browned or fried, 325
company (quick), **(mic-w)** 416
cottage, 326
crispy, 326
diet stuffed, 327
french-fried, 327

Vegetables and Misc. Dishes (cont.)
mashed, 273
and onions **(mic-w)**, 416
scalloped, 327
scalloped (old-fashioned), 328
scalloped (quick), 568
scalloped supreme, 328
and turnips, creamed, 326
Rice, how to cook, 329
Rice, browned, 329
Rice casserole, 330
Rice, wild (and hamburger), 309
Rice, easy oven-cooked 329
Salsify, baked, 330
Sauerkraut, tasty 330
Slaw, hot, 331
Soybeans, favorite, 331
Spinach balls (party), 536
Spinach casserole, 332
Spinach, delicious and savory, 332
Spinach soufflé, quick, 570
Squash (butternut) casserole, 333
Squash, fried, 331
Squash onion casssserole, 333
Squash, vegetable spgahetti, 333
Stuffed cabbage (cabbage rolls), 318
Sweet potato bake, 334
Sweet potatoes, candied, 334
Sweet potatoes, orange-glazed, 334
Turnips and potatoes, creamed, 326
Vegetable bowl (party), 537
Vegetable casserole, 335
Vegetable dip, 539
Vegetable salad, crunchy, 497
Vegetable skillet soufflé, 573
Vegetable soups, 522, 574
Vegetable stir-fry, 574
Vegetable tomato soup, 574
Vegetable trays, 528
Vegetables and cheese sauce, 320, 573
Zucchini casserole (favorite), 336
Zucchini squash, baked, 336
Zucchini squash, fried, 331
Zucchini stir-fry (Mexican), 574
Zucchini stir-fry, ten minute, 575
Zucchini vegetable pot, 335
Venison (see Meats)

Waffles, 86, 555
Waldorf salads, 487
Watermelon magnifique, 208
Ways to save, 640
Wedding reception punch, 37
Weights and measures, 662
White sauce, 338, **(mic-w)** 419
Whole wheat biscuit mix, 68
Whole wheat bread, 60
Whole wheat orange bread, 61
Whole wheat pancakes, 85
Whole wheat rolls (angel flake), 53
Wild meats, information about, 349
Window cleaner, 655
Windshield washer cleaner, 655

Yogurt, 254
Yogurt salad dressings, 475, 504

Zucchini bars, 157
Zucchini bread, 81
Zucchini cakes, 81, 136
Zucchini casseroles 310, 336
Zucchini chocolate chip cookies, 173

Zucchini lasagna, 310
Zucchini omelet, 261
Zucchini pie, 311
Zucchini pizza, 311
Zucchini squash, baked, 336

Zucchini squash, fried, 331
Zucchini stir-fry (Mexican), 574
Zucchini stir-fry, ten minute, 575
Zucchini vegetable pot, 335

CANNING, FREEZING, AND PRESERVING INDEX

Canning, methods and information about, 591
Freezing, information about, 595
—Fruits, procedure for processing, 597
—Fruits, timetable for processing, 611
—Fruits, yield when processed, 609
—Meats, procedure for processing, 610, 356
—Meats, timetable for processing, 612
—Vegetables, procedure for processing, 602
—Vegetables, timetable for blanching, 612
—Vegetables, timetable for processing, 611
—Vegetables, yield when processed, 610
—Tips for, 614
Fruits, 598-602
—Sugar syrup for, 597
Apple cider, 598
Apples, 598
Applesauce, 598
Apricots, 599
Berries, 599
Cherries, 599
Cranberries, 600
Grape juice concentrate, 600
Grape juice, quick, 600
Melons, 600
Peaches, 600
Pears, 601
Pineapple, 601
Plums, 601
Rhubarb, 601
Strawberries, 601
Tomato juice, 602
Tomatoes, 602
Vegetables, 603-609
Asparagus, 603
Beans (green or wax), 604
Beans (lima), 604
Beets, 604
Broccoli, 605
Brussels sprouts, 604
Cabbage, 605
Carrots, 605
Cauliflower, 605
Corn, 606
Greens, 606
Okra, 606
Peas, green, 607
Peas, snow or sugar, 607
Peppers, green, 607
Pimiento peppers, 607
Potatoes, Irish, 607
Pumpkin, 608
Salsify, 608
Sauerkraut, 608 (see also 620)
Soybeans, green, 608
Squash, 609
Sweet potatoes, 609

Recipes, 615-632
Apple pie filling, 615
Apple rings, spiced, 615
Beans, dried, 616
Beans, pork and, 617
Bologna, hamburger, 616
Catsup, 617
Catsup, smooth, 618
Coleslaw, 618
Corn, easy frozen, 618
Fruit pie filling, 616
Jam and Jelly, 628-632 (see also page
       432 for **(mic-w)** recipes)
Apple butter, large amount, 628
Apple butter, oven method, 628
Apple butter, small amount, 629
Blackberry 630
Cider-cinnamon jelly, 629
Grape jelly, 629
Orange marmalade, 630
Peach butter (old-fashioned), 630
Peach jam, 631
Raspberry jelly, 630
Red beet jelly, 631
Strawberry freezer jam, 632
Strawberry honey, 631
Strawberry, uncooked, 632
Mincemeat, 618
Pickle and Relish, 622-627
Beet, 622
Bread and butter, 623
Corn relish, 623
Cucumber (old-fashioned), 622
Dill, 624
Lime, 625
Refrigerator, 626
Sweet, crisp, 626
Sweet, seven-day, 625
Watermelon rind, 627
Zucchini relish, 627
Pie filling, apple, 615
Pie filling, fruit, 616
Pizza sauce, 619
Sauerkraut, 620 (see also 608)
Spaghetti sauce, 619
Tomato juice cocktail, 620
Tomato soup, 620
Vegetable juice cocktail, 621
Vegetable soup, 621
Zucchini "crushed pineapple," 619
Zucchini, sliced, 622
Storing Vegetables, 613
Cabbage, 613
Carrots, 613
Onions, 613
Potatoes, 613
Tomatoes, 613

ESTHER HEATWOLE SHANK

The author was born and raised on a dairy farm in the Shenandoah Valley of Virginia near Bridgewater, not far from Harrisonburg.

She and her twin brother were the fifth and sixth children of their parents. Six more brothers and sisters followed! With this many mouths to feed and so much work to be done on the farm, the children were given major domestic responsibilities at a young age. Esther and her four sisters helped with the cooking, gardening, and canning for as far back as she can remember.

Since her father was a minister, there was a continual flow of guests into their home for meals. As a nonsalaried Mennonite preacher, he operated a dairy farm to support his growing family. Lacking modern equipment, farmers in those days banded together to help each other during harvest season. When threshing grain or filling silo, there would be a dozen to 20 men at the Heatwole table. This gave Esther opportunity for much experience in food preparation.

Esther married Rawley J. Shank. They purchased their own dairy farm near Harrisonburg, where they raised their three daughters—Linda Sue, Donna Elaine, and Nancy Lou. With no sons, Esther continued over the years to cook for farmhands as well as for her family.

Esther frequently invited persons for meals as a way to reach out to others in her church and social circles. Hundreds of guests have fellowshiped around the Shank table, many from other states and some from foreign countries. Since one of her hobbies was collecting good recipes and cooking tips, this gave her many opportunities to gather and share information from a wide variety of places.

Esther and Rawley are members of Zion Hill Mennonite Church near Singers Glen. She has been active in her church women's group, in teaching Sunday school, and in many service and community projects.

Esther is a graduate of Eastern Mennonite High School, Harrisonburg, Virginia, where she studied business. She did secretarial work for a number of years for Mennonite Broadcasts, Inc. (now Media Ministries). The Shanks have moved from their farm to Park View, where she continues her efforts as a volunteer.

In this book Esther is happy to share with her daughters and others her extensive collection of time-tested recipes and kitchen secrets—the heritage of good Mennonite country-style cooking!